BIRDS
OF EASTERN
CANADA

BIRDS
OF EASTERN
CANADA

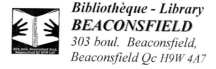

CONSULTANT EDITOR
DAVID M. BIRD, PH.D.
Emeritus Professor of Wildlife Biology
McGill University

DK | Penguin Random House

DORLING KINDERSLEY

FIRST EDITION

Senior Art Editors
Caroline Hill, Ina Stradins

Senior Editors
Angeles Gavira Guerrero,
Ankush Saikia

Canadian Editor
Barbara Campbell

Project Editor
Nathan Joyce

Project Designer
Mahua Sharma

Designers
Sonia Barbate, Helen McTeer

Editors
Jamie Ambrose, Lori Baird, Tamlyn
Calitz, Marcus Hardy, Patrick
Newman, Siobhan O'Connor,
Garima Sharma, David Summers,
Miezan van Zyl, Rebecca Warren

Design Assistant
Becky Tennant

Editorial Assistants
Elizabeth Munsey, Jaime Tenreiro

Creative Technical Support
John Goldsmid

DTP Manager
Sunil Sharma

Senior DTP Designers
Pushpak Tyagi, Tarun Sharma

DTP Designers
Manish Chandra Upreti, Rajdeep
Singh, Anurag Tiwari, Satish
Chandra Gaur

Production Editor
Maria Elia

Production Controller
Rita Sinha

Jacket Designer
Mark Cavanagh

Illustrators
John Cox, Andrew Mackay

Picture Editor
Neil Fletcher

Picture Researchers
Laura Barwick, Will Jones

Managing Art Editor
Phil Ormerod

Managing Editors
Glenda Fernandes, Sarah Larter

Publishing Manager
Liz Wheeler

Art Director
Bryn Walls

Publishers
Jonathan Metcalf, Aparna Sharma

THIS EDITION

Senior Editor
Dharini Ganesh

Art Editor
Anjali Sachar

Assistant Editor
Ishita Jha

Assistant Art Editor
Nobina Chakravorty

Managing Art Editor
Sudakshina Basu

Senior Managing Editor
Rohan Sinha

DTP Designer
Sachin Gupta

Jacket Designer
Priyanka Bansal

Senior DTP Designer
Harish Aggarwal

**Jackets Editorial
Coordinator**
Priyanka Sharma

Managing Jackets Editor
Saloni Singh

Canadian Editor
Barbara Campbell

**Jacket Design
Development Manager**
Sophia MTT

AMERICAN MUSEUM OF NATURAL HISTORY

Editor-in-chief
François Vuilleumier

Project Coordinators
Caitlin Roxby, Molly Leff

CONTRIBUTORS

David M. Bird
Nicholas L. Block
Peter Capainolo
Matthew Cormons
Malcolm Coulter
Joseph DiCostanzo
Shawneen Finnegan
Neil Fletcher
Ted Floyd
Jeff Groth
Paul Hess
Brian Hiller
Rob Hume
Thomas Brodie Johnson

Kevin T. Karlson
Stephen Kress
William Moskoff
Bill Pranty
Michael L. P. Retter
Noah Strycker
Paul Sweet
Rodger Titman
Elissa Wolfson

Map Editor Paul Lehman

Project Coordinator
Joseph DiCostanzo

This Canadian Edition, 2019
First Canadian Edition, 2013

DK Canada
320 Front Street West, Suite 1400
Toronto, Ontario M5V 3B6

Copyright © 2013, 2019 Dorling Kindersley Limited
DK, a Division of Penguin Random House LLC
19 20 21 22 23 10 9 8 7 6 5 4 3 2 1
001—313674—Mar/2019

Published in Great Britain by Dorling Kindersley Limited.

**Library and Archives Canada
Cataloguing in Publication**
    Birds of eastern Canada / consultant editor, David M. Bird.
—2nd edition.
Includes index.
ISBN 978-1-55363-296-2 (softcover)
    1. Birds—Canada, Eastern—Identification. 2. Bird
watching—Canada, Eastern—Guidebooks. 3. Canada,
Eastern—Guidebooks. I. Bird, David M. (David Michael),
1949–, editor
QL685.B583 2019   598.072'34713   C2018-902671-5

DK books are available at special discounts when
purchased in bulk for corporate sales, sales promotions,
premiums, fund-raising, or educational use. For details,
please contact specialmarkets@dk.com.

Printed in China

A WORLD OF IDEAS:
SEE ALL THERE IS TO KNOW

www.dk.com

CONTENTS

PREFACE

SUMMER SINGER
Male Indigo Buntings sing from the highest available perch all summer long.

Publishing an all-inclusive, up-to-date reference book on the bird species that are found in any delineated geographical entity, such as a country like Canada, is a constantly evolving chore. With never-ending new data on morphology and behavior coupled with rapidly changing molecular technology and innovative Citizen Science programs like eBird, taxonomists are incessantly making alterations to the official list of the birds of the world. But that's not the whole story. Changing weather patterns are causing more and more bird species to shift their breeding and wintering ranges further north, and extreme weather events like hurricanes and tropical storms are blowing more and more birds across entire continents and oceans, leading to newly established populations in regions where they did not exist before. So, if birders and ornithologists want to have the latest and correct information at their fingertips, that means putting new editions of reference books and field guides on their library shelves every few years or so. And that is exactly what we have done with these 2nd editions of *Birds of Eastern Canada* and *Birds of Western Canada*.

These two handy regional guides offer, for almost all Canadian bird species, profiles with detailed information, including beautiful photographs and precise distribution maps; readable accounts of notable characteristics; data on identification, behavior, habitat, voice, nest construction, breeding season, and food; diagrams of flight patterns; statistics of size, wingspan, weight, clutch size, number of broods per year, and lifespan; and geographical information about breeding, wintering, and migration. While the use of scientific jargon has been minimized, a glossary identifies concepts that benefit from an explanation. The user-friendly format should permit readers to enjoy either studying one species account at a time or browsing to make cross comparisons.

As before, the Eastern and Western ranges are split along the 100th Meridian, or around Winnipeg, an invisible barrier located in a transitional zone between habitats that represents Eastern versus Western landscape types or biomes. While almost all of the bird species residing in Canada are included, a handful of birds that spend most of their time in a Canadian range far out to sea, for example, were left out of these volumes.

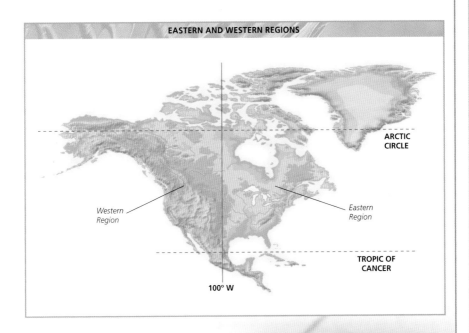

EASTERN AND WESTERN REGIONS

ARCTIC CIRCLE

Western Region

Eastern Region

TROPIC OF CANCER

100° W

During my tenure as a professor of ornithology for over 35 years, I have come to realize the real value of a concise reference work that can be conveniently carried around. I hope that these books will be useful to all persons interested in birds, whether young or older, enthusiastic birder or novice. If you are going birding, don't leave home without it!

David M. Bird
Emeritus Professor of Wildlife Biology
McGill University

TRAVELING BIRD
The Bohemian Waxwing is named for its nomadic lifestyle in the winter, as it travels around looking for fruit to eat.

HOW THIS BOOK WORKS

THIS GUIDE COVERS JUST over 350 eastern Canadian bird species. The species are organized into two sections: the first profiles common Canadian species found in the east, with each given full-page treatment; the second covers rarer birds in quarter-page entries.

COLOR BAND
The information bands at the top and bottom of each entry are color-coded for each family.

▽ INTRODUCTION
The species are organized conventionally by order, family, and genus. Related birds appear together, preceded by a group introduction. The book follows the most up-to-date avian classification system, based on the latest scientific research.

GROUP NAME
The common name of the group the species belongs to is at the top of each page.

COMMON NAME

IN FLIGHT
Illustrations show the bird in flight, from above and/or below —differences of season, age, or sex are not always visible.

PHOTOGRAPHS
These illustrate the species in different views and plumage variations. Significant differences relating to age, sex, and season (breeding/nonbreeding) are shown and the images labelled accordingly; if there is no variation, the images have no label. Unless stated otherwise, the bird shown is an adult.

FLIGHT PATTERNS
This feature briefly describes the way the species flies. See panel opposite.

SIMILAR SPECIES
Similar-looking species are identified and key differences pointed out.

LENGTH, WINGSPAN, AND WEIGHT
Length is tip of tail to tip of bill; measurements are averages or ranges.

SOCIAL
The social unit the species is usually found in.

LIFESPAN
The average or maximum life expectancy.

STATUS
The conservation status of the species; the symbol (p) means the data available can only suggest a provisional status. The term "Localized" suggests that the species may be widespread but restricted to smaller areas of suitable habitat and climatic conditions.

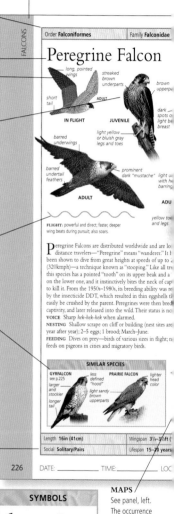

Order **Falconiformes** | Family **Falconidae**

Peregrine Falcon

long, pointed wings — streaked brown underparts — brown upperpar

short tail | ADULT

IN FLIGHT | **JUVENILE**

dark spots on light bre breast

light yellow or bluish gray legs and toes

barred underwings

barred undertail feathers | prominent dark "mustache" | light un with he barring

ADULT | **ADU**

yellow toe and legs

FLIGHT: powerful and direct; faster, deeper wing beats during pursuit; also soars.

Peregrine Falcons are distributed worldwide and are lo distance travelers—"Peregrine" means "wanderer." It h been shown to dive from heights of up to (320kmph)—a technique known as "stooping." Like all tr this species has a pointed "tooth" on its upper beak and a on the lower one, and it instinctively bites the neck of cap to kill it. From the 1950s–1980s, its breeding ability was re by the insecticide DDT, which resulted in thin eggshells t easily be crushed by the parent. Peregrines were then bred captivity, and later released into the wild. Their status is no
VOICE Sharp *hek-hek-hek* when alarmed.
NESTING Shallow scrape on cliff or building (nest sites are year after year); 2–5 eggs; 1 brood; March–June.
FEEDING Dives on prey—birds of various sizes in flight; n feeds on pigeons in cities and migratory birds.

SIMILAR SPECIES

GYRFALCON see p.225 | larger and stockier longer tail | less defined "hood" light sandy brown upperparts | **PRAIRIE FALCON** | lighter head color

Length 16in (41cm) | Wingspan 3¼–3⁷⁄ (
Social **Solitary/Pairs** | Lifespan **15–20 years**

226 | DATE: _____ TIME: _____ LOC

MAPS

In this book, North America is the region from the southern tip of Florida and the US–Mexico border to the Canadian High Arctic. Each profile includes a map showing the range of the species, with colors reflecting seasonal movements.

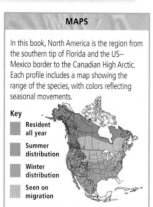

Key
- Resident all year
- Summer distribution
- Winter distribution
- Seen on migration

SYMBOLS

♂ Male	☘ Spring
♀ Female	☼ Summer
◑ Juvenile	🍂 Autumn
◐ Immature	❄ Winter

MAPS
See panel, left. The occurrence caption describes the bird's preferred habitats and range within the North American region.

▽ COMMON SPECIES

The main section of the book features the 330 most commonly seen bird species in the region of eastern Canada. Each entry is clear and detailed, following the same easy-to-access structure.

Species *Falco peregrinus*

yellow eye-ring

wood ed

bluish gray upperparts

PARENTAL CARE
An adult Peregrine gently feeds a hatchling bits of meat; the remaining egg is likely to hatch soon.

OCCURRENCE
A variety of habitats across northern North America, ranging from open valleys to cities with tall buildings. Peregrines prefer to inhabit cliffs along sea coasts, in addition to inland mountain ranges, but also occur in open country such as scrubland and salt marshes.

| Weight | 22–35oz (620–1000g) |
| Status | **Secure** |

HABITAT/BEHAVIOR
Additional photographs reveal the species in its typical habitat or show the bird exhibiting typical behavior.

CLASSIFICATION
The top band of each entry provides the scientific order, family, and species names (see glossary, pp. 389–392 for full definitions of these terms).

DESCRIPTION
Conveys the main features and essential character of the species.

VOICE
A description of the species' calls and songs, given phonetically where possible.

NESTING
The type of nest and its usual location; the number of eggs in a clutch; the number of broods in a year; the breeding season.

FEEDING
How, where, and what the species feeds on.

△ RARE SPECIES

Twenty-four less common birds are presented on pp. 383–388. Arranged in the same group order used in the main section, these entries consist of one clear photograph of the species accompanied by a description of the bird.

FLIGHT PATTERNS

Simple line diagrams are used to illustrate eight basic flight patterns.

wingbeats

Woodpecker-like: bursts of wingbeats between deeply undulating glides.

Finch-like: light, bouncy action with flurries of wingbeats between deep, undulating glides.

Grouse-like: bursts of wing beats between short, straight glides.

Hawk-like: straight, with several quick, deep beats between short, flat glides.

Gull-like: continually flapping, with slow, steady wingbeats.

Duck-like: continually flapping, with fast wingbeats.

Kite-like: deep, slow wingbeats between soaring glides.

Swallow-like: swooping, with bursts of wingbeats between glides.

EVOLUTION

Ornithologists agree that birds evolved from dinosaurs about 150 million years ago, but there is still debate about the dinosaur group from which they descended. Around 10,000 species of birds exist today, living in many different kinds of habitats across the world, from desert to Arctic tundra.

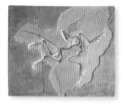

MISSING LINK?
Archaeopteryx, shown here as a 145-million-year-old fossil, had dinosaur-like teeth, but birdlike feathers.

SPECIATION

What are species and how do they evolve? Species are biological entities. When two species of a genus overlap they rarely interbreed and produce hybrids. The North American Flicker has an eastern (yellow-shafted) and a western (red-shafted) form; after the discovery that these two forms interbreed in the Great Plains, the flickers are now considered one species. In other cases, a previously single species, such as the Northern Oriole, has been divided into the Baltimore Oriole and the Bullock's Oriole. Such examples illustrate how species evolve, first by geographic separation, followed in time by overlap. This process can take millions of years.

BIRD GENEALOGY

The diagram below is called a phylogeny, and shows how selected groups of birds are related to each other. The timescale at the top of the diagram is derived from both fossil and DNA evidence, which allows ornithologists to estimate when different lineages of birds diverged. The names of groups shown in bold are those living in Canada.

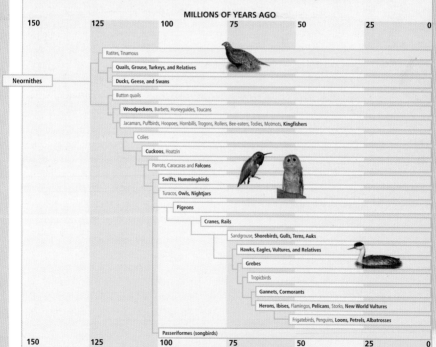

MILLIONS OF YEARS AGO

150   125   100   75   50   25   0

Neornithes

Ratites, Tinamous
Quails, Grouse, Turkeys, and Relatives
Ducks, Geese, and Swans
Button quails
Woodpeckers, Barbets, Honeyguides, Toucans
Jacamars, Puffbirds, Hoopoes, Hornbills, Trogons, Rollers, Bee-eaters, Todies, Motmots, **Kingfishers**
Colies
Cuckoos, Hoatzin
Parrots, Caracaras and **Falcons**
Swifts, Hummingbirds
Turacos, **Owls, Nightjars**
Pigeons
Cranes, Rails
Sandgrouse, **Shorebirds, Gulls, Terns, Auks**
Hawks, Eagles, Vultures, and Relatives
Grebes
Tropicbirds
Gannets, Cormorants
Herons, Ibises, Flamingos, **Pelicans**, Storks, New World Vultures
Frigatebirds, Penguins, **Loons, Petrels, Albatrosses**
Passeriformes (songbirds)

150   125   100   75   50   25   0

BLENDING IN
This magnificent species is diurnal, unlike most other owls, which are nocturnal. The Snowy Owl breeds in the Arctic tundra and if the ground is covered with snow, it blends in perfectly.

CONVERGENCE

The evolutionary process during which birds of two distantly related groups develop similarities is called convergence. Carrion-eating birds of prey are one example. Old World vultures belong to the hawk family (Accipitridae), while New World vultures are more closely related to storks. However, both groups are characterized by hooked bills, bare heads, and weak talons.

PARALLEL EVOLUTION
The African longclaws (family Motacillidae) and North American meadowlarks (family Icteridae) show convergence in plumage color and pattern.

CAPE LONGCLAW

WESTERN MEADOWLARK

EXTINCTION

During the last 150 years, North America has lost the Passenger Pigeon, the Great Auk, the Carolina Parakeet, the Labrador Duck, and the Eskimo Curlew. Humans hunted them out of existence and/or destroyed their habitat. Some species that seemed doomed have had a reprieve. Thanks to a breeding and release program, the Whooping Crane still makes its annual migration from Canada to the US.

OVERHUNTING
The Passenger Pigeon was eradicated as a result of relentless hunting.

CLASSIFYING BIRDS
All past and present animal life is named and categorized into groups. Classifications reflect the genealogical relationships among groups, based on traits such as color, bones, or DNA. Birds make up the class "Aves," which includes "orders;" each "order" is made up of one or more "families." "Genus" is a subdivision of "family," which contains one or more "species." A species is a unique group of similar organisms that interbreed and produce fertile offspring. Some species have distinct populations, which are known as subspecies.

Aves (Birds) — Class

Passeriformes (songbirds) — Order

Parulidae (Wood Warblers) — Family

Setophaga — Genus

Setophaga castanea | Setophaga palmarum | Setophaga tigrina — Species

S. p. palmarum — Subspecies

ANATOMY AND FLIGHT

I**N SPITE OF THEIR EXTERNAL DIVERSITY**, birds are
remarkably similar internally. To allow flight, birds
require a skeleton that is both rigid and light. Rigidity
is achieved by the fusion of some bones, especially
the lower vertebrae, while lightness is maintained
by having hollow limb bones.
These are connected to air sacs,
which, in turn, are connected
to the bird's lungs.

SKELETON
Avian skeletal features include
the furcula (wishbone), the
keeled sternum (breastbone),
and the fused tail vertebrae.

"hand"

"forearm"

neck
vertebrae

bill

furcula

fused tail
vertebrae

keeled
sternum

secondaries

FLIGHT ADAPTATIONS
For birds to be able to fly, they need light and rigid bones, a
lightweight skull, and hollow wing and leg bones. In addition,
pouch-like air sacs are connected to hollow bones, which
reduce a bird's weight. The air sacs also function as a cooling
system, which birds need because they have a high metabolic
rate. The breast muscles, which are crucial for flight,
attach to the keeled sternum (breastbone).

tail
feathers

uppertail
coverts

rump

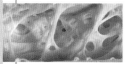

BIRD BONE STRUCTURE
Most bird bones, except those of
penguins and other flightless birds,
are hollow, which reduces their weight.
A honeycomb of internal struts makes
the bones remarkably strong.

tertials

LEGS, FEET, AND TOES
When you look at a bird's leg, you do not see its
thigh, which is inside the body cavity, but the leg
from the knee down. When we talk about a bird's
feet we really mean its toes. The shin is a fused tibia
and fibula. This fused bone plus the heel are known
as the "tarso-metatarsus."

primaries

enables
grip on
ground

WALKING
Ground-foraging birds usually
have a long hind claw.

enables
strong grip
on branches

CLIMBING
Most climbers have two toes
forward and two backward.

UNDERPARTS
Underwing coverts
have a regular pattern
of overlapping rows.
Short feathers cover
the head, breast, belly,
and flanks. In most birds,
the toes are unfeathered.

axillaries

breast

webbing
provides
thrust in
water

SWIMMING
Water-loving birds have
webbing between their toes.

used to
grasp prey

HUNTING
Birds of prey have powerful toes
and strong, sharp claws.

undertail
coverts

bill

belly

toes

FEATHERS

All birds, by definition, have feathers. These remarkable structures, which are modified scales, serve two main functions: insulation and flight. Special muscles allow birds to raise their feathers or to flatten them against the body. In cold weather, fluffed-out feathers keep an insulating layer of air between the skin and the outside. This insulating capacity is why humans often find wearing loose-fitting "down" jackets so effective against the cold. The first feathers that chicks have after hatching are down feathers. The rigidity of the flight feathers helps to create a supporting surface that birds use to generate thrust and lift.

primary coverts

secondary coverts

coverts

neck

nape

crown

chin

throat

mantle

scapulars

alula (bastard wing)

UPPERPARTS
The wing feathers from the "hand" of the bird are the primaries and those on the "forearm" are the secondaries. Each set has its accompanying row of coverts. The tertials are adjacent to the secondaries.

TYPES OF FEATHERS
Birds have three main kinds of feathers: down, contour, and flight feathers. The rigid axis of all feathers is called the "rachis."

DOWN FEATHER   **CONTOUR FEATHER**   **FLIGHT FEATHER**

WING FUNCTIONS

Flapping, soaring, gliding, and hovering are among the ways birds can use their wings. They also exhibit colors or patterns as part of territorial and courtship displays. Several birds, such as herons, open their wings like an umbrella when foraging in water for fish. An important aspect of wings is their relationship to a bird's weight. The ratio of a bird's wing area to weight is called wing loading, but this may also be affected by wing shape. An eagle has a large wing area to weight ratio, which means it has lower wing loading, whereas a swallow has a small wing area to weight ratio, and therefore high wing loading. This means that the slow, soaring eagle is capable of much more energy-efficient flight than the fast, agile swallow.

LONG AND BROAD
The broad, long, rectangular wings of an eagle allow it to soar. The outstretched alulae (bastard wings) give it extra lift.

POINTED
Broad at their base and tapering toward a point, and bent at the wrist, a swallow's wings enable fast flight and sharp turns.

SHORT AND ROUND
Short, broad, and round wings enable warblers to move between perches and to migrate long distances.

WING AERODYNAMICS

The supporting surface of a bird's wing enables it to take off and stay aloft. Propulsion and lift are linked in birds—which use their wings for both—unlike in airplanes in which these two functions are separate. Large and heavy birds, like swans, flap their wings energetically to create propulsion, and need a long, watery runway before they can fly off. The Golden Eagle can take off from a cliff with little or no wing flapping, but the Black and Turkey Vultures hop up from carrion then flap vigorously and finally use air flowing across their wings to soar. This diagram shows how air flow affects lift.

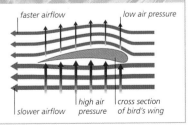

faster airflow   low air pressure

slower airflow   high air pressure   cross section of bird's wing

MIGRATION

Until recently, the mechanics, or the "how" of migration was poorly understood. Today, however, ornithologists know that birds use a variety of cues including visual and magnetic, whether they migrate by day or by night. Birds do not leave northern breeding areas because of the winter cold, but because day-length is getting shorter and food scarcer.

NIGHT MIGRANTS
During migration, ornithologists can point a telescope on the moon and count the birds that cross its surface.

REFUELING
Red Knots make a stop on their long journey to eat horseshoe crab eggs.

INSTINCTIVE MOVE

Even though many birds use visual cues and landmarks during their migration, for example birds of prey flying along the Appalachians, "instinctive" behavior must control much of how and where they move. Instinct is a loose term that is hard to define, but ornithologists generally understand it as a genetically programmed activity. They assume that natural selection has molded a behavior as complex as migration by acting on birds' DNA; this hypothesis is reasonable but hard to prove. Nevertheless, it would seem to be the only explanation why many juvenile shorebirds leave their breeding grounds after their parents and yet find their way to their final destination.

NAVIGATION

One of the most puzzling aspects of migration is understanding how birds make their way from their breeding grounds to their destination. Ornithologists have devised experiments to determine how the different components of a navigation system work. For example, if visual landmarks are hidden by fog, a faint sun can give birds a directional clue; if heavy clouds hide the sun, then the birds' magnetic compass may be used to ascertain their direction.

FINDING THE WAY
Birds coordinate information their brains receive from the sun, moon, stars, landmarks, and magnetite, or iron oxide, and use it as a compass.

OVERLAND FLIERS
Sandhill Cranes migrate over hills and mountains from their Arctic tundra breeding grounds to the marshes of the Platte River in the midwestern US.

GLOBETROTTERS

Some bird species in Canada are year-round residents, although a few individuals of these species move away from where they hatched at some time in the year. However, a large number of Canadian species are migratory. A few species breed in Labrador, but winter in the Gulf of the Caribbean. Others breed in the Canadian Arctic Archipelago, fly over land and the Pacific Ocean, and spend the winter at sea off the coast of Peru. Many songbirds fly from Canada's boreal forests to Mexico and northern South America. The most amazing globetrotters, such as the Red Knot, fly all the way to Tierra del Fuego, making only a few stops along the way after their short breeding season in the Arctic tundra. The return journeys of some of these travelers are not over the same route—instead, their entire trip is elliptical in shape.

EPIC JOURNEY
The Arctic Tern is an amazing long-distance migrant, breeding in northern regions and wintering in the pack ice of Antarctica after flying a round-trip distance of about 25,000 miles (40,000km).

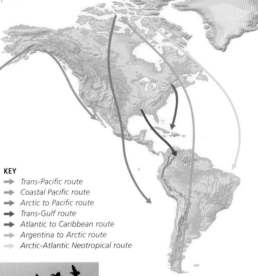

KEY
➡ Trans-Pacific route
➡ Coastal Pacific route
➡ Arctic to Pacific route
➡ Trans-Gulf route
➡ Atlantic to Caribbean route
➡ Argentina to Arctic route
⇢ Arctic-Atlantic Neotropical route

NEOTROPICAL MIGRANT
Many wood warblers, such as this Blackpoll Warbler, breed in boreal forests before migrating to their wintering grounds in the Caribbean, or Central or South America.

MIGRATION ROUTES
The map above shows the range of migration routes that some North American species take to and from their breeding grounds.

V-FORMATION
Geese and other large waterfowl fly in a v-formation to allow following birds to gain lift from those in front, thereby saving energy. The lead bird is regularly replaced.

PARTIAL MIGRANT

The American Robin is a good example of a partial migrant, a species in which the birds of some populations are resident whereas others migrate out of their breeding range. Most Canadian populations of the American Robin fly south, US populations are largely resident, and quite a few from either population spend the winter in the Southwest, Florida, or Mexico.

KEY
▇ Breeding distribution
▇ Resident all year
▇ Nonbreeding distribution

15

COURTSHIP AND MATING

WHETHER MONOGAMOUS OR NOT, males and females need to mate for their species to perpetuate itself. With most species, the male plays the dominant role of advertising a territory to potential mates using vocal or visual displays. Females then select a male and if the two respond positively to each other, a period of courtship follows ending in mating. The next step is nest-building, egg-laying, and rearing the young.

DISPLAYS

Mutual attraction between the sexes starts with some sort of display, usually performed by the male. These displays can take a number of forms, from flashing dazzling breeding plumage, conducting elaborate dancing rituals, performing complex songs, offering food or nesting material, or actually building a nest. Some birds, such as grebes, have fascinatingly intricate ceremonies, in which both male and female simultaneously perform the same movements.

WELCOME HOME
Northern Gannets greet their mates throughout the breeding season by rubbing bills together and opening their wings.

DANCING CRANES
During courtship, Sandhill Cranes perform spectacular dances, the two birds of a pair leaping into the air with wings opened and legs splayed.

COURTSHIP FEEDING

In some species, males offer food to their mate to maintain the pair-bond. The male Common Tern routinely brings small fish to a mate in a nesting colony, spreading his wings and tail until she accepts the fish.

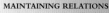

MAINTAINING RELATIONS
A male Northern Cardinal offers food to the female, which is a way of reinforcing their pair bond.

BREEDING

After mating, a nest is made, often by the female, where she lays from one to a dozen eggs. Not all birds make nests. Nightjars, for example lay their eggs directly on the ground. In many species incubation doesn't start until the female has laid all the eggs. Incubation, again usually done by the female, varies from twelve days to about 45 days. Songbirds ranging from the temperate zone to the Arctic show a range in clutch size with more eggs produced in the North than in the South. The breeding process can fail at any stage, for example a predator can eat the eggs or the chicks. Some birds will nest again but others give up breeding for the season.

MATING
Mating is usually brief, and typically takes place on a perch or on the ground, but a few species like swifts and swallows can mate in the air. This male Black Tern balances himself by opening his wings.

POLYGAMY
This Winter Wren collects nesting material for one of the several nests he will build.

MONOGAMOUS BONDS
Some birds, such as Snow Geese, mostly remain paired for life after establishing a bond.

SINGLE FATHER

A male Red-necked Phalarope incubates eggs in the Arctic tundra. Phalaropes are well known for their reversal of breeding roles. The female, who is the larger and more colorful of the two sexes, aggressively competes for males, and after mating with several of them, plays no role in nest building, incubation, or caring for chicks, but tends to her territory instead. Although the chicks can feed by themselves immediately after hatching, they remain with a male before growing feathers and living on their own.

NESTS AND EGGS

MOST BIRD SPECIES BUILD THEIR OWN NEST, which is a necessary container for their eggs. Exceptions include cowbirds, which lay their eggs in other species' nests. Nest-building is often done by the female alone, but in some species the male may help or even build it himself. Eggs are incubated either by females alone, or by males or females, depending on the species. Eggshells are thick enough to sustain the weight of incubating parents, yet thin enough for a chick to break its way out. Eggs, consisting of 60 percent water, contain a fatty yolk as well as sugars and proteins for nourishment of the embryo.

NEST TYPES

In addition to the four types shown below, nests range from a simple scrape in the ground with a few added pebbles to an elaborate woven basket-like structure. Plant matter forms basic nest material. This includes twigs, grass stems, bark, lichens, mosses, plant down, and rootlets. Some birds add mud to their nest for strength. Others incorporate animal hair or feathers to improve its softness and insulation. Female eider ducks pluck down feathers from their belly. Some birds include bits of plastic or threads in their nests. Many birds make their nest or lay their eggs deep inside the empty burrows of other animals, or in already-excavated cavities in trees.

UNTIDY NEST
Huge stick nests, built on top of dead trees, are the hallmark of Ospreys. They also use a wide variety of artificial structures, including nesting platforms built for them by humans.

EGG CUP
A clutch of blue robin's eggs in a cup lined with grass stems. Robins build their nests either in shrubs or trees, and sometimes on artificial structures like porch lights.

NATURAL CAVITY
This Northern Saw-whet Owl is nesting at the bottom of a tree cavity that has probably been excavated by a woodpecker.

NEST BOX
Cavity-nesting bluebirds have been affected by habitat loss, and compete with other birds for nest sites, which may include human-made structures.

COMPLEX WEAVE
New World orioles weave intricate nests from dried grass stems and other plant material, and hang them from the tip of branches, often high up in trees.

EGG SHAPES

There are six basic egg shapes among birds, as illustrated to the right. The most common egg shapes are longitudinal or elliptical. Murres lay pear-shaped eggs, an adaptation for nesting on the narrow ledges of sea cliffs; if an egg rolls, it does so in a tight circle and remains on the ledge. Spherical eggs with irregular red blotches are characteristic of birds of prey. Pigeons and doves lay white oval eggs, usually two per clutch. The eggs of many songbirds, including sparrows and buntings, are conical and have a variety of dark markings on a pale background.

COLOR AND SHAPE
Birds' eggs vary widely in terms of shape, colors, and markings. The American Robin's egg on the left is a beautiful blue.

PEAR SHAPED   **LONGITUDINAL**   **ELLIPTICAL**

CONICAL

OVAL

SPHERICAL

NEAT ARRANGEMENT
Many shorebirds, such as plovers and sandpipers, lay four conical eggs with the narrow ends pointed in toward each other.

HATCHING CONDITION

After a period of incubation, which varies from species to species, chicks break the eggshell, some of them using an egg tooth, a special bill feature that falls off after hatching. After a long and exhausting struggle, the chick eventually tumbles out of the shell fragments. The transition from the watery medium inside the egg to the air outside is a tremendous physiological switch. Once free of their shell, the hatchlings recover from the exertion and either beg food from their parents or feed on their own.

FOOD DELIVERY
Tern chicks, although able to move around, cannot catch the fish they need to survive and must rely on their parents to provide food until they can fly.

PARENTAL GUIDANCE
Birds of prey, such as these Snowy Owl owlets, need their parents to care for them longer than some other bird species, and do not leave the nest until their feathers are sufficiently developed for their first flight.

BROOD PARASITISM

Neither cowbirds in the New World nor cuckoos in the Old World make a nest. Female cowbirds deposit up to 20 eggs in the nests of several other species. If the foster parents accept the foreign egg, they will feed the chick of the parasite until it fledges. In the picture below, a tiny wood warbler feeds its adopted chick, a huge cowbird hatchling that has overgrown the nest.

FAST FEEDER
Coots, gallinules, and rails hatch with a complete covering of down and can feed themselves immediately after birth.

IDENTIFICATION

S OME SPECIES ARE EASY TO IDENTIFY, but in many cases, species identification is tricky. In Canada, a notoriously difficult group in terms of identification is the wood warblers, especially in the fall, when most species have similar greenish and/or yellowish plumage.

GEOGRAPHIC RANGE

Each bird species in Canada lives in a particular area that is called its geographic range. Some species have a restricted range; for example, the Whooping Crane breeds only in Wood Buffalo National Park in Alberta and the Northwest Territories. Other species, such as the Red-tailed Hawk, range from coast to coast and from northern Canada to Mexico. Species with a broad range usually breed in a variety of vegetation types, while species with narrow ranges often have a specialized habitat; for example, steep, rocky shores for the Northern Gannet.

BLUEBIRD VARIATIONS
Species of the genus Sialia, such as the Mountain Bluebird above and the Eastern Bluebird below, are easy to identify.

bright blue wings

white belly

chestnut flanks

SIZE AND WEIGHT

From hummingbird to Tundra Swan and from extra-light to heavy, such is the range of sizes and weights found among the bird species of Canada. Size can be measured in several ways, for example the length of a bird from bill-tip to tail-tip, or its wingspan. Size can also be estimated for a given bird in relationship with another that is familiar. For example, the less familiar Bicknells' Thrush can be compared with the well-known American Robin.

SIZE MATTERS
Smaller shorebirds, with shorter legs and bills, forage in shallow water, but larger ones have longer legs and bills and can feed in deeper water.

SEMIPALMATED SANDPIPER   LESSER YELLOWLEGS   HUDSONIAN GODWIT   WHIMBREL

GENERAL SHAPE

Just as birds come in all sizes, their body shapes vary, but size and shape are not necessarily correlated. In the dense reed beds in which it lives, the American Bittern's long and thin body blends in with stems. The round-bodied Sedge Wren hops in shrubby vegetation or near the ground where slimness is not an advantage. In dense forest canopy, the slender and long-tailed Yellow-billed Cuckoo can maneuver easily. Mourning Doves inhabit rather open habitats and their plumpness is irrelevant when it comes to their living space.

tall, narrow body

long tail

short tail

AMERICAN BITTERN

thickset body

YELLOW-BILLED CUCKOO

small head

slender shape

tiny tail

round body

MOURNING DOVE   SEDGE WREN

BILL SHAPE

These images show a range of bill shapes and sizes relative to the bird's head size. In general, bill form, including length or thickness, corresponds to the kinds of food a birds consumes. With its pointed bill, the Black-capped Chickadee picks tiny insects from crevices in tree bark. At another extreme, dowitchers probe mud with their long thin bills, feeling for worms. The willet swishes its bill back and forth in water in search of aquatic insects.

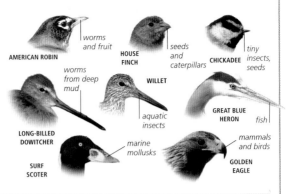

AMERICAN ROBIN — *worms and fruit*

HOUSE FINCH — *seeds and caterpillars*

CHICKADEE — *tiny insects, seeds*

WILLET

LONG-BILLED DOWITCHER — *worms from deep mud*

aquatic insects

GREAT BLUE HERON — *fish*

SURF SCOTER — *marine mollusks*

GOLDEN EAGLE — *mammals and birds*

WING SHAPE

Birds' wing shapes are correlated with their flight style. The long, round-tipped wings of the Red-tailed Hawk are perfect for soaring, while the tiny wings of hummingbirds are exactly what is needed to hover in front of flowers and then to back away after a meal of nectar. When flushed, partridges flutter with their round wings and briefly drop down.

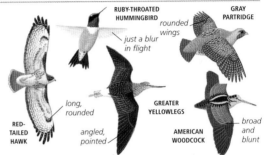

RUBY-THROATED HUMMINGBIRD — *just a blur in flight*

GRAY PARTRIDGE — *rounded wings*

RED-TAILED HAWK — *long, rounded*

angled, pointed

GREATER YELLOWLEGS

AMERICAN WOODCOCK — *broad and blunt*

TAIL SHAPE

It is not clear why some songbirds, like the American Goldfinch, have a notched tail while other similarly sized birds do not. Tail shapes vary as much as wing shapes, but are not so easily linked to a function. Irrespective of shape, tails are needed for balance. In some birds, tail shape, color, and pattern are used in courtship displays or in defensive displays when threatened.

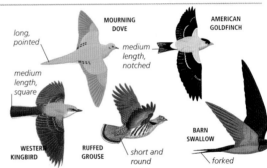

MOURNING DOVE — *long, pointed*

AMERICAN GOLDFINCH — *medium length, notched*

medium length, square

WESTERN KINGBIRD

RUFFED GROUSE — *short and round*

BARN SWALLOW — *forked*

COLORS AND MARKINGS

Melanin and carotenoid pigments determine color. Gray and brown birds have melanin (under hormonal influence), yellow and red ones have carotenoid (derived from food). House Finches are reddish because they eat a carotenoid-rich diet. Diversity in color and markings also results from scattering of white light by feathers (producing blue colors) and optical interference (iridescence) due to the structural properties of some feathers.

BALTIMORE ORIOLE — *orange-yellow shoulder patch*

BLACK AND WHITE WARBLER — *black-and-white streaks*

WOOD THRUSH — *black spots*

WHITE-CROWNED SPARROW — *black-and-white head pattern*

BARRED OWL — *streaking on belly*

BLUE-HEADED VIREO — *white eye-ring*

SPECIES GUIDE

DUCKS, GEESE, AND SWANS

RECENT SCIENTIFIC studies indicate that waterfowl are closely related to gamebirds. Most species of waterfowl molt all their flight feathers at once after breeding, making them flightless for several weeks until they grow new ones.

feeding, a swan stretches its long neck to reach water plants at the bottom, submerging up to half its body as it does so. The Trumpeter Swan is North America's largest native waterfowl, growing up to 6ft (1.8m) long, and weighing up to 30lb (13.6kg).

GEESE

Ornithologists group geese and swans together into the subfamily Anserinae. Intermediate in body size and neck length between swans and ducks, geese are more terrestrial than either, often being seen grazing on dry land. Like swans, geese tend to mate for life, but do occasionally divorce. They are also highly social, and most species are migratory, flying south for the winter in large flocks.

SWANS

Swans are essentially large, long-necked geese. Their heavier weight makes them ungainly on land, and they tend to be more aquatic than their smaller relatives. On water, however, they are extremely graceful. When

DUCKS

Classified in their own subfamily, called the Anatinae, ducks are more varied than swans or geese, with many more species. They are loosely grouped by their feeding habits. Dabblers, or puddle ducks, such as the Mallard, teals, and wigeons, eat plants and other edible matter like

INSTANT TAKEOFF
Puddle ducks like the Mallard can shoot out of the water and into the air.

snails. They feed by upending on the surface of shallow water. By contrast, diving ducks, a group that includes scaups, scoters, eiders, mergansers, and the Ruddy Duck, dive deep underwater for their food.

GAGGLING GEESE
Gregarious Snow Geese form large, noisy flocks during migration and on winter feeding grounds.

Order **Anseriformes**	Family **Anatidae**	Species *Anser caerulescens*

Snow Goose

dark flight feathers

gray bill

ADULT (BLUE)

gray upperparts

blackish brown back

pale wing feathers

elongated, white head

long neck

black patch on long bill

gray wing patch

gray legs and feet

pale underparts

IMMATURE (BLUE FORM)

dark belly

ADULT (BLUE FORM)

ADULT (WHITE)

white upperparts

IN FLIGHT

gray-brown all over

IMMATURE (WHITE FORM)

grayish legs

ADULT (WHITE FORM)

pink legs

FLIGHT: direct, strong flight with moderate wing beats in either V-shaped or bunched flocks.

The abundant Snow Goose has two subspecies. The "Greater" (*A. c. atlantica*) is slightly larger and breeds further east. The smaller "Lesser" (*A. c. caerulescens*) breeds further west. Snow Geese have two color forms—white and "blue" (actually dark grayish brown with a white head), and there are also intermediate forms.

VOICE Basic a call nasal *whouk, kowk,* or *kow-luk,* also higher-pitched *heenk*; feeding call a series of *hu-hu-hur.*

NESTING Scrapes on hummock, lined with plant material and down; 2–6 eggs; 1 brood; May–July.

FEEDING Grazes on aquatic and terrestrial vegetation, including stems, seeds, leaves, tubers, and roots; also grain and young leaves in agricultural fields in winter.

TOUCHING DOWN
Snow Geese are well known for migrating in flocks that number in tens of thousands.

OCCURRENCE
Breeding colonies in High Arctic from Wrangel Island in the West to Greenland in the East; a population of "lesser" Snow Geese breeds near Hudson Bay. Winters along interior valleys westward to coastal lowlands and central plateau of Mexico; Atlantic populations winter in coastal marshes.

SIMILAR SPECIES

GREATER WHITE-FRONTED GOOSE
see p.26

dark head and neck

barred underparts

ROSS'S GOOSE
see p.25

white forehead

shorter bill

much smaller overall

Length **27–33in (69–83cm)**	Wingspan **4¼–5½ft (1.3–1.7m)**	Weight **3¾–6½lb (1.7–3kg)**
Social **Flocks**	Lifespan **Up to 27 years**	Status **Secure**

DATE: _____ TIME:_____ LOCATION:_____

| Order **Anseriformes** | Family **Anatidae** | Species *Anser rossii* |

Ross's Goose

ADULT (WHITE)
black wing tips

light gray crown

dusky line through eye

gray wash on upperparts

round head

short, triangular bill

short, deeply furrowed neck

IN FLIGHT

IMMATURE (WHITE FORM)

clean white upperparts

mostly dark brown upperparts

white rump and tail

ADULT (BLUE FORM)

ADULT (WHITE FORM)

reddish pink legs

FLIGHT: strong and direct, with rapid wing beats.

T his diminutive white goose is not much bigger than a Mallard, and half the weight of a Snow Goose; like its larger relative, it also has a rare "blue" form. About 95 percent of Ross's Geese once nested at a single sanctuary in Arctic Canada, and breeding pairs have spread eastwards along Hudson Bay and at several island locations. Hunting reduced the population to just 6,000 in the early 1950s, but since then the numbers have increased to around 2 million individuals.

VOICE Call a *keek keek keeek*, higher-pitched than Snow Goose; also a harsh, low *kork* or *kowk*; quiet when feeding.

NESTING Plant materials placed on ground, usually in colonies with Lesser Snow Geese; 3–5 eggs; 1 brood; June–August.

FEEDING Grazes on grasses, sedges, and small grains.

TRAVELING IN FAMILIES
Family groups migrate thousands of miles together, usually from northern Canada to central California.

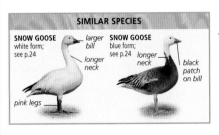

SIMILAR SPECIES

SNOW GOOSE
white form;
see p.24

larger bill

longer neck

pink legs

SNOW GOOSE
blue form;
see p.24

longer neck

black patch on bill

OCCURRENCE
Breeding grounds are amidst tundra in a number of scattered, High Arctic locations. Main wintering areas in California. On the wintering grounds, it feeds in agricultural fields, and also grasslands. Roosts overnight in several types of wetlands.

| Length **22½–25in (57–64cm)** | Wingspan **3¼ft (1.1m)** | Weight **1¾–4½lb (0.85–2kg)** |
| Social **Flocks** | Lifespan **Up to 21 years** | Status **Localized** |

DATE: _____ TIME: _____ LOCATION: _____

| Order **Anseriformes** | Family **Anatidae** | Species *Anser albifrons* |

Greater White-fronted Goose

gray wing feathers

ADULT

white rump band

IN FLIGHT

white tip to tail

pink bill with white base

brownish gray head

white flank streak

darker chocolate-brown upperparts

dull yellowish orange bill

brown underparts with black bands

larger body

longer legs, bill, and neck

bright orange legs

MALE
A. a. frontalis (TUNDRA)

A. a gambeli (TULE)

no belly barring

JUVENILE

The Greater White-fronted Goose is the most widespread goose in the Northern Hemisphere. It is easily distinguished by its black-barred belly and the patch of white at the base of its bill. There are five subspecies, two of which are most commonly seen in North America. The "Tundra" (*A. a. frontalis*), makes up the largest population, breeding across northwestern Canada and western Alaska. The "Tule" (*A. a. gambeli*), while the largest in stature, occurs in the fewest numbers, and is restricted in range to northwest Canada.

VOICE Laugh-like *klow-yo* or *klew-yo-yo*; very musical in a flock.

NESTING Bowl-shaped nest made of plant material, lined with down, constructed near water; 3–7 eggs; 1 brood; May–August.

FEEDING Eats sedges, grasses, berries, and plants on both land and water in summer; feeds on grasses, seeds, and grains in winter.

FLIGHT: strong, direct flight; flies alone, in multiple lines, or in a V-formation.

FLIGHT FORMATIONS
This heavy-bodied, powerful flier can often be seen in tightly packed flocks.

SIMILAR SPECIES

CANADA GOOSE
see p.29

black head, neck, and bill

white chin strap

HEAVY GRAZER
Grass is the major component of this goose's diet.

OCCURRENCE
Different habitats are utilized, both for breeding and wintering. Nesting areas include tundra ponds and lakes, dry rocky fields, and grassy slopes in Alaska and northern Canada. In winter, coastal marshes, inland wetlands, agricultural fields, and refuges are used along Pacific Coast, southern US, and Mexico.

Length **25–32in (64–81cm)**	Wingspan **4¼–5¼ft (1.3–1.6m)**	Weight **4–6½lb (1.8–3kg)**
Social **Flocks**	Lifespan **Up to 22 years**	Status **Secure**

DATE: _____ TIME:_____ LOCATION:_____

| Order **Anseriformes** | Family **Anatidae** | Species *Branta bernicla* |

Brant

pale bars across wings

ADULT (WESTERN)

ADULT (EASTERN)

white rump

black neck and head

IN FLIGHT

grayish white flank patch

bold, white rump

small, white "necklace" not crossing throat

barred flanks with pale belly

black neck stops abruptly at breast

broad white necklace crosses throat

dark gray-brown upperparts

black chest

bold, barred flanks

very dark belly

ADULT
B. b. nigricans
(WESTERN)

***B. b. hrota* (EASTERN)**

A small-billed, dark, stocky sea goose, the Brant winters on both the east and west coasts of North America. There are two subspecies named in North America—the pale-bellied "Atlantic" Brant (*B. b. hrota*), found in the east, and the darker "Black" Brant (*B. b. nigricans*), found in the west; an intermediate gray-bellied form, not yet named, breeds in the Canadian archipelago and winters in Boundary Bay, British Columbia. Unlike other North American geese, the Brant feeds mainly on eelgrass in winter.

VOICE Nasal *cruk*, harsh-sounding in tone; rolling series of *cut cut cut cronk*, with an upward inflection at end.

NESTING Scrape lined with grass, plant matter, and down on islands or gravel spits; 3–5 eggs; 1 brood; May–July.

FEEDING Eats grass and sedges when nesting; eelgrass in winter; also green algae, salt marsh plants, and mollusks.

FLIGHT: rapid and strong; low, irregular flight formations.

GRASSY MEAL
In winter, Brants forage almost exclusively on eelgrass between the high and low tide marks.

OCCURRENCE
Breeds in colonies in northern Canada and Alaska, and winters along both Pacific and Atlantic coasts. The western breeding population of the Brant ("Black") winters from the Aleutian Islands to northern Mexico, while the pale-bellied form ("Atlantic") is restricted in range to the East Coast.

SIMILAR SPECIES

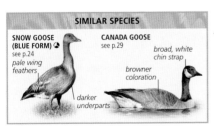

SNOW GOOSE (BLUE FORM) ☻
see p.24
pale wing feathers

darker underparts

CANADA GOOSE
see p.29
broad, white chin strap

browner coloration

| Length **22–26in (56–66cm)** | Wingspan **3½–4ft (1.1–1.2m)** | Weight **2½–4lb (1–1.8kg)** |
| Social **Flocks** | Lifespan **Up to 25 years** | Status **Secure** |

| Order **Anseriformes** | Family **Anatidae** | Species **Branta hutchinsii** |

Cackling Goose

plain grayish
brown wings

ADULT

small, black
head

white "u"-shaped patch on rump   **IN FLIGHT**

black tail

broad, white
neck ring

black line
separates white
chin strap

darker breast

ADULT
B. h. leucopareia

dark
brown
breast

ADULT
B. h. minima

small
stubby
bill

white
chin
strap

no black
under
chin

pale
breast

ADULT
B. h. hutchinsii

The Cackling Goose has recently been split from the Canada Goose; it can be distinguished from the latter by its short stubby bill, steep forehead, and short neck. There are four subspecies of Cackling Goose, which vary in breast color, ranging from dark on *B. h. minima,* and fairly dark on *B. h. leucopareia,* to pale on *B. h. hutchinsii.* The Cackling Goose is much smaller than all subspecies of Canada Goose, except the "Lesser" Canada Goose, which has a longer neck and a less sloped forehead.
VOICE Male call a *honk* or *bark;* females have higher pitched *hrink;* also high-pitched yelps.
NESTING Scrape lined with available plant matter and down; 2–8 eggs; 1 brood; May–August.
FEEDING Consumes plants in summer; in winter, grazes on grass in livestock and dairy pastures; also in agricultural fields.

FLIGHT: strong with rapid wing beats; flies in bunched V–formations.

LITTLE GEESE
Cackling Geese are tiny when seen together with the larger Canada Goose.

SIMILAR SPECIES

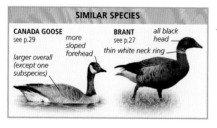

CANADA GOOSE
see p.29

more
sloped
forehead

larger overall
(except one
subspecies)

BRANT
see p.27

all black
head

thin white neck ring

OCCURRENCE
At the northernmost fringe of the Canada Goose's range, in the tundra, it breeds on rocky tundra slopes from the Aleutians east to Baffin Island and Hudson Bay. Winters from British Columbia to California, also central US, Texas, and New Mexico in pastures and agricultural fields.

| Length **21½–30in (55–75cm)** | Wingspan **4¼–5ft (1.3–1.5m)** | Weight **2–6½lb (0.9–3kg)** |
| Social **Flocks** | Lifespan **Unknown** | Status **Secure** |

DATE: _____ TIME: _____ LOCATION: _____

| Order **Anseriformes** | Family **Anatidae** | Species *Branta canadensis* |

Canada Goose

plain grayish brown wings with darker flight feathers

ADULT

IN FLIGHT

white u-shaped patch on rump

very long neck

black head

grayish brown upperparts and sides

broad white chin strap

paler upper breast

white undertail feathers

ADULT

smaller, white chin strap

dark brown overall

ADULT

ADULT

The Canada Goose is the most common, widespread, and familiar goose in North America. Given its colossal range, it is not surprising that the Canada Goose has much geographic variation, and 12 subspecies have been recognized. With the exception of the Cackling Goose, from which it has recently been separated, it is difficult to confuse it, with its distinctive white chin strap, black head and neck, and grayish brown body, with any other species of goose. It is a monogamous species, and once pairs are formed, they stay together for life.

VOICE Males mostly *honk* or *bark*; females have high pitched *hrink*.
NESTING Scrape lined with available plant matter and down, near water; 1–2 broods; 2–12 eggs; May–August.
FEEDING Grazes on grasses, sedges, leaves, seeds, agricultural crops and berries; also insects.

FLIGHT: strong and direct with fairly slow, deep wing beats; often flies in V-formation.

TRICK OF THE LIGHT
A low sun can play tricks—these birds are actually pale grayish underneath.

OCCURRENCE
Variety of inland breeding habitats near water, including grassy urban areas, marshes, prairie, parkland, coastal temperate forest, northern coniferous forest, and Arctic tundra. Winters in agricultural fields, mudflats, saltwater marshes, lakes, and rivers.

SIMILAR SPECIES

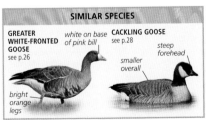

GREATER WHITE-FRONTED GOOSE see p.26

white on base of pink bill

bright orange legs

CACKLING GOOSE see p.28

steep forehead

smaller overall

Length **2¼–3½ft (0.7–1.1m)**	Wingspan **4¼–5½ft (1.3–1.7m)**	Weight **6½–9¾lb (3–4.4kg)**
Social **Flocks**	Lifespan **Up to 25 years**	Status **Secure**

DATE: _____ TIME: _____ LOCATION: _____

Order **Anseriformes**	Family **Anatidae**	Species **Cygnus olor**

Mute Swan

ADULT

extended neck

IN FLIGHT

long, pointed tail extends past toes

black-based dusky bill

blotchy brown body

JUVENILE

white overall

small knob on bill

FEMALE

swollen knob during breeding

MALE

conspicuous black knob at base of orange bill

long, "S" shaped neck

ADULT

often arches wings over back

large, heavy body

One of the heaviest birds in North America, the Mute Swan was introduced from Europe due to its graceful appearance on water, if not on land, and easy domestication. However, this is an extremely territorial and aggressive bird. When threatened, it points its bill downwards, arches its wings, hisses, and then attacks. Displacement of native waterfowl species and overgrazing by this species have led to efforts to reduce its numbers in North America.

VOICE Not mute; hisses, grunts, snorts, and snores; during courtship, trumpets, although more quietly than other swans.
NESTING Platform nest of plant materials, built on ground near water; 4–8 eggs; 1–2 broods; March–October.
FEEDING Dabbles, dips, and upends, mainly for underwater plants, but occasionally for small creatures too.

FLIGHT: strong, steady wing beats; creating a distinctive whirring and throbbing sound.

FORMATION FLYING
Groups of Mute Swans will sometimes fly in a line, and at other times, as here, they will arrange themselves in a "V" formation.

SIMILAR SPECIES

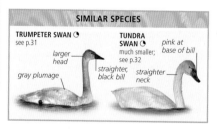

TRUMPETER SWAN ◑
see p.31

larger head

gray plumage

TUNDRA SWAN ◑
much smaller; see p.32

pink at base of bill

straighter, black bill

straighter neck

OCCURRENCE
Bulk of population is found along the Atlantic Coast from Maine to North Carolina; smaller populations around the Great Lakes and southern British Columbia. Breeds and lives year-round on sluggish rivers, ponds, or lakes, preferring still water with emergent vegetation.

Length **4–5ft (1.2–1.5m)**	Wingspan **6¹⁄₂–7¹⁄₂ft (2–2.3m)**	Weight **12–32lb (5.5–14.5kg)**
Social **Pairs/Family groups**	Lifespan **Up to 21 years**	Status **Localized**

DATE: _____ TIME:_____ LOCATION:_____

| Order **Anseriformes** | Family **Anatidae** | Species **Cygnus buccinator** |

Trumpeter Swan

huge wingspan

ADULT

long neck

IN FLIGHT

gray plumage; retained until late spring

JUVENILE

mostly black bill

eye blends in with black facial skin

elongated head

straight, black bill

neck usually straight

all-white plumage

ADULT

Northern America's quintessential swan and heaviest waterfowl, the Trumpeter Swan is a magnificent sight to behold. This species has made a remarkable comeback after numbers were severely reduced by hunting in the 1600–1800s; by the mid-1930s, fewer than a hundred were known to exist. Active reintroduction efforts were made in the upper Midwest and Ontario to re-establish the species to its former breeding range. The Trumpeter Swan's characteristic far-reaching call is usually the best way to identify it.

VOICE Call nasal, resonant *oh-OH* reminiscent of French horn.
NESTING Large mound made of plant matter on raised areas near or in freshwater; 3–6 eggs; 1 brood; April–September.
FEEDING Eats algae and aquatic plants, including moss, at or below the surface; feeds on grain in pastures and fields.

FLIGHT: slow, heavy, ponderous wing beats; "runs" on water's surface when taking off.

RUSTY STAINING
Trumpeter Swans often have rufous-stained heads and necks due to probing in iron-rich mud.

OCCURRENCE
Alaskan and northern Canadian breeders go south to winter; others remain year-round at local places such as Yellowstone National Park. Found on freshwater lakes and marshes with plenty of vegetation on which to feed. Also found on estuaries in winter.

MUTE SWAN ☾ see p.30

TUNDRA SWAN see p.32

SIMILAR SPECIES

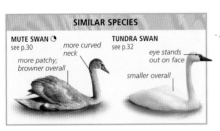

more curved neck

more patchy; browner overall

eye stands out on face

smaller overall

| Length **4¼–5ft (1.3–1.5m)** | Wingspan **6½ft (2m)** | Weight **17–28lb (7.5–12.5kg)** |
| Social **Flocks** | Lifespan **Up to 24 years** | Status **Secure** |

DATE: _____ TIME:_____ LOCATION:_____

Order **Anseriformes**	Family **Anatidae**	Species ***Cygnus columbianus***

Tundra Swan

ADULT

small head
and bill

fairly thick
neck

dark
legs **IN FLIGHT**

dull grayish
body

dirty
pink bill

JUVENILE

eye stands out
from face at
close range

yellow
facial skin
next to eye

large
yellow
bill patch

BEWICK'S SWAN

all-white
plumage

ADULT

Nesting in the Arctic tundra, this well-named species is North America's most widespread and smallest swan. Two populations exist, with one wintering in the West, and the other along the East Coast. The Tundra Swan can be confused with the Trumpeter Swan, but their different calls immediately distinguish the two species. When they are silent, weight and bill structure are the best way to tell them apart. In Eurasia, this species is known as Bewick's Swan and possesses a larger yellow patch at the base of its bill.

VOICE Clear, high-pitched yodelling *whoo-hooo* calls mixed with garbles, yelping, and barking sounds.

NESTING Mound-shaped nest made of plant matter near water; 3–6 eggs; 1 brood; May–September.

FEEDING Eats aquatic vegetation, insects, mollusks; also grain.

FLIGHT: flight pattern like that of other swans but with slightly faster wing beats.

LARGE WINTER FLOCKS
Its size, white plumage, and flocking habits make the Tundra Swan a conspicuous species.

SIMILAR SPECIES

MUTE SWAN ↻
see p.30

pointed
tail

heavier
bodied

TRUMPETER SWAN
see p.31

all-black bill

more
curved
neck

straighter
edge from
eye to bill

OCCURRENCE
Nests around lakes and pools in northern tundra from the Aleutians to the Yukon, and east to northwest Quebec. Winters in southern British Columbia, western US, and mid-Atlantic states, mostly New Jersey to south Carolina. Winter habitat includes shallow coastal bays, ponds, and lakes.

Length **4–5ft (1.2–1.5m)**	Wingspan **6¼–7¼ft (1.9–2.2m)**	Weight **12–18lb (5.5–8kg)**
Social **Flocks**	Lifespan **Up to 21 years**	Status **Secure**

DATE: _____ TIME: _____ LOCATION: _____

Order **Anseriformes**	Family **Anatidae**	Species *Aix sponsa*

Wood Duck

MALE
blue wing patch
long wings
IN FLIGHT
head held high

bold, tear-shaped eye-ring
smaller crest
brownish breast
white-edged feathers
FEMALE

brown eye
subdued facial pattern
grayish bill
IMMATURE

red eye
complex, white facial markings
helmet-like head profile

burgundy flanks
black tip of bill

long, dark tail
MALE

white-flecked maroon breast appears black at a distance

white, vertical breast stripe

The male Wood Duck is perhaps the most striking of all North American ducks. With its bright plumage, red eye and bill, and its long sleek crest that gives its head a helmet-shaped profile, the male is unmistakable. It is related to the Mandarin Duck of Asia. The Wood Duck is very dependent on mature swampy forestland, and is typically found on swamps, shallow lakes, ponds, and park settings that are surrounded by trees. Although it adapts to human activity, it is quite shy. When swimming, the Wood Duck can be seen jerking its head front to back. Of all waterfowl, this is the only species that regularly raises two broods each season.

VOICE Male gives a wheezy upslurred whistle *zweeet*; female's call a double-note, rising *oh-eek oh-eek*.

NESTING Nests in natural tree cavities or nest boxes in close proximity to water; 10–13 eggs; 2 broods; April–August.

FEEDING Forages for seeds, tree fruit, and small acorns; also spiders, insects, and crustaceans.

FLIGHT: rapid flight with deep wing beats; flies with head up; leaps straight off the water.

PLAIN BELLY
Wings raised, a male reveals one of the only plain areas of its plumage—its pale belly and undertail.

OCCURRENCE
Usually found throughout the year, along rivers, streams, and creeks, in swamps, and marshy areas. Has a preference for permanent bodies of water. If good aquatic feeding areas are unavailable, the Wood Duck feeds in open areas, including agricultural fields.

SIMILAR SPECIES

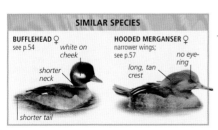

BUFFLEHEAD ♀
see p.54
white on cheek
shorter neck
shorter tail

HOODED MERGANSER ♀
narrower wings;
see p.57
long, tan crest
no eye-ring

Length **18½–21½in (47–54cm)**	Wingspan **26–29in (66–73cm)**	Weight **16–30oz (450–850g)**
Social **Small flocks**	Lifespan **Up to 18 years**	Status **Secure**

DATE: _____ TIME: _____ LOCATION: _____

| Order **Anseriformes** | Family **Anatidae** | Species **Spatula discors** |

Blue-winged Teal

powdery blue forewing
with green patch

**MALE
(BREEDING)**

white facial
crescent

white
underwing
stripe

IN FLIGHT

broken,
contrasting,
white eye-ring

grayish brown
overall

pale eyebrow,
dark cape,
and eye-line

FEMALE

pale spot
at base
of bill

white facial
crescent

dark grayish
head

black
bill

MALE (FALL)

black spots
on rich, buff-
brown breast
and flanks

white facial
crescent

long,
blackish
bill

rich tan
flanks

warmer
brown overall

**MALE
(BREEDING)**

conspicuous
white patch

This small dabbling duck is a common and widespread North American breeding species. With a bold white crescent between bill and eye on its otherwise slate-gray head and neck, the male Blue-winged Teal is quite distinctive. The Blue-winged and Cinnamon Teals, along with the Northern Shoveler, constitute the three "blue-winged" ducks; this is a conspicuous feature when the birds are flying. The Cinnamon and the Blue-winged Teals are almost identical genetically and interbreed to form hybrids. The Blue-winged Teal winters mostly south of the US and migrates north in spring.

VOICE Male a high-pitched, raspy *peew* or low-pitched *paay* during courtship; female a loud single *quack*.

NESTING Bowl-shaped depression lined with grasses, close to water's edge, in meadows; 6–14 eggs; 1 brood; April–September.

FEEDING Eats seeds of a variety of plants; feeds heavily on insect larvae, crustaceans, and snails, when breeding.

FLIGHT: fast, twisting flight; flies in compact, small groups.

OUTSTRETCHED WING
Wing stretch behavior shows the white feathers between the blue forewing and green rearwing.

SIMILAR SPECIES		

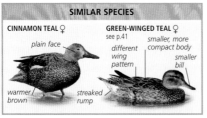

CINNAMON TEAL ♀

plain face

warmer
brown

GREEN-WINGED TEAL ♀
see p.41

different
wing
pattern

smaller, more
compact body

smaller
bill

streaked
rump

OCCURRENCE
Nests across North America, with highest numbers in the prairie and parkland regions of the midcontinent. Prefers shallow ponds or marshes during nesting; freshwater to brackish water and (less so) saltwater marshes during migration. In winter, prefers saline environments, including mangroves.

Length **14½–16in (37–41cm)**	Wingspan **23½–25in (60–64cm)**	Weight **11–18oz (300–500g)**
Social **Flocks**	Lifespan **Up to 17 years**	Status **Secure**

DATE: _____ TIME: _____ LOCATION: _____

Order **Anseriformes**	Family **Anatidae**	Species *Spatula clypeata*

Northern Shoveler

IN FLIGHT

grayish blue wing patch

pale blue wing patch

whitish tail

FEMALE

long bill

MALE

heavy fronted

dark green head

dark, narrow eye-line

brown overall

dusky olive-gray to orange bill

pale-edged, brown flank feathers

FEMALE

yellow eye

large, dark spatula-shaped bill

MALE

white breast

chestnut belly and flanks

black-and-white rump

The Northern Shoveler is a common, medium-sized, dabbling duck found in North America and Eurasia. It is monogamous—pairs remain together longer than any other dabbler species. Its distinctive long bill is highly specialized; it is wider at the tip and contains thin, comb-like structures (called "lamellae") along the sides, used to filter food items from the water. Shovelers often form tight feeding groups, swimming close together as they sieve the water for prey.

VOICE Male call a nasal, muffled *thuk thuk…thuk thuk*; also a loud, nasal *paaaay*; female call a variety of *quacks*, singly or in a series of 4–5 descending notes.

NESTING Scrape lined with plant matter and down, in short plants, near water; 6–19 eggs; 1 brood; May–August.

FEEDING Forages for seeds; filters small crustaceans and mollusks out of the water.

FLIGHT: strong direct flight; male's wings make a rattling noise when taking off.

UPSIDE DOWN FEEDER
This male upends to feed below the water's surface, revealing his orange legs.

FILTER FEEDING
Their bills open, these ducks sieve small invertebrates from the water.

OCCURRENCE
Widespread across North America, south of the tundra. Breeds in a variety of wetlands, in edges of shallow pools with nearby tall and short grasslands. Occurs in fresh- and saltmarshes, ponds, and other shallow bodies of water in winter; does not feed on land.

SIMILAR SPECIES

MALLARD ♀
larger; see p.38

darker blue wing patch

CINNAMON TEAL ♀

slimmer bill

plainer plumage

plainer face

longer tail

Length **17½–20in (44–51cm)**	Wingspan **27–33in (69–84cm)**	Weight **14–29oz (400–825g)**
Social **Flocks**	Lifespan **Up to 18 years**	Status **Secure**

DATE: _____ TIME: _____ LOCATION: _____

Order **Anseriformes**	Family **Anatidae**	Species *Mareca strepera*

Gadwall

conspicuous white patch

mostly white underwings

MALE (WINTER)

white belly

IN FLIGHT

silvery gray area

rusty sides

MALE (ECLIPSE)

brown, scalloped back

dark eyestripe

white wing patch

FEMALE

brown, rounded head

dark grayish overall

black bill

black uppertail

MALE (WINTER)

orange-yellow legs

finely patterned gray flanks and breast

Although the Gadwall's appearance is somewhat somber, many birders consider this duck one of North America's most elegant species because of the subtlety of its plumage. Despite being common and widespread, Gadwalls are often overlooked because of their retiring behavior and relatively quiet vocalizations. This dabbling duck is slightly smaller and more delicate than the Mallard, yet female Gadwalls are often mistaken for female Mallards. Gadwalls associate with other species, especially in winter.

VOICE Low, raspy *meep* or *reb* given in quick succession; female *quack* similar to that of female Mallard, but higher-pitched and more nasal; high-pitched *peep*, or *pe-peep*; both sexes give *tickety-tickety-tickety* chatter while feeding.

NESTING Bowl nest made of plant material in a scrape; 8–12 eggs; 1 brood; April–August.

FEEDING Dabbles on the surface or below for seeds, aquatic vegetation, and invertebrates, including mollusks and insects.

FLIGHT: direct flight with fast wing beats; leaps straight off the water.

BROOD ON THE MOVE
Females lead their ducklings from their nest to a brood-rearing habitat that provides cover and ample food for the ducklings to forage.

SIMILAR SPECIES

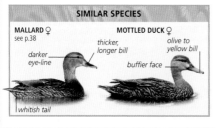

MALLARD ♀
see p.38

darker eye-line

thicker, longer bill

whitish tail

MOTTLED DUCK ♀

olive to yellow bill

buffier face

OCCURRENCE
From the western prairie pothole country of Canada and the northern US, the Gadwall's range has expanded as it has adapted to man-made bodies of water, such as reservoirs and ponds. In winter, mostly found on lakes, marshes, and along rivers.

Length **18–22½in (46–57cm)**	Wingspan **33in (84cm)**	Weight **18–45oz (500–1,250g)**
Social **Winter flocks**	Lifespan **Up to 19 years**	Status **Secure**

DATE: _____ TIME:_____ LOCATION:_____

Order **Anseriformes**	Family **Anatidae**	Species *Mareca americana*

American Wigeon

MALE (BREEDING)

white underwing patch

gray head contrasts with pinkish brown breast and flanks

long, pointed tail

IN FLIGHT

rufous-edged wing feathers

dark smudge around eye

gray head

narrow, black line along bill

warm brown breast and flanks

FEMALE

cream forehead and crown

green band from eye to nape

black-tipped bill

MALE (BREEDING)

black rump

pinkish brown flanks

Often found in mixed flocks with other ducks, the American Wigeon is a common and widespread, medium-sized dabbling duck. This bird is an opportunist that loiters around other diving ducks and coots, feeding on the vegetation they dislodge. It is more social during migration and in the nonbreeding season than when breeding.

VOICE Slow and fast whistles; male's most common call a slow, high-pitched, wheezy, three-syllable *whew-whew-whew*, with middle note loudest; also, a faster *whee* whistle.

NESTING Depression lined with plant material and down, usually in tall grass away from water; 5–10 eggs; 1 brood; May–August.

FEEDING Grazes on grass, clover, algae, and in agricultural fields; feeds on many seeds, insects, mollusks, and crustaceans during the breeding season.

FLIGHT: rapid, fairly deep wing beats; leaps almost vertically off the water.

COMING IN FOR A LANDING
This male's cream-colored forehead is clearly visible, as is the sharp contrast between the white belly, and the pinkish breast and flanks.

FLAPPING WINGS
This bird has a white patch on its underwing, while the Eurasian Wigeon has a gray patch.

OCCURRENCE
The northernmost breeder of the dabbling ducks, occurs from Alaska to the Maritimes. Prefers pothole and grassland habitats; found almost anywhere near water in winter. Winters south to northern South America and the Caribbean, in freshwater and coastal bay habitats.

SIMILAR SPECIES

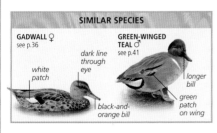

GADWALL ♀
see p.36

white patch

GREEN-WINGED TEAL ♂
see p.41

dark line through eye

longer bill

green patch on wing

black-and-orange bill

Length **17½–23in (45–58cm)**	Wingspan **33in (84cm)**	Weight **1⅛–3lb (0.5–1.3kg)**
Social **Flocks**	Lifespan **Up to 21 years**	Status **Secure**

DATE: _____ TIME: _____ LOCATION: _____

| Order **Anseriformes** | Family **Anatidae** | Species *Anas platyrhynchos* |

Mallard

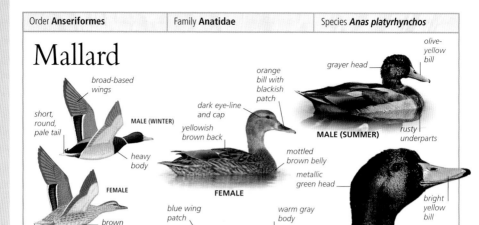

broad-based wings

short, round, pale tail

MALE (WINTER)

heavy body

FEMALE

orange bill with blackish patch

dark eye-line and cap

yellowish brown back

olive-yellow bill

grayer head

MALE (SUMMER)

rusty underparts

mottled brown belly

metallic green head

blue wing patch

warm gray body

bright yellow bill

narrow, white neck collar

brown underparts

IN FLIGHT

whitish outer tail feathers

short, black curls above white tail

MALE (WINTER)

chestnut-brown breast

The Mallard is perhaps the most familiar of all ducks, and occurs in the wild all across the Northern Hemisphere. It is the ancestor of most domestic ducks, and hybrids between the wild and domestic forms are frequently seen in city lakes and ponds, often with patches of white on the breast. Mating is generally a violent affair, but outside the breeding season the wild species is strongly migratory and gregarious, sometimes forming large flocks that may join with other species.
VOICE Male's call a quiet raspy *raab*; during courtship a high-pitched whistle; female call a *quack* or repeated in series.
NESTING Scrape lined with plant matter, usually near water, often on floating vegetation; 6–15 eggs; 1 brood; February–September.
FEEDING Feeds omnivorously on insects, crustaceans, mollusks, and earthworms when breeding; otherwise largely vegetarian; takes seeds, acorns, agricultural crops, aquatic vegetation, and bread.

FLIGHT: fast, shallow, and regular; often flies in groups.

STICKING TOGETHER
The mother leads her ducklings to water soon after they hatch. She looks after them until they can fend for themselves.

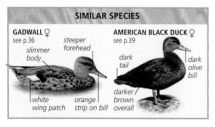

SIMILAR SPECIES

GADWALL ♀
see p.36

slimmer body

steeper forehead

white wing patch

orange strip on bill

AMERICAN BLACK DUCK ♀
see p.39

dark tail

dark olive bill

darker brown overall

OCCURRENCE
Occurs throughout the region, choosing shallow water in natural wetlands, such as marshes, prairie potholes, ponds, and ditches; can also be found in man-made habitats such as city parks and reservoirs, preferring more open habitats in winter.

| Length **19½–26in (50–65cm)** | Wingspan **32–37in (82–95cm)** | Weight **1⅞–3lb (0.9–1.4kg)** |
| Social **Flocks** | Lifespan **Up to 29 years** | Status **Secure** |

DATE: _____ TIME:_____ LOCATION:_____

| Order **Anseriformes** | Family **Anatidae** | Species *Anas rubripes* |

American Black Duck

rich violet patch

white underwing

MALE

dark tail **IN FLIGHT**

heavily streaked head and neck

olive bill

FEMALE

cinnamon-edged flank feathers

dark cap

pale head

narrow, dark eye-line

greenish yellow bill

dark body

MALE

The American Black Duck, a large dabbling duck, is closely related to the Mallard. In the past, the two species were separated by different habitat preferences—the American Black Duck preferring forested locations, and the Mallard favoring more open habitats. Over the years, these habitats became less distinct as the East was deforested and trees were planted in the Midwest. As a result, there are now many hybrids between the two species. It has also been argued that the introduction of Mallards to various areas in the East has further increased interbreeding. The American Black Duck breeds throughout a wide area in the northern part of its range. When breeding, males can be seen chasing away other males to maintain their territories.

VOICE Male's call a reedy *raeb*, given once or twice; female *quack* sounds very similar to Mallard.

NESTING Scrape lined with plant material and down, usually on ground or close to water; 4–10 eggs; 1 brood; March–September.

FEEDING An omnivore, the American Black Duck eats plant leaves and stems, roots, seeds, grains, fruit, aquatic plants, fish, and amphibians.

FLIGHT: fast, shallow, and regular; often flies in groups.

DARK PLUMAGE
This species is the darkest of all the Mallard-type ducks that occur in North America.

OCCURRENCE
Nests in eastern Canada and adjacent areas of the US in a variety of habitats including northerly and mixed hardwood forest, wooded uplands, bogs, salt- and freshwater marshes, and on islands. Resident in the central part of its range, but large numbers winter in saltwater marshes.

SIMILAR SPECIES

MALLARD ♀
see p.38

orange bill

whitish tail

paler body

MOTTLED DUCK ♀

mottled brown upperparts

unstreaked face

| Length **21½–23in (54–59cm)** | Wingspan **35–37in (88–95cm)** | Weight **1½–3½lb (0.7–1.6kg)** |
| Social **Flocks** | Lifespan **Up to 26 years** | Status **Secure** |

DATE: _____ TIME:_____ LOCATION:_____

Order **Anseriformes**	Family **Anatidae**	Species *Anas acuta*

Northern Pintail

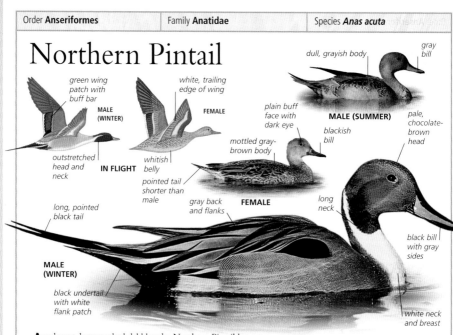

green wing patch with buff bar

MALE (WINTER)

white, trailing edge of wing

FEMALE

outstretched head and neck   **IN FLIGHT**

whitish belly

pointed tail shorter than male

long, pointed black tail

gray back and flanks   **FEMALE**

dull, grayish body

gray bill

plain buff face with dark eye

MALE (SUMMER)

blackish bill

pale, chocolate-brown head

mottled gray-brown body

long neck

white neck and breast

black bill with gray sides

MALE (WINTER)

black undertail with white flank patch

An elegant, long-necked dabbler, the Northern Pintail has extremely distinctive marking and a very long tail—in fact, the longest tail to be found on any freshwater duck. One of the earliest breeders in the year, these ducks begin nesting soon after the ice thaws. Northern Pintails were once one of the most abundant prairie breeding ducks. However, in recent decades, droughts, combined with the reduction of habitat on both their wintering and breeding grounds, have resulted in a significant decline in their population.

VOICE Male call a high-pitched rolling *prrreep prrreep;* lower-pitched wheezy *wheeeee,* which gets louder then drops off; female call a quiet, harsh *quack* or *kuk* singularly or as short series; also a loud *gaak,* often repeated.

NESTING Scrape lined with plant materials and down, usually in short grass, brush, or even in the open; 3–12 eggs; 1 brood; April–August.

FEEDING Feeds on grains, rice, seeds, aquatic weeds, insect larvae, crustaceans, and snails.

FLIGHT: fast, direct flight; can be very acrobatic in the air.

FEEDING TIME
Even when tipping up to feed, these pintails can be identified by their long, black, pointed tails.

SIMILAR SPECIES

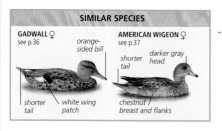

GADWALL ♀
see p.36

orange-sided bill

shorter tail   white wing patch

AMERICAN WIGEON ♀
see p.37

darker gray head

shorter tail

chestnut breast and flanks

OCCURRENCE
Widely distributed in North America; breeding in open country in shallow wetlands or meadows in mountainous forest regions. Found in tidal wetlands and saltwater habitats in migration and winter; dry harvested and flooded agricultural fields in autumn and winter.

Length **20–30in (51–76cm)**	Wingspan **35in (89cm)**	Weight **18–44oz (500–1250g)**
Social **Flocks**	Lifespan **Up to 21 years**	Status **Declining**

DATE: _____ TIME:_____ LOCATION:_____

| Order **Anseriformes** | Family **Anatidae** | Species *Anas crecca* |

Green-winged Teal

MALE
green-and-black patch on hindwing

short neck

IN FLIGHT   gray flanks

rufous head

horizontal, white line on sides

lacks white wing bar

dark green ear patch

small, narrow, black bill

A. c. crecca
(EURASIAN)

black-spotted breast

darker face

steeper forehead

white vertical bar

FEMALE

finely detailed pattern

shoulder feathers with narrow pale edge

weaker face pattern

yellowish buff undertail feathers

MALE

JUVENILE

The Green-winged Teal, the smallest North American dabbling duck, is slightly smaller than the Blue-winged and Cinnamon Teals, and lacks their blue wing patch. Its population is increasing, apparently because it breeds in more pristine habitats, and farther north, than the prairie ducks. The species has three subspecies, *A. c. crecca* (Eurasia), *A. c. carolinensis* (North America), and *A. c. nimia* (Aleutian Islands). *Carolinensis* males have a conspicuous vertical white bar, whereas Eurasian *crecca* males do not.

VOICE Male call a high-pitched, slightly rolling *crick crick*, similar to cricket; female call a quiet *quack*.

NESTING Shallow scrape on ground lined with nearby vegetation, often placed in dense vegetation near water; 6–9 eggs; 1 brood; April–September.

FEEDING Eats seeds, aquatic insects, crustaceans, and mollusks year-round; also feeds in grain fields in winter.

FLIGHT: fast flight; often flying in twisting, tight groups reminiscent of shorebird flocks.

SINGLE PARENT
The female duck is deserted by her partner during incubation, so she must provide all parental care.

SIMILAR SPECIES

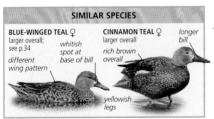

BLUE-WINGED TEAL ♀
larger overall;
see p.34

different wing pattern

whitish spot at base of bill

CINNAMON TEAL ♀
larger overall

rich brown overall

longer bill

yellowish legs

OCCURRENCE
Breeds north of the tree line in Alaska and Canada—around ponds in forest and deciduous woodlands. Prefers shallow wetlands with vegetation. In winter and migration, inland marshes, sloughs, agricultural fields, and coastal marshes. Winters south of the Caribbean and in southern Mexico.

Length **12–15½in (31–39cm)**	Wingspan **20½–23in (52–59cm)**	Weight **7–16oz (200–450g)**
Social **Flocks**	Lifespan **Up to 20 years**	Status **Secure**

| Order **Anseriformes** | Family **Anatidae** | Species *Aythya valisineria* |

Canvasback

light gray forewing

black rump and tail

MALE

belly appears white

long neck, held horizontally in flight

IN FLIGHT

dark with mottled gray patches

distinct white eye-ring

dingy brown underparts

IMMATURE

dingy brownish gray upperparts and sides

extended tear drop

FEMALE

brown breast

rich chestnut head and neck

white to pale gray back and flanks

black at both ends

high, peaked black crown

bright red eye

black breast

MALE

A large, elegant, long-billed diving duck, the Canvasback is a bird of prairie pothole country. Its specialized diet of aquatic plants has resulted in a smaller population than other ducks. With legs set toward the rear, it is an accomplished swimmer and diver, and is rarely seen on land. Weather conditions and brood parasitism by Redheads determine how successful the Canvasback's nesting is from year to year.
VOICE Mostly silent except during courtship when males make soft *cooing* noises; females emit a grating *krrrrr krrrrrr krrrrr*; females give loud *quack* when taking off; during winter, both sexes make soft wheezing series of *rrrr rrrr rrrr* sounds.
NESTING Platform over water built of woven vegetation; occasionally on shore; 8–11 eggs; 1 brood; April–September.
FEEDING Mainly eats aquatic tubers, buds, root stalks, and shoots, particularly those of wild celery; also eats snails when preferred plants are unavailable.

FLIGHT: direct strong flight; one of the fastest ducks; forms V-shaped flocks.

DEEP WATER
Canvasbacks prefer deeper-bodied waters that support the aquatic vegetation they eat.

SIMILAR SPECIES

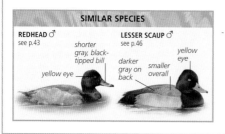

REDHEAD ♂
see p.43

shorter gray, black-tipped bill

yellow eye

LESSER SCAUP ♂
see p.46

yellow eye

darker gray on back

smaller overall

OCCURRENCE
Found in potholes, marshes, and ponds in prairie parkland, tundra; northerly forests preferred where their favorite foods grow. Winters in large numbers in large bays and lakes, and deltas, with smaller numbers scattered across North America and Mexico.

| Length **19–22in (48–56cm)** | Wingspan **31–35in (79–89cm)** | Weight **1¾–3½lb (0.8–1.6kg)** |
| Social **Flocks** | Lifespan **Up to 22 years** | Status **Secure** |

DATE: _____ TIME: _____ LOCATION: _____

| Order **Anseriformes** | Family **Anatidae** | Species *Aythya americana* |

Redhead

dark-gray forewing

MALE

brick-red head

black breast

IN FLIGHT

dark crown

tawny brown overall

gray bill with black tip

FEMALE

yellow eye

MALE (ECLIPSE)

white band

yellow eye

brick-red upper neck and head

long blue bill with black tip

medium-gray mantle and sides

black rump

black lower neck

MALE

The Redhead, a medium-sized diving duck belonging to the Pochard group, is native only to North America. Only when seen up close is it apparent that the male's seemingly gray upperparts and flanks are actually white, with dense, black, wavy markings. The Redhead often feeds at night and forages mostly around dusk and dawn, drifting during the day. It parasitizes other duck nests more than any other duck species, particularly those of the Canvasback and even other Redheads.

VOICE Male courtship call a wheezy rising then falling *whee ough*, also *meow*; female call a low, raspy *kurr kurr kurr*.

NESTING Weaves solid nest over water in dense vegetation such as cattails, lined with down; 7–14 eggs; 1 brood; May–September.

FEEDING Omnivorous; feeds on aquatic plants, seeds, tubers, algae, insects, spiders, fish eggs, snails, and insect larvae; diet is variable depending on location.

FLIGHT: direct flight; runs on water prior to takeoff.

MALE DISPLAY
This male is performing a spectacular courtship display called a head throw, while remaining otherwise completely still on the water.

EASY IDENTIFICATION
The long blue bill with a whitish band and black tip is clearly visible in males.

SIMILAR SPECIES

CANVASBACK ♀
see p.42
wedge-shaped black bill
grayish back

RING-NECKED DUCK ♀
see p.44
peaked head shape
dark-brown back

OCCURRENCE
Breeds in shallow wetlands across the Great Basin and Prairie Pothole region, very densely in certain marsh habitats. The bulk of the population winters in coastal lagoons along the Atlantic Coast and the Gulf of Mexico.

| Length **17–21in (43–53cm)** | Wingspan **30–31in (75–79cm)** | Weight **1⅜–3¼lbs (0.6–1.5kg)** |
| Social **Flocks** | Lifespan **Up to 21 years** | Status **Secure** |

DATE: _____ TIME: _____ LOCATION: _____

| Order **Anseriformes** | Family **Anatidae** | Species *Aythya collaris* |

Ring-necked Duck

dark forewing

MALE

bold white underwing

IN FLIGHT

dark brown back

bold white eye-ring

white band on bill

yellow eye

FEMALE

rounded gray sides

tall, peaked head

gray bill with white band at base

thin chestnut ring

black neck and breast

MALE

A resident of freshwater ponds and lakes, the Ring-necked Duck is a fairly common medium-sized diving duck. A more descriptive and suitable name might have been Ring-billed Duck as the bold white band on the bill tip is easy to see whereas the thin chestnut ring around the neck can be very difficult to observe. The tall, pointed head is quite distinctive, peaking at the rear of the crown. When it sits on the water, this bird typically holds its head high.

VOICE Male normally silent; female makes low *kerp kerp* call.

NESTING Floating nest built in dense aquatic vegetation, often in marshes; 6–14 eggs; 1 brood; May–August.

FEEDING Feeds in water at all times, either by diving, tipping up, or dabbling for aquatic plant tubers and seeds; also eats aquatic invertebrates such as clams and snails.

FLIGHT: strong flier with deep, rapid wing beats; flight somewhat erratic.

UNIQUE BILL
A white outline around the base of the bill and the white band on the bill are unique markings.

FLAPPING WINGS
Bold white wing linings are apparent when the Ring-necked Duck flaps its wings.

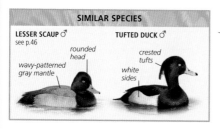

SIMILAR SPECIES

LESSER SCAUP ♂
see p.46
wavy-patterned gray mantle
rounded head

TUFTED DUCK ♂
crested tufts
white sides

OCCURRENCE
Breeds across Canada, south of the Arctic zone, in shallow freshwater marshes and bogs; sporadically in the western US. Winters in freshwater and brackish habitats such as swamps, lakes, estuaries, reservoirs, and flooded fields. Migrants are found in the Midwest near stands of wild rice.

| Length **15–18in (38–46cm)** | Wingspan **24–25in (62–63cm)** | Weight **1⅛–2lbs (500–900g)** |
| Social **Flocks** | Lifespan **Up to 20 years** | Status **Secure** |

DATE: _____ TIME: _____ LOCATION: _____

| Order **Anseriformes** | Family **Anatidae** | Species *Aythya marila* |

Greater Scaup

IN FLIGHT

gray forewing

broad, white wing stripe

MALE (NONBREEDING)

gray-brown sides

JUVENILE

little or no white around bill

medium to dark brown overall

bold white patches at base of bill

FEMALE (NONBREEDING)

smooth, round, black head with purple-green gloss

wavy-patterned gray back

blue-gray bill, wider at tip

gray-frosted shoulder feathers and sides

reduced white around bill

FEMALE (BREEDING)

dark brown overall

MALE (BREEDING)

almost all white sides

gray-and-brown back

blackish brown head

MALE (ECLIPSE)

A great swimmer and diver, the Greater Scaup is the only diving duck (genus *Aythya*) that breeds both in North America and Eurasia. Due to its more restricted coastal breeding and wintering habitat preference, it is far less numerous in North America than its close relative, the Lesser Scaup. The Greater Scaup forms large, often sexually segregated flocks outside the breeding season. If both scaup species are present together, they will also segregate within the flocks according to species. Correct identification is difficult.

VOICE During courtship, male call a soft, fast, wheezy *week week wheew*; female gives a series of growled monotone *arrrr* notes.

NESTING Simple depression lined with grasses and down, nest sites need to have dense cover of vegetation from previous year; 6–10 eggs; 1 brood; May–September.

FEEDING Dives for aquatic plants, seeds, insects, crustaceans, snails, shrimp, and bivalves.

FLIGHT: strong, fast, and agile; flocks shift and twist during prolonged flight.

FOND OF FLOCKING
Male Greater Scaups, with distinct black and white markings, flock together on the water.

SIMILAR SPECIES

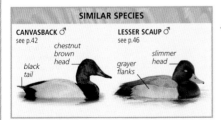

CANVASBACK ♂
see p.42

black tail

chestnut brown head

LESSER SCAUP ♂
see p.46

grayer flanks

slimmer head

see p.42 ... see p.46

OCCURRENCE
Majority breed in western coastal Alaska on tundra wetlands; also in lower densities in northwest and eastern Canada. Almost all birds winter offshore, along the Atlantic and Pacific coasts, or on the Great Lakes due to increased food availability. Small groups found inland and midcontinent, on unfrozen water bodies.

| Length **15–22in (38–56cm)** | Wingspan **28–31in (72–79cm)** | Weight **1¼–3lb (0.6–1.4kg)** |
| Social **Flocks** | Lifespan **Up to 22 years** | Status **Declining** |

DATE: _____ TIME: _____ LOCATION: _____

Order **Anseriformes**	Family **Anatidae**	Species ***Aythya affinis***

Lesser Scaup

MALE

whitish underwings

black head

IN FLIGHT

whitish belly

brown back

rich brown head and neck

white patch around base of gray bill

brown flank feathers with gray fringes

FEMALE

pale brown flanks

brown rear end

MALE (1ST WINTER)

narrow head with bump at the rear

purple-green gloss on head

narrow, thin, blue-gray bill

dark wavy pattern on upperparts

black rear end

MALE

pale flanks

black breast and neck

The Lesser Scaup, far more numerous than its somewhat larger relative (their size and weight ranges overlap), is also the most abundant diving duck in North America. The two species are very similar in appearance and are best identified by shape. Identification must be done cautiously as head shape changes with position. For example, the crown feathers are flattened just before diving in both species; thus, scaups are best identified when they are not moving.
VOICE Males mostly silent except during courtship when they make a wheezy *wheeow wheeow wheeow* sound; females give repetitive series of grating *garrrf garrrf garrrf* notes.
NESTING Nest built in tall vegetation or under shrubs, sometimes far from water, also on islands and mats of floating vegetation; 8–11 eggs; 1 brood; May–September.
FEEDING Feeds mainly on leeches, crustaceans, mollusks, aquatic insects, and aquatic plants and seeds.

FLIGHT: rapid, direct flight; can jump off water more easily than other diving ducks.

PREENING SCAUP
Ducks are meticulous preeners, and the Lesser Scaup is no exception.

SIMILAR SPECIES		
RING-NECKED DUCK ♀ see p.44	**GREATER SCAUP** ♀ see p.45	

prominent white eye-ring

solid dark back

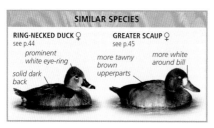

more tawny brown upperparts

more white around bill

OCCURRENCE
Breeds inland from Alaska to eastern Canada in open northern forests and forest tundra, most farther north. Winters in the Caribbean, southern US, and south to northern South America. Majority winter along coasts; others winter inland on lakes and reservoirs.

Length **15½–17½in (39–45cm)**	Wingspan **27–31in (68–78cm)**	Weight **1–2¾lb (0.45–1.2kg)**
Social **Flocks**	Lifespan **Up to 18 years**	Status **Secure**

DATE: _____ TIME: _____ LOCATION: _____

King Eider

MALE (BREEDING)

white underwing

IN FLIGHT short neck

brown-black upperparts

long-billed profile

scalloped breast

"V"-shaped markings on sides

FEMALE

white patch on face

MALE MOLTING (2ND WINTER)

white breast

pale blue crown and nape

long feathers form triangular "sails"

orange to reddish frontal shield, outlined in black

green cheek

reddish orange bill

rose blush on breast

MALE (BREEDING)

white flank patch

black underparts

The scientific name of the King Eider, *spectabilis*, means "worth seeing," and its gaudy marking and coloring around the head and bill make it hard to mistake. Females resemble the somewhat larger and paler Common Eider. The female King Eider has a more rounded head, more compact body, and a longer bill than the male. King Eiders may dive down to 180ft (55m) when foraging.

VOICE Courting males give a repeated series of low, rolled dove-like *arrrrooooo* calls, each rising, then falling, followed by softer *cooos*; females give grunts and croaks.

NESTING Slight depression in tundra lined with nearby vegetation and down; 4–7 eggs; 1 brood; June–September.

FEEDING Dives for mollusks; other food items include crustaceans, starfish, and when breeding, insects and plants.

FLIGHT: direct and rapid flight; migrates in long lines, abreast in a broad front, or in clusters.

GROUP FLIGHT
Migratory King Eiders move in large groups to their northern breeding habitats.

SIMILAR SPECIES

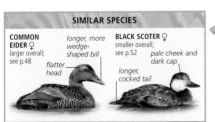

COMMON EIDER ♀
larger overall; see p.48

longer, more wedge-shaped bill

flatter head

BLACK SCOTER ♀
smaller overall; see p.52

pale cheek and dark cap

longer, cocked tail

OCCURRENCE
Nests along coasts and farther inland than Spectacled or Steller's Eiders in the high Arctic, on a variety of habitats; around low marshes, lakes, and islands; prefers well-drained areas. During winter, found mostly along the southern edge of the ice pack, in coastal waters up to 66ft (20m) deep.

Length **18½–25in (47–64cm)**	Wingspan **37in (94cm)**	Weight **2¾–4¾lb (1.2–2.1kg)**
Social **Flocks**	Lifespan **Up to 15 years**	Status **Secure**

DATE: _____ TIME:_____ LOCATION:_____

| Order **Anseriformes** | Family **Anatidae** | Species **Somateria mollissima** |

Common Eider

black cap

dark brown overall

MALE (SUMMER)

FEMALE

brown overall

olive-green wash on nape

greenish olive bill

white flecking

MALE (WINTER)

whitish underwing

IN FLIGHT

MALE (2ND WINTER)

black rump and tail

white breast, with rose tinge

long, sloping forehead

mottled, black-and-brown upperparts

MALE (WINTER)

FEMALE

The largest duck in North America, the Common Eider, is also the most numerous, widespread, and variable of the eiders. Four of its seven subspecies occur in North America, and vary in the markings and color of their heads and bills. Male Common Eiders also have considerable seasonal plumage changes, and do not acquire their adult plumage until the third year.

VOICE Repeated hoarse, grating notes *korr-korr-korr*; male's owl-like *ah-WOO-ooo*; female's low, guttural notes *krrrr-krrrr-krrrr*.

NESTING Depression on ground lined with down and plant matter, often near water; 2–7 eggs; 1 brood; June–September.

FEEDING Forages in open water and areas of shallow water; dives in synchronized flocks for mollusks and crustaceans, but consumes its larger prey above the surface.

FLIGHT: strong flight with relatively slow wing beats; flies in undulating lines, low over the water.

BROODING FEMALE
Females line their nests with down plucked from their bellies, and cover the eggs with their bodies.

OCCURRENCE
Arctic breeder on coastal islands, peninsulas, seldom along freshwater lakes and deltas near coast. One population is sedentary in the Hudson Bay and James Bay regions. Other populations winter in the Bering Sea, Hudson Bay, north British Columbia, Gulf of St. Lawrence, and along the Atlantic Coast.

SIMILAR SPECIES		
KING EIDER ♀ smaller overall; see p.47	flatter crown	**SURF SCOTER** ♀ see p.50
thicker neck		shorter, wedge-shaped bill
	shorter, more concave bill	dark brown overall

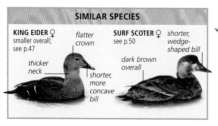

| Length **19½–28in (50–71cm)** | Wingspan **31–42in (80–108cm)** | Weight **2¾–5¾lb (1.2–2.6kg)** |
| Social **Flocks/Colonies** | Lifespan **Up to 21 years** | Status **Secure** |

DATE: _____ TIME:_____ LOCATION:_____

Harlequin Duck

MALE

dark wings above and below

short neck

pointed **IN FLIGHT** tail

dark sooty brown overall

broad face with whitish patches

scaly, pale brown lower breast and belly

FEMALE

slate-blue with bright rusty sides

two white bands perpendicular to breast and neck

white bands down either side of back

two white facial spots

rust crown stripes

very round head

steep forehead

small dark bill

white crescent

MALE

This small, hardy duck is a superbly skillful swimmer, diving to forage on the bottom of turbulent streams for its favorite insect prey. Despite the male's unmistakable plumage at close range, it looks very dark from a distance. With head and long tail held high, it can be found among crashing waves, alongside larger and bigger-billed Surf and White-winged Scoters, which feed in the same habitat.

VOICE Male a high-pitched squeak earning it the nickname "sea mouse"; female's call a raspy *ekekekekekek*.

NESTING Nests near water under vegetation or base of tree; also tree cavities; 3–9 eggs; 1 brood; April–September.

FEEDING Dives for insects and their larvae, and fish roe when breeding; in winter, eats mollusks, crustaceans, crabs, snails, fish roe, and barnacles.

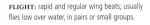

FLIGHT: rapid and regular wing beats; usually flies low over water, in pairs or small groups.

MALE GROUPS
After the breeding season, many males may gather and forage together.

PAIR IN FLIGHT
Note the crisp white markings on the slate-blue male in flight.

OCCURRENCE
Breeds near rushing coastal, mountain, or subalpine streams. During winter, found in small groups or mixed in with other sea ducks close to the shore, particularly along shallow rocky shorelines, jetties, rocky beaches, and headlands.

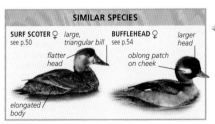

SIMILAR SPECIES

SURF SCOTER ♀
see p.50

large, triangular bill

flatter head

elongated body

BUFFLEHEAD ♀
see p.54

larger head

oblong patch on cheek

Length **13–21½in (33–54cm)**	Wingspan **22–26in (56–66cm)**	Weight **18–26oz (500–750g)**
Social **Small flocks**	Lifespan **Unknown**	Status **Secure**

DATE: _____ TIME: _____ LOCATION: _____

Order **Anseriformes**	Family **Anatidae**	Species ***Melanitta perspicillata***

Surf Scoter

MALE — black wings overall

IN FLIGHT — compact body

whitish facial patches — dark brown overall

all-dark bill

FEMALE

small, white patch on nape — black forehead

IMMATURE MALE (2ND WINTER)

white eye — white forehead — large, black spot on bill

velvety black feathers — white nape — swollen, orange bill with white base

long tail feathers

MALE

S urf Scoters, one of three species of scoters living in North America, migrate up and down both coasts, often with the other species. They take their name from the way they dive for mollusks on the sea floor, in shallow coastal waters, through heavy surf. Groups often dive and resurface in unison. Black and Surf Scoters can be difficult to tell apart as both have all-black wings. The underside of the Surf Scoter's wings are uniform black, whereas the Black Scoter's have gray flight feathers, which contrast with the black underwing feathers.

VOICE Normally silent; courting male's variety of calls includes liquid gurgled *puk-puk*, bubbled whistles, and low croaks; female call a harsh *crahh*, reminiscent of a crow.

NESTING Ground nest lined with down and vegetation on brushy tundra, often under low branches of a conifer tree; 5–10 eggs; 1 brood; May–September.

FEEDING Dives for mollusks and other aquatic invertebrates.

FLIGHT: strong wing beats; flies in bunched up groups; male's wings hum or whistle in flight.

DISTINGUISHING FEATURES
The white forehead and bright orange bill, in addition to its red-orange legs and feet, identify male Surf Scoters.

OCCURRENCE
Nests on lake islands in forested regions of interior Alaska and northern Canada. Nonbreeders in summer and adults in winter are strictly coastal, with numbers decreasing from north to south along the Pacific coast. In the East, most overwinter in the mid-Atlantic coast region.

SIMILAR SPECIES

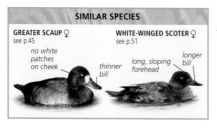

GREATER SCAUP ♀ see p.45 — no white patches on cheek — thinner bill

WHITE-WINGED SCOTER ♀ see p.51 — long, sloping forehead — longer bill

Length **19–23½in (48–60cm)**	Wingspan **30in (77cm)**	Weight **1¾–2¾lb (0.8–1.2kg)**
Social **Flocks/Pairs**	Lifespan **Unknown**	Status **Declining**

DATE: _____ TIME: _____ LOCATION: _____

| Order **Anseriformes** | Family **Anatidae** | Species **Melanitta fusca** |

White-winged Scoter

long, sloping head

blackish bill

two distinct pale patches on face

IMMATURE FEMALE

white wing patch

ADULT

appears all-black in flight

IN FLIGHT

dark brown overall

feathers extend onto the bill

FEMALE

all black with brownish sides

black knob at base of bill

upturned white "comma" around white eye

pinkish red to yellow-orange bill

MALE

The White-winged Scoter is the largest of the three scoters. When visible, the white wing patch makes identification easy. Females are quite similar to immature male and female Surf Scoters and can be identified by head shape, extent of bill feathering, and shape of white areas on the face. When diving, this scoter leaps forward and up, arching its neck, and opens its wings when entering the water. Underwater, White-winged Scoters open their wings to propel and stabilize themselves.

VOICE Mostly silent; courting males emit a whistling note; female call a growly *karr*.

NESTING Depression lined with twigs and down in dense thickets, often far from water; 8–9 eggs; 1 brood; June–September.

FEEDING Dives for mollusks and crustaceans; sometimes eats fish and aquatic plants.

FLIGHT: direct with rapid wing beats; flies low over the water in small groups.

WHITE FLASH IN FLIGHT
Scoters often migrate or feed in mixed flocks. The white wing patches are striking in flight.

OCCURRENCE
Majority breed in dense colonies in interior Alaska and western Canada on large freshwater or brackish lakes or ponds, sometimes on saltwater lakes. Winters along both coasts, large bays, inlets, and estuaries. Rarely winters inland, except on the Great Lakes.

SIMILAR SPECIES

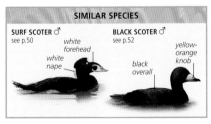

SURF SCOTER ♂
see p.50

white forehead

white nape

BLACK SCOTER ♂
see p.52

yellow-orange knob

black overall

| Length **19–23in (48–58cm)** | Wingspan **31in (80cm)** | Weight **2¾–4¾lb (0.9–1.9kg)** |
| Social **Flocks/Colonies** | Lifespan **Up to 18 years** | Status **Vulnerable** |

Order **Anseriformes**	Family **Anatidae**	Species *Melanitta americana*

Black Scoter

pale, silvery gray flight feathers

black lining on underwings

ADULT

IN FLIGHT

dark cap

pale brownish gray cheeks

black bill with small yellow patch

smaller bill

dark brown overall **FEMALE**

dark brown eye

entirely black, heavily built body

conspicuous yellow-orange knob on black bill

MALE

B lack Scoters, the most vocal of the scoters, are medium-sized sea ducks that winter along both coasts of North America. Riding high on the waves, they form dense flocks, often segregated by gender. While swimming, the Black Scoter sometimes flaps its wings and while doing so drops its neck low down, unlike the other two scoters. This scoter breeds in two widely separated sub-Arctic breeding areas and is one of the least studied ducks in North America. The Eurasian subspecies, known as the Common Scoter, has much less orange on its bill with a smaller knob at the base.

VOICE Male call a high-whistled *peeew*; female a low raspy *kraaa*.

NESTING Depression lined with grass and down, often in tall grass on tundra; 5–10 eggs; 1 brood; May–September.

FEEDING Dives in saltwater for mollusks, crustaceans, and plant matter; feeds on aquatic insects and freshwater mussels.

FLIGHT: strong wing beats; male's wings make whistling sound during takeoff.

YELLOW BILL
Male Black Scoters are distinctive with their black plumage and yellow bill-knob.

SIMILAR SPECIES

SURF SCOTER ♀
see p.50

flatter crown

two whitish patches

larger bill

WHITE-WINGED SCOTER ♀
see p.51

more sloping head

longer bill

OCCURRENCE
Breeding habitat is somewhat varied, but is generally close to fairly shallow, small lakes. Winters along both coasts. Populations wintering farther north prefer water over cobbles, gravel, or offshore ledges, whereas in southern locations, sandier habitats are chosen.

Length **17–21in (43–53cm)**	Wingspan **31–35in (79–90cm)**	Weight **1¾–2¾lb (0.8–1.2kg)**
Social **Flocks**	Lifespan **Unknown**	Status **Declining**

DATE: _____ TIME: _____ LOCATION: _____

| Order **Anseriformes** | Family **Anatidae** | Species ***Clangula hyemalis*** |

Long-tailed Duck

smudgy face pattern

MALE (WINTER) — *mostly dark brown back, flanks, head, and breast* — *small, dark bill*

chunky body

JUVENILE (WINTER) — *gray face* — *blackish head, neck, and breast*

IN FLIGHT

FEMALE (SUMMER)

MALE (SUMMER) — *dark back* — *brown breastband* — *white head* — *white eye-ring*

FEMALE (WINTER) — *short tail* — *whitish underparts* — *large, brown spot on side of head*

long dark tail — *all-dark wings* — *white shoulder feathers* — *pinkish band on bill* — *black breastband*

MALE (WINTER)

The Long-tailed Duck, which used to be called the Oldsquaw, is a small, pudgy sea duck. The male has two extremely long tail feathers, which are often held up in the air like a pennant. The male's loud calls are quite musical, and, when heard from a flock, have a chorus-like quality, hence the name Clangula, which is Latin for "loud." The Long-tailed Duck is capable of diving for a prolonged period of time, and can reach depths of 200ft (60m), making it one of the deepest diving ducks. Its three-part molt is more complex than that of other ducks.

VOICE Male call a *ang-ang-eeeooo* with yodelling quality; female barking *urk* or *uk* alarm call.

NESTING Shallow depression in ground lined with plant matter; 6–9 eggs; 1 brood; May–September.

FEEDING Dives to bottom of freshwater or saltwater habitats for mollusks, crustaceans, insects, fish, and roe.

FLIGHT: flies low over the water, somewhat erratically, with fast, fluttering wing beats.

UNMISTAKABLE MALE
In winter, dark wings, a white body with black breast-band, and a long tail make this male unmistakable.

SIMILAR SPECIES

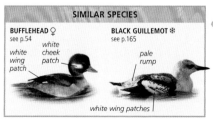

BUFFLEHEAD ♀ see p.54 — *white wing patch* — *white cheek patch*

BLACK GUILLEMOT ❀ see p.165 — *pale rump* — *white wing patches*

OCCURRENCE
Breeds in Arctic and sub-Arctic, nesting in small groups on islands and peninsulas on lakes, less commonly on tundra and freshwater ponds on islands. Winters mostly along rocky coasts and headlands, protected bays, or on large freshwater lakes.

| Length **14–23in (35–58cm)** | Wingspan **28in (72cm)** | Weight **18–39oz (500–1,100g)** |
| Social **Flocks** | Lifespan **Up to 22 years** | Status **Declining** |

Order **Anseriformes**	Family **Anatidae**	Species **Bucephala albeola**

Bufflehead

black-and-white outer wings

MALE

gray underwings with white patch

pinkish orange legs

IN FLIGHT

oval, white cheek patch

dark brown head

dark, unmarked back

all-dark wings

grayish brown sides

FEMALE

front part of head and neck has iridescent green-and-purple gloss

large, triangular, white patch on head

angled forehead

black back

small, narrow, gray bill

white breast and flanks

MALE

The smallest diving duck in North America, the Bufflehead is a close relative of the Common and Barrow's Goldeneye. Males make a bold statement with their striking head pattern. In flight, males resemble the larger Common Goldeneye, yet the large white area on their head makes them easy to distinguish. The Common Goldeneye's wings create a whirring sound in flight whereas the Bufflehead's do not. The northern limit of the Bufflehead's breeding range corresponds to that of the Northern Flicker, as the ducks usually nest in abandoned flicker cavities.

VOICE Male a low growl or squeal; chattering during breeding; female mostly silent except during courtship or calling to nestlings.

NESTING Cavity nester, no nesting material added, near water; 7–9 eggs; 1 brood; April–September.

FEEDING Dives for aquatic invertebrates: usually insects in freshwater, mollusks and crustaceans in saltwater; also eats seeds.

FLIGHT: very rapid wing beats; no flight sound, unlike Goldeneyes.

IMMEDIATE TAKE OFF
Unlike other diving ducks, the small, compact Bufflehead can take off almost vertically.

SIMILAR SPECIES

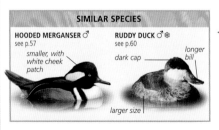

HOODED MERGANSER ♂
see p.57

smaller, with white cheek patch

RUDDY DUCK ♂ ✳
see p.60

dark cap

longer bill

larger size

OCCURRENCE
Breeds in forest from Alaska to eastern Canada, in woodlands near small lakes and permanent ponds, where young are raised. Winters largely along the Pacific and Atlantic Coasts with lower densities scattered across the continent, south to northern Mexico, and in Bermuda.

Length **12½–15½in (32–39cm)**	Wingspan **21½–24in (54–61cm)**	Weight **10–18oz (275–500g)**
Social **Flocks**	Lifespan **Up to 15 years**	Status **Secure**

DATE: _____ TIME: _____ LOCATION: _____

| Order **Anseriformes** | Family **Anatidae** | Species ***Bucephala clangula*** |

Common Goldeneye

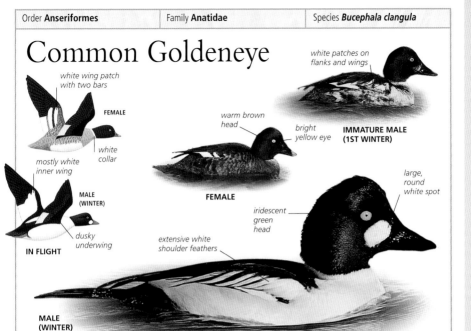

white wing patch with two bars

FEMALE

white patches on flanks and wings

white collar

mostly white inner wing

MALE (WINTER)

warm brown head

bright yellow eye

IMMATURE MALE (1ST WINTER)

FEMALE

large, round white spot

iridescent green head

dusky underwing

IN FLIGHT

extensive white shoulder feathers

MALE (WINTER)

Common Goldeneyes closely resemble Barrow's Goldeneyes. Found in North America and Eurasia, this is a medium-sized, compact, diving duck. It is aggressive and very competitive with members of its own species, as well as other cavity-nesting ducks. It regularly lays eggs in the nests of other species—a behavior that is almost parasitic. Before diving, the Common Goldeneye flattens its feathers in preparation for underwater foraging. The female's head shape changes according to her posture.

VOICE Courting males make a faint *peent* call; females a harsh *gack* or repeated *cuk* calls.

NESTING Cavity nester in holes made by other birds, including Pileated Woodpeckers, in broken branches or hollow trees; also commonly uses nest boxes; 4–13 eggs; 1 brood; April–September.

FEEDING Dives during breeding season for insects; in winter, mollusks and crustaceans; sometimes eats fish and plant matter.

FLIGHT: rapid with fast wing beats; male's wings make a tinkling sound in flight.

MALE TAKING OFF
Quite a long takeoff, involving energetically running on the water, leaves a trail of spray.

OCCURRENCE
Breeds along wetlands, lakes, and rivers with clear water in northern forests, where large trees provide appropriate nest cavities. Winters across continent, with highest densities located from north New England to the mid-Atlantic on coastal bays and in the West from coastal southeast Alaska to British Columbia.

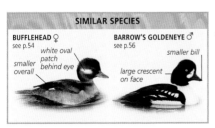

SIMILAR SPECIES

BUFFLEHEAD ♀
see p.54

smaller overall

white oval patch behind eye

BARROW'S GOLDENEYE ♂
see p.56

smaller bill

large crescent on face

| Length **15½–20in (40–51cm)** | Wingspan **30–33in (77–83cm)** | Weight **19–44oz (550–1,300g)** |
| Social **Flocks** | Lifespan **Up to 15 years** | Status **Secure** |

DATE: _____ TIME: _____ LOCATION: _____

| Order **Anseriformes** | Family **Anatidae** | Species ***Bucephala islandica*** |

Barrow's Goldeneye

white wing patch

MALE

dark underwings

narrow, white wing patch

FEMALE (BREEDING)

darker brown head

steep forehead

small, yellow bill

black head with purple gloss

sloping crown

IN FLIGHT

grayish brown wing feathers

IMMATURE MALE (1ST WINTER)

white neck

white "piano key" markings on sides

bold, white facial crescent

MALE

Barrow's Goldeneye is a slightly larger, darker version of the Common Goldeneye. Although the female can be identified by its different head structure and bill color, the bill color varies seasonally and geographically. Eastern Barrow's have blacker bills with less yellow, and western populations have entirely yellow bills, which darken in summer. During the breeding season, the majority of Barrow's Goldeneyes are found in mountainous regions of northwest North America.

VOICE Males normally silent; courting males grunt *ka-KAA*; females *cuc* call, slightly higher pitched than Common Goldeneye.

NESTING Tree cavity in holes formed by Pileated Woodpeckers, often broken limbs or hollow trees; also uses nest boxes; 6–12 eggs; 1 brood; April–September.

FEEDING Dives in summer for insects, some fish, and roe; in winter, mainly mollusks and crustaceans; some plant matter.

FLIGHT: rapid flight with fast, deep wing beats; flies near water surface on short flights.

COURTING DISPLAY
A male thrusts his head back and gives a guttural call. His feet then kick back, driving him forward.

SIMILAR SPECIES

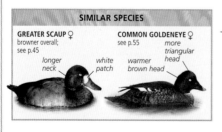

GREATER SCAUP ♀
browner overall;
see p.45

longer neck

white patch

COMMON GOLDENEYE ♀
see p.55

more triangular head

warmer brown head

OCCURRENCE
Winters along the Pacific Coast between southeast Alaska and Washington, with small populations in east Canada. Smaller numbers found inland from the lower Colorado River to Yellowstone National Park. Eastern population is localized in winter with the highest count in St. Lawrence estuary.

Length **17–19in (43–48cm)**	Wingspan **28–30in (71–76cm)**	Weight **17–46oz (475–1,300g)**
Social **Flocks**	Lifespan **Up to 18 years**	Status **Secure**

DATE: _____ TIME: _____ LOCATION: _____

Order **Anseriformes**	Family **Anatidae**	Species *Lophodytes cucullatus*

Hooded Merganser

small, gray-brown crest (raised)

triangular-shaped wings

black-and-white inner wing patch

long **IN FLIGHT**

long tail

MALE (BREEDING)

reddish-tinged crest (folded)

brownish buff eye

striking yellow eye

brownish gray flanks

yellow-based, thin, black bill

FEMALE

MALE (ECLIPSE)

longish tail, often raised

crested black-and-white head (crest not raised)

black back

yellow eye

thin, black, serrated bill

white breast

MALE (BREEDING)

warm brown flanks

bold vertical bars

This dapper, miniature fish-eater is the smallest of the three mergansers. Both male and female Hooded Mergansers have crests that they can raise or flatten. When the male raises his crest, the thin horizontal white stripe turns into a gorgeous white fan, surrounded by black. Although easily identified when swimming, the Hooded Merganser and the Wood Duck can be confused when seen in flight since they both are fairly small with bushy heads and long tails.

VOICE Normally silent; during courtship, males produce a low, growly, descending *pah-hwaaaaa*, reminiscent of a frog; females give a soft *rrrep*.

NESTING Cavity nester; nest lined with down feathers in a tree or box close to or over water; 6–15 eggs; 1 brood; February–June.

FEEDING Dives for fish, aquatic insects, and crayfish, preferably in clear and shallow fresh waters, but also in brackish waters.

FLIGHT: low, fast, and direct; shallow wing beats; quiet whirring noise produced by wings.

FANHEAD SPECTACULAR
The male's magnificent black-and-white fan of a crest is like a beacon in the late afternoon light.

OCCURRENCE
Prefers forested small ponds, marshes, or slow-moving streams during the breeding season. During winter, occurs in shallow water in both fresh- and saltwater bays, estuaries, rivers, streams, ponds, freshwater marshes, and flooded sloughs.

SIMILAR SPECIES

WOOD DUCK ♀ see p.33

bold, white eye-ring

blue wing patch

RED-BREASTED MERGANSER ♀ see p.59

steel gray-and-white plumage

rustier head with ragged crest

Length **15½–19½in (40–49cm)**	Wingspan **23½–26in (60–66cm)**	Weight **16–31oz (450–875g)**
Social **Small flocks**	Lifespan **Unknown**	Status **Secure**

DATE: _____ TIME: _____ LOCATION: _____

Order **Anseriformes**	Family **Anatidae**	Species **Mergus merganser**

Common Merganser

dark outer wing

gray-and-white inner wing

reddish brown head

FEMALE

bright, rusty brown head

silver-gray upperparts

black-tipped red bill

small white spot above eye

short, ragged crest

JUVENILE

thin, black bar

gray rump and tail

MALE (NONBREEDING)

black head

FEMALE

iridescent blackish green head

long nape feathers

black eye

reddish orange hooked bill

IN FLIGHT

all-white or tinged pink underparts

black center

serrated sides on bill

MALE (BREEDING)

white breast and underparts

The largest of the three merganser species in North America, the Common Merganser is called a Goosander in the UK. This large fish-eater is common and widespread, particularly in the northern portion of its range. It is often found in big flocks on lakes or smaller groups along rivers. It spends most of its time on the water, using its serrated bill to catch fish underwater.

VOICE Mostly silent, except when alarmed or during courtship; females give a low-pitched harsh *karr* or *gruk*, the latter also given in series; during courtship, males emit a high-pitched, bell-like note and other twangy notes; alarm call a hoarse *grrr* or *wak*.

NESTING Cavity nester sometimes high in trees; uses nest boxes, nests on ground; 6–17 eggs; 1 brood; April–September.

FEEDING Eats mostly fish (especially fond of trout and salmon, but also carp and catfish), aquatic invertebrates, frogs, small mammals, birds, and plants.

FLIGHT: fast with shallow wing beats; often flying low over the water.

FEEDING ON THE MOVE
This female Common Merganser is trying to swallow, head-first, a rather large fish.

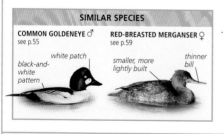

SIMILAR SPECIES

COMMON GOLDENEYE ♂
see p.55

black-and-white pattern

white patch

RED-BREASTED MERGANSER ♀
see p.59

smaller, more lightly built

thinner bill

OCCURRENCE
Breeds in the northerly forests from Alaska to Newfoundland; winters south to north central Mexico. Being very hardy, it will winter farther north than most other waterfowl as long as water remains open. Prefers fresh- to saltwater locations.

Length 21½–28in (54–71cm)	Wingspan 34in (86cm)	Weight 1¾–4¾lb (0.8–2.1kg)
Social **Flocks**	Lifespan **Up to 13 years**	Status **Secure**

DATE: _____ TIME: _____ LOCATION: _____

| Order **Anseriformes** | Family **Anatidae** | Species ***Mergus serrator*** |

Red-breasted Merganser

bill more reddish than females

long, thin, ragged double crest

dull rufous-brown head and neck

two wing bars

white-inner wing patches

MALE (WINTER)

brownish gray sides and flanks

smaller crest

gray sides and flanks

MALE (ECLIPSE)

single wing bar

white belly with gray flanks

FEMALE

IN FLIGHT

FEMALE

gray underparts with white belly

bold white line between black back and gray flanks

wispy crest on green-black head

black-and-white checkered pattern on back

red eye

slightly upturned, thin, reddish-orange bill

crisp, white collar

MALE (BREEDING)

The Red-breasted Merganser, like the other saw-billed mergansers, is an elegant fish-eating duck. Both sexes are easily recognized by their long, sparse, somewhat ragged-looking double crest. Red-breasted Mergansers are smaller than Common Mergansers, but much larger than the Hooded. The Red-breasted Merganser, unlike the other two mergansers, nests on the ground, in loose colonies, often among gulls and terns, and is protected by its neighbors.

VOICE During courtship males make a raucous *yeow-yeow* call; females emit a raspy *krrr-krrr*.

NESTING Shallow depression on ground lined with down and plant material, near water; 5–11 eggs; 1 brood; May–July.

FEEDING Dives for small fish such as herring and minnows; also salmon eggs; at times flocks coordinate and drive fish together.

FLIGHT: fast flying duck with very rapid, regular, and shallow flapping.

KEEPING CLOSE
Red-breasted Mergansers are gregarious at all times of year, often feeding in loose flocks.

OCCURRENCE
Most northerly range of all the mergansers, nests across Arctic and sub-Arctic regions, tundra and northerly forests, along coasts, inland lakes, river banks, marsh edges, and coastal islands. Winters farther south than other mergansers, mostly in protected bays, estuaries, or on the Great Lakes.

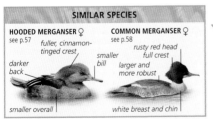

SIMILAR SPECIES

HOODED MERGANSER ♀
see p.57
fuller, cinnamon-tinged crest
darker back
smaller overall

COMMON MERGANSER ♀
see p.58
rusty red head
full crest
smaller bill
larger and more robust
white breast and chin

| Length **20–25in (51–64cm)** | Wingspan **26–29in (66–74cm)** | Weight **1¾–2¾lb (0.8–1.3kg)** |
| Social **Flocks/Colonies** | Lifespan **Up to 9 years** | Status **Secure** |

DATE: _____ TIME: _____ LOCATION: _____

Order **Anseriformes**	Family **Anatidae**	Species *Oxyura jamaicensis*

Ruddy Duck

broad, short wings with whitish wing linings

dull gray-brown two-tone body

duller head

blackish bill

pale belly

MALE (BREEDING)
IN FLIGHT

**MALE
(NONBREEDING)**

arched dark line on cheek

dark bill

brownish upperparts

paler flanks

FEMALE

black cap and nape

large head

bright blue bill, slightly knobby at base

rich cinnamon body and neck

large, white cheek patches

long tail, often erect

**MALE
(BREEDING)**

Small and stiff-tailed, the Ruddy Duck is comical in both its appearance and behavior. Both sexes often hold their tail in a cocked position, especially when sleeping. During courtship displays, the male points its long tail skyward while rapidly thumping its electric blue bill against its chest, ending the performance with an odd, bubbling sound. In another display, males make a popping sound by slapping their feet on the water's surface. Large feet, on legs set far back on its body, make the Ruddy Duck an excellent swimmer and diver; however, on land it is perhaps one of the most awkward of diving ducks. Females are known to push themselves along instead of walking.

VOICE Females give a nasal *raanh* and high pitched *eeek*; males vocally silent, but make popping noises with feet.

NESTING Platform, bowl-shaped nest built over water in thick emergent vegetation, rarely on land; 6–10 eggs; 1 brood; May–September.

FEEDING Dives for aquatic insects, larvae, crustaceans, and other invertebrates, particularly when breeding; during winter, also eats plants.

FLIGHT: rapid and direct, with fast wing beats; not very agile in flight, which seems labored.

HEAVY HEAD
A female "sitting" on the water streamlines her body ready to dive, making her look large-headed.

SIMILAR SPECIES

MASKED DUCK ♂
black tip to bill
black face
ruddy-colored back with black streaks

OCCURRENCE
Breeds in the prairie pothole region in wetland habitats; marshes, ponds, reservoirs, and other open shallow water with emergent vegetation and open areas. Majority winter on freshwater habitats from ponds to large lakes; smaller numbers found on brackish coastal marshes, bays, and estuaries.

Length **14–17in (35–43cm)**	Wingspan **22–24in (56–62cm)**	Weight **11–30oz (300–850g)**
Social **Flocks**	Lifespan **Up to 13 years**	Status **Secure**

DATE: _____ TIME: _____ LOCATION: _____

QUAILS, GROUSE, TURKEYS, AND RELATIVES

THIS DIVERSE AND ADAPTABLE group of birds thrives in habitats ranging from hot desert to frozen tundra. They spend most of the time on the ground, springing loudly into the air when alarmed.

QUAILS

Among the most terrestrial of all gamebirds, quails are also renowned for their great sociability, often forming large family groups, or "coveys," of up to 100 birds. The five species found in western North America each live in a specific habitat or at a particular elevation, although the California Quail is becoming more common in parks and suburban areas.

GROUSE

The most numerous and widespread of gamebirds, the different species of grouse can be divided into three groups based on their preferred habitats. Forest grouse include the Ruffed Grouse and the Spruce

Grouse across Canada, and the Sooty Grouse and Dusky Grouse

found only in the West. Prairie grouse, including the Sharp-tailed Grouse, are found throughout the middle of the continent. All tundra and mountaintop grouse or Ptarmigan are found in the extreme North and the Rockies. Grouse often possess patterns that match their surroundings, providing camouflage from enemies both animal and human.

DRESSED TO THRILL
With its striking plumage, the Ring-necked Pheasant is an impressive sight when flushed out of its cover.

GRASSLAND GROUSE
The aptly named Sharp-tailed Grouse is particularly common in the western prairies, strutting in search of grasshoppers.

PHEASANTS & PARTRIDGES

These Eurasian gamebirds were introduced into North America in the 19th and 20th centuries to provide additional targets for recreational hunters. While some introductions failed, species such as the colorful Ring-necked Pheasant adapted well in the new environment and now thrive in established populations.

SNOW BIRD
The Rock Ptarmigan's white winter plumage camouflages it against the snow, helping to hide it from predators.

| Order **Galliformes** | Family **Odontophoridae** | Species *Colinus virginianus* |

Northern Bobwhite

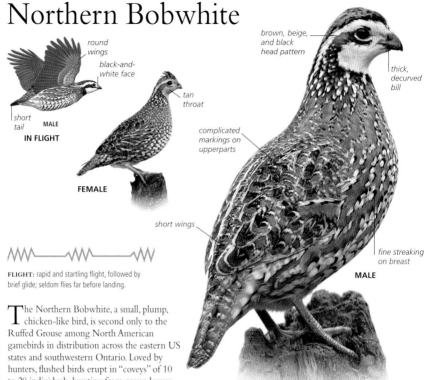

round wings

black-and-white face

MALE IN FLIGHT

short tail

tan throat

FEMALE

complicated markings on upperparts

brown, beige, and black head pattern

thick, decurved bill

short wings

fine streaking on breast

MALE

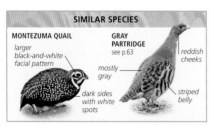

FLIGHT: rapid and startling flight, followed by brief glide; seldom flies far before landing.

The Northern Bobwhite, a small, plump, chicken-like bird, is second only to the Ruffed Grouse among North American gamebirds in distribution across the eastern US states and southwestern Ontario. Loved by hunters, flushed birds erupt in "coveys" of 10 to 20 individuals, bursting from groundcover and dispersing in many directions. Large numbers are raised in captivity and released to supplement wild populations for hunting.
VOICE Characteristic *bob-WHITE* or *bob-bob-WHITE* whistled by males in breeding season; call to reunite flock includes *hoi-lee* and *hoi* following dispersal.
NESTING Shallow depression lined with plant matter, located on ground within sight of an opening; 10–15 eggs; sometimes multiple broods per season; January–March.
FEEDING Forages for wide variety of plant matter (seeds, buds, leaves), and insects, snails, and spiders, depending on the season.

COVEY LIFE
Male, female, and immature Northern Bobwhites live together in tight flocks called coveys.

SIMILAR SPECIES

MONTEZUMA QUAIL
larger
black-and-white facial pattern

dark sides with white spots

GRAY PARTRIDGE
see p.63

mostly gray

reddish cheeks

striped belly

OCCURRENCE
Widely distributed but only locally common in much of the eastern US and southwestern Ontario, and in Mexico, southward to Guatemala. Most often associated with agricultural fields, it thrives in a patchwork of mixed young forests, fields, and brushy hedges. A permanent resident.

| Length **8–10in (20–25cm)** | Wingspan **11–14in (28–35cm)** | Weight **6oz (175g)** |
| Social **Small flocks** | Lifespan **Up to 6 years** | Status **Declining** |

DATE: _____ TIME: _____ LOCATION: _____

| Order **Galliformes** | Family **Phasianidae** | Species ***Perdix perdix*** |

Gray Partridge

ADULT

rusty head

cinnamon face

gray neck and chest with fine black barring

brown, rounded wings

dark cinnamon tail

IN FLIGHT

gray back with fine barring

underparts gray overall

horseshoe-shaped belly patch

ADULT

ADULT

chestnut barred gray flanks

FLIGHT: erupts from cover on loud, rapid wing beats; levels off, flaps and glides; flies low.

A member of the pheasant family, the Gray Partridge is native to Eurasia. Introduced to North America in the late 18th century, it became a resident after repeated re-introductions. Hunters call it the Hungarian Partridge or "Hun" for short. This species has benefited from the mixture of agricultural and fallow fields, which resulted from long-term conservation programs, and its population is stable or expanding in the west. The isolated eastern populations, however, are declining due to changes in land use. This species is popular with hunters in both North America and Europe.

VOICE Short *kuk-kuk-kuk*, quickly and in a series when alarmed; *prruk-prruk* between adults and young when threatened.

NESTING Shallow depression in soil lined with vegetation, usually in hedgerows; 14–18 eggs; 1 brood; March–May.

FEEDING Eats mostly seeds and row crops such as corn and wheat; succulent green leaves in spring; insects when breeding.

NOISY TAKEOFF
When the Gray Partridge takes flight its wings make a loud, whirring sound.

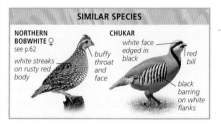

SIMILAR SPECIES

NORTHERN BOBWHITE ♀
see p.62

white streaks on rusty red body

CHUKAR

white face edged in black

buffy throat and face

red bill

black barring on white flanks

OCCURRENCE
Primarily agricultural fields of crops including corn, wheat, and oats, as well as associated hedgerows and fallow grasslands. Most birds are nonmigratory, but there is some movement by eastern birds after breeding.

| Length **11–13in (28–33cm)** | Wingspan **17–20in (43–51cm)** | Weight **12–18oz (350–500g)** |
| Social **Family groups** | Lifespan **Up to 4 years** | Status **Declining** |

DATE: _____ TIME: _____ LOCATION: _____

Ring-necked Pheasant

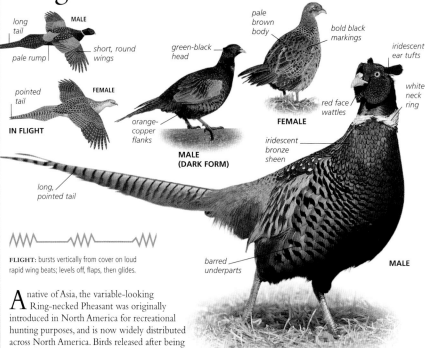

long tail

MALE

short, round wings

pale rump

pointed tail

FEMALE

IN FLIGHT

long, pointed tail

pale brown body

bold black markings

green-black head

orange-copper flanks

MALE (DARK FORM)

iridescent bronze sheen

red face wattles

FEMALE

iridescent ear tufts

white neck ring

barred underparts

MALE

FLIGHT: bursts vertically from cover on loud rapid wing beats; levels off, flaps, then glides.

A native of Asia, the variable-looking Ring-necked Pheasant was originally introduced in North America for recreational hunting purposes, and is now widely distributed across North America. Birds released after being bred in captivity are used to supplement natural reproduction for hunting purposes. In the wild, several females may lay eggs in the same nest—a phenomenon called "egg-dumping." There is a less common dark form, which can be distinguished principally because it lacks the distinctive white band around the neck.

VOICE Male emits a loud, raucous, explosive double note, *Karrk-KORK*, followed by loud wing-flapping; both sexes cackle when flushed.

NESTING Shallow bowl composed of grasses, usually on ground in tall grass or among low shrubs; 7–15 eggs; 1 brood; March–June.

FEEDING Feeds on corn and other grain, seeds, fruit, row crops, grass, leaves and shoots; eats insects when available.

OCCURRENCE
Widespread across southern Canada and the US; prefers mixture of active agricultural crops (especially corn fields), fallow fields, and hedgerows; also cattail marshes and wooded river bottoms. The Ring-necked Pheasant is native to Asia from the Caucasus east to China.

SIMILAR SPECIES

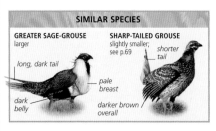

GREATER SAGE-GROUSE
larger

long, dark tail

dark belly

SHARP-TAILED GROUSE
slightly smaller; see p.69

shorter tail

pale breast

darker brown overall

FLUSHED OUT
The Ring-necked Pheasant is a powerful flier when alarmed or flushed out of its cover.

Length **19½–28in (50–70cm)**	Wingspan **30–34in (76–86cm)**	Weight **1¼–6½lb (0.5–3kg)**
Social **Solitary/Flocks**	Lifespan **Up to 4 years**	Status **Secure**

DATE: _____ TIME: _____ LOCATION: _____

| Order **Galliformes** | Family **Phasianidae** | Species ***Bonasa umbellus*** |

Ruffed Grouse

ADULT (RUFOUS FORM)

heavy white spotting on brown upperparts

raised crest

dark patch on neck

IN FLIGHT

brown-barred underparts

rusty tail with black band

ADULT (RUFOUS FORM)

feathered legs

spotted gray upperparts

gray-barred underparts

ADULT (GRAY FORM)

The Ruffed Grouse is perhaps the most widespread gamebird in North America. There are two color forms, rufous and gray, both allowing the birds to remain camouflaged and undetected on the forest floor, until they eventually burst into the air in an explosion of whirring wings. The male is well known for his extraordinary wing beating or "drumming" display, which he performs year-round, but most frequently in the spring.

VOICE Hissing notes, and soft *purrt, purrt, purrt* when alarmed, by both sexes; males "drumming" display when heard from distance resembles small engine starting, *thump…thump…thump…thump… thump…thuthuthuth.*

NESTING Shallow, leaf-lined bowl set against a tree trunk, rock or fallen log in forest; 6–14 eggs; 1 brood; March–June.

FEEDING Forages on ground for leaves, buds, and fruit; occasionally insects.

FLIGHT: an explosive take-off, usually at close range, glides for a short distance before landing.

OCCURRENCE
Found in young, mixed habitat forests throughout northern US and Canada. Southern edge of range extends along higher elevations of the Appalachians and middle levels of the Rocky Mountains, if suitable habitat is available.

SIMILAR SPECIES

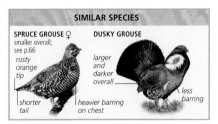

SPRUCE GROUSE ♀
smaller overall; see p.66

rusty orange tip

shorter tail

DUSKY GROUSE

larger and darker overall

heavier barring on chest

less barring

WARM RED
The rufous form of the Ruffed Grouse is more common in hotter parts of the continent.

| Length **17–20in (43–51cm)** | Wingspan **20–23in (51–58cm)** | Weight **20–22oz (575–625g)** |
| Social **Solitary/Small flocks** | Lifespan **Up to 10 years** | Status **Secure** |

DATE: _____ TIME:_____ LOCATION:_____

| Order **Galliformes** | Family **Phasianidae** | Species *Falcipennis canadensis* |

Spruce Grouse

MALE
(FRANKLIN'S)

ADULT

paler
overall

**FEMALE
(TAIGA)**

heavy barring
on underparts

mottled
gray-brown
upperparts

bright red comb
above eye

black
throat

IN FLIGHT

white spots
on black tail

gray
upperparts

heavily
barred
underparts

black
breast

white spots
on underparts

**MALE
F. c. canadensis
(TAIGA)**

**FEMALE
F. c. franklinii
(FRANKLIN'S)**

mostly blackish tail

Perhaps because of the remoteness of their habitat and lack of human contact, Spruce Grouse are not afraid of humans. This lack of wariness when approached has earned them the name "fool hens." Their specialized diet of pine needles causes the intestinal tract to expand in order to accommodate a larger volume of food to compensate for its low nutritional value. There are two subspecies of Spruce Grouse (*F. c. canadensis* and *F. c. franklinii*), both of which have red and gray forms.

VOICE Mostly silent; males clap their wings during courtship display; females often utter long cackle at dawn and dusk.

NESTING Lined with moss, leaves, feathers; often at base of tree; naturally low area in forest floor; 4–6 eggs; 1 brood; May–July.

FEEDING Feeds mostly on pine but also spruce needles; will eat insects, leaves, fruit, and seeds when available.

FLIGHT: generally avoids flying; when disturbed, bursts into flight on whirring wings.

RUFOUS BAND
The male "Taiga" subspecies displays the thin rufous band on the tip of his tail.

SIMILAR SPECIES

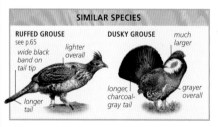

RUFFED GROUSE
see p.65

wide black
band on
tail tip

lighter
overall

longer
tail

DUSKY GROUSE

much
larger

longer,
charcoal-
gray tail

grayer
overall

OCCURRENCE
Present year-round in forests dominated by conifers, including Jack, Lodgepole, Spruce, Red Spruce, Black Spruce, Balsam Fir, Subalpine Fir, Hemlock, and Cedar. Found from western Alaska to the Atlantic Coast.

| Length **14–17in (36–43cm)** | Wingspan **21–23in (53–58cm)** | Weight **16oz (450g)** |
| Social **Solitary** | Lifespan **Up to 10 years** | Status **Secure** |

DATE: _____ TIME: _____ LOCATION: _____

| Order **Galliformes** | Family **Phasianidae** | Species ***Lagopus lagopus*** |

Willow Ptarmigan

red comb

reddish brown body

black tail

white between eye and black bill

black bill

black bill

rich reddish brown body

all-white body

ADULT (WINTER)

IN FLIGHT

MALE (SUMMER)

yellow-brown body

lacks red comb

ADULT (WINTER)

dark, scaly bars

white belly

FEMALE (SUMMER)

MALE (SUMMER)

feathered feet

FLIGHT: strong, rapid wing beats before gliding; prefers to walk.

The most common of the three ptarmigan species, the Willow Ptarmigan also undertakes the longest migration of the group. The Willow Ptarmigan is an unusual gamebird species, as male and female remain bonded throughout the chick-rearing process, in which the male is an active participant. The "Red Grouse" of British moors is a subspecies (*L. l. scoticus*) of the Willow Ptarmigan.

VOICE Variety of purrs, clucks, hissing, meowing noises; *Kow-Kow-Kow* call given before flushing, possibly alerting others.
NESTING Shallow bowl scraped in soil, lined with plant matter, protected by overhead cover; 8–10 eggs; 1 brood; March–May.
FEEDING Mostly eats buds, stems, and seeds, but also flowers, insects, and leaves when available.

PERFECT BLEND-IN
Its reddish brown upperparts camouflage this summer ptarmigan in the shrubby areas it inhabits.

SIMILAR SPECIES

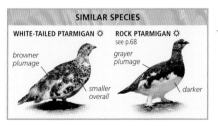

WHITE-TAILED PTARMIGAN ☼

browner plumage

smaller overall

ROCK PTARMIGAN ☼
see p.68

grayer plumage

darker

OCCURRENCE
Prefers tundra in Arctic, sub-Arctic, and sub-alpine regions. Thrives in willow thickets along low, moist river corridors; also in the low woodlands of the sub-Arctic tundra.

Length **14–17½in (35–44cm)**	Wingspan **22–24in (56–61cm)**	Weight **15–28oz (425–800g)**
Social **Winter flocks**	Lifespan **Up to 9 years**	Status **Secure**

DATE: _____ TIME: _____ LOCATION: _____

Order **Galliformes**	Family **Phasianidae**	Species **Lagopus muta**

Rock Ptarmigan

brown-and-black barring

MALE (WINTER)
black tail
white wings
small bill
all-white wings

mostly gray upperparts

small, round head
red comb

mottled belly

FEMALE (SUMMER)

gray wing patch
IN FLIGHT

MALE (SUMMER)

black line between eye and bill

FEMALE (WINTER)
white plumage

"salt-and-pepper" barring on gray upperparts

small, delicate bill

MALE (WINTER)

white belly

MALE (SUMMER)

feathered feet

FLIGHT: bursts into flight with rapid wing beats, followed by gliding and shallow flapping.

The Rock Ptarmigan is the most northerly of the three ptarmigan species found in North America. Although some birds make a short migration to more southern wintering grounds, many remain on their breeding grounds year-round. This species is well known for its distinctive seasonal variation in plumage, which helps to camouflage it against its surroundings. The Rock Ptarmigan is the official bird of Nunavut Territory.

VOICE Quiet; male call a raspy *krrrh*, also growls and clucks.
NESTING Small scrape or natural depression, lined with plant matter, often away from cover; 8–10 eggs; 1 brood; April–June.
FEEDING Feeds on buds, seeds, flowers, and leaves, especially birch and willow; eats insects in summer.

IN BETWEEN PLUMAGE
Various transitional plumage patterns can be seen on the Rock Ptarmigan in spring and fall.

SIMILAR SPECIES

WHITE-TAILED PTARMIGAN ☼
all-white tail in winter

WILLOW PTARMIGAN ☼
see p.67

smaller overall

larger overall

lighter brown upperparts

OCCURRENCE
Prefers dry, rocky tundra and shrubby ridge tops; will use edges of open meadows and dense evergreen stands along fairly high-elevation rivers and streams during winter. Occurs throughout the Northern Hemisphere in Arctic tundra from Iceland to Kamchatka in far east Russia.

Length **12½–15½in (32–40cm)**	Wingspan **19½–23½in (50–60cm)**	Weight **16–23oz (450–650g)**
Social **Winter flocks**	Lifespan **Up to 8 years**	Status **Secure**

DATE: _____ TIME:_____ LOCATION:_____

| Order **Galliformes** | Family **Phasianidae** | Species *Tympanuchus phasianellus* |

Sharp-tailed Grouse

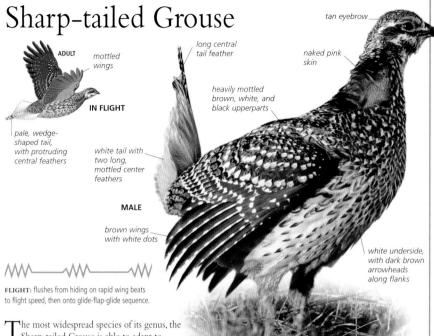

tan eyebrow

ADULT

mottled wings

long central tail feather

naked pink skin

heavily mottled brown, white, and black upperparts

IN FLIGHT

pale, wedge-shaped tail, with protruding central feathers

white tail with two long, mottled center feathers

MALE

brown wings with white dots

white underside, with dark brown arrowheads along flanks

FLIGHT: flushes from hiding on rapid wing beats to flight speed, then onto glide-flap-glide sequence.

The most widespread species of its genus, the Sharp-tailed Grouse is able to adapt to the greatest variety of habitats. It is not migratory, but undertakes seasonal movements between grassland summer habitats and woodland winter habitats. Elements of this grouse's spectacular courtship display have been incorporated into the culture and dance of Native American people, including foot stomping and tail feather rattling. The Sharp-tailed Grouse is the provincial bird of Saskatchewan.

VOICE Male calls a variety of unusual clucks, cooing, barks, and gobbles during courtship; females cluck with different intonations.

NESTING Shallow depression lined with plant matter close at hand as well as some feathers from female, usually near overhead cover; 10–12 eggs; 1 brood; March–May.

FEEDING Forages primarily for seeds, leaves, buds, and fruit; also takes insects and flowers when available.

PRAIRIE DANCER
The courtship dance of the Sharp-tailed Grouse heralds the arrival of spring to the grasslands.

SIMILAR SPECIES

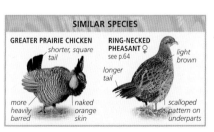

GREATER PRAIRIE CHICKEN
shorter, square tail
more heavily barred
naked orange skin

RING-NECKED PHEASANT ♀
see p.64
longer tail
light brown
scalloped pattern on underparts

OCCURRENCE
Has a northern and western distribution in North America, from Alaska (isolated population) southward across Canada to northern prairie states. Prefers a mixture of fallow and active agricultural fields combined with brushy forest edges and woodlots along river beds.

| Length **15–19in (38–48cm)** | Wingspan **23–26in (58–66cm)** | Weight **26–34oz (750–950g)** |
| Social **Flocks** | Lifespan **Up to 7 years** | Status **Declining (p)** |

DATE: _____ TIME: _____ LOCATION: _____

| Order **Galliformes** | Family **Phasianidae** | Species *Meleagris gallopavo* |

Wild Turkey

MALE (EAST)

IN FLIGHT

tail fanned in display

humped back

no feathers on head

long legs

IMMATURE

rusty tail with black band

black-and-white barred wings

unfeathered blue-and-red head

large red wattles

hair-like "beard" on breast

dark overall

iridescent bronze-and-purplish body

dark body, with bronze iridescence

FEMALE

MALE (WEST)

Once proposed by Benjamin Franklin as the national emblem of the US, the Wild Turkey—the largest gamebird in North America—was eliminated from most of its original range by the early 1900s due to over-hunting and habitat destruction. Since then, habitat restoration and the subsequent reintroduction of Wild Turkeys has been very successful.

VOICE Well-known gobble, given by males especially during courtship; female makes various yelps, clucks, and purrs, based on mood and threat level.

NESTING Scrape on ground lined with grass; placed against or under protective cover; 10–15 eggs; 1 brood; March–June.

FEEDING Omnivorous, it scratches in leaf litter on forest floor for acorns and other food, mostly vegetation; also takes plants and insects from agricultural fields.

FLIGHT: after running, leaps into the air with loud, rapid wing beats, then glides.

COLLECTIVE DISPLAY
Once the population expands into new areas, numerous males will be seen displaying together.

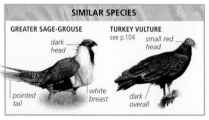

SIMILAR SPECIES

GREATER SAGE-GROUSE
dark head
pointed tail
white breast

TURKEY VULTURE
see p.104
small red head
dark overall

OCCURRENCE
Found in mixed mature woodlands, fields with agricultural crops; also in various grasslands, close to swamps, but adaptable and increasingly common in suburban and urban habitats. Quite widespread, but patchily distributed across the US and southern Canada.

| Length **2¾–4ft (0.9–1.2m)** | Wingspan **4–5ft (1.2–1.5m)** | Weight **10–24lb (4.5–11kg)** |
| Social **Flocks** | Lifespan **Up to 9 years** | Status **Secure** |

DATE: _____ TIME: _____ LOCATION: _____

Family **Gaviidae**

LOONS

Worldwide there are only five species of loon, comprising a single genus (*Gavia*), a single family (the Gaviidae), and a single order (the Gaviiformes). The five species are limited to the Northern Hemisphere, where they are found in both northern North America and northern Eurasia. One feature of loons is that their legs are positioned so far to the rear of their body that they must shuffle on their bellies when they go from water to land. Not surprisingly, therefore, loons are almost entirely aquatic birds. In summer they are found on rivers, lakes, and ponds, where they nest close to the water's edge. After breeding, they occur along coasts, often after flying hundreds of miles away from their freshwater breeding grounds.

Excellent swimmers and divers, loons are unusual among birds in that their bones are less hollow than those of other groups. Consequently, they can expel air from their lungs and compress their body feathers until they slowly sink beneath the surface. They can remain submerged like this for several minutes. A loon's wings are relatively small in proportion to its body weight. This means that they have to run a long way across the surface of the water, flapping energetically, before they can get airborne. Once in the air they keep on flapping and can fly at up to 60mph (95kmh).

LOON RANGER
The Common Loon has a wider range than any other in North America, as its name suggests.

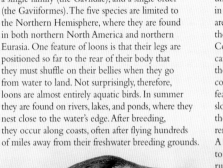

FLIGHT SHAPE
The humped back and drooping neck of this Red-throated Loon are typical of a loon in flight.

PROVIDING FOR THE FUTURE
A Red-throated Loon gives a fish to its chick to gulp down headfirst and whole.

| Order **Gaviiformes** | Family **Gaviidae** | Species **Gavia stellata** |

Red-throated Loon

white speckled back

white face

ADULT (NONBREEDING)

humped back

head lower than body

white underparts

ADULT (BREEDING)

ADULT (NONBREEDING)

IN FLIGHT

upturned bill

pale dusky face

IMMATURE

upturned gray bill

gray face and neck

all-brown back

striped gray nape

tapering dark reddish brown throat patch

ADULT (BREEDING)

E ven when seen from a distance, this elegant loon is almost unmistakable, with a pale, slim body, upward tilted head, and a thin, upturned bill. Unlike other Loons, the Red-throated Loon can leap straight into the air from both land and water, although most of the time it needs a "runway." The Red-throated Loon has an elaborate breeding ritual—side by side, a pair of birds races upright across the surface of water. Downy chicks climb onto the parents back only when very young.

VOICE High gull-like or even cat-like wail and low goose-like growl; vocal on breeding grounds, otherwise silent.

NESTING Scrape with mud and vegetation added during incubation, placed at water's edge in coastal and lake bays, shallow ponds, often at high altitudes; 2 eggs; 1 brood; April–July.

FEEDING Mainly eats fish; also spiders, crustaceans, and mollusks; flies long distances from shallow ponds when food is scarce.

FLIGHT: very direct; fast, with constant wing beats; head held lower than other loons.

TAKING OFF
While this bird is using the water's surface to take off, it can leap directly into flight from water and land.

SIMILAR SPECIES

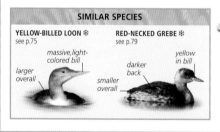

YELLOW-BILLED LOON ✳
see p.75

larger overall

massive, light-colored bill

RED-NECKED GREBE ✳
see p.79

darker back

smaller overall

yellow in bill

OCCURRENCE
Lives in open areas within northern boreal forest, muskeg, and tundra; in Canadian Arctic Archipelago, sometimes in areas almost devoid of vegetation. Winters on the Great Lakes, and both coasts southwards to Florida and northern Mexico.

| Length **24–27in (61–69cm)** | Wingspan **3½ft (1.1m)** | Weight **3¼lb (1.5kg)** |
| Social **Solitary/Loose flocks** | Lifespan **Up to 23 years** | Status **Declining** |

DATE: _____ TIME: _____ LOCATION: _____

Order **Gaviiformes**	Family **Gaviidae**	Species **Gavia pacifica**

Pacific Loon

pale crown

paler bill

red eye

neck droops less than other loons

ADULT (BREEDING)

IN FLIGHT

ADULT (MOLTING)

dark gray upperparts

dark, partial throat band

white stripes on side of neck

slim, black bill

dark throat

ADULT (BREEDING)

checkered pattern on upperparts

ADULT (NONBREEDING)

brownish black tail feathers

A lthough the Pacific Loon's breeding range is about a third of that of the Common Loon, it is believed to be the most abundant loon species in North America. It shares its habitat in northern Alaska with the nearly identical, but slightly larger and darker Arctic Loon. It is a conspicuous migrant along the Pacific Coast in spring, but disappears to its remote breeding grounds in summer. The Pacific Loon is an expert diver and swimmer, capable of remaining underwater for sustained periods of time, usually in pursuit of fish. However, on its terrestrial nesting site, its chicks are vulnerable to a number of mammalian predators.
VOICE Deep barking *kowk*; high-pitched wail, croaks, and growls when breeding; makes a yelping noise when diving.
NESTING Simple scrape in flat area close to water, vegetation and mud added during incubation; 1–2 eggs; June–July.
FEEDING Eats fish, aquatic insects, and mollusks in breeding lake or nearby waters; may dip or dive, depending on the depth.

FLIGHT: swift and direct with constant wing beats; humped back, but head in line with body.

LEVEL GROUND
As loons cannot take off from land, nest sites need to be on flat land close to the water.

SIMILAR SPECIES

ARCTIC LOON ✿

darker nape

bolder black-and-white stripes on neck

ARCTIC LOON ❉

heavier bill

brownish neck and head

OCCURRENCE
Breeds across Arctic and sub-Arctic North America, from Alaska and northern Canadian provinces to Hudson Bay and on some of the islands of the Canadian Arctic; tundra lakes and muskeg. Small numbers in Great Lakes and along East coast from Quebec to Florida. Vagrant elsewhere.

Length **23–29in (58–74cm)**	Wingspan **2¾–4¼ft (0.9–1.3m)**	Weight **2½–5½lb (1–2.5kg)**
Social **Flocks**	Lifespan **Up to 25 years**	Status **Secure**

DATE: _____ TIME: _____ LOCATION: _____

| Order **Gaviiformes** | Family **Gaviidae** | Species *Gavia immer* |

Common Loon

barely
visible eye

brownish
head

scalloped pattern
on back

checkered
back pattern

light,
partial
collar

JUVENILE

ADULT (BREEDING)   humped back   **ADULT (NONBREEDING)**

iridescent
green on
head and
neck

head held
low

**ADULT
(NONBREEDING)**

white lines on
sides of neck

white "necklace"
on throat

IN FLIGHT

spotted wings

**ADULT
(BREEDING)**

The Common Loon has the largest range of all loons in North America and is the only species to nest in a few of the northern states. It is slightly smaller than the Yellow-billed Loon but larger than the other three loons. It can remain underwater for well over 10 minutes, although it usually stays submerged for 40 seconds to 2 minutes while fishing, or a few more minutes if it is being pursued. Evidence shows that, occasionally, it interbreeds with its closest relative, the Yellow-billed Loon, in addition to the Arctic and Pacific Loons. The Common Loon is the provincial bird of Ontario.

FLIGHT: fast, direct, with constant wing beats; head and neck held just above belly.

VOICE Most recognized call a 3–10 note falsetto yodel, rising, then fading; other calls similar in quality.

NESTING Simple scrape in large mound of vegetation, a few feet from open water; 2 eggs; 1 brood; April–June.

FEEDING Feeds primarily on fish underwater; also eats crustaceans, mollusks, amphibians, leeches, insects, and aquatic plants.

COZY RIDE
Downy Common Loon chicks climb up the backs of male and female adults for a safe ride.

BATHING RITUAL
Common Loons often shake their wings after bathing.

OCCURRENCE
Breeds across North America, Canada, and south to northern US. Winters on large ice-free lakes in Canada and the US, and along the Pacific and Atlantic Coasts, south to Baja California and Florida.

SIMILAR SPECIES

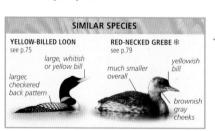

YELLOW-BILLED LOON
see p.75

large, whitish
or yellow bill

larger,
checkered
back pattern

RED-NECKED GREBE ❋
see p.79

much smaller
overall

yellowish
bill

brownish
gray
cheeks

Length **26–36in (66–91cm)**		Wingspan **4¼–5ft (1.3–1.5m)**		Weight **4½–18lb (2–8kg)**
Social **Family groups**		Lifespan **Up to 30 years**		Status **Vulnerable**

DATE: _____ TIME: _____ LOCATION: _____

Order **Gaviiformes**	Family **Gaviidae**	Species *Gavia adamsii*

Yellow-billed Loon

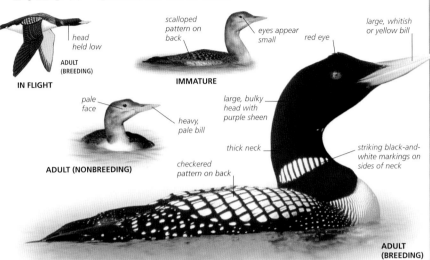

IN FLIGHT
head held low
ADULT (BREEDING)

scalloped pattern on back
eyes appear small
red eye
large, whitish or yellow bill
IMMATURE

pale face
heavy, pale bill
large, bulky head with purple sheen
thick neck
striking black-and-white markings on sides of neck

ADULT (NONBREEDING)
checkered pattern on back

ADULT (BREEDING)

The largest of the loons, the Yellow-billed Loon has the most restricted range and smallest global population. About three-quarters of the estimated 16,000–30,000 birds live in North America, and unsustainable levels of harvesting have caused recent declines. It makes the most of the short nesting season, arriving at its breeding grounds already paired and breeding immediately, although extensive ice formation can prevent it from breeding in some years. Yellow-billed Loons have more rugged proportions than other loons; their feet, for example, extend further away from their bodies.

VOICE Tremulous call much like Common Loon's, but louder, harsher, and even more "mournful"; yodels, wails, and "laughs."

NESTING Depression in mass of mud and vegetation, on shores of tundra lakes and ponds, and on river islands at high altitudes; 1–2 eggs; 1 brood; June–July.

FEEDING Dives underwater to catch small fish; also eats crustaceans, worms, and some vegetation.

FLIGHT: rapid and direct; head and neck held lower than body.

BOLDLY PATTERNED
The adult Yellow-billed Loon is strikingly patterned, like a checkerboard.

SIMILAR SPECIES

COMMON LOON ❋
see p.74
dark crown and pale cheeks

RED-NECKED GREBE ❋
see p.79
heavy, dark bill
shorter bill, yellowish at base
smaller overall

OCCURRENCE
Breeds from extreme northern edge of Alaska to eastern Northwest Territories and Nunavut. Also breeds in northern Siberia. Winters along the Pacific Coast of Alaska and British Columbia, and has been sighted in a number of US states.

Length **30–36in (77–92cm)**	Wingspan **4–5ft (1.2–1.5m)**	Weight **8³⁄₄–14lb (4–6.5kg)**
Social **Solitary/Pairs/Family groups**	Lifespan **Up to 30 years**	Status **Vulnerable**

GREBES

GREBES RESEMBLE LOONS and share many of their aquatic habits, but anatomical and molecular features show that they are actually unrelated; and they are placed in a different order: the Podicipediformes. Grebe bodies are streamlined, offering little resistance when diving and swimming. Underwater, their primary means of propulsion is the sideways motion of their lobed toes. The legs are placed far back on the body, which greatly aids the bird when swimming above or below the surface. Grebes have short tails, and their trailing legs and toes serve as rudders when they fly. The position of the legs makes it impossible, however, for grebes to stand upright for long or to easily walk on land. Thus, even when breeding they are tied to water; and their nests are usually partially floating platforms, built on beds of water plants. Grebes' toes have broad lobes that splay when the bird thrusts forward through the water with its feet. They dive to catch fish with a short, forward arching spring. Unusual among birds, they swallow feathers, supposedly to trap fish bones and protect their stomachs, then periodically disgorge them. Like loons, grebes can control their buoyancy by exhaling air and compressing their plumage so that they sink quietly below the surface. They are strong fliers, as well as migratory.

A FINE DISPLAY
This Horned Grebe reveals the colorful plumes on its head, as part of its elaborate courtship display.

PIED BILL
The black-and-white bill pattern clearly distinguishes this bird as the Pied-billed Grebe.

| Order **Podicipediformes** | Family **Podicipedidae** | Species **Podilymbus podiceps** |

Pied-billed Grebe

outstretched neck

ADULT (BREEDING)

lighter flight feathers

IN FLIGHT

yellowish bill

whitish throat

ADULT (NONBREEDING)

brown eye

whitish, hooked bill with a black ring

brownish gray body

reddish brown neck and breast

black throat patch

ADULT (BREEDING)

white undertail

The widest ranging of the North American grebes, the Pied-billed Grebe is tolerant of highly populated areas and is often seen breeding on lakes and ponds across North America. It is a powerful swimmer and can remain submerged for 16–30 seconds when it dives. In contrast to some of the elaborate displays from other grebe species, its courtship ritual is more vocal than visual and a pair usually duet-call in the mating season. Migration, conducted at night, is delayed until its breeding area ices up and food becomes scarce. The Pied-billed Grebe is capable of sustained flights of over 2,000 miles (3,200km).

VOICE Various grunts and wails; in spring, call a cuckoo-like repeated gobble *kup-kup-Kaow-Kaow-kaow*, gradually speeding up.

NESTING Floating nest of partially decayed plants and clipped leaves, attached to emergent vegetation in marshes and quiet waters; 4–7 eggs; 2 broods; April–October.

FEEDING Dives to catch a variety of crustaceans, fish, amphibians, insects, and other invertebrates; also picks prey from emergent vegetation, or catches them mid-air.

FLIGHT: strong, direct flight with rapid wing beats, but rarely seen.

BACK OFF
When alarmed, a Pied-billed Grebe will flap its wings in a defensive display.

OCCURRENCE
Breeds on a variety of water bodies, including coastal brackish ponds, seasonal ponds, marshes, and even sewage ponds. Winters in the breeding area if food and open water are available, otherwise chooses still waters resembling its breeding habitat.

SIMILAR SPECIES

LEAST GREBE ✿

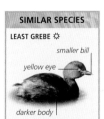

smaller bill

yellow eye

darker body

| Length **12–15in (31–38cm)** | Wingspan **18–24in (46–62cm)** | Weight **13–17oz (375–475g)** |
| Social **Family groups** | Lifespan **At least 3 years** | Status **Vulnerable** |

DATE: _____ TIME: _____ LOCATION: _____

| Order **Podicipediformes** | Family **Podicipedidae** | Species **Podiceps auritus** |

Horned Grebe

IN FLIGHT

ADULT
(SUMMER)

neck and head in line with body

white cheek

flattish top of head

white sides to neck

ADULT
(WINTER)

gold streak from eye to nape

black crown

red eye

ADULT
(SPRING MOLT)

rufous neck

short, dark bill with whitish tip

black throat

**ADULT
(SUMMER)**

The timing of the Horned Grebe's migration depends largely on the weather—this species may not leave until its breeding grounds get iced over, nor does it arrive before the ice melts. Its breeding behavior is well documented since it is approachable on nesting grounds and has an elaborate breeding ritual. This grebe's so-called "horns" are in fact yellowish feather patches located behind its eyes, which it can raise at will.

VOICE At least 10 calls, but descending *aaanrrh* call most common in winter, ends in trill; muted conversational calls when birds are in groups.

NESTING Floating, soggy nest, hidden in vegetation, in small ponds and lake inlets; 3–9 eggs; 1 brood; May–July.

FEEDING Dives in open water or forages among plants, mainly for small crustaceans and insects, but also leeches, mollusks, amphibians, fish, and some vegetation.

FLIGHT: strong, rapid wing beats; runs on water to become airborne; rarely takes off from land.

HITCHING A RIDE
In common with other grebes, Horned Grebe chicks often ride on the back of a swimming parent.

SIMILAR SPECIES

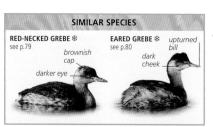

RED-NECKED GREBE ❋
see p.79

brownish cap

darker eye

EARED GREBE ❋
see p.80

dark cheek

upturned bill

OCCURRENCE
Breeds in small freshwater, even slightly brackish, ponds and marshes, including man-made ponds. Prefers areas with open water and patches of sedges, cattails, and other wetland vegetation in any ecosystem. Winters on saltwater close to shore; also on large bodies of freshwater.

| Length **12–15in (30–38cm)** | Wingspan **18–24in (46–62cm)** | Weight **11–20oz (300–575g)** |
| Social **Pairs/Loose flocks/Colonies** | Lifespan **Up to 5 years** | Status **Declining** |

DATE: _____ TIME: _____ LOCATION: _____

Order **Podicipediformes**	Family **Podicipedidae**	Species ***Podiceps grisegena***

Red-necked Grebe

head and neck in line with body

white-edged inner wing

ADULT (BREEDING)

IN FLIGHT

brownish cap

pale, reddish brown crescent near ear

ADULT (NONBREEDING)

broad stripes on cheek and ear

mostly yellowish bill

JUVENILE

broad head with crest at rear

grayish white cheeks and throat

black cap

brown eye

gray flanks

chestnut brown neck and chest

ADULT (BREEDING)

The Red-necked Grebe is smaller than Western and Clark's Grebes, but larger than the other North American grebes. It migrates over short to medium distances and spends the winter along both coasts, where large flocks may be seen during the day. It runs along the water's surface to become airborne, although it rarely flies. This grebe doesn't come ashore often; it stands erect, but walks awkwardly, and prefers to sink to its breast and shuffle along. **VOICE** Nasal, gull-like call on breeding grounds, evolves into bray, ends with whinny; also honks, rattles, hisses, purrs, and ticks. **NESTING** Compact, buoyant mound of decayed and fresh vegetation in sheltered, shallow marshes and lakes, or artificial wetlands; 4–5 eggs; 1 brood; May–July. **FEEDING** An opportunistic hunter, eats fish, crustaceans, aquatic insects, worms, mollusks, salamanders, and tadpoles.

FLIGHT: fast, direct, wing beats, with head and outstretched neck mostly level with line of body.

COURTSHIP DISPLAY
This courting pair face each other, with outstretched necks and raised chests.

SIMILAR SPECIES

RED-THROATED LOON ❊
see p.72

no yellow on bill

white spots on back *white neck*

HORNED GREBE ❊
see p.78

reddish eye
paler neck

OCCURRENCE
Breeds from northern prairies and forests, almost to the tree line in the northwest; limited to suitable interior bodies of water such as large marshes and small lakes. Winters primarily in estuaries, inlets, bays, and offshore shallows along Atlantic and Pacific Coasts; can also be found on the Great Lakes.

Length **16½–22in (42–56cm)**	Wingspan **24–35in (61–88cm)**	Weight **1¾–3½lb (0.8–1.6kg)**
Social **Pairs/Loose flocks**	Lifespan **Up to 6 years**	Status **Vulnerable**

DATE: _____ TIME: _____ LOCATION: _____

Order **Podicipediformes**	Family **Podicipedidae**	Species ***Podiceps nigricollis***

Eared Grebe

darker flanks

white patch on wing

browner plumage

ADULT (SUMMER)

outstretched neck

dusky white flanks

dusky cheek

IN FLIGHT

upturned bill

grayish neck

JUVENILE

large, wispy gold patch behind red eye

dark back

ADULT (WINTER)

black neck

black crest

red eye

thin, upturned bill

rufous breast and sides

ADULT (SUMMER)

The most abundant grebe in North America, the Eared Grebe is quite remarkable in terms of physiology. After breeding, it undergoes a complex and drastic reorganization of body-fat stores, along with changes in muscle, heart, and digestive organ mass to prepare it for fall migration. All of this increases the bird's energy reserves and body mass, but renders it flightless. It may have the longest periods of flightlessness of any flying bird—up to 10 months.

VOICE Various trills during courtship, including squeaky, rising *poo-eep*; sharp *chirp* when alarmed; usually silent at other times.

NESTING Sodden nest of decayed bottom plants anchored in thinly spaced reeds or submerged vegetation in shallow water of marshes, ponds, and lakes; 1 brood; 1–8 eggs; May–July.

FEEDING Forages underwater for small crustaceans and aquatic insects; also small fish and mollusks; consumes worms in winter.

FLIGHT: flies with neck outstretched, held at a low angle; rarely flies except during migration.

SALTY WATER
The Eared Grebe prefers salty water at all times except when breeding.

SIMILAR SPECIES

RED-NECKED GREBE ❊
see p.79

browner cap

thicker bill

HORNED GREBE ❊
see p.78

more distinct white cheek

white tip on bill

OCCURRENCE
Breeds in marshes, shallow lakes, and ponds in the four western provinces. After breeding, many birds seek highly saline, slow-to-freeze waters, such as Mono Lake, where their favorite foods thrive—brine shrimp and alkali flies. Winters in coastal bays of Pacific coast and is a vagrant on the Atlantic coast.

Length **12–14in (30–35cm)**	Wingspan **22¹/₂–24in (57–62cm)**	Weight **7–26oz (200–725g)**
Social **Flocks**	Lifespan **Up to 12 years**	Status **Secure**

DATE: _____ TIME: _____ LOCATION: _____

TUBENOSES

THE TUBENOSES ARE DIVIDED INTO several families, but all are characterized by the tubular nostrils for which the order is named. These nostrils help to get rid of excess salt, and may enhance their sense of smell.

FLAP AND GLIDE
Shearwaters alternate stiff-winged flapping with gliding just over the ocean's surface.

SHEARWATERS

Shearwaters and gadfly petrels (family Procellariidae) are smaller than albatrosses (found only in western Canada). Like their larger relatives they are excellent gliders, but their lighter weight and proportionately shorter wings mean that they use more powered flight than albatrosses. They range over all the world's oceans. With its far more numerous islands, the Pacific Ocean is home to a greater variety of these seabirds than the Atlantic. During and after storms are the best times to look for these birds, as this is when they have been drifting away from the deep sea due to wind and waves.

STORM-PETRELS

The smallest tubenoses in North American waters, the storm-petrels (family Hydrobatidae) are also the most agile fliers. They often patter or "dance" as they fly low to the surface of the ocean in search of small fish, squid, and crustaceans. Storm-petrels spend most of their lives flying over the open sea, only visiting land in the breeding season, when they form huge colonies.

HOOKED BILL
In addition to the tubular nostrils all tubenoses have strongly hooked bills.

OLD BIRD
The Northern Fulmar is one of the longest-lived birds, with a lifespan of up to 50 years.

| Order **Procellariiformes** | Family **Procellariidae** | Species ***Fulmarus glacialis*** |

Northern Fulmar

white patch on wing

paddle-like wings

gray back

white head

**ADULT
(ATLANTIC FORM)**

small dark patch in front of eye

**ADULT
(ATLANTIC
FORM)**

IN FLIGHT

thick, yellow bill

short, rounded, gray tail

ADULT (LIGHT PACIFIC FORM)

white underparts

FLIGHT: snappy wing beats and long glides near the surface of the ocean.

dark gray overall

ADULT (DARK PACIFIC FORM)

Possessing paddle-shaped wings and distinctive color patterns ranging from almost all-white to all-gray, the Northern Fulmar is among the most common seabirds in places like the Bering Sea. It breeds at high latitudes, then disperses south to offshore waters on both coasts of the continent. The Northern Fulmar can often be seen in large mixed flocks containing albatrosses, shearwaters, and petrels. Fulmars often follow boats, eager to pounce on the offal thrown overboard by fishermen.
VOICE Mostly silent at sea; occasionally utters cackles and grunts.
NESTING Scrape in rock or soil on edge of cliff; 1 egg; 1 brood; May–October.
FEEDING Picks fish and offal from the surface of the ocean; also dives underwater to catch fish.

FEEDING FRENZY
Large numbers of Northern Fulmars compete for the offal discarded by fishing trawlers.

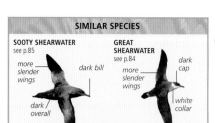

SIMILAR SPECIES

SOOTY SHEARWATER
see p.85

more slender wings

dark bill

dark overall

GREAT SHEARWATER
see p.84

more slender wings

dark cap

white collar

OCCURRENCE
Breeds on remote, high, coastal cliffs in Alaska and northern Canada; winters at sea in offshore Pacific and Atlantic waters, generally farther north than most other seabirds. Breeds in Europe, to Greenland, Svalbard; also parts of Russia.

| Length **17½–19½in (45–50cm)** | Wingspan **3¼–3½ft (1–1.1m)** | Weight **16–35oz (0.45–1kg)** |
| Social **Flocks** | Lifespan **Up to 50 years** | Status **Secure** |

DATE: _____ TIME: _____ LOCATION: _____

Cory's Shearwater

dark wingtip and trailing edge

long, pointed wings

clean white underwing

all white belly

pale rump **ADULT**

grayish head and chin

ADULT

yellow bill with dark tip

IN FLIGHT

scalloped pattern

ADULT

white breast, with sooty-gray sides

FLIGHT: slow, deliberate wing beats interspersed with long glides; often arcs strongly on bent wings.

Close studies of a group of Cory's Shearwaters off the Atlantic coast suggest the presence of two forms. The more common form, *C. d. borealis*, nests in the eastern Atlantic and is chunkier, with less white in the wing from below. The other form, *C. d. diomedea*, breeds in the Mediterranean, has a more slender build (including a thinner bill), and has more extensive white under the wing. Cory's Shearwater has a distinctive, relatively languid flight style that is different from the other shearwaters regularly found in North American waters.

VOICE Mostly silent at sea; descending, lamb-like bleating.

NESTING Nests in burrow or rocky crevice; 1 egg; 1 brood; May–September.

FEEDING Dives into water or picks at surface for small schooling fish, and marine invertebrates such as squid.

LAZY FLIERS
In calm weather Cory's Shearwaters look heavy and fly low, swooping higher in strong winds.

SIMILAR SPECIES

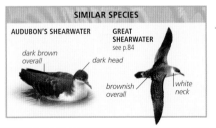

AUDUBON'S SHEARWATER
dark brown overall

GREAT SHEARWATER
see p.84
dark head
brownish overall
white neck

OCCURRENCE
This species breeds in the Mediterranean and on islands of the eastern Atlantic, including the Azores, the Salvages, Madeira, and the Canaries. When nonbreeding, Cory's Shearwaters disperse widely over the Atlantic Ocean, including off the east coast of Canada.

| Length **18in (46cm)** | Wingspan **3½ft (1.1m)** | Weight **28oz (800g)** |
| Social **Flocks** | Lifespan **Unknown** | Status **Secure** |

DATE: _____ TIME: _____ LOCATION: _____

Great Shearwater

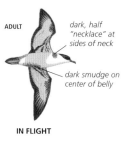

ADULT

dark, half "necklace" at sides of neck

dark smudge on center of belly

IN FLIGHT

thin, white band on rump

darker outer wing feathers

brownish upperwings

white collar

dark cap

thin, black bill

ADULT

A common species in North Atlantic waters, from northern Canada to Florida, the Great Shearwater is similar in size to Cory's Shearwater and the birds scavenge together for scraps around fishing boats. However, their plumages and flight styles are quite different. While Cory's Shearwater has slow, labored wing beats, and glides high on broad, bowed, swept-back wings, Great Shearwaters keep low, flapping hurriedly between glides on straight, narrow wings. The brown smudges on the belly (not always visible) and paler underwings of the Great Shearwater also help distinguish the species.

VOICE Silent at sea; descending, lamb-like bleating at breeding sites.

NESTING Digs deep burrow in peaty or boggy soil; 1 egg; 1 brood; September–March.

FEEDING Feeds either from the surface, picking up items such as fish and squid, or makes shallow dives with open wings.

FLIGHT: fast, stiff wing beats interspersed with gliding; arcs high in windy conditions.

WHITE COLLAR
The Great Shearwater's white collar is highly visible between its black cap and sooty back.

SIMILAR SPECIES

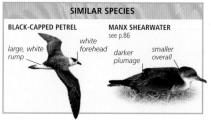

BLACK-CAPPED PETREL

large, white rump

white forehead

MANX SHEARWATER
see p.86

darker plumage

smaller overall

OCCURRENCE
Nests on just a few islands in the middle of the South Atlantic. Total population probably well over 200 million. Postbreeding birds make a very long 8-shaped migration around the Atlantic, spending late July–September in North Atlantic waters, usually offshore.

Length **18in (46cm)**	Wingspan **3½ft (1.1m)**	Weight **30oz (850g)**
Social **Flocks**	Lifespan **At least 25 years**	Status **Secure**

DATE: _____ TIME:_____ LOCATION:_____

Order **Procellariiformes**	Family **Procellariidae**	Species *Puffinus griseus*

Sooty Shearwater

silvery white patch along underwing

ADULT

all-dark underparts

IN FLIGHT

ADULT

long, slender wings

ADULT

all-dark upperparts

sooty head

long, hooked bill

FLIGHT: rapid, stiff wing beats, interspersed with glides; arcs up highly in strong winds.

Sooty Shearwaters are extremely long-distance migrants, with both Atlantic and Pacific populations undergoing lengthy circular migrations. Pacific birds in particular travel as far as 300 miles (480km) per day and an extraordinary 45,000 miles (72,500km) or more per year. Huge flocks of this species are often seen off the coast of California. It is fairly easy to identify off the East Coast of North America, as it is the only all-dark shearwater found there.
VOICE Silent at sea; occasionally gives varied, agitated vocalizations when feeding, very loud calls at breeding colonies.
NESTING In burrow or rocky crevice; 1 egg; 1 brood; October–May.
FEEDING Dives and picks at surface for small schooling fish and mollusks such as squid.

HUGE FLOCKS
Sooty Shearwaters are often found in "rafts" numbering many thousands of birds.

TUBENOSE
Shearwaters are tubenoses, so-called for the salt-excreting tubes on their bills.

OCCURRENCE
Sooty Shearwaters breed on islands in the southern Ocean and nearby waters, some colonies numbering in the thousands of pairs. Postbreeding movements take them north into the Pacific and Atlantic Ocean, on 8-shaped migrations.

SIMILAR SPECIES

SHORT-TAILED SHEARWATER
dark upperparts

GREAT SHEARWATER
see p.84
dark cap
white tail band
shorter bill
pale throat
white collar

Length **18in (46cm)**	Wingspan **3ft 3in (1m)**	Weight **27oz (775g)**
Social **Flocks**	Lifespan **Unknown**	Status **Secure**

| Order **Procellariiformes** | Family **Procellariidae** | Species **Puffinus puffinus** |

Manx Shearwater

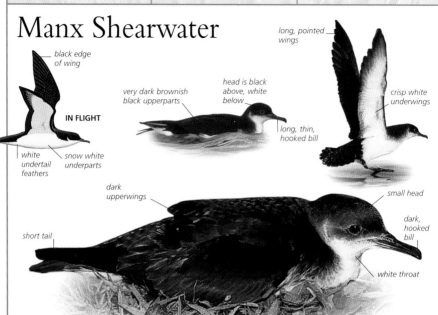

long, pointed wings

black edge of wing

very dark brownish black upperparts

head is black above, white below

crisp white underwings

IN FLIGHT

long, thin, hooked bill

white undertail feathers

snow white underparts

dark upperwings

small head

dark, hooked bill

short tail

white throat

M ost shearwaters are little known because of their nocturnal and oceanic ways, but the Manx is an exception. It is common in the British Isles, and ornithologists have been studying it there for decades. Long-term banding programs revealed one bird that flew over 3,000 miles (4,800km) from Massachusetts to its nesting burrow in Wales in just 12½ days, and another that was captured 56 years after it was first banded, making its accumulated migration-only mileage around 600,000 miles (1,000,000km).

VOICE Usually silent at sea, but at breeding sites, produces loud and raucous series of cries, *kah-kah-kah-kah-kah-HOWW*.

NESTING In burrow, in peaty soil, or rocky crevice; 1 egg; 1 brood; April–October.

FEEDING Dives into water, often with open wings and stays underwater, or picks at surface for small schooling fish and squid.

FLIGHT: rapid, stiff wing beats interspersed with glides; arcs high in strong winds.

PITTER-PATTER
Unlike gulls, shearwaters have to patter along the surface with their feet to achieve lift-off speed.

SIMILAR SPECIES

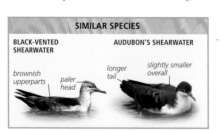

BLACK-VENTED SHEARWATER

brownish upperparts

paler head

AUDUBON'S SHEARWATER

longer tail

slightly smaller overall

OCCURRENCE
Breeds on many islands in eastern North Atlantic; restricted to islands off Newfoundland in North America. Regularly occurs off east coast as far south as Florida. Rare in Gulf of Mexico and off the West Coast. Rarely seen from shore; cold-water shearwater.

| Length **13½in (34cm)** | Wingspan **33in (83cm)** | Weight **14–20oz (400–575g)** |
| Social **Migrant flocks** | Lifespan **Up to 55 years** | Status **Secure** |

DATE: _____ TIME: _____ LOCATION: _____

| Order **Procellariiformes** | Family **Hydrobatidae** | Species *Oceanites oceanicus* |

Wilson's Storm-Petrel

broad, pointed wings

white rump and lower flanks

pale bar on upperwing

ADULT

IN FLIGHT

dark wings and body

"walking" on water

small, black "tube nose"

ADULT

short, square tail

yellow webbing between toes

Named after Alexander Wilson, often called the "father of North American ornithology," Wilson's Storm-Petrel is the quintessential small oceanic petrel. It is an extremely abundant species and breeds in the many millions on the Antarctic Peninsula and islands in Antarctica. After breeding, many move north to spend the summer off the Atlantic coast of North America. Here, they are a familiar sight to fishermen and birders at sea. By August they can be seen lingering, but by October they have flown south.

VOICE At sea, soft rasping notes; at breeding sites a variety of *coos*, *churrs*, and twitters during the night.

NESTING Mostly in rock crevices; also burrows where there is peaty soil; 1 egg; 1 brood; November–March.

FEEDING Patters on the water's surface, legs extended, picking up tiny crustaceans; also carrion, droplets of oil.

FLIGHT: flutters, low to ocean's surface, often "stalling" to drop to the surface and glean food.

FEEDING FLOCK
While flying, this bird "walks" on water, simultaneously picking food from the surface.

SIMILAR SPECIES

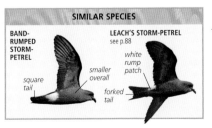

BAND-RUMPED STORM-PETREL

square tail

smaller overall

LEACH'S STORM-PETREL
see p.88

white rump patch

forked tail

OCCURRENCE
Breeds on the Antarctic Peninsula, many sub-Antarctic islands, and islands in the Cape Horn Archipelago. April–September or October, moves north, and is abundant off the coasts of Atlantic Canada and the US in July–September. With inshore winds, can often be seen from land.

| Length **6³/₄in (17cm)** | Wingspan **16in (41cm)** | Weight **1¹/₁₆–1⁷/₁₆oz (30–40g)** |
| Social **Flocks** | Lifespan **Up to 10 years** | Status **Secure** |

DATE: _____ TIME: _____ LOCATION: _____

| Order **Procellariiformes** | Family **Hydrobatidae** | Species *Oceanodroma leucorhoa* |

Leach's Storm-Petrel

long, angled wings

white rump with thin, dark line down center

ADULT

IN FLIGHT

brown bar across blackish wings

ADULT

dark sooty black underwings

dark smudge beside eye

forked tail

dark sooty brown underparts

ADULT

FLIGHT: buoyant, deep wing beats low over ocean's surface, interrupted by twists and turns.

Leach's Storm-Petrel is widespread in both the Atlantic and Pacific Oceans, unlike most other storm-petrels. It breeds in colonies on islands off the coasts, coming to land at night and feeding offshore during the day, often many miles from the colony. This wide-ranging storm-petrel has both geographical and individual variation; most populations show a white rump, but others have a dark rump that is the same color as the rest of the body. Leach's Storm-Petrel can be distinguished from the similar Band-rumped Storm-Petrel by its notched tail and swooping flight.

VOICE At nesting sites, often from burrows, calls are long series of soft purring and chattering sounds.

NESTING Underground burrow on island free of predators such as rats; 1 egg; 1 brood; May–November.

FEEDING Gleans small crustaceans and small fish from the water's surface while in flight.

BALANCING ACT
Leach's Storm-Petrel will often balance itself with its wings while walking.

SIMILAR SPECIES

BAND-RUMPED STORM-PETREL

white of rump extends toward belly

BLACK STORM-PETREL

dark rump

OCCURRENCE
Breeds on islands in the Pacific Ocean from Alaska and the Aleutian Islands south to California; in the Atlantic Ocean, from Newfoundland to Maine. After breeding, it wanders widely on both oceans, keeping well out of sight of land.

Length **7–8¹⁄₂in (18–22cm)**	Wingspan **17¹⁄₂–19in (45–48cm)**	Weight **1⁹⁄₁₆–1¾oz (45–50g)**
Social **Colonies**	Lifespan **Up to 36 years**	Status **Secure**

DATE: _____ TIME: _____ LOCATION: _____

GANNETS AND CORMORANTS

UNTIL RECENTLY, GANNETS AND CORMORANTS were grouped with pelicans under the order Pelicaniformes. Now they are part of the order Suliformes, which also includes frigatebirds, boobies, and anhingas. Only gannets and cormorants are found in Canada.

HALF AND HALF
This Northern Gannet shows the distinctive mottled black-and-white plumage of an immature bird.

GANNETS
Gannets are large white seabirds with yellowish heads, long bills, and black-tipped wings. They are fish eaters that hunt by diving from heights of up to 98ft (30m) into the water. Gannets breed in colonies, usually on islands and coasts, and lay one egg per season. These birds take five years to become fully mature—first-year birds are dark overall, and gradually show more white through subsequent moultings.

CORMORANTS
With 36 species worldwide, cormorants are medium to large waterbirds—some are marine, others are freshwater. They have broad and long wings, rounded tails, short and strong legs, and hookedtipped bills often tilted upwards while swimming. In flight, the neck is extended but noticeably kinked. When hunting for fish, cormorants dive from the surface of the water, rolling smoothly under or with a noticeable forward leap; they then swim underwater with closed wings, using their webbed toes for propulsion. Most cormorants are dark birds, apart from some distinctive facial patterns on areas of bare skin which become more colorful in spring. Many of these birds nest on cliff ledges, although some prefer trees, while others are happy to use both cliffs and trees. There is one flightless cormorant species in the Galápagos.

DARK PLUMAGE
Grooming for this Double-crested Cormorant includes spreading its wings to dry them in the sun.

| Order **Suliformes** | Family **Sulidae** | Species ***Morus bassanus*** |

Northern Gannet

black wing tip

light blue eye

yellow tinge to back of head

dark brown overall

upper wings and white back mottled with black

IMMATURE (3RD YEAR)

pointed gray bill

black wing tip

ADULT

JUVENILE (1ST YEAR)

white upperparts

long, pointed wing

IN FLIGHT

yellow-orange nape

black-and-white mottled upperparts

white underparts

ADULT

pointed tail

IMMATURE (2ND YEAR)

FLIGHT: strong, direct flight with deep, powerful wing beats and short glides.

The Northern Gannet is known for its spectacular headfirst dives during frantic, voracious foraging in flocks of hundreds to thousands for surface-schooling fish. This bird nests in just six locations in northeastern Canada. The Northern Gannet was the first species to have its total world population estimated, at 83,000 birds in 1939. Numbers have since increased.

VOICE Loud landing call by both sexes *arrrr, arrah*, or *urrah rah rah*; hollow groan *oh-ah* uttered during take-off; *krok* call at sea.

NESTING Large pile of mud, seaweed, and rubbish, glued with guano, on bare rock or soil; 1 egg; 1 brood; April–November.

FEEDING Plunge-dives headfirst into water and often swims underwater to catch fish; eats mackerel, herring, capelin, and cod.

NESTING SITE
Northern Gannets prefer to nest in huge, noisy colonies on isolated rocky slopes or cliffs.

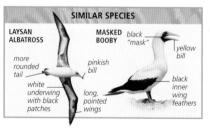

SIMILAR SPECIES

LAYSAN ALBATROSS

more rounded tail

white underwing with black patches

MASKED BOOBY

pinkish bill

long, pointed wings

black "mask"

yellow bill

black inner wing feathers

OCCURRENCE
Breeds on isolated rock stacks, on small uninhabited islands in the eastern North Atlantic, or on steep, inaccessible cliffs in marine areas of northeast North America; during migration and in winter, can be found in the waters of the continental shelf of the Gulf and Atlantic coast.

| Length **2¾–3½ft (0.8–1.1m)** | Wingspan **5½ft (1.7m)** | Weight **5–8lb (2.2–3.6kg)** |
| Social **Flocks** | Lifespan **Up to 20 years** | Status **Localized** |

DATE: _____ TIME:_____ LOCATION:_____

Double-crested Cormorant

white crest

bluish eye

ADULT (BREEDING)

no crest

long neck

pale neck and breast

browner plumage overall

orange facial skin

ADULT (NONBREEDING)

black overall

JUVENILE

black underparts

blackish crest

pale throat and chest

JUVENILE

IN FLIGHT

ADULT
P. a. auritus
(EASTERN; BREEDING)

FLIGHT: regular wing beats, occasional glides; over water, flies close to the surface; often soars.

This species is the most widespread of the North American cormorants. It often flies high over land in V-shaped flocks, but is mostly seen swimming in the water with its head and neck visible, or resting on trees and rocks, sometimes with its wings spread. While fishing, it dives from the surface of the water and chases fish underwater, using its webbed toes for propulsion.

VOICE Deep gruntlike calls while nesting, roosting, and fishing; *t-t-t-t* call before taking off and *urg-urg-urg* before landing; prolonged *arr-r-r-r-r-t-t* while mating, and *eh-hr* as threat.

NESTING Nests of twigs and sticks, seaweed, and trash, lined with grass; built on ground, cliffs, or in trees usually in colonies; 3-5 eggs; 1 brood; April–August.

FEEDING Pursues slow-moving or schooling fish; feeds on insects, crustaceans, amphibians, and, rarely, on voles and snakes.

ADULT
P. a. cincinatus
(WESTERN; BREEDING)

DRYING OFF
Like all cormorants, the Double-crested usually perches with wings spread to dry its feathers.

SIMILAR SPECIES

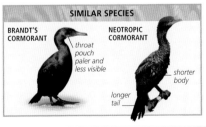

BRANDT'S CORMORANT

throat pouch paler and less visible

NEOTROPIC CORMORANT

shorter body

longer tail

OCCURRENCE
Breeds in a wide range of aquatic habitats, including ponds, artificial and natural lakes, slow-moving rivers, estuaries, lagoons, and seashores; winters on coastlines and sandbars in coastal inlets; roosts near catfish farms in some areas.

| Length **28–35in (70–90cm)** | Wingspan **3½–4ft (1.1–1.2m)** | Weight **2¾–5½lb (1.2–2.5kg)** |
| Social **Flocks** | Lifespan **Up to 18 years** | Status **Secure** |

DATE: _____ TIME: _____ LOCATION: _____

| Order **Suliformes** | Family **Phalacrocoracidae** | Species **Phalacrocorax carbo** |

Great Cormorant

large head with flat forehead

thick bill with hooked tip

JUVENILE

whitish gray belly

orange-yellow patch of skin near bill

long, black neck

brown neck

ADULT

white throat

outstretched head

mostly white underparts

neck kinked in flight

glossy black underparts with greenish scalloping

IN FLIGHT

ADULT (BREEDING)

JUVENILE

long body with glossy black upperparts

short, black legs and webbed feet

FLIGHT: regular, shallow wing beats; sometimes glides and soars; flocks often fly in V-shape.

long, broad tail

A s its name suggests, the Great Cormorant is the largest of the North American cormorants and is also the most widely distributed cormorant species in the world. It sometimes breeds in mixed colonies with Double-crested Cormorants. From a distance, the two can be confused, especially outside breeding areas. However, Great Cormorants can be distinguished by their stouter bill, larger size, and their white throat when breeding. It is a coastal species in North America, but in Europe, it is more likely to be found inland. Like other cormorants, its plumage retains water, which effectively reduces buoyancy so that it is able to dive more easily. The Great Cormorant can dive to depths of 115ft (35m) to catch prey.

VOICE Deep, guttural calls at nesting and roosting site; otherwise silent.

NESTING Mound of seaweed, sticks, and debris added to previous year's nest, built on cliff ledges and flat tops of rocks above high-water mark on islands; 3–5 eggs; 1 brood; April–August.

FEEDING Dives to pursue fish and small crustaceans; smaller prey swallowed underwater, while larger prey brought to surface.

SIMILAR SPECIES

DOUBLE-CRESTED CORMORANT see p.91
thinner bill
black throat

RARE EVENT
Great Cormorants usually nest on sea cliffs; tree breeding is rare in North America.

OCCURRENCE
Breeds on cliff ledges of islands along rocky coasts, in northeast US and Maritimes of Canada; feeds in protected inshore waters. Winters in shallow coastal waters similar to breeding habitat, but not restricted to rocky shoreline; winter habitat extends to the Carolinas in the US.

| Length **33–35in (84–90cm)** | Wingspan **4¼–5¼ft (1.3–1.6m)** | Weight **5¾–8¼lb (2.6–3.7kg)** |
| Social **Colonies** | Lifespan **Up to 14 years** | Status **Secure** |

DATE: _____ TIME:_____ LOCATION:_____

PELICANS, HERONS, IBISES, AND RELATIVES

T HESE RELATED WATERBIRDS exploit a diversity of water and waterside habitats in different ways, from plunge-diving in the ocean to wading at the edge of mangroves and freshwater marshes, from scooping up fish to stealthy and patient hunting from overhanging branches.

PELICANS

Pelicans are large fish-eating birds, bulky but buoyant on water. Brown Pelicans, vagrants in Canada, dive headfirst to catch fish, while White Pelicans work together to herd fish into shallow bays, and scoop them up in their large, flexible bill pouches unique to pelicans.

HERONS, EGRETS, AND BITTERNS

These waterside birds have long toes, which enable them to walk on wet mud and wade among reed stems. Their long toes also aid their balance as they lean forward in search of fish and when catching prey in their long, pointed bills. Herons and egrets have slender, feathered necks with a distinct kink that gives a lightning forward thrust when catching prey. Most herons and egrets make bulky nests in treetop colonies, whereas bitterns nest on the ground in marshes. Unlike storks and cranes, they all fly with their heads withdrawn into their shoulders.

POISED AND READY
This Green Heron is ready to make a strike for its prey.

IBISES

Waterside or dry-land birds, ibises are long-legged, and walk with great strides. They have long, decurved bills that are adapted to picking insects, worms, small mollusks, and crustaceans from wet mud. Ibises often fly in long lines or V-formations.

DANCING ON AIR
The Great Egret's courtship display often involves spreading its wings and leaping in a kind of aerial dance.

American White Pelican

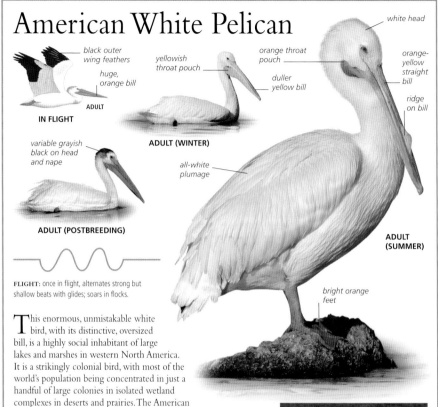

white head

black outer wing feathers

huge, orange bill

ADULT
IN FLIGHT

yellowish throat pouch

orange throat pouch

duller yellow bill

orange-yellow straight bill

ridge on bill

ADULT (WINTER)

variable grayish black on head and nape

all-white plumage

ADULT (POSTBREEDING)

ADULT (SUMMER)

bright orange feet

FLIGHT: once in flight, alternates strong but shallow beats with glides; soars in flocks.

This enormous, unmistakable white bird, with its distinctive, oversized bill, is a highly social inhabitant of large lakes and marshes in western North America. It is a strikingly colonial bird, with most of the world's population being concentrated in just a handful of large colonies in isolated wetland complexes in deserts and prairies. The American White Pelican forms foraging flocks, which beat their wings in coordinated movements to drive fish into shallow water, where they can be caught more easily.

VOICE Usually silent except around nesting colonies; around the nest, young and adults exchange various grunts and hisses.

NESTING Depression in the ground, both sexes incubate; 1–2 eggs; 1 brood; April–August.

FEEDING Mainly gulps down small fish, occasionally eats small amphibians, and crayfish.

LARGE COLONIES
The White Pelican is highly social and is usually seen feeding or roosting in large groups.

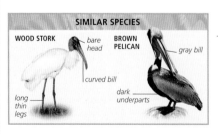

SIMILAR SPECIES

WOOD STORK
bare head

BROWN PELICAN
gray bill

curved bill

dark underparts

long thin legs

OCCURRENCE
Breeds on islands in freshwater lakes in south-central Canada, mountainous areas of the western US, and in coastal northeast Mexico; an early spring migrant, often returning to breeding grounds in early March. Winters in coastal regions from California and Texas to Mexico and Central America.

Length 4¼–5½ft (1.3–1.7m)	Wingspan 7¾–9½ft (2.4–2.9m)	Weight **12–20lb (5.5–9kg)**
Social **Colonies**	Lifespan **Up to 26 years**	Status **Vulnerable**

DATE: _____ TIME: _____ LOCATION: _____

Order **Pelecaniformes**	Family **Ardeidae**	Species *Botaurus lentiginosus*

American Bittern

rusty brown crown

long, straight bill

dark outer wing feathers

trailing legs

ADULT

black streak on side of neck

duller crown

IN FLIGHT

brown back

no large black patch on neck

short tail

brown streaks on chest

JUVENILE

ADULT

greenish legs

The American Bittern's camouflaged plumage and secretive behavior help it to blend into the thick vegetation of its freshwater wetland habitat. It is heard much more often than it is seen; its call is unmistakable and has given rise to many evocative colloquial names, such as "thunder pumper."

VOICE Deep, resonant *pump-er-unk*, *pump-er-unk*; calls mainly at dawn, dusk, and night time, but also during the day in the early mating season.

NESTING Platform or mound constructed of available marsh vegetation, usually over shallow water; 2–7 eggs; 1 brood; April–August.

FEEDING Stands still or moves slowly, then strikes downward with bill to catch prey; eats fish, insects, crustaceans, snakes, amphibians, and small mammals.

FLIGHT: steady, deep, slightly stiff wing beats; usually flies relatively low and direct.

SIMILAR SPECIES

LEAST BITTERN
see p.96

black back

smaller overall

yellowish legs

BLACK-CROWNED NIGHT-HERON ☾
see p.101

white spots

thicker bill

LOOKING UP
Bitterns are secretive birds, but can occasionally be found walking slowly through reeds.

OCCURRENCE
Breeds in heavily vegetated freshwater wetlands across the northern US and southern Canada; also occasionally in estuarine wetlands; winters in southern and coastal wetlands where temperatures stay above freezing; can appear in any wetland habitat during migration.

Length **23½–31in (60–80cm)**	Wingspan **3½–4¼ft (1.1–1.3m)**	Weight **13–20oz (375–575g)**
Social **Solitary**	Lifespan **At least 8 years**	Status **Declining**

DATE: _____ TIME: _____ LOCATION: _____

| Order **Pelecaniformes** | Family **Ardeidae** | Species *Ixobrychus exilis* |

Least Bittern

brown back

buff and black pattern on wings

MALE

IN FLIGHT

dark-brown back

streaked underparts

dark-brown cap

pale wing feathers

FEMALE

JUVENILE

black back

short tail

yellowish legs and toes

black cap

long, yellow bill

brown streaks on chest

MALE

The smallest heron in North America, the Least Bittern is also one of the most colorful, but its secretive nature makes it easy to overlook in its densely vegetated marsh habitat. A dark color form, which was originally described in the 1800s as a separate species named Cory's Bittern, has rarely been reported in recent decades.

VOICE Soft *ku, ku, ku, ku, ku* display call; year-round, a loud *kak, kak, kak*.

NESTING Platform of marsh vegetation with sticks and stems added, usually within 30ft (9m) of open water; 2–7 eggs; 1 brood; April–August.

FEEDING Feeds on small fish, insects including dragonflies; also crustaceans; clings quietly to vegetation before striking prey, or stalks slowly.

FLIGHT: rapid wing beats; weak, direct flight; flies low, around top of vegetation.

REED CREEPER
With its small, thin body, this species easily creeps through dense reeds in search of prey.

SIMILAR SPECIES

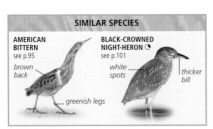

AMERICAN BITTERN
see p.95

brown back

greenish legs

BLACK-CROWNED NIGHT-HERON ☾
see p.101

white spots

thicker bill

OCCURRENCE
Breeds in summer in lowland freshwater marshes; less commonly in brackish and rarely in saltwater marshes; frequents similar habitat on migration; winters in brackish and saltwater marshes. Wide distribution in the Americas, south to Argentina.

| Length **11–14in (28–36cm)** | Wingspan **15½–18in (40–46cm)** | Weight **2⅝–3³⁄₈oz (75–95g)** |
| Social **Solitary/Small flocks** | Lifespan **Unknown** | Status **Secure** |

DATE: _____ TIME: _____ LOCATION: _____

| Order **Pelecaniformes** | Family **Ardeidae** | Species *Ardea herodias* |

Great Blue Heron

ADULT

dark wing tips

dark tail

brownish body

IN FLIGHT

crooked neck

JUVENILE

blue-gray body

white face

dark bill

gray neck

yellowish bill

lighter-colored neck, almost beige

light bill

large, white bird

overall similar to Great Blue

shaggy plumes

light legs

MALE

dark legs

WURDEMANN'S HERON (WHITE-HEADED FORM)

GREAT WHITE HERON (WHITE FORM)

FLIGHT: deep-flapping, regular wing beats.

T his is the largest heron in North America and one of the largest herons in the world. The Great Blue Heron is a common inhabitant of a variety of North American waterbodies, from marshes to swamps, as well as along sea coasts. Its majestic, deliberate flight is a highly wonderful sight to behold; look for the characteristic tight s-shaped neck and long, trailing legs.

VOICE Mostly silent; gives a loud, barking squawk or *crank* in breeding colonies or when disturbed.

NESTING Nest of twigs and branches; usually in colonies, but also singly; in trees, often over water, but also over ground; 2–4 eggs; 1–2 broods; February–August.

FEEDING Catches prey, sometimes spearing, with quick jab of bill; primarily fish.

LOFTY ABODE
Great Blue Herons nest in small colonies in trees, and often roost in them.

SIMILAR SPECIES

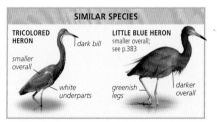

TRICOLORED HERON

smaller overall

dark bill

white underparts

LITTLE BLUE HERON
smaller overall; see p.383

greenish legs

darker overall

OCCURRENCE
Across southern Canada and the US in wetlands, such as marshes, lake edges, and along rivers and swamps; also in marine habitats, especially tidal grass flats. The Great White Heron is primarily found in marine habitats.

| Length 2¾–4¼ft (0.9–1.3m) | Wingspan 5¼–6½ft (1.6–2m) | Weight 4¾–5½lb (2.1–2.5kg) |
| Social **Solitary/Flocks** | Lifespan **Up to 20 years** | Status **Secure** |

DATE: _____ TIME: _____ LOCATION: _____

Order **Pelecaniformes**	Family **Ardeidae**	Species ***Ardea alba***

Great Egret

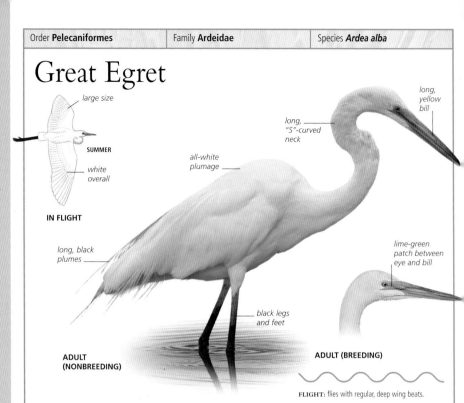

large size

SUMMER

white overall

IN FLIGHT

long, "S"-curved neck

long, yellow bill

all-white plumage

long, black plumes

black legs and feet

lime-green patch between eye and bill

ADULT (NONBREEDING)

ADULT (BREEDING)

FLIGHT: flies with regular, deep wing beats.

This large white heron is found on every continent except Antarctica. When feeding, the Great Egret apparently prefers to forage alone rather than in flocks—it maintains space around itself, and will defend a territory of 10ft (3m) in diameter from other wading birds. This territory "moves" with the bird as it feeds. In years of scarce food supplies, a chick may kill a sibling, permitting the survival of at least one bird.

VOICE Largely vocal during courtship and breeding; otherwise, *kraak* or *cuk-cuk-cuk* when disturbed or in a combative encounter.

NESTING Nest of twigs in trees, over land or water; 2–4 eggs; 1 brood; March–July.

FEEDING Catches prey with quick thrust of bill; feeds on aquatic prey, primarily fish, also crustaceans.

TREE PERCHES
Great Egrets nest in trees and regularly perch in them when not feeding.

SIMILAR SPECIES		
LITTLE BLUE HERON ☾ see p.383	**SNOWY EGRET** black bill; see p.383	
two-toned bill	smaller overall	
smaller overall	yellow-green legs	yellow feet

OCCURRENCE
Breeds in trees over water or on islands; forages in freshwater and marine wetlands from marshes and ponds to rivers. Migratory over much of its North American range; more southerly populations resident. Range has expanded northward into Canada. Distance migrated depends on severity of winter.

Length **3¼ft (1m)**	Wingspan **6ft (1.8m)**	Weight **1¾–3¼lb (0.8–1.5kg)**
Social **Solitary**	Lifespan **Up to 25 years**	Status **Secure**

DATE: _____ TIME: _____ LOCATION: _____

Order **Pelecaniformes**	Family **Ardeidae**	Species *Bubulcus ibis*

Cattle Egret

rich buff on back

ADULT (BREEDING)

IN FLIGHT

all-white body

yellow bill

ADULT (NONBREEDING)

looks all-white in flight at long range

dark legs and feet

ADULT (BREEDING)

rich buff crown

yellow bill, reddish in spring

short neck

white body and wings

rich buff on breast in spring

ADULT (BREEDING)

yellow legs and feet

FLIGHT: flies with regular wing beats; neck crooked and legs extended.

Unlike most other herons, the Cattle Egret is a grassland species that rarely wades in water, and is often seen with livestock, feeding on the insects disturbed by their feet. It is thought to have originated in the shortgrass prairies of Africa and is now found worldwide. It was first seen in Florida in 1941, but expanded rapidly and has now bred in over 40 US states and up into the southern provinces of Canada.

VOICE Generally silent; vocal at the nest: *rick-rack* common.

NESTING Nest of branches or plants placed in trees over ground; also in trees or shrubs over water; 2–5 eggs; 1 brood; March–October.

FEEDING Eats in groups, consumes insects, spiders as well as larger animals such as frogs; insects stirred up in grasslands by cattle.

VOCAL BREEDERS
This bird almost never calls away from a breeding colony, but is vocal near its nests.

OCCURRENCE
Since the 1940s, it has expanded to many habitats in much of North America, primarily in grasslands and prairies, but also wetland areas. In tropical regions, the Cattle Egrets flock around the cattle feeding in shallow wetlands.

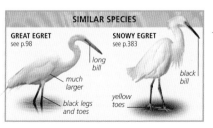

SIMILAR SPECIES

GREAT EGRET
see p.98

much larger

black legs and toes

SNOWY EGRET
see p.383

long bill

black bill

yellow toes

Length **20in (51cm)**	Wingspan **31in (78cm)**	Weight **13oz (375g)**
Social **Colonies**	Lifespan **Up to 17 years**	Status **Secure**

DATE: _____ TIME: _____ LOCATION: _____

| Order **Pelecaniformes** | Family **Ardeidae** | Species *Butorides virescens* |

Green Heron

ADULT (BREEDING)

greenish back

IN FLIGHT

short, rufous neck

greenish black cap

white speckles on wings

paler bill

JUVENILE

white chin

thin, straight, black bill

cream streak extends from throat to belly

long back plumes

yellowish legs and feet

ADULT (NONBREEDING)

glossy orange legs

ADULT (BREEDING)

A small, solitary, and secretive bird of dense thicketed wetlands, the Green Heron can be difficult to observe. This dark, crested heron is most often seen flying away from a perceived threat, emitting a loud squawk. While the Green Heron of North and Central America has now been recognized as a separate species, it was earlier grouped with what is now the Striated Heron (*B. striata*), which is found in the tropics and subtropics throughout the world.

VOICE Squawking *keow* when flying from disturbance.
NESTING Nest of twigs often in bushes or trees, often over water but also on land; 1–2 broods; 3–5 eggs; March–July.
FEEDING Mainly fish, but also frogs, insects, and spiders; lays insects and other items on the water's surface as bait to attract fish.

FLIGHT: direct, a bit plodding, and usually over short distances.

READY TO STRIKE
Green Herons usually catch their prey by lunging forward and downward with their whole body.

SIMILAR SPECIES

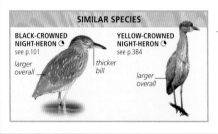

BLACK-CROWNED NIGHT-HERON ◑
see p.101

larger overall

thicker bill

YELLOW-CROWNED NIGHT-HERON ◑
see p.384

larger overall

OCCURRENCE
An inhabitant of swampy thickets, but occasionally dry land close to water across much of the lower half of North America, but missing in the plains, the Rocky Mountains, and the western deserts that do not provide appropriate wetlands. Winters in coastal wetlands.

| Length **14½–15½in (37–39cm)** | Wingspan **25–27in (63–68cm)** | Weight **7–9oz (200–250g)** |
| Social **Solitary/Pairs/Small flocks** | Lifespan **Up to 10 years** | Status **Secure** |

DATE: _____ TIME: _____ LOCATION: _____

Black-crowned Night-Heron

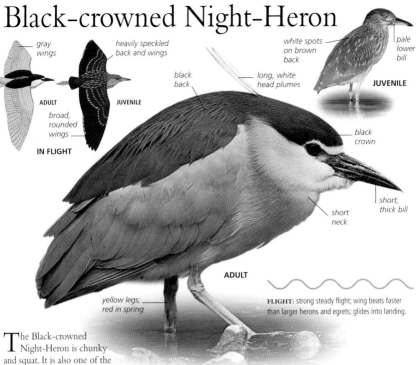

gray wings

heavily speckled back and wings

ADULT

JUVENILE

broad, rounded wings

IN FLIGHT

black back

long, white head plumes

white spots on brown back

pale lower bill

JUVENILE

black crown

short, thick bill

short neck

ADULT

yellow legs; red in spring

FLIGHT: strong steady flight; wing beats faster than larger herons and egrets; glides into landing.

The Black-crowned Night-Heron is chunky and squat. It is also one of the most common and widespread herons in North America and in the world. But because, as its name suggests, it is mainly active at twilight and at night, many people have never seen one. However, its distinctive barking call can be heard at night—even at the center of large cities.

VOICE Loud, distinctive *quark* or *wok*, often given in flight and around colonies.

NESTING Large stick nests built usually 20–40ft (6–12m) up in trees; 3–5 eggs; 1 brood; November–August.

FEEDING Feeds primarily on aquatic animals, such as fish, crustaceans, insects, and mollusks; also eggs and chicks of colonial birds, such as egrets, ibises, and terns.

LONG PLUMES
In breeding plumage, the plumes of the male of this species are longer than the female's.

OCCURRENCE
Widespread; can be found wherever there are waterbodies, such as lakes, ponds, streams; generally absent from higher elevations. Colonies often on islands or in marshes; colony sites may be used for decades. In winter, found in areas where water remains open.

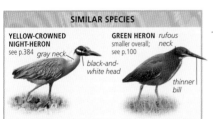

SIMILAR SPECIES

YELLOW-CROWNED NIGHT-HERON
see p.384 gray neck

GREEN HERON *rufous*
smaller overall; *neck*
see p.100

black-and-white head

thinner bill

Length **23–26in (58–65cm)**	Wingspan **3¹/₂–4ft (1.1–1.2m)**	Weight **1¹/₂–2¹/₂lb (0.7–1kg)**
Social **Colonies**	Lifespan **Up to 21 years**	Status **Secure**

DATE: _____ TIME: _____ LOCATION: _____

| Order **Pelecaniformes** | Family **Threskiornithidae** | Species *Plegadis falcinellus* |

Glossy Ibis

finely streaked head and neck

iridescent crown

dark brown eye

outstretched neck

dark maroon neck

ADULT (NONBREEDING)

trailing legs

ADULT (BREEDING)

iridescent bronze-green feathers on inner wing

curved, gray-brown bill

IN FLIGHT

chestnut or maroon underparts

ADULT (BREEDING)

gray-green legs and feet

FLIGHT: alternate wing beats and glides; flies with neck outstretched, legs extended beyond tail.

With its long, curved bill, the dark, long-legged Glossy Ibis is similar to the White-faced Ibis. It is well known for its wandering tendencies and can also be found in southern Europe, Asia, Australia, and Africa. Despite being found in the US in the mid-19th century, the Glossy Ibis was not discovered nesting in Florida until 1886. Confined to Florida until the mid-20th century, it then started spreading northward, eventually as far as southern Ontario and across into Nova Scotia.

VOICE Crow-like croak; subdued nasal chatter in flocks; mostly silent.

NESTING Platform of twigs and reeds in trees, shrubs, or reeds, on ground or over water; 3–4 eggs; 1 brood; April–July.

FEEDING Forages by feel, puts bill in soil and mud to catch prey, including snails, insects, leeches, frogs, and crayfish.

MARSH FEEDER
The Glossy Ibis regularly feeds in shallow pools and along the waterways of coastal marshes.

SIMILAR SPECIES

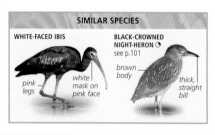

WHITE-FACED IBIS

pink legs

white mask on pink face

BLACK-CROWNED NIGHT-HERON see p.101

brown body

thick, straight bill

OCCURRENCE
Common from New England south to Florida but has spread north into the eastern provinces. Occurs in brackish and freshwater marshes and in flooded or plowed fields; feeds with other waders in inland freshwater wetlands as well as coastal lagoons and estuaries.

| Length **23in (59cm)** | Wingspan **36in (92cm)** | Weight **13oz (375g)** |
| Social **Flocks/Colonies** | Lifespan **15–20 years** | Status **Secure (p)** |

DATE: _____ TIME: _____ LOCATION: _____

HAWKS, EAGLES, VULTURES, AND RELATIVES

MANY BIRDS OF PREY grasp their victims with strong feet that have sharp, hooked claws, and tear their food with hooked bills, but they are a remarkably varied group and a common description does not apply to all of them.

HAWKS, EAGLES, AND RELATIVES

This group covers a range of raptors with varied hunting methods. Bald Eagles scavenge fish while Golden Eagles prey on small to medium-sized mammals and larger-sized birds. Harriers scrutinize the ground while flying low on raised wings across open spaces. Ospreys are exclusively fish-eaters and hover over water before diving in to catch prey with their strong feet, which have spiny scales to help hold slippery fish. Forest-dwelling hawks rely more on speed and stealth, ambushing small birds, although Northern Goshawks occasionally "stoop" from a height to catch big birds and medium-sized mammals.

VULTURES

Primarily feeding on carrion, vultures rarely kill prey and find food by using exceptionally acute vision, covering large areas of land in wide-ranging, soaring flights. They use updrafts of warm air to stay aloft on long, broad, "fingered" wings. Turkey Vultures help Black Vultures (rare in Canada) find carcasses, as they not only have excellent vision, but also one of the world's best olfactory senses that help them find dead animals hidden under the forest canopy. Turkey Vultures can be seen flying solo but also roosting in large groups in trees and on artificial structures. Each bird keeps an eye on other widely scattered birds—should one drop to the ground, others quickly follow. Turkey Vultures can also be found foraging for carrion washed up on beaches.

WEAK TOOL
In spite of its sharp beak, the Turkey Vulture cannot always break the skin of carcasses.

DOUBLE SHOT
With lots of fish running in a tight school, this Osprey has the strength and skill to catch two with one dive.

Order **Accipitriformes**	Family **Cathartidae**	Species *Cathartes aura*

Turkey Vulture

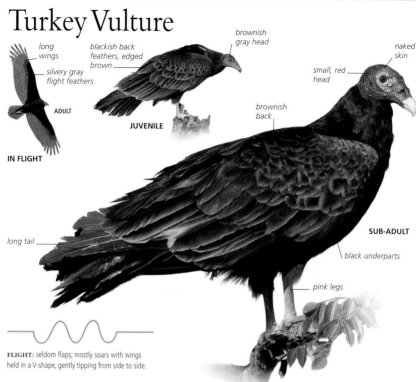

long wings

silvery gray flight feathers

ADULT

IN FLIGHT

blackish back feathers, edged brown

brownish gray head

JUVENILE

naked skin

small, red head

brownish back

SUB-ADULT

long tail

black underparts

pink legs

FLIGHT: seldom flaps; mostly soars with wings held in a V-shape, gently tipping from side to side.

The most widely distributed vulture in North America, the Turkey Vulture is found in most of the US and has expanded its range into southern Canada from coast to coast. It possesses an excellent sense of smell and uses it to locate carcasses sometimes hidden from view. The Turkey Vulture's habit of defecating down its legs, which it shares with the Wood Stork, may serve to cool it or to kill bacteria with its ammonia content.

VOICE Silent, but will hiss at intruders; also grunts.

NESTING Dark recesses, such as under large rocks or stumps, on rocky ledges in caves, and crevices, in mammal burrows and hollow logs, and abandoned buildings; 1–3 eggs; 1 brood; March–August.

FEEDING Feeds on a wide range of wild and domestic carrion, mostly mammals, but also birds, reptiles, amphibians, and fish; occasionally takes live prey such as nestlings or trapped birds.

SOAKING UP THE SUN
Turkey Vultures often spread their wings to sun themselves and increase their body temperature.

SIMILAR SPECIES

BLACK VULTURE see p.384

shorter tail

all-black body

OCCURRENCE
Generally forages and migrates over mixed farmland and forest; prefers to nest in forested or partly forested hillsides offering hidden ground protected from disturbance; roosts in large trees such as cottonwoods, on rocky outcrops, and on power line transmission towers; some winter in urban areas and near landfills. Also seen on beaches.

Length **25–32in (64–81cm)**	Wingspan **5¹/₂–6ft (1.7–1.8m)**	Weight **4¹/₂lb (2kg)**
Social **Flocks**	Lifespan **At least 17 years**	Status **Secure**

DATE: _____ TIME: _____ LOCATION: _____

| Order **Accipitriformes** | Family **Pandionidae** | Species *Pandion haliaetus* |

Osprey

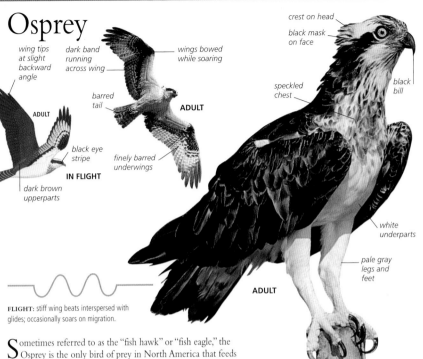

wing tips at slight backward angle

dark band running across wing

wings bowed while soaring

barred tail

ADULT

ADULT

crest on head

black mask on face

speckled chest

black bill

black eye stripe

finely barred underwings

IN FLIGHT

dark brown upperparts

dark brown upperparts

white underparts

pale gray legs and feet

ADULT

FLIGHT: stiff wing beats interspersed with glides; occasionally soars on migration.

Sometimes referred to as the "fish hawk" or "fish eagle," the Osprey is the only bird of prey in North America that feeds almost exclusively on live fish. Sharp spicules (tiny, spike-like growths) on the pads of its feet, reversible outer toes, and an ability to lock its talons in place enable it to hold onto slippery fish. Some populations declined between the 1950s and 1980s due to the use of organochlorine pesticides. However, the ban on use of these chemicals, along with availability of artificial nest sites and a tolerance of nearby human activity, has allowed the Osprey to return to its former numbers. The Osprey is the provincial bird of Nova Scotia.

VOICE Slow, whistled notes, falling in pitch: *tiooop, tioooop, tiooop*; also screams by displaying male.

NESTING Twig nest on tree, rock pinnacles, and a wide variety of artificial structures; 1–4 eggs; 1 brood; March–August.

FEEDING Dives to catch fish up to top 3ft (90cm) of water.

IMPROVING AERODYNAMICS
Once caught, a fish is held with its head pointing forward, reducing drag as the bird flies.

SIMILAR SPECIES		
BALD EAGLE (2ND YEAR) see p.106	**GOLDEN EAGLE** see p.115	dark brown head

no crook in wings during flight

paler tail

brown, feathered legs

OCCURRENCE
Breeds in a wide variety of habitats: northern forests, near shallow reservoirs, along freshwater rivers and large lakes, estuaries and salt marshes, coastal deserts and desert saltflat lagoons. Migrates through and winters in similar habitats.

| Length **21–23in (53–58cm)** | Wingspan **5–6ft (1.5–1.8m)** | Weight **3–4½lb (1.4–2kg)** |
| Social **Solitary/Pairs** | Lifespan **Up to 25 years** | Status **Secure** |

| Order **Accipitriformes** | Family **Accipitridae** | Species *Haliaeetus leucocephalus* |

Bald Eagle

JUVENILE

dark head, jutting out

ADULT

white head

brown body

white tail

IN FLIGHT

dark brown eyes

white belly and underwings mottled brown

dark brown overall

pure white head with yellow eyes

IMMATURE (2ND YEAR)

dark bill starting to turn yellow at base

yellow, hooked bill

dark eyestripe on whitish face

JUVENILE (1ST YEAR)

IMMATURE (4TH YEAR)

dark chocolate-brown overall

long, wedge-shaped, white tail

yellow legs and feet

ADULT

FLIGHT: slow, powerful wing beats; soars and glides on broad, wide wings held at a right angle.

With its white head and tail, the Bald Eagle, although an opportunist, prefers to scavenge on carrion and steal prey from other birds, including Ospreys. It was nearing extinction because the use of DDT led to reproductive failure. Declared endangered in 1967, its populations have rebounded to high numbers, especially on the coasts. The Bald Eagle was selected by an act of Congress in 1782 as the national emblem of the US.
VOICE Surprisingly high-pitched voice, 3–4 notes followed by a rapidly descending series.
NESTING Huge stick nest, usually in tallest tree; 1–3 eggs; 1 brood; March–September.
FEEDING Favors carrion, especially fish, also eats birds, mammals, reptiles; steals fish from Osprey.

SIMILAR SPECIES

FERRUGINOUS HAWK
dark head

whitish underparts

GOLDEN EAGLE ◑
white in flight feathers;
see p.115

feathered legs

SUBSTANTIAL ABODE
Bald eagles make the largest stick nest of all raptors; it can weigh up to two tons.

OCCURRENCE
Widespread across Canada and much of the US. Breeds in forested areas near water; also shoreline areas ranging from undeveloped to relatively well-developed with marked human activity; winters along major river systems and in coastal areas and occasionally even in arid regions of southwest US.

| Length **28–38in (71–96cm)** | Wingspan **6½ft (2m)** | Weight **6½–14lb (3–6.5kg)** |
| Social **Solitary/Pairs** | Lifespan **Up to 28 years** | Status **Secure** |

DATE: _____ TIME:_____ LOCATION:_____

Order **Accipitriformes** | Family **Accipitridae** | Species *Circus hudsonius*

Northern Harrier

MALE — black wing tips; wings held in V-shape; white rump — **IN FLIGHT**

FEMALE — dark barring on silver-gray underwings; bluish gray upperparts

dark bill with yellow skin near bluish base

bluish gray head; reddish underparts — **JUVENILE**

white ring around face; brown upperparts — **FEMALE**

white underparts with reddish brown markings

gray uppertail with light undertail feathers

MALE

Found nearly all over North America, the Northern Harrier is most often seen flying buoyantly low in search of food. A white rump, V-shaped wings, and tilting flight make this species easily identifiable. The blue-gray males are strikingly different from the dark-brown females. The bird's most recognizable characteristic is its owl-like face, which contains stiff feathers to help channel in sounds from prey. Northern Harriers are highly migratory throughout their range.

VOICE Call given by both sexes in rapid succession at nest: *kek* becomes more high-pitched when intruders are spotted.
NESTING Platform of sticks on ground in open, wet field; 4–6 eggs; 1 brood; April–September.
FEEDING Mostly hunts rodents like mice and muskrats; also birds, frogs, reptiles; occasionally takes larger prey such as rabbits.

FLIGHT: low and slow with lazy flaps, alternating with buoyant, brusquely tilting glides.

WATERY DWELLING
To avoid predators, Northern Harriers prefer to raise their young on wet sites in tall, dense vegetation.

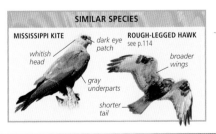

SIMILAR SPECIES

MISSISSIPPI KITE — whitish head; gray underparts

ROUGH-LEGGED HAWK see p.114 — dark eye patch; broader wings; shorter tail

OCCURRENCE
Breeds in a variety of open wetlands: marshes, meadows, pastures, fallow fields across most of North America; winters in open habitats like deserts, coastal sand dunes, cropland, grasslands, marshy, and riverside areas.

| Length **18–20in (46–51cm)** | Wingspan **3½–4ft (1.1m–1.2m)** | Weight **11–26oz (300–750g)** |
| Social **Solitary/Pairs/Colonies** | Lifespan **Up to 16 years** | Status **Secure** |

DATE: _____ TIME: _____ LOCATION: _____

| Order **Accipitriformes** | Family **Accipitridae** | Species *Accipiter striatus* |

Sharp-shinned Hawk

square-tipped tail

short, rounded wings

grayish blue upperparts

head appears small

JUVENILE

wide, dark, horizontal bars on gray tail

IN FLIGHT

rounded head

slightly browner upperparts than male

yellow legs and toes

MALE

grayish blue crown

reddish yellow eye

reddish brown bars on underparts

dark brown upperparts

light yellowish eye

wide, brown streaks on underparts

ADULT

white, fluffy undertail feathers

FEMALE

JUVENILE FEMALE

This small and swift hawk is quite adept at capturing birds, occasionally even taking species larger than itself. The Sharp-shinned Hawk's short, rounded wings and long tail allow it to make abrupt turns and lightning-fast dashes in thick woods and dense shrubby terrain. With needle-like talons, long, spindle-thin legs, and long toes, this hawk is well adapted to snatching birds in flight. The prey is plucked before being consumed or fed to the nestlings.

VOICE High-pitched, repeated *kiu kiu kiu* call; sometimes makes squealing sound when disturbed at nest.

NESTING Sturdy nest of sticks lined with twigs or pieces of bark; sometimes an old crow or squirrel nest; 3–4 eggs; 1 brood; March–June.

FEEDING Catches small birds, such as sparrows and wood warblers, on the wing, or takes them unaware while perched.

FLIGHT: rapid, direct, and strong; nimble enough to maneuver in dense forest; soars during migration.

HUNTING BIRDS
A Sharp-shinned Hawk pauses on the ground with a freshly captured sparrow in its talons.

SIMILAR SPECIES

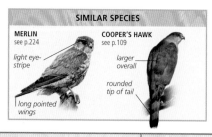

MERLIN
see p.224

light eye-stripe

long pointed wings

COOPER'S HAWK
see p.109

larger overall

rounded tip of tail

OCCURRENCE
Deep coniferous forests and mixed hardwood–conifer woodlands across North America from the tree limit in northern Canada to the Gulf states. During fall migration sometimes seen in flocks of hundreds of individuals. Winters in Central America from Guatemala to Panama.

| Length **11in (28 cm)** | Wingspan **23in (58cm)** | Weight **3½–6oz (100–175g)** |
| Social **Solitary/Flocks** | Lifespan **At least 10 years** | Status **Secure** |

DATE: _____ TIME: _____ LOCATION: _____

| Order **Accipitriformes** | Family **Accipitridae** | Species *Accipiter cooperii* |

Cooper's Hawk

dark crown and flatter head

reddish eye

grayish blue upperparts

broad, rounded wings

JUVENILE

long, barred tail with rounded tip

IN FLIGHT

yellowish eyes

light underparts, with brown streaks

mottled dark brown upperparts

grayish blue overall

yellow legs and toes

brown tail

head extends beyond leading edge of wings

JUVENILE

ADULT

ADULT

gray tail with wide, dark bands

FLIGHT: fast with rapid wing beats interspersed with glides; sometimes soars.

white band at tip of tail

A secretive and inconspicuous bird, Cooper's Hawk, was named by Charles Bonaparte, nephew of French Emperor Napoleon Bonaparte, for William C. Cooper, a noted New York naturalist. It is a typical woodland hawk, capable of quickly maneuvering through dense vegetation. Although it prefers to stay close to cover, it will venture out in search of food. Should a human approach the nest of a Cooper's Hawk, the brooding adult will quietly glide down and away from the nest tree rather than attack the intruder.

VOICE Most common call a staccato *ca-ca-ca-ca*; other vocalizations include as many as 40 different calls.

NESTING Medium-sized, stick nest, usually in a large deciduous tree; 4–5 eggs; 1 brood; April–May.

FEEDING Catches birds, such as robins and blackbirds; larger females can capture grouse; also eats chipmunks, small squirrels, and even bats.

DENSE BARRING
This hawk has characteristic fine, reddish brown, horizontal barring on its undersides.

OCCURRENCE
Breeds in woodlands across northern North America, southern Canada, and the northern US, south to Florida, Texas, and northwestern Mexico. Likes mature deciduous forests with leaf cover; also roosts in conifers, and has adapted to urban environments. Winters in southwestern US and Mexico.

SIMILAR SPECIES	
NORTHERN HARRIER ♀ see p.107 — larger overall	**SHARP-SHINNED HAWK** see p.108 — whitish underparts, square-tipped tail, much smaller head

Length **15½–17½in (40–45cm)**	Wingspan **28–34in (70–86cm)**	Weight **13–19oz (375–525g)**
Social **Solitary/Pairs**	Lifespan **At least 10 years**	Status **Secure**

DATE: _____ TIME: _____ LOCATION: _____

Order **Accipitriformes** | Family **Accipitridae** | Species *Accipiter gentilis*

Northern Goshawk

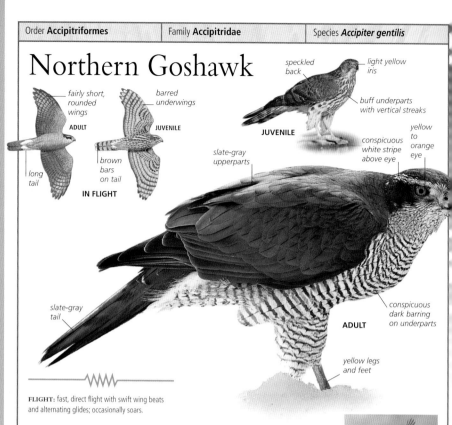

fairly short, rounded wings

ADULT

barred underwings

JUVENILE

long tail

brown bars on tail

IN FLIGHT

speckled back

light yellow iris

buff underparts with vertical streaks

JUVENILE

conspicuous white stripe above eye

yellow to orange eye

slate-gray upperparts

slate-gray tail

conspicuous dark barring on underparts

ADULT

yellow legs and feet

FLIGHT: fast, direct flight with swift wing beats and alternating glides; occasionally soars.

The powerful and agile Northern Goshawk is secretive by nature and not easily observed, even in regions where it is common. It has few natural enemies, but will defend its territories, nests, and young fiercely by repeatedly diving and screaming at intruders that get too close. Spring hikers and turkey-hunters occasionally discover Northern Goshawks by wandering into their territory and being driven off by the angry occupants.

VOICE Loud, high-pitched *gek-gek-gek* when agitated.

NESTING Large stick structures lined with bark and plant matter in the mid- to lower region of tree; 1–3 eggs; 1 brood; May–June.

FEEDING Sits and waits on perch before diving rapidly; preys on birds as large as grouse and pheasants; also mammals, including hares and squirrels.

OCCASIONAL SOARER
A juvenile Northern Goshawk takes advantage of a thermal, soaring during migration.

OCCURRENCE
Breeds in deep deciduous, coniferous, and mixed woodlands in northern North America, from the tundra–taiga border south to California, northern Mexico, and Pennsylvania in the eastern US, absent from east central US. Likes to nest in monoculture forests.

SIMILAR SPECIES

GYRFALCON (GRAY FORM) see p.225

longer, pointed wings

COOPER'S HAWK see p.109

brownish upperparts

no streaks on underparts

streaked underparts

Length **21in (53cm)**	Wingspan **3½ft (1.1m)**	Weight **2–3lb (0.9–1.4kg)**
Social **Solitary/Pairs**	Lifespan **Up to 20 years**	Status **Secure**

DATE: _____ TIME: _____ LOCATION: _____

Order **Accipitriformes**	Family **Accipitridae**	Species **Buteo lineatus**

Red-shouldered Hawk

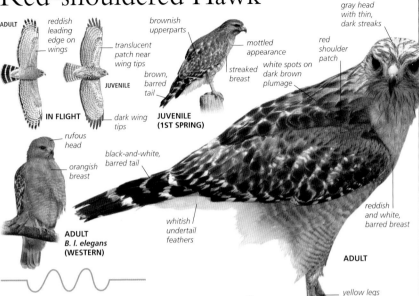

ADULT

reddish leading edge on wings

translucent patch near wing tips

IN FLIGHT

dark wing tips

brownish upperparts

JUVENILE

brown, barred tail

streaked breast

JUVENILE (1ST SPRING)

mottled appearance

white spots on dark brown plumage

gray head with thin, dark streaks

red shoulder patch

rufous head

orangish breast

black-and-white, barred tail

whitish undertail feathers

ADULT
B. l. elegans
(WESTERN)

reddish and white, barred breast

ADULT

yellow legs and feet

FLIGHT: occasional rapid flapping; soars in lazy circles over treetops with wings and tail spread.

The Red-shouldered Hawk has a remarkable distribution, with widespread populations in the East and northeast, and in the Midwest Great Plains and the West, from Oregon to Baja California, despite a geographical gap of 1,000 miles (1,600km) between the two regions Eastern birds are divided into four subspecies; western populations belong to the subspecies *B. l. elegans*. The red shoulder patches are not always evident, but the striped tail and translucent "windows" in the wings are easily identifiable.
VOICE Call a whistled *kee-aah*, accented on first syllable, descending on second.
NESTING Platform of sticks, dried leaves, bark, moss, and lichens in trees not far from water; 3–4 eggs; 1 brood; March–July.
FEEDING Catches mice, chipmunks, and voles; also snakes, toads, frogs, crayfish, and small birds.

SIMILAR SPECIES

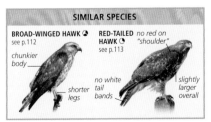

BROAD-WINGED HAWK ♂
see p.112

chunkier body

shorter legs

RED-TAILED HAWK ♂
see p.113

no red on "shoulder"

no white tail bands

slightly larger overall

CHESTNUT WING
When seen from below, the reddish forewing of this adult hawk is clearly visible.

OCCURRENCE
Eastern populations breed in woodlands and forest, deciduous or mixed, whereas those in the West occur in oak woodlands and eucalyptus groves. Some pairs nest in parks and near backyards in suburban areas. Eastern birds migrate to Mexico.

Length **17–24in (43–61cm)**	Wingspan **3–3½ft (0.9–1.1m)**	Weight **17–27oz (475–775g)**
Social **Solitary/Flocks**	Lifespan **Up to 18 years**	Status **Declining (p)**

| Order **Accipitriformes** | Family **Accipitridae** | Species *Buteo platypterus* |

Broad-winged Hawk

dark border on edges of wings

one to two broad, white bands visible on tail

ADULT

ADULT

upperparts brown with white flecking

JUVENILE

pale tan wings with dark tips

pale outer wing feathers

IN FLIGHT

finely barred, all-brown tail

JUVENILE

pale underparts, with conspicuous, tear-shaped, brown spots

short, yellow feet

JUVENILE

One of the most numerous of all North American birds of prey, the Broad-winged Hawk migrates in huge flocks or "kettles," with thousands of birds gliding on rising thermals. Some birds winter in Florida, but the majority average about 70 miles (110km) a day to log more than 4,000 miles (6,500km) before ending up in Brazil, Bolivia, and even some of the Caribbean islands. Compared to its two cousins, the Red-shouldered and Red-tailed Hawks, the Broad-winged Hawk is slightly smaller, but stockier. Adults are easily identified by a broad, white-and-black band on their tails. Broad-winged Hawks have two color forms, the light one being more common than the dark, sooty brown one.

VOICE High-pitched *peeoweee* call, first note shorter and higher-pitched.

NESTING Platform of fresh twigs or dead sticks, often on old squirrel, hawk, or crow nest in tree; 2–3 eggs; 1 brood; April–August.

FEEDING Eats small mammals, toads, frogs, snakes, grouse chicks, insects, and spiders; crabs in winter.

FLIGHT: circles above forest canopy with wings and tail spread; short flights from branch to branch.

SIMILAR SPECIES

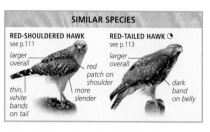

RED-SHOULDERED HAWK
see p.111

larger overall

thin, white bands on tail

red patch on shoulder

more slender

RED-TAILED HAWK ◐
see p.113

larger overall

dark band on belly

WATCHING FOR PREY
From an elevated perch, this hawk scans for vertebrate prey such as rodents.

OCCURRENCE
Breeds across Canada (but not the Rockies) and in the eastern US (not west of the 100th meridian), in forested areas with deciduous, conifers, and mixed trees, with clearings and water nearby. Concentrations of migrants can be seen at bottlenecks such as the Isthmus of Tehuantepec and Panama.

| Length **13–17in (33–43cm)** | Wingspan **32–39in (81–100cm)** | Weight **10–19oz (275–550g)** |
| Social **Flocks** | Lifespan **Up to 14 years** | Status **Secure** |

DATE: _____ TIME: _____ LOCATION: _____

Order **Accipitriformes**	Family **Accipitridae**	Species ***Buteo jamaicensis***

Red-tailed Hawk

FLIGHT: soaring flight punctuated with lazy, slow wing flaps; hangs motionless in the wind.

The Red-tailed Hawk is the most widely distributed and commonly seen hawk in North America. As many as 16 subspecies have been described to date, varying in coloration, tail markings, and size. The very dark Harlan's Hawk, which breeds in Alaska and northwestern Canada, is so distinctive that it was at one time thought of as a separate species, but recent research suggests otherwise. While it occasionally stoops on prey, the Red-tailed Hawk usually adopts a sit-and-wait approach.

VOICE Call *kee-eee-arrr* that rises then descends over a period of 2–3 seconds.

NESTING Large platform of sticks, twigs on top of tall tree, cliff, building, ledge, or billboard; 2 eggs; 1 brood; February–September.

FEEDING Captures small mammals such as voles, mice, rats; birds including pheasant, quail; small reptiles; carrion also eaten.

FLYING HIGH
A Red-tailed Hawk soaring over an open field is a very common sight in North America.

SIMILAR SPECIES

FERRUGINOUS HAWK (LIGHT FORM)

ROUGH-LEGGED HAWK (DARK FORM)
see p.114

OCCURRENCE
Breeds, forages in open areas in wide range of habitats and altitudes: scrub desert, grasslands, agricultural fields and pastures, coniferous and deciduous woodland, and tropical rainforest. Prefers areas with tall perch sites; can be found in suburban woodlots.

Length **18–26in (46–65cm)**	Wingspan **3½–4¼ft (1.1–1.3m)**	Weight **1½–3¼lb (0.7–1.5kg)**
Social **Solitary/Pairs**	Lifespan **Up to 21 years**	Status **Secure**

DATE: ____________ TIME: ____________ LOCATION: ____________

| Order **Accipitriformes** | Family **Accipitridae** | Species *Buteo jamaicensis* |

Red-tailed Hawk

| Order **Accipitriformes** | Family **Accipitridae** | Species *Buteo lagopus* |

Rough-legged Hawk

dark wing tips

bold black patch

FEMALE

black trailing edge

one line before tail tip

pale head

ADULT

dark tail band

IN FLIGHT

short, broad head

MALE

JUVENILE

black belly

barred underparts

thin bands near tail tip

FLIGHT: strong wing beats; usually soars on thermals; frequently hovers in one spot.

white tail with faint black band at tip

plain gray brown or frosty feather edges

MALE

The Rough-legged Hawk is known for its extensive variation in plumage—some individuals are almost completely black, whereas others are much paler, very nearly cream or white. The year to year fluctuation in numbers of breeding pairs in a given region strongly suggests that this species is nomadic, moving about as a response to the availability of its rodent prey.

VOICE Wintering birds silent; breeding birds utter loud, cat-like mewing or thin whistles, slurred downward when alarmed.

NESTING Bulky mass of sticks, lined with grasses, sedges, feathers and fur from prey, constructed on cliff ledge; 2–6 eggs; 1 brood; April–August.

FEEDING Hovers in one spot over fields in search of prey; lemmings and voles in spring and summer; mice and shrews in winters; variety of birds, ground squirrels, and rabbits year-round.

ABUNDANT FOOD SUPPLY
When small mammals are abundant, these hawks produce large broods on cliff ledges in the tundra.

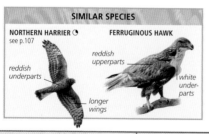

SIMILAR SPECIES

NORTHERN HARRIER ♀
see p.107

FERRUGINOUS HAWK

reddish upperparts

reddish underparts

white underparts

longer wings

OCCURRENCE
Breeds in rough, open country with low crags and cliffs, in high subarctic and Arctic regions; found on the edge of extensive forest or forest clearings, and in treeless tundra, uplands, and alpine habitats. Winters in open areas with fields, marshes, and rough grasslands.

| Length **19–20in (48–51cm)** | Wingspan **4¼–4½ft (1.3–1.4m)** | Weight **1½–3lb (0.7–1.4kg)** |
| Social **Solitary** | Lifespan **Up to 18 years** | Status **Secure** |

DATE: _____ TIME:_____ LOCATION:_____

| Order **Accipitriformes** | Family **Accipitridae** | Species *Aquila chrysaetos* |

Golden Eagle

holds wings in distinctive "V"

long, narrow white wing patches

JUVENILE

ADULT

head tucked in

brown overall

dark brown underparts

black tail band

IN FLIGHT

flat, broad head merges into heavy bill

golden feathers on long neck

large, powerful bill

pale head

dark plumage with variable white

white tail feathers

ADULT

heavy feathering on legs

white tail feathers

JUVENILE

FLIGHT: slow, steady wing beats; most often seen gliding or soaring.

The most formidable of all North American birds of prey, the Golden Eagle is more numerous in the western part of Canada. It defends large territories ranging from 8 to 12 square miles (20–30 square kilometers), containing up to 14 nests. Although it appears sluggish, it is amazingly swift and agile, and employs a variety of hunting techniques to catch specific prey. Shot and poisoned by ranchers and trappers, it is unfortunately also faced with dwindling habitat and food sources due to human development.

VOICE Mostly silent, but breeding adults yelp and mew.

NESTING Large pile of sticks and vegetation on cliffs, in trees, and on manmade structures; 1–3 eggs; 1 brood; April–August.

FEEDING Eats mammals, such as hares, rabbits, ground squirrels, prairie dogs, marmots, foxes, and coyotes; also birds.

POWER AND STRENGTH
With its sharp talons and strong wings, legs, and feet, the Golden Eagle can take prey as large as a coyote.

SIMILAR SPECIES

BALD EAGLE ♂
see p.106

white head and neck

some pale wing feathers

FERRUGINOUS HAWK ♂
(DARK FORM)

no golden tinge

smaller overall

OCCURRENCE
In North America occurs mostly in grasslands, wetlands, and rocky areas; breeds south to Mexico, in open and semi-open habitats from sea level to 12,000ft (3,500m) including tundra, shrublands, grasslands, coniferous forests, farmland, areas close to streams or rivers; winters in open habitat.

| Length **28–33in (70–84cm)** | Wingspan **6–7¼ft (1.8–2.2m)** | Weight **6½–13lb (3–6kg)** |
| Social **Solitary/Pairs** | Lifespan **Up to 39 years** | Status **Declining (p)** |

DATE: _____ TIME: _____ LOCATION: _____

RAILS, CRANES, AND RELATIVES

THESE BIRDS OF THE MARSHES AND WETLANDS include many distinctive groups. The Rallidae, or rail family, is a diverse group of small- to medium-sized marsh birds, represented in Canada by two long-billed rails, two short-billed rails, two gallinules (one a rare species in Canada), and a coot. The cranes, or Gruidae, include very large to huge birds, superficially similar to storks and larger than the tallest herons and egrets. However, genetic and anatomical differences place cranes in a different order from storks, and herons and egrets.

RAILS AND COOTS

Rails are mostly secretive, solitary, and inconspicuous in dense marsh vegetation, whereas coots are seen on open water. Rails are all somewhat chicken-like birds with stubby tails and short, rounded wings, looking round-bodied from the side but very slender head-on. The rails of the genus *Rallus* have excellent camouflage, and are long-legged, long-toed, long-billed, and narrow-bodied—the origin of the saying "as thin as a rail." The short-billed species are similar, but with shorter necks and stout, stubby bills. Both groups walk through wet marsh vegetation, though they can swim well. The American Coot has broad lobes along the sides of its toes, making it a more proficient swimmer and diver in deeper water. Neither has a particularly specialized diet; they eat insects, small crabs, slugs, snails, and plant matter. Breeding pairs of rails keep in close contact in dense vegetation by calling out loudly.

THIN AS A RAIL
This marsh-dwelling Virginia Rail's narrow body enables it to slip easily through reed beds.

CRANES

The two North American species of cranes have long necks, small heads, and short bills. The long plumes on their inner wing feathers form a bustle, cloaking the tail on a standing crane, thereby giving them a different profile than any heron. Cranes fly with their necks straight out, rather than in the tight S-curve that is regularly seen in similar-sized herons. Cranes are long-distance migrants. The western-dwelling Whooping Crane, one of the world's rarest birds, is the tallest bird in North America, standing nearly 5ft (1.5m) high.

CRANE RALLY
Large numbers of Sandhill Cranes gather on feeding grounds in winter, groups arriving in V-formation.

Yellow Rail

dangling legs

ADULT

white patch on inner wing feathers

IN FLIGHT

long tan stripes on blackish background

dark brown crown

stubby yellow to olive-gray bill

dark stripe runs from cheek to bill

buff or yellow breast

ADULT

short tail

FLIGHT: low, weak, short, and direct with stiff wing beats; dangling legs.

Although widespread, the diminutive, secretive, nocturnal Yellow Rail is extremely difficult to observe in its dense, damp, grassy habitat, and is detected mainly by its voice. The Yellow Rail, whose Latin name of *noveboracensis* means "New Yorker," has a small head, almost no neck, a stubby bill, a plump, almost tail-less body, and short legs. The bill of the male turns yellow in the breeding season; for the rest of the year, it is olive-gray like the female's. Although the Yellow Rail tends to dart for cover when disturbed, when it does fly, it reveals a distinctive white patch on its inner wing.

VOICE Two clicking calls followed by three more given by males, usually at night, reminiscent of two pebbles being struck together; also descending cackles, quiet croaking, and soft clucking.

NESTING Small cup of grasses and sedges, on the ground or in a plant tuft above water, concealed by overhanging vegetation; 8–10 eggs; 1 brood; May–June.

FEEDING Plucks seeds, aquatic insects, various small crustaceans, and mollusks (primarily small freshwater snails) from vegetation or ground; forages on the marsh surface or in shallow water, hidden by grass.

CURIOUS LISTENER
Imitating the "tick" calls of the Yellow Rail is often an effective way to lure it out into the open.

OCCURRENCE
Breeds in brackish and freshwater marshes and wet sedge meadows in Canada and the north central US; there is an isolated breeding population in Oregon. Winters predominantly in coastal marshes along the eastern seaboard.

SIMILAR SPECIES

SORA see p.120

black streaks on brown upperparts

gray underparts

Length **7¼in (18.5cm)**	Wingspan **11in (28cm)**	Weight **1¾oz (50g)**
Social **Pairs**	Lifespan **Unknown**	Status **Endangered**

DATE: _____ TIME:_____ LOCATION:_____

| Order **Gruiformes** | Family **Rallidae** | Species ***Rallus elegans*** |

King Rail

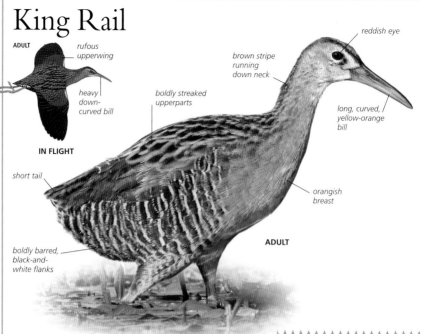

ADULT

rufous upperwing

heavy down-curved bill

IN FLIGHT

short tail

boldly barred, black-and-white flanks

brown stripe running down neck

boldly streaked upperparts

reddish eye

long, curved, yellow-orange bill

orangish breast

ADULT

T his chicken-like marsh bird is the freshwater version of the Clapper Rail. These two species are known to interbreed where their ranges overlap. A scattered and localized breeder across eastern North America, the King Rail depends on extensive freshwater marsh habitats with tall, emergent reeds and cattails. Concealed by this vegetation, the King Rail is rarely seen and is most often detected by its distinctive calls.

VOICE Male call similar to Clapper Rail but lower; emits a loud *kik kik kik* during breeding season.

NESTING Cup of vegetation, often hidden by bent stems that form a canopy; 6–12 eggs; 2 broods; February–August.

FEEDING Forages in concealed locations for insects, snails, spiders, and crustaceans such as shrimps, crabs, and barnacles; also fish, frogs, and seeds.

FLIGHT: somewhat clumsy and labored; legs dangling; prefers to run.

LARGEST RAIL
Easily confused with the closely related Clapper Rail, this is the largest North American rail.

OCCURRENCE
Mostly breeds in freshwater marshes in the eastern US and in extreme southern Ontario. Also found throughout the year along the southern coast of the US, including Florida, and in central Mexico and Cuba.

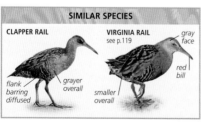

SIMILAR SPECIES

CLAPPER RAIL

grayer overall

flank barring diffused

VIRGINIA RAIL
see p.119

gray face

red bill

smaller overall

| Length **15in (38cm)** | Wingspan **20in (51cm)** | Weight **13oz (375g)** |
| Social **Pairs** | Lifespan **Unknown** | Status **Endangered** |

DATE: _____ TIME: _____ LOCATION: _____

| Order **Gruiformes** | Family **Rallidae** | Species *Rallus limicola* |

Virginia Rail

gray cheeks

rufous upperwing

streaked black and brown upperparts

ADULT (BREEDING)

dark outer wing feathers

IN FLIGHT

white undertail

curved, red bill

reddish brown breast

black-and-white barring on flanks

reddish legs and toes

ADULT (BREEDING)

diffused streaking

dark bill

dark, blotchy breast

ADULT (NONBREEDING)

A smaller version of the King Rail, this freshwater marsh dweller is similar to its other relatives, more often heard than seen. Distributed in a wide range, the Virginia Rail spends most of its time in thick, reedy vegetation, which it pushes aside using its "rail thin" body and flexible vertebrae. Although it spends most of its life walking, it can swim and even dive to escape danger. The Virginia Rail is a partial migrant that leaves its northern breeding grounds in winter.

VOICE Series of pig-like grunting *oinks* that start loud and sharp, becoming steadily softer; also emits a series of double notes *ka-dik ka-dik*.

NESTING Substantial cup of plant material, concealed by bent-over stems; 5–12 eggs; 1–2 broods; April–July.

FEEDING Actively stalks prey or may wait and dive into water; primarily eats snails, insects, and spiders, but may also eat seeds.

FLIGHT: weak and struggling with outstretched neck and legs trailing behind.

HARD TO SPOT
The secretive Virginia Rail is difficult to spot in its reedy habitat.

OCCURRENCE
Breeds in freshwater habitats across North America, though is found throughout the year along the West Coast of the US. In winter, moves to saltwater and freshwater marshes in the southern US, including Florida, and in northern and central Mexico.

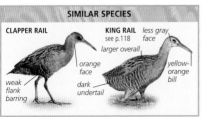

SIMILAR SPECIES

CLAPPER RAIL

KING RAIL see p.118

less gray face

larger overall

orange face

yellow-orange bill

weak flank barring

dark undertail

| Length **9½in (24cm)** | Wingspan **13in (33cm)** | Weight **3oz (85g)** |
| Social **Pairs** | Lifespan **Unknown** | Status **Secure** |

DATE: _____ TIME: _____ LOCATION: _____

| Order **Gruiformes** | Family **Rallidae** | Species **Porzana carolina** |

Sora

reduced black on face

white markings on back

ADULT (NONBREEDING)

no black mask

buffy breast

JUVENILE

long, trailing legs

ADULT (BREEDING)

short tail

white barring on flanks

IN FLIGHT

brown cheek patch

yellow bill

black mask

yellowish green legs

gray breast

ADULT (BREEDING)

Despite being the most widely distributed rail in North America, the Sora is rarely seen. It breeds in freshwater marshes and migrates hundreds of miles south in winter despite its weak and hesitant flight. It swims well, with a characteristic head-bobbing action. The Sora can be spotted walking at the edge of emergent vegetation—its yellow bill and black mask distinguish it from other rails.

VOICE Call a long, high, and loud, descending, horse-like whinny *ko-wee-hee-hee-hee-hee*; has an upslurred whistle.

NESTING Loosely woven basket of marsh vegetation suspended above water or positioned in clumps of vegetation on the water's surface; 8–11 eggs; 1 brood; May–June.

FEEDING Rakes vegetation with feet or pulls with bill in search of seeds of wetland plants, insects, spiders, and snails.

FLIGHT: appears weak, yet strenuous; wing beats hurried and constant.

CHICKEN-LIKE WALK
A rare sight, the Sora walks chicken-like through a marsh, its body in a low crouch.

SIMILAR SPECIES

YELLOW RAIL see p.117
buffy streaks
buffy breast

VIRGINIA RAIL see p.119
longer bill
reddish legs

OCCURRENCE
Breeds in freshwater marshes with emergent vegetation across most of temperate North America; rarely in salt marshes along the Atlantic Coast. Winters in freshwater, saltwater, and brackish marshes with spartina grass from the southern US to northern South America.

| Length **8¹/₂in (22cm)** | Wingspan **14in (36cm)** | Weight **2⁵/₈oz (75g)** |
| Social **Solitary** | Lifespan **Unknown** | Status **Secure** |

DATE: _____ TIME: _____ LOCATION: _____

| Order **Gruiformes** | Family **Rallidae** | Species *Gallinula galeata* |

Common Gallinule

small, round wings

ADULT

long trailing feet

IN FLIGHT

glossy brown back

square-topped, red facial shield

shiny slate-gray breast

white patch on side of tail

pale gray-brown body

dull bill

white streaks on flanks

JUVENILE

pale green legs with very long toes

ADULT

FLIGHT: rather weak and labored with legs trailing.

The Common Gallinule is fairly widespread in southeastern Canada and the eastern US; its distribution is more scattered in the western states. It has similarities in behavior and habitat to both the true rails and the coots. Equally at home on land and water, its long toes allow it to walk easily over floating vegetation and soft mud. When walking or swimming, the Common Gallinule nervously jerks its short tail, revealing its white undertail feathers, and bobs its head.

VOICE A variety of rapid, raucous, cackling phrases and an explosive *krrooo*.
NESTING Bulky platform of aquatic vegetation with growing plants pulled over to conceal it, or close to water; 5–11 eggs, 1–3 broods; May–August, maybe year round in Florida.
FEEDING Forages mainly on aquatic and terrestrial plants and aquatic vegetation; also eats snails, spiders, and insects.

DUAL HABITAT
A walker and a swimmer, the gallinule is equally at home on land and in water.

OCCURRENCE
Breeds in freshwater habitats in the eastern US and Canada; more localized in the West. Winters in warmer areas with open water such as the southern US, and Mexico. Also found in Central and South America.

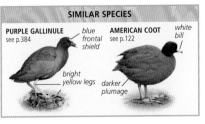

SIMILAR SPECIES

PURPLE GALLINULE see p.384

blue frontal shield

bright yellow legs

AMERICAN COOT see p.122

white bill

darker plumage

| Length **14in (36cm)** | Wingspan **21in (53cm)** | Weight **11oz (325g)** |
| Social **Pairs** | Lifespan **Up to 10 years** | Status **Secure** |

| Order **Gruiformes** | Family **Rallidae** | Species *Fulica americana* |

American Coot

ADULT (BREEDING)

black head

red eye

dark gray body

white bill

white-edged feathers

IN FLIGHT

black ring on bill

ADULT (BREEDING)

dull grayish plumage

long, greenish yellow legs

lobed toes

JUVENILE

This duck-like species of rail is the most abundant and widely distributed of North American rails. Its lobed toes make it well adapted to swimming and diving, but they are somewhat of an impediment on land. Its flight is clumsy; it becomes airborne with difficulty, running along the water surface before taking off. American Coots form large flocks on open water in winter, often associating with ducks—an unusual trait for a member of the rail family.

VOICE Various raucous clucks, grunts, and croaks and an explosive *keek*.

NESTING Bulky cup of plant material placed in aquatic vegetation on or near water; 5–15 eggs; 1–2 broods; April–July.

FEEDING Forages on or under shallow water and feeds on land; primarily herbivorous, but also eats snails, insects, spiders, tadpoles, fish, and even carrion.

FLIGHT: low and labored; runs for quite a long distance to take off.

SWIMMING AWAY
The red-headed, baldish-looking American Coot chicks leave the nest a day after hatching.

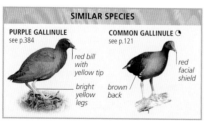

SIMILAR SPECIES

PURPLE GALLINULE
see p.384

red bill with yellow tip

bright yellow legs

COMMON GALLINULE ☾
see p.121

brown back

red facial shield

OCCURRENCE
Breeds in open water habitats west of the Appalachians and in Florida. Moves from the northern parts of its range in winter to the southeastern US, where open water persists; also migrates to western and southern Mexico.

| Length **15½in (40cm)** | Wingspan **24in (61cm)** | Weight **16oz (450g)** |
| Social **Flocks** | Lifespan **Up to 22 years** | Status **Secure** |

DATE: _____ TIME: _____ LOCATION: _____

| Order **Gruiformes** | Family **Gruidae** | Species **Grus canadensis** |

Sandhill Crane

black wing tips

head held straight

ADULT

IN FLIGHT

trailing legs

red crown

long, black bill

pale cheek

long neck

brownish head

body with pale brown smudges

JUVENILE

ADULT

rusty body

shaggy feathers

long, black legs

"IRON-STAINED" PLUMAGE

FLIGHT: alternates slow, steady flapping with periods of gliding; flocks in single-file.

These large, slender, and long-necked birds are famous for their elaborate courtship dances, far-carrying vocalizations, and remarkable migrations. Their bodies are sometimes stained with a rusty color, supposedly because they probe into mud which contains iron; when a bird preens, this is transferred from the bill to its plumage. Sandhill Cranes are broadly grouped into "Lesser" and "Greater" populations that differ in the geographical location of their breeding grounds and migration routes.

VOICE Call loud, wooden, hollow bugling, audible at great distances; noisy in flight and courtship.

NESTING Mound of sticks and grasses placed on ground; 1 egg; 1 brood; April–September.

FEEDING Eats shoots, grain; also aquatic mollusks and insects.

MEMORABLE IMAGE
Its long neck, large wings, and distinctive red crown make it difficult to mistake.

OCCURRENCE
Breeds in muskeg, tundra, and forest clearings across northwestern North America, east to Quebec and the Great Lakes; large wintering and migratory flocks often densely packed, roosting in or near marshes. Winters south to northern Mexico.

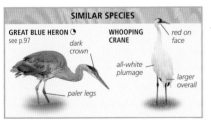

SIMILAR SPECIES

GREAT BLUE HERON ◑
see p.97

dark crown

paler legs

WHOOPING CRANE

red on face

all-white plumage

larger overall

| Length **2³/₄–4ft (0.8–1.2m)** | Wingspan **6–7¹/₂ft (1.8–2.3m)** | Weight **7³/₄–11lb (3.5–5kg)** |
| Social **Flocks** | Lifespan **Up to 25 years** | Status **Secure** |

DATE: _____ TIME: _____ LOCATION: _____

SHOREBIRDS, GULLS, AUKS, AND RELATIVES

SHOREBIRDS, GULLS, AUKS, AND RELATIVES

THE DIVERSE SHOREBIRD, gull, and auk families together form the order Charadriiformes. They are tiny to medium-sized, mostly migratory birds, associated with aquatic habitats. Over 100 species are found in North America.

DISTANCE TRAVELER
The Arctic Tern is well known for its long yearly migration of around 25,000 miles (40,000km).

SHOREBIRDS

The various species popularly known as shorebirds belong to several different families. In Eastern Canada there are the plovers (Charadriidae), and the sandpipers and the phalaropes (Scolopacidae). They have long legs in proportion to their bodies, and a variety of bills, ranging from short to long, thin, thick, straight, down-curved and up-curved.

GULLS

The over 20 species of Canadian gulls in the family Laridae all share a similar stout body shape, sturdy bills, and webbed toes. Nearly all are scavengers. Closely associated with coastal areas, few gulls venture far out to sea. Some species are seen around fishing ports and harbors, or inland, especially in urban areas, landfills, and farm fields.

TERNS

Terns are specialized, long-billed predators that dive for fish. More slender and elegant than gulls, nearly all are immediately recognizable when breeding, due to their black caps and long, pointed bills. The related but differently billed Black Simmer, a vagrant in Canada, also catches fish.

AUKS, MURRES, AND PUFFINS

Denizens of the northern oceans, these birds come to land only to breed. Most nest in colonies on sheer cliffs overlooking the ocean, but puffins excavate burrows in the ground, and some murrelets nest away from predators high up in treetops far inland.

ON THE MOVE
Dunlins and other sandpipers gather in large, highly coordinated flocks on migration.

| Order **Charadriiformes** | Family **Charadriidae** | Species *Pluvialis squatarola* |

Black-bellied Plover

white-edged, dark-centered feathers

checkered upperparts

white rump

black outer wing feathers

white wing stripe

MALE (BREEDING)

markedly streaked breast

JUVENILE

ADULT (NONBREEDING)

diffused streaks to upper breast

whitish underparts

whitish crown

black cheeks

ADULT (NONBREEDING)

checkered, black-and-white upperparts

black underwing patch

IN FLIGHT

darker crown

black belly

duller plumage than male

MALE (BREEDING)

FEMALE (MOLTING TO BREEDING PLUMAGE)

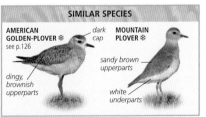

FLIGHT: straight and fast; powerful wing beats.

The Black-bellied Plover is the largest and most common of the three North American *Pluvialis* plovers. Its preference for open feeding habitats, its bulky structure, and very upright stance make it a fairly conspicuous species. The Black-bellied Plover's black underwing patches, visible in flight, are present in both its breeding and nonbreeding plumages and distinguish it from the other *Pluvialis* plovers.

VOICE Typical call a three-syllabled, clear, plaintive, whistled *whEE-er-eee*, with middle note lower; flight song of male during breeding softer, with accent on second syllable.

NESTING Shallow depression lined with mosses and lichens in moist to dry lowland tundra; 1–5 eggs; 1 brood; May–July.

FEEDING Forages mainly along coasts in typical plover style: run, pause, and pluck; eats insects, worms, bivalves, and crustaceans.

CASUAL WADING
The Black-bellied Plover wades in shallow water but does most of its foraging in mudflats.

SIMILAR SPECIES

AMERICAN GOLDEN-PLOVER ✷ see p.126

dark cap

MOUNTAIN PLOVER ✷

sandy brown upperparts

dingy, brownish upperparts

white underparts

OCCURRENCE
Breeds in High Arctic habitats from western Russia across the Bering Sea to Alaska, and east to Baffin Island; winters primarily in coastal areas from southern Canada and US, south to southern South America. Found inland during migration. Migrates south all the way to South America.

| Length **10½–12in (27–30cm)** | Wingspan **29–32in (73–81cm)** | Weight **5–9oz (150–250g)** |
| Social **Flocks** | Lifespan **Up to 12 years** | Status **Secure** |

DATE: _____ TIME: _____ LOCATION: _____

| Order **Charadriiformes** | Family **Charadriidae** | Species *Pluvialis dominica* |

American Golden-Plover

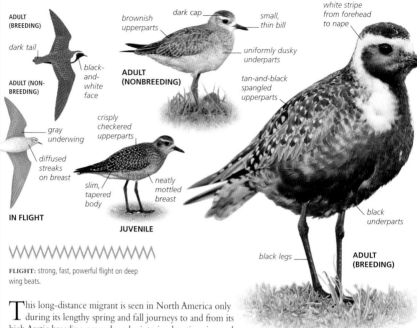

ADULT (BREEDING)

dark tail

ADULT (NON-BREEDING)

black-and-white face

gray underwing

diffused streaks on breast

IN FLIGHT

brownish upperparts

dark cap

small, thin bill

ADULT (NONBREEDING)

uniformly dusky underparts

tan-and-black spangled upperparts

white stripe from forehead to nape

crisply checkered upperparts

slim, tapered body

neatly mottled breast

JUVENILE

black underparts

black legs

ADULT (BREEDING)

FLIGHT: strong, fast, powerful flight on deep wing beats.

This long-distance migrant is seen in North America only during its lengthy spring and fall journeys to and from its high Arctic breeding grounds and wintering locations in southern South America. An elegant, slender, yet large plover, it prefers inland grassy habitats and plowed fields to coastal mudflats. The American Golden-Plover's annual migration route includes a feeding stop at Labrador, then a 1,550–1,860 miles (2,500–3,000km) flight over the Atlantic Ocean to South America.

VOICE Flight call a whistled two-note *queE-dle*, or *klee-u*, with second note shorter and lower pitched; male flight song a strong, melodious whistled *kid-eek*, or *kid-EEp*.

NESTING Shallow depression lined with lichens in dry, open tundra; 4 eggs; 1 brood; May–July.

FEEDING Forages in run, pause, and pluck sequence on insects, mollusks, crustaceans, and worms; also berries and seeds.

DISTRACTION TECHNIQUE
This breeding American Golden-Plover is feigning an injury to its wing to draw predators away from its chicks or eggs in its nest.

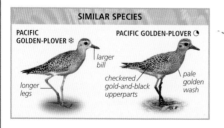

SIMILAR SPECIES

PACIFIC GOLDEN-PLOVER ❄

longer legs

PACIFIC GOLDEN-PLOVER ☾

larger bill

checkered gold-and-black upperparts

pale golden wash

OCCURRENCE
Breeds in Arctic tundra habitats. In migration, it occurs in prairies, tilled farmlands, golf courses, pastures, airports; also mudflats, shorelines, and beaches. In spring, seen in Texas and Great Plains; in fall, uncommon in northeast Maritimes and New England; scarce along the Pacific Coast.

| Length **9½–11in (24–28cm)** | Wingspan **23–28in (59–72cm)** | Weight **4–7oz (125–200g)** |
| Social **Solitary/Small flocks** | Lifespan **Unknown** | Status **Secure** |

DATE: _____ TIME: _____ LOCATION: _____

| Order **Charadriiformes** | Family **Charadriidae** | Species *Charadrius semipalmatus* |

Semipalmated Plover

pointed wings

scalloped feather edges

pale base of bill

brownish breastband

white eyestripe

brownish crown

brownish upperparts

ADULT (BREEDING)

JUVENILE

black tail band

IN FLIGHT

diffused brownish collar

yellow eye-ring

black forecrown

white underparts

black bill with orange base

black breastband

yellowish legs

ADULT (NONBREEDING)

orange legs

ADULT (BREEDING)

S imilar in appearance to the Common Ringed Plover in Eurasia, the Semipalmated Plover is a small bird with a tapered shape. It is a familiar sight in a wide variety of habitats during migration and in winter, when these birds gather in loose flocks. A casual walk down a sandy beach between fall and spring might awaken up to 100 Semipalmated Plovers, sleeping in slight depressions in the sand, though flocks of up to 1,000 birds may also be encountered.

VOICE Flight call a whistled abrupt *chu-WEEp*, with soft emphasis on second syllable; courtship display song quick version of flight call followed by rough *r-r-r-r-r-r*, ending with a slurred, descending *yelp*.

NESTING Simple scrape on bare or slightly vegetated ground in Arctic tundra; 3–4 eggs; 1 brood; May–June.

FEEDING Forages in typical plover style: run, pause, and pluck; eats aquatic mollusks, crustaceans, flies, beetles, and spiders.

FLIGHT: straight, fast; with fluttering wing beats.

BY SIGHT AND TOUCH
Semipalmated Plovers locate prey by sight or through the sensitive soles of their feet.

OCCURRENCE
Breeding habitat is Arctic or sub-Arctic tundra with well-drained gravel, shale, or other sparsely vegetated ground. During migration, mudflats, saltwater marshes, lake edges, tidal areas, and flooded fields. During winter, coastal or near coastal habitats.

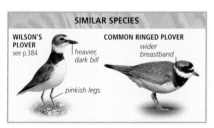

SIMILAR SPECIES

WILSON'S PLOVER
see p.384

heavier, dark bill

pinkish legs

COMMON RINGED PLOVER
wider breastband

| Length **6³⁄₄–7¹⁄₂in (17–19cm)** | Wingspan **17–20¹⁄₂in (43–52cm)** | Weight **1¹⁄₁₆–2¹⁄₂oz (30–70g)** |
| Social **Solitary/Flocks** | Lifespan **Up to 6 years** | Status **Secure** |

DATE: _____ TIME: _____ LOCATION: _____

| Order **Charadriiformes** | Family **Charadriidae** | Species *Charadrius melodus* |

Piping Plover

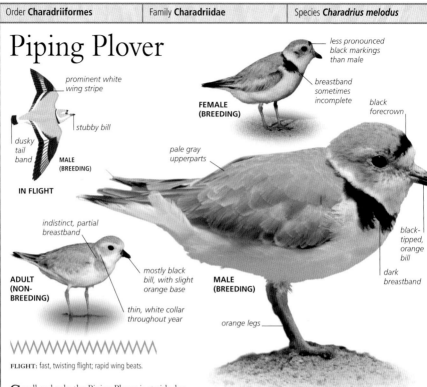

IN FLIGHT

prominent white wing stripe

stubby bill

dusky tail band

MALE (BREEDING)

FEMALE (BREEDING)

less pronounced black markings than male

breastband sometimes incomplete

black forecrown

pale gray upperparts

black-tipped, orange bill

dark breastband

ADULT (NON-BREEDING)

indistinct, partial breastband

mostly black bill, with slight orange base

thin, white collar throughout year

MALE (BREEDING)

orange legs

WWWWWWWWWWWWWW

FLIGHT: fast, twisting flight; rapid wing beats.

Small and pale, the Piping Plover is at risk due to eroding coastlines, human disturbance, and predation by foxes, raccoons, and cats. With its pale gray back, it is well camouflaged along beaches or in dunes, but conservation measures, such as fencing off nesting beaches and control of predators, are necessary to restore populations. Two subspecies of the Piping Plover are recognized; one nests on the Atlantic Coast, and the other inland.
VOICE Clear, whistled *peep* call in flight; quiet *peep-lo* during courtship and contact; high-pitched *pipe-pipe-pipe* song.
NESTING Shallow scrape in sand, gravel, dunes, or salt flats; 4 eggs; 1 brood; April–May.
FEEDING Typical run, pause, and pluck plover feeding style; diet includes marine worms, insects, and mollusks.

VULNERABLE NESTS
The fragile nature of their preferred nesting sites has led to this species becoming endangered.

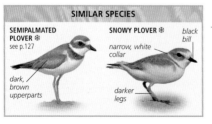

SIMILAR SPECIES

SEMIPALMATED PLOVER ❀
see p.127

dark, brown upperparts

SNOWY PLOVER ❀

narrow, white collar

black bill

darker legs

OCCURRENCE
Found along beaches, in saline sandflats, and adjacent mudflats; during winter, found exclusively along the Atlantic and Gulf Coasts, sandflats, and mudflats. Inland subspecies nests on sand or gravel beaches adjacent to large lakes, rivers, and saline lakes.

| Length **6½–7in (17–18cm)** | Wingspan **18–18½in (45–47cm)** | Weight **1⅝–2⅜oz (45–65g)** |
| Social **Small flocks** | Lifespan **Up to 11 years** | Status **Endangered** |

DATE: _____ TIME: _____ LOCATION: _____

| Order **Charadriiformes** | Family **Charadriidae** | Species *Charadrius vociferus* |

Killdeer

long wings

white wing bar

ADULT

reddish orange tail and rump

IN FLIGHT

long tail

brownish upperparts

rufous wash to back and wings

black collar encircling neck

red eye-ring

brownish crown

small, thin, black bill

MALE

second neck band crosses upper breast

white underparts

pinkish legs, sometimes with yellowish tinge

FLIGHT: fast, twisting flight with fluid wing beats.

This loud and vocal shorebird is the most widespread plover in North America, nesting in all southern Canadian provinces and across the US. The Killdeer's piercing call carries for long distances, sometimes causing other birds to fly away in fear of imminent danger. These birds often nest near human habitation, allowing a close observation of their vigilant parental nature with young chicks.

VOICE Flight call a rising, drawn out *deeee*; alarm call a loud, penetrating *dee-ee*, given repetitively; agitated birds also give series of *dee* notes, followed by rising trill.

NESTING Scrape on ground, sometimes in slight depression; 4 eggs; 1 brood (north), 2–3 broods (south); March–July.

FEEDING Forages in typical plover style: run, pause, and pick; eats a variety of invertebrates such as worms, snails, grasshoppers, and beetles; also small vertebrates and seeds.

CLEVER MANEUVER
The Killdeer lures intruders away from its nest with a "broken wing" display.

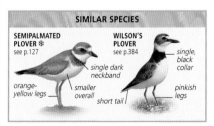

SIMILAR SPECIES

SEMIPALMATED PLOVER ❋
see p.127

single dark neckband

orange-yellow legs

smaller overall

WILSON'S PLOVER
see p.384

single, black collar

pinkish legs

short tail

OCCURRENCE
Widespread across Canada and the US, the Killdeer occurs in a wide variety of habitats. These include shorelines, mudflats, lake and river edges, sparsely grassy fields and pastures, golf courses, roadsides, parking lots, flat rooftops, driveways, and other terrestrial habitats.

| Length **9–10in (23–26cm)** | Wingspan **23–25in (58–63cm)** | Weight **2¼–3⅛ oz (65–90g)** |
| Social **Small flocks** | Lifespan **Up to 10 years** | Status **Declining** |

DATE: _____ TIME: _____ LOCATION: _____

| Order **Charadriiformes** | Family **Scolopacidae** | Species *Bartramia longicauda* |

Upland Sandpiper

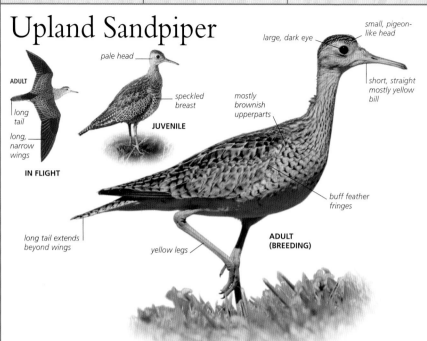

ADULT

pale head

long tail

long, narrow wings

IN FLIGHT

speckled breast

JUVENILE

large, dark eye

small, pigeon-like head

mostly brownish upperparts

short, straight mostly yellow bill

buff feather fringes

ADULT (BREEDING)

long tail extends beyond wings

yellow legs

Unlike other sandpipers, this graceful bird spends most of its life away from water in grassy habitats. The Upland Sandpiper's coloration helps it camouflage itself in the grasslands, especially while nesting on the ground. It is well known for landing on fence posts and raising its wings while giving its tremulous, whistling call. The bird is currently listed as endangered in many of its breeding states due to the disappearance of its grassland habitat.

VOICE Flight call a low *qui-pi-pi-pi*; song consists of gurgling notes followed by long, descending "wolf whistle" *whooooleeeeee, wheeelooooo-ooooo.*

NESTING Simple depression in ground among grass clumps; 4 eggs; 1 brood; May.

FEEDING Feeds with head-bobbing motion on adult and larval insects, spiders, worms, centipedes; occasionally seeds.

FLIGHT: strong and swift; rapid, fluttering flight in breeding display.

DRY GROUND WADER
A true grassland species, the Upland Sandpiper is rarely found away from these habitats.

OCCURRENCE
Breeds in native tallgrass or mixed-grass prairies. Airports make up large portion of its breeding habitat in the northeast US. During migration and in winter it prefers shortgrass habitats such as grazed pastures, turf farms, cultivated fields.

SIMILAR SPECIES

WHIMBREL
see p.131

long, curved bill

dull bluish gray legs

LONG-BILLED CURLEW ♂

very long, curved bill

much larger overall

| Length **11–12½in (28–32cm)** | Wingspan **25–27in (64–68cm)** | Weight **4–7oz (150–200g)** |
| Social **Migrant flocks** | Lifespan **Unknown** | Status **Declining** |

DATE: _____ TIME: _____ LOCATION: _____

| Order **Charadriiformes** | Family **Scolopacidae** | Species *Numenius phaeopus* |

Whimbrel

striped crown

long, pointed wings

ADULT

long, decurved, mostly black bill; orange base in winter

brownish patterned upperparts

finely streaked neck, breast, and underparts

all-dark rump

coarsely streaked face, neck, and breast

light brown spotting to upper breast

large, heavy body

IN FLIGHT

brownish tail and rump

ADULT

long, grayish legs

FLIGHT: steady and moderate wing beats; often glides.

This large, conspicuous shorebird is the most widespread of the curlew species, with four subspecies across North America and Eurasia. Its bold head stripes and clearly streaked face, neck, and breast make the species distinctive. The Whimbrel's fairly long, decurved bill allows it to probe into fiddler crab burrows, a favorite food item.
VOICE Characteristic call is a loud, staccato *pi-pi-pi-pi-pi*; flight song a series of haunting melodious whistles, followed by long trill.
NESTING Depression in hummock, mound, grass, sedge, or gravel; 4 eggs; 1 brood; May–August.
FEEDING Probes for crabs, in addition to worms, mollusks, and fish; also eats insects and berries.

LARGE MOUTHFUL
The Whimbrel often rinses muddy crabs in water before swallowing them whole.

UP CLOSE
A close look at the Whimbrel shows this bird's beautiful, fine patterning.

OCCURRENCE
Several populations breed in northern, sub-Arctic, and low-Arctic regions of North America; during migration and in winter, found mostly in coastal marshes, tidal creeks, flats, and mangroves; also at inland Salton Sea, California. Winters along rocky coasts in South America.

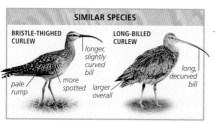

SIMILAR SPECIES

BRISTLE-THIGHED CURLEW — longer, slightly curved bill — more spotted — pale rump

LONG-BILLED CURLEW — long, decurved bill — larger overall

| Length **15½–16½in (39–42cm)** | Wingspan **30–35in (76–89cm)** | Weight **11–18oz (300–500g)** |
| Social **Flocks** | Lifespan **Up to 19 years** | Status **Secure** |

DATE: _____ TIME: _____ LOCATION: _____

| Order **Charadriiformes** | Family **Scolopacidae** | Species *Limosa haemastica* |

Hudsonian Godwit

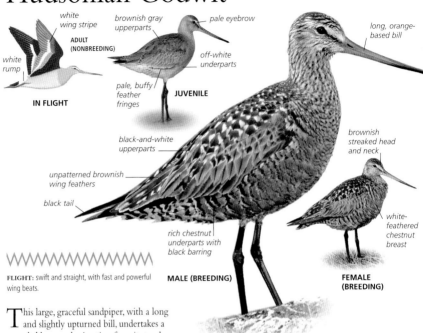

white wing stripe

brownish gray upperparts

pale eyebrow

ADULT (NONBREEDING)

long, orange-based bill

white rump

off-white underparts

JUVENILE

pale, buffy feather fringes

IN FLIGHT

black-and-white upperparts

brownish streaked head and neck

unpatterned brownish wing feathers

black tail

white-feathered chestnut breast

rich chestnut underparts with black barring

MALE (BREEDING)

FEMALE (BREEDING)

FLIGHT: swift and straight, with fast and powerful wing beats.

This large, graceful sandpiper, with a long and slightly upturned bill, undertakes a remarkable annual migration from its tundra breeding grounds in Alaska and Canada all the way to extreme southern South America, a distance probably close to 10,000 miles (16,000km) in one direction, with very few stopovers. There are perhaps 50,000–80,000 breeding pairs. Counts in Tierra del Fuego indicate a total of perhaps 30,000 to 40,000 birds wintering there, all found in two areas of tidal mudflats. Between the far North and the far South, North American stops are few, and only in the spring, along a central route mid-continent. Hudsonian Godwits spend six months wintering, two months breeding, and four months flying between the two locations.

VOICE Flight call emphatic *peed-wid*; also high *peet* or *kwee*; display song *to-wida to-wida to-wida*, or *to-wit, to-wit, to-wit*.

NESTING Saucer-shaped depression on dry hummock or tussocks under cover; 4 eggs; 1 brood; May–July.

FEEDING Probes in mud for insects, insect grubs, worms, crustaceans and mollusks; also eats plant tubers in fall.

LONG-HAUL BIRD
Hudsonian Godwits only make a few stops on their long flights to and from South America.

SIMILAR SPECIES

BAR-TAILED GODWIT ☽
more streaks

shorter legs

longer bill

OCCURRENCE
Breeds in the High Arctic, in sedge meadows and bogs in scattered tundra; scarce along the Atlantic Coast in fall near coastal freshwater reservoirs; but locally common in flooded rice fields, pastures, and reservoirs in spring. Winters in extreme southern Chile and Argentina.

| Length **14–16in (35–41cm)** | Wingspan **27–31in (68–78cm)** | Weight **7–12oz (200–350g)** |
| Social **Flocks** | Lifespan **Up to 29 years** | Status **Vulnerable** |

DATE: _____ TIME: _____ LOCATION: _____

| Order **Charadriiformes** | Family **Scolopacidae** | Species *Limosa fedoa* |

Marbled Godwit

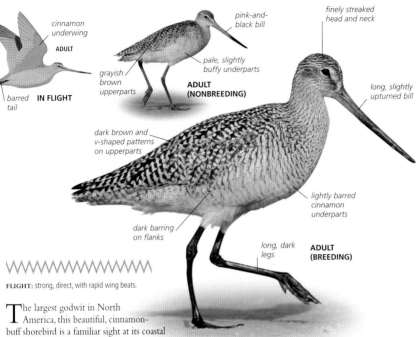

cinnamon underwing

ADULT

barred tail **IN FLIGHT**

pink-and-black bill

pale, slightly buffy underparts

grayish brown upperparts

ADULT (NONBREEDING)

finely streaked head and neck

long, slightly upturned bill

dark brown and v-shaped patterns on upperparts

lightly barred cinnamon underparts

dark barring on flanks

long, dark legs

ADULT (BREEDING)

FLIGHT: strong, direct, with rapid wing beats.

The largest godwit in North America, this beautiful, cinnamon-buff shorebird is a familiar sight at its coastal wintering areas. Its distinctive brown-and-cinnamon plumage and the fact that it chooses open habitats, such as mudflats and floodplains, to feed and roost, make the Marbled Godwit a conspicuous species. A monogamous bird, the Marbled Godwit is also long-lived—the oldest bird recorded was 29 years old.

VOICE Call a nasal *ah-ahk*, and single *ahk*; breeding call, *goddWhit*, *wik-wik*; other calls include *rack-a, karatica, ratica, ratica*.
NESTING Depression in short grass in Alaska; also nests on vegetation in water; 4 eggs; 1 brood; May–July.
FEEDING Probes mudflats, beaches, short grass for insects, especially grasshoppers; also crustaceans, mollusks, and small fish.

EASILY RECOGNIZED
Its large size and buffy to cinnamon color make this godwit a very distinctive shorebird.

SIMILAR SPECIES

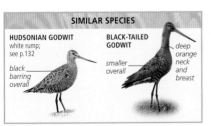

HUDSONIAN GODWIT
white rump;
see p.132

black barring overall

BLACK-TAILED GODWIT

smaller overall

deep orange neck and breast

OCCURRENCE
Breeds in the grassy marshes of the Great Plains. During migration and in winter, prefers sandy beaches and coastal mudflats with adjoining meadows or savannas in California and the Gulf of Mexico. Also seen on inland wetlands and lake edges.

| Length **16½–19in (42–48cm)** | Wingspan **28–32in (70–81cm)** | Weight **10–16oz (275–450g)** |
| Social **Winter flocks** | Lifespan **Up to 29 years** | Status **Secure** |

DATE: _____ TIME: _____ LOCATION: _____

| Order **Charadriiformes** | Family **Scolopacidae** | Species *Arenaria interpres* |

Ruddy Turnstone

bold red patches
on back and
wings

black-and-
white head
and breast
pattern

short, dark,
chisel-like bill

brownish
head
markings

variably
streaked,
whitish face

brownish
upperparts

**ADULT
(BREEDING)**

dark flight
feathers

IN FLIGHT

black
breast

**ADULT
(NONBREEDING)**

bright white
underparts,
at all ages

white-edged,
dark feathers

**ADULT
(BREEDING)**

short,
orange legs

orange
legs

**JUVENILE
(FALL)**

This tame, medium-sized, and stocky sandpiper with a chisel-shaped bill is a common visitor along the shorelines of North and South America. On its high-Arctic breeding grounds, it is bold and aggressive and is able to drive off predators as large as the Glaucous Gull and Parasitic Jaeger. The Ruddy Turnstone was given its name due to its reddish back color and because of its habit of flipping and overturning items like mollusk shells and pebbles, or digging in the sand and looking for small crustaceans and other marine invertebrates. Two subspecies live in Arctic North America: *A. i. interpres* in northeast Canada and *A. i. morinellas* elsewhere in Canada and Alaska.

VOICE Rapid chatter on breeding ground: *TIT-wooo TIT-woooRITititititititit*; flight call a low, rapid *kut-a-kut*.

NESTING Simple scrape lined with lichens and grasses in dry, open areas; 4 eggs; 1 brood; June.

FEEDING Forages along shoreline for crustaceans, insects, including beetles, spiders; also eats plants.

FLIGHT: swift and strong flight, with quick wing beats.

WINTER GATHERINGS
Ruddy Turnstones often congregate in large winter flocks on rocky shorelines.

SIMILAR SPECIES

BLACK TURNSTONE

darker
overall

duller
legs

no rust
color in
plumage

OCCURRENCE
Breeds in high Arctic: wide-open, barren, and grassy habitats and rocky coasts, usually near water. In winter, on sandy or gravel beaches and rocky shorelines, from northern California to South America, and from northern Massachusetts south along Atlantic and Gulf Coasts.

| Length **8–10½in (20–27cm)** | Wingspan **20–22½in (51–57cm)** | Weight **3½–7oz (100–200g)** |
| Social **Flocks** | Lifespan **Up to 7 years** | Status **Secure** |

DATE: _____ TIME: _____ LOCATION: _____

| Order **Charadriiformes** | Family **Scolopacidae** | Species **Calidris canutus** |

Red Knot

white wing stripe

white eyebrow

ADULT (WINTER)

IN FLIGHT

grayish upperparts

pale fringes to wing feathers

JUVENILE

mostly pale gray upperparts

gray spots on upper breast

yellowish green legs

pale underparts

ADULT (WINTER)

boldly marked black, rust, and white upperparts

dark, straight, stocky bill

salmon-colored face and breast

white lower belly with dark V-shaped marks

short, dark legs

ADULT (SUMMER)

A substantial, plump sandpiper, the Red Knot is the largest North American shorebird in the genus *Calidris*. There are two North American subspecies—*C. c. rufa* and *C. c. roselaari*. Noted for its extraordinary long-distance migration, *C. c. rufa* flies about 9,300 miles (15,000km) between its high-Arctic breeding grounds and wintering area in South America, especially in Tierra del Fuego, at the tip of South America. Recent declines have occurred in this population, attributed to over-harvesting of horseshoe crab eggs—its critical food source. With the population of *C. c. rufa* having declined from over 100,000 birds in the mid-1980s to below 15,000 today, the Red Knot is now listed as endangered in New Jersey, and faces possible extinction.

VOICE Flight call a soft *kuEEt* or *kuup*; display song *eerie por-meeee por-meeee*, followed by *por-por por-por*.

NESTING Simple scrape in grassy or barren tundra, often lined; 4 eggs; 1 brood; June.
FEEDING Probes mud or sand for insects, plant material, small mollusks, crustaceans, especially small snails, worms, and other invertebrates.

FLIGHT: powerful, swift, direct flight with rapid wing beats.

STAGING AREAS
Red Knots form colossal flocks during migration and on their wintering grounds.

OCCURRENCE
Breeds in flat, barren tundra in high-Arctic islands and peninsulas. Mostly coastal during migration and winter, preferring sandbars, beaches, and tidal flats, where it congregates in huge flocks.

SIMILAR SPECIES

BLACK-BELLIED PLOVER see p.125

large, dark eye

longer, dark legs

| Length **9–10in (23–25cm)** | Wingspan **23–24in (58–61cm)** | Weight **3⅜–8oz (95–225g)** |
| Social **Large flocks** | Lifespan **Unknown** | Status **Declining** |

Order **Charadriiformes**	Family **Scolopacidae**	Species **Calidris himantopus**

Stilt Sandpiper

plain grayish brown upperparts

ADULT (NONBREEDING)

greenish leg

whitish belly

white rump

long, pointed wing

whitish eyebrow extends behind eye

scaly look to upperparts

crisp, white-and-rust-fringed upperparts

ADULT (NONBREEDING)

dusky tail band

IN FLIGHT

long, dark, straight bill

slightly diffused gray streaks to breast and neck

JUVENILE (FALL)

long, yellowish legs

long wings and tail

rusty cheek patch

rusty cap

ADULT (BREEDING)

chocolate-brown barring on white underparts

The slender Stilt Sandpiper is uncommon and unique to North America, where it breeds in several small areas of northern tundra. It favors shallow, freshwater habitats, where it feeds in a distinctive style, walking slowly through belly-deep water with its neck outstretched and bill pointed downward. It either picks at the surface, or submerges itself, keeping its tail raised up all the while. During migration it forms dense, rapidly moving flocks that sometimes include other sandpiper species.
VOICE Flight or alarm call low, muffled *chuf*; also *krrit* and sharp *kew-it*; display call *xxree-xxree-xxree-xxree-ee-haw, ee-haw*.
NESTING Shallow depression on raised knolls or ridges in tundra; 4 eggs; 1 brood; June.
FEEDING Eats mostly adult and larval insects; also some snails, mollusks, and seeds.

FLIGHT: fast and direct, with rapid beats of its long wings.

SIMILAR SPECIES

DUNLIN ❊ see p.138

shorter neck

shorter, black legs

CURLEW SANDPIPER ❊

black legs

curved bill

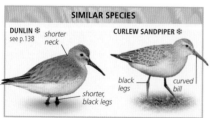

PALE BELOW
Wading through shallow water, this Stilt Sandpiper displays its whitish underparts.

OCCURRENCE
Breeds in moist to wet coastal tundra on well-drained, raised knolls or ridges in Alaska, Yukon, and northwestern territories and Hudson Bay. During migration and in winter, prefers freshwater habitats, such as flooded fields, marsh pools, reservoirs, and sheltered lagoons to tidal mudflats.

Length **8–9in (20–23cm)**	Wingspan **17–18½in (43–47cm)**	Weight **1¾–2⅛oz (50–60g)**
Social **Pairs/Flocks**	Lifespan **At least 3 years**	Status **Secure**

DATE: _____ TIME: _____ LOCATION: _____

Order **Charadriiformes**	Family **Scolopacidae**	Species **Calidris alba**

Sanderling

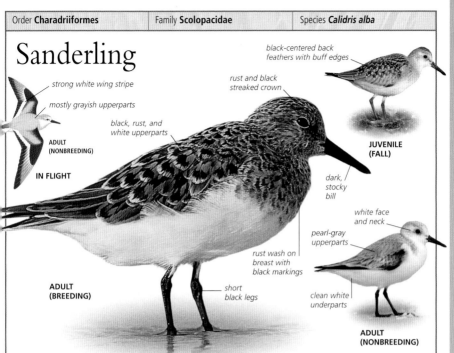

strong white wing stripe

mostly grayish upperparts

black, rust, and white upperparts

**ADULT
(NONBREEDING)**

IN FLIGHT

rust and black streaked crown

black-centered back feathers with buff edges

**JUVENILE
(FALL)**

dark, stocky bill

pearl-gray upperparts

white face and neck

rust wash on breast with black markings

**ADULT
(BREEDING)**

short black legs

clean white underparts

**ADULT
(NONBREEDING)**

The Sanderling is probably the best-known shorebird in the world. It breeds in some of the most remote, high-Arctic habitats, from Greenland to Siberia, but occupies just about every temperate and tropical shoreline in the Americas whennot breeding. Indeed, its wintering range spans both American coasts, from Canada to Argentina. Feeding in flocks, it is a common sight in winter on sandy beaches. In many places, though, the bird is declining rapidly, with pollution of the sea and shore, and the disturbance caused by people using beaches for various recreational purposes, the main causes.

VOICE Flight call squeaky *pweet*, threat call *sew-sew-sew*; display song harsh, buzzy notes and chattering *cher-cher-cher*.

NESTING Small, shallow depression on dry, stony ground; 4 eggs; 1–3 broods; June–July.

FEEDING Probes along the surf-line in sand for insects, small crustaceans, small mollusks, and worms.

FLIGHT: rapid, free-form; birds in flocks twisting and turning as if they were one.

CHASING THE WAVES
The Sanderling scampers after retreating waves to pick up any small creatures stranded by the sea.

OCCURRENCE
Breeds in barren high-Arctic coastal tundra of northernmost Canada, including the islands, north to Ellesmere Island. During winter months and on migration, found along all North American coastlines, but especially sandy beaches; inland migrants found along lake and river edges.

SIMILAR SPECIES

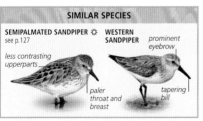

SEMIPALMATED SANDPIPER ☼ see p.127

less contrasting upperparts

WESTERN SANDPIPER

prominent eyebrow

paler throat and breast

tapering bill

Length **7½–8in (19–20cm)**	Wingspan **16–18in (41–46cm)**	Weight **1⁷⁄₁₆–3½oz (40–100g)**
Social **Small flocks**	Lifespan **Up to 10 years**	Status **Declining**

DATE: _____ TIME: _____ LOCATION: _____

Order **Charadriiformes**	Family **Scolopacidae**	Species *Calidris alpina*

Dunlin

JUVENILE

black-and-cream stripes on back

black streaks on buff underside

JUVENILE

dull gray-brown head and back

white sided rump

thin white wing bar

IN FLIGHT

long, tapered, black bill

dull, gray-streaked breast

rich chestnut-and-black back

fine dark streaks on whitish breast

large, squarish, black belly patch

ADULT (BREEDING)

ADULT (NONBREEDING)

FLIGHT: swift and direct flight, with rapid wing beats.

The Dunlin is one of the most abundant and widespread of North America's shorebirds, but of the ten officially recognized subspecies, only two breed in Canada: *C. a. arcticola* and *C. a. hudsonia*. The Dunlin is unmistakable in its striking, red-backed, black-bellied breeding plumage. In winter it sports much drabber colors, but more than makes up for this by gathering in spectacular flocks of many thousands of birds on its favorite, coastal mudflats.

VOICE Call accented trill, *drurr-drurr*, that rises slightly, then descends; flight call *jeeezp*; song *wrraah-wrraah*.

NESTING Simple cup lined with grasses, leaves, and lichens in moist to wet tundra; 4 eggs; 1 brood; June–July.

FEEDING Probes for marine, freshwater, terrestrial invertebrates: clams, worms, insect larvae, crustaceans; also plants and small fish.

OLD RED BACK
The Dunlin was once known as the Red-backed Sandpiper due to its distinct breeding plumage.

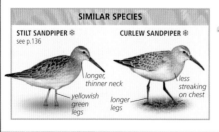

SIMILAR SPECIES		
STILT SANDPIPER ❁ see p.136	**CURLEW SANDPIPER** ❁	
longer, thinner neck	less streaking on chest	
yellowish green legs	longer legs	

OCCURRENCE
Breeds in Arctic and sub-Arctic moist, wet tundra, often near ponds, with drier islands for nest sites. In migration and winter, prefers coastal areas with extensive mudflats and sandy beaches; also feeds in flooded fields and seasonal inland wetlands.

Length **6¹/₂–8¹/₂in (16–22cm)**	Wingspan **12¹/₂–17¹/₂in (32–44cm)**	Weight **1⁹/₁₆–2¹/₄oz (45–65g)**
Social **Large flocks**	Lifespan **Up to 24 years**	Status **Declining**

DATE: _____ TIME: _____ LOCATION: _____

Purple Sandpiper

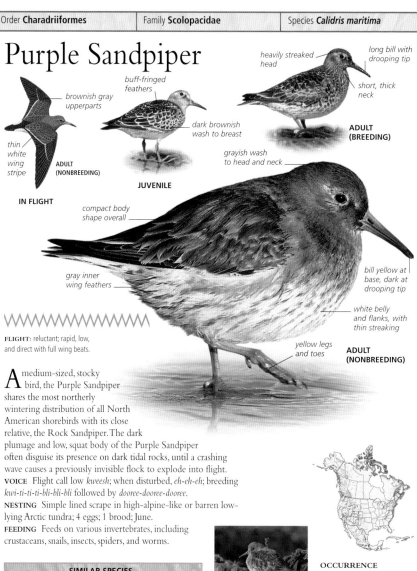

brownish gray
upperparts

thin
white
wing
stripe

**ADULT
(NONBREEDING)**

IN FLIGHT

buff-fringed
feathers

dark brownish
wash to breast

JUVENILE

heavily streaked
head

long bill with
drooping tip

short, thick
neck

**ADULT
(BREEDING)**

grayish wash
to head and neck

compact body
shape overall

gray inner
wing feathers

bill yellow at
base, dark at
drooping tip

white belly
and flanks, with
thin streaking

yellow legs
and toes

**ADULT
(NONBREEDING)**

FLIGHT: reluctant; rapid, low,
and direct with full wing beats.

A medium-sized, stocky
bird, the Purple Sandpiper
shares the most northerly
wintering distribution of all North
American shorebirds with its close
relative, the Rock Sandpiper. The dark
plumage and low, squat body of the Purple Sandpiper
often disguise its presence on dark tidal rocks, until a crashing
wave causes a previously invisible flock to explode into flight.
VOICE Flight call low *kweesh*; when disturbed, *eh-eh-eh*; breeding
kwi-ti-ti-ti-bli-bli-bli followed by *dooree-dooree-dooree*.
NESTING Simple lined scrape in high-alpine-like or barren low-
lying Arctic tundra; 4 eggs; 1 brood; June.
FEEDING Feeds on various invertebrates, including
crustaceans, snails, insects, spiders, and worms.

SIMILAR SPECIES

ROCK SANDPIPER
slightly
smaller bill

darker, plainer
upperparts

less
orange color
to base of bill

DUNLIN
see p.138
longer
black bill

plain, pale
gray-brown
upperparts

WINTER EXPOSURE
The Purple Sandpiper winters
mainly on exposed rocky shores
along the eastern seaboard.

OCCURRENCE
On breeding grounds, found on
barren Arctic and alpine tundra
habitats in the Canadian Arctic
Archipelago. On migration and in
winter, predominantly found on
rocky, wave-pounded shores on
the eastern seaboard.

Length 8–8½in (20–21cm)	Wingspan 16½–18½in (42–47cm)	Weight 1¾–3½oz (50–100g)
Social **Small flocks**	Lifespan **Up to 20 years**	Status **Declining**

DATE: _____ TIME: _____ LOCATION: _____

Order **Charadriiformes**	Family **Scolopacidae**	Species ***Calidris bairdii***

Baird's Sandpiper

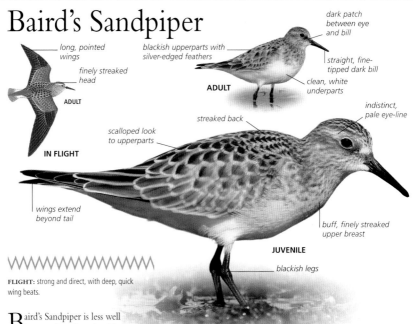

long, pointed wings

finely streaked head

ADULT

IN FLIGHT

dark patch between eye and bill

blackish upperparts with silver-edged feathers

ADULT

straight, fine-tipped dark bill

clean, white underparts

indistinct, pale eye-line

streaked back

scalloped look to upperparts

wings extend beyond tail

buff, finely streaked upper breast

JUVENILE

blackish legs

FLIGHT: strong and direct, with deep, quick wing beats.

Baird's Sandpiper is less well known than the other North American *Calidris* sandpipers. It was described in 1861, later than its relatives, by the famous North American ornithologist Elliott Coues, a former surgeon in the US Army, in honor of Spencer Fullerton Baird. Both men were founding members of the AOU (the American Ornithologists' Union). From its high-Arctic tundra habitat, Baird's Sandpiper moves across North America and the Western USA, into South America, and all the way to Tierra del Fuego, a remarkable biannual journey of 6,000–9,000 miles (9,700–14,500km).

VOICE Flight call a low, dry *preep*; song on Arctic breeding ground: *brraay, brray, brray*, followed by *hee-aaw, hee-aaw, hee-aaw*.

NESTING Shallow depression in coastal or upland tundra; 4 eggs; 1 brood; June.

FEEDING Picks and probes for insects and larvae; also spiders and pond crustaceans.

FEEDING IN FLOCKS
Flocks of this sandpiper rush about in search of food in shallow water and muddy areas.

SIMILAR SPECIES		

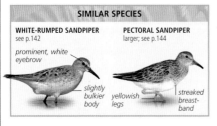

WHITE-RUMPED SANDPIPER
see p.142

prominent, white eyebrow

slightly bulkier body

PECTORAL SANDPIPER
larger; see p.144

yellowish legs

streaked breast-band

OCCURRENCE
Breeds in tundra habitats of High Arctic Alaska and Canada. During migration and winter, inland freshwater habitats: lake and river margins, wet pastures, rice fields; also tidal flats at coastal locations. In winter, common in the high Andes of South America, and sometimes all the way to Tierra del Fuego.

Length 5¾–7¼in (14.5–18.5cm)	Wingspan 16–18½in (41–47cm)	Weight 1¹⁄₁₆–2oz (30–55g)
Social **Flocks**	Lifespan **Unknown**	Status **Secure**

DATE: _____ TIME:_____ LOCATION:_____

Least Sandpiper

ADULT

faint
tail
band

IN FLIGHT

buff to
rust fringed
inner wing

JUVENILE

uniform
brownish gray
upperparts

short tail
and wings

small, rounded head

dark patch
between eye
and bill

**ADULT
(BREEDING)**

short,
yellowish
legs

pale, whitish
eyebrow

**ADULT
(NONBREEDING)**

white
chin and
belly

streaked, brownish
breast and head

yellow to yellowish
green legs

FLIGHT: level flight; fast and direct
on quick wing beats; in mixed flocks.

The little Least Sandpiper is often
overlooked because of its muted
plumage and preference for feeding
unobtrusively near vegetative cover. With its brown
or brownish gray plumage, the Least Sandpiper virtually disappears
in the landscape when feeding crouched down on wet margins of
water bodies. The bird is often found in small to medium flocks,
members of which typically are nervous when foraging, and
frequently burst into flight, only to alight a short way off.
VOICE Its flight call, *kreeeep*, rises in pitch, often repeated
two-syllable *kree-eep*; display call trilled *b-reeee, b-reeee, b-reeee.*
NESTING Depression in open, sub-Arctic habitat near water;
4 eggs; 1 brood; May–June.
FEEDING Forages for variety of small terrestrial and aquatic
prey, especially sand fleas, mollusks, and flies.

FLOCK IN FLIGHT
The narrow pointed wings of the Least Sandpiper
allow it to fly fast and level.

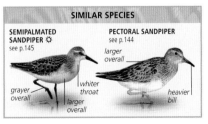

SIMILAR SPECIES

**SEMIPALMATED
SANDPIPER** ☼
see p.145

grayer
overall

whiter
throat

larger
overall

PECTORAL SANDPIPER
see p.144

larger
overall

heavier
bill

OCCURRENCE
Breeds in wet low-Arctic areas
from Alaska and the Yukon to
Quebec and Newfoundland.
During migration and in winter,
uses muddy areas such as lake
shores, riverbanks, flooded fields,
and tidal flats. Winters from
southern North America south
to Peru and Brazil.

| Length **4¾in (12cm)** | Wingspan **13–14in (33–35cm)** | Weight **⁵⁄₁₆–1oz (9–27g)** |
| Social **Flocks** | Lifespan **Up to 16 years** | Status **Declining** |

| Order **Charadriiformes** | Family **Scolopacidae** | Species *Calidris fuscicollis* |

White-rumped Sandpiper

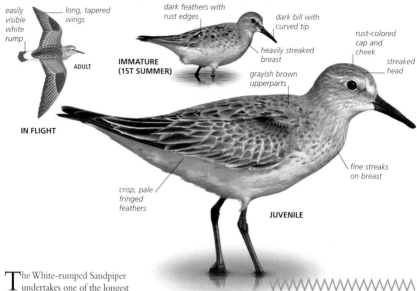

easily visible white rump

long, tapered wings

IN FLIGHT

ADULT

dark feathers with rust edges

IMMATURE (1ST SUMMER)

dark bill with curved tip

heavily streaked breast

grayish brown upperparts

rust-colored cap and cheek

streaked head

fine streaks on breast

crisp, pale fringed feathers

JUVENILE

The White-rumped Sandpiper undertakes one of the longest migrations of any bird in the Western Hemisphere. From its high-Arctic breeding grounds in Alaska and Canada, it migrates in several long jumps to extreme southern South America—about 9,000–12,000 miles (14,500–19,300km), twice a year. Almost the entire population migrates through the central US and Canada in spring, with several stopovers, which are critical to the success of its journey. While associating with other shorebird species during migration and winter, it can be overlooked in the crowd. Its insect-like call and white rump aid identification.
VOICE Call a very high-pitched, insect-like *tzeet*; flight song an insect-like, high-pitched, rattling buzz, interspersed with grunts.
NESTING Shallow depression in usually wet but well-vegetated tundra; 4 eggs; 1 brood; June.
FEEDING Picks and probes for insects, spiders, earthworms, and marine worms; also some plant matter.

FLIGHT: fast, strong, and direct flight with deep wing beats.

WING POWER
Long narrow wings enable this species to migrate to and from the Arctic and Tiera del Fuego.

SIMILAR SPECIES

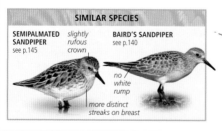

SEMIPALMATED SANDPIPER see p.145

slightly rufous crown

BAIRD'S SANDPIPER see p.140

no white rump

more distinct streaks on breast

OCCURRENCE
Breeds in wet but well-vegetated tundra, usually near ponds, lakes, or streams. In migration and winter, grassy areas: flooded fields, grassy lake margins, rivers, ponds, grassy margins of tidal mudflats, and roadside ditches. On wintering grounds, often associates with Baird's Sandpiper.

| Length **6–6¾in (15–17cm)** | Wingspan **16–18in (41–46cm)** | Weight **⅞–1¾oz (25–50g)** |
| Social **Flocks** | Lifespan **Unknown** | Status **Secure** |

DATE: _____ TIME:_____ LOCATION:_____

| Order **Charadriiformes** | Family **Scolopacidae** | Species *Calidris subruficollis* |

Buff-breasted Sandpiper

pale central band

streaked and spotted brown hind neck

buff head and face with spotted brown crown

buff-edged brown upperparts

short, dark bill

scaly upperparts

dark rump

ADULT (NONBREEDING)

bright yellowish orange legs

ADULT (BREEDING)

IN FLIGHT

more white-fringed upperpart feathers than adult

rich buff wash to breast

JUVENILE

dull, yellow legs

FLIGHT: fast, straight, and low, with rapid wing beats.

S leek and elegant, this sandpiper is unique among North American shorebirds in terms of its mating system. On the ground in the Arctic, each male flashes his white underwings to attract females for mating. After mating, the female leaves to perform all nest duties alone, while the male continues to display and mate with other females. Once nesting is over, the Buff-breasted Sandpiper migrates an astonishing 16,000 miles (26,000km) from its breeding grounds to winter in temperate South America.

VOICE Flight call soft, short *gert*, or longer, rising *grriit*.
NESTING Simple depression on well-drained moss or grass hummock; 4 eggs; 1 brood; June.
FEEDING Forages on land for insects, insect larvae, and spiders; occasionally eats seeds.

LANDLUBBER
The Buff-breasted Sandpiper is very much a shorebird of dry land; it doesn't swim or dive.

OCCURRENCE
Breeds in moist to wet, grassy or sedge coastal tundra; during migration, favors short grass areas such as pastures, sod farms, meadows, rice fields, or agricultural areas. Winters in the pampas region of South America in short, wet grass habitats.

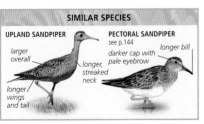

SIMILAR SPECIES

UPLAND SANDPIPER

larger overall

longer wings and tail

PECTORAL SANDPIPER
see p.144

longer, streaked neck

darker cap with pale eyebrow

longer bill

| Length **7¼–8in (18.5–20cm)** | Wingspan **17–18½in (43–47cm)** | Weight **1⁷⁄₁₆–3⅜oz (40–95g)** |
| Social **Large flocks** | Lifespan **Unknown** | Status **Declining** |

DATE: _____ TIME: _____ LOCATION: _____

| Order **Charadriiformes** | Family **Scolopacidae** | Species *Calidris melanotos* |

Pectoral Sandpiper

long, graceful, pointed wings

rust-edged, dark-centered feathers

rust crown and cheeks with black streaks

streaked crown and face

curved bill with orange base

ADULT

JUVENILE

darker flight feathers

brownish upperparts, with buff fringes

IN FLIGHT

medium length, stocky bill

ADULT

heavily streaked breast

yellowish legs

white belly

This medium-sized sandpiper is a true champion of long-distance migration. From their breeding grounds in the high-Arctic to their wintering grounds on the pampas of southern South America, some birds travel up to 30,000 miles (48,000km) each year. The Pectoral Sandpiper is a promiscuous breeder, with males keeping harems of females in guarded territories. Males mate with as many females as they can attract with a display that includes a deep, booming call, and flights, but take no part in nest duties. Males migrate earlier than females, with both sexes prefer wet, grassy habitats during migration and in winter.

VOICE Flight call low, trilled *chrrk*; display song deep, hollow, hooting: *whoop, whoop, whoop.*

NESTING Shallow depression on ridges in moist to wet sedge tundra; 4 eggs; 1 brood; June.

FEEDING Probes or jabs mud for larvae, and forages for insects and spiders on tundra.

FLIGHT: fast and direct, with rapid, powerful wing beats; flocks zig-zag when flushed.

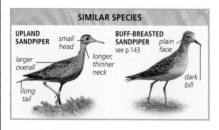

SIMILAR SPECIES

UPLAND SANDPIPER small head

larger overall

longer, thinner neck

long tail

BUFF-BREASTED SANDPIPER plain face see p.143

dark bill

LONG JOURNEYS
This species migrates long distances to arrive in southern South America for the winter.

OCCURRENCE
In North America, breeds in northern Alaska, northern Yukon, Northern Territories, and some islands of the Canadian Arctic Archipelago, in wet, grassy tundra, especially near coasts. On migration and in winter favors wet pastures, the grassy margins of ponds and lakes, and saltmarshes.

| Length **7½–9in (19–23cm)** | Wingspan **16½–19½in (42–49cm)** | Weight **1¾–4oz (50–125g)** |
| Social **Migrant flocks** | Lifespan **Up to 4½ years** | Status **Secure** |

DATE: _____ TIME: _____ LOCATION: _____

Semipalmated Sandpiper

white eyebrow

crisp, pale fringed feathers

short, straight bill with blunt tip

streaked black and rust crown

slightly paler grayish nape

pale grayish black legs

dark-centered back feathers with buff fringes

JUVENILE

short, dark bill

pale wing stripe along flight feathers

SUMMER

IN FLIGHT

wing tips extend to tail tip

ADULT (SUMMER)

lightly streaked breast

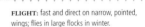

This is the most abundant of the so-called "peep" *Calidris* sandpipers, breeding in Canada's Arctic tundra. Flocks of up to 300,000 birds gather on migration staging areas. As a species, though, it can be hard to identify, due to plumage variation between juveniles and breeding adults, and a bill that varies markedly in size and shape from west to east. Semipalmated sandpipers from northeasterly breeding grounds may fly nonstop to their South American wintering grounds in the fall.

VOICE Flight call *chrrk* or higher, sharper *chit*; display song monotonous, droning trill, often repeated for minutes at a time.

NESTING Shallow, lined scrape in short grass habitat; 4 eggs; 1 brood; May–June.

FEEDING Probes mud for aquatic and terrestrial invertebrates such as mollusks, worms, and spiders.

FLIGHT: fast and direct on narrow, pointed, wings; flies in large flocks in winter.

SLEEPING TOGETHER
Semipalmated Sandpipers form large feeding or resting flocks on migration and in winter.

OCCURRENCE
Breeds in Arctic and sub-Arctic tundra habitats near water; in Alaska, on outer coastal plain. Migrants occur in shallow fresh- or saltwater and open muddy areas with little vegetation, such as intertidal flats or lake shores. Winters in Central and South America, south to Brazil and Peru.

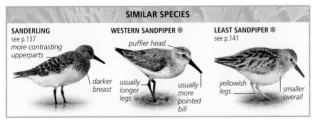

SIMILAR SPECIES

SANDERLING
see p.137
more contrasting upperparts

darker breast

WESTERN SANDPIPER ❊
puffier head
usually longer legs
usually more pointed bill

LEAST SANDPIPER ❊
see p.141
yellowish legs
smaller overall

Length **5¼–6in (13.5–15cm)**	Wingspan **13½–15in (34–38cm)**	Weight **½–1⁷⁄₁₆oz (14–40g)**
Social **Large flocks**	Lifespan **Up to 12 years**	Status **Secure**

| Order **Charadriiformes** | Family **Scolopacidae** | Species ***Limnodromus griseus*** |

Short-billed Dowitcher

white slash from rump to mid-back

ADULT (BREEDING)

orange-fringed feathers

flanks less heavily streaked

orange wash to face, neck, breast, and underparts

long, stout bill

JUVENILE

long, pointed wings

IN FLIGHT

dark-centered upperpart feathers

ADULT
L. g. griseus

variable spotting on upper breast

slightly larger bill

ADULT
L. g. hendersoni

greenish yellow legs

streaked flanks

plain gray upperparts

white belly

ADULT (NONBREEDING)

FLIGHT: swift, powerful with quick wing beats.

T he Short-billed Dowitcher is a common visitor along the
Atlantic, Gulf, and Pacific Coasts. Its remote and bug-infested
breeding areas in northern bogs have hindered the study of its
breeding behavior until recent years. There are three subspecies
(*L. g. griseus*, *L. g. hendersoni*, and *L. g. caurinus*), which differ in
plumage, size, and respective breeding areas. Recent knowledge
about shape and structure has helped ornithologists distinguish
the Short-billed from the Long-billed Dowitcher.

VOICE Flight call low, plaintive *tu-tu-tu*, 3–4 notes; flight
song *tu-tu, tu-tu, toodle-ee, tu-tu*, ending with low *anh-anh-anh*.
NESTING Simple depression, typically in sedge hummock;
4 eggs; 1 brood; May–June.
FEEDING Probes in "sewing machine" feeding style with water
up to belly for aquatic mollusks, crustaceans, and insects.

ORANGE UNDERPARTS
In complete breeding plumage, the Short-billed
Dowitcher is orange, even in late afternoon light.

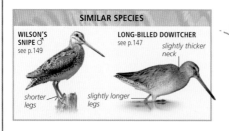

SIMILAR SPECIES

WILSON'S SNIPE ♂
see p.149

LONG-BILLED DOWITCHER
see p.147

slightly thicker neck

shorter legs

slightly longer legs

OCCURRENCE
Breeds mostly in sedge
meadows or bogs with
interspersed spruce and
tamaracks between subarctic
tundra and boreal forest.
Migrates south to Central
and South America, preferring
coastal mudflats, salt marshes
or adjacent freshwater pools.

| Length **9–10in (23–25cm)** | Wingspan **18–20in (46–51cm)** | Weight **2½–5½oz (70–155g)** |
| Social **Pairs/Flocks** | Lifespan **Up to 20 years** | Status **Secure (p)** |

DATE: _____ TIME: _____ LOCATION: _____

| Order **Charadriiformes** | Family **Scolopacidae** | Species *Limnodromus scolopaceus* |

Long-billed Dowitcher

bands on tail

ADULT (BREEDING)

dark upperparts with reddish markings

ADULT (BREEDING)

brick-red underparts

white rump patch

long, pointed wings

IN FLIGHT

lightly streaked head

white belly

black-centered feathers

JUVENILE

mostly dusky gray upperparts

short but distinct white eyebrow

long, stout bill

dark patch between eye and bill

variable dark barring on flanks

white belly

ADULT (NONBREEDING)

It was not until 1950 that museum and field studies identified two separate species of dowitcher in North America. The Long-billed Dowitcher is usually slightly larger, longer-legged, and heavier in the chest and neck than the Short-billed Dowitcher. The breeding ranges of the two species are separate, but their migration and en route stop-over areas overlap. The Long-billed Dowitcher is usually found in freshwater wetlands, and in the fall most of its population occurs west of the Mississippi River.

VOICE Flight and alarm call sharp, whistled *keek*, given singly or in series when agitated; song buzzy *pipipipipipi-chi-drrr*.

NESTING Deep sedge or grass-lined depression in sedge or grass; 4 eggs; 1 brood; May–June.

FEEDING Probes wet ground with "sewing-machine" motion for spiders, snails, worms, insects, and seeds.

FLIGHT: swift, direct flier with fast, powerful wing beats.

TOUCHY FEELY
Sensitive touch-receptors at the tip of the bird's bill enable it to feel in the mud for food.

SIMILAR SPECIES

WILSON'S SNIPE
see p.149

pale, central crown stripe

shorter legs

SHORT-BILLED DOWITCHER
see p.146

slightly smaller overall

orangish underparts

OCCURRENCE
Breeds in wet, grassy meadows or coastal sedge tundra near freshwater pools. Migrates to Mexico and Central America, south to Panama, when found in freshwater habitats, including ponds, flooded fields, lake shores, also sheltered lagoons, salt marsh pools, and tidal mudflats.

| Length **9½–10in (24–26cm)** | Wingspan **18–20½in (46–52cm)** | Weight **3–4oz (85–125g)** |
| Social **Pairs/Flocks** | Lifespan **Unknown** | Status **Vulnerable** |

| Order **Charadriiformes** | Family **Scolopacidae** | Species *Scolopax minor* |

American Woodcock

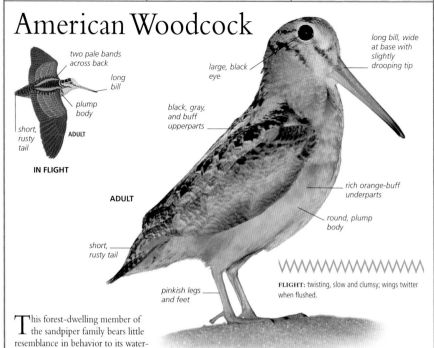

two pale bands across back

long bill

plump body

short, rusty tail

ADULT

IN FLIGHT

large, black eye

long bill, wide at base with slightly drooping tip

black, gray, and buff upperparts

ADULT

rich orange-buff underparts

round, plump body

short, rusty tail

pinkish legs and feet

FLIGHT: twisting, slow and clumsy; wings twitter when flushed.

This forest-dwelling member of the sandpiper family bears little resemblance in behavior to its water-favoring relatives, but slightly resembles Wilson's Snipe and the dowitchers. Although widespread, the American Woodcock is very secretive and seldom seen, except during its twilight courtship displays. It is largely nocturnal, and feeds in mature fields or woodlands. Its noisy, repetitive display flights are a welcome sign of spring in northern breeding areas.

VOICE Low, nasal *peen* call by male during dawn and dusk display; variety of chirping and twittering sounds given by male in display flight, made by air passing through narrow outer wing feathers.

NESTING Shallow depression in existing leaf and twig litter in young, mixed growth woodlands; 4 eggs; 1 brood; January (southern populations) and April (northern populations).

FEEDING Probes deep in damp soil or mud; mostly for earthworms, but also insects, snails, and some plants.

STAYING PUT
A foraging American Woodcock "caught" in an open field will freeze before it flies off.

SIMILAR SPECIES

WILSON'S SNIPE
see p.149

smaller head

longer legs

streaked breast and flanks

LONG-BILLED DOWITCHER
see p.147

more slender shape

smaller head

OCCURRENCE
Breeds from southern Canada to southeastern US states, in damp, second growth forest, overgrown fields and bogs. In winter, found in similar habitat; also found along marsh edges, swamps, and damp, grassy roadsides in Texas and Florida in the southern US.

| Length **10–12in (25–31cm)** | Wingspan **16–20in (41–51cm)** | Weight **4–7oz (125–200g)** |
| Social **Solitary** | Lifespan **Up to 9 years** | Status **Secure** |

DATE: _____ TIME: _____ LOCATION: _____

| Order **Charadriiformes** | Family **Scolopacidae** | Species *Gallinago delicata* |

Wilson's Snipe

high-set large, dark eye

streaked face

long, thick, tapered bill, slightly drooping at tip

white, vertical streaks

long, pointed, angled wings

long bill

ADULT

short tail

IN FLIGHT

mostly brown upperparts

brown spots on breast and neck

white underparts with barring on flanks

short russet tail

MALE

FLIGHT: extremely fast and zig-zagging, rapid wing beats; erratic-looking changes of direction.

This secretive and well camouflaged member of the sandpiper family has an unsettled taxonomic history, but is now classified individually. On its breeding grounds Wilson's Snipe produces rather eerie sounds during its aerial, mainly nocturnal, display flights. The birds fly up silently from the ground, and then, from about 330ft (100m) up, they descend quickly, with their tail feathers spread, producing a unique, loud and vibrating sound through modified feathers.

VOICE Alarm and overhead flight call raspy *kraitsch*; perched and low flying breeding birds give repetitive, monotonous *kup-kup-kup-kup* in alarm or aggression; distinctive whistling sound during territorial displays.

NESTING Elaborate woven nest lined with fine grass on ground, sedge, or moss; 4 eggs; 1 brood; May–June.

FEEDING Forages in mud or shallow water; probes deep into subsoil; diet includes mostly insect larvae, but also crustaceans, earthworms, and mollusks.

RUSSET TAIL
Wilson's Snipe's russet-colored tail is usually hard to see, but it is evident on this preening bird.

OCCURRENCE
Widespread from Alaska to Quebec and Labrador south of the tundra zone; breeds in a variety of wetlands, including marshes, bogs, and open areas with rich soil. Winters further south, where it prefers damp areas with vegetative cover, such as marshes, wet fields, and other bodies of water.

SIMILAR SPECIES

AMERICAN WOODCOCK
see p.148

plump body

buffy orange underparts

SHORT-BILLED DOWITCHER
see p.146

smaller eye

orange tint to breast

LONG-BILLED DOWITCHER
see p.147

no white streaks on back

longer legs

| Length **10–11in (25–28cm)** | Wingspan **17–19in (43–48cm)** | Weight **2⅞–5oz (80–150g)** |
| Social **Solitary** | Lifespan **Up to 10 years** | Status **Secure** |

DATE: _____ TIME: _____ LOCATION: _____

| Order **Charadriiformes** | Family **Scolopacidae** | Species **Actitis macularius** |

Spotted Sandpiper

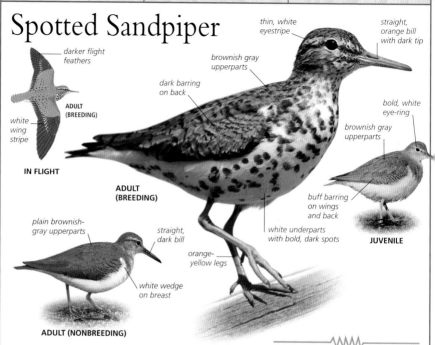

darker flight feathers

ADULT (BREEDING)

white wing stripe

IN FLIGHT

thin, white eyestripe

straight, orange bill with dark tip

brownish gray upperparts

dark barring on back

bold, white eye-ring

brownish gray upperparts

ADULT (BREEDING)

buff barring on wings and back

white underparts with bold, dark spots

JUVENILE

plain brownish-gray upperparts

straight, dark bill

orange-yellow legs

white wedge on breast

ADULT (NONBREEDING)

One of only two species of the genus *Actitis*, from the Latin meaning "a coastal inhabitant," this small, short-legged sandpiper is the most widespread shorebird in North America. It is characterized by its quick walking pace, its habit of constantly teetering and bobbing its tail, and its unique style of flying low over water. Spotted Sandpipers have an unusual mating behavior, in which the females take on an aggressive role, defending territories and mating with three or more males per season.

VOICE Call a clear, ringing note *tee-tee-tee-tee*; flight song a monotonous *cree-cree-cree*.

NESTING Nest cup shaded by or scrape built under herbaceous vegetation; 3 eggs; 1–3 broods; May–June.

FEEDING Eats many items, including adult and larval insects, mollusks, small crabs, and worms.

FLIGHT: mostly shallow, rapidly, stiffly fluttering wing beats, usually low above water.

BEHAVIORAL QUIRKS
This sandpiper "teeters," raising and lowering its tail while walking along the water's edge.

SIMILAR SPECIES

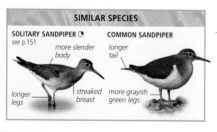

SOLITARY SANDPIPER ◐
see p.151

more slender body

longer legs

streaked breast

COMMON SANDPIPER

longer tail

more grayish green legs

OCCURRENCE
Breeds across North America in a wide variety of grassy, brushy, forested habitats near water, but not High Arctic tundra. During migration and in winter found in habitats near freshwater, including lake shores, rivers, streams, beaches, sewage ponds, ditches, seawalls, sometimes estuaries.

| Length **7¼–8in (18.5–20cm)** | Wingspan **15–16in (38–41cm)** | Weight **1⁹⁄₁₆–1¾oz (45–50g)** |
| Social **Small flocks** | Lifespan **Up to 12 years** | Status **Secure** |

DATE: _____ TIME:_____ LOCATION:_____

| Order **Charadriiformes** | Family **Scolopacidae** | Species *Tringa solitaria* |

Solitary Sandpiper

long, pointed wings

ADULT (BREEDING)

dark flight feathers

IN FLIGHT

brown-and-white checkered upperparts

brownish streaked crown and head

JUVENILE

dark-and-white checkered upperparts

conspicuous white eye-ring

roundish forehead

straight, dark, tapered bill

finely streaked breast

ADULT (BREEDING)

greenish olive legs

FLIGHT: graceful and strong, with deep, stiff wing beats.

Alexander Wilson described this species in 1813, naming it, quite appropriately, "Solitary." This Sandpiper seldom associates with other shorebirds as it moves nervously along margins of wetlands. When feeding, the Solitary Sandpiper constantly bobs its head like the Spotted Sandpiper. When disturbed, the Solitary Sandpiper often flies directly upward, and when landing, it keeps its wings upright briefly, flashing the white underneath, before carefully folding them to its body.

VOICE Flight and alarm call a high-pitched *weet-weet-weet* or *pit*; display song a *pit-pit-pit-pit*; *kik-kik-kik*.

NESTING Abandoned nests in trees (a unique behavior for a North American shorebird); 4 eggs; 1 brood; May–June.

FEEDING Eats insects, small crustaceans, snails, and small frogs.

LONE RANGER
This sandpiper is often solitary and is found in quiet, sheltered habitats and along river shores.

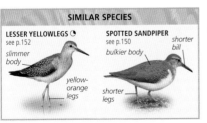

SIMILAR SPECIES

LESSER YELLOWLEGS ☾
see p.152
slimmer body
yellow-orange legs

SPOTTED SANDPIPER
see p.150
bulkier body
shorter legs
shorter bill

OCCURRENCE
Breeds primarily in bogs in northern forests; in winter and during migration, occurs in sheltered pools or muddy areas near forests. Winters from Mexico down to South America, sometimes in tiny pools at high altitude in the Andes; also riverbanks, streams, rain pools, and ditches.

| Length **7½–9in (19–23cm)** | Wingspan **22–23in (56–59cm)** | Weight **1¹⁄₁₆–2¹⁄₄oz (30–65g)** |
| Social **Solitary/Small flocks** | Lifespan **Unknown** | Status **Secure** |

DATE: _____ TIME: _____ LOCATION: _____

| Order **Charadriiformes** | Family **Scolopacidae** | Species ***Tringa flavipes*** |

Lesser Yellowlegs

small head

gray back with delicate scalloping pattern

dark, slender bill

ADULT (BREEDING)

long, pointed, dark wings

diffused, pale streaks on breast

IN FLIGHT

diffused spots on neck

black-and-brown upperparts with white spotting

white underparts

brownish upperparts

ADULT (BREEDING)

heavily streaked head, neck, and breast

ADULT (NONBREEDING)

crisp whitish spotting on wings

JUVENILE

long, yellow-orange legs

yellow legs

FLIGHT: straight and fast; with gliding and sideways banking; legs trail behind body.

With its smaller head, thinner bill, and smoother body shape, the Lesser Yellowlegs has a more elegant profile than the Greater Yellowlegs. It prefers smaller, freshwater, or brackish pools to open saltwater habitats, and it walks quickly and methodically while feeding. Although this species is a solitary feeder, it is often seen in small to large loose flocks in migration and winter.

VOICE Low, whistled *tu-tu* call; series of *tu* or *cuw* notes when agitated; display song a *pill-e-wee, pill-e-wee, pill-e-wee.*

NESTING Depression in ground or moss, lined with grass and leaves; 4 eggs; 1 brood; May–June.

FEEDING Eats a wide variety of aquatic and terrestrial insects, mollusks, and crustaceans, especially flies and beetles; also seeds.

BALANCING ACT
The Lesser Yellowlegs uses its long, raised wings for balance while feeding in soft mud.

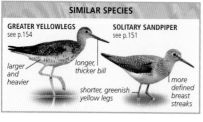

SIMILAR SPECIES

GREATER YELLOWLEGS
see p.154

larger and heavier

longer, thicker bill

SOLITARY SANDPIPER
see p.151

shorter, greenish yellow legs

more defined breast streaks

OCCURRENCE
Breeds in northerly forest with clearings, and where forest meets tundra. In migration and in winter, uses wide variety of shallow wetlands, including flooded pastures and agricultural fields, swamps, lake and river shores, tidal creeks, and brackish mudflats. Winters from Mexico to Argentina.

| Length **9–10in (23–25cm)** | Wingspan **23–25in (58–64cm)** | Weight **2–3⅜oz (55–95g)** |
| Social **Flocks** | Lifespan **Unknown** | Status **Secure** |

DATE: _____ TIME:_____ LOCATION:_____

| Order **Charadriiformes** | Family **Scolopacidae** | Species **Tringa semipalmata** |

Willet

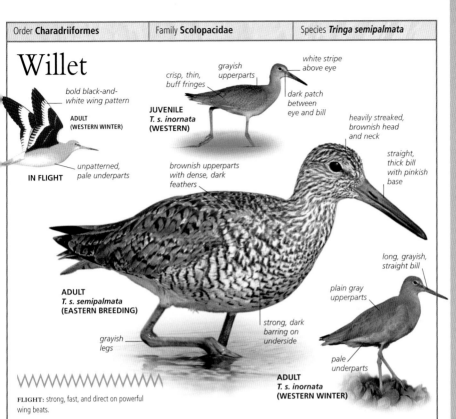

bold black-and-white wing pattern

ADULT (WESTERN WINTER)

IN FLIGHT
unpatterned, pale underparts

crisp, thin, buff fringes

grayish upperparts

JUVENILE
T. s. inornata
(WESTERN)

white stripe above eye

dark patch between eye and bill

heavily streaked, brownish head and neck

straight, thick bill with pinkish base

brownish upperparts with dense, dark feathers

ADULT
T. s. semipalmata
(EASTERN BREEDING)

grayish legs

strong, dark barring on underside

long, grayish, straight bill

plain gray upperparts

pale underparts

ADULT
T. s. inornata
(WESTERN WINTER)

FLIGHT: strong, fast, and direct on powerful wing beats.

The two distinct subspecies of the Willet, Eastern (*T. s. semipalmata*) and Western (*T. s. inornata*), differ in breeding habits, plumage coloration, vocalizations, and migratory habits. The Eastern Willet leaves North America from September to March; whereas the Western Willet winters along southern North American shorelines south to South America.

VOICE Flight call a loud *kyah-yah*; alarm call a sharp, repeated *kleep*; song an urgent, rapid *pill-will-willet*.

NESTING Depression in vegetated dunes, wetlands, prairies, or saltmarshes; 4 eggs; 1 brood; April–June.

FEEDING Picks, probes, or swishes for crustaceans such as fiddler and mole crabs, aquatic insects, marine worms, small mollusks, and fish.

EXPOSED PERCH
Willets roost on exposed perches at breeding grounds.

OCCURRENCE
Eastern subspecies breeds in coastal saltwater habitats: salt marshes, barrier islands, beaches, mangroves; winters in similar habitats. Western subspecies breeds near sparsely vegetated prairie wetlands or adjacent semiarid grasslands; winters in coastal regions.

SIMILAR SPECIES

GREATER YELLOWLEGS see p.154
longer neck
yellowish orange legs

WANDERING TATTLER 1ST
stockier body
yellowish legs

| Length **12½–16½in (32–42cm)** | Wingspan **21½–28½in (54–72cm)** | Weight **7–12oz (200–350g)** |
| Social **Flocks** | Lifespan **Up to 10 years** | Status **Secure** |

DATE: _____ TIME: _____ LOCATION: _____

Greater Yellowlegs

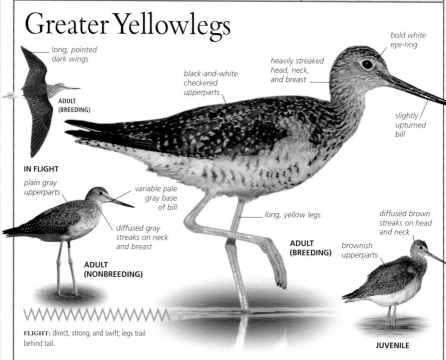

long, pointed
dark wings

**ADULT
(BREEDING)**

black-and-white
checkered
upperparts

bold white
eye-ring

heavily streaked
head, neck,
and breast

slightly
upturned
bill

IN FLIGHT

plain gray
upperparts

variable pale
gray base
of bill

diffused gray
streaks on neck
and breast

**ADULT
(NONBREEDING)**

long, yellow legs

**ADULT
(BREEDING)**

diffused brown
streaks on head
and neck

brownish
upperparts

JUVENILE

FLIGHT: direct, strong, and swift; legs trail
behind tail.

This fairly large shorebird often runs frantically in many
directions while pursuing small prey. It is one of the first
northbound spring shorebird migrants, and one of the first to
return south in late June or early July. Its plumage, a mixture
of brown, black, and white checkered upperparts, and streaked
underparts, is more streaked during the breeding season.
VOICE Call a loud, penetrating *tew-tew-tew*; agitated birds
make repetitive *keu* notes; song a continuous *too-whee*.
NESTING Simple scrape in moss or peat, usually close to water;
4 eggs; 1 brood; May–June.
FEEDING Picks water surface and mud for small aquatic and
terrestrial crustaceans and worms; also eats small fish, frogs,
seeds, and berries.

EFFECTIVE METHOD
The Greater Yellowlegs often catches small fish
by sweeping its bill sideways through water.

SIMILAR SPECIES

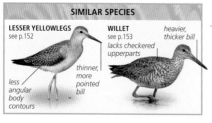

LESSER YELLOWLEGS
see p.152

less
angular
body
contours

thinner,
more
pointed
bill

WILLET
see p.153
lacks checkered
upperparts

heavier,
thicker bill

OCCURRENCE
Breeds in openings in northerly
forests with bogs and wet
meadows, a habitat called
muskeg. In migration and
winter, uses a wide variety
of shallow water habitats,
including freshwater and
saltwater marshes, reservoirs,
and tidal mudflats.

Length **11½–13in (29–33cm)**	Wingspan **28–29in (70–74cm)**	Weight **4–8oz (125–225g)**
Social **Solitary/Flocks**	Lifespan **Unknown**	Status **Secure**

DATE: _____ TIME:_____ LOCATION:_____

| Order **Charadriiformes** | Family **Scolopacidae** | Species **Phalaropus tricolor** |

Wilson's Phalarope

reddish-brown markings on sides of back

FEMALE (BREEDING)

grayish brown wings

IN FLIGHT

plain gray upperparts

yellowish legs

largely white face

white cheek

white underparts

JUVENILE (MOLTING TO 1ST WINTER)

gray and reddish brown back

paler head markings

plain gray-and-black upperparts

MALE

white eyebrow

fairly long, straight bill

black stripe from bill to nape

rust neck and throat

FEMALE (BREEDING)

A truly American phalarope, Wilson's is the largest of the three phalarope species. Unlike its two relatives, it does not breed in the Arctic, but in the shallow wetlands of western North America, and winters mainly in continental habitats of Bolivia and Argentina instead of in the ocean. This species can be found employing the feeding technique of spinning in shallow water to churn up adult and larval insects, or running in various directions on muddy wetland edges with its head held low to the ground while chasing and picking up insects. This bird is quite tolerant of humans on its breeding grounds, but this attitude changes immediately before migration, as it has gained weight and its movement is sluggish.

VOICE Flight call a low, nasal *werpf*; also higher, repetitive *emf, emf, emf, emf*, or *luk, luk, luk*.

NESTING Simple scrape lined with grass; 4 eggs; 1 brood; May–June.

FEEDING Eats brine shrimp, various insects, and insect larvae.

FLIGHT: fast and direct with quick wing beats.

ODD ONE OUT
Unlike its two essentially oceanic cousins, Wilson's Phalarope is also found in freshwater habitats.

OCCURRENCE
Breeds in shallow, grassy wetlands of interior North America; during migration and winter, occurs in salty lakes and saline ponds as well as inland waterbodies. In winter, tens of thousands can be seen in the middle of Titicaca Lake in Bolivia.

SIMILAR SPECIES

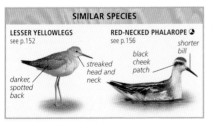

LESSER YELLOWLEGS
see p.152

darker, spotted back

streaked head and neck

RED-NECKED PHALAROPE ♀
see p.156

black cheek patch

shorter bill

| Length **8½–9½in (22–24cm)** | Wingspan **15½–17in (39–43cm)** | Weight **1¼–3oz (35–85g)** |
| Social **Large flocks** | Lifespan **Up to 10 years** | Status **Secure** |

Order **Charadriiformes**	Family **Scolopacidae**	Species *Phalaropus lobatus*

Red-necked Phalarope

pointed wings

narrow, white wing stripe

FEMALE (BREEDING)

IN FLIGHT

dark cap and cheek patch

black back with dull, white lines

JUVENILE (WORN PLUMAGE)

dark upperparts with buff or rust feather edges

dark upperparts with buff stripes

JUVENILE

dark gray crown and face

white throat

needle-like, dark bill

rust neck and upper breast

FEMALE (BREEDING)

white underparts with dusky streaked flanks

This aquatic sandpiper spends much of its life in deep ocean waters feeding on tiny plankton; each year, after nine months at sea, it comes to nest in the Arctic. Its Latin name *lobatus* reflects the morphology of its feet, which are webbed (lobed). Both the Red-necked Phalarope and the Red Phalarope are oceanic birds that are found in large flocks or "rafts" far from shore. However, both species are occasionally found swimming inland in freshwater habitats. Like the other two phalaropes, the Red-necked has a fascinating and unusual reversal of typical sex roles. The female is more brightly colored and slightly larger than the male; she will also pursue the male, compete savagely for him, and will migrate shortly after laying her eggs, leaving him to care for them.

VOICE Flight call a hard, squeaky *puit* or *kit*; on breeding grounds, vocalizations include variations of flight call notes.

NESTING Depression in wet sedge or grass; 3–4 eggs; 1–2 broods; May–June.

FEEDING Eats plankton; also insects, brine shrimp, and mollusks.

FLIGHT: fast and direct, with rapid wing beats.

SINGLE FATHER
Male phalaropes perform all nesting and rearing duties after the female lays the eggs.

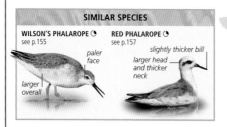

SIMILAR SPECIES

WILSON'S PHALAROPE ♀
see p.155

paler face

larger overall

RED PHALAROPE ♀
see p.157

slightly thicker bill

larger head and thicker neck

OCCURRENCE
Breeds in wet tundra, on raised ridges, or hummocks, but during migration and in winter, occurs far out to sea and away from shores, although sometimes found in a number of freshwater habitats.

Length **7–7½in (18–19cm)**	Wingspan **12½–16in (32–41cm)**	Weight **1¹⁄₁₆–1⁹⁄₁₆oz (30–45g)**
Social **Flocks**	Lifespan **Unknown**	Status **Declining**

DATE: _____ TIME: _____ LOCATION: _____

Red Phalarope

bold white wing bar

FEMALE (BREEDING)

white rump with black line in center, and white edges

broad, pointed wings

IN FLIGHT

buff feather fringes

scalloped upperparts

dull rust crown with black streaks

brick-red underparts; paler than female

MALE (BREEDING)

black cheek patch and nape

mostly gray upperparts

white underparts

white neck and head

ADULT (NONBREEDING)

bold white cheek patch

black crown

tan-fringed feathers on upperparts

stout, yellow bill with black tip

deep brick-red neck, throat, and underparts

FEMALE (BREEDING)

The Red Phalarope spends over ten months each year over deep ocean waters. It also migrates across the ocean, which explains why few birds of this species are ever seen inland. Many Red Phalaropes winter in tropical waters, with concentrations in the Humboldt Current off Peru and Chile, and in the Benguela current off southwestern Africa. During migration over Alaskan waters, flocks of Red Phalaropes feed on crustaceans in the mud plumes that are created by the foraging of gray and bowhead whales on the ocean floor.

VOICE Flight call a sharp *psip* or *pseet*, often in rapid succession; alarm call a drawn-out, 2-syllabled *sweet*.

NESTING Depression on ridge or hummock in coastal sedge; 3–4 eggs; 1 brood; June.

FEEDING Plucks prey from sea; marine crustaceans, fish eggs, larval fish; adult or larval insects.

FLIGHT: direct with rapid wing beats, birds in flocks often synchronize.

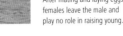

DIFFERENT COLOR
In nonbreeding plumage, phalaropes are gray and white.

NO TIES
After mating and laying eggs, females leave the male and play no role in raising young.

OCCURRENCE
Breeds in coastal Arctic tundra; during migration and in winter, occurs in deep ocean waters; small numbers are seen near the shore in coastal California in fall and winter. The Red Phalarope is rare inland.

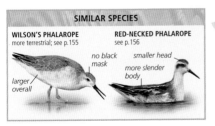

SIMILAR SPECIES

WILSON'S PHALAROPE
more terrestrial; see p.155

larger overall

RED-NECKED PHALAROPE
see p.156

no black mask

smaller head

more slender body

Length 8–8½in (20–22cm)	Wingspan 16–17½in (41–44cm)	Weight 1¼–2⅝oz (35–75g)
Social **Large flocks**	Lifespan **Unknown**	Status **Secure**

DATE: _____ TIME: _____ LOCATION: _____

| Order **Charadriiformes** | Family **Stercorariidae** | Species **_Stercorarius pomarinus_** |

Pomarine Jaeger

ADULT
(BREEDING;
PALE FORM)

prominent
white "flash"
in feathers

white
wing flash

barred
flanks

ADULT
(NONBREEDING;
PALE FORM)

dusky
breastband

ADULT
(DARK
FORM)

dark overall

blunt
tail
spike

IN FLIGHT

twisted, spoon-like
central tail feathers

all-dark
body

JUVENILE
(FALL;
DARK FORM)

deep,
barrel
breast

gray-brown
back

blackish
cap

pale
based,
thick bill

cream
cheeks

dusky
breast-
band

ADULT
(BREEDING;
PALE FORM)

The intimidating Pomarine Jaeger uses its size and strength to overpower larger seabirds, such as gulls and shearwaters, in order to steal their food. Thought to be nomadic during the breeding season, it only nests opportunistically, when populations of lemmings are at their peak to provide food for its young. Although larger and more powerful than the Parasitic Jaeger, the Pomarine Jaeger is not as acrobatic in the air and is readily driven away from breeding territories by the more dynamic Parasitic Jaeger. Interestingly, research suggests that the Pomarine Jaeger is actually more closely related to the large skuas—such as the Great and South Polar Skuas—than to other jaegers.

VOICE Nasal _cow-cow-cow_ and various sharp, low whistles.
NESTING Shallow unlined depression on a rise or hummock in open tundra; 2 eggs; 1 brood; June–August.
FEEDING Hunts lemmings and other rodents; eats fish or scavenges refuse from fishing boats during nonbreeding season; often steals fish from other seabirds, such as gulls.

FLIGHT: powerful, deep, quick wing beats, with glides; rapid twists and turns in pursuit of prey.

SIMILAR SPECIES

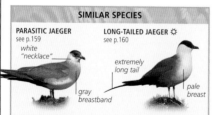

PARASITIC JAEGER
see p.159

white
"necklace"

gray
breastband

LONG-TAILED JAEGER ✿
see p.160

extremely
long tail

pale
breast

OBVIOUS FEATURE
The twisted, spoon-like central tail feathers are clearly visible when the Pomarine Jaeger flies.

OCCURRENCE
Breeds on open tundra in the Canadian Arctic. Migrates north in spring and south in fall, along coasts and also far offshore. Most often seen when brought close to land by gales. Storm-driven birds very occasionally found inland. More commonly seen on West Coast than East Coast; winters far out at sea.

| Length **17–20in (43–51cm)** | Wingspan **4ft (1.2m)** | Weight **23–26oz (650–750g)** |
| Social **Solitary** | Lifespan **Unknown** | Status **Secure** |

DATE: _____ TIME: _____ LOCATION: _____

Order **Charadriiformes**	Family **Stercorariidae**	Species *Stercorarius parasiticus*

Parasitic Jaeger

pale cheek patch

ADULT (DARK FORM)

barring on wings

white wing patch

IN FLIGHT

mostly dark brown overall

dark cap

pale cheek

dark upperparts

ADULT (PALE FORM) **ADULT (DARK FORM)**

long, pointed, central feathers

ADULT (PALE FORM)

dark legs and toes

gray breastband

white wing patch

FLIGHT: swift wing beats interspersed with fast glides, interrupted by twisting and climbing.

A true avian pirate of the high seas, the Parasitic Jaeger routinely seeks food by chasing, bullying, and forcing other seabirds to drop or regurgitate fish or other food they have caught. Unlike most jaegers, the Parasitic Jaeger is adaptable in its feeding habits so that it can forage and raise its young under a wide range of environmental conditions. Breeding on the Arctic tundra, it migrates to offshore areas during the nonbreeding season.

VOICE Variety of terrier-like yelps and soft squeals, often during interactions with other jaegers or predators, usually around nesting territories.

NESTING Shallow unlined depression on a rise or hummock in open tundra; 2 eggs; 1 brood; May–August.

FEEDING Steals fish and other aquatic prey from gulls and terns; catches small birds, eats eggs, or hunts small rodents on breeding grounds.

PARASITIC PIRATE
This Parasitic Jaeger is harrying a gull by pecking at it, to make it disgorge its hard-won meal.

SIMILAR SPECIES

POMARINE JAEGER
see p.158

two long, central, twisted tail feathers

LONG-TAILED JAEGER
see p.160

black cap

heavy hooked bill

longer pointed tail

OCCURRENCE
Breeds on tundra in northern Canada and Alaska (breeds farther south than other jaegers); during migration and in winter, uses both nearshore and offshore waters; rarely found inland outside the breeding season.

Length **16–18½in (41–47cm)**	Wingspan **3ft 3in–3½ft (1–1.1m)**	Weight **13–18oz (375–500g)**
Social **Solitary/Small flocks**	Lifespan **Up to 18 years**	Status **Secure**

DATE: _____ TIME: _____ LOCATION: _____

Order **Charadriiformes**	Family **Stercorariidae**	Species *Stercorarius longicaudus*

Long-tailed Jaeger

gray-and-black upperwing

ADULT (BREEDING)

IN FLIGHT

slim, long body

thin wings

IMMATURE (2ND SUMMER)

dark cap

yellowish cream cheeks

dark, grayish back

grayish brown

JUVENILE (DARK FORM)

extremely long tail streamers

ADULT (BREEDING)

pale breast, with no breastband

FLIGHT: direct, swift glides with rapid wing beats; more buoyant and light than other jaegers.

This elegant and striking species is a surprisingly fierce Arctic and marine predator. Though the Long-tailed Jaeger occasionally steals food from small gulls and terns, it is much less proficient at such piracy than its larger relatives, and usually hunts for its own food. Indeed, the Long-tailed Jaeger is so dependent on there being an abundance of lemmings in the Arctic that in years when lemming numbers dip low, the bird may not even attempt to nest, because there would not be enough lemmings with which to feed its chicks.

VOICE Calls include a chorus of *kreek*, a loud *kreer* warning call, whistles, and high-pitched, sharp clicks.

NESTING Shallow, unlined depression on a rise or hummock in open tundra; 2 eggs; 1 brood; May–August.

FEEDING Hunts lemmings on tundra breeding grounds; takes fish, beetles, and mayflies from water surface; occasionally steals small fish from terns.

DEFENSIVE MOVES
This species protects its territory with angry calls, aggressive swoops, and distraction displays.

SIMILAR SPECIES

POMARINE JAEGER
see p.158

long twisted feathers

PARASITIC JAEGER
see p.159

thin bill

hooked bill

shorter tail

OCCURRENCE
Breeds on tundra in northern Canada and Alaska—generally the most northern breeding jaeger; on migration and in winter uses mostly offshore waters; very rarely seen inland in winter.

Length **19–21in (48–53cm)**	Wingspan **3½ft (1.1m)**	Weight **10–11oz (275–300g)**
Social **Solitary/Flocks**	Lifespan **Up to 8 years**	Status **Secure**

DATE: _____ TIME: _____ LOCATION: _____

Order **Charadriiformes**	Family **Alcidae**	Species *Alle alle*

Dovekie

short, dark tail

dark wings

ADULT (BREEDING)

IN FLIGHT

dark head and upper breast

white triangle on side of breast

ADULT (BREEDING)

white collar at back of head

dark back

dark crown

small bill

white throat

white undertail

ADULT (NONBREEDING)

A lso known widely as the Little Auk, the stocky and diminutive black-and-white Dovekie is a bird of the high Arctic. Most Dovekies breed in Greenland in large, noisy, crowded colonies (the largest one containing 15–20 million birds), but some breed in northeastern Canada, and others on a few islands in the Bering Sea off Alaska. On their breeding grounds, both adult and immature Dovekies are hunted ruthlessly by Glaucous Gulls, as well as mammalian predators, such as the Arctic Fox. Vast numbers of Dovekies winter on the low-Arctic waters off the northeastern North American seaboard, in immense flocks. Occasionally, severe onshore gales cause entire flocks to become stranded along the East Coast of North America.

VOICE Variety of calls at breeding colony, including high-pitched trilling that rises and falls; silent at sea.

NESTING Pebble nest in crack or crevice in boulder field or rocky outcrop; 1 egg; 1 brood; April–August.

FEEDING Mostly picks tiny crustaceans from just below the sea's surface.

FLIGHT: rapid, whirring wing beats; flies in flocks low over the water's surface.

SOCIABLE LITTLE AUK
After initial squabbles over nest sites, Dovekies in breeding colonies become highly sociable.

SIMILAR SPECIES

BLACK GUILLEMOT ◐
see p.165

black-and-white barring on wing

whitish head

longer bill

OCCURRENCE
Breeds on islands inside the Arctic Circle; in Greenland, mostly, but also in northeastern Canada and the Bering Sea. Many birds remain just south of the Arctic pack ice throughout the winter; others fly south to winter off the northeastern seaboard of North America.

Length **8½in (21cm)**	Wingspan **15in (38cm)**	Weight **6oz (175g)**
Social **Colonies**	Lifespan **Unknown**	Status **Secure**

DATE: _____ TIME: _____ LOCATION: _____

Order **Charadriiformes**	Family **Alcidae**	Species *Uria aalge*

Common Murre

ADULT (BREEDING)
black wing
slender head and bill

IN FLIGHT

white eye-ring
white line extending backwards from eye
dark brown upperparts and breast

ADULT (WHITE BRIDLED FORM)

curved, black line droops behind eye
white face and throat

ADULT (NONBREEDING)

black head
long, straight, black bill
white underparts
black back

ADULT (BREEDING)

grayish legs and feet

FLIGHT: fairly quick with rapid wing beats; close to water's surface.

Abundant, penguin-like birds of the cooler northern oceans, Common Murres are often seen standing upright on cliffs. They are strong fliers and adept divers, to a depth of 500ft (150m). Their large nesting colonies, on rocky sea cliff ledges, are so densely packed that incubating adults may touch each other on both sides. Common Murre eggs are pointed at one end—when pushed, they roll around in a circle, reducing the risk of rolling off the nesting ledge. It has been suggested that unique egg markings may help adults recognize their own eggs.
VOICE Low-pitched, descending call given from cliffs or water, reminiscent of trumpeting elephant.
NESTING Directly on bare rock near shore, on wide cliff ledge, or large crevice; 1 egg; 1 brood; May–July.
FEEDING Pursues small schooling fish, such as herring, sand lance, and haddock; also crustaceans, marine worms, and squid.

BREEDING COLONY
Crowded together, Common Murres are not territorial but will defend a personal space.

SIMILAR SPECIES

THICK-BILLED MURRE
see p.163
thick, pale line between eye and bill

RAZORBILL ☼
see p.164
bill with white bar near tip

OCCURRENCE
Breeds close to rocky shorelines, nesting on coastal cliff ledges or flat rocks on top of sea stacks on both East and West coasts. Found further offshore during nonbreeding season, spending extended periods on the open ocean and in large bays. Winters at sea.

Length **17½in (44cm)**	Wingspan **26in (65cm)**	Weight **35oz (1000g)**
Social **Colonies**	Lifespan **At least 40 years**	Status **Localized**

DATE: _____ TIME: _____ LOCATION: _____

| Order **Charadriiformes** | Family **Alcidae** | Species *Uria lomvia* |

Thick-billed Murre

ADULT (BREEDING)

IN FLIGHT

short, black tail

hunched in flight

brownish black sides of head

white breast and underparts

white line along bill

all-blackish upperparts

ADULT (BREEDING)

reduced or absent white line on bill

more extensive white on throat

ADULT (NONBREEDING)

FLIGHT: near the water surface with strong, rapid wing beats.

Large and robust, the Thick-billed Murre is one of the most abundant seabirds in the whole of the Northern Hemisphere. Its dense, coastal cliff breeding colonies can be made up of around a million birds each. Chicks leave the colony when they are only about 25 percent of the adult's weight. Their growth is completed at sea, while being fed by the male parent alone. The Thick-billed Murre can dive to a remarkable 600ft (180m) to catch fish and squid.

VOICE Roaring, groaning, insistent sounding *aoorrr*; lower-pitched than the Common Murre.

NESTING Rocky coast or narrow sea cliff ledge in dense colony; 1 egg; 1 brood; March–September.

FEEDING Cod, herring, capelin, and sand lance in summer; also crustaceans, worms, and squid.

SIMILAR SPECIES

COMMON MURRE see p.162

more upright posture

longer, thinner bill

RAZORBILL see p.164

flat, dark bill

thick neck

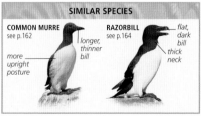

CLIFF HANGER
Thick-billed Murres breed in dense colonies on steep cliffs, often in very remote areas.

OCCURRENCE
Breeds on rocky shorelines, using the same nest each year. Winters at sea, spending extended periods of time on very cold, deep, and often remote ocean waters and pack ice edges or openings.

| Length **18in (46cm)** | Wingspan **28in (70cm)** | Weight **34oz (975g)** |
| Social **Colonies** | Lifespan **At least 25 years** | Status **Secure** |

Order **Charadriiformes**	Family **Alcidae**	Species *Alca torda*

Razorbill

IN FLIGHT

long, black, pointed tail

thick, black bill

ADULT (BREEDING)

bill smaller than in breeding birds

brownish head

white underparts up to chin

ADULT (NONBREEDING)

thin white line extends from bill to eye

large, round head

short neck

black upperparts

ADULT (BREEDING)

snowy white underparts

blackish legs and feet

FLIGHT: agile with rapid wing beats; long, pointed, black tail streamlines shape in flight.

This stocky, heavy-billed bird is the closest living relative of the extinct Great Auk. One of the rarest breeding seabirds in North America, the Razorbill is a strong flier and more agile in flight than many related species. Razorbills typically feed at depths of about 20ft (6m), but are sometimes known to dive to depths of more than 450ft (140m). On shore, Razorbills walk upright like penguins. They carry small fish at once to their chick, later male razorbills escort their flightless young to the sea to feed.

VOICE Deep, guttural, resonant croak, *hey al.*

NESTING Enclosed sites often built in crevices, among boulders, or in abandoned burrows; 1 egg; 1 brood; May–July.

FEEDING Dives for schooling fish, including capelin, herring, and sand lance; also consumes marine worms and crustaceans; sometimes steals fish from other auks.

IN FLIGHT
The razorbill flaps its wings constantly in flight as they are too small for the bird to glide.

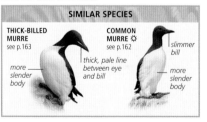

SIMILAR SPECIES

THICK-BILLED MURRE see p.163

more slender body

thick, pale line between eye and bill

COMMON MURRE ☼ see p.162

slimmer bill

more slender body

OCCURRENCE
Breeds on rocky islands and shorelines, or steep mainland cliffs in northeast North America; most of the world's population breeds in Iceland. Winters south of breeding range on ice-free coastal waters reaching New Jersey and Virginia. Forages in cool, shallower water, near shore.

Length **17in (43cm)**	Wingspan **26in (65cm)**	Weight **26oz (725g)**
Social **Colonies**	Lifespan **At least 30 years**	Status **Localized**

DATE: _____ TIME: _____ LOCATION: _____

Black Guillemot

ADULT (BREEDING)

gray bars in white wing patch

gray cap

gray neck

broad, rounded wings

oval, snowy white upperwing patch

JUVENILE

thin, straight bill

large white patch

dark belly

IN FLIGHT

scarlet legs and feet

ADULT (BREEDING)

round, black body

B lack Guillemots, also known as "sea pigeons," are medium-sized auks with distinctive black plumage and white wing patches. Their striking scarlet legs and mouth lining help attract a mate during the breeding season. Like the other two species of the *Cepphus* genus, Black Guillemots prefer shallow, inshore waters to the open ocean. They winter near the shore, sometimes moving into the mouths of rivers.

VOICE Very high-pitched whistles and squeaks given on land and water near nesting habitat that resonate like an echo.

NESTING Shallow scrape in soil or pebbles within cave or crevice; site may be reused; 1–2 eggs; 1 brood; May–August.

FEEDING Dives under water near shore to hunt small, bottom-dwelling fish, such as rock eels, sand lance, and sculpin; propels down to depths of 59ft (18m) using partly opened wings, webbed feet as a rudder; feeds close to nesting islands.

FLIGHT: flies low over the water with very rapid wing beats.

FOOD FOR CHICKS
The birds carry food for the chicks in their bills and often pause near the nest before dashing home.

OCCURRENCE
Primarily an Atlantic species. Breeds in crevices on remote rocky islands and cliffs that provide protection from predators. At sea prefers shallow waters, close to rocky coasts. At end of breeding season, adults and young move closer to shore to avoid pack ice.

SIMILAR SPECIES

DOVEKIE ❊
see p.161
smaller

dark back

white patch behind eye

PIGEON GUILLEMOT ☼
dusky underwings in flight

black bar on white wing patch

| Length **13in (33cm)** | Wingspan **21in (53cm)** | Weight **15oz (425g)** |
| Social **Colonies** | Lifespan **At least 20 years** | Status **Localized** |

DATE: _____ TIME: _____ LOCATION: _____

| Order **Charadriiformes** | Family **Alcidae** | Species ***Fratercula arctica*** |

Atlantic Puffin

IN FLIGHT — short tail — ADULT (BREEDING)

black back, collar, and underwings

blue-gray, orange, and red stripes on bill

orange legs and feet

ADULT (BREEDING)

dusky gray face — dull bill

ADULT (NONBREEDING)

gray face — red eye-ring

thick black line

stocky, rounded body

large, colorful, triangular bill

white breast

ADULT (BREEDING)

With its black-and-white "tuxedo," ungainly upright posture, and enormous, colorful bill, the Atlantic Puffin is often known as the "clown of the sea." It is seen in summer, when large breeding colonies gather on remote, rocky islands. To feed itself and its young, it can dive down to 200ft (60m) with partly folded wings, essentially "flying" underwater in pursuit of small schooling fish. The Atlantic Puffin is the provincial bird of Newfoundland and Labrador.

VOICE Rising and falling buzzy growl, resembling a chainsaw.
NESTING Underground burrow or deep rock crevice lined with grass and feathers; 1 egg; 1 brood; June–August.
FEEDING Dives deep for capelin, herring, hake, sand lance, and other small fish, which it swallows underwater, or stores crossways in its bill to take back to its chicks.

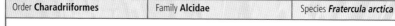

FLIGHT: swift and direct, with rapid wing beats; often circles breeding islands.

CATCH AND CARRY
When returning to breeding colonies to feed chicks, most birds carry more than one fish in their bill.

SIMILAR SPECIES

LONG-TAILED DUCK ♂ ❄
see p.53
long tail
white eye-ring
dark flanks

HORNED PUFFIN
fleshy "horn" above eye
yellow base to bill
stubby bill

OCCURRENCE
This northern North Atlantic seabird (found on both sides of the ocean) breeds in colonies on small, rocky, offshore islands, where it excavates nesting burrows or nests under boulders. Between breeding seasons, it heads for the high seas and remains far offshore, favoring cold, open waters.

| Length **12½in (32cm)** | Wingspan **21in (53cm)** | Weight **12oz (350g)** |
| Social **Colonies** | Lifespan **At least 30 years** | Status **Localized** |

DATE: _____ TIME: _____ LOCATION: _____

Black-legged Kittiwake

pale outer wing feathers
black "M" pattern in wings
pale gray upperparts
black bill
black tip to tail
ADULT
JUVENILE
IN FLIGHT
black wing tip

yellow bill
white head
pale gray back feathers

ADULT

dark neck collar
dark wing bar
black legs and feet

JUVENILE

A kittiwake nesting colony is an impressive sight, with sometimes thousands of birds lined up along steep cliff ledges overlooking the sea. The ledges are often so narrow that the birds' tails stick out over the edge. Kittiwakes have sharper claws than other gulls, probably to give them a better grip on their ledges. In the late 20th century, the Black-legged Kittiwake population expanded greatly in the Canadian maritime provinces, with numbers doubling in the Gulf of St. Lawrence.

VOICE Repeated, nasal *kit-ti-wake, kit-ti-wake* call; vocal near nesting cliffs; usually silent in winter.
NESTING Mound of mud and vegetation on narrow cliff ledge; 1–3 eggs; 1 brood; April–August.
FEEDING Snatches small marine fish and invertebrates from the surface, or dives just below the water's surface; feeds in flocks.

FLIGHT: very stiff-winged; rapid, shallow wing beats; overall more buoyant than most gulls.

LIVING ON THE EDGE
Young and adult kittiwakes pack together tightly on their precariously narrow cliff ledges.

OCCURRENCE
Rarely seen far from the ocean; common in summer around sea cliffs, with ledges suitable for nesting, and nearby offshore waters; winters at sea; most likely to be seen from land during and after storms; strays have appeared throughout the interior.

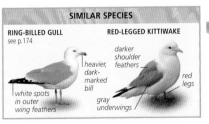

SIMILAR SPECIES

RING-BILLED GULL see p.174
heavier, dark-marked bill
white spots in outer wing feathers

RED-LEGGED KITTIWAKE
darker shoulder feathers
red legs
gray underwings

| Length **15–16in (38–41cm)** | Wingspan **3ft 1in–4ft (0.95m–1.2m)** | Weight **11–18oz (300–500g)** |
| Social **Colonies** | Lifespan **Up to 26 years** | Status **Secure** |

DATE: _____ TIME: _____ LOCATION: _____

| Order **Charadriiformes** | Family **Laridae** | Species *Xema sabini* |

Sabine's Gull

IN FLIGHT

ADULT — white triangle on wing

JUVENILE — black outer wing feathers

black band on tail

gray back

gray hood

red eye-ring

black border

yellow-tipped black bill

white underparts

black legs

ADULT (BREEDING)

JUVENILE

barring on gray-brown back

black bill

This strikingly patterned gull was discovered in Greenland by the English scientist Edward Sabine during John Ross's search for the Northwest Passage in 1818 (it was described in 1819). The distinctive wing pattern and notched tail make it unmistakable in all plumages—only juvenile kittiwakes are superficially similar. Previously thought to be related to the larger, but similarly patterned, Swallow-tailed Gull of the Galapagos, recent research indicates that Sabine's Gull is more closely related to the Ivory Gull. This species breeds in the Arctic and winters at sea, off the coasts of the Americas (south to Peru) and Africa (south to the Cape region).

VOICE Raucous, harsh *kyeer, kyeer, kyeer,* tern-like.

NESTING Shallow depression in marsh or tundra vegetation usually near water, lined with grass or unlined; 3–4 eggs; 1 brood; May–August.

FEEDING Catches aquatic insects from the water surface while swimming, wading, or flying during breeding season; winter diet mainly includes crustaceans, small fish, and plankton.

FLIGHT: wing beats shallow and stiff; tern-like, buoyant.

STRIKING WING PATTERN
Juvenile Sabine's Gulls have a muted version of the distinctive triangular wing pattern seen in the adults.

SIMILAR SPECIES

BLACK-LEGGED KITTIWAKE ☾
see p.167

partial black collar

black wing bar

OCCURRENCE
In the summer, breeds near the Arctic coast and on wet tundra in freshwater and brackish habitats, but also occurs near saltwater. Winters far off-shore in tropical and subtropical waters; widespread in Pacific and Atlantic oceans on migration.

| Length **13–14in (33–36 cm)** | Wingspan **35in–3ft 3in (90–100cm)** | Weight **5–9oz (150–250g)** |
| Social **Colonies** | Lifespan **At least 8 years** | Status **Secure** |

DATE: _____ TIME: _____ LOCATION: _____

| Order **Charadriiformes** | Family **Laridae** | Species *Chroicocephalus philadelphia* |

Bonaparte's Gull

black wing tips

ADULT (NONBREEDING)

white flash on outer wings

IN FLIGHT

gray back

brown patches on wing

IMMATURE (1ST WINTER)

blackish "ear" spot

white head

black hood

gray neck

ADULT (NONBREEDING)

gray back and wings

short bill

white wedge on wing

ADULT (BREEDING)

orange-red legs

white underparts with rosy glow when breeding

L ighter and more delicate than the other North American gulls, Bonaparte's Gull is commonly distinguished in winter by the blackish smudge behind each eye and the large, white wing patch. It is one of North America's most common and widespread gulls. During migration and in winter, flocks of this species can number in the thousands. This species was named after the 19th century French ornithologist Charles Lucien Bonaparte (nephew of Napoleon).

VOICE Harsh *keek, keek*; can be vocal in feeding flocks, *kew, kew, kew*.

NESTING Stick nest of twigs, branches, tree bark, lined with mosses or lichens; usually in conifers 5–20ft (1.5–6m) above ground; also in rushes over water; 1–4 eggs; 1 brood; May–July.

FEEDING Catches insects in flight on breeding grounds; picks crustaceans, mollusks, and small fish from water's surface; also plunge-dives.

FLIGHT: graceful, light, and agile; rapid wing beats; can be mistaken for a tern in flight.

TERN-LIKE GULL
Bonaparte's Gulls are very social and, flying in flocks, these pale, delicate birds look like terns.

WHITE UNDERWINGS
In all plumages, Bonaparte's Gull have white underwings, unlike other similar small gulls.

OCCURRENCE
During breeding season, found in northern forest zone, in lakes, ponds, or bogs; on migration, may be found anywhere where there is water: ponds, lakes, sewage pools, or rivers. Winters on Great Lakes and along the coast; often found in large numbers at coastal inlets.

SIMILAR SPECIES

BLACK-HEADED GULL
see p.170
dark outer wing feathers

larger overall

LITTLE GULL
see p.171
smaller overall

uniform gray upperwing

red bill

| Length **11–12in (28–30cm)** | Wingspan **35in–3ft 3in (90–100cm)** | Weight **6–8oz (175–225g)** |
| Social **Flocks** | Lifespan **Up to 18 years** | Status **Secure** |

DATE: _____ TIME: _____ LOCATION: _____

| Order **Charadriiformes** | Family **Laridae** | Species ***Chroicocephalus ridibundus*** |

Black-headed Gull

white flash on outer wings

black trailing edge of wing

ADULT (NONBREEDING)

IN FLIGHT

black-tipped, red bill

brownish "crown-collar"

dark "ear" spot

reddish bill

gray back

white underparts

bright red legs

ADULT (NONBREEDING)

brown spots on feathers

black-tipped orange bill

very pale gray back

white nape

chocolate brown hood

dark red bill

black tail tip

dark red legs

IMMATURE (1ST WINTER)

ADULT (BREEDING)

An abundant breeder in Eurasia, the Black-headed Gull colonized North America in the 20th century. It was first seen in the 1920s, not long after nests were discovered in Iceland in 1911. It has become common in Newfoundland after being found nesting there in 1977, and has nested as far south as Cape Cod. However, it has not spread far to the West and remains an infrequent visitor or stray over most of the continent.

VOICE Loud laughing (its French name is Laughing Gull) or a chattering *kek kek keeaar*; very vocal at breeding sites.
NESTING Loose mass of vegetation, on ground or on top of other vegetation; may be a large mound in wet areas; 2–3 eggs; 1 brood; April–August.
FEEDING Picks insects, small crustaceans, and mollusks off water's surface while flying or hovering; eats some vegetation; also forages in plowed farm fields; raids garbage dumps.

FLIGHT: graceful, light, and buoyant; agile.

BEAUTIFUL BREEDING PLUMAGE
Most North American birders never see the elegant summer plumage of the Black-headed Gull.

OCCURRENCE
Rare breeder in northeastern North America; singles or a few individuals may be found along the coast, often with Bonaparte's Gulls, at harbors, inlets, bays, rivers, lakes, sewage outlets, or garbage dumps; strays may occur anywhere. One of the most common European gulls.

SIMILAR SPECIES

BONAPARTE'S GULL
see p.169
smaller and more delicate

white underwing

black bill

LITTLE GULL
see p.171
much smaller overall

all gray upperwing

| Length **13½–14½in (34–37cm)** | Wingspan **3ft 3in–3½ft (1–1.1m)** | Weight **7–14oz (200–400g)** |
| Social **Colonies** | Lifespan **Up to 18 years** | Status **Localized** |

DATE: _____ TIME: _____ LOCATION: _____

| Order **Charadriiformes** | Family **Laridae** | Species *Hydrocoloeus minutus* |

Little Gull

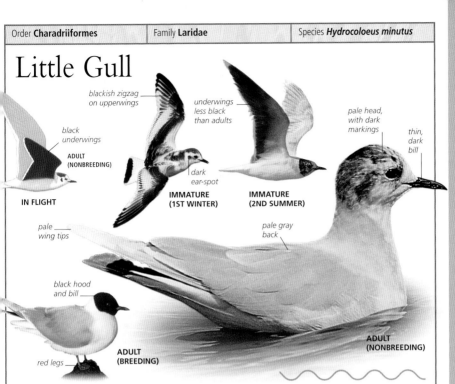

blackish zigzag
on upperwings

underwings
less black
than adults

pale head,
with dark
markings

thin,
dark
bill

black
underwings

**ADULT
(NONBREEDING)**

dark
ear-spot

**IMMATURE
(1ST WINTER)**

**IMMATURE
(2ND SUMMER)**

IN FLIGHT

pale
wing tips

pale gray
back

black hood
and bill

**ADULT
(NONBREEDING)**

red legs

**ADULT
(BREEDING)**

A Eurasian species distributed from the Baltic to China, the
Little Gull is the smallest gull in the world. Whether it is a
recent immigrant to North America or has actually been here,
unnoticed, in small numbers for many years remains a mystery.
It was first recorded in North America in the early 1800s, but
a nest was not found until 1962, in Ontario, Canada. Known
nesting areas are still few, but winter numbers have been
increasing steadily in recent decades.

VOICE Nasal *kek, kek, kek, kek*, reminiscent of a small tern.
NESTING Thick, floating mass of dry cattails, reeds, or other
vegetation, in marshes and ponds; 3 eggs; 1 brood; May–August.
FEEDING Seizes prey from water's surface, while swimming
or plunge-diving; typical prey includes flying insects, aquatic
invertebrates such as shrimps, and small fish.

FLIGHT: quick wing beats; light, nimble,
and agile.

SIMPLE ELEGANCE
Its long, pale gray wings with a thin white border
place this bird among the most elegant of gulls.

OCCURRENCE
Breeds in extensive freshwater
marshes in Hudson Bay and
Great Lakes region, but the full
extent of its breeding range in
North America is unknown; can
appear almost anywhere while
migrating. Winters primarily
along sea coasts, at sewage
outfalls; often with groups
of Bonaparte's Gulls.

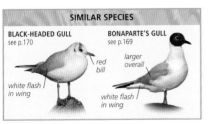

SIMILAR SPECIES

BLACK-HEADED GULL
see p.170

BONAPARTE'S GULL
see p.169

red
bill

larger
overall

white flash
in wing

white flash
in wing

| Length **10–12in (25–30cm)** | Wingspan **23½–26in (60–65cm)** | Weight **3½–5oz (100–150g)** |
| Social **Colonies** | Lifespan **Up to 6 years** | Status **Secure** |

DATE: _____ TIME: _____ LOCATION: _____

| Order **Charadriiformes** | Family **Laridae** | Species *Leucophaeus atricilla* |

Laughing Gull

broken white eye-ring

black head

white forehead

long, slightly drooped bill

ADULT (WINTER)

dark gray wings

brown wing feathers

white neck

IMMATURE (1ST WINTER)

IN FLIGHT

dark gray back

white underparts

black wing tips

long, dark legs

ADULT (BREEDING)

gray nape

ADULT (WINTER)

The distinctive call of the Laughing Gull is a familiar sound in spring and summer along the East Coast. Already abundant when the Europeans arrived in North America, it was greatly reduced in the 19th century by egg collectors and the millinery trade. Its numbers increased in the 1920s, following protection, but declined again due to competition with larger gulls from the North. With the closing of landfills however, the Laughing Gull population has recovered. It has been known to hybridize with the Ring-billed Gull.

VOICE Typical call strident laugh, *ha...ha...ha...ha...ha*; very vocal in breeding season; quiet in winter.

NESTING Mass of grass on dry land with heavy vegetation, sand, rocks, and salt marshes; 2–4 eggs, 1 brood; April–July.

FEEDING Picks from surface while walking and swimming; feeds on various invertebrates: insects, earthworms, squid, crabs, crab eggs, and larvae; also eats small fish, garbage, and berries.

FLIGHT: strong and direct; graceful for a gull; agile enough to catch flying insects.

DARK WING TIPS
Unlike many gulls, the Laughing Gull usually shows little or no white in the wing tips.

SIMILAR SPECIES

FRANKLIN'S GULL
see p.173

white band in wing tips

short, straight bill

FRANKLIN'S GULL ☀
see p.173

short, straight bill

darker head

pink blush on underparts

OCCURRENCE
During breeding season usually found near saltwater. Post-breeders and juveniles wander widely; strays can turn up anywhere, including parking lots. Rare in winter in the Northeast. On occasion, they show up as far north as Newfoundland.

| Length **15½–18in (39–46cm)** | Wingspan **3¼–4ft (1–1.2m)** | Weight **7–13oz (200–375g)** |
| Social **Colonial** | Lifespan **Up to 20 years** | Status **Secure** |

DATE: _____ TIME: _____ LOCATION: _____

| Order **Charadriiformes** | Family **Laridae** | Species *Leucophaeus pipixcan* |

Franklin's Gull

black wing tips set-off by white band

dark gray wings

ADULT (WINTER)

IN FLIGHT

dark back of head

gray back

short, straight bill

ADULT (WINTER)

partial hood

IMMATURE (1ST SUMMER)

dark gray back

broken white eye crescent

black head

red bill

white in outer wing feathers

pink blush underneath

ADULT (SUMMER)

~~~~~~~~

FLIGHT: stiff and direct; relatively fast wing beats; agile flier.

Since its discovery, Franklin's Gull has carried a number of names: Prairie Dove, Rosy Dove, and Franklin's Rosy Gull—"Dove" alluding to its dainty appearance and "rosy" to the pink blush of its undersides. Its official name honors British Arctic explorer, John Franklin, on whose first expedition, the bird was discovered in 1823. Unlike other gulls, this species has two complete molts each year. As a result, its plumage usually looks fresh and it rarely has the scruffy look of some other gulls.

VOICE Nasal *weeh-a, weeh-a*; shrill *kuk kuk kuk kuk*; extremely vocal around breeding colonies.

NESTING Floating mass of bulrushes or other plants; material added as nest sinks; 2–4 eggs; 1 brood; April–July.

FEEDING Feeds mainly on earthworms and insects during breeding and some seeds, taken while walking or flying; opportunistic feeder during migration and winter.

PROMINENT EYES
In all plumages, Franklin's Gull has much more prominent white eye-crescents than similar species.

OCCURRENCE
In summer, a bird of the high prairies; always nests over water. On migration often found in agricultural areas; large numbers frequent plowed fields or follows plows. Winters mainly along the Pacific Coast of South America.

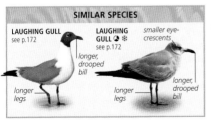

SIMILAR SPECIES

LAUGHING GULL
see p.172

longer, drooped bill

longer legs

LAUGHING GULL ♂ ❄
see p.172

longer legs

smaller eye-crescents

longer, drooped bill

| Length **12½–14in (32–36cm)** | Wingspan **33in–3ft 1in (85–95cm)** | Weight **8–11oz (225–325g)** |
| Social **Colonial** | Lifespan **At least 10 years** | Status **Declining** |

Order **Charadriiformes**	Family **Laridae**	Species *Larus delawarensis*

Ring-billed Gull

white wing spots

ADULT (BREEDING)

dark eye

mottled gray back

black-tipped, pink bill

white neck

IMMATURE (1ST WINTER)

heavily mottled back

mottled underparts

pink legs

JUVENILE

black band on yellow bill

fine streaks on head

IN FLIGHT

gray back

pale gray back

IMMATURE (2ND WINTER)

pale eye, with red eye-ring

pale gray back

olive-yellow legs

ADULT (NONBREEDING)

white markings on outer wing feathers

ADULT (BREEDING)

white underparts

yellowish or greenish legs

FLIGHT: quick, deep wing beats; strong, direct flight, soaring on thermals.

One of the most common birds in North America, the medium-sized Ring-billed Gull is distinguished by the black band on its yellow bill. From the mid-19th to the early 20th century, population numbers crashed due to shooting and habitat loss. Protection allowed the species to make a spectacular comeback, and in the 1990s, there were an estimated 3–4 million birds. It can often be seen scavenging in parking lots at malls and following farmers' tractors.

VOICE Call a slightly nasal and whiny *kee-ow* or *meee-ow*; series of 4–6 *kyaw* notes, higher pitched than Herring Gull.

NESTING Shallow cup of plant matter on ground in open areas, usually near low vegetation; 1–5 eggs; 1 brood; April–August.

FEEDING Picks food while walking; also dips and plunges in water; eats small fish, insects, grain, small rodents; also scavenges.

BLACK WING MARKING
The sharply demarcated black wing tips are prominent from both above and below.

SIMILAR SPECIES

MEW GULL

darker mantle

round head

small bill

MEW GULL 1ST

less distinct streaks

round head

small bill

OCCURRENCE
Breeds in freshwater habitats in the interior of the continent. In winter, switches to mostly saltwater areas and along both the East and West Coasts; also along major river systems and reservoirs. Found year-round near the southern Great Lakes.

Length **17–21½in (43–54cm)**	Wingspan **4–5ft (1.2–1.5m)**	Weight **11–25oz (300–700g)**
Social **Colonies**	Lifespan **Up to 32 years**	Status **Secure**

DATE: _____ TIME:_____ LOCATION:_____

| Order **Charadriiformes** | Family **Laridae** | Species *Larus argentatus* |

Herring Gull

white spots near wing tips

ADULT (BREEDING)

light head

barred gray-brown overall

mottled brown back

barred brown body

large, yellow bill with red spot

white head and neck

IMMATURE (1ST WINTER)

gray wings

IMMATURE (2ND WINTER)

gray back

streaked head

ADULT (NONBREEDING)

black outer wing feathers

white underparts

IN FLIGHT

streaked head and neck

pink legs

white underparts

ADULT (BREEDING)

ADULT (NONBREEDING)

The Herring Gull is the archetypal, large "white-headed" gull that nearly all other gulls are compared with. When people mention "seagulls" they usually refer to the Herring Gull. The term "seagull" is actually misleading because the Herring Gull, like most other gulls, does not commonly go far out to sea—it is a bird of near-shore waters, coasts, lakes, rivers, and inland waterways. Now very common, the Herring Gull was nearly wiped out in the late 19th and early 20th century by plumage hunters and egg collectors.

VOICE Typical call a high-pitched, shrill, repeated *heyaa…heyaa… heyaa…heyaa*; vocal throughout the year.

NESTING Shallow bowl on ground lined with feathers, vegetation, detritus; 2–4 eggs; 1 brood; April–August.

FEEDING Eats fish, crustaceans, mollusks, worms; eggs and chicks of other seabirds; scavenges carrion, garbage; steals from other birds.

FLIGHT: steady, regular, slow wing beats; also commonly soars and glides.

MASTER SCAVENGER
A common sight near any water body, the Herring Gull is an expert scavenger of carrion and trash.

OCCURRENCE
Found throughout North America along coasts and inland on lakes, rivers, and reservoirs; also frequents garbage dumps. Breeds in northeastern US and across Canada. Migrates southward across much of the continent to winter in coastal areas and along lakes and major rivers.

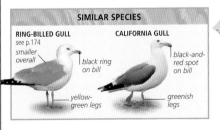

SIMILAR SPECIES

RING-BILLED GULL
see p.174
smaller overall

black ring on bill

yellow-green legs

CALIFORNIA GULL

black-and-red spot on bill

greenish legs

| Length **22–26in (56–66cm)** | Wingspan **4–5ft (1.2–1.5m)** | Weight **28–42oz (800–1200g)** |
| Social **Colonies** | Lifespan **At least 35 years** | Status **Secure** |

DATE: _____ TIME: _____ LOCATION: _____

Order **Charadriiformes**	Family **Laridae**	Species *Larus glaucoides*

Iceland Gull

gray wing tips

pale brown plumage

ADULT (WINTER)

IMMATURE (1ST WINTER)

IN FLIGHT

pale or gray wing tip

short, pale yellow bill with red spot

markedly streaked head

gray back

white belly

ADULT (WINTER)

pink legs

brown barred plumage

blackish bill

head mostly white

IMMATURE (1ST WINTER)

IMMATURE (2ND WINTER)

pale, barred underparts

FLIGHT: light and graceful; wings long in proportion to body.

The Iceland Gull is the smallest "white-winged" gull. Similar to the larger Glaucous Gull, it is a common sight in winter, and immatures are seen more often than adults. North American breeding birds have gray wing tips, and have been considered a separate species called the "Kumlien's Gull." *L. g. thayeri*, previously considered a separate species under the name "Thayer's Gull," breeds in the Canadian High Arctic and winters primarily on the Pacific Coast, but is also found in the interior and along the East Coast.

VOICE Call a *clew, clew, clew* or *kak-kak-kak*; vocal around breeding colonies; virtually silent on wintering grounds.

NESTING Loose nest of moss, vegetation, and feathers, usually on narrow rock ledge; 2–3 eggs; 1 brood; May–August.

FEEDING Grabs small fish from surface while in flight; also eats small fish, crustaceans, mollusks, carrion, and garbage.

WING TIP COLOR VARIATION
Some adult Iceland Gulls found in North America have wing tips that are almost pure white.

SIMILAR SPECIES

GLAUCOUS GULL
see p.196

much larger body

larger bill

white wing tips

OCCURRENCE
Uncommon far from sea coast; usually nests on ledges on vertical cliffs overlooking the sea; winters where it finds regions of open water in frozen seas and along coast. A few wander to open water areas in the interior, such as the Great Lakes and major rivers; Niagara Falls.

Length **20½–23½in (52–60cm)**	Wingspan **4½–5ft (1.4–1.5m)**	Weight **21–39oz (600–1,100g)**
Social **Colonies**	Lifespan **Up to 33 years**	Status **Secure**

DATE: _____ TIME: _____ LOCATION: _____

| Order **Charadriiformes** | Family **Laridae** | Species *Larus fuscus* |

Lesser Black-backed Gull

black wing tips
with white spot

**ADULT
(NONBREEDING)**

IN FLIGHT

back turns
dark gray

**IMMATURE
(2ND WINTER)**

mottled, dark
brown body

**IMMATURE
(1ST WINTER)**

black
bill

yellow
eye

streaked
head and
neck

slate-gray
back

white underparts

yellow
head

white
head

yellow bill
with red spot

bright
yellow legs

ADULT (BREEDING)

dull yellow
legs

**ADULT
(NONBREEDNG)**

This European visitor was first discovered in North America on the New Jersey coast on September 9, 1934 and in New York City a few months later. In recent decades, it has become an annual winter visitor. Nearly all the Lesser Black-backed Gulls found in North America are of the Icelandic and western European subspecies *L. f. graellsii*, with a slate-gray back. Another European subspecies, with a much darker back, has rarely been reported in North America, but it is probably only a matter of time before it nests here.

VOICE A *kyow…yow…yow…yow* call, similar to that of Herring Gull; also a deeper and throaty, repeated *gah-gah-gah-gah*.

NESTING Scrape on ground lined with dry lichens, dry grass, and feathers; 3 eggs; 1 brood; April–September.

FEEDING Eats mollusks, crustaceans, and various insects; also scavenges carrion and garbage.

FLIGHT: powerful and direct; regular wing beats; long wings make it appear graceful.

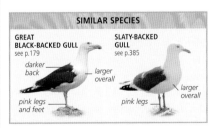

SIMILAR SPECIES

**GREAT
BLACK-BACKED GULL**
see p.179

darker
back

larger
overall

pink legs
and feet

**SLATY-BACKED
GULL**
see p.385

larger
overall

pink legs

EXCITING FIND
In recent years, gull enthusiasts and birdwatchers have found these birds visiting from Europe.

OCCURRENCE
Regular and increasingly common winter visitor to eastern North America, usually along the coast, but also in the interior; wherever gulls commonly concentrate such as harbors, lakeshores, landfills, and around fishing boats.

| Length **20½–26in (52–67cm)** | Wingspan **4¼–5ft (1.3–1.5m)** | Weight **22–35oz (625–1000g)** |
| Social **Colonies** | Lifespan **Up to 26 years** | Status **Secure** |

DATE: _____ TIME: _____ LOCATION: _____

| Order **Charadriiformes** | Family **Laridae** | Species *Larus hyperboreus* |

Glaucous Gull

ADULT (WINTER)

streaking on head

mottled white plumage

IMMATURE (1ST WINTER, FADED)

IN FLIGHT

white wing tips

light brownish plumage

IMMATURE (1ST WINTER)

mottled, pale brown back

IMMATURE (1ST WINTER)

white head

pale brown underparts

pale gray upperparts

yellow bill with distinct red spot

pale gray upperparts

white underparts

pink legs

ADULT (SUMMER)

FLIGHT: heavy, slow, and powerful; often glides and soars.

The Glaucous Gull is the largest of the "white-winged" gulls. Its large, pale shape is immediately apparent in a group of gulls as it appears like a large white spectre among its smaller, darker cousins. In the southern part of its US winter range, pale immatures are encountered more frequently than adults. In the Arctic, successful pairs of Glaucous Gulls maintain the bonds with their mates for years, often returning to the same nest site year after year.

VOICE Similar to that of the Herring Gull, but slightly harsher and deeper; hoarse, nasal *ku-ku-ku*.

NESTING Shallow cup lined with vegetation on ground, at edge of tundra pools, on cliffs and ledges and islands; 1–3 eggs; 1 brood; May–July.

FEEDING Eats fish, crustaceans, mollusks; also eggs and chicks of waterfowl, small seabirds, and small mammals.

NORTHERN VISITOR
This large gull is an uncommon visitor over most of North America during the winter months.

SIMILAR SPECIES

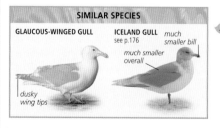

GLAUCOUS-WINGED GULL

dusky wing tips

ICELAND GULL see p.176

much smaller bill

much smaller overall

OCCURRENCE
Breeds along the high-Arctic coast, rarely inland; winters along northern Atlantic and Pacific coasts and the Great Lakes; frequently seen at Niagara Falls. Strays, usually immatures, can occur inland anywhere where concentrations of gulls are found, such as landfill sites and dumps.

| Length **26–30in (65–75cm)** | Wingspan **5–6ft (1.5–1.8m)** | Weight **2¾–6lb (1.2–2.7kg)** |
| Social **Colonies** | Lifespan **Up to 21 years** | Status **Secure** |

DATE: _____ TIME: _____ LOCATION: _____

| Order **Charadriiformes** | Family **Laridae** | Species *Larus marinus* |

Great Black-backed Gull

red eye-ring

large white spot on wing tips

ADULT (BREEDING)

white head with faint streaks

white underwings

white head and neck

yellow bill with red spot

ADULT (BREEDING)

black upperparts

IN FLIGHT

ADULT (NONBREEDING)

white tips to outer feathers

white underparts

whitish head

black bill

speckled back

ADULT (BREEDING)

pale pink legs and feet

IMMATURE (1ST WINTER)

The largest gull in North America, the Great Black-backed Gull is known for its bullying disposition. In breeding colonies, it is especially aggressive in the morning and early evening, and after chicks hatch; adults dive at ground predators and strike them with their wings and feet. For other birds, there are advantages and disadvantages to this behavior: while eiders nesting in Great Black-backed gull colonies might suffer low predation from other predators, they lose many of their ducklings to the predatory gulls.

VOICE Low, growling flight call, often repeated, low-pitched *heyaa… heyaa…heyaa…heyaa*, similar to the Herring Gull.

NESTING Shallow bowl on ground, lined with vegetation, feathers, and trash; 2–3 eggs; 1 brood; April–August.

FEEDING Scavenges and hunts fish, marine invertebrates, small mammals, eggs, chicks, adult seabirds, and waterfowl.

FLIGHT: heavy lumbering with deep wing beats.

SOLITARY BIRDS
While all gulls are social animals, the Great Black-backed Gull is the most solitary.

OCCURRENCE
Breeds on natural and artificial islands, barrier beaches, salt marshes, sand dunes; during winter, found along the coast, near shore water, major rivers, landfills, and harbors; in all seasons, often found together with Herring Gulls and Ring-billed Gulls. Also occurs in Europe.

SIMILAR SPECIES

LESSER BLACK-BACKED GULL ❄
see p.177

smaller body

slate-gray back

yellow legs

SLATY-BACKED GULL
see p.385

gray back

bright pink legs

| Length **28–31in (71–79cm)** | Wingspan **5–5¼ft (1.5–1.6m)** | Weight **2¾–4½lb (1.3–2kg)** |
| Social **Pairs/Colonies** | Lifespan **Up to 27 years** | Status **Secure** |

| Order **Charadriiformes** | Family **Laridae** | Species **Hydroprogne caspia** |

Caspian Tern

streaked
dark crown

dark markings
on upperparts

JUVENILE

**ADULT
(BREEDING)**

**ADULT
(NONBREEDING)**

slightly
crested
black cap

short
tail

dark-tipped outer
wing feathers

IN FLIGHT

light gray back

thick, red
bill with
dark tip

**ADULT
(BREEDING)**

white underparts

black legs and feet

FLIGHT: strong, swift flier; heavy, powerful wing
beats; the most gull-like of North American terns.

Rivalling some of the gulls in size, the Caspian
Tern is the world's largest tern. Unlike other
"black-capped" terns, it never has a completely
white forehead, even in winter. In non-breeding
plumage, the cap is very heavily streaked. The Caspian Tern
is known for its predatory habits, stealing prey from other seabirds, as
well as snatching eggs and eating the chicks of other gulls and terns.
It is aggressive in defending its nesting
territory, giving hoarse alarm calls, and rhythmically opening
and closing its beak in a threatening display to intruders.
VOICE Hoarse, deep *kraaa, kraaa*; also barks at intruders;
male's wings vibrate loudly in courtship flight.
NESTING Shallow scrape on ground; 2–3 eggs; 1 brood;
May–August.
FEEDING Plunges into water to snatch fish, barnacles, and snails.

AGGRESSIVE BIRDS
The Caspian Tern is one of the most aggressive
terns, though actual physical contact is rare.

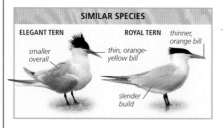

SIMILAR SPECIES

ELEGANT TERN

smaller
overall

ROYAL TERN

thin, orange-
yellow bill

thinner,
orange bill

slender
build

OCCURRENCE
Found in a variety of aquatic
habitats, freshwater and
marine; rare offshore; breeds
on interior lakes, salt marsh,
and on coastal barrier islands;
winters on and near the coast.
May be seen on marshes and
wetlands during migration.

| Length **18½–21½in (47–54cm)** | Wingspan **4¼–5ft (1.3–1.5m)** | Weight **19–27oz (525–775g)** |
| Social **Colonies/Pairs** | Lifespan **Up to 30 years** | Status **Secure** |

DATE: _____ TIME: _____ LOCATION: _____

Order **Charadriiformes**	Family **Laridae**	Species **Chlidonias niger**

Black Tern

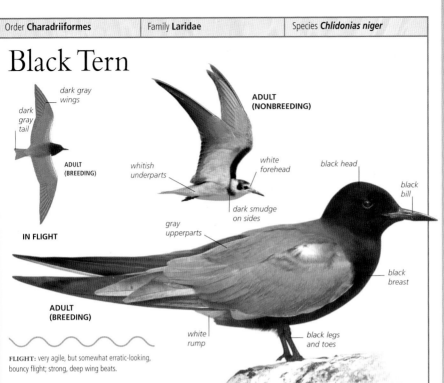

dark gray wings

dark gray tail

ADULT (BREEDING)

ADULT (NONBREEDING)

whitish underparts

white forehead

black head

black bill

dark smudge on sides

gray upperparts

black breast

IN FLIGHT

ADULT (BREEDING)

white rump

black legs and toes

FLIGHT: very agile, but somewhat erratic-looking, bouncy flight; strong, deep wing beats.

The Black Tern is a small, elegant, marsh-dwelling tern that undergoes a remarkable change in appearance from summer to winter—more so than any other regularly occurring North American tern. The Black Tern's breeding plumage can cause the bird to be confused with the closely related White-winged Tern, which is an accidental visitor to North America. The Black Tern's nonbreeding plumage is much paler than its breeding plumage—the head turns white with irregular black streaks, and the neck, breast, and belly become whitish gray.

VOICE Call nasal and harsh *krik, kip,* or *kik*; most vocal during breeding, but calls throughout the year.

NESTING Shallow cup on top of floating mass of vegetation, sometimes on top of muskrat lodges; usually 3 eggs; 1 brood; May–August.

FEEDING Picks prey off water's surface or vegetation; rarely plunge-dives; in summer, feeds on mainly insects, caught from the air or ground, also freshwater fish; in winter, eats mainly small sea fish.

FLOATING NEST
A floating nest is a dry place to lay eggs and raise chicks in a watery environment.

SIMILAR SPECIES

SOOTY TERN

white spots on back

much larger overall

OCCURRENCE
Freshwater marshes in summer, but nonbreeding plumaged birds—probably young—occasionally seen along the coast. During migration, can be found almost anywhere near water. Winters in the marine coastal waters of Central and South America.

Length **9–10in (23–26cm)**	Wingspan **25–35in (63–88cm)**	Weight **1¾ –2½ oz (50–70g)**
Social **Colonies**	Lifespan **Up to 9 years**	Status **Vulnerable**

DATE: _____ TIME: _____ LOCATION: _____

Order **Charadriiformes**	Family **Laridae**	Species *Sterna dougallii*

Roseate Tern

scalloped appearance to upperparts

dark legs

JUVENILE

long tail feathers

red base to black bill

ADULT (LATE SUMMER)

pale gray underwings

IN FLIGHT

ADULT (SPRING)

pale gray upperparts

black cap

black bill

long, forked tail

white underparts

ADULT (SPRING)

FLIGHT: strong and fairly swift; stiffer-winged than terns of similar size.

Mostly found nesting with Common Terns, the Roseate Tern is paler and more slender. Its slim bill is black only for a short time in the spring before turning at least half red during the nesting season. At breeding colonies, these terns engage in distinctive courtship flights, with pairs gliding down from hundreds of feet in the air, swaying side to side with each other. Some birds nest as trios—two females and a male—all taking part in incubating the eggs and raising the young.

VOICE Most common calls *keek* or *ki-rik* given in flight and around nesting colony.

NESTING Simple scrape, often under vegetation or large rocks; adds twigs and dry grass during incubation; 1–3 eggs; 1 brood; May–August.

FEEDING Catches small fish with its bill by diving from a height of 3–20ft (1–6m); carries whole fish to young.

GRACEFUL COURTSHIP
Roseate Tern pairs engage in elegant, graceful courtship displays before mating.

SIMILAR SPECIES

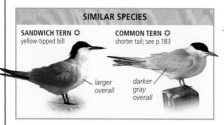

SANDWICH TERN ☼
yellow-tipped bill

COMMON TERN ☼
shorter tail; see p.183

larger overall

darker gray overall

OCCURRENCE
Breeds almost exclusively in coastal areas in the Northeast from Long Island, New York, to Nova Scotia, with another small population in the outer Florida Keys. Typically nests on beaches and offshore islands. Not often seen far from breeding sites.

Length **13–16in (33–41cm)**	Wingspan **28in (70cm)**	Weight **3–5oz (85–150g)**
Social **Colonies**	Lifespan **Up to 26 years**	Status **Endangered**

DATE: _____ TIME: _____ LOCATION: _____

| Order **Charadriiformes** | Family **Laridae** | Species **Sterna hirundo** |

Common Tern

dark wedge on outer feathers

brown bars on upperparts

whitish forehead

dark bill with red-orange base

black wing bar

JUVENILE

ADULT (BREEDING)

IN FLIGHT

white forehead

bill mostly dark

blackish leg

ADULT (NONBREEDING)

black cap

gray upperparts

forked tail

pale gray-white underparts

black-tipped red bill

red leg

ADULT (BREEDING)

FLIGHT: graceful, steady and strong; wing beats relatively deep.

One of North America's most widespread terns, the Common Tern was nearly wiped out in the late 19th century by hunters seeking its feathers. The 1918 Migratory Bird Treaty helped protect it, and numbers increased, but populations have declined again in recent decades due to human disturbance, habitat loss, and pollution.

VOICE Common call loud *keee-aarr* descending at end; emits *kek-kek-kek-kek* call when attacking intruders; vocal in colonies; also calls elsewhere.

NESTING Shallow scrape on bare sand, often gravel or similar surface, dry vegetation and debris used during incubation; 2–3 eggs; 1 brood; May–August.

FEEDING Plunges for prey, snatches from water's surface, catches insects in flight; mainly eats fish but also crustaceans, squid, and insects.

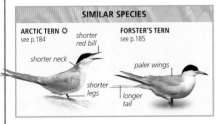

SIMILAR SPECIES

ARCTIC TERN ☼
see p.184

shorter red bill

shorter neck

shorter legs

FORSTER'S TERN
see p.185

paler wings

longer tail

FEEDING FLOCK
A flock of Common Terns focus on a school of fish, diving to catch them. Fishermen watch for such flocks to locate fish.

OCCURRENCE
Found almost anywhere with water during migration. Winters in Central and South America. One population breeds along the barrier beaches and coasts northwards from the Carolinas; a second population occurs around lakes and wetland areas in the northern interior.

| Length **12–14in (31–35cm)** | Wingspan **30–31in (75–80cm)** | Weight **3⅜–5oz (95–150g)** |
| Social **Colonies** | Lifespan **Up to 26 years** | Status **Endangered** |

DATE: _____ TIME: _____ LOCATION: _____

SHOREBIRDS, GULLS, AUKS, AND RELATIVES

Arctic Tern

barring on upperparts

white forehead

short, dark bill

black cap extends to nape

short, blood-red bill

JUVENILE

ADULT (BREEDING)

dark tips to translucent outer wing feathers

long, forked tail

short neck

white cheek

IN FLIGHT

short, red bill

gray upperparts

ADULT (BREEDING)

long wings

pale gray underparts

short, red legs and feet

The majority of these remarkable birds breed in the Arctic, then migrate to the Antarctic seas for the Southern Hemisphere summer before returning north. On this round-trip, the Arctic Tern travels at least 25,000 miles (40,000km). Apart from during migration, it spends its life in areas of near continuous daylight and rarely comes to land, except to nest. It looks fairly similar to the Common Tern, but the former has a comparatively smaller bill, shorter legs, and a shorter neck.

VOICE Descending *keeyaar* call; nearly all calls similar to Common Tern, but higher-pitched and harsher.
NESTING Shallow scrape on bare ground or low vegetation in open areas; 2 eggs; 1 brood; May–August.
FEEDING Mostly plunge-dives for small fish and crustaceans, including crabs and shrimps; will also take prey from surface, sometimes catches insects in flight.

FLIGHT: downstroke slower than upstroke; buoyant and elegant with regular wing beats.

FEEDING THE YOUNG
Both parents feed chicks—males bring more food than females, especially right after hatching.

TRANSLUCENT FEATHERS
The translucent outer wing feathers of the Arctic Tern are evident on these two flying birds.

SIMILAR SPECIES

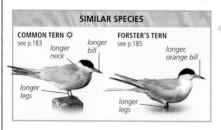

COMMON TERN ☼
see p.183
longer neck
longer bill
longer legs

FORSTER'S TERN
see p.185
longer, orange bill
longer legs

OCCURRENCE
Breeds in far North, mostly in open, unforested areas near water and along the coast; generally migrates far offshore. Spends more time away from land than other northern terns. Winters on edge of pack ice in Antarctica.

| Length **11–15½in (28–39cm)** | Wingspan **26–30in (65–75cm)** | Weight **3⅛–4oz (90–125g)** |
| Social **Colonies** | Lifespan **Up to 34 years** | Status **Vulnerable** |

DATE: _____ TIME: _____ LOCATION: _____

Forster's Tern

gray wings with slightly darker wing tips

deeply forked tail

IN FLIGHT

ADULT (NONBREEDING)

large, black ear patch

shorter tail

JUVENILE

plain gray wings

dark bill

ADULT (NONBREEDING)

black cap and nape

pale gray upperparts

orange-red bill with dark tip

ADULT (BREEDING)

long, gray tail with white outer margins extending beyond wing tips

snowy white underparts

orange legs

FLIGHT: graceful and agile, with shallow wing beats.

This medium-sized tern is very similar in appearance to the Common Tern. The features that differentiate it from the Common Tern are its lighter outer wing feathers and longer tail. Early naturalists could not tell the two species apart until 1834 when English botanist Thomas Nuttall made the distinction. He named this tern after Johann Reinhold Forster, a naturalist who accompanied the English explorer Captain Cook on his epic second voyage (1772–75).
VOICE Harsh, descending *kyerr*; more nasal than Common Tern.
NESTING Shallow scrape in mud or sand, but occasionally nests on top of muskrat lodge or on old grebe nest; sometimes constructs raft of floating vegetation; 2–3 eggs; 1 brood; May–August.
FEEDING Catches fish and crustaceans with shallow plunge-diving, often only head submerges; also catches insects in flight.

BLACK EARS
With its black ear patch, Forster's Tern is more distinctive in nonbreeding than breeding plumage.

SIMILAR SPECIES

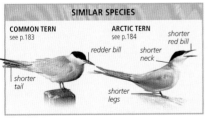

COMMON TERN see p.183

shorter tail

ARCTIC TERN see p.184

redder bill

shorter neck

shorter red bill

shorter legs

OCCURRENCE
Breeds in prairie provinces and southern Ontario, in freshwater and saltwater marshes with large stretches of open water. Winters on both coasts and across southern US states, unlike the Common Tern, which primarily winters in South America.

Length **13–14in (33–36cm)**	Wingspan **29–32in (73–82cm)**	Weight **4–7oz (125–190g)**
Social **Colonies**	Lifespan **Up to 16 years**	Status **Secure**

DATE: _____ TIME: _____ LOCATION: _____

PIGEONS AND DOVES

THE LARGER SPECIES WITHIN the family Columbidae are known as pigeons, and the smaller ones as doves, although there is no actual scientific basis for the distinction. They are all fairly heavy, plump birds with relatively small heads and short necks. They also possess slender bills with their nostrils positioned in a fleshy mound at the base. Among other things, members of this family have strong wing muscles, making them powerful and agile fliers. When alarmed, they burst into flight with their wings emitting a distinctive clapping or swishing sound. Pigeons and doves produce a nutritious "crop-milk," which they secrete to feed their young. Despite human activity having severely affected members of this family in the past (the leading cause of the Passenger Pigeon's extinction in the 19th century is thought to be overhunting), the introduced Rock Pigeon has adapted and proliferated worldwide. Rock Pigeons, featuring an amazing array of plumages from all-white, reddish, and gray to all-black, can be found in habitatas ranging from downtown city centers and suburban neighborhoods to open farmlands. Among the species native to North America, only the elegant Mourning Dove is as widespread as the various species of introduced birds of its kind.

URBAN DWELLER
Rock pigeons are a common sight in cities around the world.

DOVE IN THE SUN
The Mourning Dove sunbathes each side of its body in turns, its wings and tail outspread.

| Order **Columbiformes** | Family **Columbidae** | Species **Columba livia** |

Rock Pigeon

black wing bars

white underwings

white rump

ADULT

IN FLIGHT

gray back

iridescence on neck

short bill

no wing bars

variably colored body

two black wing bars

ADULT (FERAL)

ADULT (ANCESTRAL FORM)

dark-tipped tail

The Rock Pigeon was introduced to the Atlantic coast of North America by 17th century colonists. Now feral, this species is found all over the continent, especially around farms, cities, and towns. This medium-sized pigeon comes in a wide variety of plumage colors and patterns, including bluish gray, checkered, rusty red, and nearly all-white. Its wings usually have two dark bars on them—unique among North American pigeons. The variability of the Rock Pigeon influenced Charles Darwin as he developed his theory of natural selection.
VOICE Soft, gurgling *coo*, *roo-c'too-coo*, for courtship and threat.
NESTING Twig nest on flat, sheltered surface, such as caves, rocky outcrops, and buildings; 2 eggs; several broods; year-round.
FEEDING Eats seeds, fruit, and rarely insects; human foods such as popcorn, bread, peanuts; various farm crops in rural areas.

FLIGHT: strong, direct; can reach speeds up to around 60mph (95kph).

CITY PIGEONS
Most Rock Pigeons in North America descend from domesticated forms and exhibit many colors.

SIMILAR SPECIES

WHITE-CROWNED PIGEON mangroves

white crown

dark gray overall

BAND-TAILED PIGEON western

white band on nape

yellow bill with dark tip

OCCURRENCE
Across southern Canada and North America; nests in human structures of all sorts; resident. Original habitat in the Old World was (and still is) sea cliffs and inland canyons; found wild in some places, such as dry regions of North Africa, but feral in much of the world.

| Length **11–14in (28–36cm)** | Wingspan **20–26in (51–67cm)** | Weight **9–14oz (250–400g)** |
| Social **Solitary/Flocks** | Lifespan **Up to 6 years** | Status **Secure** |

DATE: _____ TIME: _____ LOCATION: _____

| Order **Columbiformes** | Family **Columbidae** | Species ***Zenaida macroura*** |

Mourning Dove

mostly uniform gray wings

pointed tail

ADULT

IN FLIGHT

faint mottling on neck and underparts

JUVENILE

blue eye-ring

thin, dark bill

black dot on side of face

dark spots on wings

long, pointed tail

ADULT

plump, gray body

pink legs and toes

One of the most familiar, abundant, and widespread North American birds, the Mourning Dove is a long, plump, medium-sized dove with an undersized head. It has a grayish tan body with a pale, rosy breast and black spots on folded wings. While coveted by hunters—as many as 70 million are shot annually—the Mourning Dove is also well known to those who live on farms and in suburbia. Found all across North America, the species is divided into two subspecies—the larger grayish brown *Z. m. carolinensis*, east of the Mississippi River, and the smaller, paler *Z. m. marginella* in the west.

VOICE Mellow, owl-like call: *hoO-Oo-oo, hoo-hoo-hoo.*
NESTING Flat, flimsy twig platform, mostly in trees, sometimes on the ground; 2 eggs; 2 broods; February–October.
FEEDING Forages mainly for seeds on the ground; obtains food quickly and digests it later at roost.

FLIGHT: swift, direct flight, with fairly quick wing beats; twists and turns sometimes.

FAMILIAR SIGHT
The Mourning Dove is North America's most widespread member of this family.

OCCURRENCE
Breeds in a wide variety of habitats but shuns extensive forests; human-altered vegetation favored for feeding, including farmland and suburbia. Winters in small to medium sheltered woodland while feeding in grain fields; winters in southern Mexico and Central America.

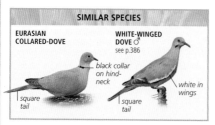

SIMILAR SPECIES

EURASIAN COLLARED-DOVE

black collar on hind-neck

square tail

WHITE-WINGED DOVE ♂
see p.386

white in wings

square tail

| Length **9–13½in (23–34cm)** | Wingspan **14½–17½in (37–45cm)** | Weight **3–6oz (85–175g)** |
| Social **Pairs/Winter flocks** | Lifespan **Up to 19 years** | Status **Secure** |

DATE: _____ TIME: _____ LOCATION: _____

CUCKOOS

CUCKOOS ARE NOTORIOUS for laying eggs in other birds' nests, but the two species found in Canada seldom do so. Their close relatives on the continent are the Greater Roadrunner, and two species of Ani. The Groove-billed Ani sometimes shows up in Ontario.

Generally shy and reclusive, the Black-billed Cuckoo and Yellow-billed Cuckoo favor dense, forested habitats. They are more often heard than seen. Both species usually build a nest and raise their own offspring. However, sometimes the Black-billed Cuckoo and the Yellow-billed Cuckoo lay their eggs in other birds' nest, including each other's, and even the nests of their own species. In flight, cuckoos are often mistaken for small birds of prey. They do sometimes pounce on lizards, frogs, and other small animals—even small birds—but mostly they glean insects from the foliage of trees. Both cuckoos regularly feed on caterpillars; the Black-billed

STRONG STOMACH
The Black-billed Cuckoo can safely eat caterpillars that are poisonous to other birds.

Cuckoo especially relishes tent caterpillars and gypsy moth larvae. The numbers of both species vary from year to year in a given locale in response to prey abundance. Besides their slender bodies and long tails, cuckoos have zygodactyl feet, with the two inner toes pointing forward and the two outer toes pointing backward. Cuckoos in North America are vulnerable to pollutants, and the Yellow-billed Cuckoo is declining rapidly to the point of arousing serious concerns over its future.

WEATHER BIRD
Folklore has it that the Yellow- billed Cuckoo, or "Raincrow," calls most on cloudy days.

NIGHT SINGER
During the breeding season, the Black-billed Cuckoo will often call throughout the night.

| Order **Cuculiformes** | Family **Cuculidae** | Species *Coccyzus americanus* |

Yellow-billed Cuckoo

ADULT

large white spots on tips of tail feathers

bright rufous on wings

IN FLIGHT

JUVENILE

more black on bill

slightly shorter tail

bare yellow skin around eye

grayish brown back

mostly yellow bill

ADULT

rufous outer wing feathers

long tail

FLIGHT: flight is swift using long strokes to maintain level pattern.

The Yellow-billed Cuckoo is a shy, slow-moving bird, with a reputation for fairly odd behaviors, including its habit of calling more often on cloudy days. This tendency has earned it the nickname "rain crow" in some areas. In addition to raising young in its own nest, females often lay eggs in the nests of more than a dozen other species, especially during years with abundant food. The host species may be chosen on the basis of how closely the color of its eggs matches those of the cuckoo's. This brood parasitism is the rule in the Yellow-billed Cuckoo, which is an Old World species, and occurs in North America as a widespread vagrant.

VOICE Call a series of 10–12 low notes that slow down as it progresses, *ca ca ca ca coo coo coo cowl cowl cowl.*

NESTING Flimsy oval-shaped platform of small sticks and branches, often lined with leaves and strips of plants; 2–4 eggs; 1–2 broods; May–August.

FEEDING Mostly consumes insects such as grasshoppers, crickets, katydids, and caterpillars of several moth species; also eats seeds.

RARE SIGHT
Given the habitat they prefer and their skittish nature, a clear view of a Yellow-billed Cuckoo is rare.

OCCURRENCE
Has a wide range in the US; extends into southeastern Canada. Found primarily in open forests with a mix of openings and thick understory cover, especially those near water. Winters in similar habitats in Central and South America.

SIMILAR SPECIES

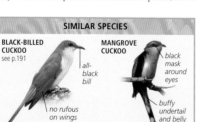

BLACK-BILLED CUCKOO
see p.191

all-black bill

no rufous on wings

MANGROVE CUCKOO

black mask around eyes

buffy undertail and belly

| Length **10–12in (26–30cm)** | Wingspan **17–20in (43–51cm)** | Weight **2–2¼oz (55–65g)** |
| Social **Small winter flocks** | Lifespan **Up to 4 years** | Status **Declining** |

DATE: _____ TIME: _____ LOCATION: _____

| Order **Cuculiformes** | Family **Cuculidae** | Species *Coccyzus erythropthalmus* |

Black-billed Cuckoo

long tail

ADULT

small white spots on tips of tail feathers

long wings

IN FLIGHT

bare red skin around eye

grayish brown back

long, black, decurved bill

pale grayish white underparts

grayish feet

ADULT

long tail

Although common, the Black-billed Cuckoo is usually difficult to spot because of its secretive nature and dense, leafy habitat. This species feeds mainly on spiny caterpillars, but the spines of these insects can become lodged in the cuckoo's stomach, obstructing digestion, so the bird periodically empties its stomach to clear any such blockage. The decline of this species is probably an indirect result of the chemical control of caterpillar outbreaks in forests throughout their range. During the breeding season, the birds call throughout the night, which leads some to believe erroneously that the cuckoo is nocturnal.

VOICE Series of 2–5 repeatedly whistled notes, *coo-coo-coo-coo*, with short breaks between series.

NESTING Shallow cup of sticks lined with moss, leaves, grass, and feathers; 2–4 eggs; 1 brood; May–July.

FEEDING Almost exclusively eats caterpillars, especially tent caterpillars and gypsy moths.

FLIGHT: flight is swift, direct, and graceful, with long, smooth wing beats.

SEARCHING FOR FOOD
These cuckoos spend a lot of their time in trees as they search for their favorite hairy caterpillars.

SIMILAR SPECIES

YELLOW-BILLED CUCKOO
see p.190

yellow bill

rufous outer wing feathers

MANGROVE CUCKOO
specialized habitat

black mask around eyes

buffy undertail and belly

OCCURRENCE
Widespread northern and eastern North American species, lives in thickly wooded areas close to water, but can also be found in brushy forest edges and evergreen woods. Winters in South America in evergreen woodlands, scrub, and humid forests.

| Length **11–12in (28–31cm)** | Wingspan **16–19in (41–48cm)** | Weight **1⁹⁄₁₆–2oz (45–55g)** |
| Social **Solitary** | Lifespan **Up to 5 years** | Status **Declining** |

191

OWLS

Partly because of their nocturnal habits and eerie cries, owls have fascinated humans throughout history. They are placed in the order Strigiformes, and two families are represented in North America: the Barn Owl is classified in Tytonidae, while the rest of the owl species are the Strigidae. Most owls are active primarily at night and have developed adaptations for living in low-light environments. Their large eyes are sensitive enough to see in the dark and face forward to maximize binocular vision. Since the eyes are fixed in their sockets, a flexible neck helps owls turn the head up to 270° toward

OWL IN DAYLIGHT
The habits of the Barn Owl remain secretive, because it is not often seen in daylight.

a direction of interest. Ears are offset on each side of the head to help identify the source of a sound; "ear tufts" on some species, however, are for visual effect and unrelated to hearing. Many owls have serrations on the forward edges of their flight feathers to cushion airflow, so their flight is silent while stalking prey. All North American owls are predatory to some degree and they inhabit most areas of the continent. The western Burrowing Owl is unique in that it hunts during the day and nests underground.

BIG HORNS
The "ear" tufts of the Great Horned Owl are taller than those of other "tufted" owls.

SNOW SWOOP
The Great Gray Owl can hunt by sound alone, allowing it to locate and capture prey hidden even beneath a thick snow cover.

| Order **Strigiformes** | Family **Tytonidae** | Species *Tyto alba* |

Barn Owl

barring on wings and tail

head lacks "ear" tufts

ADULT

IN FLIGHT

ADULT

relatively small eyes

rounded, heart-shaped facial disc

long wings

pale buff upperparts

white underparts

dark eyes

gray and black spots

ruff surrounds facial disk

ADULT

feathered legs

FLIGHT: irregular bursts of flapping, interspersed with short glides, banking, doubling back, fluttering.

Aptly named, the Barn Owl inhabits old sheds, sheltered rafters, and empty buildings in rural fields. With its affinity for human settlement, and 32 subspecies, this owl has an extensive range covering every continent except Antarctica. Although widespread, the Barn Owl is secretive. Primarily nocturnal, it can fly undetected until its screeching call pierces the air. The Barn Owl has expanded its range northward into the southern parts of provinces where winter weather is more mild.

VOICE Typical call loud, raspy, screeching shriek, *shkreee,* often given in flight; also clicking sounds associated with courtship.

NESTING Unlined cavity in tree, cave, building, hay bale, or nest box; 5–7 eggs; 1–2 broods; March–September.

FEEDING Hunts on the wing for small rodents such as mice; research reveals it can detect the slightest rustle made by prey even in total darkness.

NOCTURNAL HUNTER
The Barn Owl hunts at night for small rodents, but may be seen before sunset feeding its young.

OCCURRENCE
In North America breeds from northwestern and northeastern US south to Mexico. Small Canadian range in southern Ontario and British Columbia. Resident in all except very north of range. Prefers open habitats, such as desert, grassland, and fields, wherever prey and suitable nest sites are available.

SIMILAR SPECIES

SNOWY OWL
see p.196
black markings on female and juvenile

SHORT-EARED OWL
see p.201
dark patches on outer wing

dark barring on underparts

| Length **12½–15½in (32–40cm)** | Wingspan **3ft 3in (100cm)** | Weight **14–25oz (400–700g)** |
| Social **Solitary** | Lifespan **Up to 8 years** | Status **Declining** |

Order **Strigiformes**	Family **Strigidae**	Species **Megascops asio**

Eastern Screech-Owl

"ear" tufts

dark gray bars on short, rounded wings

ADULT

yellow eyes

white spots on inner wing feathers

streaked underparts

IN FLIGHT

short tail

ADULT (GRAY FORM)

feathered legs

FLIGHT: direct, purposeful flight; straight with steady wing beats, typically below tree cover.

This widespread little owl has adapted to suburban areas, and its distinctive call is a familiar sound across the eastern US and southern Canada at almost any time of the year. Although it is an entirely nocturnal species, it may be found roosting during the day in a birdhouse or tree cavity. With gray and red color forms, this species shows more plumage variation than the Western Screech-Owl. The relatively high mortality rate of Eastern Screech-Owls, especially juveniles, is caused in part by predation by Great Horned Owls and collisions with motor vehicles.

VOICE Most familiar call a descending whinny and often used in movie soundtracks; also an even trill; occasional barks and screeches; female higher-pitched than male.

NESTING No nest; lays eggs in cavity in tree, woodpecker hole, rotted snag, nest box; 2–6 eggs; 1 brood; March–August.

FEEDING Captures prey with toes; eats insects, earthworms, rodents, songbirds, crayfish, small fish, tadpoles, snakes, and lizards.

STANDING OUT
The striking red color form of the Eastern Screech-Owl is less common than the gray.

SIMILAR SPECIES

BOREAL OWL
see p.202

brown back

no ear tufts

white spots

NORTHERN SAW-WHET OWL
see p.203

long brown streaks

OCCURRENCE
In the US and southern Canada, breeds in a variety of different lowland wooded areas east of the Rockies. Also breeds south to northeast Mexico. Can be found in suburban and urban parks and gardens; usually avoids mountain forests.

Length **6½–10in (16–25cm)**	Wingspan **19–24in (48–61cm)**	Weight **5–7oz (150–200g)**
Social **Solitary**	Lifespan **Up to 13 years**	Status **Secure**

DATE: _____ TIME: _____ LOCATION: _____

Great Horned Owl

ADULT

long, broad wing

dark arc on wing

IN FLIGHT

mottled, barred, brownish and gray upperparts

ADULT

large "ears"

yellow eye

rusty facial disk

white throat and chin

barred underparts

ADULT

heavy barring of underparts

barring on undertail

FLIGHT: fairly slow with heavy wing beats alternating with short glides; swoops when hunting.

The Great Horned Owl is perhaps the archetypal owl. Large and adaptable, it is resident from Alaska to Tierra del Fuego and is the provincial bird of Alberta. With such a big range, geographical variation occurs; atleast 13 subspecies have been described. The southernmost populations —*B. v. magellanicus*, from Peru to Patagonia—are often considered a distinct species. The Great Horned Owl's deep hoots are easily recognized, and can often be heard in movie soundtracks. The bird is the top predator in its food chain, often killing and eating other owls, and even skunks. An early breeder, it starts hooting in the middle of winter, and often lays its eggs in January.

VOICE Series of hoots *whoo-hoo-oo-o*; also screams, barks, and hisses; female higher-pitched.

NESTING Old stick nest, in tree, exposed cavity, cliff, human structure, or on the ground; 1–5 eggs; 1 brood; January–April.

FEEDING Hunts mammals, reptiles, amphibians, birds, and insects; mostly nocturnal.

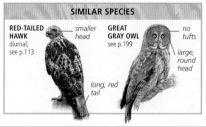

SIMILAR SPECIES

RED-TAILED HAWK diurnal; see p.113

smaller head

long, red tail

GREAT GRAY OWL see p.199

no tufts

large, round head

RECYCLING
The Great Horned Owl breeds in old stick nests constructed by other large birds, like crows.

OCCURRENCE
In North America, found in nearly every type of habitat, except Arctic tundra. Prefers fragmented landscapes: desert, swamp, prairie, woodland, and urban areas. Rare only in the Appalachian Mountains in the East and in the Sonoran and Mohave Deserts in the West.

Length **18–25in (46–63cm)**	Wingspan **3–5ft (0.9–1.6m)**	Weight **1⅞–5½lb (0.9–2.5kg)**
Social **Solitary**	Lifespan **Up to 28 years**	Status **Secure**

DATE: _____ TIME:_____ LOCATION:_____

| Order **Strigiformes** | Family **Strigidae** | Species ***Bubo scandiacus*** |

Snowy Owl

white face

flecked gray-brown

IMMATURE

IN FLIGHT

large round head

yellow eyes

dusky barring

variably barred underparts

JUVENILE

variable barring on wings

nearly all-white breast

feathered legs

ADULT

FLIGHT: slow, steady flight with strong, deep wing beats; flaps interspersed with glides.

An icon of the far north, the Snowy Owl is a bird of the open tundra, where it hunts from headlands or hummocks and nests on the ground. In such a harsh environment, the Snowy Owl largely depends on lemmings for prey. It is fiercely territorial, and will valiantly defend its young in the nest even against larger animals, such as the Arctic Fox. The Snowy Owl is the provincial bird of Quebec.

VOICE Deep hoots, doubled or given in a short series, usually by male; also rattles, whistles, and hisses.

NESTING Scrape in ground vegetation or dirt, with no lining; 3–12 eggs; 1 brood; May–September.

FEEDING Mostly hunts lemmings, but takes whatever other small mammals, birds, and occasionally fish, it can find.

SNOWY MALE
Some adult males display no barring at all and have entirely pure white plumage.

SIMILAR SPECIES

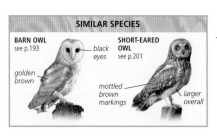

BARN OWL
see p.193

golden brown

black eyes

SHORT-EARED OWL
see p.201

mottled brown markings

larger overall

OCCURRENCE
Breeds in the tundra of Eurasia and northern North America, north to Ellesmere Island; North American birds winter south to the Great Plains. In some years, many North American birds winter south of their normal range, including in dunes, marshes, and airfields, as far south as Idaho and New Jersey.

| Length **20–27in (51–68cm)** | Wingspan **4¼–5¼ft 1.3–1.6m)** | Weight **3½–6½lb (1.6–2.9kg)** |
| Social **Solitary** | Lifespan **Up to 9 years** | Status **Vulnerable** |

DATE: _____ TIME: _____ LOCATION: _____

Order **Strigiformes**	Family **Strigidae**	Species *Surnia ulula*

Northern Hawk Owl

fine spotting on forehead and crown

yellowish eyes

black line around white face

brownish black upperparts

heavy white marking

ADULT long wings

patterned face

IN FLIGHT

long tail

whitish facial discs

ADULT

heavy barring below

ADULT

regularly barred underparts

Whether swooping low through a bog or perching at the tip of a branch, the Northern Hawk Owl is as falcon-like as it is owl-like, being streamlined, a powerful flier, and an active daytime hunter. It is patchily distributed across the northern North American forests, far from most human settlements, so is seldom seen—and is not well studied—on its breeding grounds. In winter, though, the bird is somewhat nomadic, and is occasionally seen south of its breeding range for a few days or weeks in southern Canada and the northern US.

VOICE Ascending, whistled, drawn-out trill; also chirps, screeches, and yelps.

NESTING Cavities, hollows, broken-off branches, old stick nests, nest boxes; 3–13 eggs; 1 brood; April–August.

FEEDING Swoops like a falcon, from an elevated perch, to pounce on prey; preys mainly on rodents in summer, and on grouse, ptarmigan, and other birds in summer.

FLIGHT: powerful, deep wing beats; glides; highly maneuverable, occasionally soars.

KEEN-EYED OWL
The Northern Owl hunts mainly by sight, swooping on prey spotted from a high perch.

OCCURRENCE
Breeds across the forests of northern Canada, from Alaska to Québec and Newfoundland, in sparse woodland or mixed conifer forest with swamps, bogs, burnt areas, or storm damage. In winter occasionally moves south to southern Canada, Great Lakes region and New England.

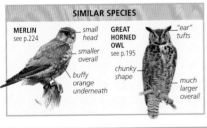

SIMILAR SPECIES

MERLIN
see p.224

small head

smaller overall

buffy orange underneath

GREAT HORNED OWL
see p.195

"ear" tufts

chunky shape

much larger overall

Length **14–17½in (36–44cm)**	Wingspan **31in (80cm)**	Weight **11–12oz (300–350g)**
Social **Family groups**	Lifespan **Up to 10 years**	Status **Secure**

DATE: _____ TIME: _____ LOCATION: _____

| Order **Strigiformes** | Family **Strigidae** | Species **Strix varia** |

Barred Owl

rounded wings

ADULT

IN FLIGHT

large, round head

dark eyes

conspicuously yellowish bill

brown upperparts

heavy white spotting

barring on breast

streaking on belly

ADULT

barred tail

ADULT

FLIGHT: glides silently among trees, interspersed with flaps; rarely hovers.

The Barred Owl is more adaptable and aggressive than its close relative, the Spotted Owl. Recent range expansions have brought the two species into closer contact, which has resulted in the Barred Owl displacing the Spotted Owl, as well as occasional interbreeding. The Barred Owl is mostly nocturnal, but may also call or hunt during the day.
VOICE Series of hoots in rhythm: *who-cooks-for-you, who-cooks-for-you-all*; also pair duetting (at different pitches), cawing, cackling, and guttural sounds.
NESTING No nest; lays eggs in broken-off branches, cavities, old stick nests; 1–5 eggs; 1 brood; January–September.
FEEDING Perches quietly and waits to spot prey below, then pounces; eats small mammals, birds, amphibians, reptiles, insects, and spiders.

WOODED HABITATS
The Barred Owl is very much at home in deep woodlands, including conifer forests.

OCCURRENCE
Widespread, though not evenly so, across North America from British Columbia across to the Maritimes and much of the eastern US. Found in a variety of wooded habitats—from cypress swamps in the south to conifer rainforest in the northwest—and in mixed hardwoods.

SIMILAR SPECIES

GREAT HORNED OWL see p.195

"ear" tufts

SPOTTED OWL

yellow eyes

larger overall

horizontal barring on underparts

longer tail

pale oval bars

| Length **17–19½in (43–50cm)** | Wingspan **3½ft (1.1m)** | Weight **17–37oz (475–1,050g)** |
| Social **Solitary** | Lifespan **Up to 18 years** | Status **Secure** |

DATE: _____ TIME:_____ LOCATION:_____

| Order **Strigiformes** | Family **Strigidae** | Species **Strix nebulosa** |

Great Gray Owl

white crescents between small yellow eyes

gray and white facial disks

long wings

round facial pattern

ADULT

long tail

black and white chin

long wings

ADULT

mottled gray upperparts

heavily streaked underparts

IN FLIGHT

thickset body

ADULT

With a thick layer of feathers that insulate it against cold northern winters, the Great Gray Owl is North America's tallest owl, although it weighs less than the Great Horned Owl or Snowy Owl. Its excellent hearing makes it an efficient rodent hunter. Often able to detect prey by sound alone, it will often plunge through deep snow, or into a burrow, to snatch unseen prey. This bird is primarily nocturnal, but may also hunt by daylight, usually at dawn or dusk. The Great Gray Owl is the provincial bird of Manitoba.

FLIGHT: deep, methodical wing beats, interspersed with glides; hovers while hunting.

VOICE Slow series of deep hoots, evenly spaced; also variety of hisses and chattering noises around nest site.

NESTING Reuses old eagle or hawk nests, broken-off trees; 2–5 eggs; 1 brood; March–July.

FEEDING Eats rodents and other small mammals; waits to pounce from perch or hunts in flight.

SIMILAR SPECIES

GREAT HORNED OWL see p.195

"ear" tufts

barring on breast

barring on belly

BARRED OWL see p.198

dark eyes

MAKESHIFT NEST
The Great Gray Owl often utilizes hollow snags as nesting sites, besides reusing deserted nests.

OCCURRENCE
In North America, resident across northern forests from Alaska to Québec, south to Montana and Wyoming. Also resident in Eurasia from Scandinavia to the Russian Far East. Found in taiga, and muskeg (peat bogs), in fir, spruce, and pine forests.

| Length **24–33in (61–84cm)** | Wingspan **4½ft (1.4m)** | Weight **1½–3¾lb (0.7–1.7kg)** |
| Social **Solitary** | Lifespan **Up to 14 years** | Status **Secure** |

DATE: _____ TIME: _____ LOCATION: _____

Order **Strigiformes**	Family **Strigidae**	Species *Asio otus*

Long-eared Owl

tan patch on outer wing

rusty face disks

long "ear" tufts

dark wrist patch

gray tips

IN FLIGHT

slender body

finely streaked underparts

ADULT

white "eyebrows"

dark eye-ring

yellow eye

black bill

mottled upperwings

ADULT

FLIGHT: quick, deep wing beats and long glides; often hovers while hunting.

Although widely distributed across North America, the Long-eared Owl is seldom seen, being secretive and nocturnal. By day it roosts high up and out of sight in thick cover. Only at nightfall does it fly out to hunt on the wing over open areas, patrolling for small mammals. Its wing feathers, like those of many other owls, have sound-suppressing structures that allow it to fly almost silently, so it can hear the slightest rustle on the ground below.

VOICE Evenly spaced *hooo* notes, continuously repeated, about 3 seconds apart, typically 10–50 per series, sometimes more; barks when alarmed.

NESTING Old stick nests of ravens, crows, magpies, and hawks; 2–7 eggs; 1 brood; March–July.

FEEDING Preys mainly on mice and other small rodents, occasionally small birds.

OWL ON THE WING
In flight this bird's "ear" tufts are flattened back and not visible, but the face and underwing markings are clearly revealed.

SIMILAR SPECIES

GREAT HORNED OWL see p.195

tufts farther apart

much larger overall

horizontal barring on underparts

SHORT-EARED OWL see p.201

patterned buffy above

pale below

larger overall

OCCURRENCE
Breeds in old nests, especially in dense stands of cottonwood, willow, juniper, and conifers by open areas suitable for hunting. Occasionally uses old nests in tree holes, cliffs, or on ground in dense vegetation; in winter, up to 100 birds in roosts. Northern birds move south for winter; some western birds resident.

Length **14–15½in (35–40cm)**	Wingspan **34–39in (86–98cm)**	Weight **8–15oz (225–425g)**
Social **Solitary/Winter flocks**	Lifespan **Up to 27 years**	Status **Secure**

DATE: _____ TIME: _____ LOCATION: _____

| Order **Strigiformes** | Family **Strigidae** | Species **Asio flammeus** |

Short-eared Owl

short ear tufts

large, round head

blackish eye-ring

yellow eyes

pale face disks

black wing tips

row of pale spots along sides of back

whitish underwing

narrow, dark bar

dark wrist patch

orange-buff to yellowish outer wings

white belly

complex, buff marbling on upperparts

ADULT

IN FLIGHT

black wing tips

fine dark streaks

whitish buff underparts

ADULT

FLIGHT: light, slow, buoyant, harrier-like, maneuverable; often hovers, sometimes soars.

This owl is often seen on cloudy days or toward dusk, floating above and patrolling low back and forth over open fields, looking and listening for prey, sometimes with Northern Harriers. Although territorial in the breeding season, it sometimes winters in communal roosts of up to 200 birds, occasionally alongside Long-eared Owls. About 10 subspecies are widely distributed across five continents and numerous islands, including the Greater Antilles, Galápagos, the Falklands and Hawaii. Unlike other North American owls, the Short-eared Owl builds its own nest.

VOICE Usually silent; male courtship call a rapid *hoo hoo hoo*, often given during display flights; about 16 notes in 3 seconds; also barking, *chee-oww*.
NESTING Scrape lined with grass and feathers on ground; 4–7 eggs; 1–2 broods; March–June.
FEEDING Eats small mammals and some birds.

SIMILAR SPECIES

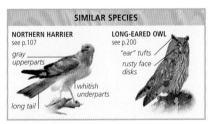

NORTHERN HARRIER
see p.107

gray upperparts

whitish underparts

long tail

LONG-EARED OWL
see p.200

"ear" tufts

rusty face disks

LOOKOUT POST
Perched on a branch, a Short-eared Owl keeps a wary eye on any intruder on its territory.

OCCURRENCE
Breeds in open areas, including prairie, grasslands, tundra, fields, and marshes, across northern North America, from Alaska, the Yukon, and British Columbia to Québec, and Newfoundland, south to the western and central prairies, and east to New England. Partial migrant.

| Length **13½–16in (34–41cm)** | Wingspan **2¾–3½ft (0.9–1.1m)** | Weight **11–13oz (325–375g)** |
| Social **Solitary/Winter flocks** | Lifespan **Up to 13 years** | Status **Vulnerable** |

DATE: _____ TIME: _____ LOCATION: _____

| Order **Strigiformes** | Family **Strigidae** | Species *Aegolius funereus* |

Boreal Owl

usually flat-topped head, with fine white spots

yellow eyes

pale bill

IN FLIGHT

ADULT

rounded wings

finely spotted crown

black border around face

white and brown streaked underparts

ADULT

short tail

ADULT

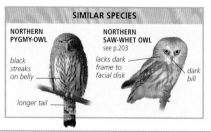

FLIGHT: quick, strong wing beats; adept at maneuvering; glides down to attack prey.

Unusually, the female Boreal Owl is much bigger than the male. Males will mate with two or three females in years when voles and other small rodents are abundant. The Boreal Owl roosts on an inconspicuous perch by day and hunts at night, detecting its prey by sound. In the US and Canada it is elusive and rarely seen, since it breeds at high elevations in isolated western mountain ranges. White spotting on the crown, a grayish bill, and a black facial disk distinguish the Boreal Owl from the Northern Saw-whet Owl.

VOICE Prolonged series of whistles, usually increasing in volume and intensity toward the end; also screeches and hisses; can be heard from afar.

NESTING Natural and woodpecker-built tree cavities, also nest boxes; 3–6 eggs; 1 brood; March–July.

FEEDING Mainly eats small mammals, occasionally birds and insects; pounces from elevated perch; sometimes stores prey.

DAYTIME ROOSTING
The Boreal Owl roosts in dense vegetation by day, even when the branches are laden with snow.

SIMILAR SPECIES

NORTHERN PYGMY-OWL

black streaks on belly

longer tail

NORTHERN SAW-WHET OWL
see p.203

lacks dark frame to facial disk

dark bill

OCCURRENCE
Breeds in northern forests from Alaska to Newfoundland and Québec, south into the Rockies to Colorado and New Mexico. Largely sedentary, but irregular movements take place south of the breeding range, southward to New England and New York.

| Length **8½–11in (21–28cm)** | Wingspan **21½–24in (54–62cm)** | Weight **3⅜–8oz (90–225g)** |
| Social **Solitary** | Lifespan **Up to 11 years** | Status **Secure** |

DATE: _____ TIME: _____ LOCATION: _____

Northern Saw-whet Owl

ADULT

rounded wings

thin white streaks on forehead and crown

whitish eyebrows

white patch between eyes

yellow eyes

dark bill

chestnut-brown upperparts with white spots

short tail
IN FLIGHT

brown streaks

ADULT

ADULT

FLIGHT: swift and direct; low to ground with quick wing beats; swoops up to perch.

unmarked white undertail feathers

One of the most secretive yet common and widespread owls in North America, the Northern Saw-whet Owl is much more often heard than seen. Strictly nocturnal, it is concealed as it sleeps by day in thick vegetation, usually in conifers. Although the same site may be used for months if it remains undisturbed, it is never an easy bird to locate and, like most owls, it is elusive, even though it sometimes roosts in large garden trees. When it is discovered, the Northern Saw-whet Owl "freezes," and relies on its camouflage rather than flying off. At night it watches intently from a perch, before swooping down to snatch its prey.

VOICE Series of rapid whistled notes, on constant pitch; can continue for minutes on end; also whines and squeaks.

NESTING Unlined cavity in tree, usually old woodpecker hole or nest box; 4–7 eggs; 1 brood; March–July.

FEEDING Hunts from elevated perch; eats small mammals, including mice and voles; also eats insects and small birds.

RARE SIGHT
Despite being abundant in its range, this species is quite shy and is rarely seen by humans.

SIMILAR SPECIES

ELF OWL

gray back

smaller overall

BOREAL OWL
see p.202

darker face

spotted crown

black facial border

OCCURRENCE
Breeds from Alaska and British Columbia to Maritimes; in west, south to Mexico; in east, south to Appalachians; coniferous and mixed deciduous forests, swampy forests, wooded wetlands, bogs. Winters in south to central states, in open woodlands, pine plantations, shrubby areas.

Length **7–8½in (18–21cm)**	Wingspan **16½–19in (42–48cm)**	Weight **3½oz (100g)**
Social **Solitary**	Lifespan **Up to 10 years**	Status **Secure**

Family **Caprimulgidae**

NIGHTJARS

Aaaa LTHOUGH WIDESPREAD and common throughout North America, species of the family Caprimulgidae are heard more often than they are seen. The exceptions to this rule are the two species of nightjars that regularly forage for insects at dawn and dusk. All members of this group are medium-sized birds that use their long wings and wide tails to make rapid and graceful turns to capture their insect prey in the air. They feed predominantly on large flying insects such as moths. Their wide, gaping mouths are surrounded by bristles that greatly aid in foraging efforts. They have very small legs and toes. Nightjars are generally similar in coloration and pattern, having a mottled mixture of various browns, grays, and blacks that provides impeccable camouflage when they remain hidden during daylight hours. This ability to hide in plain sight is useful during the nesting season when all nightjars lay their patterned eggs directly on the ground, without any nest material. The nature of the camouflage pattern of their feathers makes it difficult to distinguish between species when they rest in trees or on the ground. The most reliable means of telling species apart is their voice. If seen, the placement and nature of white markings, combined with the style of flight are the best means of identification. Most members of the family migrate and move southward as insects become dormant in the North. Nightjars are also known as "Goatsuckers," because it was believed in ancient Greece that these birds sucked blood from goats.

NIGHT HUNTER
The nocturnal Whip-poor-will hunts from the ground, looking up to spot its flying insect prey.

SITTING PRETTY
Unusually for birds, members of the nightjar family, such as this Common Nighthawk, often perch lengthwise on branches.

| Order **Caprimulgiformes** | Family **Caprimulgidae** | Species *Chordeiles minor* |

Common Nighthawk

pointed wings

MALE

white bars on outer wing feathers

narrow wings

long wings

IN FLIGHT

delicate, gray-black pattern overall

white throat

white wing patch **MALE**

very small bill

large, dark eye

barring on gray underparts

FEMALE

FLIGHT: erratic flight with deep wing beats interrupted by banking glides.

Common Nighthawks are easy to spot as they swoop over parking lots, city streets, and athletics fields during the warm summer months. They are more active at dawn and dusk than at night, pursuing insect prey up to 250ft (76m) in the air. The species once took the name Booming Nighthawk, a reference to the remarkable flight display of the male birds, during which they dive rapidly towards the ground, causing their feathers to vibrate and produce a characteristic "booming" sound.

VOICE Nasal *peeent*; also soft clucking noises from both sexes.

NESTING Nests on ground on rocks, wood, leaves, or sand, also on gravel-covered rooftops in urban areas; 2 eggs; 1 brood; May–July.

FEEDING Catches airborne insects, especially moths, mayflies, and beetles, also ants; predominantly active at dusk and dawn.

A RARE SIGHT
Common Nighthawks are seen in flight more often than other caprimulgids, and it is a rare treat to see one resting on a perch.

OCCURRENCE
Wide variety of open habitats such as cleared forests, fields, grassland, beaches, and sand dunes; also common in urban areas, including cities. The most common and widespread North American nighthawk, this species also occurs in Central and South America.

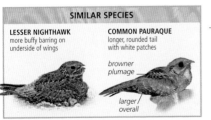

SIMILAR SPECIES

LESSER NIGHTHAWK
more buffy barring on underside of wings

COMMON PAURAQUE
longer, rounded tail with white patches

browner plumage

larger overall

Length **9–10in (23–26cm)**	Wingspan **22–24in (56–61cm)**	Weight **2⅞oz (80g)**
Social **Solitary/Flocks**	Lifespan **Up to 9 years**	Status **Declining**

DATE: _____ TIME: _____ LOCATION: _____

| Order **Caprimulgiformes** | Family **Caprimulgidae** | Species *Antrostomus vociferus* |

Eastern Whip-poor-will

rounded wings

MALE

IN FLIGHT

buffy throat stripe

FEMALE

black-and-gray bands across back

buffy corners to tail

flat, wide bill with long bristles

huge eye

tawny patch on cheeks

whitish throat stripe

MALE

cinnamon barring on dark wings

white corners to tail

A s with many of the nightjars, the Eastern Whip-poor-will is heard more often than seen. Its camouflage makes it extremely difficult to spot on the forest floor and it usually flies away only when an intruder is very close—sometimes within a few feet. This species apparently has an unusual breeding pattern—while the male feeds the first brood until fledging, the female lays eggs for a second brood. Both eggs from one brood may hatch simultaneously during full moon, when there is most light at night, allowing the parents more time to forage for their young.

VOICE Loud, three-syllable whistle *WHIP-perrr-WIIL*.

NESTING Lays eggs on leaf litter on forest floor, often near overhead plant cover; 2 eggs; 2 broods; April–July.

FEEDING Flies upward quickly from perch to capture passing moths and other insects, such as mosquitoes.

FLIGHT: slow, erratic flight, with alternating bouts of flapping and gliding.

WAITING IN AMBUSH
Like other nightjars, this species waits in ambush for its prey from a perch on the forest floor.

SIMILAR SPECIES

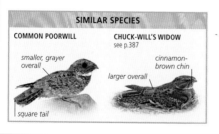

COMMON POORWILL

smaller, grayer overall

square tail

CHUCK-WILL'S WIDOW
see p.387

larger overall

cinnamon-brown chin

OCCURRENCE
Mixed mature forests with open understory, especially oak and pine forests on dry upland sites. Breeds north to southern Canada and south to Mexico.

| Length **9–10in (23–26cm)** | Wingspan **17–20in (43–51cm)** | Weight **1⁹⁄₁₆–2¹⁄₄oz (45–65g)** |
| Social **Solitary** | Lifespan **Up to 15 years** | Status **Secure** |

DATE: _____ TIME: _____ LOCATION: _____

Family **Apodidae**

SWIFTS

S WIFTS SPEND VIRTUALLY ALL their daylight hours and many night hours as well, plying the skies. The most aerial birds in North America—if not the world—swifts eat, drink, court, mate, and even sleep on the wing. Unsurprisingly, swifts also are some of the fastest and most acrobatic flyers of the bird world. Several species have been clocked at over 100mph (160kph). They feed on insects caught in zooming, zigzagging and dashing pursuits. The family name, based on the Greek *apous*, which means "without feet," originates from the ancient belief that swifts had no feet and lived their entire lives in the air.

APTLY NAMED
Chimney Swifts will build their nest inside chimneys when they can get access.

Family **Trochilidae**

HUMMINGBIRDS

F OUND ONLY IN THE AMERICAS, hummingbirds are sometimes referred to as the crown jewels of the bird world. The first sight of a glittering hummingbird can be a life-changing experience. The amount of iridescence in their plumages varies from almost none to seemingly every feather. Most North American male hummingbirds have a colorful throat patch called a gorget, but most females lack this gorgeous attribute. Because iridescent colors are structural and not pigment-based, a gorget can often appear blackish until seen at the correct angle towards the light.

Hummingbirds are the only birds that can fly backwards, an adaptation that allows them to move easily between flowers. Flying sideways, up, down, and hovering are also within hummingbirds' abilities, and all are achieved by their unique figure-eight, rapid wing strokes and reduced wing bone structure. Their long, thin bills allow them access to nectar in tubular flowers.

AGGRESSIVE MALES
This male Ruby-throated Hummingbird defends his territory from a perch.

| Order **Apodiformes** | Family **Apodidae** | Species ***Chaetura pelagica*** |

Chimney Swift

large eyes

short bill

dark brown upperparts

pale brown throat

long, sickle-shaped wings

ADULT

short, square tail

throat slightly paler than body

IN FLIGHT

very long, black wings

stiff spined tail

Nicknamed "spine-tailed," the Chimney Swift is a familiar summer sight and sound, racing through the skies east of the Rockies, its rolling twitters often heard. These birds do almost everything on the wing—feeding, drinking, and even bathing. Chimney Swifts have adapted to nest in human structures, including chimneys, although they once nested in tree holes. It remains a common bird, although local populations have declined; and it has expanded its range west and south.

VOICE High, rapid chips and twittering; notes from individuals in a flock run together into a rapid, descending chatter.

NESTING Shallow cup of twigs and saliva attached to inside of chimney or other artificial structure, rarely hollow tree; 4–5 eggs; 1 brood; April–August.

FEEDING Pursues a large variety of small aerial insects.

FLIGHT: fast, acrobatic, and erratic; very rapid, vibrating wing beats; soars with tail fanned.

HIGH FLYER
Swifts feed at heights on sunny days, and only feed near the ground when it is cold and cloudy.

OCCURRENCE
Widespread in eastern North America, over many habitats: urban and suburban areas, small towns; in sparsely populated areas nests in hollow trees and caves; regular in summer in southern California, present late March to early November. Winters in Amazonian South America.

SIMILAR SPECIES

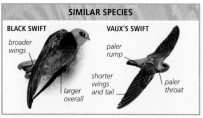

BLACK SWIFT
broader wings
larger overall

VAUX'S SWIFT
paler rump
shorter wings and tail
paler throat

| Length **5in (13cm)** | Wingspan **14in (36cm)** | Weight **⅝–1¹⁄₁₆oz (17–30g)** |
| Social **Flocks** | Lifespan **Up to 15 years** | Status **Declining** |

DATE: _____ TIME:_____ LOCATION:_____

| Order **Apodiformes** | Family **Trochilidae** | Species *Archilochus colubris* |

Ruby-throated Hummingbird

MALE

IN FLIGHT (MALE)

dark, forked tail

bronzy green upperparts

pale-tipped crown feathers

greenish speckling on throat

IMMATURE MALE

green crown

black face

straight, black bill

orange-red throat

white chest

greenish sides and flanks

glittering green upperparts

white chin and throat

FEMALE

white underparts with buff wash on sides and flanks

rounded tail

grayish white underparts

MALE

The only hummingbird to breed east of the Mississippi River, the Ruby-throated Hummingbird is a welcome addition to gardens throughout its range. It is easily identified in most of its range, though more difficult to distinguish in areas where other species are found, particularly during migration. Males perform a deep diving display for females. Before migration, these birds add about 1/16oz (2g) of fat to their weight to provide enough fuel for their nonstop 800-mile (1,300km) flight across the Gulf of Mexico.

VOICE Call a soft, thick *chic*, sometimes doubled; twittered notes in interactions; chase call a fast, slightly buzzy *tsi-tsi-tsi-tsi-tsi-tsi-tsi-tsi*; soft, rattling song very rarely heard.

NESTING Tiny cup of plant down, with bud scales and lichen on the exterior, bound with spider's silk, usually in deciduous trees; 2 eggs; 1–2 broods; April–September.

FEEDING Drinks nectar from many species of flowers; feeds on small insects and spiders, caught aerially or gleaned from foliage.

FLIGHT: swift, forward flight with very fast wing beats; hovers at flowers and darts after insects.

CATCHING THE LIGHT
Although the throat patch often appears all black, the right lighting sets it afire with color.

SIMILAR SPECIES

BLACK-CHINNED HUMMINGBIRD ♀

broader outer feathers

longer bill

ANNA'S HUMMINGBIRD ♀
harder, sharper call notes

thicker neck

grayer underparts

OCCURRENCE
Favors a variety of woodlands, and gardens; earliest migrants appear in the South as early as late February; most leave by November; regular in winter in south Florida; small numbers winter elsewhere on the Gulf Coast; vagrant to the West. The bulk of the population migrates to Central America in winter.

Length **3½in (9cm)**	Wingspan **4¼in (11cm)**	Weight **1/16–7/32oz (2–6g)**
Social **Solitary**	Lifespan **Up to 9 years**	Status **Secure**

DATE: _____ TIME: _____ LOCATION: _____

KINGFISHERS

KINGFISHERS ARE PRIMARILY a tropical family that apparently originated in the Australasian region. There are approximately 90 species of kingfisher in the world, and most have large heads with long pointed bills, short legs, stubby tails, and bright plumage. Three species of Alcedinidae are found in North America, but only one, the Belted Kingfisher, is widespread and found in Canada. Like most species of kingfishers, these birds are large-headed and large-billed but have comparatively short legs and toes. Although lacking the array of bright blues, greens, and reds associated with their tropical and European counterparts, Belted Kingfishers are striking birds, distinguished by shaggy head crests, breastbands, and white underparts. The females of the species are more brightly colored than the males, sporting chestnut-colored breastbands. While they also eat amphibians, reptiles, insects, and crustaceans, Belted

Kingfishers are primarily fish-eaters. They will frequent a favorite perch along a waterway for hunting, or hover if no perch is available, and will plunge headfirst into the water to catch their prey. After catching a fish, they routinely stun their prey by beating it against a perch before turning the fish around so that it can be eaten head first. Mating pairs dig a burrow in a bank about 3–6ft (1–2m) long. The female lays 6–7 eggs; both adults share the task of incubating the eggs and feeding the young. Parents entice the young to leave the burrow by perching outside with a fish in their bill and calling to them. A week usually passes before the fledglings are able to capture live fish. Migration depends on the availability of open water—kingfishers will stay in an area year-round if they have access to fishing grounds.

FISH DINNER
A Belted Kingfisher uses its large bill to catch and hold slippery prey.

SEDATE MALE
Unlike many birds, the male Belted Kingfisher is not as colorful as the female.

| Order **Coraciiformes** | Family **Alcedinidae** | Species ***Megaceryle alcyon*** |

Belted Kingfisher

MALE — large head

single blue breastband

barred tail

IN FLIGHT

bluish gray head with shaggy crest

bluish slate upperparts

white collar

white belly

MALE

prominent crest

long, thick, powerful bill

chestnut band across breast

chestnut flanks

FEMALE

double crest

white collar

single dark breastband

IMMATURE MALE

FLIGHT: strongly flaps its wings and then glides after two or three beats; frequently hovers.

I ts stocky body, double-pointed crest, large head, and contrasting white collar distinguish the Belted Kingfisher from other species in its range. This kingfisher's loud and far-carrying rattles are heard more often than the bird is seen. Interestingly, it is one of the few birds in North America in which the female is more colorful than the male. The Belted Kingfisher can be found in a large variety of aquatic habitats, both coastal and inland, vigorously defending its territory, all year round.
VOICE Harsh mechanical rattle given in flight or from a perch; sometimes emits screams or trill-like warble during breeding.
NESTING Unlined chamber in subterranean burrow 3–6ft (1–2m) deep, excavated in earthen bank usually over water, but sometimes in ditches, sand, or gravel pits; 6–7 eggs; 1 brood; March–July.
FEEDING Plunge-dives from branches or wires to catch a wide variety of fish near the surface, including sticklebacks and trout; also takes crustaceans, such as crayfish.

CATCH OF THE DAY
The female's chestnut belly band and flanks are clearly visible here as she perches with her catch.

SIMILAR SPECIES

RINGED KINGFISHER ♂

larger overall

chestnut belly

OCCURRENCE
Breeds and winters around clear, open waters of streams, rivers, lakes, estuaries, and protected marine shorelines, where perches are available and prey is visible. Avoids water with emergent vegetation. Northern populations migrate south to Mexico, Central America, and the West Indies.

Length **11–14in (28–35cm)**	Wingspan **19–23in (48–58cm)**	Weight **5–6oz (150–175g)**
Social **Solitary**	Lifespan **Unknown**	Status **Secure**

DATE: _____ TIME: _____ LOCATION: _____

WOODPECKERS

T HE THREE GROUPS of closely related species that constitute the family Picidae are found throughout North America. They are a physically striking group adapted to living on tree trunks.

WOODPECKERS

The species that constitute the typical woodpeckers of North America share a distinct set of physical characteristics and behaviors. Their pecking and drumming, which they use for purposes of constructing nest cavities, communication, and feeding, is made possible by a very thick skull, adapted to withstand the shock that results from continual pecking on wood.

Woodpeckers nest in cavities in dead trees, and they are vulnerable to the loss of their specialized habitats through forest clearing.

SAPSUCKERS

This group of birds feeds on tree sap as a primary source of nourishment for both adults and their young. Sapsuckers have tongues tipped with stiff hairs to allow sap to stick to them. The holes the birds create in trees in order to extract the sap also attract insects, which make up the main protein source in the sapsucker diet. Because they damage living trees, some orchard growers consider sapsuckers to be pests.

BALANCING ACT
The Yellow-bellied Sapsucker rests its stiff tail against a tree to maintain its balance.

FLICKERS

Flickers are relatively large members of the family Picidae and spend more time feeding on the ground than other woodpeckers, consuming ants and other insects. Flickers often forage in open areas around human habitation. They are notable for their colorful underwing feather plumages and their distinctive white rump.

RED ALERT
With its crimson head, the Red-headed Woodpecker is an instantly recognizable bird in North America.

COMMON BIRD
The Northern Flicker can be found across the entire North American continent.

Red-headed Woodpecker

white rump

red head

ADULT

IN FLIGHT

bright red hood

bluish gray bill

brownish head

upperparts black with bluish sheen

narrow black "necklace"

ADULT

wing feathers white with black barring

JUVENILE

white wing feathers

The Red-headed Woodpecker is the only member of this family that has a completely red head, and is therefore easy to identify. Unlike most other woodpecker species, it forages for food—both insects and nuts—and stores it for eating at a later time. It is one of the most skilled flycatchers in the woodpecker family. Its numbers have declined, largely because of the destruction of its habitat, especially the removal of dead trees in urban and rural areas, and clearing and cutting of trees for firewood in rural areas. The Red-headed Woodpecker is a truly North American bird, not extending south of the Rio Grande.

VOICE Primary call an extremely harsh and loud *churr*, also produces breeding call and alarm; no song; active drummer.

NESTING Excavates cavity in dead wood; 3–5 eggs; 1–2 broods; May–August.

FEEDING Forages in flight, on ground, and in trees; feeds on a variety of insects, spiders, nuts seeds, berries, and fruit, and, in rare cases, small mammals such as mice.

WORK IN PROGRESS
The Red-headed Woodpecker excavates its breeding cavities in tree trunks and stumps.

FLIGHT: strong flapping; undulation not as marked as in other woodpecker species.

OCCURRENCE
Breeds in a variety of habitats, especially open deciduous woodlands, including riverine areas, orchards, municipal parks, agricultural areas, forest edges, and forests affected by fire. Uses the same habitats during the winter as in the breeding season.

Length 8½–9½ in (22–24cm)	Wingspan 16–18in (41–46cm)	Weight 2–3oz (55–85g)
Social **Solitary**	Lifespan **At least 10 years**	Status **Declining**

DATE: _____ TIME: _____ LOCATION: _____

| Order **Piciformes** | Family **Picidae** | Species *Melanerpes carolinus* |

Red-bellied Woodpecker

white patches at base of outer wing

MALE

IN FLIGHT

gray crown

red crown

red nape

FEMALE

red crown

pale grayish tan face

pale grayish tan underparts

regular black-and-white barring

MALE

FLIGHT: undulating flight, as with other woodpecker species.

This attractive, abundant woodpecker is found throughout the eastern half of the US, and has expanded its range both northward into Canada and westward in the last decade or two. Despite its common name, it does not actually possess a red belly. The male is distinguished by its red forehead, crown, and nape, while the female only has a red nape; both have pale-colored underparts and regularly barred upperparts. Male Red-bellied Woodpeckers excavate several holes in trees, one of which the female chooses. They also use previously available cavities, but often lose them to aggressive starlings. Unlike many woodpecker species, although the Red-bellied eats insects, it does not excavate trees to find them.

VOICE Rather soft, clearly rolling, slightly quivering *krrurrr* call.

NESTING Cavity nester; 4–5 eggs; 1–3 broods; May–August.

FEEDING Eats insects, fruit, seeds, acorns, and other nuts; in winter, eats mainly vegetable matter.

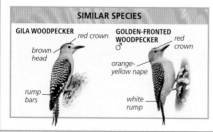

SIMILAR SPECIES		
GILA WOODPECKER brown head rump bars red crown	**GOLDEN-FRONTED WOODPECKER** ♂ orange-yellow nape white rump red crown	

SUBURBAN SPECIES
These birds can be seen and heard on tree trunks in suburban and urban woods.

OCCURRENCE
Resident in southeastern Canada and eastern and southeastern US, where it breeds in a wide range of habitats; found in forests, swamps, suburban wooded areas, open woodlands, and parks. Winter habitats resemble the breeding areas.

Length **9–10½in (23–27cm)**	Wingspan **16in (41cm)**	Weight **2½oz (70g)**
Social **Solitary/Pairs**	Lifespan **Up to 12 years**	Status **Secure**

DATE: _____ TIME:_____ LOCATION:_____

| Order **Piciformes** | Family **Picidae** | Species *Sphyrapicus varius* |

Yellow-bellied Sapsucker

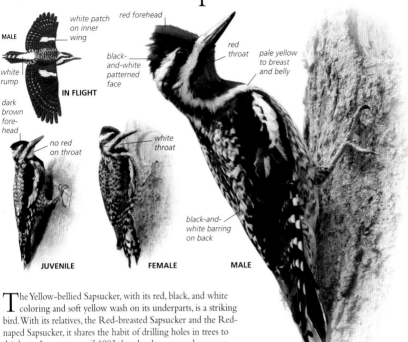

MALE

white patch on inner wing

red forehead

IN FLIGHT

white rump

black-and-white patterned face

red throat

pale yellow to breast and belly

dark brown forehead

no red on throat

white throat

black-and-white barring on back

JUVENILE

FEMALE

MALE

The Yellow-bellied Sapsucker, with its red, black, and white coloring and soft yellow wash on its underparts, is a striking bird. With its relatives, the Red-breasted Sapsucker and the Red-naped Sapsucker, it shares the habit of drilling holes in trees to drink sap. It was not until 1983 that the three sapsuckers were allocated to separate species. This is the only North American woodpecker that is completely migratory, with females moving farther south than males.

VOICE Primary call a mewing *wheer-wheer-wheer*.

NESTING Cavities in dead trees; 5–6 eggs; 1 brood; May–June.

FEEDING Drinks sap; eats ants and other small insects; feeds on the inner bark of trees, also a variety of fruit.

FLIGHT: typical woodpecker, undulating flight pattern with intermittent flapping and gliding.

STRIKING SPECIES
The Yellow-bellied Sapsucker's white rump and black-and-white forked tail are clearly evident here.

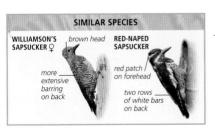

SIMILAR SPECIES

WILLIAMSON'S SAPSUCKER ♀

brown head

more extensive barring on back

RED-NAPED SAPSUCKER

red patch on forehead

two rows of white bars on back

OCCURRENCE
Breeds in eastern Alaska, Canada, and south to the Appalachians. Prefers either deciduous or mixed deciduous-coniferous forests; prefers young forests. In winter, it is found in open wooded areas in southeastern states, Caribbean islands, and Central America.

| Length **8–9in (20–23cm)** | Wingspan **16–18in (41–46cm)** | Weight **1¾oz (50g)** |
| Social **Solitary/Pairs** | Lifespan **Up to 7 years** | Status **Secure** |

DATE: _____ TIME: _____ LOCATION: _____

| Order **Piciformes** | Family **Picidae** | Species **Picoides pubescens** |

Downy Woodpecker

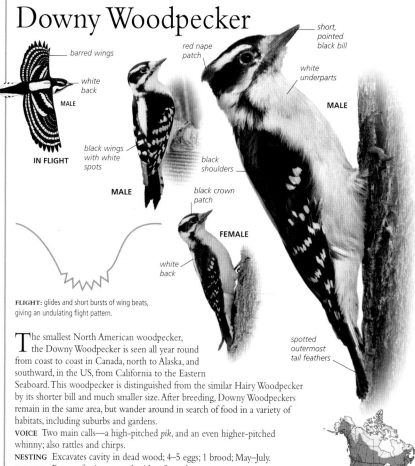

barred wings

red nape patch

short, pointed black bill

white back

MALE

white underparts

MALE

black wings with white spots

IN FLIGHT

black shoulders

MALE

black crown patch

FEMALE

white back

spotted outermost tail feathers

FLIGHT: glides and short bursts of wing beats, giving an undulating flight pattern.

The smallest North American woodpecker, the Downy Woodpecker is seen all year round from coast to coast in Canada, north to Alaska, and southward, in the US, from California to the Eastern Seaboard. This woodpecker is distinguished from the similar Hairy Woodpecker by its shorter bill and much smaller size. After breeding, Downy Woodpeckers remain in the same area, but wander around in search of food in a variety of habitats, including suburbs and gardens.

VOICE Two main calls—a high-pitched *pik*, and an even higher-pitched whinny; also rattles and chirps.

NESTING Excavates cavity in dead wood; 4–5 eggs; 1 brood; May–July.

FEEDING Forages for insects and spiders from the surfaces and bark crevices of live and dead trees, but also eats fruit, seeds, and other vegetable matter, depending on the season.

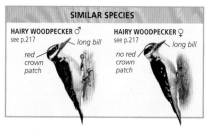

SIMILAR SPECIES

HAIRY WOODPECKER ♂
see p.217

long bill

red crown patch

HAIRY WOODPECKER ♀
see p.217

long bill

no red crown patch

SUET LOVERS
Downy Woodpeckers will feed on suet provided in feeders during the winter.

OCCURRENCE
Breeds in a wide variety of habitats, including deciduous and mixed deciduous-coniferous woodlands, parks, wooded suburban areas, and areas near rivers. While using nature's bounty of dead trees, it will also use manmade objects such as fence posts. Resident, but local movements occur.

| Length **6–7in (15–18cm)** | Wingspan **10–12in (25–30cm)** | Weight **1¹⁄₁₆oz (30g)** |
| Social **Solitary/Flocks** | Lifespan **Up to 11 years** | Status **Secure** |

DATE: _____ TIME: _____ LOCATION: _____

Hairy Woodpecker

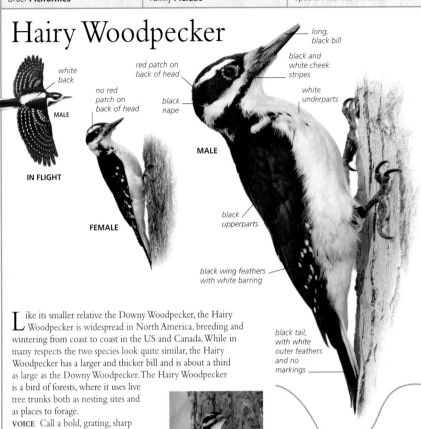

long, black bill

black and white cheek stripes

white underparts

red patch on back of head

white back

no red patch on back of head

black nape

MALE

MALE

IN FLIGHT

FEMALE

black upperparts

black wing feathers with white barring

black tail, with white outer feathers and no markings

L ike its smaller relative the Downy Woodpecker, the Hairy Woodpecker is widespread in North America, breeding and wintering from coast to coast in the US and Canada. While in many respects the two species look quite similar, the Hairy Woodpecker has a larger and thicker bill and is about a third as large as the Downy Woodpecker. The Hairy Woodpecker is a bird of forests, where it uses live tree trunks both as nesting sites and as places to forage.

VOICE Call a bold, grating, sharp *Peek,* similar to that of the Downy Woodpecker, but lower in pitch, and louder. Drumming a rather loud, even series of taps.

NESTING Excavates cavity in live trees; 4 eggs; 1 brood; May–July.

FEEDING Eats mainly insects and their larvae; also nuts and seeds.

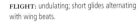

FLIGHT: undulating; short glides alternating with wing beats.

HOME SWEET HOME
The Hairy Woodpecker is generally found in forests and prefers mature woodland areas, using both deciduous and coniferous trees.

OCCURRENCE
Breeds primarily in forests, both deciduous and coniferous, but also in more open woodlands, swamps, suburban parks, and wooded areas. Resident in North America all the year-round, though in the far north of its range it may move south for the winter.

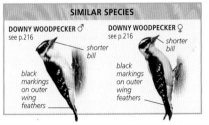

SIMILAR SPECIES

DOWNY WOODPECKER ♂
see p.216

shorter bill

black markings on outer wing feathers

DOWNY WOODPECKER ♀
see p.216

shorter bill

black markings on outer wing feathers

| Length **9–9½in (23–24cm)** | Wingspan **15–16in (38–41cm)** | Weight **2½oz (70g)** |
| Social **Solitary/Winter flocks** | Lifespan **At least 16 years** | Status **Secure** |

| Order **Piciformes** | Family **Picidae** | Species *Picoides dorsalis* |

American Three-toed Woodpecker

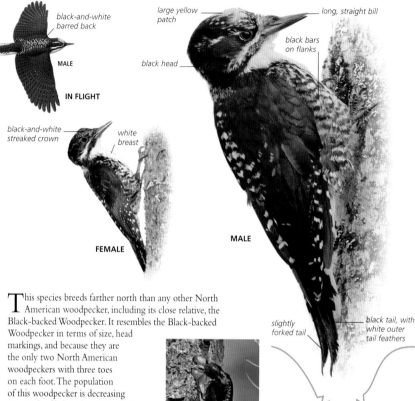

black-and-white barred back

MALE

IN FLIGHT

large yellow patch

long, straight bill

black head

black bars on flanks

black-and-white streaked crown

white breast

FEMALE

MALE

This species breeds farther north than any other North American woodpecker, including its close relative, the Black-backed Woodpecker. It resembles the Black-backed Woodpecker in terms of size, head markings, and because they are the only two North American woodpeckers with three toes on each foot. The population of this woodpecker is decreasing as a result of habitat loss. This species and its relative require mature forests with old or dead trees.

VOICE Call notes *queep*, *quip*, or *pik*; generally quiet, likened to the Yellow-bellied Sapsucker.

NESTING Excavates cavity mainly in dead or dying wood, sometimes in live wood; 4 eggs; 1 brood; May–July.

FEEDING Flakes off bark and eats insects underneath, mainly the larvae of Bark Beetles.

slightly forked tail

black tail, with white outer tail feathers

FLIGHT: undulating flight with rapid wing beats typical of other woodpeckers.

COLOR VARIATION
The streaks on this species' back are highly variable; some populations have nearly all-white backs.

SIMILAR SPECIES

BLACK-BACKED WOODPECKER
shorter call;
see p.219

solid black back

OCCURRENCE
Breeds in mature northerly coniferous forests across Canada and through the Rockies. Since it is largely nonmigratory, this is also the winter habitat for most populations, although it is found in more open areas in winter.

Length **8–9in (20–23cm)**	Wingspan **15in (38cm)**	Weight **2¼–2½oz (65–70g)**
Social **Solitary/Pairs**	Lifespan **Unknown**	Status **Vulnerable**

DATE: _____ TIME:_____ LOCATION:_____

Order **Piciformes**	Family **Picidae**	Species **Picoides arcticus**

Black-backed Woodpecker

white spots on outer wings

black back

MALE

IN FLIGHT

long, black bill

yellow cap on black head

white stripe on head

white underparts

black cap

black back and wings

MALE

FEMALE

Formerly called the Black-backed Three-toed Woodpecker, this species has a black back and heavily barred flanks. Despite being widespread across the northern US, southern Canada, and southern Alaska, this bird is difficult to find. The Black-backed Woodpecker often occurs in areas of burned forest, eating wood-boring beetles that occur after outbreaks of fire. This diet is very restrictive, and the species is greatly affected by forestry programs, which prevent the spread of fire. Although it overlaps geographically with the American Three-toed Woodpecker, the two are rarely found together in the same locality.

VOICE Main call a single *pik*.
NESTING Cavity excavated in tree; 3–4 eggs; 1 brood; May–July.
FEEDING Eats beetles, especially larvae of wood-boring beetles, by flaking off bark.

FLIGHT: typical undulating flight of woodpeckers.

FREQUENT MOVING
This bird excavates a new nest cavity each year, rarely returning in subsequent years.

OCCURRENCE
Inhabitant of northerly and mountainous coniferous forests that require fire for renewal. Breeding occurs soon after sites are burned as new colonies are attracted to the habitat. Occasional irruptive movements into the Great Lakes region and the Maritimes in response to outbreaks of wood-boring beetles.

SIMILAR SPECIES

AMERICAN THREE-TOED WOODPECKER
see p.218

black-and-white barred upperparts

Length **9–9½in (23–24cm)**	Wingspan **15–16in (38–41cm)**	Weight **2½oz (70g)**
Social **Pairs**	Lifespan **Unknown**	Status **Secure**

DATE: _____ TIME: _____ LOCATION: _____

| Order **Piciformes** | Family **Picidae** | Species **Colaptes auratus** |

Northern Flicker

gray crown

buffy forehead

red "mustache"

bright yellow underwings

IN FLIGHT

black crescent

MALE (YELLOW-SHAFTED FORM)

MALE (RED-SHAFTED FORM)

orangish red underwings

brownish back with black barring

no "mustache"

gray fore-head and crown

black "mustache"

red crescent

FEMALE (YELLOW-SHAFTED FORM)

MALE (YELLOW-SHAFTED FORM)

MALE (RED-SHAFTED FORM)

In contrast to other North American woodpeckers, the Northern Flicker is a ground forager. The two subspecies, the Yellow-shafted Flicker in the East, and Red-shafted Flicker in the West, interbreed in a wide area in the Great Plains. They can be distinguished when in flight, as the underwing feathers will either be a vivid yellow or a striking red, as their names indicate.

VOICE Two main calls; loud *kew-kew-kew*, each note ascending at the end; the other, softer call, described as *wicka-wicka-wicka*.

NESTING Cavity usually in dead wood, but sometimes in live wood; 6–8 eggs; 1 brood; May–June.

FEEDING Feeds mainly on ants in breeding season; also fruits in winter.

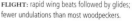

FLIGHT: rapid wing beats followed by glides; fewer undulations than most woodpeckers.

SHARING CHORES
The Northern Flicker nests in tree cavities, where parents take turns incubating eggs.

SIMILAR SPECIES

GILDED FLICKER

cinnamon crown

paler brown back

FEET ON THE GROUND
Unlike other woodpeckers, flickers can be found foraging for ants on the ground.

OCCURRENCE
A common species found in woodland in every part of theUS, the southern half of Canada, and north into Alaska. During breeding season, prefers open woodlands and forest edge; also suburbs. Little is known about this bird's winter habitat.

| Length **12–13in (31–33cm)** | Wingspan **19–21in (48–53cm)** | Weight **4oz (125g)** |
| Social **Solitary** | Lifespan **9 years** | Status **Secure** |

DATE: _____ TIME: _____ LOCATION: _____

| Order **Piciformes** | Family **Picidae** | Species ***Dryocopus pileatus*** |

Pileated Woodpecker

large overall

MALE

large white patch

long tail

IN FLIGHT

red crest

red forehead

red crest

large black bill

white chin

scarlet "mustache"

black forehead

black "mustache"

black back

white patch on wing

FEMALE

MALE

The largest woodpecker in North America, the Pileated Woodpecker is instantly recognizable by its spectacular large, tapering, bright-red crest. A mated pair of Pileated Woodpeckers defends their breeding territory all year—even if one bird dies, the other does not desert the territory. Indeed, a pair may live in the same old, dead tree every year, but will hammer out a new nest cavity with their powerful bills each season. The abandoned nest cavities created by the Pileated Woodpecker are sometimes reused by other birds, and occasionally inhabited by mammals.

VOICE Two primary calls, both high-pitched and quite loud— *yuck-yuck-yuck*, and *yuka-yuka-yuka*.

NESTING Excavates cavity, usually in dead tree; 3–5 eggs; 1 brood; May–July.

FEEDING Bores deep into trees and peels off large strips of bark to extract carpenter ants and beetle larvae; also digs on ground and on fallen logs, and opportunistically eats fruit and nuts.

EASY PICKINGS
This Pileated Woodpecker readily visits feeders to supplement its natural diet.

FLIGHT: slow, deep wing beats, with occasional undulation when wings briefly folded.

OCCURRENCE
Breeds and lives year-round in northwestern North America and throughout the eastern half of the US, in deciduous and coniferous forest and woodlands; also found in swampy areas. In some areas, chooses young forests with dead trees but in other places, old-growth conifers.

| Length **16–18in (41–46cm)** | Wingspan **26–30in (66–76cm)** | Weight **10oz (275g)** |
| Social **Pairs** | Lifespan **Up to 9 years** | Status **Secure** |

DATE: _____ TIME: _____ LOCATION: _____

FALCONS

R ECENTLY SEPARATED FROM other diurnal birds of prey such as eagles and hawks, falcons and caracaras form a distinctive group of raptors. Caracaras are found in the New World but not in Canada, while falcons have a worldwide distribution, with a much larger number of species.

Falcons are known for their speed and agility in flight, but paradoxically spend long periods perched on a rock ledge or tree branch. The larger, bird-hunting species, such as the Peregrine Falcon, draw attention to their presence by creating panic among other birds when they fly over, ready to chase prey as large as ducks and pigeons. Falcons include birds that catch and eat insects on the wing, those that hover in one place searching for small prey below, and yet others that are more dramatic aerial hunters. Falcons in dramatic pursuits, or in high-speed "stoops" from above, seize birds up to their own size. Large species such as the Gyrfalcon may kill prey bigger than themselves. Falcons are distinguished from bird-eating hawks belonging to the genus *Accipiter* by their dark eyes. They also have a notch, or tooth, on the upper mandible, possibly to help them to dispatch and dismember their prey. Unlike the Accipiters, they do not build nests, but many falcons use abandoned nests of other birds and some lay eggs on a bare ledge or in an unlined cavity.

ARCTIC GIANT
The Arctic-bred Gyrfalcon is the largest of the falcons.

PRECISION LANDING
A Peregrine Falcon swoops down to settle on the branch, thrusting out its feet to absorb the shock of landing.

| Order **Falconiformes** | Family **Falconidae** | Species *Falco sparverius* |

American Kestrel

gray crown with reddish cap

rufous upperparts

dark barring or spots on blue-gray wings

light undertail with partial barring

small head

FEMALE   **MALE**

light undertail feathers

long wings

MALE

bold "mustache"

tan to cinnamon breast

spotted underparts

yellow to yellowish orange legs and toes

IN FLIGHT

dark, outer flight feathers

barred, rufous upperparts

heavy checks on belly

FEMALE

JUVENILE MALE

dark, barred, rufous tail

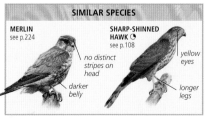

The smallest of the North American falcons, the American Kestrel features long pointed wings, a "tooth and notch" bill structure, and the dark brown eyes typical of falcons, though kestrels have shorter toes than other falcons. This may be due to the fact that kestrels often dive into long grass to capture insects and small mammals, which would be more difficult with long, thin toes. Male and female American Kestrels show differences in plumage, and also in size: females are slightly larger.
VOICE Common call a high-pitched *killy-killy-killy*.
NESTING Natural cavities, crevices, holes in dead trees, woodpeckers' holes, crevices in barns, manmade nest boxes, buildings; 4–5 eggs; 1 brood; April–June.
FEEDING Plunges for grasshoppers and crickets in spring and summer; small birds and mice in fall and winter; lizards and snakes.

FLIGHT: delicate and almost mothlike; may hover in one place for long, searching for prey.

HIGH FLIER
A male American Kestrel hovers over a field, its sharp eyes scanning the ground for insects and rodents.

SIMILAR SPECIES

MERLIN see p.224

no distinct stripes on head

darker belly

SHARP-SHINNED HAWK see p.108

yellow eyes

longer legs

OCCURRENCE
From near the northern tree line in Alaska and Canada south, east, and west throughout most of North America. Occurs also in Central and South America. Habitat ranges from semi-open tree groves to grasslands, cultivated and fallow farmland, and open desert.

| Length **9in (23cm)** | Wingspan **22in (56cm)** | Weight **3½–4oz (100–125g)** |
| Social **Family groups** | Lifespan **10–15 years** | Status **Secure** |

| Order **Falconiformes** | Family **Falconidae** | Species *Falco columbarius* |

Merlin

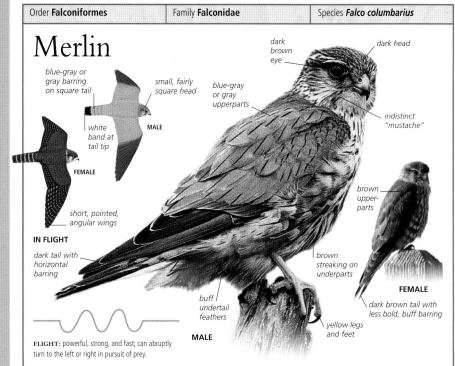

dark brown eye

dark head

blue-gray or gray barring on square tail

small, fairly square head

blue-gray or gray upperparts

indistinct "mustache"

MALE

white band at tail tip

FEMALE

brown upper-parts

short, pointed, angular wings

IN FLIGHT

dark tail with horizontal barring

brown streaking on underparts

FEMALE

dark brown tail with less bold, buff barring

buff undertail feathers

MALE

yellow legs and feet

FLIGHT: powerful, strong, and fast; can abruptly turn to the left or right in pursuit of prey.

Merlins are small, fast-flying falcons that were formerly known as "pigeon hawks," because their shape and flight are similar to those strong fliers. Merlins can overtake and capture a wide variety of prey, but mostly small birds. They can turn on a dime, and use their long, thin middle toes, typical of falcons, to pluck birds from the air after launching a direct attack. The smaller males are different in color. Both males and females show geographical color variations.

VOICE Male call a high-pitched *ki-ki-ki-ki*; female call a low-pitched *kek-ek-ek-ek-ek*.

NESTING Small scrapes on ground in open country, or abandoned nests of other species, such as crows, in forested areas and more recently in suburban green spaces; 4–6 eggs; 1 brood; April–June.

FEEDING Catches small birds in midair, and occasionally birds as large as doves; also feeds on small mammals, including bats.

ABOUT TO ROUSE
An adult female Merlin sits on a moss-covered rock, about to "rouse," or fluff out and shake her feathers.

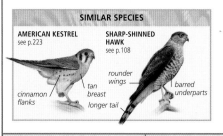

SIMILAR SPECIES

AMERICAN KESTREL
see p.223

SHARP-SHINNED HAWK
see p.108

rounder wings

tan breast

cinnamon flanks

barred underparts

longer tail

OCCURRENCE
Breeds from northern Alaska and the Pacific Northwest across Canada to Newfoundland. Winters mostly in western states down into Mexico. Merlins can be seen hunting along coastlines, over marshlands and open fields, and in desert areas.

| Length **10in (25cm)** | Wingspan **24in (61cm)** | Weight **5–7oz (150–200g)** |
| Social **Pairs/Family groups** | Lifespan **10–15 years** | Status **Secure** |

DATE: _____ TIME: _____ LOCATION: _____

Gyrfalcon

pointed tips

dark brown to black all over

almost completely white

JUVENILE (GRAY FORM)

darker wing linings

paler flight feathers

ADULT (DARK FORM)

yellow bill

ADULT (WHITE FORM)

IN FLIGHT

paler upperparts with brown barring

dark brown iris

yellow patch of skin near bill

gray, barred upperparts

heavily streaked head

blue bill with dark tip

yellow toes and legs

ADULT (GRAY FORM)

long, barred tail

lighter underparts with spots

ADULT (GRAY FORM)

Arctic-bred, the Gyrfalcon is used to harsh environments. It is the largest of all the falcons and one of the most majestic species of bird in the world. For centuries, the Gyrfalcon has been sought by both the nobility and falconers for its power, beauty, and gentle nature; it is also the official bird of the Northwest Territories. It uses its speed to pursue prey in a "tail chase," sometimes striking its quarry on the ground, but also in flight. Three forms are known, ranging from almost pure white to gray and blackish.

VOICE Loud, harsh *KYHa-KYHa-KYHa*.

NESTING Scrape on cliff, or old Common Ravens' nests; 2–7 eggs; 1 brood; April–July.

FEEDING Feeds mostly on large birds such as ptarmigan, pigeons, grouse; may also hunt mammals, such as Arctic hare.

FLIGHT: powerful and direct; continuous, rapid, stiff wing beats.

SNOWY PLUMAGE
A Gyrfalcon stands on an Arctic hillside. From a distance, it might be mistaken for a patch of snow.

SIMILAR SPECIES

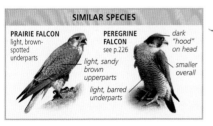

PRAIRIE FALCON
light, brown-spotted underparts

PEREGRINE FALCON
see p.226

light, sandy brown upperparts

light, barred underparts

dark "hood" on head

smaller overall

OCCURRENCE
Found in Arctic North America. Sometimes seen in northern regions of the US. A truly Arctic species found in the most barren regions of the tundra, high mountains and foothills of the tundra, and Arctic and sub-Arctic evergreen forests and woodlands. Not common outside its breeding range.

| Length **22in (56cm)** | Wingspan **4ft (1.2m)** | Weight **2¾–4lb (1.2–1.8kg)** |
| Social **Solitary/Pairs** | Lifespan **15–30 years** | Status **Localized** |

Order **Falconiformes**	Family **Falconidae**	Species *Falco peregrinus*

Peregrine Falcon

long, pointed wings

streaked brown underparts

ADULT

short tail

IN FLIGHT

JUVENILE

brown upperparts

dark "hood" on head

yellow eye-ring

bluish gray upperparts

dark spots on light buff breast

light yellow or bluish gray legs and toes

barred underwings

barred undertail feathers

prominent dark "mustache"

light underparts with horizontal barring

ADULT

ADULT

yellow toes and legs

FLIGHT: powerful and direct; faster, deeper wing beats during pursuit; also soars.

Peregrine Falcons are distributed worldwide and are long-distance travelers—"Peregrine" means "wanderer." It has been shown to dive from great heights at speeds of up to 200mph (320kmph)—a technique known as "stooping." Like all true falcons, this species has a pointed "tooth" on its upper beak and a "notch" on the lower one, and it instinctively bites the neck of captured prey to kill it. From the 1950s–1980s, its breeding ability was reduced by the insecticide DDT, which resulted in thin eggshells that could easily be crushed by the parent. Peregrines were then bred in captivity, and later released into the wild. Their status is now secure.

VOICE Sharp *hek-hek-hek* when alarmed.

NESTING Shallow scrape on cliff or building (nest sites are used year after year); 2–5 eggs; 1 brood; March–June.

FEEDING Dives on prey—birds of various sizes in flight; now feeds on pigeons in cities and migratory birds.

PARENTAL CARE
An adult Peregrine gently feeds a hatchling bits of meat; the remaining egg is likely to hatch soon.

SIMILAR SPECIES

GYRFALCON see p.225

less defined "hood"

larger and stockier

longer tail

PRAIRIE FALCON

lighter head color

light sandy brown upperparts

OCCURRENCE
A variety of habitats across northern North America, ranging from open valleys to cities with tall buildings. Peregrines prefer to inhabit cliffs along sea coasts, in addition to inland mountain ranges, but also occur in open country such as scrubland and salt marshes.

Length **16in (41cm)**	Wingspan **3¼–3½ft (1–1.1m)**	Weight **22–35oz (620–1000g)**
Social **Solitary/Pairs**	Lifespan **15–20 years**	Status **Secure**

DATE: _____ TIME: _____ LOCATION: _____

NEW WORLD FLYCATCHERS

BIRDS POPULARLY KNOWN AS "flycatchers" occur in many parts of the world, but several different families of songbird have this name. With the exception of some Old World species that may stray into Alaska, the North American species are all members of a single family—the Tyrant Flycatchers (Tyrannidae). With about 400 species, this is the largest bird family in the New World. The North American species are uniform in appearance with only a hint of the family's diversity found in Central and South America. Most are drab-colored, olive-green or gray birds, sometimes with yellow on the underparts, but an exception is the Scissor-tailed Flycatcher, seen on rare occasions in

Canada. The members of the genus *Empidonax* include some of the most difficult birds to identify in North America; they are best distinguished by their songs. Typical flycatcher feeding behavior is to sit on a branch or exposed perch sallying forth to catch flying insects. Tyrannid flycatchers are found across North America, except in Arctic regions. Many live in wooded habitats, though the kingbirds (genus *Tyrannus*) prefer woodland edges and deserts. Nearly all flycatchers are long-distance migrants and spend the winter in Central and South America.

KEEPING WATCH
This Alder Flycatcher is on the alert to spot a potential meal.

ERECT STANCE
A large-headed look and erect posture are typical of this Eastern Phoebe.

CATCHY TUNE
The Eastern Wood-pewee would be difficult to spot if not for its distinctive *pee-ah-wee* song.

| Order **Passeriformes** | Family **Tyrannidae** | Species **Contopus cooperi** |

Olive-sided Flycatcher

short tail

ADULT (SUMMER)

pointed wings

IN FLIGHT

large, dark head

lower base of bill often dull orange

brownish gray back

dull white throat

brownish olive flanks

white belly

ADULT (SUMMER)

FLIGHT: fast and direct, with deep, rapid wing beats; turns sharply to chase prey.

The Olive-sided Flycatcher is identified by its distinctive song, large size, and contrasting belly and flank colors, which make its underside appear like a vest with the buttons undone. Both members of a breeding pair are known to aggressively defend their territory. This flycatcher undertakes a long journey from northern parts of North America to winter in Panama and the Andes.

VOICE Call an evenly spaced *pip-pip-pip*; song a loud 3-note whistle: *quick-THREE-BEERS* or *whip-WEE-DEER*.

NESTING Open cup of twigs, rootlets, lichens; 2–5 eggs; 1 brood; May–August.

FEEDING Sits and waits for prey to fly past its perch before swooping after it; eats flying insects, such as bees, wasps, and flying ants.

BUILDING THE NEST
The female Olive-sided Flycatcher usually constructs the nest on her own.

EXPOSED PERCH
This species can often be found singing from an exposed twig emerging from the canopy.

OCCURRENCE
Breeds in mountainous, northern coniferous forests at edges or openings around ponds, bogs, meadows where standing dead trees occur. Also found in post-fire forests with abundant stumps. Winters in forest edges with tall trees and stumps.

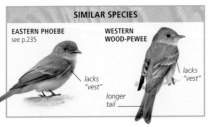

SIMILAR SPECIES

EASTERN PHOEBE
see p.235

lacks "vest"

WESTERN WOOD-PEWEE

lacks "vest"

longer tail

| Length **7–8in (18–20cm)** | Wingspan **13in (33cm)** | Weight **1¹⁄₁₆–1¹⁄₄oz (30–35g)** |
| Social **Solitary** | Lifespan **Up to 7 years** | Status **Declining** |

| Order **Passeriformes** | Family **Tyrannidae** | Species *Contopus virens* |

Eastern Wood-Pewee

slightly ragged crest

partial eye-ring

yellow lower mandible

pale gray

pale throat

pointed wings

ADULT

thin, white wing bars

yellowish wash on underparts

IN FLIGHT

thin, white edges to wing feathers

ADULT

FLIGHT: flies out from perch to catch flying insects; direct, steady wing beats.

The Eastern Wood-Pewee is found in many types of woodland in the eastern US and southern and eastern Canada. The male is slightly larger than the female, but their plumage is practically identical. Recent population declines in this species have been attributed to heavy browsing by White-tailed Deer. This has been compounded by the Eastern Wood-Pewee's susceptibility to brood parasitism by Brown-headed Cowbirds.

VOICE Call terse *chip*; song slurred *pee-ah-wee*, plaintive *wee-ooo*, or *wee-ur*, and slurred *ah di dee*.

NESTING Shallow cup of grass, lichens on horizontal limb; 2–4 eggs; 1 brood; May–September.

FEEDING Consumes mainly flying insects, such as flies, beetles, and bees; occasionally forages for insects on foliage on the ground.

SEARCHING FOR PREY
Holding its tail perfectly still, this Wood-Pewee is perched upright, scanning for prey.

COLORATION
The Eastern Wood-Pewee has yellowish underparts and a yellow lower mandible.

OCCURRENCE
Widely distributed in eastern US and adjacent Canadian provinces. Breeds in deciduous and coniferous forests, often near clearings or edges; uses waterside areas in Midwest, less so in the East. Late-arriving migrant. Winters in shrubby, second-growth forests of South America.

SIMILAR SPECIES

WESTERN WOOD-PEWEE
range barely overlaps

dark gray back

WILLOW FLYCATCHER
tendency to wag tail; see p.233

stronger eye-ring

smaller size

lighter breast and head

| Length **6in (15cm)** | Wingspan **9–10in (23–26cm)** | Weight **⅜–¹¹⁄₁₆oz (10–19g)** |
| Social **Solitary** | Lifespan **Up to 7 years** | Status **Secure** |

DATE: _____ TIME: _____ LOCATION: _____

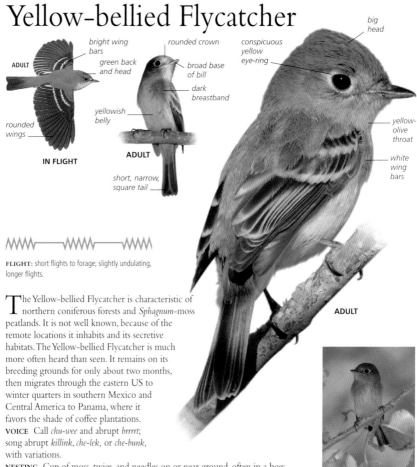

| Order **Passeriformes** | Family **Tyrannidae** | Species *Empidonax flaviventris* |

Yellow-bellied Flycatcher

ADULT

bright wing bars

green back and head

rounded crown

broad base of bill

dark breastband

conspicuous yellow eye-ring

big head

yellowish belly

rounded wings

IN FLIGHT

ADULT

short, narrow, square tail

yellow-olive throat

white wing bars

ADULT

FLIGHT: short flights to forage; slightly undulating, longer flights.

The Yellow-bellied Flycatcher is characteristic of northern coniferous forests and *Sphagnum*-moss peatlands. It is not well known, because of the remote locations it inhabits and its secretive habitats. The Yellow-bellied Flycatcher is much more often heard than seen. It remains on its breeding grounds for only about two months, then migrates through the eastern US to winter quarters in southern Mexico and Central America to Panama, where it favors the shade of coffee plantations.

VOICE Call *chu-wee* and abrupt *brrrrt*; song abrupt *killink*, *che-lek*, or *che-bunk*, with variations.

NESTING Cup of moss, twigs, and needles on or near ground, often in a bog; 3–5 eggs; 1 brood; June–July.

FEEDING Catches insects in the air or gleans mosquitoes, midges, and flies from foliage; sometimes eats berries and seeds.

ANISODACTYL FOOT
Note the bird's foot arrangement—three toes point forward and one backward.

OCCURRENCE
Breeds from Alaska to Quebec, Newfoundland, and the northeast US (New England) in boreal forests and bogs dominated by spruce trees. Winters in Mexico and Central America to Panama, in lowland forests, second-growth, and riverside habitats.

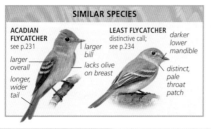

SIMILAR SPECIES

ACADIAN FLYCATCHER
see p.231

larger bill

larger overall

longer, wider tail

LEAST FLYCATCHER
distinctive call; see p.234

lacks olive on breast

darker lower mandible

distinct, pale throat patch

| Length **5½in (14cm)** | Wingspan **8in (20cm)** | Weight **9⁄32–½oz (8–15g)** |
| Social **Solitary** | Lifespan **At least 4 years** | Status **Secure** |

DATE: _____ TIME:_____ LOCATION:_____

| Order **Passeriformes** | Family **Tyrannidae** | Species *Empidonax virescens* |

Acadian Flycatcher

ADULT

IN FLIGHT

prominent wing bars

slight crest

narrow, eye-ring

greenish nape and back

broad bill with yellowish lower mandible

two wing bars

white-edged flight feathers

pale belly

yellowish wash on lower belly

broad tail

ADULT

Its often-drooped wings and minimal wing and tail flicking give the Acadian Flycatcher an outwardly calm appearance compared to other flycatchers. It bathes by diving into water, then preens on a perch. It suffers more parasitism from Brown-headed Cowbirds in small woodlots than in large forests. Where cowbirds lay their eggs in the flycatcher's nest, they displace the flycatcher's young.

FLIGHT: direct, fast with quick wing beats; short flights to and from perches; hovers while foraging.

VOICE Contact call soft *peet*, one of many calls; territorial song *tee-chup*, *peet-sah* or *flee-sick*, loud and "explosive" sounding.

NESTING Shallow, open cup in tree fork or shrub near water; 3 eggs; 2 broods; May–August.

FEEDING Takes insects from undersides of leaves, also catches them in the air and occasionally on the ground; eats berries.

SIMILAR SPECIES

WILLOW FLYCATCHER flicks tail; see p.233

lacks distinct eye-ring

LEAST FLYCATCHER smaller overall; see p.234

smaller bill

more gray overall

TOP PERFORMER This flycatcher is seen typically perched on a treetop from where it sings forcefully.

OCCURRENCE
Breeds in eastern US and southern Ontario in mature deciduous forests associated with water; prefers large undisturbed tracts. Winters in Nicaragua, Costa Rica, and Panama, and in South America along the Andes from Venezuela and Colombia to Ecuador, in tropical forests and woodlands with evergreen trees.

| Length **6in (15cm)** | Wingspan **9in (23cm)** | Weight **⅜–½oz (11–14g)** |
| Social **Solitary** | Lifespan **Up to 10 years** | Status **Secure** |

DATE: _____ TIME: _____ LOCATION: _____

| Order **Passeriformes** | Family **Tyrannidae** | Species **Empidonax alnorum** |

Alder Flycatcher

white eye-ring

brownish olive head

dark upper mandible

paler lower mandible

whitish throat and breast

brownish olive upperparts

ADULT

dark legs and toes

ADULT

two white wing bars

rounded wings

IN FLIGHT

FLIGHT: short bursts, with twists and turns; weak over long distances.

long, dark tail

Until 1973 the Alder Flycatcher and the Willow Flycatcher were considered to be one species called Traill's Flycatcher. The two species cannot be reliably identified by sight, but they do have distinctive songs. The Alder Flycatcher also breeds farther north than the Willow Flycatcher, arriving late in spring and leaving early in fall. Its nests are extremely hard to locate, and much remains to be learned about this bird's breeding habits.

VOICE Calls include flat *pit* or *pip-peep-tip*, also *wee-oo* and *churr*; male sings characteristic *fee-bee-o* song while breeding, and occasionally during spring migration.

NESTING Coarse and loosely structured nest low in fork of deciduous shrub; 3–4 eggs; 1 brood; June–July.

FEEDING Mostly eats insects, caught mainly in flight, but some gleaned from foliage; eats fruit in winter.

ON THE ALERT
Attentive to potential meals, an Alder Flycatcher will swiftly pursue prey as soon as it flies by.

SIMILAR SPECIES

ACADIAN FLYCATCHER see p.231
greener back
longer, deeper bill

WILLOW FLYCATCHER see p.233
fainter eye-ring
slightly longer bill

OCCURRENCE
Breeds at low density across northern North America, in wet shrubby habitats with alder or willow thickets, often close to streams. Winters at low elevations in South America in tropical second-growth forest and forest edges.

| Length 5¾in (14.5cm) | Wingspan 8½in (22cm) | Weight ½oz (14g) |
| Social **Solitary** | Lifespan **At least 3 years** | Status **Secure** |

DATE: _____ TIME:_____ LOCATION:_____

| Order **Passeriformes** | Family **Tyrannidae** | Species *Empidonax traillii* |

Willow Flycatcher

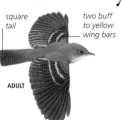

ADULT

IN FLIGHT

square tail

two buff to yellow wing bars

thin eye-ring

brown eye

dark upper mandible

paler lower mandible

grayish green upperparts

yellow-tinged flanks

whitish belly

ADULT

dark legs and toes

dark tail

FLIGHT: weak and fluttering; swoops and hovers when pursuing insects.

The Willow Flycatcher is only distinguished from the nearly identical Alder Flycatcher by its song. It is a strongly territorial bird, spreading its tail and flicking it upward during aggressive encounters. The Willow Flycatcher is, however, a frequent victim of brood parasitism by the Brown-headed Cowbird, which lays its eggs in the flycatcher's nest and removes the eggs that were already inside. Compounded by loss of suitable breeding habitat, this may be a major reason for the Willow Flycatcher's decline, especially in the case of the southwestern subspecies, *E. t. extimus*, which is now considered endangered.

VOICE Calls include soft, dry *whit* and several buzzy notes; song sharp *fitz-bew* with accent on the first syllable; also *creet*.

NESTING Rather loose and untidy cup in base of shrub near water; 3–4 eggs; 1 brood; May–August.

FEEDING Eats insects, mostly caught in flight; eats fruit in winter.

UNEVEN WORKLOAD
Although both parents feed their young, the female Willow Flycatcher does so the most.

SIMILAR SPECIES

ALDER FLYCATCHER different song; see p.232

bolder wing bars

LEAST FLYCATCHER see p.234

larger head

bold white eye-ring

OCCURRENCE
Breeds from southern Canada to eastern and southwestern US, mainly in willow thickets and other moist shrubby areas along watercourses. On winter grounds, it favors lighter woodland, shrubby clearings, and brush near water in coastal areas.

| Length **5–6¾in (13–17cm)** | Wingspan **7½–9½in (19–24cm)** | Weight **⅜–⁹⁄₁₆oz (11–16g)** |
| Social **Solitary** | Lifespan **Up to 11 years** | Status **Declining** |

Order **Passeriformes**	Family **Tyrannidae**	Species *Empidonax minimus*

Least Flycatcher

short, narrow tail

large head

ADULT

two wing bars

IN FLIGHT

short, broad-based bill

pale throat

buffy wing bars

JUVENILE

marked, white eye-ring

greenish brown back

short wings

ADULT

pale yellow belly

FLIGHT: direct, short forays with rapid wing beats to catch prey; sometimes hovers briefly.

The smallest eastern member of the *Empidonax* genus is a solitary bird and is very aggressive towards intruders encroaching upon its breeding territory. This combative behavior reduces the likelihood of acting as unwitting host parents to eggs laid by the Brown-headed Cowbird. The Least Flycatcher is very active, and frequently flicks its wings and tail upward. Common in the eastern US and across Canada in mixed and deciduous woodland, especially at the edges, it spends a short time—up to only two months—on its northern breeding grounds before migrating south. Adults molt in winter, while young molt before and during fall migration.

VOICE Call soft, short *whit*; song frequent, persistent, characteristic *tchebeck*, sings during spring migration and breeding season.

NESTING Compact cup of tightly woven bark strips and plant fibers in fork of deciduous tree; 3–5 eggs; 1 brood; May–July.

FEEDING Feeds principally on insects, such as flies, midges, beetles, ants, butterflies, and larvae; occasionally eats berries and seeds.

YELLOW TINGE
The subtle yellow tinge to its underparts and white undertail feathers are evident here.

OCCURRENCE
Breeds in coniferous and mixed deciduous forests across North America, east of Rockies to East Coast; occasionally in conifer groves or wooded wetlands, often near openings or edges. Winters in Central America in varied habitat from second-growth evergreen woodland to arid scrub.

SIMILAR SPECIES

WILLOW FLYCATCHER
see p.233

larger body

longer bill

ALDER FLYCATCHER
see p.232

larger overall

wider tail

Length **5¼ in (13.5cm)**	Wingspan **7¾ in (19.5cm)**	Weight **⁹⁄₃₂–⁷⁄₁₆ oz (8–13g)**
Social **Solitary**	Lifespan **Up to 6 years**	Status **Secure**

DATE: _____ TIME: _____ LOCATION: _____

| Order **Passeriformes** | Family **Tyrannidae** | Species *Sayornis phoebe* |

Eastern Phoebe

rounded wings with two faint wing bars

ADULT

white throat

IN FLIGHT

ADULT (FALL)

yellowish tint on lower belly

round, dark-capped head

dark eye

olive tint to sides and breast

long, dark tail

ADULT (BREEDING)

The Eastern Phoebe is an early spring migrant that tends to nest under bridges, culverts, and on buildings, in addition to rocky outcroppings. Not shy, it is also familiar because of its *fee-bee* vocalization and constant tail wagging. By tying a thread on the leg of several Eastern Phoebes, ornithologist John James Audubon established that individuals return from the south to a previously used nest site. Although difficult to tell apart, males tend to be slightly larger and darker than females.

VOICE Common call a clear, weak *chip*; song an emphatic *fee-bee* or *fee-b-be-bee*.

NESTING Open cup of mud, moss, and leaves, almost exclusively on manmade structures; 3–5 eggs; 2 broods; April–July.

FEEDING Feeds mainly on flying insects; also consumes small fruits from fall through winter.

FLIGHT: direct, with steady wing beats; hovers occasionally; approaches nest with a low swoop.

PALE EDGES
Perched on a twig, a male shows off the pale margins of his wing feathers.

LIGHTER FEMALE
They are difficult to distinguish, but the female is slightly lighter overall than the male.

OCCURRENCE
Found in open woodland and along deciduous or mixed forest edges, in gardens and parks, near water. Breeds across Canada from the Northwest Territories south of the tundra belt and in the eastern half of the US. Winters in the southeast US and Mexico.

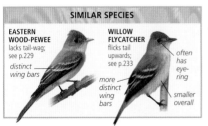

SIMILAR SPECIES

EASTERN WOOD-PEWEE
lacks tail-wag; see p.229

distinct wing bars

WILLOW FLYCATCHER
flicks tail upwards; see p.233

often has eye-ring

more distinct wing bars

smaller overall

| Length 5½–7in (14–17cm) | Wingspan 10½in (27cm) | Weight ¹¹/₁₆oz (20g) |
| Social **Solitary** | Lifespan **Up to 9 years** | Status **Secure** |

DATE: _____ TIME: _____ LOCATION: _____

| Order **Passeriformes** | Family **Tyrannidae** | Species *Myiarchus crinitus* |

Great Crested Flycatcher

ADULT

rusty edges to outer wing feathers

whitish wing bars

IN FLIGHT

brown crest

olive-brown back

long, thin bill

gray breast and face

ADULT

yellow belly

brownish legs and feet

The Great Crested Flycatcher is locally common and geographically quite widespread from Alberta and the Maritimes to Florida and Texas, but is often overlooked because it remains in the forest canopy,

long tail

FLIGHT: fast and direct; can glide between perches; will also hover.

though it visits the ground for food and nest material. Its presence is usually given away by its loud, sharp, double-syllabled notes. It lines its nest with shed snakeskins like other *Myiarchus* flycatchers.

VOICE Principal call a loud, abrupt *purr-it* given by both sexes; male song repeated *whee-eep*, occasionally *wheeyer*.

NESTING In deep cavity, usually woodpecker hole, lined with leaves, bark, trash, and snakeskins; 4–6 eggs; 1 brood; May–July.

FEEDING Picks flying insects, moths, and caterpillars mainly from leaves and branches in the canopy; also small berries and fruit.

TRICOLORED SPECIES
Viewed from the front, the eastern Great Crested Flycatcher is tricolored.

OCCURRENCE
Widespread in eastern North America, from Alberta to the Maritimes in Canada, and, in the US, south to Texas and Florida. Migrates to Mexico, Central America, and northern South America. Breeds in deciduous and mixed woodlands with clearings.

SIMILAR SPECIES

ASH-THROATED FLYCATCHER
silvery white throat
paler yellow belly

BROWN-CRESTED FLYCATCHER
more rufous wings
heavier bill
paler yellow belly

| Length **7–8in (18–20cm)** | Wingspan **13in (33cm)** | Weight **⅞–1⁷⁄₁₆oz (25–40g)** |
| Social **Solitary** | Lifespan **Up to 13 years** | Status **Secure** |

DATE: _____ TIME: _____ LOCATION: _____

| Order **Passeriformes** | Family **Tyrannidae** | Species *Tyrannus verticalis* |

Western Kingbird

olive-gray back

strong, dark eye-line

small bill

white chin

ADULT

white-edged tail

dark wing with no wing bars

IN FLIGHT

gray head

gray chest

gray back

yellow belly

white edge to outer tail feathers

ADULT

notched tail

ADULT

A conspicuous summer breeder in the US and lower parts of the western provinces, the Western Kingbird occurs in open habitats in much of western North America. The white outer edges on its outer tail feathers distinguish it from other kingbirds. Its population has expanded eastward over the last 100 years. A large, loosely defined territory is defended against other kingbirds when breeding begins in spring; a smaller core area is defended as the season progresses.

VOICE Calls include *whit*, *pwee-t*, and chatter; song, regularly repeated sharp *kip* notes and high-pitched notes.

NESTING Open, bulky cup of grass, rootlets, and twigs in tree, shrub, utility pole; 2–7 eggs; 1 brood; April–July.

FEEDING Feeds on insects and fruit.

FLIGHT: agile, fast, direct, flapping flight; flies to catch insects; hovers to pick bugs on vegetation.

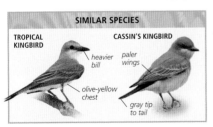

FENCE POST
A favorite place for the Western Kingbird to perch, and look around, is on fenceposts.

QUENCHING THIRST
A juvenile Western Kingbird drinks at the edge of a shallow pool of water.

SIMILAR SPECIES

TROPICAL KINGBIRD

CASSIN'S KINGBIRD

heavier bill

paler wings

olive-yellow chest

gray tip to tail

OCCURRENCE
Widespread in southwestern Canada and the western US, in open habitats such as grasslands, savannah, desert shrub, pastures, and cropland, near elevated perches; particularly near water. Winters in similar habitats and in tropical forest and shrubbery from Mexico to Costa Rica.

| Length **8–9in (20–23cm)** | Wingspan **15–16in (38–41cm)** | Weight **1¼–1⁹⁄₁₆oz (35–45g)** |
| Social **Solitary** | Lifespan **Up to 6 years** | Status **Secure** |

| Order **Passeriformes** | Family **Tyrannidae** | Species *Tyrannus tyrannus* |

Eastern Kingbird

ADULT

IN FLIGHT

white-tipped tail

white throat

pale edges to wing feathers

dark crown and cheeks, almost black

dark eyes

faint gray "necklace"

white throat and underparts

relatively short, thick bill

slate-gray back

ADULT

white belly

black legs and toes

white undertail feathers

black tail with white tip

ADULT

The Eastern Kingbird is a tame and widely distributed bird. It is a highly territorial species and is known for its aggressive behavior toward potential predators, particularly crows and hawks, which it pursues relentlessly. It is able to identify and remove the eggs of the Brown-headed Cowbird when they are laid in its nest. The Eastern Kingbird is generally monogamous and pairs will return to the same territory in subsequent years. This species winters in tropical South America, where it forages for fruit in the treetops of evergreen forests.

VOICE Principal call is loud, metallic *chatter-zeer*; song rapid, electric *kdik-kdik-kdik-pika-pika-pika-kzeeeer*.

NESTING Open cup of twigs, roots, stems in hawthorn, elm, stump, fence, or post; 2–5 eggs; 1 brood; May–August.

FEEDING Catches flying insects from elevated perch or gleans insects from foliage; eats berries and fruit, except in spring.

FLIGHT: strong, direct, and very agile with vigorous, rapid wing beats; hovers and sails.

WHITE-TIPPED
The white-tipped tails of these two Eastern Kingbirds are conspicuous as they sit on a budding twig.

SIMILAR SPECIES

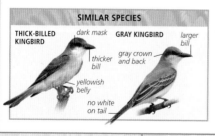

THICK-BILLED KINGBIRD
dark mask
thicker bill
yellowish belly

GRAY KINGBIRD
larger bill
gray crown and back
no white on tail

OCCURRENCE
Breeds across much of North America in a variety of open habitats, including urban areas, parks, golf courses, fields with scattered shrubs, beaver ponds, and along forest edges. Long-distance migrant; winters in South America, south to Argentina.

| Length **7–9in (18–23cm)** | Wingspan **13–15in (33–38cm)** | Weight **1¹⁄₁₆–2oz (30–55g)** |
| Social **Solitary/Pairs** | Lifespan **Up to 7 years** | Status **Secure** |

DATE: _____ TIME: _____ LOCATION: _____

Family **Vireonidae**

VIREOS

Vireos are a family of songbirds restricted to the New World, with 15 species occurring in Canada and the United States. The classification of vireos has long been problematic—traditionally they were associated with warblers, but recent molecular studies suggest that they are actually related to crow-like birds. Vireo plumage is drab, often predominantly greenish or grayish above and whitish below, augmented by eye-rings, "spectacles," eyestripes, and wingbars. Most vireos have a preference for broad-leaved habitats, where they move about deliberately, hopping and climbing as they slowly forage for their prey. Because they are mainly insect-eaters, most are mid- to long-distance migrants, retreating to warmer climes in winter, when insects are dormant. Vireos are most often detected by the male's loud and clear territorial song, which is repetitive and persistent.

SEPARATE SPECIES
The Blue-headed Vireo is one of three species, formerly known as just one species, the Solitary Vireo.

KEEN SONGSTER
The White-eyed Vireo sings almost continuously, even on the hottest days of summer.

Family **Corvidae**

JAYS, CROWS, RAVENS, AND MAGPIES

Although jays and crows belong to a highly diverse family, the corvids, most members share some important characteristics. They are remarkably social, some species even breed cooperatively, but at the same time they can be quiet and stealthy. Always the opportunists, corvids use strong bills and toes to obtain a varied, omnivorous diet. Ornithologists have shown that ravens, magpies, jays, and crows are among the most intelligent birds. They exhibit self-awareness when looking into mirrors, can make tools, and successfully tackle difficult counting and problem-solving. As a rule, most corvid plumage comes in shades of blue, black, and/or white. The plumage of adult corvids does not vary by season. Corvidae are part of an ancient bird lineage (Corvoidea) that originated in Australasia. Crows and jays were among the birds most affected by the spread of West Nile virus in the early 2000s, but most populations seem to have recovered quickly.

BRAINY BIRD
Common Ravens are one of the smartest birds, known for their problem-solving skills.

| Order **Passeriformes** | Family **Laniidae** | Species *Lanius ludovicianus* |

Loggerhead Shrike

ADULT

white flash in wings

white edges to tail

IN FLIGHT

black wings

pale undertail feathers

JUVENILE

gray crown

hooked bill

black "mask"

unstreaked, gray underparts

ADULT

rounded tail

FLIGHT: fast with rapid wing beats, sometimes interspersed with glides; swoops from perches.

Although a songbird, the Loggerhead Shrike is superficially raptor-like in several ways, particularly its prominent black face mask and powerful, hooked bill. It sits atop posts or tall trees, swooping down to catch prey on the ground. It has the unusual habit of then impaling its prey on thorns, barbed wire, or sharp twigs, which is thought to be the reason for the nickname "butcher bird." Unfortunately, the Loggerhead Shrike is declining, possibly because of human alteration of its habitat and/or food resources.

VOICE Quiet warbles, trills, and harsh notes; song harsh notes singly or in series: *chaa chaa chaa.*

NESTING Open cup of vegetation, placed in thorny tree; 5 eggs; 1 brood; March–June.

FEEDING Kills large insects and small vertebrates—rodents, birds, reptiles—with its powerful bill.

GEARED FOR HUNTING
The Loggerhead Shrike perches upright on tall shrubs or small trees, where it scans for prey.

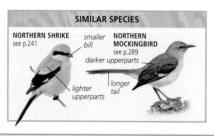

SIMILAR SPECIES

NORTHERN SHRIKE see p.241

smaller bill

NORTHERN MOCKINGBIRD see p.289

darker upperparts

lighter upperparts

longer tail

OCCURRENCE
Found in semi-open country with scattered perches, but its distribution is erratic, occurring in relatively high densities in certain areas, absent from seemingly suitable habitat. Occurs in congested residential areas in some regions (south Florida), but generally favors fairly remote habitats.

| Length **9in (23cm)** | Wingspan **12in (31cm)** | Weight **1¼–2⅛oz (35–60g)** |
| Social **Solitary** | Lifespan **Unknown** | Status **Endangered** |

DATE: _____ TIME:_____ LOCATION:_____

Order **Passeriformes** | Family **Laniidae** | Species *Lanius borealis*

Northern Shrike

large head

narrow black mask

pale gray upperparts

conspicuous white wing bar

ADULT

pale gray upperparts

IN FLIGHT

strongly hooked bill

delicately barred breast

brownish underparts

IMMATURE

long tail

black wings

ADULT

gray-white underparts

black tail, with white outer tail feathers

FLIGHT: short flights between hunting perches; pounces on prey.

This northern version of the familiar Loggerhead Shrike is an uncommon winter visitor to the northern US and southern Canada. In some winters, this species is widespread across the mid-latitudes of North America; in other winters it is nearly absent. The Northern Shrike is paler, larger bodied, and larger billed than the Loggerhead Shrike, which enables it to attack and subdue larger prey than the Loggerhead. Many Northern Shrike populations worldwide are in decline, but to date there is no sign of a similar decline in North America.

VOICE Variety of short warbles, trills, and harsh notes; generally silent on wintering grounds.

NESTING Open, bulky cup in low tree or large shrub, lined with feathers and hair; 4–6 eggs; 1 brood; May–June.

FEEDING Swoops down on prey, such as rodents, small birds, and insects, which it impales on thorns or pointed branches.

BLACK-AND-WHITE DISPLAY
The Northern Shrike flashes its distinctive black-and-white markings while in flight.

SIMILAR SPECIES

LOGGERHEAD SHRIKE
see p.240

shorter bill

darker, smaller overall

NORTHERN MOCKINGBIRD
see p.289

straight, white-edged tail

less black in wings

thin bill

OCCURRENCE
Breeds in sub-Arctic coniferous forests, across Canada and Alaska. Winters in more southerly open country with sufficient perches. Avoids built-up and residential districts, but spends much time perching on fence posts and roadside signs.

Length **10in (25cm)**	Wingspan **14in (35cm)**	Weight **1¾–2⅝oz (50–75g)**
Social **Solitary**	Lifespan **Unknown**	Status **Vulnerable**

DATE: _____ TIME: _____ LOCATION: _____

| Order **Passeriformes** | Family **Vireonidae** | Species **Vireo griseus** |

White-eyed Vireo

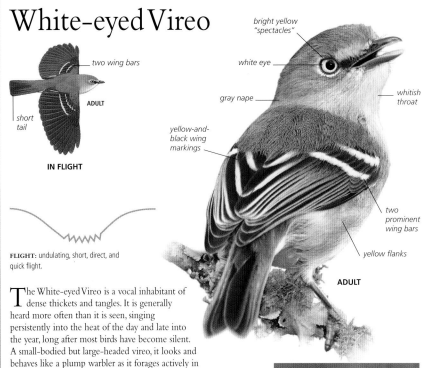

bright yellow "spectacles"

white eye

gray nape

whitish throat

yellow-and-black wing markings

two wing bars

ADULT

short tail

IN FLIGHT

two prominent wing bars

yellow flanks

ADULT

FLIGHT: undulating, short, direct, and quick flight.

The White-eyed Vireo is a vocal inhabitant of dense thickets and tangles. It is generally heard more often than it is seen, singing persistently into the heat of the day and late into the year, long after most birds have become silent. A small-bodied but large-headed vireo, it looks and behaves like a plump warbler as it forages actively in shrubbery. It is heavily parasitized by the Brown-headed Cowbird, and as many as half of the White-eyed Vireo's offsprings do not survive.

VOICE Call a raspy, angry scold; male's song a highly variable and complex repertoire of over a dozen distinct songs.

NESTING Deep cup in dense vegetation, outer layer composed of coarse material, lined with finer fibers, often near water, suspended from twigs by the rim; 3–5 eggs; 2 broods; March–July.

FEEDING Hops from branch to branch pursuing bees, flies, beetles, and bugs, plucking them from leaves or sallying out to snatch them in the air; feeds primarily on fruit in winter.

WHITE EYE, WHITE WING BARS
The White-eyed Vireo's distinctive markings ensure that it is highly conspicuous.

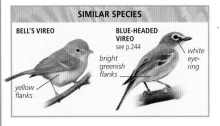

SIMILAR SPECIES

BELL'S VIREO

yellow flanks

BLUE-HEADED VIREO
see p.244

bright greenish flanks

white eye-ring

OCCURRENCE
A common breeder in dense brush and scrub across the eastern US and southern Ontario, from Texas to the Great Lakes region and southern New England. Retreats to southern states of the US, the Atlantic slope of Mexico, Cuba, and the Bahamas in winter.

| Length **5in (13cm)** | Wingspan **7½in (19cm)** | Weight **⅜oz (10g)** |
| Social **Solitary** | Lifespan **Up to 7 years** | Status **Secure** |

DATE: _____ TIME: _____ LOCATION: _____

Yellow-throated Vireo

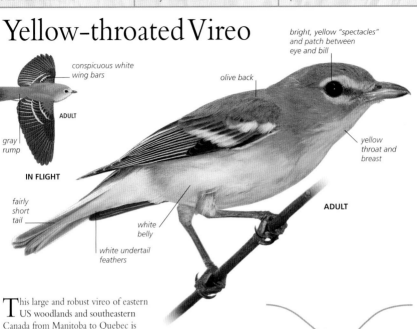

bright, yellow "spectacles" and patch between eye and bill

conspicuous white wing bars

olive back

ADULT

gray rump

IN FLIGHT

yellow throat and breast

fairly short tail

ADULT

white belly

white undertail feathers

This large and robust vireo of eastern US woodlands and southeastern Canada from Manitoba to Quebec is usually found foraging and singing high in the canopy. It is distinctly patterned, with a bright yellow throat, breast, and "spectacles," and a white belly and flanks. The fragmentation of forests, spraying of insecticides, and cowbird parasitism have led to regional declines in Yellow-throated Vireo populations, but the bird's range, as a whole, has actually expanded.

VOICE Scolding, hoarse, rapid calls; male song a slow, repetitive, two- or three-note phrase, separated by long pauses.

NESTING Rounded cup of plant and animal fibers bound with spider webs, usually located towards the top of a large tree and hung by the rim; 3–5 eggs; 1 brood; April–July.

FEEDING Forages high in trees, picking insects from the branches; also eats fruit when available.

FLIGHT: direct, but jerky, alternating rapid wing beats with brief pauses.

CANOPY SINGER
The Yellow-throated Vireo sings from the very tops of tall trees.

HIGH FORAGER
This bird finds much of its food in the peeling bark of mature trees.

OCCURRENCE
Breeds in extensive, mature deciduous, and mixed woodlands in the eastern half of the US, and extreme southern Canada. Winters mainly from southern Mexico to northern South America, primarily in wooded areas.

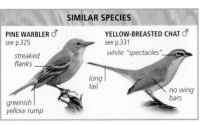

SIMILAR SPECIES

PINE WARBLER ♂
see p.325

streaked flanks

greenish yellow rump

YELLOW-BREASTED CHAT ♂
see p.331

white "spectacles"

long tail

no wing bars

Length **5½in (14cm)**	Wingspan **9½in (24cm)**	Weight **⅝oz (18g)**
Social **Solitary/Pairs**	Lifespan **Up to 6 years**	Status **Secure**

DATE: _____ TIME: _____ LOCATION: _____

Blue-headed Vireo

gray head

conspicuous white "spectacles"

looks "big-headed"

contrasting white throat

two wing bars

ADULT

greenish back

IN FLIGHT

ADULT

white belly

bright greenish flanks

relatively short tail

Closely related to the Cassin's Vireo and Plumbeous Vireo, the fairly common Blue-headed Vireo is the brightest and most colorful of the three. Its blue-gray, helmeted head, adorned with striking white "spectacles" around its dark eyes also helps to distinguish it from other vireos in its range. This stocky and slow-moving bird is heard more often than it is seen in its forest breeding habitat. However, during migration it can be more conspicuous, and it is the first vireo to return in spring.

VOICE Call a harsh, scolding chatter; male's song a series of rich, sweet, high phrases of two to six notes slurred together.

NESTING Shallow, rounded cup loosely constructed of animal and plant fibers, lined with finer material and suspended from twigs by the rim; 3–5 eggs; 2 broods; May–July.

FEEDING Gleans insects from branches and leaves, usually high in shrubs and trees; often makes short sallies after prey.

FLIGHT: slow, heavy, undulating flight with a series of deep wing beats followed by short pauses.

SPECTACLED VIREO
Its rather thick head with conspicuous "spectacles" and gray color are distinctive field marks.

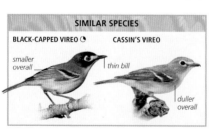

SIMILAR SPECIES

BLACK-CAPPED VIREO ☾

smaller overall

CASSIN'S VIREO

thin bill

duller overall

OCCURRENCE
Breeds in large tracts of undisturbed coniferous and mixed forests with a rich understory, largely across eastern North America. It winters in woodlands across the southeastern US from Virginia to Texas, as well as in Mexico and northern Central America to Costa Rica.

Length **5½in (14in)**	Wingspan **9½in (24cm)**	Weight **⁹⁄₁₆oz (16g)**
Social **Solitary/Pairs**	Lifespan **Up to 7 years**	Status **Secure**

DATE: _____ TIME: _____ LOCATION: _____

| Order **Passeriformes** | Family **Vireonidae** | Species **Vireo gilvus** |

Warbling Vireo

pale brownish crown contrasts with darker back

white eyebrow

grayish behind eye

grayish green upperparts

blackish bill

ADULT

ADULT (FALL)

IN FLIGHT

grayish overall

pale patch between eye and bill

yellowish flanks

ADULT

FLIGHT: fast and undulating; rapid wing beats followed by brief, closed-winged glides.

Widely distributed across North America, this rather drab vireo is better known for its cheerful warbling song than for its plumage, and coincidentally, its thin bill and longish tail give this rather active vireo a somewhat warbler-like appearance. The eastern subspecies (*V.g. gilvus*), which is heavier and has a larger bill, and the western subspecies (*V.g. swainsonii*) are quite different and may in fact be separate species. Of all the vireos, the Warbling Vireo is most likely to breed in human developments, such as city parks, suburbs, and orchards.

VOICE Harsh, raspy scold call; male's persistent song a high, rapid, and highly variable warble.

NESTING Rough cup placed high in a deciduous tree, hung from the rim between forked twigs; 3–5 eggs; 2 broods; March–July.

FEEDING Gleans a variety of insects, including grasshoppers, aphids, and beetles from leaves; eats fruit in winter.

PLAIN-LOOKING SONGSTER
The Warbling Vireo makes up for its plain appearance by its colorful voice, full of rounded notes and melodious warbles.

SIMILAR SPECIES

BELL'S VIREO

faint wing bar

longer tail

PHILADELPHIA VIREO
see p.246

no wing bar

dark line extends to bill

shorter bill

yellow on breast and throat

OCCURRENCE
Extensive distribution across most of temperate North America, from Alaska, around the northern limit of the northerly zone, and through western, central, and eastern North America. Breeds in deciduous and mixed forests, particularly near water. Winters in southern Mexico and Central America.

| Length **5½in (14cm)** | Wingspan **8½in (21cm)** | Weight **⁷/₁₆oz (12g)** |
| Social **Solitary/Pairs** | Lifespan **Up to 13 years** | Status **Secure** |

DATE: _____ TIME: _____ LOCATION: _____

Order **Passeriformes**	Family **Vireonidae**	Species *Vireo philadelphicus*

Philadelphia Vireo

gray cap

slightly hooked, black bill

ADULT

IN FLIGHT

white eyebrow

dark line through eye

greenish upperparts

yellow throat

yellowish underparts

ADULT

FLIGHT: fast, bouncy, undulating flight with strong wing beats.

Despite being widespread, the Philadelphia Vireo remains rather poorly studied. It shares its breeding habitat with the similar looking, but larger and more numerous, Red-eyed Vireo, and, interestingly, it modifies its behavior to avoid competition. It is the most northerly breeding vireo, with its southernmost breeding range barely reaching the US. Its scientific and English names derive from the fact that the bird was first discovered near Philadelphia in the mid-19th century.

VOICE Song a series of two- and four-note phrases, remarkably similar to the song of the Red-eyed Vireo.

NESTING Rounded cup of plant fibers bound by spider webs, hanging between forked twigs that narrows at the rim; 3–5 eggs; 1–2 broods; June–August.

FEEDING Gleans caterpillars, bees, flies, and bugs from leaves; usually forages high in trees, moving with short hops and flights.

DISTINGUISHED APPEARANCE
The Philadelphia Vireo's gentle expression and pudgy appearance help separate it from its neighbor, the Red-eyed Vireo.

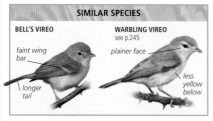

SIMILAR SPECIES

BELL'S VIREO

faint wing bar

longer tail

WARBLING VIREO
see p.245

plainer face

less yellow below

OCCURRENCE
Breeds in deciduous woodlands, mixed woodlands, and woodland edges, in a wide belt across Canada, reaching the Great Lakes and northern New England. The Philadelphia Vireo winters from Mexico to Panama and northern Colombia.

Length **5¼in (13.5cm)**	Wingspan **8in (20cm)**	Weight **⁷⁄₁₆oz (12g)**
Social **Solitary/Pairs**	Lifespan **Up to 8 years**	Status **Secure**

DATE: _____ TIME: _____ LOCATION: _____

| Order **Passeriformes** | Family **Vireonidae** | Species *Vireo olivaceus* |

Red-eyed Vireo

generally olive above

head held at downward angle

bird appears long and slender

ADULT

IN FLIGHT

gray crown

white eyestripe with black upper border

heavy eye-line

long bill

deep red eye

ADULT

whitish underparts

bluish legs and toes

Probably the most common songbird of northern and eastern North America, the Red-eyed Vireo is perhaps the quintessential North American vireo, although it is heard far more often than it is seen. It sings persistently and monotonously all day long and late into the season, long after other species have stopped singing. It generally stays high in the canopy of the deciduous and mixed woodlands where it breeds. The entire population migrates to central South America in winter. To reach their Amazonian winter habitats, Red-eyed Vireos migrate in fall (August–October) through Central America, Caribbean Islands, and northern South America to Educador, Peru, and Brazil.

VOICE Nasal mewing call; male song consists of slurred short, robin-like, three-note phrases.

NESTING Open cup nest hanging on horizontal fork of tree branch; built with plant fibers bound with spider's web; exterior is sometimes decorated with lichen; 3–5 eggs; 1 brood; May–July.

FEEDING Gleans insects from leaves, hopping methodically in the canopy and sub-canopy of deciduous trees; during fall and winter, primarily feeds on fruit.

FLIGHT: fast, strong, and undulating with the body angled upwards.

HOPPING BIRD
The Red-eyed Vireo's primary form of locomotion is hopping; at ground level and in trees.

OCCURRENCE
Breeds across North America from the Yukon and British Columbia east to the Canadian maritimes, southward from Washington to south central Texas, and west to Canada in central and northern states. Inhabits the canopy of deciduous forests and pine hardwood forests.

SIMILAR SPECIES

BLACK-WHISKERED VIREO

faint black "mustache"

duller green upperparts

BROWN EYES
Immature Red-eyed Vireos have brown eyes, but those of the adult birds are red.

| Length **6in (15cm)** | Wingspan **10in (25cm)** | Weight ⅝oz (17g) |
| Social **Solitary/Pairs** | Lifespan **Up to 10 years** | Status **Secure** |

DATE: _____ TIME: _____ LOCATION: _____

| Order **Passeriformes** | Family **Corvidae** | Species *Perisoreus canadensis* |

Canada Jay

ADULT

brownish back
with white
streaks

P. c. obscurus
(NORTHWESTERN)

dark crown

white
forehead

white collar

short
bill

dark gray
upperparts

long,
tail
with
white
corners

IN FLIGHT

gray overall,
darker
upperparts

whitish
"mustache"

uniform medium
to dark gray

JUVENILE

dark, smoky gray
tail and wings

P. c. canadensis
(NORTHERN)

black legs
and toes

Fearless and cunning, the Canada Jay's inquisitive behavior and skill at stealing food have earned it the colloquial name of "Camp Robber." Its habit of storing food for later use by sticking it to trees with its viscous saliva is thought to be one of the reasons that enable this non-migratory bird to survive the long northern winters. Canada Jays can often collect in noisy groups of three to six birds in order to investigate intruders encroaching upon their territory. This species has been known by several different names over the years, including Whiskey Jack and Gray Jay, but a recent decision has restored the original name of Canada Jay.
VOICE Mostly silent, but also produces variety of odd clucks and screeches; sometimes Blue Jay-like *jay!* and eerie warning whistles, including bisyllabic *whee-oo* or *ew*.
NESTING Bulky platform of sticks with cocoons on south side of coniferous tree; 2–5 eggs; 1 brood; February–May.
FEEDING Forages for insects and berries; also raids birds' nests.

FLIGHT: hollow-sounding wing beats followed by slow, seemingly awkward, rocking glides.

BUILT FOR COLD
The Canada Jay's short extremities and dense, fluffy plumage are perfect for long, harsh winters.

OCCURRENCE
Northerly forests, especially lichen-festooned areas with firs and spruces. Found in coniferous forests across northern North America from Alaska to Newfoundland, the Maritimes, and north New York and New England; south to the western mountains.

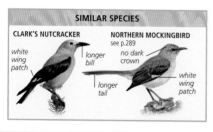

SIMILAR SPECIES

CLARK'S NUTCRACKER

white
wing
patch

longer
bill

longer
tail

NORTHERN MOCKINGBIRD
see p.289

no dark
crown

white
wing
patch

| Length **10–11½in (25–29cm)** | Wingspan **18in (46cm)** | Weight **2⅛–2⅞oz (60–80g)** |
| Social **Family groups** | Lifespan **Up to 10 years** | Status **Secure** |

DATE: _____ TIME:_____ LOCATION:_____

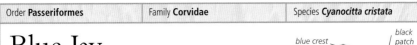

| Order **Passeriformes** | Family **Corvidae** | Species **Cyanocitta cristata** |

Blue Jay

long tail with white corners

white streak in blue wings

ADULT

white trailing edge feathers

blue wings and tail

IN FLIGHT

black bars on tail

blue crest

black collar

plain blue mantle

black patch between eye and bill

long, black bill

whitish throat

ADULT

grayish underparts

black legs and feet

The Blue Jay is common in rural and suburban backyards across Canada and the eastern US. Beautiful as it is, the Blue Jay has a darker side. It often raids the nests of smaller birds for eggs and nestlings. Although usually thought of as a nonmigratory species, some Blue Jays undergo impressive migrations, with loose flocks sometimes numbering in the hundreds visible overhead in spring and fall. The Blue Jay is the provincial bird of Prince Edward Island.

VOICE Harsh, screaming *jay! jay!;* other common call an odd ethereal, chortling *queedle-ee-dee;* soft clucks when feeding.

NESTING Cup of strong twigs at variable height in trees or shrubs; 3–6 eggs; 1 brood; March–July.

FEEDING Eats insects, acorns, small vertebrates, such as lizards, rodents, bird eggs, birds, tree frogs; fruit and seeds.

FLIGHT: bursts of flapping followed by long glides on flat wings.

UNIQUE FEATURES
The Blue Jay is unique among American jays, in having white patches on its wings and tail.

VERSATILE BIRD
Blue Jays are true omnivores, eating almost anything they can find. They are also excellent imitators of other bird calls.

OCCURRENCE
Native to eastern deciduous, coniferous, and mixed woodlands, but also at home in suburban vegetation; found extensively in backyards; the Blue Jay is especially fond of oak trees and their acorns.

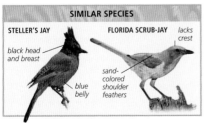

SIMILAR SPECIES

STELLER'S JAY

black head and breast

blue belly

FLORIDA SCRUB-JAY

lacks crest

sand-colored shoulder feathers

| Length **9½–12in (24–30cm)** | Wingspan **16in (41cm)** | Weight **2¼–3½oz (65–100g)** |
| Social **Small flocks** | Lifespan **Up to 7 years** | Status **Secure** |

DATE: _____ TIME:_____ LOCATION:_____

| Order **Passeriformes** | Family **Corvidae** | Species *Pica hudsonia* |

Black-billed Magpie

ADULT

large, white patches on outer wings

white shoulder feathers

IN FLIGHT

blue-green iridescence to wings and tail

black back and head

thick, black bill

black breast

ADULT

white belly

long, dark tail

L oud, flashy, and conspicuous, the Black-billed Magpie is abundant in the northwestern quarter of the continent, from Alaska to the interior of the US. It has adapted to suburbia, confidently strutting across front lawns in some places. Until recently, it was considered the same species as the Eurasian Magpie (*P. pica*), and even though they look nearly identical, scientific evidence points instead to a close relationship with the other North American magpie, the Yellow-billed Magpie. Its long tail enables it to make rapid changes in direction in flight. The male will also use his tail to perform a variety of displays while courting a female. Black-billed Magpies are rarely found in large flocks, but they form them sometimes in fall.

VOICE Common call a questioning, nasal *ehnk*; also raspy *shenk, shenk, shenk*, usually in series.

NESTING Large, domed, often made of thorny sticks; 5–8 eggs; 1 brood; March–June.

FEEDING Omnivorous; forages on ground, mainly for insects, worms, seeds and carrion; even picks ticks from mammals.

FLIGHT: direct, with slow, steady, and often shallow wing beats; occasional shallow glides.

IRIDESCENT SHEEN
In bright sunlight, beautiful iridescent blues, greens, golds, and purples appear on the wings and tail.

SIMILAR SPECIES

YELLOW-BILLED MAGPIE

yellow bill

yellow patch around eye

OCCURRENCE
Found in open habitats, foothills, and plains of the western US and Canada; nests in streamside vegetation; persecution has made it wary and restricted to wilderness in some areas, but in others it has adapted to suburbs of towns and cities.

| Length **17–19½in (43–50cm)** | Wingspan **25in (63cm)** | Weight **6–7oz (175–200g)** |
| Social **Small flocks** | Lifespan **Up to 15 years** | Status **Secure** |

DATE: _____ TIME:_____ LOCATION:_____

| Order **Passeriformes** | Family **Corvidae** | Species *Corvus brachyrhynchos* |

American Crow

black overall **ADULT**

IN FLIGHT

black overall, with greenish sheen

long, black bill

ADULT

strong legs and feet

shorter bill

dull black overall

JUVENILE

One of the most widespread and familiar of North American birds, the American Crow is common in almost all habitats—from wilderness to urban centers. Like most birds with large ranges, there is substantial geographical variation in this species. Birds are black across the whole continent, but size and bill shape vary from region to region. The birds of the coastal Pacific Northwest (*C. b. hesperis*), are on average smaller and have a lower-pitched voice; Floridian birds (*C. b. pascuus*) are more solitary and warier than most.

VOICE Call a loud, familiar *caw!*; juveniles' call higher-pitched.
NESTING Stick base with finer inner cup; 3–7 eggs; 1 brood; April–June.
FEEDING Feeds omnivorously on fruit, carrion, garbage, insects, spiders; raids nests.

FLIGHT: direct and level with slow, steady flapping; does not soar.

LOOKING AROUND
Extremely inquisitive, American Crows are always on the look-out for food or something of interest.

OCCURRENCE
Often seen converging on favored roosting areas; most numerous in relatively open areas with widely spaced, large trees; has become abundant in some cities; a partial migrant, some populations are more migratory than others.

SIMILAR SPECIES

NORTHWESTERN CROW
range, voice differ

bluish black upperparts

smaller overall

COMMON RAVEN
see p.252

larger, curved bill

much larger overall

shaggy throat feathers

| Length **15½–19½in (39–49cm)** | Wingspan **3ft (1m)** | Weight **15–22oz (425–625g)** |
| Social **Social** | Lifespan **Up to 15 years** | Status **Secure** |

DATE: _____ TIME: _____ LOCATION: _____

| Order **Passeriformes** | Family **Corvidae** | Species **Corvus corax** |

Common Raven

ADULT

long, black wings

flared outer wing feathers

IN FLIGHT

large, protruding head

wedge-shaped tail

thick, long bill, with pronounced curvature

black upperparts, with purplish gloss

shaggy throat

dark gray neck and underparts

ADULT

long, black legs and feet

The Common Raven is twice the size of the American Crow, a bird of Viking legend, literature, and scientific wonder. Its Latin name, *Corvux corax*, means "crow of crows." Ravens are perhaps the most brilliant of all birds: they learn quickly, adapt to new circumstances with remarkable mental agility, and communicate with each other through an array of vocal and motional behaviors. The Common Raven is the official bird of the Yukon Territory.

VOICE Varied vocalizations, including hoarse, rolling *krruuk*, twangy peals, guttural clicks, and resonant *bonks*.

NESTING Platform of sticks with fine inner material on trees, cliffs, or man-made structure; 4–5 eggs; 1 brood; March–June.

FEEDING Feeds omnivorously on carrion, small crustaceans, fish, rodents, fruit, grain, and garbage; also raids nests.

FLIGHT: slow, steady, and direct; can also be quite acrobatic; commonly soars.

SHARING INFORMATION
Ravens in flocks can communicate information about food sources.

SIMILAR SPECIES

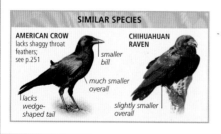

AMERICAN CROW
lacks shaggy throat feathers; see p.251

smaller bill

lacks wedge-shaped tail

CHIHUAHUAN RAVEN

much smaller overall

slightly smaller overall

OCCURRENCE
Found in almost every kind of habitat, including tundra, mountainous areas, northern forest, woodlands, prairies, arid regions, coasts, and around human settlements; has recently recolonized areas on southern edge of range, from which it was once expelled by humans.

| Length **23½–27in (60–69cm)** | Wingspan **4½ft (1.4m)** | Weight **2½–3¼lb (1–1.5kg)** |
| Social **Solitary/Pairs/Small flocks** | Lifespan **Up to 15 years** | Status **Secure** |

DATE: _____ TIME: _____ LOCATION: _____

SWALLOWS

Swallows are a cosmopolitan family of birds with species found nearly everywhere, except in the polar regions and some of the largest deserts, although during migration they fly over some of the world's harshest deserts, including the Sahara and Atacama. Ornithologists usually call the short-tailed species martins and the long-tailed ones swallows. For example, the bird known as a Bank Swallow in most of North America is called a Sand Martin in southern states such as Mississippi and Alabama, as well as in the UK. The Bank Swallow and the Barn Swallow, which is also found across Eurasia, are the most widespread. All North American swallows are migratory, and most of them winter in Central and South America, where they feed on flying insects that occur year-round. They are all superb fliers, and skilled at aerial pursuit and capture of flying insects. They are sometimes confused with swifts, which belong to a different group, and have a different style of flight. Swallows have relatively shorter, broader wings and less stiff wing beats.

SURFACE SKIMMER
This Tree Swallow flies low over fresh water to catch insects as they emerge into the air.

CHICKADEES AND TITMICE

Chickadees and titmice may be some of the most well-known and widespread birds in North America. Scientific studies have shown that more than one genus exists, despite the bird's plumage similarities.

Regardless of their genus, chickadees are frequent visitors to backyards and are readily distinguished from titmice by their smooth-looking dark caps and black bibs. The name "chickadee" is derived from the common calls of several species. Highly social outside the breeding season and generally tolerant of people, these energetic little birds form flocks in winter. Some species, such as the Black-capped Chickadee, can lower their body temperature to survive the cold, but others, like the similar-looking Carolina Chickadee (a vagrant species in Canada), have a high winter mortality rate. Most species eat a combination of insects and plant material.

TITMICE
Titmice are distinguished from chickadees by their crests; most, like the familiar Tufted Titmouse, also have plain throats. Like chickadees, titmice are highly territorial and insectivorous during the breeding season, then become gregarious seed-eaters afterwards. At that time they often form mixed-species flocks with other small birds, like Kinglets, as they move through woodlands searching for food. Titmice are nonmigratory.

TAME BIRDS
Black-capped Chickadees have distinctive black-and-white markings and are often very tame.

| Order **Passeriformes** | Family **Alaudidae** | Species *Eremophila alpestris* |

Horned Lark

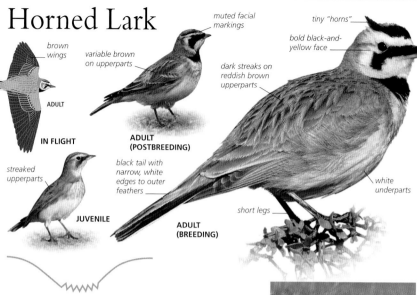

brown wings

ADULT

IN FLIGHT

variable brown on upperparts

muted facial markings

tiny "horns"

bold black-and-yellow face

dark streaks on reddish brown upperparts

ADULT (POSTBREEDING)

white underparts

streaked upperparts

JUVENILE

black tail with narrow, white edges to outer feathers

short legs

ADULT (BREEDING)

FLIGHT: undulating, with wings folded in after every few beats.

The Horned Lark is a bird of open country, especially places with extensive bare ground. The species is characteristic of arid, alpine, and Arctic regions; in these areas, it flourishes in the bleakest of habitats imaginable, from sun-scorched, arid lakes in the Great Basin to windswept tundra above the timberline. In some places, the only breeding bird species are the Horned Lark and the equally resilient Common Raven. In Europe and Asia, this species is known as the Shore Lark.

VOICE Flight call a sharp *sweet* or *soo-weet*; song, either in flight or from the ground, pleasant, musical tinkling series, followed by *sweet… suit… sweet… s'sweea'weea'witta'swit.*

NESTING In depression in bare ground, somewhat sheltered by grass or low shrubs, lined with plant matter; 2–5 eggs; 1–3 broods; March–July.

FEEDING Survives exclusively on seeds of grasses and sedges in winter; eats mostly insects in summer.

GROUND FORAGER
With its short legs bent under its body, an adult looks for insects and seeds.

OCCURRENCE
Breeds widely, in any sort of open, even barren habitat with extensive bare ground, especially short-grass prairies and deserts. Winters wherever there are snow-free openings, including places along beaches and roads. Winters from southern Canada southward to Florida and Mexico.

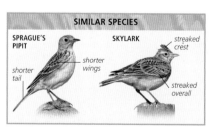

SIMILAR SPECIES

SPRAGUE'S PIPIT

SKYLARK

shorter tail

shorter wings

streaked crest

streaked overall

VERY VOCAL
The Horned Lark is a highly vocal bird, singing from the air, the ground, or low shrubs.

| Length **7in (18cm)** | Wingspan **12in (30cm)** | Weight **1¹/₁₆oz (30g)** |
| Social **Winter flocks** | Lifespan **Up to 8 years** | Status **Secure** |

DATE: _____ TIME: _____ LOCATION: _____

| Order **Passeriformes** | Family **Hirundinidae** | Species **Progne subis** |

Purple Martin

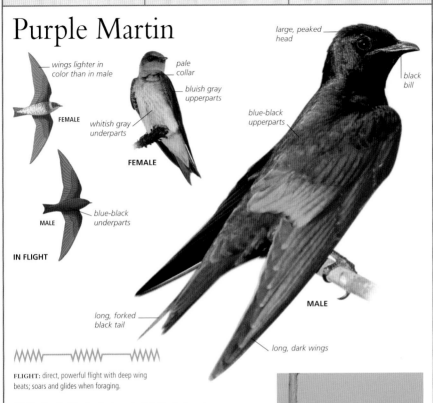

large, peaked head

wings lighter in color than in male

pale collar

bluish gray upperparts

FEMALE

whitish gray underparts

blue-black upperparts

black bill

FEMALE

blue-black upperparts

MALE

blue-black underparts

IN FLIGHT

long, forked black tail

MALE

long, dark wings

FLIGHT: direct, powerful flight with deep wing beats; soars and glides when foraging.

The Purple Martin, the largest of all North American swallows, is one of the most popular of all backyard birds. Thousands of devoted Purple Martin-lovers belong to two national organizations that publish magazines and newsletters devoted to the species. Found mostly in the eastern half of the continent, with local populations scattered across the West, this glossy-blue swallow is common in some areas and yet quite scarce in others. In the West it nests in abandoned woodpecker holes, but in the East the Purple Martin now depends almost entirely on the provisioning of "apartment-type" birdhouses for breeding.

VOICE Alarm call a *zwrack* or *zweet*; other calls are a variety of rolling, bubbling sounds; song a series of gurgles, chortles, and croaking phrases.
NESTING Loose mat of vegetation and mud in birdhouse compartments, rarely in natural cavities; 4 eggs; 1 brood; April–August.
FEEDING Captures flying insects at 150–500ft (45–150m) in the air; sometimes gleans insects from foliage or the ground.

FLOCK TOGETHER
Purple Martins are social birds; they breed in colonies and roost in flocks, as shown.

OCCURRENCE
In North America, eastern birds found almost exclusively in towns and cities where nestboxes are provided; western populations occur in more rural areas such as mountain and coastal forests where woodpecker holes are abundant; also uses Saguaro cactus for nesting in the Southwest.

| Length **7–8in (18–20cm)** | Wingspan **15–16in (38–41cm)** | Weight **1⁷⁄₁₆–2¹⁄₈oz (40–60g)** |
| Social **Large flocks/Colonies** | Lifespan **Up to 13 years** | Status **Secure** |

DATE: _____ TIME: _____ LOCATION: _____

| Order **Passeriformes** | Family **Hirundinidae** | Species *Tachycineta bicolor* |

Tree Swallow

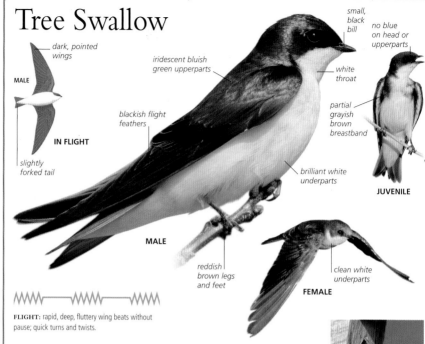

MALE

dark, pointed wings

IN FLIGHT

slightly forked tail

iridescent bluish green upperparts

blackish flight feathers

MALE

reddish brown legs and feet

small, black bill

no blue on head or upperparts

white throat

partial grayish brown breastband

brilliant white underparts

JUVENILE

clean white underparts

FEMALE

FLIGHT: rapid, deep, fluttery wing beats without pause; quick turns and twists.

One of the most common North American swallows, the Tree Swallow is found from coast to coast in the upper half of the continent all the wayup to Alaska. As its Latin name *bicolor* suggests, it has iridescent bluish green upperparts and white underparts. Juveniles can be confused with the smaller Bank Swallow, which has a more complete breastband. The Tree Swallow lives in a variety of habitats, but its hole-nesting habit makes it completely dependent on abandoned woodpecker cavities in dead trees and on artificial "housing" such as nestboxes. The size of the population fluctuates according to the availability of the nesting sites.

VOICE Ranges from variable high, chirping notes to chatters and soft trills; also complex high and clear two-note whistle phrases.

NESTING Layer of fine plant matter in abandoned woodpecker hole or nest box, lined with feathers; 4–6 eggs; 1 brood; May–July.

FEEDING Swoops after flying insects from dawn to dusk; also takes bayberries.

KEEPING LOOKOUT
This species uses artificial nestboxes, which the males defend as soon as they arrive.

OCCURRENCE
Typically breeds close to water in open habitat such as fields, marshes, lakes, and swamps, especially those with standing dead wood for cavity-nesting. Winters in large roosts in hundreds of thousands of birds in tall marsh vegetation.

SIMILAR SPECIES

BANK SWALLOW
paler brown rump; see p.258

distinct dusky breastband

VIOLET-GREEN SWALLOW
white flank patch

white eye patch

violet-green upperparts

| Length **5–6in (13–15cm)** | Wingspan **12–14in (30–35cm)** | Weight **⅝–⅞oz (17–25g)** |
| Social **Large flocks** | Lifespan **Up to 11 years** | Status **Secure** |

DATE: _____ TIME: _____ LOCATION: _____

| Order **Passeriformes** | Family **Hirundinidae** | Species *Stelgidopteryx serripennis* |

Northern Rough-winged Swallow

dark brown overall

ADULT

dark face

IN FLIGHT

JUVENILE

black eye

tan-buffy wing bars

pale underparts

light crescent from cheek to crown

brown head

pale brown breast

pale, grayish brown belly

ADULT

long, brown wings

square tail

G iven the name *serripennis*, "saw-like," by Audubon in 1888, and characterized by the serrations on its outer wing feathers, this species is otherwise somewhat drab in color and aspect. The Northern Rough-winged Swallow has a broad distribution in North America, being found across southern Canada and throughout the US. Often overlooked by birdwatchers, this brown-backed, dusky-throated swallow can be spotted hunting insects over water. In size and habit, the Northern Rough-winged Swallow shares many similarities with the Bank Swallow, including breeding habits and color, but the latter's notched tail and smaller size makes it easy to tell them apart.

VOICE Steady repetition of short, rapid *brrrt* notes inflected upward; sometimes a buzzy *jee-jee-jee* or high-pitched *brzzzzzt*.

NESTING Loose cup of twigs and straw in a cavity or burrow in a bank, such as road cuts; 4–7 eggs; 1 brood; May–July.

FEEDING Captures flying insects, including flies, wasps, bees, damselflies, and beetles in the air; more likely to feed over water and at lower altitudes than other swallows.

FLIGHT: slow, deliberate wing beats; short to long glides; long, straight flight, ends in steep climb.

BROWN BIRD
This swallow is brownish above and pale grayish below, with just a brown smudge on its neck.

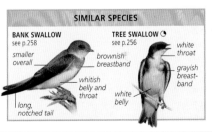

SIMILAR SPECIES

BANK SWALLOW
see p.258

smaller overall

whitish belly and throat

long, notched tail

TREE SWALLOW ☾
see p.256

brownish breastband

white throat

grayish breast-band

white belly

OCCURRENCE
In North America, widespread from coast to coast. Nests at a wide variety of altitudes, prefers exposed banks of clay, sand, or gravel such as gorges, shale banks, and gravel pits. Forages along watercourses where aerial insects are plentiful. Breeds south to Costa Rica. Winters in Central America.

Length 4¾–6in (12–15cm)	Wingspan **11–12in (28–30cm)**	Weight ⅜–⅝oz (10–18g)
Social **Solitary**	Lifespan **Unknown**	Status **Secure**

DATE: _____ TIME: _____ LOCATION: _____

| Order **Passeriformes** | Family **Hirundinidae** | Species *Riparia riparia* |

Bank Swallow

dark brown head

dark brown upperparts

ADULT

dark breastband

white belly

IN FLIGHT

whitish chin and throat

brownish cheeks

ADULT

forked tail

whitish underparts

ADULT

wings dark underneath

The Bank Swallow, known in the UK as the Sand Martin, is the slimmest and smallest of North American swallows. As its scientific name *riparia* (meaning "riverbanks") and common name suggest, the Bank Swallow nests in the banks and bluffs of rivers, streams, and lakes. It also favors sand and gravel quarries in the East. It is widely distributed across North America, breeding from south of the tundra–taiga line down to the central US. The nesting colonies can range from as few as 10 pairs to as many as 2,000, which are quite noisy when all the birds are calling or coming in to feed the young.

VOICE Call a soft *brrrrr* or *breee* often issued in pairs; song a harsh twittering or continuous chatter.

NESTING Burrow in soft, sandy bank containing a flat platform of grass, feathers, and twigs; 2–6 eggs; 1 brood; April–August.

FEEDING Catches insects, such as flies, moths, dragonflies, and bees in flight, but occasionally skims aquatic insects or their larvae off the water or terrestrial insects from the ground.

FLIGHT: fast, frantic, butterfly-like flight with glides, twists, and turns; shallow, rapid wing beats.

WAITING FOR MOM
Hungry youngsters still expect to be fed, even when they're ready to fledge.

SIMILAR SPECIES

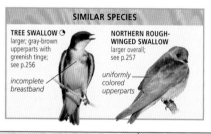

TREE SWALLOW ♀
larger; gray-brown upperparts with greenish tinge; see p.256

incomplete breastband

NORTHERN ROUGH-WINGED SWALLOW
larger overall; see p.257

uniformly colored upperparts

OCCURRENCE
Widespread in North America. Breeds in lowland habitats associated with rivers, streams, lakes, reservoirs, and coasts, as well as in sand and gravel quarries. Often prefers manmade sites; winters in grasslands, open farm habitat, and freshwater areas in South America.

| Length **4¾–5½in (12–14cm)** | Wingspan **10–11in (25–28cm)** | Weight **⅜–¹¹⁄₁₆oz (10–19g)** |
| Social **Colonies** | Lifespan **Up to 9 years** | Status **Secure** |

DATE: _____ TIME: _____ LOCATION: _____

| Order **Passeriformes** | Family **Hirundinidae** | Species **Petrochelidon pyrrhonota** |

Cliff Swallow

long, roundish wings

brown-tinged, black back

rusty cheek patch

mottled throat

JUVENILE

bluish-black back

ADULT

IN FLIGHT

rusty-brown cheeks

bluish black cap

pale hind neck collar

whitish forehead

dark throat

ADULT

pale underparts

slight notch in squared tail

pale reddish rump

The Cliff Swallow is one of North America's most social land birds, sometimes nesting in colonies of over 3,500 pairs, especially in the western US. It is more locally distributed across the east. It can be distinguished from other North American swallows by its square tail and orange rump, but it resembles its close relative, the Cave Swallow, in color, pattern, and in affixing its mud nests to the sides of highway culverts, bridges, and buildings. The considerable increase in such structures has allowed the species to expand its range from the west to breed almost everywhere on the continent, south of the tundra forest.

VOICE Gives *purr* and *churr* calls when alarmed; song a low, squeaky, 6-second twitter given in flight and near nests.

NESTING Domed nests of mud pellets on cave walls, buildings, culverts, bridges, and dams; 3–5 eggs; 1–2 broods; April–August.

FEEDING Catches flying insects (often swarming varieties) while on the wing; sometimes forages on the ground; ingests grit to aid digestion.

FLIGHT: strong, fast wing beats; glides more often but less acrobatically than other swallows.

GATHERING MUD
The Cliff Swallow gathers wet mud from puddles, pond edges, and streamsides to build its nests.

SIMILAR SPECIES

CAVE SWALLOW

brighter orange cheek

paler overall

INDIVIDUAL HOMES
In a Cliff Swallow colony, each nest has a single opening.

OCCURRENCE
Breeds almost anywhere in North America from Alaska to Mexico, except deserts, tundra, and unbroken forest; prefers concrete or cliff walls, culverts, buildings, cliffs, and undersides of piers on which to affix mud nests; feeds over grasslands, marshes, lakes, and reservoirs. Migrates to South America.

| Length **5in (13cm)** | Wingspan **11–12in (28–30cm)** | Weight **$^{11}/_{16}$–1$^{1}/_{4}$oz (20–35g)** |
| Social **Colonies** | Lifespan **Up to 11 years** | Status **Secure** |

DATE: _____ TIME:_____ LOCATION:_____

Order **Passeriformes**	Family **Hirundinidae**	Species *Hirundo rustica*

Barn Swallow

long, pointed wings

ADULT

IN FLIGHT

reddish orange underparts

duller plumage than adult

JUVENILE

shiny blue head and upperparts

chestnut forehead

deep, chestnut-brown throat

reddish orange belly

slender wings

deeply forked tail

ADULT

long tail "streamers"

The most widely distributed and abundant swallow in the world, the Barn Swallow is found just about everywhere in North America south of the Arctic timberline. Originally a cave-nester before Europeans settlers came to the New World, the Barn Swallow readily adapted to nesting under the eaves of houses, under bridges, and inside buildings such as barns. It is now rare to find this elegant swallow breeding in a natural site. Steely blue upperparts, reddish underparts, and a deeply forked tail identify the Barn Swallow. North American breeders have deep, reddish orange underparts, but birds from Eurasia are white-bellied.

VOICE High-pitched, squeaky *chee-chee* call; song a long series of chatty, pleasant churrs, squeaks, chitterings, and buzzes.

NESTING Deep cup of mud and grass-stems attached to vertical surfaces or on ledges; 4–6 eggs; 1–2 broods; May–September.

FEEDING Snatches flying insects, such as flies, mosquitoes, wasps, and beetles in the air at lower altitudes than other swallows; sometimes eats wild berries and seeds.

FLIGHT: bursts of straight flight; close to the ground; weaves left and right, with sharp turns.

WELL PROTECTED
Whether in a barn or other structure, a Barn Swallow nest is protected from wind and rain.

SIMILAR SPECIES

TREE SWALLOW ♂
see p.256

lacks forked tail and dark breast band

white underparts

OCCURRENCE
Breeds across North America, except in the tundra zone; south as far as central Mexico. Found in most habitats, but prefers agricultural regions, towns, and highway overpasses; migrates over coastal marshes; winters near sugarcane fields, grain fields, and marshes.

Length **6–7½in (15–19cm)**	Wingspan **11½–13in (29–33cm)**	Weight **⅝–¹¹⁄₁₆oz (17–20g)**
Social **Small colonies/flocks**	Lifespan **Up to 8 years**	Status **Secure**

DATE: _____ TIME: _____ LOCATION: _____

| Order **Passeriformes** | Family **Paridae** | Species **Poecile atricapillus** |

Black-capped Chickadee

white on wings and tail

black-and-white head

ADULT

grayish brown upperparts

white edges on wing feathers

IN FLIGHT

bright white cheeks

short black bill

black cap and bib

white edges on outer tail feathers

faded buff flanks

ADULT

The Black-capped Chickadee is the most widespread chickadee in North America, equally at home in the cold far north and in warm Appalachian valleys. To cope with the harsh northern winters, this species can decrease its body temperature, entering a controlled hypothermia to conserve energy. There is some variation in appearance according to geographical location, with northern birds being slightly larger and possessing brighter white wing edgings than southern birds. Although it is a nonmigratory species, in winter flocks occasionally travel south of their traditional range in large numbers. The Black-capped Chickadee is the provincial bird of New Brunswick.

VOICE Raspy *tsick-a-dee-dee-dee* call; song loud, clear whistle *bee-bee* or *bee-bee-be*, first note higher in pitch.

NESTING Cavity in rotting tree stump, lined with hair, fur, feathers, plant fibers; 6–8 eggs; 1 brood; April–June.

FEEDING Forages for insects and their eggs, and spiders in trees and bushes; mainly seeds in winter; may take seeds from an outstretched hand.

FLIGHT: swift and undulating, with fast wing beats.

ROUGH-EDGED BIB
The Black-capped Chickadee has a smaller bib than the Chestnut-backed Chickadee.

OCCURRENCE
Variety of wooded habitats, from vast forests in the far north to small woodlands in urban parks and suburbs. In years of poor seed crops in northern parts of the range, large numbers migrate sometimes as far south as Texas.

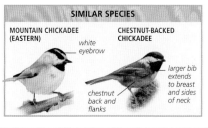

SIMILAR SPECIES

MOUNTAIN CHICKADEE (EASTERN)

white eyebrow

CHESTNUT-BACKED CHICKADEE

larger bib extends to breast and sides of neck

chestnut back and flanks

| Length **5¼in (13.5cm)** | Wingspan **8½in (22cm)** | Weight **⅜oz (11g)** |
| Social **Mixed flocks** | Lifespan **Up to 12 years** | Status **Secure** |

DATE: _____ TIME: _____ LOCATION: _____

| Order **Passeriformes** | Family **Paridae** | Species *Poecile hudsonicus* |

Boreal Chickadee

ADULT

IN FLIGHT

brown cap

grayish brown back

gray cheeks

gray tail

gray wings

black bib

rich brown flanks and belly

ADULT

FLIGHT: bouncy, fast wing beats with brief glides.

The Boreal Chickadee was previously known by other names, including Hudsonian Chickadee, referring to its northernrange, and the Brown-capped Chickadee, due to its appearance. In the past, this species made large, irregular journeys south of its usual range during winters of food shortage, but this pattern of invasions has not occurred in recent decades. Its back color is an interesting example of geographic variation—grayish in the West and brown in the central and eastern portions of its range.

VOICE Call a low-pitched, buzzy, lazy *tsee-day-day*; also a high-pitched trill, *didididididi*; no whistled song.

NESTING Cavity lined with fur, hair, plant down; in natural, excavated, or old woodpecker hole; 4–9 eggs; 1 brood; May–June.

FEEDING Gleans insects, conifer seeds; hoards larvae and seeds in bark crevices in fall in preparation for winter.

IDENTIFICATION TIP
A brown back or flank help distinguish a Boreal Chickadee from a Black-capped Chickadee.

OCCURRENCE
Found across the vast northern spruce-fir forests, from Alaska to Newfoundland, and from the treeline at the tundra south to the northeastern and northwestern states. The southern edge of the range appears to be retracting for unknown reasons.

SIMILAR SPECIES

CHESTNUT-BACKED CHICKADEE *narrow, white cheeks*

chestnut sides

ACROBATIC FORAGER
This acrobatic feeder is able to cling on to conifer needles as it searches for insects and spiders.

| Length **5½in (14cm)** | Wingspan **8½in (21cm)** | Weight **⅜oz (10g)** |
| Social **Flocks** | Lifespan **Up to 5 years** | Status **Secure** |

DATE: _____ TIME: _____ LOCATION: _____

| Order **Passeriformes** | Family **Paridae** | Species **Baeolophus bicolor** |

Tufted Titmouse

ADULT

crest may be flattened

gray wings

IN FLIGHT

gray tail

tufted dark gray head

black fore-head

conspicuous black eye in whitish face

prominent orange flanks

ADULT

gray underparts

gray-black legs and feet

FLIGHT: swift and undulating, with irregular wing beats; usually across short distances.

A familiar and friendly sight, the Tufted Titmouse is the most widespread of the North American titmice, and one of the two largest and most fearless; this lack of fear, particularly around people, has enabled it to adapt very well to human habitations. In the last century, its range has expanded significantly northward up to southern Canada, probably due to the increased numbers of birdfeeders, which allow the Tufted Titmouse to survive the cold northern winters.

VOICE Call a loud, harsh *pshurr, pshurr, pshurr*; song a ringing, far-carrying *peto peto peto,* sometimes shortened to *peer peer peer.*
NESTING Tree cavities, old woodpecker holes, and nest boxes, lined with damp leaves, moss, grass, hair; 5–6 eggs; 1 brood; March–May.
FEEDING Forages actively in trees and shrubs for insects, spiders, and their eggs; in winter, corn kernels, seeds, and small fruit; can split an acorn by hammering it with its bill.

COLOR VARIATION
The orange on the flanks varies between bright on freshly molted feathers and dull on worn adults.

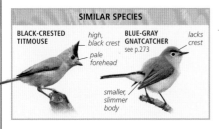

SIMILAR SPECIES

BLACK-CRESTED TITMOUSE — high, black crest; pale forehead

BLUE-GRAY GNATCATCHER see p.273 — lacks crest; smaller, slimmer body

OCCURRENCE
Lives year-round in areas of large and small deciduous and coniferous woodlands in the eastern half of the US and southeastern Canada. It has flourished in parks and gardens and can often be found using nest boxes in suburban backyards.

| Length **6½ in (16cm)** | Wingspan **10in (25cm)** | Weight **¹¹⁄₁₆ oz (20g)** |
| Social **Mixed flocks** | Lifespan **Up to 13 years** | Status **Secure** |

DATE: _____ TIME: _____ LOCATION: _____

Family **Sittidae**

NUTHATCHES

ACROBATIC POSE
Downward-facing nuthatches, such as this White-breasted Nuthatch, often lift their heads in a characteristic pose.

COMMON WOODLAND BIRDS, NUTHATCHES are easily recognized by their distinctive shape and characteristic feeding techniques, and often located by loud squeaky calls. They are tree-dwellers, feeding around branches and nesting in small tree holes. Nuthatches are quite plump-bodied, short-tailed but large-headed birds, with strong, pointed bills and short legs, strong toes, and arched claws. Unlike woodpeckers and creepers, which mostly climb in an upward direction, they do not need to use the tail as a prop when exploring a tree's bark. These birds rely solely on their strong and secure grip to hop and shuffle in all directions, frequently hanging upside down. They feed on spiders and also probe for insects and their larvae in the cracks of tree bark. They also eat seeds and nuts, which they may wedge into a crevice and break open with noisy taps of the bill—hence, the name "nuthatch."

Family **Troglodytidae**

WRENS

COCKED TAIL
As they sing, Winter Wrens often hold their tails upward, in a near-vertical position.

WITH ONE EXCEPTION, THE EURASIAN Winter Wren, wrens are North American songbirds. They are sharp-billed birds with short- or medium-length tails that are frequently cocked. Wrens are intricately patterned, mostly with dark bars and streaks, and pale spots on buff and rusty backgrounds. Their family name, *Troglodytidae,* derives from a Greek word for "cave-dweller" —while they do not really inhabit caves, the description is apt as some North American species, such as the Winter Wren, forage deep inside thick cover of all kinds, from scrub to upturned tree roots and overgrown stumps, or in dense growth inside ditches. Marsh Wrens are found in marshes and Sedge Wrens in sedge meadows. Wrens are often best located by their calls, which are fairly loud for such small birds. There are species that sing precisely synchronized duets.

Red-breasted Nuthatch

rounded wings

MALE

white bands on tail

IN FLIGHT

slightly muted head pattern

dark blue-gray crown and eyestripe

bold black-and-white head pattern

pointed, chisel-like bill

pale orange underparts

FEMALE

black eyestripe

blue-gray upperparts

blue-gray, short tail, with black side feathers

white cheeks

rusty underparts

compact body shape

MALE

FLIGHT: short, swift dashes across forest clearings; irregular, undulating motion.

This aggressive, inquisitive nuthatch, with its distinctive black eyestripe, breeds in conifer forests across North America. The bird inhabits mountains in the West; in the East, it is found in lowlands and hills. However, sometimes it breeds in conifer groves away from its core range. Each fall, birds move from their main breeding grounds, but the extent of this exodus varies from year to year, depending on population cycles and food availability.
VOICE Call a one-note tooting sound, often repeated, with strong nasal yet musical quality: *aaank, enk, ink,* rather like a horn.
NESTING Excavates cavity in pine tree; nest of grass lined with feathers, with sticky pine resin applied to entrance; 5–7 eggs, 1 brood; May–July.
FEEDING Probes bark for beetle grubs; also eats insect larvae found on conifer needles; seeds in winter.

TASTY GRUB
This nuthatch has just extracted its dinner from the bark of a tree, a favorite foraging habitat.

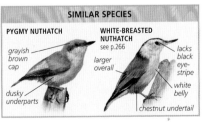

SIMILAR SPECIES

PYGMY NUTHATCH

grayish brown cap

dusky underparts

WHITE-BREASTED NUTHATCH
see p.266

larger overall

lacks black eye-stripe

white belly

chestnut undertail

OCCURRENCE
Found year-round in coniferous and mixed hardwood forests. During breeding season, absent from southeastern pine forests, except in the Appalachians. In the west, shares its habitat with Pygmy Nuthatch, but ranges to higher elevations.

| Length **4¼in (11cm)** | Wingspan **8½in (22cm)** | Weight **⅜–⁷⁄₁₆oz (10–13g)** |
| Social **Solitary/Pairs** | Lifespan **Up to 7 years** | Status **Secure** |

DATE: _____ TIME: _____ LOCATION: _____

| Order **Passeriformes** | Family **Sittidae** | Species *Sitta carolinensis* |

White-breasted Nuthatch

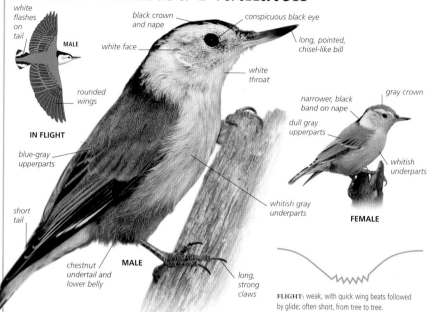

white flashes on tail

MALE

white face

IN FLIGHT

rounded wings

blue-gray upperparts

short tail

chestnut undertail and lower belly

MALE

black crown and nape

conspicuous black eye

long, pointed, chisel-like bill

white throat

whitish gray underparts

long, strong claws

gray crown

narrower, black band on nape

dull gray upperparts

whitish underparts

FEMALE

FLIGHT: weak, with quick wing beats followed by glide; often short, from tree to tree.

The amiable White-breasted Nuthatch inhabits residential neighborhoods across southern Canada and the US, and often visits birdfeeders in winter. The largest of our nuthatches, it spends more time probing furrows and crevices on trunks and boughs than other nuthatches do. It walks irregularly on trees: forward, backward, upside-down, or horizontally. Of the eleven subspecies in its Canada-to-Mexico range, five occur in Canada and in the US. They differ in call notes and, to a lesser extent, in plumage.

VOICE Calls vary geographically: eastern birds nasal *yank yank*; interior birds stuttering *st't't't't*; Pacific-slope birds tremulous *yiiirk*; song of all populations a mellow *tu tu tu tu*, like a flicker, but softer.

NESTING Tree cavity, once used by woodpeckers, lined with grass and hair, adds mud to cavity opening; 5–9 eggs, 1 brood; April–June.

FEEDING Scours bark methodically for insects such as beetle larvae.

UNUSUAL DESCENT
Nuthatches are unusual in that they routinely descend branches and trunks head-first.

OCCURRENCE
More liberal than other nuthatches in use of forest types; overlaps with the smaller species in coniferous forest ranges, but also common in broadleaf deciduous or mixed forests; weakly migratory: little movement in most falls, but moderate departures from breeding grounds in some years.

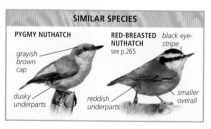

SIMILAR SPECIES

PYGMY NUTHATCH

grayish brown cap

dusky underparts

RED-BREASTED NUTHATCH
see p.265

reddish underparts

black eye-stripe

smaller overall

| Length **5³/₄ in (14.5cm)** | Wingspan **11in (28cm)** | Weight **¹¹/₁₆–⁷/₈ oz (19–25g)** |
| Social **Solitary/Pairs** | Lifespan **Up to 9 years** | Status **Secure** |

DATE: _____ TIME: _____ LOCATION: _____

Order **Passeriformes**	Family **Certhiidae**	Species **Certhia americana**

Brown Creeper

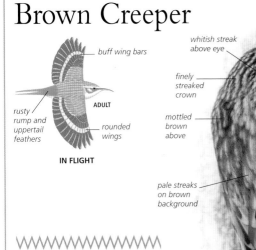

buff wing bars

ADULT

rusty rump and uppertail feathers

rounded wings

IN FLIGHT

thin, downward-curving bill

whitish streak above eye

finely streaked crown

mottled brown above

white chin, throat, and breast

pale streaks on brown background

FLIGHT: short, floppy flights from one tree to another; also capable of sustained migration.

ADULT (SUMMER)

rusty tint to belly and undertail

long, forked tail

Although distinctive, widespread, and fairly common, the Brown Creeper is one of the most understated of the forest birds, with its soft vocalizations and cryptic plumage. As it forages, it hops up a tree trunk, then flies down to another tree, starts again from near the ground, hops up, and so on. These birds have adapted to habitat changes in the Northeast and their numbers have increased in regenerating forests. Mid- and southwestern populations, by contrast, have declined because forest cutting has reduced their breeding habitat. The Brown Creeper is a partial migrant—some individuals move south in the fall, and head north in the spring; others remain close to their breeding grounds.

VOICE High-pitched and easily overlooked call a buzzy *zwisss*, flight call an abrupt *tswit*; song a wheezy jumble of thin whistles and short buzzes.

NESTING Unique hammock-shaped nest, behind piece of peeling bark; 5–6 eggs, 1 brood; May–July.

FEEDING Probes bark for insects, especially larvae, eggs, pupae, and aphids.

SIMILAR SPECIES

PYGMY NUTHATCH

blue-gray upperparts

smaller overall

straight bill

smaller overall

BROWN-HEADED NUTHATCH

blue-gray upperparts

shorter tail

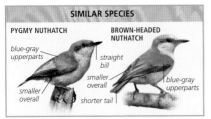

STRONG TAIL
The Brown Creeper uses its forked tail to prop it against the trunk of this tree.

OCCURRENCE
The only North American creeper, it breeds in a variety of forests, particularly fairly moist coniferous or mixed hardwood forests, also large stands with snags and standing dead trees. In winter, it is seen in small groves without coniferous trees; also in residential districts or suburbs.

Length **5¼in (13.5cm)**	Wingspan **8in (20cm)**	Weight **¼–⅜oz (7–10g)**
Social **Solitary**	Lifespan **Up to 4 years**	Status **Secure**

DATE: _____ TIME: _____ LOCATION: _____

Order **Passeriformes**	Family **Troglodytidae**	Species ***Troglodytes aedon***

House Wren

plain brown
crown

faintly barred
wings

browner
upperparts

pale buffy
throat

thin, indistinct
eyebrow

thin, slightly
curved bill

narrow, pale
eye-ring

**ADULT
(EASTERN)**

**ADULT
T. a. aedon
(EASTERN)**

grayish
brown
back

IN FLIGHT

narrow, black
barring on tail

**ADULT
T. a. parkmanii
(WESTERN)**

pale gray-brown
underparts

FLIGHT: straight, with fast wing beats;
typically over short distances.

Of all the North American wrens, the
House Wren is the plainest, yet one of
the most familiar and endearing, especially when making its home in a backyard
nest box. However, it can be a fairly aggressive species, driving away nearby
nesting birds of its own species and others by destroying nests, puncturing eggs,
and even killing young. In the 1920s, distraught bird lovers mounted a campaign
calling for the eradication of House Wrens, though
the campaign did not last long as most were in
favor of letting nature take its course.
VOICE Call a sharp *chep* or *cherr*; song opens
with several short notes, followed by bubbly
explosion of spluttering notes.
NESTING Cup lined
with soft material on
stick platform in natural,
manmade cavities, such
as nest boxes; 5–8 eggs;
2–3 broods; April–July.
FEEDING Forages for
insects and spiders in
trees and shrubs,
gardens, and yards.

SIMILAR SPECIES

WINTER WREN *dark brown*
see p.269 *overall*
*shorter
tail*

*heavily
barred
flanks*

NESTING MATERIAL
This small bird has brought an
unusually large twig to its nest
inside an old woodpecker hole.

OCCURRENCE
Breeds in cities, towns, parks,
farms, yards, gardens, and
woodland edges. Rarely seen
during migration period (late
July to early October). Winters
south of its breeding range,
from southern US to Mexico, in
woodlands, shrubby areas, and
weedy fields. Nests, or is resident
as far south as Tierra del Fuego.

Length 4½in (11.5cm)	Wingspan 6in (15cm)	Weight ⅜oz (11g)
Social **Solitary**	Lifespan **Up to 9 years**	Status **Secure**

DATE: _____ TIME:_____ LOCATION:_____

| Order **Passeriformes** | Family **Troglodytidae** | Species ***Troglodytes hiemalis*** |

Winter Wren

distinct, tan
eyebrow

stubby tail, usually
cocked straight up

dark brown,
barred back

small,
thin bill

short,
barred
tail

ADULT

ADULT

barred,
rounded
wings

flanks
strongly
barred

IN FLIGHT

The Winter Wren has one of the loudest songs of any small North American species. Once considered more widespread, it has recently been split from the Pacific Wren, which occupies much of the western fringe of the continent. It is a bird of low undergrowth and tangled roots, often foraging in the upturned roost and broken branches of fallen trees, appearing mouse-like as it creeps amid the shadows. It frequently appears in full view, gives a few harsh, scolding calls, then dives back out of sight into the low cover. It can survive periods of intense cold and even snow cover by finding insects and spiders in bark crevices and soil-encrusted roots. Several Winter Wrens may roost together in small cavities for warmth.

VOICE Call a double *chek-chek* or *chimp-chimp*; song a loud, extremely long, complex series of warbles, trills, and single notes.
NESTING Well-hidden in a cavity near ground with dead wood and crevices; nest a messy mound lined with feathers; 4–7 eggs; 1–2 broods; April–July.
FEEDING Forages for insects in low, dense undergrowth, often in wet areas along streams; sometimes thrusts its head into water to capture prey.

FLIGHT: fast and direct, with rapid beats of its short, broad wings.

VOCAL VIRTUOSO
The Winter Wren is a skulker, but in the breeding season singing males show up on lower perches.

OCCURRENCE
Breeds in northerly and mountain forests dominated by evergreen trees with a dense understory, fallen trees, and banks of streams. In the Appalachians, breeds in treeless areas with grass near cliffs. Northernmost birds migrate south to winter in woodlands, brush piles, tangles, and secluded spots.

SIMILAR SPECIES

HOUSE WREN
see p.268
pale brown
back

long
tail

plain,
unbarred
flanks

NERVOUS REACTION
When alarmed, this wren cocks its tail almost vertically, before escaping into a mossy thicket.

| Length **4in (10cm)** | Wingspan **5½in (14cm)** | Weight **5/16oz (9g)** |
| Social **Solitary/Family groups** | Lifespan **At least 4 years** | Status **Secure** |

| Order **Passeriformes** | Family **Troglodytidae** | Species **Cistothorus platensis** |

Sedge Wren

streaked cap · short bill
buffy eyebrow
streaked back and inner wing feathers
ADULT
reddish tan rump
streaked back
short, round wings
IN FLIGHT
barred wings and tail
faint, white barring on chest
buffy underparts
ADULT

FLIGHT: short bursts, from cover to cover, with fast wing beats.

The Sedge Wren, formerly named the Short-billed Marsh Wren, is an extremely shy bird. It stays out of sight in dense cover except when singing atop a sedge stalk or a shrub. If discovered, it flies a short distance, drops down, and runs out of sight through the vegetation. The Sedge Wren has two geographically distinct breeding seasons—May–June in the north central region of its range, and July–September in the southern and eastern regions. A feature of its breeding behavior, also found in other species of wrens, is the male's habit of building up to 8–10 unlined "dummy" nests before the female builds the better-concealed, real nest.

VOICE Call a loud *chap*; song a dry, staccato two-part chatter: *cha cha cha cha ch'ch'ch ch'ch'ch'ch'*.

NESTING Globular, woven structure of sedges with side entrance; lined with plant matter, down, and hair; 4–8 eggs; 1–2 broods; May–August.

FEEDING Forages for spiders and insects, such as grasshoppers, flies, mosquitoes, and bugs, close to or on ground in cover of sedges and grass.

LOOK CLOSELY
Close study is necessary to appreciate the Sedge Wren's subtle patterning, which is plainer than the Marsh Wren's.

OCCURRENCE
In North America, breeds in wet meadows and sedge marshes with low water levels. Widely distributed in the Americas from the Canadian prairies, east to Quebec and from northern US, to the south central states. Winters from Texas to Florida in drier habitats including grassy fields and coastal-plain prairies.

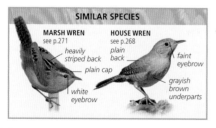

SIMILAR SPECIES

MARSH WREN see p.271 — heavily striped back, plain cap, white eyebrow

HOUSE WREN see p.268 — plain back, faint eyebrow, grayish brown underparts

| Length **4½in (11.5cm)** | Wingspan **5½–6in (14–15.5cm)** | Weight **⁵⁄₁₆oz (9g)** |
| Social **Loose colonies** | Lifespan **Unknown** | Status **Secure** |

DATE: _____ TIME: _____ LOCATION: _____

Order **Passeriformes**	Family **Troglodytidae**	Species *Cistothorus palustris*

Marsh Wren

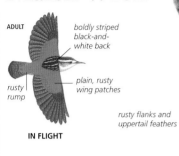

ADULT

boldly striped black-and-white back

rusty rump

plain, rusty wing patches

IN FLIGHT

barred tail feathers

heavily streaked, black-and-white back

whitish eyebrow

brown cap

rusty flanks and uppertail feathers

dull whitish, buff underparts

long bill

ADULT

FLIGHT: straight, with rapid wing beats over short distances, from one reed patch to another.

The Marsh Wren, a common resident of saltwater and freshwater marshes, is known for singing loudly through both day and night. The males perform fluttery, aerial courtship flights while singing, and are polygamous, mating with two or more females. Like the Sedge Wren, the male builds several dummy nests before his mate constructs one herself. The Marsh Wren nests in taller vegetation than the Sedge Wren and over deeper water. Eastern (*C. p. palustris*) and Western (*C. p. paludicola*) Marsh Wrens differ in voice and behavior, and some ornithologists classify them as separate species.

VOICE Calls a low *chek* and a raspy *churr*; song a loud *chuk chuk chuk*, then fast *tih-tih-tih-rih-tih-tih*, an enthusiastic singer.
NESTING Oblong structure with side entrance, woven of reeds and lined with soft materials; 4–5 eggs; 2 broods; March–July.
FEEDING Forages acrobatically for insects, such as mosquitoes, dragonflies, and beetles, within dense clusters of cattails and reeds.

DELICATELY PERCHED
This wren perches on vertical reeds and often holds itself up by spreading its legs across two stalks.

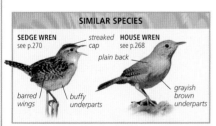

SIMILAR SPECIES

SEDGE WREN see p.270

streaked cap

HOUSE WREN see p.268

plain back

barred wings

buffy underparts

grayish brown underparts

OCCURRENCE
Breeds across North America from Canada to the mountains of the western and central northern states. Inhabits freshwater and saltwater marshes with tall vegetation, above water, sometimes more than 3ft (1m) deep. It is irregularly distributed in its range. Winters in grassy marshes and wetlands.

Length **5in (13cm)**	Wingspan **6in (15cm)**	Weight **⅜oz (11g)**
Social **Loose colonies**	Lifespan **Unknown**	Status **Localized**

DATE: _____ TIME: _____ LOCATION: _____

Order **Passeriformes**	Family **Troglodytidae**	Species *Thryothorus ludovicianus*

Carolina Wren

white eyebrow bordered by black above

huge head

tiny tail

ADULT

rufous upperparts

duller overall

white wing spots

thin, black barring on tail

IN FLIGHT

FLEDGLING

powerful-looking, bluish bill

white spots on wing

ADULT

buffy underparts

pinkish legs and toes

The Carolina Wren is a popular and common backyard bird in most of its range. It is rarely still, often flicking its tail and looking around nervously. Extremely harsh winters at the northernmost fringe of the Carolina Wren's range in New England and southeastern Canada can cause a sudden decline in numbers, as food resources are covered for long periods by ice and heavy snow. At such times, survival may depend on human help for food and shelter.

VOICE Calls variable; often a sharp *chlip* or long, harsh chatter; song a loud, long, fast *whee'dle-dee whee'dle-dee whee'dle-dee*.

NESTING Cup of weeds, twigs, leaves in natural or human-made cavity; 4–8 eggs; 2–3 broods; April–July.

FEEDING Forages for insects in shrubs and on ground; in winter, favorite foods are peanut butter or suet at a feeder.

FLIGHT: fast and straight over short distances, with rapid wing beats.

DISTINCTIVE BORDER
A unique feature of this wren, not always noticed but visible here, is the black border on the eyebrow.

SIMILAR SPECIES

BEWICK'S WREN *dull brown or gray upperparts*

longer tail

TIRELESS SINGER
Unlike many birds, the male Carolina Wren sings all year long, even on cold winter days.

OCCURRENCE
Breeds in a variety of bushy woodland habitats, such as thickets, parks with shrubby undergrowth, suburban yards with dense, low trees or bushes, and gardens; from northeastern Mexico to the Great Lakes and up into southeastern Canada. A separate population can be found from Mexico to Nicaragua.

Length **5¼ in (13.5cm)**	Wingspan **7½ in (19cm)**	Weight **¹¹⁄₁₆ oz (19g)**
Social **Pairs/Family groups**	Lifespan **At least 9 years**	Status **Secure**

DATE: _____ TIME: _____ LOCATION: _____

| Order **Passeriformes** | Family **Polioptilidae** | Species **Polioptila caerulea** |

Blue-gray Gnatcatcher

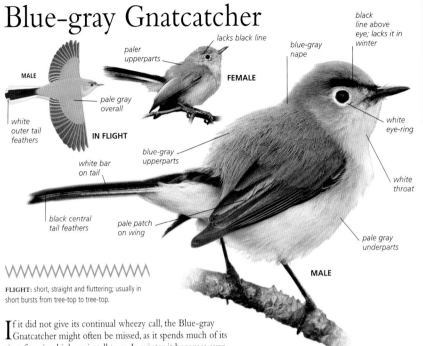

MALE

paler upperparts

lacks black line

FEMALE

pale gray overall

black line above eye; lacks it in winter

blue-gray nape

white outer tail feathers

IN FLIGHT

pale gray underparts

white bar on tail

blue-gray upperparts

white eye-ring

black central tail feathers

pale patch on wing

white throat

pale gray underparts

MALE

FLIGHT: short, straight and fluttering; usually in short bursts from tree-top to tree-top.

If it did not give its continual wheezy call, the Blue-gray Gnatcatcher might often be missed, as it spends much of its time foraging high up in tall trees. In winter it becomes even harder to find as it is generally silent. This species is the most northerly of the North American gnatcatchers and is also the only one to migrate. It can exhibit aggressive behavior and is capable of driving off considerably larger birds than itself. The range of the Blue-gray Gnatcatcher appears to be expanding and populations are increasing.

VOICE Call soft, irregular *zhee, zhee*, uttered constantly while foraging; song soft combination of short notes and nasal wheezes.

NESTING Cup of plant fibers, spider webs, mosses; usually high on branch; lined with soft plant material; 4–5 eggs; 1–2 broods; April–June.

FEEDING Forages for small insects and spiders by acrobatically flitting from twig to twig, while twitching long tail.

LISTEN CLOSELY
The complex song is rather faint; it is heard best when the bird is singing on a low perch.

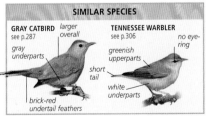

SIMILAR SPECIES

GRAY CATBIRD see p.287
larger overall
gray underparts
short tail
brick-red undertail feathers

TENNESSEE WARBLER see p.306
greenish upperparts
no eye-ring
white underparts

OCCURRENCE
In eastern North America, breeds in deciduous or pine woodlands; in the West, in scrubby habitats, often near water. Winters in brushy habitats in southern US, Mexico, and Central America. Also breeds in Mexico, Belize, and the Bahamas.

| Length 4¼in (11cm) | Wingspan 6in (15cm) | Weight ⁷⁄₃₂oz (6g) |
| Social **Solitary/Flocks** | Lifespan **At least 4 years** | Status **Secure** |

DATE: _____ TIME: _____ LOCATION: _____

| Order **Passeriformes** | Family **Regulidae** | Species *Regulus satrapa* |

Golden-crowned Kinglet

whitish wing bars

MALE

IN FLIGHT

yellow crown patch, with black border

FEMALE

orange-and-yellow patch on crown, with black border

broad whitish stripe above eye

olive-green upperparts

short, straight bill

MALE

white wing bar

notched tail

pale buff to whitish underparts

FLIGHT: quick and erratic, but not direct; high in the air; can hover while foraging.

This hardy little bird, barely more than a ball of feathers, breeds in northern and mountainous coniferous forests in Canada and the US, after a considerable hiatus in mountain forests of Mexico and Guatemala. The planting of spruce trees has been quite beneficial to the Golden-crowned Kinglet, allowing it to expand its range southward into the US Midwest.

VOICE Call a thin, high-pitched and thread-like *tsee* or *see see*; song a series of high-pitched ascending notes for 2 seconds; complex song *tsee-tsee-tsee-tsee-teet-leetle*, followed by brief trill.

NESTING Deep, cup-shaped nest with rims arching inward, made of moss, lichen, and bark, and lined with finer strips of the same; 8–9 eggs; 1–2 broods; May–August.

FEEDING Gleans flies, beetles, mites, spiders, and their eggs from tips of branches, under bark, tufts of conifer needles; eats seeds, and persimmon fruit.

CONIFER CONNOISEUR
This bird particularly favors coniferous forests for foraging for insects and seeds.

SIMILAR SPECIES

RUBY-CROWNED KINGLET see p.275

white eye-ring

no eye-stripe

olive underparts

HIGHER VOICE
The Golden-crowned has a higher-pitched and less musical song than the Ruby-crowned.

OCCURRENCE
Breeds in remote northern and subalpine spruce or fir forests, mixed coniferous–deciduous forests, single-species stands, and pine plantations; winters in a wide variety of habitats— coniferous and deciduous forests, pine groves, low-lying hardwood forests, swamps, and urban and suburban habitats.

| Length 3¼–4¼in (8–11cm) | Wingspan 5½–7in (14–18cm) | Weight ⁵/₃₂–⁹/₃₂oz (4–8g) |
| Social **Solitary/Pairs** | Lifespan **Up to 5 years** | Status **Secure** |

DATE: _____ TIME: _____ LOCATION: _____

Ruby-crowned Kinglet

red patch on crown

ADULT

white wing bars

patch on crown often concealed

incomplete white eye-ring

olive-green upperparts

notched tail

IN FLIGHT

no red patch on crown

FEMALE

MALE

MALE

olive underparts

small, upturned bill

brown legs with paler brown feet

T he Ruby-crowned Kinglet is perhaps one of the most easily recognizable songbirds in North America because of its very small size, white eye-ring, two white wing bars, and habit of incessantly flicking its wings while foraging. This bird is renowned for its loud, complex song and for laying up to 12 eggs in a clutch—probably the highest of any North American songbird. Despite local declines resulting from logging and forest fires, the Ruby-crowned Kinglet is common across the continent. It will sometimes join mixed-species flocks in winter with nuthatches and titmice.

VOICE Call a low, husky *jidit*; song, remarkably loud for such a small bird, begins with 2–3 high, clear notes *tee* or *zee* followed by 5–6 lower *tu* or *turr* notes, and ends with ringing galloping notes *tee-da-leet*, *tee-da-leet*, *tee-da-leet*.

NESTING Globular or elongated nest hanging from or on large branch with an enclosed or open cup, made of mosses, feathers, lichens, spider's silk, bark, hair, and fur; 5–12 eggs; 1 brood; May–October.

FEEDING Gleans a wide variety of insects, spiders, and their eggs among the leaves on the outer tips of higher, smaller branches; eats fruit and seeds; often hovers to catch prey.

FLIGHT: short bursts of rapid wing beats, but overall quick and direct flight.

CONCEALED COLOR
This bird's red patch is often concealed unless the bird is agitated or excited.

OCCURRENCE
Within the northerly forest zone, breeds near water in Black Spruce and tamarack forests, muskegs, forests with mixed conifers and northern hardwoods; in the mountainous West, spruce-fir, Lodgepole Pine, and Douglas Fir forests. Winters in a broad range of forests, thickets, and borders.

SIMILAR SPECIES

HUTTON'S VIREO larger head
stouter bill
heavier overall

ALWAYS FLICKING
Ruby-crowned Kinglets are easily identified by their habit of constantly flicking their wings.

| Length 3½–4¼in (9–11cm) | Wingspan 6–7in (15–18cm) | Weight ³⁄₁₆–³⁄₈oz (5–10g) |
| Social **Winter flocks** | Lifespan **Up to 5 years** | Status **Secure** |

DATE: _____ TIME: _____ LOCATION: _____

Family **Muscicapidae, Turdidae**

THRUSHES

GROUND BIRDS
Though they perch to sing, thrushes, including this Gray-cheeked Thrush, spend a lot of their time on or near the ground.

Thrushes, chats (Wheatears and Bluethroats), and their relatives are small- to medium-sized birds, frequenting forests but feeding largely on the ground. Many are brownish in color, with more or less obvious spotting underneath, lacking vivid hues but often exquisitely patterned. They make up for their lack of color with their beautiful, musical songs. The American Robin and the bluebirds are clear exceptions as they are highly recognizable birds.

Family **Mimidae, Sturnidae**

THRASHERS

DISTINCTIVE BILL
This Brown Thrasher is characterized by its slender, curved bill, long, thin legs, and long, rounded tail.

Thrush-like in form, thrashers have longer tails and are distinguished by their distinctly curved bills. Catbirds and mockingbirds are found across southern Canada—the Northern Mockingbird's range is spreading northward. Thrashers are mainly insect-eaters, but they also feed on a variety of seeds and berries. They are well known for their ability to mimic the songs of other species in their own song sequences: Mimidae is derived from the Latin for "to imitate."

Family **Motacillidae**

PIPITS

COUNTRY-LOVERS
Pipits, such as this American Pipit, live in open country, including beaches, dunes, and tundra.

This group of ground-dwelling songbirds occurs across most of the world, although only two are found in Canada, and only one—the American Pipit—is Canada-wide. The two species of pipit that breed in North America also winter there. Very much birds of open, treeless country, both pipit species are likely to be seen on their widespread wintering grounds more often than in their breeding range.

276

Order **Passeriformes**	Family **Muscicapidae**	Species *Oenanthe oenanthe*

Northern Wheatear

MALE (BREEDING)

tail has a black "T"

IN FLIGHT

long, black wings

FEMALE (BREEDING)

mouse-brown back

black mask

tan eyebrow

tan throat and breast

FEMALE (BREEDING)

gray back

white forehead and eyebrow

black bill

white underparts

MALE (BREEDING)

long, thin, black legs

similar to female, but duller

JUVENILE

Although widely distributed in Europe, the Middle East and Africa, the Northern Wheatear is present in North America only during its brief breeding season, where it is confined to Alaska and northeastern Canada. The two subspecies that breed in North America, the larger *O. o. leucorhoa* in the Northeast and *O. o. oenanthe* in the Northwest, migrate to wintering grounds in sub-Saharan Africa. The Northern Wheatear can be distinguished by its black-and-white tail, which bobs when the bird walks.
VOICE Multiple calls, a sharp *tuc* or *tek* common; three types of songs—territorial, conversational, and perched—consisting of mixtures of sweet and harsh notes; imitates other species.
NESTING Under rocks or in abandoned burrows; nests have coarse outer foundation, with cradle and cup within of finer material; 5–6 eggs; 1 brood; June–July.
FEEDING Eats insects, but also takes berries; diet in North America not well known.

FLIGHT: undulating when flying long distances; fluttering from perch to perch.

KEEP YOUR DISTANCE
Northern Wheatears are highly territorial, so neighbors get yelled at if they come too close.

OCCURRENCE
Breeds in rocky tundra of Alaska and northern Canada, including the Yukon (*O. o. oenanthe*) and the Arctic archipelago (*O. o. leucorhoa*). Both subspecies winter in Africa, *O. o. oenanthe* by flying across Asia, *O. o. leucorhoa* by flying across the Atlantic.

Length **5½–6in (14–15cm)**	Wingspan **10¾in (27cm)**	Weight **½oz (14g)**
Social **Solitary/Flocks**	Lifespan **Up to 7 years**	Status **Secure**

DATE: _____ TIME:_____ LOCATION:_____

THRUSHES

Order **Passeriformes**	Family **Turdidae**	Species *Sialia sialis*

Eastern Bluebird

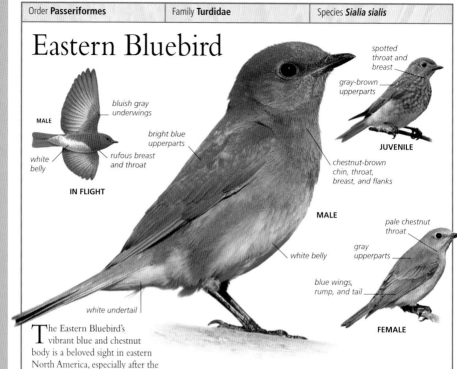

MALE

bluish gray underwings

bright blue upperparts

white belly

rufous breast and throat

IN FLIGHT

white undertail

spotted throat and breast

gray-brown upperparts

JUVENILE

chestnut-brown chin, throat, breast, and flanks

MALE

white belly

pale chestnut throat

gray upperparts

blue wings, rump, and tail

FEMALE

The Eastern Bluebird's vibrant blue and chestnut body is a beloved sight in eastern North America, especially after the remarkable comeback of the species in the past 30 years. After much of the bird's habitat was eliminated by agriculture in the mid-1900s, volunteers offered the bluebirds nest boxes asalternatives to their tree cavities, and they took to these like ducks to water. The Eastern Bluebird's mating system involves males seeking (or not minding) multiple partners.

VOICE Main song a melodious series of soft, whistled notes; *churr-wi* or *churr-li*; songs for mating and asserting territoriality.
NESTING Cavity nester, in trees or man-made boxes; nest of grass lined with grass, weeds, and twigs; uses old nests of other species; 3–7 eggs; 2 broods; February–September.
FEEDING Feeds on insects, like grasshoppers, and caterpillars in breeding season; in winter, also takes fruit and plants.

FLIGHT: shallow wing beats; slow and easy.

HOME DELIVERY
A female bluebird delivers food to a nest box.

SIMILAR SPECIES

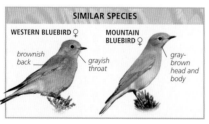

WESTERN BLUEBIRD ♀

brownish back

grayish throat

MOUNTAIN BLUEBIRD ♀

gray-brown head and body

OCCURRENCE
Found in eastern Canada and the eastern US, where it lives in clearings and woodland edges; occupies multiple open habitats in rural, urban, and suburban areas: woodlands, plains, orchards, parks, and spacious lawns. Breeds and winters across the eastern half of North America.

Length **6–8in (15–20cm)**	Wingspan **10–13in (25–33cm)**	Weight **1¹/₁₆oz (30g)**
Social **Flocks**	Lifespan **8–10 years**	Status **Secure**

DATE: _____ TIME:_____ LOCATION:_____

Order **Passeriformes**	Family **Turdidae**	Species *Myadestes townsendi*

Townsend's Solitaire

ADULT

dark gray outer flight feathers

long tail

wide, buff bands on flight feathers

short head

IN FLIGHT

plain gray

upright posture

ADULT

black legs and feet

large, black eye

white eye-ring

gray upperparts and head

short, black bill

paler underparts

ADULT

pale chestnut-tan patches

spotted back

heavily spotted breast

JUVENILE

long tail

long, dark tail with white outer feathers

The rather shy Townsend's Solitaire inhabits most of western North America, especially high-elevation coniferous forests of the Sierras and Rockies. Its drab gray plumage, with a chestnut-tan wing pattern, remains the same throughout the year, and the sexes look alike. From a perch high on a branch, Townsend's Solitaire darts after flying insects and snaps its bill shut after catching its prey, unlike other thrush-like birds.
VOICE Calls are single-note, high-pitched whistles; sings all year, but especially when establishing territories; main song robin-like, full of rolled or trilled sounds, interspersed with squeaky notes.
NESTING Cup of pine needles, dry grass, weed stems, and bark on ground or under overhang; 4 eggs; 1–2 broods; May–August.
FEEDING Forages for a wide variety of insects and spiders during breeding season; feeds on fruit and berries after breeding, particularly junipers.

FLIGHT: unhurried motion, usually over short distances, with slow, steady wing beats.

JUNIPER LOVER
Solitaires love the berry-like cones of junipers, which they eat to supplement their winter diet.

SIMILAR SPECIES

MOUNTAIN BLUEBIRD ♀

dull bluish back

blue in wings and tail

short tail

GRAY PLUMAGE
Townsend's Solitaire is a drab gray overall, but a conspicuous white eye-ring.

OCCURRENCE
During breeding season, found in open conifer forests along steep slopes or areas with landslides; during winter, at lower elevations, in open woodlands where junipers are abundant. Partial-migrant northern populations move south in winter, as far as central Mexico.

Length **8–8½in (20–22cm)**	Wingspan **13–14½in (33–37cm)**	Weight **1¹⁄₁₆–1¼oz (30–35g)**
Social **Solitary**	Lifespan **Up to 5 years**	Status **Secure**

DATE: _____ TIME: _____ LOCATION: _____

Order **Passeriformes**	Family **Turdidae**	Species ***Catharus fuscescens***

Veery

pale, reddish brown upperparts

inconspicuous, pale eye-ring

black upper bill

less distinct spotting on breast

creamy pink at base of bill

brownish tan upperparts

ADULT

IMMATURE
C. f. fuscescens
(EASTERN)

IN FLIGHT

poorly marked brown spots on buff breast and throat

white underparts

tan wash on flanks

creamy pink legs and feet

ADULT
C. f. salicicola
(WESTERN)

The least spotted of the North American *Catharus* thrushes, the Veery is medium-sized, like the others, but browner overall. It has been described as "dusky," but there is a geographical variation in duskiness; four subspecies have been described to reflect this. Eastern birds (*C. f. fuscescens*) are ruddier than their western relations (*C. f. salicicola*). The Veery is a long-distance migrant, spending the northern winter months in central Brazil, in a variety of tropical habitats.
VOICE A series of descending *da-vee-ur, vee-ur, veer, veer*, somewhat bi-tonal, sounding like the name Veery; call a rather soft *veer*.
NESTING Cup of dead leaves, bark, weed stems, and moss on or near ground; 4 eggs; 1–2 broods; May–July.
FEEDING Forages on the ground for insects, spiders, snails; eats fruit and berries after breeding.

FLIGHT: rapid and straight, with intermittent hops and glides; makes long hops when on ground.

DAMP DWELLINGS
The Veery breeds in damp habitats such as moist wooded areas or in trees near or in swamps.

SIMILAR SPECIES

GRAY-CHEEKED THRUSH
see p.281

gray face

bold black-brown breast spots

BICKNELL'S THRUSH
see p.282

bold brown breast spots

grayish brown upperparts

SWAINSON'S THRUSH
see p.283

buffy-colored face

bold brown-black breast spots

OCCURRENCE
In summer, mainly found in damp deciduous forests, preferring the canopy, but in some places habitat near rivers preferred. In winter, choice of habitat flexible; found in tropical broadleaf evergreen forest, on forest edges, in open woodlands, and in second-growth areas regenerating after fires or clearing.

Length **7in (18cm)**	Wingspan **11–11½in (28–29cm)**	Weight **1¹⁄₁₆–2oz (28–54g)**
Social **Pairs**	Lifespan **Up to 10 years**	Status **Declining**

DATE: _____ TIME:_____ LOCATION:_____

Order **Passeriformes**	Family **Turdidae**	Species *Catharus minimus*

Gray-cheeked Thrush

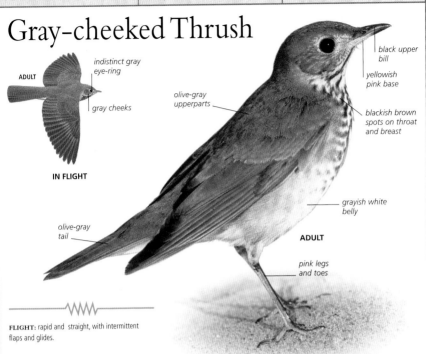

ADULT

IN FLIGHT

indistinct gray eye-ring

gray cheeks

olive-gray upperparts

black upper bill

yellowish pink base

blackish brown spots on throat and breast

grayish white belly

olive-gray tail

ADULT

pink legs and toes

FLIGHT: rapid and straight, with intermittent flaps and glides.

The Gray-cheeked Thrush is the least known of the four North American *Catharus* thrushes because it breeds in remote areas of Canada and Alaska. In fact, most of the existing information on this species is a result of research on the Bicknell's Thrush, which was considered to be a subspecies of the Gray-cheeked Thrush until 1993. During migration, the Gray-cheeked Thrush is more likely to be heard in flight at night than seen on the ground by birdwatchers.

VOICE Call a thin *kweer*, sometimes two notes; song flute-like, somewhat nasal, several notes ending on a lower pitch.

NESTING Cup of grass, twigs, moss, dead leaves, and mud, placed near ground in shrubbery; 4 eggs; 1 brood; May–July.

FEEDING Forages insects, including beetles, ants, spiders, earthworms, and fruit.

FEEDING HABITAT
A Gray-cheeked Thrush hops across the forest floor looking for prey.

OCCURRENCE
On breeding grounds, occupies densely vegetated areas with small shrubs; preference for spruce forests in northern Canada and Alaska. During migration, favors wooded areas with dense understory. In winter, prefers forested areas and secondary succession woodlands.

SIMILAR SPECIES

BICKNELL'S THRUSH see p.282

olive-brown upperparts

brownish spots

MIGRATION PATTERN
During migration, this bird can be seen near a variety of sites with trees or shrubs.

Length 6½–7in (16–18cm)	Wingspan 11½–13½in (29–34cm)	Weight ⅞–1¹⁄₁₆oz (26–30g)
Social **Mixed flocks**	Lifespan **Up to 7 years**	Status **Secure**

DATE: _____ TIME: _____ LOCATION: _____

| Order **Passeriformes** | Family **Turdidae** | Species *Catharus bicknelli* |

Bicknell's Thrush

olive-brown upperparts

ADULT

indistinct eye-ring

blackish upper bill

olive-brown head

brownish olive back

tan spots

olive-brown wings

rufous tail

IN FLIGHT

pale base to bill

brown specks and spots

buff breast

whitish to buff belly

whitish to buff undertail feathers

grayish buff wash on flanks

IMMATURE

pink legs

FLIGHT: rapid and straight, with intermittent flaps and glides.

Bicknell's Thrush was long considered a subspecies of the Gray-cheeked Thrush, until 1993 when it was shown to be a distinct species with a slight difference in color, song, habitat, and migration. In the field, it is best distinguished from the Gray-cheeked Thrush by its song, which is less full and lower in pitch. Bicknell's Thrush breeds only in dwarf conifer forests on mountain tops in eastern Canada and adjacent northeastern US, usually above 3,000ft (1,000m). Habitat loss threatens this species on its wintering grounds in Cuba, Hispaniola, and Puerto Rico. Males and females mate with multiple partners in a single season; because of this, males may care for young in multiple nests.

VOICE Call *pheeuw*, one or two notes; complicated flute-like song of about four parts, ending with rising pitch; males sing, especially during flight; females rarely sing; song varies among populations.

NESTING Cup of moss and evergreen twigs, near ground; 3–4 eggs; 1 brood; June–August.

FEEDING Feeds mainly on caterpillars and insects; in addition, fruit during migration and possibly in winter.

MOUNTAIN-TOP BREEDING
This species breeds in high-elevation woodland areas, especially in conifers.

SIMILAR SPECIES

GRAY-CHEEKED THRUSH
see p.281

olive-gray brown

grayish face

OCCURRENCE
Restricted to dense spruce or fir forest at or near the treeline, at 3,000ft (1,000m), often in disturbed areas undergoing successional changes. During migration, found in a variety of habitats, such as woodlots and beaches. In winter, strong preference for wet mountainous Caribbean forests.

| Length 6½–7in (16–18cm) | Wingspan 12in (30cm) | Weight ⅞–1¹⁄₁₆ oz (26–30g) |
| Social **Solitary/Small flocks** | Lifespan **Up to 8 years** | Status **Vulnerable** |

DATE: _____ TIME: _____ LOCATION: _____

Order **Passeriformes**	Family **Turdidae**	Species ***Catharus ustulatus***

Swainson's Thrush

ADULT

IN FLIGHT

olive-brown rump and tail

more rufous in upperparts

russet back

**ADULT
C. u. ustulatus
(WESTERN)**

smaller, less distinct, sparser spotting

buffy eye-ring

olive-brown upperparts

buff breast

distinct blackish spots

**ADULT
C. u. swainsoni
(EASTERN)**

S wainson's Thrush can be distinguished from other spotted thrushes by its buffy face and the rising pitch of its flute-like, melodious song. This species is also distinctive as it feeds higher up in the understory than most of its close relatives. The western subspecies of Swainson's Thrush is russet-backed and migrates to Central America for the winter, while the other populations are olive-backed and winter in South America.

VOICE Single-note call *whit* or *whooit*; main song delivered by males, several phrases, each one spiraling upward; flute-like song is given during breeding and migration.

NESTING Open cup of twigs, moss, dead leaves, bark, and mud, on branches near trunks of small trees or in shrubs; 3–4 eggs; 1–2 broods; April–July.

FEEDING Forages in the air, using fly-catching methods to capture a wide range of insects during breeding season; berries during migration and in winter.

FLIGHT: rapid and straight, with intermittent flaps and glides.

DISTINCTIVE SONG
This bird's song distinguishes it from other thrushes.

TREE DWELLER
Shy and retiring, Swainson's Thrush feeds in trees more than other *Catharus* thrushes.

OCCURRENCE
Breeds mainly in coniferous forests, especially spruce and fir, except in California, where it prefers deciduous riverside woodlands and damp meadows with shrubbery. During spring and fall migrations, dense understory is preferred. Winter habitat is mainly old growth forest.

SIMILAR SPECIES

VEERY
see p.280

tawny brown back

HERMIT THRUSH
see p.284

lightly spotted breast

rust-colored tail

grayish cheeks

streaks on sides of breast

Length 6½–7½in (16–19cm)	Wingspan 11½–12in (29–31cm)	Weight ⅞–1⁹⁄₁₆oz (25–45g)
Social **Pairs/Flocks**	Lifespan **Up to 11 years**	Status **Declining**

| Order **Passeriformes** | Family **Turdidae** | Species *Catharus guttatus* |

Hermit Thrush

thin, white eye-ring

gray-brown upperparts

darker brown upperparts

dark spots on whitish breast

ADULT C. G. FAXONI (EASTERN)

paler gray flanks

brownish back

IN FLIGHT

gray-brown upperparts

ADULT C. g. guttatus (NORTHWESTERN)

more extensive breast spotting

dark spots on buff breast

ADULT C. g. audoboni (ROCKIES)

reddish tail

ADULT C. g. faxoni (EASTERN)

tawny buff flanks

The Hermit Thrush's song is the signature sound of northerly and mountain forests in the West—fluted, almost bi-tonal, far-carrying, and ending up with almost a question mark. The Hermit Thrush is so named because of its solitary lifestyle, especially in winter, when birds maintain inter-individual territories. Geographical variation within the vast range of the species has led to the recognition of nine subspecies (three are shown here). It generally winters south of the US, in Mexico, Guatemala, and El Salvador.

VOICE Calls *tchek*, soft, dry; song flute-like, ethereal, falling, repetitive, and varied; several phrases delivered on a different pitch.

NESTING Cup of grasses, mosses, twigs, leaves, mud, hair, on ground or in low tree branches; 4 eggs; 1–2 broods; May–July.

FEEDING Mainly forages on ground for insects, larvae, earthworms, and snails; in winter, also eats fruit.

FLIGHT: rapid and straight, with intermittent flaps and glides.

URBAN VISITOR
This thrush is frequently seen in wooded areas in urban and suburban parks.

OCCURRENCE
Occurs in coniferous forests and mixed conifer–deciduous woodlands; prefers to nest along the edges of a forest interior, like a bog location. Found in forest and other open woodlands during winter. During migration, found in many wooded habitats.

SIMILAR SPECIES

VEERY see p.280
tawny brown back
lightly spotted breast

BICKNELL'S THRUSH see p.282
olive-brown back
yellow base of bill

SWAINSON'S THRUSH see p.283
olive-brown upperparts

| Length **6–7in (15–18cm)** | Wingspan **10–11in (25–28cm)** | Weight **⅞–1¹/₁₆ oz (25–30g)** |
| Social **Solitary** | Lifespan **Up to 9 years** | Status **Secure** |

DATE: _____ TIME:_____ LOCATION:_____

| Order **Passeriformes** | Family **Turdidae** | Species *Hylocichla mustelina* |

Wood Thrush

ADULT

rusty orange head and back

roundish, brown wings

IN FLIGHT

short, reddish brown tail

white eye-ring

rusty orange head

reddish brown lower back and rump

black bill with pink base

creamy pink legs and toes

large, black triangular spots on breast, sides, and flanks

ADULT

FLIGHT: straight, direct flight with consistent wing beats.

The Wood Thrush is perhaps the most striking of the small North American thrushes, due to the black spots that cover its underparts, and its rufous head and back. In the breeding season, its flute-like song echoes through the Northeastern hardwood forests and suburban forested areas. Wood Thrush populations have fallen over the past 30 years, largely due to forest destruction and fragmentation. Sadly, this decline has been exacerbated by the Wood Thrush's susceptibility to parasitism by the Brown-headed Cowbird.

VOICE Rapid *pip-pippipip* or *rhuu-rhuu*; a three-part flute-like song—first part indistinct, second part loudest, third part trilled; males have variations of all three parts; mainly before sunrise.

NESTING Cup-shaped nest made with dried grass and weeds in trees or shrubs; 3–4 eggs; 1–2 broods; May–July.

FEEDING Forages in leaf litter, mainly for worms, beetles, moths, caterpillars; eats fruits after breeding season.

STUNNING SOLOIST
The Wood Thrush can often be seen singing its melodious songs from a conspicuous perch.

SIMILAR SPECIES

VEERY
see p.280

smaller overall

fainter spotting

longer tail

HERMIT THRUSH
see p.284

reddish tail

spotting only on throat and upper breast

OCCURRENCE
Hardwood forests in the East, from Texas and Florida to Minnesota and the Canadian Maritimes. Breeds in interior and at edges of deciduous and mixed forests; needs dense understory, shrubbery, and moist soil. Winters in Texas, Louisiana, Florida, and south through Central America to Panama.

| Length 7½–8½in (19–21cm) | Wingspan 12–13½in (30–34cm) | Weight 1⁷⁄₁₆–1¾ oz (40–50g) |
| Social **Pairs/Flocks** | Lifespan **Up to 9 years** | Status **Declining** |

DATE: _____ TIME:_____ LOCATION:_____

Order **Passeriformes**	Family **Turdidae**	Species **Turdus migratorius**

American Robin

MALE — dark head

IN FLIGHT

more complete white eye-ring

gray back

orangish red breast

white rump

broken white eye-ring

yellow bill

dark streaks on chin

dark gray back

FEMALE

mottled gray back

spotted breast

JUVENILE

fairly long, dark tail

brick-red underparts

MALE

FLIGHT: strong, swift flights with intermittent flaps and glides.

The American Robin, the largest and most abundant of the North American thrushes, is probably the most familiar bird on the continent, and its presence on suburban lawns is an early sign of spring. Unlike other species, it has adapted and prospered in human-altered habitats. It breeds across all of Canada and the US. And it winters across the US, migrating out of most of Canada in fall. The decision to migrate is largely governed by changes in the availability of food. As the breeding season approaches, it is the males that sing first, either late in winter or early spring. The bird's brick-red breast—more vivid in males than in females—is its most distinguishing feature.

VOICE Calls a high pitch *tjip* and a multi-note, throaty *tjuj-tjuk*; primary song a melodious *cheer-up, cheer-up, cheer-wee*, one of the first birds to be heard during dawn chorus, and one of the last to cease singing in the evening.

NESTING Substantial cup of grass, weeds, twigs, occasional garbage in tree or shrub, in fork of tree, or on branch on tree; 4 eggs; 2–3 broods; April–July.

FEEDING Forages in leaf litter, mainly for earthworms and small insects; mostly consumes fruit in the winter season.

SEASONAL DIET
Robins are particularly dependent on the availability of fruit during the winter months.

SIMILAR SPECIES

VARIED THRUSH
bluish gray upperparts
orange eyebrow
wide black necklace

OCCURRENCE
Breeding habitat a mix of forest, woodland, suburban gardens, lawns, municipal parks, and farms. A partial migrant, these robins tend to be found in woodlands where berry-bearing trees are present. Nonmigrating populations' winter habitat is similar to breeding habitat.

Length **8–11in (20–28cm)**	Wingspan **12–16in (30–41cm)**	Weight **2⅝oz (75g)**
Social **Flocks**	Lifespan **Up to 13 years**	Status **Secure**

DATE: _____ TIME: _____ LOCATION: _____

| Order **Passeriformes** | Family **Mimidae** | Species ***Dumetella carolinensis*** |

Gray Catbird

dark gray to black head

straight, blackish bill

gray overall

gray upperparts

large, black eye

ADULT

long, black tail

IN FLIGHT

gray underparts

bright brick-red undertail feathers

ADULT

I n addition to the feline-like, mewing calls that earned it its common name, the Gray Catbird not only has an extraordinarily varied vocal repertoire, but it can also sing two notes simultaneously. It has been reported to imitate the vocalizations of over 40 bird species, at least one frog species, and several sounds produced by machines and electronic devices. Despite their shy, retiring nature, Gray Catbirds tolerate human presence and will rest in shrubs in suburban and urban lots. Another fascinating skill is the Gray Catbird's ability to recognize and remove eggs of the brood parasite, the Brown-headed Cowbird.
VOICE *Mew* call, like a young kitten; song a long, complex series of unhurried, often grouped notes, sometimes interspersed with whistles and squeaks.
NESTING Large, untidy cup of woven twigs, grass, and hair lined with finer material; 3–4 eggs; 1–2 broods; May–August.
FEEDING Feeds on a wide variety of berries and insects, usually whatever is most abundant in season.

FLIGHT: short flights between habitat patches with constant, medium-speed wing beats.

ANGLED ATTITUDE
Between bouts of feeding, a Gray Catbird often rests with its body and tail at a 50 degree angle.

LARGE BLACK EYES
Peering from the foliage, a Gray Catbird investigates its surroundings.

OCCURRENCE
Breeds in mixed young to mid-aged forests with abundant undergrowth, from British Columbia east to Maritimes and Newfoundland, and in the US diagonally west-east from Washington State to New Mexico, east to the Gulf Coast, north to New England. Northern population migratory.

SIMILAR SPECIES

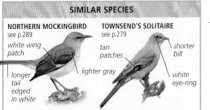

NORTHERN MOCKINGBIRD
see p.289
white wing patch
longer tail edged in white

TOWNSEND'S SOLITAIRE
see p.279
tan patches
lighter gray
shorter bill
white eye-ring

| Length **8–9½in (20–24cm)** | Wingspan **10–12in (25–30cm)** | Weight **1¼–2⅛oz (35–60g)** |
| Social **Solitary/Pairs** | Lifespan **Up to 11 years** | Status **Secure** |

DATE: _____ TIME: _____ LOCATION: _____

| Order **Passeriformes** | Family **Mimidae** | Species *Toxostoma rufum* |

Brown Thrasher

bright yellow eye

grayish cheeks

fairly straight, dark bill

indistinct "mustache"

reddish brown upperparts

dark streaking on pale underparts

rufous wings and upperparts

ADULT

long tail with pale outer tips

IN FLIGHT

two pale wing bars

long tail, paler than back

ADULT

The Brown Thrasher is usually difficult to view clearly because it keeps to dense underbrush. Like most other thrashers, this species prefers running or hopping to flying. When nesting, it can recognize and remove the eggs of brood parasites like the Brown-headed Cowbird. The current population decline is most likely the result of fragmentation of large, wooded habitats into patches, which lack the forest interior habitat this species needs.
VOICE Calls varied, including rasping sounds; song a long series of musical notes, sometimes imitating other species; repeats phrase twice before moving onto the next one.
NESTING Bulky cup of twigs, close to ground, lined with leaves, grass, bark; 3–5 eggs; 1 brood; April–July.
FEEDING Mainly insects (especially beetles) and worms gathered from leaf litter on the forest floor; will peck at cultivated grains, nuts, berries, and fruit.

FLIGHT: slow and heavy with deep wing beats; below treetops, especially in and around ground.

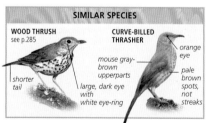

SIMILAR SPECIES

WOOD THRUSH
see p.285

shorter tail

large, dark eye with white eye-ring

CURVE-BILLED THRASHER

mouse gray-brown upperparts

orange eye

pale brown spots, not streaks

STREAKED BREAST
Displaying its heavily streaked underparts, this Brown Thrasher is perched and ready to sing.

OCCURRENCE
Widespread across central and eastern North America, from Canada to Texas and Florida, in a variety of densely wooded habitats, particularly those with thick undergrowth, but will use woodland edges, hedges, and riverside trees. A partial migrant, it winters in the southern part of its range.

| Length **10–12in (25–30cm)** | Wingspan **11–14in (28–36cm)** | Weight **2⅛–2⅞oz (60–80g)** |
| Social **Solitary/Flocks** | Lifespan **Up to 13 years** | Status **Declining** |

DATE: _____ TIME: _____ LOCATION: _____

| Order **Passeriformes** | Family **Mimidae** | Species *Mimus polyglottos* |

Northern Mockingbird

ADULT

white patches on wing

IN FLIGHT

shorter tail

speckled breast and belly

JUVENILE

gray head

pointed, curved bill

yellow eye

long tail with white outer tail feathers

white undertail feathers

FLIGHT: usually direct and level on constant, somewhat fluttering, quick wing beats.

ADULT

white patch on wing feathers

The ability of the Northern Mockingbird to imitate sounds is truly impressive: some individuals can incorporate more than 100 different phrases of as many different birds in their songs. Phrases are usually repeated, often quite a few times, and somewhat modified at each repetition. This species, once thought to be headed for extinction due to the caged-bird trade in the 1700s and 1800s, has largely recovered since then. In fact, the Northern Mockingbird's range has expanded in the last few decades, partly due to its high tolerance for humans and their habitats. A diagnostic field characteristic is its tendency to "wing flash," displaying its white outer wing feather patches on raised wings, possibly to scare insects into the open.

VOICE Long, complex repertoire often imitating other birds, non-bird noises, and the sounds of mechanical devices.

NESTING Bulky cup of twigs, lined, in shrub or tree; 3–5 eggs; 1–3 broods; March–August.

FEEDING Eats a wide variety of fruit, berries, and insects, including ants, beetles, and grasshoppers.

BERRY PICKER
Northern Mockingbirds love berries, and make good use of them during the fall.

SIMILAR SPECIES

LOGGERHEAD SHRIKE ☾
see p.240

brown mask

black wings

CLARK'S NUTCRACKER

white patch low on wing

darker gray belly

whiter sides to tail

OCCURRENCE
Widespread in the US from coast to coast south of the timberline, primarily along edges of disturbed habitats, including young forests and especially suburban and urban areas with shrubs or hedges. Breeding range has extended into southern Canada.

| Length **8½–10in (22–25cm)** | Wingspan **13–15in (33–38cm)** | Weight **1⁹⁄₁₆–2oz (45–55g)** |
| Social **Pairs** | Lifespan **Up to 20 years** | Status **Secure** |

DATE: _____ TIME:_____ LOCATION:_____

| Order **Passeriformes** | Family **Sturnidae** | Species **Sturnus vulgaris** |

European Starling

short, square tail

pointed, triangular wings

body feathers tipped whitish or buff

wing feathers edged bright orange-buff

ADULT (BREEDING)

IN FLIGHT

large spots on undertail

ADULT (NONBREEDING)

black face with hints of shiny, glossy purple

glossy black body with mostly green sheen

blue-based, sharp, yellow bill; pink-based on female

dark, glossy, blue-black belly

MALE (BREEDING)

long, pinkish brown legs and strong toes

dull brownish head

dark bill

plain brown body

IMMATURE (FALL)

JUVENILE

This distinctive non-native species is perhaps the most successful bird in North America—and probably the most maligned. In the 1890s, 60 to 100 European Starlings were successfully released in New York City's Central Park to become the ancestors of the 200 million birds now living in North America. This adaptable and aggressive bird competes with native species for nest sites, and usually wins—even against larger species such as the Northern Flicker and American Kestrel.
VOICE Highly varied; gives whooshing *ssssssheer*, often in flight; also whistled *wheeeooo*; song an elaborate pulsing series with slurred whistles and clicking notes; imitates other birds and other noises.
NESTING Natural or artificial cavity of any sort; 4–6 eggs; 1–2 broods; March–July.
FEEDING Omnivorous; picks at anything that might be edible; insects and berries are common food items; also visits birdfeeders and trashcans; often feeds on grubs in lawns.

FLIGHT: individuals fly in direct, buzzy manner; flocks bunch up tightly in flight.

INSECT EATER
Despite its parents' omnivorous diet, the nestlings are fed almost exclusively on insects and larvae.

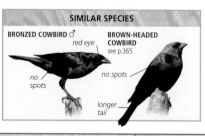

SIMILAR SPECIES

BRONZED COWBIRD ♂
red eye
no spots

BROWN-HEADED COWBIRD
see p.365
no spots
longer tail

OCCURRENCE
In North America from southern Canada to the US–Mexico border; also Puerto Rico and other Caribbean islands. Common to abundant in cities, towns, and farmlands; also occurs in relatively "wild" settings far from human habitation. Forms flocks at all times, huge in winter.

| Length **8½in (21cm)** | Wingspan **16in (41cm)** | Weight **2⅝– 3⅜oz (75–95g)** |
| Social **Colonies** | Lifespan **Up to 17 years** | Status **Secure** |

DATE: _____ TIME:_____ LOCATION:_____

Order **Passeriformes**	Family **Motacillidae**	Species **Anthus rubescens**

American Pipit

ADULT

faint streaking on gray upperparts

pale eyebrow

"mustache"

buffy eyestripe

thin, dark bill

dark "mustache"

no streaking on grayish back

wing bars

gray cheek with buffy eyestripes

whitish with heavier streaking on chest and flanks

IN FLIGHT

ADULT (NONBREEDING)

white outer tail feathers

pale edges to wing feathers

long tail with white outer tail feathers

light reddish buffy chest and flanks

ADULT (BREEDING)

long hind claw

dark legs and toes

FLIGHT: typically strong with a distinct, undulating, rise and fall pattern.

The American Pipit is divided into four subspecies, three of which breed in North America, and the fourth in Siberia. In nonbreeding plumage, the American Pipit is a drab-looking, brownish gray bird that forages for insects along water and shores, or in cultivated fields with short stems. In the breeding season, molting transforms it into a beauty—with gray upperparts and reddish underparts. American Pipits are known for pumping their tails up and down. When breeding, males display by rising into the air, then flying down with wings open and singing. Its migration takes the American Pipit as far south as Guatemala.

VOICE Alarm call a *tzeeep*; song repeated *tzwee-tzooo* from the air.
NESTING Cup in shallow depression on ground, outer frame of grass, lined with fine grass and hair; 4–6 eggs; 1 brood; June–July.
FEEDING Picks insects; also eats seeds during migration.

WINTER DRAB
Foraging in short vegetation, this bird is almost the same color as its surroundings.

OCCURRENCE
Breeds in Arctic tundra in the north, and alpine tundra in the Rockies; also breeds on treeless mountain tops in Maine and New Hampshire. Winters in open coastal areas and harvested agricultural fields across the US. Some North American migrants fly to Asia for the winter.

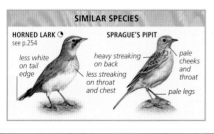

SIMILAR SPECIES

HORNED LARK ☾
see p.254

less white on tail edge

SPRAGUE'S PIPIT

heavy streaking on back

less streaking on throat and chest

pale cheeks and throat

pale legs

Length **6–8in (15–20cm)**	Wingspan **10–11in (25–28cm)**	Weight **¹¹⁄₁₆oz (20g)**
Social **Flocks**	Lifespan **Up to 6 years**	Status **Secure**

DATE: _____ TIME:_____ LOCATION:_____

| Order **Passeriformes** | Family **Bombycillidae** | Species *Bombycilla garrulus* |

Bohemian Waxwing

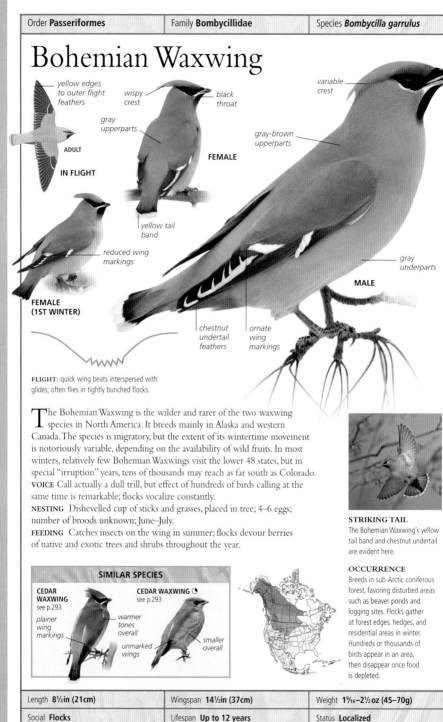

yellow edges to outer flight feathers

wispy crest

black throat

variable crest

gray upperparts

gray-brown upperparts

ADULT

IN FLIGHT

FEMALE

yellow tail band

reduced wing markings

gray underparts

FEMALE (1ST WINTER)

chestnut undertail feathers

ornate wing markings

MALE

FLIGHT: quick wing beats interspesed with glides; often flies in tightly bunched flocks.

The Bohemian Waxwing is the wilder and rarer of the two waxwing species in North America. It breeds mainly in Alaska and western Canada. The species is migratory, but the extent of its wintertime movement is notoriously variable, depending on the availability of wild fruits. In most winters, relatively few Bohemian Waxwings visit the lower 48 states, but in special "irruption" years, tens of thousands may reach as far south as Colorado.
VOICE Call actually a dull trill, but effect of hundreds of birds calling at the same time is remarkable; flocks vocalize constantly.
NESTING Dishevelled cup of sticks and grasses, placed in tree; 4–6 eggs; number of broods unknown; June–July.
FEEDING Catches insects on the wing in summer; flocks devour berries of native and exotic trees and shrubs throughout the year.

STRIKING TAIL
The Bohemian Waxwing's yellow tail band and chestnut undertail are evident here.

OCCURRENCE
Breeds in sub-Arctic coniferous forest, favoring disturbed areas such as beaver ponds and logging sites. Flocks gather at forest edges, hedges, and residential areas in winter. Hundreds or thousands of birds appear in an area, then disappear once food is depleted.

SIMILAR SPECIES

CEDAR WAXWING
see p.293

plainer wing markings

CEDAR WAXWING ◐
see p.293

warmer tones overall

unmarked wings

smaller overall

| Length **8½in (21cm)** | Wingspan **14½in (37cm)** | Weight **1⁹⁄₁₆–2½oz (45–70g)** |
| Social **Flocks** | Lifespan **Up to 12 years** | Status **Localized** |

DATE: _____ TIME: _____ LOCATION: _____

Cedar Waxwing

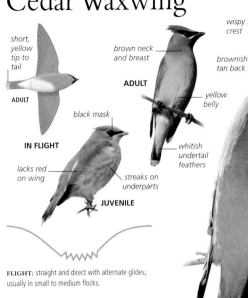

wispy crest

white bars on face

short, yellow tip to tail

brown neck and breast

ADULT

brownish tan back

black "bandit" mask

yellow belly

ADULT

black mask

IN FLIGHT

whitish undertail feathers

ADULT

lacks red on wing

streaks on underparts

JUVENILE

waxy, red tips on inner wing

FLIGHT: straight and direct with alternate glides; usually in small to medium flocks.

Flocks of Cedar Waxwings, a nomadic species, move around the US and Canada looking for berries, which are their main source of food. Common in a specific location one year, they may disappear the next and occur elsewhere. Northern breeders tend to be more migratory than southern ones. In winter, their nomadic tendencies send Cedar Waxwings as far south as South America. They can often be heard and identified by their high-pitched calls, long before the flock settles to feed.

VOICE Basic vocalization a shrill trill: *shr-r-r-r-r* or *tre-e-e-e-e-e*, which appears to serve the function of both call note and song.

NESTING Open cup placed in fork of tree, often lined with grasses, plant fibers; 3–5 eggs; 1–2 broods; June–August.

FEEDING Eats in flocks at trees and shrubs with ripe berries throughout the year; also catches flying insects in summer.

BATHING ADULT
Cedar Waxwings love to take baths, and use birdbaths in suburban gardens.

SIMILAR SPECIES

BOHEMIAN WAXWING ♂
see p.292

larger overall

BOHEMIAN WAXWING ♀ ●
see p.292

more ornate wing pattern

pale gray breast

rufous undertail

OCCURRENCE
Across northern US and southern Canada, in wooded areas. Breeds in woodlands, especially near streams and clearings. Winters anywhere where trees and shrubs have ripe fruits, especially in Mexico and South America. Spends a lot of time in treetops, but sometimes comes down to shrub level.

Length **7¹⁄₂in (19cm)**	Wingspan **12in (30cm)**	Weight **1¹⁄₁₆–1¹⁄₄oz (30–35g)**
Social **Flocks**	Lifespan **Up to 7 years**	Status **Secure**

DATE: _____ TIME: _____ LOCATION: _____

LONGSPURS AND SNOW BUNTINGS

Members of the longspur and Snow Bunting families are small, short-legged birds of open country. In eastern Canada, the family includes two species in the genus *Calcarius*, Lapland and Smith's Longspurs; and one in *Plectrophenax*, the Snow Bunting. They have recently been made into a separate family distinct from the Old World buntings and New World sparrows with which they had previously been closely linked. Longspurs derive their name from their long, curved hindclaws.

In winter, the birds belonging to this family feed in flocks—Snow Buntings are especially gregarious and eye-catching birds, justifying their colloquial name "snowflake," as they rise in a blizzard of white wings. Lapland Longspurs sometimes form immense flocks, even millions strong. Snow Buntings breed in tundra habitat, mostly in the Arctic but with a few populations found in subarctic mountain tops. Lapland and Smith's Longspurs both breed in tundra habitat. Snow Bunting and Lapland Longspur are also found in Eurasia, while the other species are found only in North America. Smith's Longspur breeds in Alaska and northern Canada, wintering in the central US.

EYE-CATCHING IN SUMMER
This breeding male Smith's Longspur has an orangish neck, chest, and belly, and a contrasting black-and-white patterned head.

CHANGING COLORS
Snow Buntings are well camouflaged against exposed rocks and snow throughout the year. Brown edges on the feathers in winter wear off, so that in spring they become pristine black and white.

| Order **Passeriformes** | Family **Calcariidae** | Species *Calcarius lapponicus* |

Lapland Longspur

thin, white edge to tail

MALE (BREEDING)

black face

IN FLIGHT

rich buffy hood

streaked crown

white eye-line

thick, yellowish bill

bright rufous nape

black streak on throat

FEMALE (BREEDING)

rusty wing panel

thick streaking on flanks

ADULT (NONBREEDING)

white underparts

MALE (BREEDING)

black flanks

FLIGHT: deeply undulating, with birds often calling in troughs as they flap.

One of the most numerous breeding birds of the Arctic tundra, the Lapland Longspur is found in huge flocks over open habitats of Canada's southern prairies and into the US in the winter. They can be seen on gravel roads and in barren countryside immediately following heavy snowfalls. Genetic (DNA) evidence suggests that the four longspur species and the two *Plectrophenax* buntings do not belong to the Emberizidae family, but rather form a distinct group of their own. This species is known as the Lapland Bunting in Great Britain and Ireland.
VOICE Flight call a dry rattle, *tyew*, unlike other longspurs; song a series of thin tinklings and whistles, often in flight.
NESTING Cup of grass and sedges placed in depression on ground next to a clump of vegetation; 4–6 eggs; 1 brood; May–July.
FEEDING Eats insects during breeding season; seeds in winter.

CONSPICUOUS SPECIES
This longspur is one of the most conspicuous breeding birds on the Arctic tundra.

OCCURRENCE
Breeds in tundra right across Arctic North America and Eurasia. Winters in open grasslands and barren fields, and on beaches across the northern and central US and parts of southern Canada.

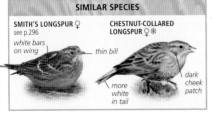

SIMILAR SPECIES

SMITH'S LONGSPUR ♀
see p.296

white bars on wing

CHESTNUT-COLLARED LONGSPUR ♀ ✳

thin bill

more white in tail

dark cheek patch

| Length 6½in (16cm) | Wingspan 10½–11½in (27–29cm) | Weight ⅞–1¹⁄₁₆oz (25–30g) |
| Social **Large flocks** | Lifespan **Up to 5 years** | Status **Secure** |

DATE: _____ TIME: _____ LOCATION: _____

Order **Passeriformes**	Family **Calcariidae**	Species *Calcarius pictus*

Smith's Longspur

MALE (BREEDING)

IN FLIGHT

white outer tail feathers

white cheek patch

relatively long wings

rich, buffy overall

wings extend past tail

FEMALE (FALL)

fine breast streaks

black-and-white "helmet"

thin bill

orange collar

white shoulder

rich pumpkin-colored underparts

MALE (BREEDING)

white undertail feathers

With its pumpkin-colored breast and black-and-white "helmet," Smith's Longspur in its breeding colors contrasts strongly with its drab winter plumage. On both its remote breeding grounds in the Arctic, and its restricted shortgrass range in winter, this bird hides on the ground at all times, making it very hard to spot. Smith's Longspur migrates through the Great Plains to reach its wintering grounds, but on the return journey it swings east, giving it an elliptical migration path. This species breeds communally: males mate with several females who, in turn, mate with other males.

VOICE Flight call a mechanical, dry, sharp rattle; also a nasal *nief* when squabbling; song a series of thin, sweet whistles.

NESTING Concealed cup of sedges, lined with feathers, placed in hummock on ground; 3–5 eggs; 1 brood; June–July.

FEEDING Eats mainly seeds and insects; migrants may rely heavily upon introduced foxtail grass.

FLIGHT: deeply undulating, with birds often calling in troughs as they flap.

LINEBACK LONGSPUR
On his breeding or spring staging grounds, the male sports a striking black-and-white "helmet."

SIMILAR SPECIES

LAPLAND LONGSPUR ♀ ❄
see p.295

thicker bill

broad, reddish edges to wings

CHESTNUT-COLLARED LONGSPUR ♀ ❄

lacks rich buff color and streaks

more white in tail

OCCURRENCE
Breeds along the tundra-taiga timberline from northern Alaska southeast to northern Ontario; also mountainous southeastern Alaska and southwestern Yukon. Migrant birds are found in shortgrass prairie. Winters in various open areas with shortgrass in Kansas, Texas, and Arkansas.

Length **6–6½in (15–16cm)**	Wingspan **10–11½in (25–29cm)**	Weight **⅞–1¹/₁₆oz (25–30g)**
Social **Large flocks**	Lifespan **Up to 5 years**	Status **Secure**

DATE: _____ TIME: _____ LOCATION: _____

Snow Bunting

less white in wings

white outer tail feathers

MALE (NONBREEDING)
white head and underparts

black back

yellow bill

IN FLIGHT
large white patches on black wings

MALE (BREEDING)
black bill

FEMALE (BREEDING)
pale rufous crown

white underparts

dark brown eyes

rusty orange cheek patch

black peeks through buffy feather edgings

FEMALE (NONBREEDING)

gray body

white eye-ring

MALE (NONBREEDING)

rusty orange breast patch

white underparts

JUVENILE

The bold white wing patches of the Snow Bunting make it immediately recognizable in a whirling winter flock of dark-winged longspurs and larks. In winter, heavy snowfall forces flocks onto roadsides, where they can be seen more easily. To secure and defend the best territories, some of the males of this remarkably hardy species arrive as early as April in their barren high-Arctic breeding grounds. The Snow Bunting is very similar in appearance to the rare and localized McKay's Bunting. Although McKay's Bunting generally has less black on the back, in the wings, and on the tail, the two species cannot always be conclusively identified. This is especially true since Snow and McKay's Buntings sometimes interbreed, producing hybrids.

VOICE Flight call a musical, liquid rattle, also *tyew* notes and short buzz; song a pleasant series of squeaky and whistled notes.

NESTING Bulky cup of grass and moss, lined with feathers, and placed in sheltered rock crevice; 3–6 eggs; 1 brood; June–August.

FEEDING Eats seeds (sedge in Arctic), flies and other insects, and buds on migration.

FLIGHT: deeply undulating; flocks "roll" along as birds at back overtake those in front.

ROCKY GROUND
About the only perches in the Snow Bunting's barren breeding grounds are large boulders.

SIMILAR SPECIES

McKAY'S BUNTING
mostly white tail, back, and wings

OCCURRENCE
Breeds in rocky areas, usually near sparsely vegetated tundra, right across the Arctic. North American birds winters in open country and on shores across the whole of southern Canada and the northern US, and in southern and western coastal areas of Alaska.

Length 6½–7in (16–18cm)	Wingspan 12½–14in (32–35cm)	Weight 1¼–2oz (35–55g)
Social **Large flocks**	Lifespan **Unknown**	Status **Declining**

DATE: _____ TIME: _____ LOCATION: _____

WOOD WARBLERS

THE FAMILY PARULIDAE IS REMARKABLE for its diversity in plumage, song, feeding, breeding biology, and sexual dimorphism. In general though, warblers share similar shapes: all are smallish birds with longish, thin bills (unlike thick vireo bills) used mostly for snapping up invertebrates. The odd, chunky, thick-billed Yellow-breasted Chat is a notable exception, but genetic data suggests what many birders have long suspected: it's not a warbler at all! Ground-dwelling warblers tend to be larger and clad in olives, browns, and yellows, while many arboreal species are small and sport bright oranges, cool blues, and even ruby reds. The color, location, and presence or absence of paler wingbars and tail spots is often a good identification aid. Warblers recently underwent an explosion of speciation in the East, and over 30 species may be seen there in a morning of spring birding. The spring arrival of beautiful

singing males is the birding highlight of the year for many birdwatchers. Eastern-breeding species utilize three different migration strategies to deal with the obstacle of the Gulf of Mexico when coming from and going to their Neotropical wintering grounds. Circum-Gulf migrants fly through Mexico, along the western shore of the Gulf of Mexico. Caribbean migrants travel through Florida and island hop through the Caribbean. And finally, trans-Gulf migrants fly directly across the Gulf of Mexico between the Yucatan Peninsula and the northern Gulf Coast. Birds flying this last and most deadly route are subject to serious predation by falcons roosting on oil rigs and to abrupt weather changes over the Gulf which sometimes yield spectacular fallout events at famed locations like High Island, Texas.

PLASTIC PLUMAGE
Many male *Setophaga* warblers (like this Blackburnian) are only brightly colored when breeding.

FEEDING STRATEGIES
Some warblers, such as this Black-and-white, probe the cracks in tree trunks for food.

STATIC PLUMAGE
In other warbler species, such as this Golden-winged, males keep their stunning plumage year-round.

Order **Passeriformes**	Family **Parulidae**	Species *Seiurus aurocapilla*

Ovenbird

orange-and-black
striped crown

bold white
eye-ring

IN FLIGHT

plain olive
overall

ADULT

olive
upperparts

white
throat

black
streaked
underparts

ADULT

FLIGHT: fast, slightly undulating, and direct with rapid wing beats.

Like members of the unrelated, tropical ovenbird family (Furnariidae), this little bird is so-called for the domed, oven-like nests it builds on the ground; unique structures for a North American bird. The Ovenbird is also noted for its singing. Males flit about boisterously, often at night, incorporating portions of their main song into a jumble of spluttering notes. In the forest, one male singing loudly to declare his territory can set off a whole chain of responses from his neighbors, until the whole forest rings.

VOICE Call variably pitched, sharp *chik* in series; flight call high, rising *siiii*; song loud, ringing crescendo of paired notes *chur-tee' chur-tee' chur-tee' chur-tee' chur-TEE chur-TEE chur-TEE*.

NESTING Domed structure of leaves and grass on ground with side entrance; 3–6 eggs; 1 brood; May–July.

FEEDING Forages mainly on the forest floor for insects and other invertebrates.

STRUTTING ITS STUFF
The Ovenbird is noted for the way it struts across the forest floor like a tiny chicken.

OCCURRENCE
Breeds in closed-canopy mixed and deciduous forests with suitable amount of fallen plant material for nest building and foraging; migrants and wintering birds use similar habitats.

SIMILAR SPECIES

NORTHERN WATERTHRUSH much slimmer; see p.301

dark brown upperparts

no eye-ring

LOUISIANA WATERTHRUSH see p.300

white eyebrow

dark brown upperparts

Length **6in (15cm)**	Wingspan **9½in (24cm)**	Weight **⁹⁄₁₆–⁷⁄₈oz (16–25g)**
Social **Solitary/Flocks**	Lifespan **Up to 7 years**	Status **Declining**

DATE: _____ TIME: _____ LOCATION: _____

| Order **Passeriformes** | Family **Parulidae** | Species **Parkesia motacilla** |

Louisiana Waterthrush

short tail

dull brown overall

ADULT

IN FLIGHT

white eyebrow flares behind eye

buffy area near bill and eye

large bill

unstreaked throat

thick, sparse breast streaking

bicolored flanks; white forward, washed cinnamon on rear

ADULT

bright, bubble gum pink legs and toes in spring

FLIGHT: fast, slightly undulating, and direct with rapid wing beats.

The Louisiana Waterthrush is one of the earliest warblers to return north in the spring; as early as March, eastern ravines are filled with cascades of its song. Both the stream-loving Louisiana Waterthrush and its still-water cousin, the Northern Waterthrush, bob their tails as they walk, but the Louisiana Waterthrush arcs its entire body at the same time. In spring, this species shows brighter pink legs than the Northern Waterthrush.

VOICE Call a round *spink*; flight call a rising, buzzy *ziiiit*; song a loud, descending, ringing, whistled cascade, ending with sputtering *see'-oh see'-oh see'-uh see'-uh tip-uh-tik-uh-tip-whee'ur-tik.*

NESTING Bulky mass of leaves, moss, and twigs, under steep stream bank over water; 4–6 eggs; 1 brood; May–August.

FEEDING Forages in streams for insect larvae, snails, and small fish; also catches flying insects such as dragonflies and stoneflies.

TAKING A LITTLE DIP
In many ways, this species is the "dipper of the East," picking invertebrates from shallow streams.

SIMILAR SPECIES

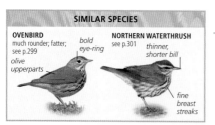

OVENBIRD
much rounder; fatter; see p.299
olive upperparts

bold eye-ring

NORTHERN WATERTHRUSH
see p.301
thinner, shorter bill

fine breast streaks

OCCURRENCE
Breeds along fast-moving streams in deciduous forests in the eastern US and southern Ontario; migrants stop over near running water, including gardens; winters along wooded streams and rivers in mountains and hills in the Caribbean, Mexico, Central America, and northern parts of South America.

| Length **6in (15cm)** | Wingspan **10in (25cm)** | Weight **⅝–⅞oz (18–25g)** |
| Social **Solitary** | Lifespan **Up to 8 years** | Status **Secure** |

DATE: _____ TIME:_____ LOCATION:_____

| Order **Passeriformes** | Family **Parulidae** | Species *Parkesia noveboracensis* |

Northern Waterthrush

pale eyebrow
narrows behind eye

dull brown
upperparts

short tail

ADULT

small,
short
bill

pale
eyebrow

streaking
on white or
yellowish
flanks

fine, dense
breast
streaking

IN FLIGHT

ADULT

dull, fleshy-colored
legs and toes

FLIGHT: fast, slightly undulating, and direct
with rapid wing beats.

The tail-bobbing Northern Waterthrush is often
heard giving a *spink!* call as it swiftly flees from
observers. Although this species may be mistaken for the closely
related Louisiana Waterthrush, there are clues that are helpful in
its identification. While the Northern Waterthrush prefers still
water, its relative greatly prefers running water; in addition, its
song is quite unlike that of the Louisiana Waterthrush.
VOICE Call a sharp, rising, ringing *spink!*; flight call a rising,
buzzy *ziiiit*; song a loud series of rich, accelerating, staccato notes,
usually decreasing in pitch *teet, teet, toh-toh toh-toh tyew-tyew!*
NESTING Hair-lined, mossy cup placed on or near ground,
hidden in roots of fallen or standing tree or in riverbank;
4–5 eggs; 1 brood; May–August.
FEEDING Mostly eats insects such as ants, mosquitoes, moths,
and beetles, both larvae and adult, plus slugs, and snails; when
migrating, also eats small crustaceans, and even tiny fish.

YELLOW FORM
Many Northern Waterthrushes have yellow
underparts, like this one, while others have white.

SIMILAR SPECIES

OVENBIRD
much rounder;
fatter; see p.299
olive
upperparts

bold
eye-ring

**LOUISIANA
WATERTHRUSH**
see p.300

orange
wash to
flanks

eyebrow
widens behind
eye

thicker,
longer
bill

OCCURRENCE
Breeds right across northern
North America in dark,
still-water swamps and bogs;
also in the still edges of rivers
and lakes; migrant birds use
wet habitats; winters in
shrubby marshes, mangroves,
and occasionally in crops, such
as rice fields and citrus groves.

| Length **6in (15cm)** | Wingspan **9½in (24cm)** | Weight **½–⅞oz (14–23g)** |
| Social **Solitary** | Lifespan **Up to 9 years** | Status **Secure** |

DATE: _____ TIME: _____ LOCATION: _____

| Order **Passeriformes** | Family **Parulidae** | Species ***Vermivora chrysoptera*** |

Golden-winged Warbler

MALE (in flight) — gray back, bright yellow wing panel, white outer tail feathers

IN FLIGHT

bright yellow wing panel

black "mask"

bright yellow crown

gray back suffused with yellow

unstreaked wings

black throat

yellow wing panel

MALE

white undertail

gray "mask"

FEMALE

greenish yellow crown

One of the continent's most beautiful warblers, this species is unfortunately being genetically swamped by the more southerly Blue-winged Warbler. This situation is worsening as more habitat is cleared and climate changes take place. The Golden-winged interbreeds with the Blue-winged, resulting in two more frequently seen hybrid forms: Brewster's Warbler, which resembles the Blue-winged Warbler, and Lawrence's Warbler, which looks like a Blue-winged Warbler with the mask and black throat of a Golden-winged.

VOICE Call a sharp *tsip*; flight call high, slightly buzzy *ziiih*; song buzzy *zee zuu zuu zuu*, first note higher; birds that deviate from this song pattern may be hybrids.

NESTING Shallow bulky cup, on or just above ground; 4–6 eggs; 1 brood; May–July.

FEEDING Hangs upside down at clusters of curled-up dead leaves; feeds on moth larvae, other winged insects, and spiders.

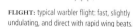

FLIGHT: typical warbler flight: fast, slightly undulating, and direct with rapid wing beats.

SMALL TREES REQUIRED
Golden-winged Warblers breed in shrubby habitats created by clearance and re-growth.

OCCURRENCE
Breeds in the northeastern US and southeastern Canada in short secondary growth habitat with dense patches of deciduous shrubs or tangles, or in marshes with a forest edge; uses any wooded habitat on migration; winters in Central America from Guatemala to north Colombia; mostly on the Caribbean side.

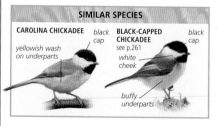

SIMILAR SPECIES

CAROLINA CHICKADEE	BLACK-CAPPED CHICKADEE
black cap	black cap
yellowish wash on underparts	see p.261
	white cheek
	buffy underparts

Length **4¾in (12cm)**	Wingspan **7½in (19cm)**	Weight **⁹⁄₃₂–³⁄₈oz (8–11g)**
Social **Migrant/Winter flocks**	Lifespan **Unknown**	Status **Declining**

DATE: _____ TIME: _____ LOCATION: _____

| Order **Passeriformes** | Family **Parulidae** | Species ***Vermivora cyanoptera*** |

Blue-winged Warbler

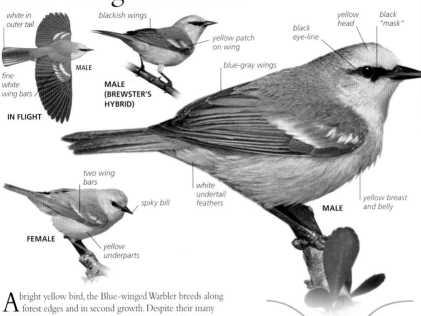

white in outer tail

blackish wings

yellow patch on wing

MALE

blue-gray wings

yellow head

black "mask"

black eye-line

fine white wing bars

IN FLIGHT

MALE (BREWSTER'S HYBRID)

two wing bars

spiky bill

white undertail feathers

yellow breast and belly

MALE

FEMALE

yellow underparts

A bright yellow bird, the Blue-winged Warbler breeds along forest edges and in second growth. Despite their many differences, Blue-winged and Golden-winged warblers are closely related and interbreed freely, producing a variety of fertile combinations. The most frequently produced hybrid, Brewster's Warbler, named in 1874, was once believed to be a different species. It is similar to the Golden-winged Warbler (yellowish breast, two yellow wing bars), but has the Blue-winged's facial pattern, without the black mask and throat.

VOICE Sharp *tsip* call, like *Spizella* sparrows; flight call: a high, slightly buzzy *ziiih;* song is a low, harsh, buzzy *beee-burrrrr,* second note very low in pitch and rattling; deviation from this song pattern may hint at hybrid origin.

NESTING Deep, bulky cup of vegetation, just off the ground in grasses; 4–5 eggs; 1 brood; May–June.

FEEDING Hangs upside down at clusters of dead leaves; probes for moth larvae and small insects.

FLIGHT: typical warbler flight: fast, slightly undulating, and direct with rapid wing beats.

SIMILAR SPECIES

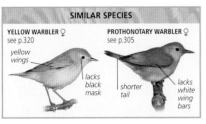

YELLOW WARBLER ♀
see p.320

yellow wings

lacks black mask

PROTHONOTARY WARBLER ♀
see p.305

shorter tail

lacks white wing bars

DECEPTIVE HYBRID
The black border to this bird's ear patch indicates a Blue- or Golden-winged ancestry.

OCCURRENCE
Breeds in areas of second-growth forest, but is less picky than the Golden-winged Warbler and can use older and taller stands. Occurs in any wooded habitat on migration. Migrates across the Gulf of Mexico to winter in southeastern Mexico and central Panama.

| Length **4¾in (12cm)** | Wingspan **7½in (19cm)** | Weight **⁹⁄₃₂–⅜oz (8–11g)** |
| Social **Loose flocks** | Lifespan **Up to 7 years** | Status **Secure** |

DATE: _____ TIME: _____ LOCATION: _____

| Order **Passeriformes** | Family **Parulidae** | Species **Mniotilta varia** |

Black-and-white Warbler

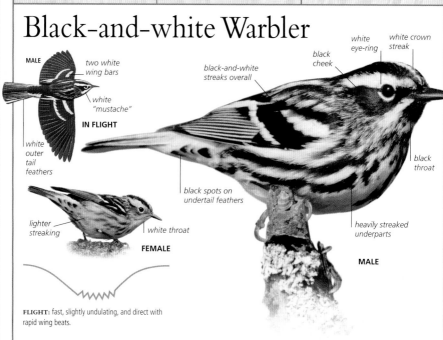

MALE

two white wing bars

white "mustache"

IN FLIGHT

white outer tail feathers

white eye-ring

white crown streak

black cheek

black-and-white streaks overall

black throat

black spots on undertail feathers

heavily streaked underparts

MALE

lighter streaking

white throat

FEMALE

FLIGHT: fast, slightly undulating, and direct with rapid wing beats.

The Black-and-white Warbler is best known for its creeper-like habit of feeding in vertical and upside-down positions as it pries into bark crevices, where its relatively long, curved bill allows it to reach into tiny nooks and crannies. These habits, combined with a streaked plumage, make this bird one of the most distinctive warblers in North America. It is a long-distance migrant, with some birds wintering in parts of northern South America.

VOICE Sharp *stik* call; flight call a very high, thin *ssiit*, often doubled; song a thin, high-pitched, wheezy series *wheesy wheesy wheesy wheesy wheesy wheesy.*
NESTING Cup on ground against stump, fallen logs, or roots; 4–6 eggs; 1 brood; April–August.
FEEDING Creeps along branches and trunks, probing into bark for insects and insect larvae.

SQUEAKY WHEEL
The high-pitched, wheezy song of this warbler is said to be reminiscent of a squeaky wheel.

UPSIDE DOWN
Black-and-white Warblers often creep head-first along trunks and branches of trees.

OCCURRENCE
Breeds in deciduous and mixed mature and second-growth woodlands; migrants occur on a greater variety of habitats; winters in a wide range of wooded habitats in southern US, Mexico and into Central and South America.

SIMILAR SPECIES

BLACKPOLL WARBLER ♂
see p.322
white cheek patch

black cap

BLACK-THROATED GRAY WARBLER ♂

yellow patch

bright orange legs

| Length **5in (13cm)** | Wingspan **8in (20cm)** | Weight **⁵⁄₁₆–½oz (9–14g)** |
| Social **Migrant/Winter flocks** | Lifespan **Up to 11 years** | Status **Secure** |

DATE: _____ TIME:_____ LOCATION:_____

| Order **Passeriformes** | Family **Parulidae** | Species **Protonotaria citrea** |

Prothonotary Warbler

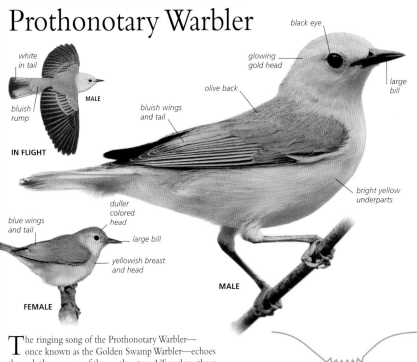

black eye

white
in tail

glowing
gold head

olive back

MALE

bluish
rump

IN FLIGHT

large
bill

bluish wings
and tail

bright yellow
underparts

duller
colored
head

blue wings
and tail

large bill

yellowish breast
and head

MALE

FEMALE

The ringing song of the Prothonotary Warbler—once known as the Golden Swamp Warbler—echoes through the swamps of the southeastern US and southern Ontario every summer. This is one of the few cavity-nesting warbler species; it will use manmade bird houses placed close to still water. Prothonotary Warblers also tend to stay fairly low over the water, making them easy to spot. This warbler's yellow head and breast reminded an early naturalist of the bright yellow robes worn by Prothonotaries (high ranking papal clerks), and he passed the name on to this colorful bird.

FLIGHT: fast, with slight undulations, and direct with rapid wing beats.

VOICE Flight call a loud, high *sviit*; call note a loud *chip*; song a loud series of penetrating and internally rising notes *tsveet tsveet tsveet tsveet tsveet tsveet tsveet*.
NESTING Over or near still water; woodpecker holes often used; 3–8 eggs; 1–2 broods; April–July.
FEEDING Mostly eats insects and small mollusks; also seeds, fruit, and nectar.

OCCURRENCE
Breeds in wooded areas over or near still water, especially in cypress swamps and bottomlands across the southeastern US and up into southern Ontario. Winters in mangroves and dry forests in Southern Mexico.

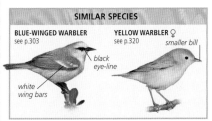

SIMILAR SPECIES

BLUE-WINGED WARBLER
see p.303

YELLOW WARBLER ♀
see p.320

smaller bill

black
eye-line

white
wing bars

GOLDEN SONGBIRD
Visible in the darkness of a southern swamp, a Prothonotary Warbler sings its ringing song.

| Length **5½in (14cm)** | Wingspan **9in (23cm)** | Weight **½–⅝oz (14–18g)** |
| Social **Winter flocks** | Lifespan **Up to 8 years** | Status **Endangered** |

DATE: _____ TIME: _____ LOCATION: _____

| Order **Passeriformes** | Family **Parulidae** | Species *Oreothlypis peregrina* |

Tennessee Warbler

gray head
white eyestripe

MALE (BREEDING)

IN FLIGHT

olive-green upperparts

olive-gray head

FEMALE

whitish belly

blue-gray crown

spiky bill

olive back and wings

olive-gray back

yellowish throat and breast

white undertail feathers

grayish white underparts

MALE (BREEDING)

MALE (FALL)

The Tennessee Warbler was named after its place of discovery, but this bird would have been on migration, as it breeds almost entirely in Canada and winters in Central America. These warblers inhabit fairly remote areas, and their nests are difficult to find. It is one of a number of species that takes advantage of outbreaks of spruce budworm; the population of Tennessee Warblers tends to increase in years when budworms are abundant.

VOICE Call a sharp *tzit*; flight call a thin slightly rolling *seet*; song usually three-part staccato series, *chip-chip-chip*, each series increasing in pitch and usually in tempo.

NESTING Nest woven of fine plant matter, in ground depression, concealed from above by shrubbery; 4–7 eggs; 1 brood; June.

FEEDING Searches outer branches of trees for caterpillars, bees, wasps, beetles, and spiders; also eats fruit in winter and drinks nectar by piercing base of flowers.

FLIGHT: fast, slightly undulating, and direct with rapid wing beats.

UNIQUE UNDERPARTS
The breeding male is the only North American warbler with unmarked grayish white underparts.

SIMILAR SPECIES

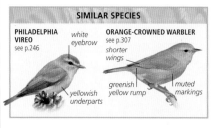

PHILADELPHIA VIREO
see p.246

white eyebrow

yellowish underparts

ORANGE-CROWNED WARBLER
see p.307
shorter wings

greenish yellow rump

muted markings

OCCURRENCE
Breeds in a variety of habitats, especially woodlands with dense understory and thickets of willows and alders. Very common in suburban parks and gardens during migration, particularly in the Midwest. Winters from southern Mexico to northern Ecuador and northern Venezuela.

| Length 4¾ in (12cm) | Wingspan 7¾ in (19.5cm) | Weight ⁹/₃₂–⁵/₈ oz (8–17g) |
| Social **Flocks** | Lifespan **Up to 6 years** | Status **Secure** |

DATE: _____ TIME: _____ LOCATION: _____

Orange-crowned Warbler

dull olive overall

MALE

IN FLIGHT

short wings

crown shows orange when bird is alarmed

pale yellow eyebrow

olive-green upperparts

greenish yellow rump

muted breast markings

ADULT (WEST)

gray head

drabber plumage overall

yellow undertail feathers

IMMATURE (EAST; 1ST WINTER)

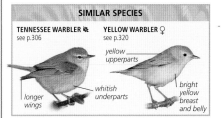

Common and relatively brightly colored in the West but uncommon and duller in the East, the Orange-crowned Warbler has a large breeding range. The 19th-century American naturalist Thomas Say described this species on the basis of specimens collected in Nebraska. He was struck by the tiny orange cap, but because it was so concealed in the plumage of the crown, he named it *celata*, which is Latin for "hidden." The orange cap is not usually visible in the field.

VOICE Call a clean, sharp *tsik*; flight call a high, short *seet*; song a loose, lazy trill; eastern birds lazier, western birds more emphatic.

NESTING Cup of grasses, fibers, and down, usually on ground under bush; 4–5 eggs; 1 brood; March–July.

FEEDING Gleans mostly arthropods such as beetles, ants, spiders, and their larvae; also eats fruit; collects nectar by piercing base of flower.

FLIGHT: fast, slightly undulating, and direct with rapid wing beats.

FACE MARKINGS
In eastern populations of this warbler, the birds have whitish facial markings during their first winter.

SIMILAR SPECIES

TENNESSEE WARBLER 🐦
see p.306

YELLOW WARBLER ♀
see p.320

yellow upperparts

longer wings

whitish underparts

bright yellow breast and belly

OCCURRENCE
Breeds in varied habitats across North America from Alaska eastward to Newfoundland, and in the West from British Columbia southward to California, New Mexico, and western Texas. Prefers streamside thickets. Some winter in the West, while others go to Mexico and Guatemala.

Length **5in (13cm)**	Wingspan **7¼in (18.5cm)**	Weight **¼–⅜oz (7–11g)**
Social **Winter flocks**	Lifespan **Up to 6 years**	Status **Secure**

DATE: _____ TIME: _____ LOCATION: _____

Order **Passeriformes**	Family **Parulidae**	Species *Oreothlypis ruficapilla*

Nashville Warbler

MALE
O. r. ruficapilla
(EASTERN)

olive-green
upperparts

IN FLIGHT

rounded
wings

rufous
crown patch

conspicuous
white eye-ring

blue-gray
helmet

grayish
green back

olive
wings

MALE
O. r. ridgwayi
(WESTERN)

yellow undertail
feathers

white
patch
on belly

duller olive
back

less contrast
between gray
and yellow

FEMALE
O. r. ruficapilla
(EASTERN)

Although often confused with the ground-walking, chunky Connecticut Warbler, the Nashville Warbler is much smaller, hops about up in trees, and has a yellow throat. Nashville has two subspecies: *O. r. ruficapilla* in the East and *O. r. ridgwayi* in the West. Differences in voice, habitat, behavior, and plumage hint that they may in fact be separate species. *O. r. ridgwayi* can be distinguished as it has more extensive white on its belly and a grayish green back.
VOICE Call sharp *tik*, sharper in West; flight call high, thin *siit*; eastern song two parts: first part lazy, second faster trill *tee-tsee tee-tsee tee-tsee titititi*; western song slightly lower and fuller with lazier second part, a seldom trilled *tee-tsee tee-tsee tee-tsee weesay weesay way*.
NESTING Cup hidden on ground in dense cover; 3–6 eggs; 1 brood; May–July.
FEEDING Gleans insects and spiders from trees.

FLIGHT: fast, slightly undulating, and direct, with rapid wing beats.

SIMILAR SPECIES

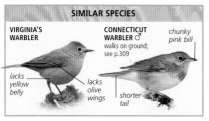

VIRGINIA'S WARBLER

lacks
yellow
belly

CONNECTICUT WARBLER ♂
walks on ground;
see p.309

chunky
pink bill

lacks
olive
wings

shorter
tail

FIELD MARKS
The white eye-ring and belly are evident on this singing male.

OCCURRENCE
Ruficapilla breeds in wet habitats of Saskatchewan east to Newfoundland and south to West Virginia; *ridgwayi* in brushy montane areas in Sierras and northern Rockies; *ridgwayi* winters in coastal California and south Texas to Guatemala; *ruficapilla* migrates to winter mainly in Mexico.

Length **4¾in (12cm)**	Wingspan **7½in (19cm)**	Weight **¼–⁷⁄₁₆oz (7–13g)**
Social **Migrant/Winter flocks**	Lifespan **Up to 7 years**	Status **Secure**

DATE: _____ TIME: _____ LOCATION: _____

| Order **Passeriformes** | Family **Parulidae** | Species *Oporornis agilis* |

Connecticut Warbler

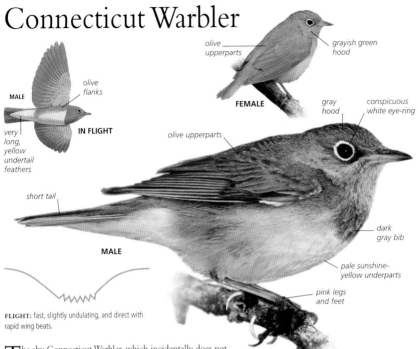

olive upperparts

grayish green hood

FEMALE

gray hood

conspicuous white eye-ring

olive flanks

MALE

IN FLIGHT

very long, yellow undertail feathers

olive upperparts

short tail

MALE

dark gray bib

pale sunshine-yellow underparts

pink legs and feet

FLIGHT: fast, slightly undulating, and direct with rapid wing beats.

The shy Connecticut Warbler, which incidentally does not breed in this state, breeds in remote, boggy habitats in Canada and is hard to spot during its spring and fall migrations. It arrives in the US in late May and leaves its breeding grounds in August. It is the only warbler that walks along the ground in a bouncy manner, with its tail bobbing up and down.

VOICE Seldom-heard call a nasal *champ*, flight call a buzzy *ziiiit*; song a loud "whippy," accelerating series, often ending with upward inflection *tweet, chuh WHIP-uh chee-uh-WHIP-uh chee-uh-WAY*.

NESTING Concealed cup of grass or leaves, lined with fine plant matter and hair; placed near or on ground in damp moss or grass clump; 3–5 eggs; 1 brood; June–July.

FEEDING Gleans a variety of adult insects, insect larvae, and spiders from under leaves; also eats small fruit.

EXCEPTIONAL UNDERTAIL
The yellow undertail feathers nearly reach the tip of the Connecticut Warbler's tail.

OCCURRENCE
Breeds across Canada from British Columbia to Quebec and in the US in Minnesota and the Great Lakes region, in bogs and pine forests. Winters in forest habitats of Amazonian Peru and Brazil.

SIMILAR SPECIES

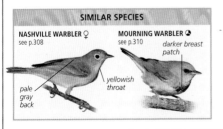

NASHVILLE WARBLER ♀
see p.308

pale gray back

MOURNING WARBLER ♂
see p.310

yellowish throat

darker breast patch

| Length **6in (15cm)** | Wingspan **9in (23cm)** | Weight **⁷/₁₆–¹¹/₁₆oz (13–20g)** |
| Social **Solitary** | Lifespan **Up to 4 years** | Status **Secure (p)** |

| Order **Passeriformes** | Family **Parulidae** | Species *Geothlypis philadelphia* |

Mourning Warbler

gray head

black mask

MALE (BREEDING)

pattern like male (breeding), but more subdued

olive upperparts

black bib and speckled throat

yellow underparts

pink toes and legs

IN FLIGHT

yellow undertail feathers

"hooded" look

IMMATURE MALE

pale gray hood

lacks speckled markings on throat

FEMALE

MALE (BREEDING)

The pleasant song of the Mourning Warbler is often used in commercials and movies as a background sound of idyllic suburban settings. It is doubtful, however, that you would find this gray-headed, black-throated warbler in a backyard, as it prefers dense, herbaceous tangles—both for breeding and during migration. These birds are late spring migrants and the leaves are fully out when they arrive in the eastern US, making it difficult to see them. The easiest way to see a Mourning Warbler is to track a male by its song.

VOICE Call a flat *tchik*; flight call a high, thin, clear *svit*; song a very burry series of paired notes with low-pitched ending: *churrr-ee churrr-ee churrr-ee churr-ee-oh.*

NESTING Well-concealed cup of leaves, lined with grass, on or near ground in dense tangle; 2–5 eggs; 1 brood; June–August.

FEEDING Mainly gleans insects and spiders in low foliage; eats some plant material in winter.

FLIGHT: fast, slightly undulating, and direct with rapid wing beats.

FOLLOW THAT BIRD
Tracking down a singing male is the easiest way to find this skulking species.

SIMILAR SPECIES

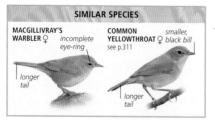

MACGILLIVRAY'S WARBLER ♀ incomplete eye-ring

longer tail

COMMON YELLOWTHROAT ♀ see p.311

smaller, black bill

longer tail

OCCURRENCE
Breeds in dense thickets of disturbed woodlands from the Yukon and British Columbia, east to Quebec and Newfoundland, south to the Great Lakes, New England, New York, and the Appalachians. Winters in dense thickets in Central and South America.

| Length **5in (13cm)** | Wingspan **7¹⁄₂in (19cm)** | Weight **³⁄₈–⁷⁄₁₆oz (10–13g)** |
| Social **Solitary** | Lifespan **Up to 8 years** | Status **Secure** |

DATE: _____ TIME:_____ LOCATION:_____

Common Yellowthroat

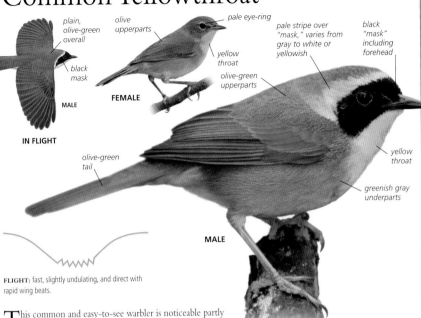

plain, olive-green overall

olive upperparts

pale eye-ring

pale stripe over "mask," varies from gray to white or yellowish

black "mask" including forehead

black mask

yellow throat

olive-green upperparts

MALE

FEMALE

IN FLIGHT

olive-green tail

yellow throat

greenish gray underparts

MALE

FLIGHT: fast, slightly undulating, and direct with rapid wing beats.

This common and easy-to-see warbler is noticeable partly because of its loud, simple song. This species varies in voice and plumage across its range and 14 subspecies have been described. In the western US, the birds have yellower underparts, brighter white head stripes, and louder, simpler songs than the eastern birds. The male often flies upwards rapidly, delivering a more complex version of its song.

VOICE Call a harsh, buzzy *tchak*, repeated into chatter when agitated; flight call a low, flat, buzzy *dzzzit*; song a variable but distinctive series of rich (often three-note) phrases: *WITCH-uh-tee WITCH-uh-tee WITCH-uh-tee WHICH*; more complex flight song.

NESTING Concealed, bulky cup of grasses just above ground or water; 3–5 eggs; 1 brood; May–August.

FEEDING Eats insects and spiders in low vegetation; also seeds.

UNFORGETABLE CALL
The song of the male Common Yellowthroat is an extremely helpful aid in its identification.

OCCURRENCE
Found south of the tundra, from Alaska and the Yukon to Quebec and Newfoundland, and south to California, Texas, and to southeastern US. Habitats dense herbaceous understory, from marshes and grasslands to pine forest and hedgerows. Winters from Mexico to Panama and the Antilles.

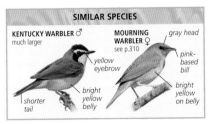

SIMILAR SPECIES

KENTUCKY WARBLER ♂
much larger

yellow eyebrow

shorter tail

bright yellow belly

MOURNING WARBLER ♀
see p.310

gray head

pink-based bill

bright yellow on belly

Length **5in (13cm)**	Wingspan **6¾in (17cm)**	Weight **⁵⁄₁₆–³⁄₈oz (9–10g)**
Social **Migrant/Winter flocks**	Lifespan **Up to 11 years**	Status **Secure**

DATE: _____ TIME: _____ LOCATION: _____

| Order **Passeriformes** | Family **Parulidae** | Species **Setophaga citrina** |

Hooded Warbler

hint of a dark hood

dark patch between eye and bill

MALE

FEMALE

whitish undertail feathers

yellow underparts

IN FLIGHT

plain, olive upperparts

black cap and hood

black eye

white markings on tail

yellow face

black bib

MALE

FLIGHT: fast, slightly undulating, and direct with rapid wing beats.

yellow underparts

The Hooded Warbler is a strikingly patterned and loud warbler, and is often particularly conspicuous over its eastern US breeding range. Both male and females frequently flash the white markings hidden on the inner webs of their tails. The extent of the black hood varies in female Hooded Warblers; it ranges from none in first fall birds to almost as extensive as males in some adult females. Genetic (DNA) and vocal information point to a close relationship with *Setophaga* warblers.

VOICE Call a metallic *tsink*; flight call a high, thin *sweep*; song a rich, whistled series, ending loudly and emphatically: *tu-wee' tu-wee' tu-wee-TEE-tee-yu.*

NESTING Bulky cup of leaves lined with hair, in shrub near eye level; 3–5 eggs; 1–2 broods; May–July.

FEEDING Eats many different kinds of insects found low in vegetation.

STRIKING MASK
The black and yellow face of the Hooded Warbler makes the male an unmistakable bird.

SIMILAR SPECIES

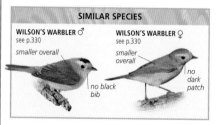

WILSON'S WARBLER ♂
see p.330
smaller overall

WILSON'S WARBLER ♀
see p.330
smaller overall

no black bib

no dark patch

OCCURRENCE
Breeds in moist deciduous forests with dense understory in eastern US and southern Ontario; has bred in some moist mountain canyons. Migrants like similar habitat. Winters in moist woodlands with good understory, especially lowland rainforest, from eastern Mexico to Panama and the West Indies.

| Length **5¼in (13.5cm)** | Wingspan **7in (17.5cm)** | Weight **⁵⁄₁₆oz–⁷⁄₁₆oz (9–12g)** |
| Social **Migrant/Winter flocks** | Lifespan **Up to 8 years** | Status **Secure (p)** |

DATE: _____ TIME: _____ LOCATION: _____

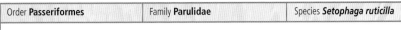

American Redstart

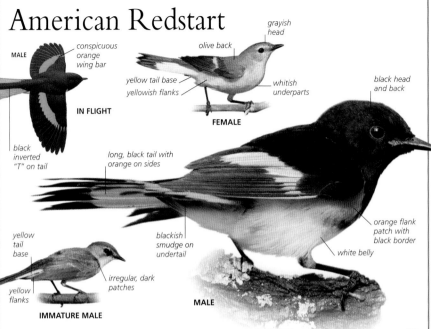

WOOD WARBLERS

Order **Passeriformes** | Family **Parulidae** | Species ***Setophaga ruticilla***

MALE · IN FLIGHT — conspicuous orange wing bar; black inverted "T" on tail

FEMALE — grayish head; olive back; yellow tail base; yellowish flanks; whitish underparts

MALE — black head and back; long, black tail with orange on sides; blackish smudge on undertail; orange flank patch with black border; white belly

IMMATURE MALE — yellow tail base; yellow flanks; irregular, dark patches

The American Redstart is a vividly colored, energetic and acrobatic warbler with a reasonably broad range across North America. One of its behavioral quirks is to fan its tail and wings while foraging, supposedly using the flashes of bold color to scare insects into moving, making them easy prey. It possesses well-developed rictal bristles, hair-like feathers extending from the corners of the mouth, which help it to detect insects.

VOICE Harsh *tsiip* call; flight call a high, thin *sveep*; song a confusingly variable, high, thin, yet penetrating series of notes; one version burry, emphatic, and downslurred *see-a see-a see-a see-a* ZEE-*urrrr*.

NESTING Cup of grasses and rootlets, lined with feathers; placed low in deciduous tree; 2–5 eggs; 1–2 broods; May–July.

FEEDING Gleans insects and spiders from leaves at mid-levels in trees; also catches moths, flies in flight; will also eat fruit.

FLIGHT: fast, slightly undulating, and direct with rapid wing beats.

COMMON SONG
This bird's short, ringing song is a common sound in the moist deciduous woods of the East and North.

MALE CARER
As with most warblers, male Redstarts help raise the young, though they may be polygamous.

OCCURRENCE
Breeds in moist deciduous and mixed woodlands across North America; migrants and wintering birds use a wide range of habitats. Winters from Baja California and south Florida through Middle America and the Caribbean to northern South America.

Length **5in (13cm)**	Wingspan **8in (20cm)**	Weight **7/32–3/8oz (6–11g)**
Social **Flocks**	Lifespan **Up to 10 years**	Status **Secure**

DATE: _____ TIME: _____ LOCATION: _____

Order **Passeriformes**	Family **Parulidae**	Species *Setophaga tigrina*

Cape May Warbler

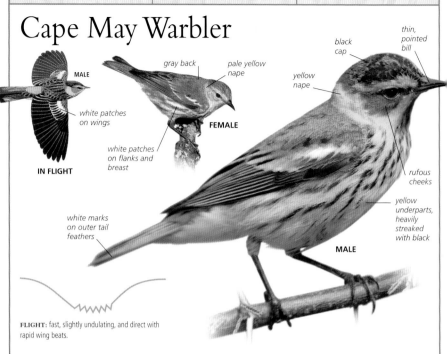

MALE

white patches on wings

IN FLIGHT

gray back

pale yellow nape

FEMALE

white patches on flanks and breast

black cap

thin, pointed bill

yellow nape

rufous cheeks

yellow underparts, heavily streaked with black

white marks on outer tail feathers

MALE

FLIGHT: fast, slightly undulating, and direct with rapid wing beats.

The Cape May Warbler is a spruce budworm specialist, and so the populations of this bird increase during outbreaks of that insect. These birds often chase other birds aggressively from flowering trees, where they use their especially thin and pointed bills and semitubular tongues to suck the nectar from blossoms. In its summer forest habitat, the Cape May Warbler uses its bill to feed on insects by plucking them from clumps of conifer needles.

VOICE Song a high, even-pitched series of whistles *see see see see*.

NESTING Cup placed near trunk, high in spruce or fir near top; 4–9 eggs; 1 brood; June–July.

FEEDING Gleans arthropods, especially spruce budworms, but also flies, moths, and beetles from mid-high levels in canopy; also fruit and nectar during the nonbreeding season.

SPRING FLASH
Magnificently colored, a male warbler displays its chestnut cheek, yellow necklace, and yellow rump.

SIMILAR SPECIES

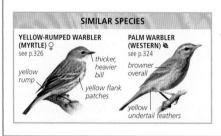

YELLOW-RUMPED WARBLER (MYRTLE) ♀
see p.326

yellow rump

thicker, heavier bill

yellow flank patches

PALM WARBLER (WESTERN)
see p.324

browner overall

yellow undertail feathers

OCCURRENCE
Breeds from the Yukon and British Columbia to the Great Lakes, the Maritimes, and New England in mature spruce–fir forests. Migrants found in varied habitats. Winters in varied habitats, especially backyard gardens, in Central America, as far south as Honduras.

Length **5in (13cm)**	Wingspan **8in (20cm)**	Weight **⁵/₁₆–⁷/₁₆oz (9–13g)**
Social **Migrant flocks**	Lifespan **Up to 4 years**	Status **Secure**

DATE: _____ TIME: _____ LOCATION: _____

Cerulean Warbler

whitish eyebrow

pale blue crown

sea-green upperparts

FEMALE

yellowish underparts

indistinct eyestripe

bright blue crown

black breastband

MALE

two white wing bars

blue upperparts

MALE

short tail with white band

MALE

IN FLIGHT

white undertail feathers

white chin and throat

MALE

black streaks on flanks

white belly

FLIGHT: fast, slightly undulating, and direct with rapid wing beats.

This unusually colored species is difficult to spot, as it spends the majority of its time foraging in the canopy of deciduous forests. It was once common across the Midwest and the Ohio River Valley, but its habitat is being cleared for agriculture and fragmented by development. In winter, this bird lives high in the canopy of the Andean foothills, but sadly this habitat is threatened by coffee cultivation.

VOICE Call a slurred *chip*; flight call a buzzy *zeet*; three-part, buzzy song consisting of a short series of low paired notes followed by a mid-range trill and upslurred high-pitched *zhree*.

NESTING Compact cup high on fork in deciduous tree, far from trunk; 2–5 eggs; 1 brood; May–July.

FEEDING Gleans insects high in canopy, especially from leaf bases.

UNIQUE COLOR
Female Cerulean Warblers have a unique blue color on their head and upperparts.

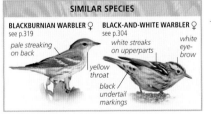

SIMILAR SPECIES

BLACKBURNIAN WARBLER ♀
see p.319

pale streaking on back

yellow throat

BLACK-AND-WHITE WARBLER ♀
see p.304

white streaks on upperparts

white eye-brow

black undertail markings

OCCURRENCE
Mainly breeds in mature deciduous forests across the northeastern US and southeastern Canada; tends to prefer dense woodlands during migration. Winters in evergreen forests in the Andes, principally from Columbia to Peru.

Length 4¾ in (12cm)	Wingspan 7¾ in (19.5cm)	Weight ⁹⁄₃₂–³⁄₈ oz (8–10g)
Social **Migrant/Winter flocks**	Lifespan **Up to 6 years**	Status **Vulnerable**

Order **Passeriformes**	Family **Parulidae**	Species **Setophaga americana**

Northern Parula

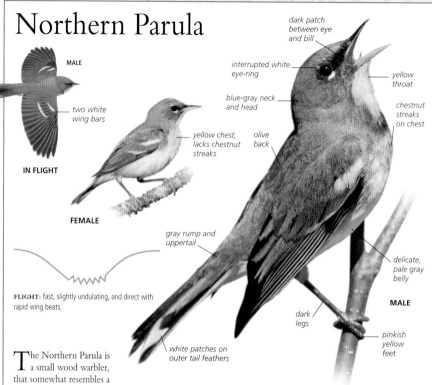

dark patch between eye and bill

interrupted white eye-ring

yellow throat

blue-gray neck and head

chestnut streaks on chest

olive back

MALE

two white wing bars

IN FLIGHT

yellow chest, lacks chestnut streaks

FEMALE

gray rump and uppertail

delicate, pale gray belly

MALE

dark legs

FLIGHT: fast, slightly undulating, and direct with rapid wing beats.

white patches on outer tail feathers

pinkish yellow feet

The Northern Parula is a small wood warbler, that somewhat resembles a chickadee in its active foraging behavior. This bird depends on very specific nesting materials—*Ushea* lichens, or "Old Man's Beard," in the north, and *Tillandsia*, or Spanish Moss, in the South. The presence of these parasitic plants on trees greatly limits the geographical range of this species. The Northern Parula interbreeds with the Tropical Parula in southern Texas where their ranges cross, producing hybrid birds.

VOICE Call a very sharp *tsip*; flight call a thin, weak, descending *tsiif*; song a variable, most common buzzy upslurred trill, variably continuous or in steps, ending very high, but then dropping off in an emphatic *zip*.

NESTING Hanging pouch in clump of lichens; 4–5 eggs; 1 brood; May–July (south) or April–August (north).

FEEDING Gleans for caterpillars, flies, moths, beetles, wasps, ants, spiders; also eats berries, nectar, some seeds.

THE AMERICAN TIT
This small yellow-and-chestnut-breasted bird was named by Carl Linnaeus in 1758.

SIMILAR SPECIES

TROPICAL PARULA

dark face

more yellow

OCCURRENCE
Nests in almost any kind of wooded area with its preferred nesting material; migrants (some of which cross the Gulf of Mexico) occur in almost any habitat; winters in varied habitats from southern Texas and Florida across Caribbean and Mexico south to Panama.

Length **4¼in (11cm)**	Wingspan **7in (18cm)**	Weight **¼–⅜oz (7–10g)**
Social **Winter flocks**	Lifespan **Up to 7 years**	Status **Secure**

DATE: _____ TIME: _____ LOCATION: _____

Magnolia Warbler

plain face with pale eye-ring

greenish back

black face

white eyebrow

incomplete eye-ring

MALE (BREEDING)

gray crown

yellow rump

white undertail feathers

IMMATURE (FALL)

broken white tail band

IN FLIGHT

large white patch on wing

greenish back with black stripes

black streaking on breast and flanks not as heavy

yellow underparts with black streaks

FEMALE (BREEDING)

MALE (BREEDING)

FLIGHT: fast, slightly undulating, and direct with rapid wing beats.

The bold, flashy, and common Magnolia Warbler is hard to miss as it flits around at eye level, fanning its uniquely marked tail. This species nests in young forests and winters in almost any habitat, so its numbers have not suffered in recent decades, unlike some of its relatives. Although it really has no preference for its namesake plant, the 19th-century ornithologist Alexander Wilson discovered a Magnolia Warbler feeding in a magnolia tree during migration, which is how it got its name.

VOICE Call a tinny *jeinf*, not particularly warbler-like; also short, simple whistled series *wee'-sa wee'-sa WEET-a-chew*; short, distinctive, flight call a high, trilled *zeep*.

NESTING Flimsy cup of black rootlets placed low in dense conifer against trunk; 3–5 eggs; 1 brood; June–August.

FEEDING Gleans mostly caterpillars, beetles, and spiders.

SPRUCE WARBLER
The conspicuous male Magnolia Warbler can be found singing its distinctive, loud song throughout the day often in a spruce tree.

SIMILAR SPECIES

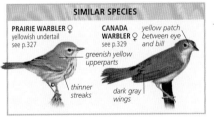

PRAIRIE WARBLER ♀
yellowish undertail
see p.327

thinner streaks

CANADA WARBLER ♀
see p.329

greenish yellow upperparts

dark gray wings

yellow patch between eye and bill

OCCURRENCE
Breeds in dense, young mixed and coniferous forests from Yukon east to Newfoundland and south into Appalachians of Tennessee; migrates across the Gulf and Caribbean; winters in varied habitats in Caribbean and from southeast Mexico to Panama; rare vagrant in the West.

Length **5in (13cm)**	Wingspan **7½in (19cm)**	Weight **$7/32$–$7/16$oz (6–12g)**
Social **Migrant/Winter flocks**	Lifespan **Up to 6 years**	Status **Secure**

DATE: _____ TIME: _____ LOCATION: _____

| Order **Passeriformes** | Family **Parulidae** | Species **Setophaga castanea** |

Bay-breasted Warbler

olive crown and back

two wing bars

greenish cheeks

IMMATURE FEMALE (FALL)

unstreaked breast

MALE (BREEDING)

two white wing bars

FEMALE (BREEDING)

chestnut crown, streaked black

bold buffy neck patch

buffy wash on flanks and under tail

dusky ear patch

gray upperparts with black streaks

chestnut brown crown

black face

white tips on outer tail feathers

IN FLIGHT

two white wing bars

chestnut brown chin and flanks

buff undertail

MALE (BREEDING)

yellowish buff belly

FLIGHT: fast, slightly undulating, and direct, with rapid wing beats.

Splashed with deep chestnut, crisp white, warm buff, and jet black, a male Bay-breasted Warbler in breeding plumage is a particularly striking bird, but fall females are very different with their dull, greenish plumage. Like the Tennessee Warbler, this species depends largely on outbreaks of spruce budworm (a major food source), so its numbers rise and fall according to those outbreaks. Overall, the Bay-breasted Warbler population has decreased because of the increased use of pesticide sprays.

VOICE Call a somewhat upslurred *tsip*; flight call a high, buzzy, short, and sharp *tzzzt;* song of very high, thin notes, often ending on lower pitch: *wee-si wee-si wee-si wee.*

NESTING Fragile-looking cup of grass and lichens on horizontal branch at mid-level in forest; 4–5 eggs; 1 brood; May–July.

FEEDING Mostly eats moths, smaller insects, worms, spiders, and caterpillars during migration and on breeding grounds; eats mainly fruit in winter.

SINGING IN THE FOREST
A brilliantly colored breeding male sings its high-pitched song on a spruce branch.

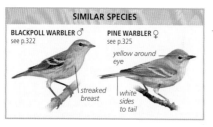

SIMILAR SPECIES

BLACKPOLL WARBLER ♂
see p.322

streaked breast

PINE WARBLER ♀
see p.325

yellow around eye

white sides to tail

OCCURRENCE
Breeds in mature spruce-fir-balsam forest across the forest belt from Yukon to the Maritimes, and south to the Great Lakes area and northern New England. Migrants occur in varied habitat, but especially woodland edges. Winters in wet forest in central America.

| Length **5½in (14cm)** | Wingspan **9in (23cm)** | Weight **⅜–½oz (11–15g)** |
| Social **Migratory/Winter flocks** | Lifespan **Up to 4 years** | Status **Vulnerable** |

DATE: _____ TIME: _____ LOCATION: _____

Blackburnian Warbler

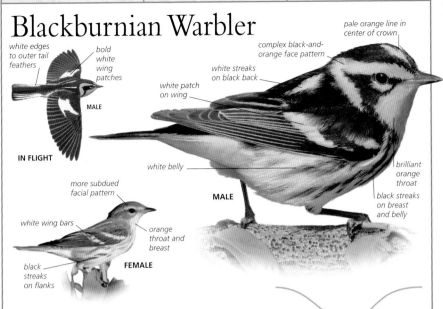

white edges to outer tail feathers

bold white wing patches

MALE

IN FLIGHT

pale orange line in center of crown

complex black-and-orange face pattern

white streaks on black back

white patch on wing

white belly

brilliant orange throat

black streaks on breast and belly

MALE

more subdued facial pattern

white wing bars

orange throat and breast

black streaks on flanks

FEMALE

This fiery beacon of the treetops is considered one of the most beautiful members of its family; its orange throat is unique among the North American warblers. The Blackburnian Warbler co-exists with many other *Setophaga* warblers in the coniferous and mixed woods of the north and east, but is able to do so by exploiting a slightly different niche for foraging—in this case the treetops. It also seeks the highest trees for nesting.
VOICE Call a slightly husky *chik*; flight-call a high, thin *zzee;* song variable, but always high-pitched; swirling series of lisps, spiraling upward to end in an almost inaudible *trill*.
NESTING Fine cup in conifer on horizontal branch away from trunk, usually high in tree; 4–5 eggs; 1 brood; May–July.
FEEDING Gleans arthropods, such as spiders, worms, and beetles; also fruit.

FLIGHT: fast, slightly undulating, and direct with rapid wing beats.

DISTINGUISHING FEATURES
The female is like a dull adult male, but with two wing bars and no black on the face.

AVIAN FIREFLY
This male in breeding plumage glows when seen against a dark forest background.

OCCURRENCE
Breeds in coniferous and mixed forests from Alberta east through the North Great Lakes to Newfoundland and south into the Appalachians of Georgia; migrants found in wooded, shrubby, or forest edge habitats. Winters in wet forests in Costa Rica and Panama, and southward as far as Peru.

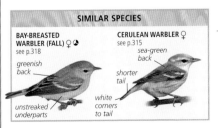

SIMILAR SPECIES

BAY-BREASTED WARBLER (FALL) ♀♂
see p.318

greenish back

unstreaked underparts

CERULEAN WARBLER ♀
see p.315

sea-green back

shorter tail

white corners to tail

| Length **5in (13cm)** | Wingspan **8½in (21cm)** | Weight **⁵⁄₁₆–⁷⁄₁₆oz (9–12g)** |
| Social **Winter flocks** | Lifespan **Up to 8 years** | Status **Vulnerable** |

| Order **Passeriformes** | Family **Parulidae** | Species ***Setophaga petechia*** |

Yellow Warbler

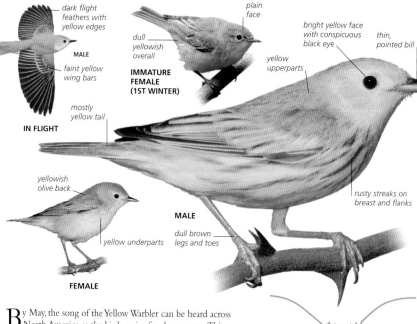

dark flight feathers with yellow edges

MALE

faint yellow wing bars

dull yellowish overall

IMMATURE FEMALE (1ST WINTER)

plain face

bright yellow face with conspicuous black eye

thin, pointed bill

yellow upperparts

mostly yellow tail

IN FLIGHT

yellowish olive back

rusty streaks on breast and flanks

MALE

yellow underparts

dull brown legs and toes

FEMALE

By May, the song of the Yellow Warbler can be heard across North America as the birds arrive for the summer. This warbler is treated as a single species with about 35 subspecies, mostly in its tropical range (West Indies and South America). The Yellow Warbler is known to build another nest on top of an old one when cowbird eggs appear in it, which can result in up to six different tiers. The Yellow Warbler does not walk, but rather hops from branch to branch.

VOICE Call a variable *chip*, sometimes given in series; flight call buzzy *zeep*; song variable series of fast, sweet notes; western birds often add an emphatic ending.

NESTING Deep cup of plant material, grasses in vertical fork of deciduous tree or shrub; 4–5 eggs; 1 brood; May–July.

FEEDING Eats mostly insects and insect larvae, plus some fruit.

FLIGHT: fast, slightly undulating, and direct, with rapid wing beats.

ONE OF A KIND
This species has more yellow in its plumage than any other North American wood warbler.

SIMILAR SPECIES

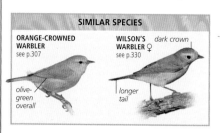

ORANGE-CROWNED WARBLER
see p.307

olive-green overall

WILSON'S WARBLER ♀
see p.330

dark crown

longer tail

OCCURRENCE
Widespread in most shrubby and second-growth habitats of North America. Migrates to southern US and southward to Mexico, Central America, and South America. Resident populations live in Florida and the West Indies.

| Length **5in (13cm)** | Wingspan **8in (20cm)** | Weight **⁹⁄₃₂–¹⁄₂oz (8–14g)** |
| Social **Flocks** | Lifespan **Up to 9 years** | Status **Secure** |

DATE: _____ TIME:_____ LOCATION:_____

Chestnut-sided Warbler

MALE (BREEDING)

two yellow wing bars

yellow cap

black "mustache"

chestnut band along flanks

yellow-and-black streaks on upperparts

conspicuous white cheeks

yellow crown

IN FLIGHT

FEMALE (BREEDING)

white throat

white outer tail feathers

white tail spots

two wing bars

olive crown

rich chestnut flanks

bright lime-green above

plain face with white eye-ring

MALE (BREEDING)

FEMALE (1ST FALL)

plain gray underside

The Chestnut-sided Warbler is one of the few wood warbler species that has benefited from deforestation, because it depends on deciduous second-growth and forest edges for breeding. Once a rare bird, it is more common now than it was in the early 19th century. These birds vary in appearance, immature females looking quite unlike adult males in breeding. In all plumages, yellowish wing bars and whitish belly are the most distinguishing characteristics. Its pleasant song has long been transcribed as *pleased pleased pleased to MEET'cha*.
VOICE Call a sweet *chip*; flight call a low, burry *brrrt*; song a series of fast, sweet notes, usually ending with emphatic *WEET-chew*.
NESTING Open, easy-to-find cup just off ground in small deciduous tree or shrub; 3–5 eggs; 1 brood; May–August.
FEEDING Eats insects, especially larvae; also berries and seeds.

FLIGHT: fast, slightly undulating, and direct with rapid wing beats.

MALE TERRITORY
This singing, territorial male prefers second-growth thickets as its habitat.

OCCURRENCE
Breeds in successive stages of regrowth in deciduous forests, from Alberta to the Great Lakes, New England, and the Appalachians; isolated populations in the Midwest. Winters in the West Indies, Mexico, and Central America, south to Venezuela and northern Colombia.

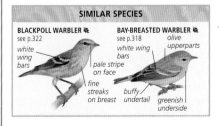

SIMILAR SPECIES

BLACKPOLL WARBLER 🦉
see p.322
white wing bars
fine streaks on breast

BAY-BREASTED WARBLER 🦉
see p.318
white wing bars
buffy undertail
olive upperparts
greenish underside
pale stripe on face

Length **5in (13cm)**	Wingspan **8in (20cm)**	Weight **⁹⁄₃₂–⁷⁄₁₆oz (8–13g)**
Social **Winter flocks**	Lifespan **Up to 7 years**	Status **Secure**

DATE: _____ TIME: _____ LOCATION: _____

| Order **Passeriformes** | Family **Parulidae** | Species *Setophaga striata* |

Blackpoll Warbler

white tail spots

MALE

greenish upperparts with fine black streaks

black cap

white cheek

faint, fine streaking on underparts

two white wing bars

FEMALE (BREEDING)

IN FLIGHT

greenish overall

bold black streaks on gray back

streaking on breast

MALE (FALL)

streaked underparts

pale feet contrasting with darker legs

white undertail feathers

orange legs

MALE (BREEDING)

The Blackpoll Warbler is well known for undergoing a remarkable fall migration that takes it over the Atlantic Ocean from southern Canada and the northeastern US to northern Venezuela. Before departing, it almost doubles its body weight with fat to serve as fuel for the nonstop journey. In spring, most of these birds travel the shorter Caribbean route back north.
VOICE Call piercing *chip*; flight call high, buzzy yet sharp *tzzzt*; common song crescendo of fast, extremely high-pitched ticks, ending with a decrescendo *tsst tsst TSST TSST TSST tsst tsst;* less commonly, ticks run into even faster trill.
NESTING Well-hidden cup placed low against conifer trunk; 3–5 eggs; 1–2 broods; May–July.
FEEDING Gleans arthropods, such as worms and beetles, but will take small fruit in fall and winter.

FLIGHT: fast, slightly undulating, and direct, with rapid wing beats.

REACHING THE HIGH NOTES
The song of the male Blackpoll is so high-pitched that it is inaudible to many people.

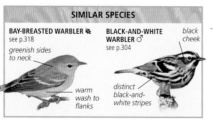

SIMILAR SPECIES		
BAY-BREASTED WARBLER 🦜 see p.318	**BLACK-AND-WHITE WARBLER** ♂ see p.304	*black cheek*
greenish sides to neck		
	distinct black-and-white stripes	
warm wash to flanks		

OCCURRENCE
Breeds in spruce-fir forests across the northern boreal forest zone from Alaska eastward to Newfoundland, southward to coastal coniferous forests in the Maritimes and northern New England. Migrants gather in the Atlantic Ocean to landfall in the Caribbean and northern South America.

Length **5½in (14cm)**	Wingspan **9in (23cm)**	Weight **⅜–⅝oz (10–18g)**
Social **Flocks**	Lifespan **Up to 8 years**	Status **Secure**

DATE: _____ TIME: _____ LOCATION: _____

| Order **Passeriformes** | Family **Parulidae** | Species *Setophaga caerulescens* |

Black-throated Blue Warbler

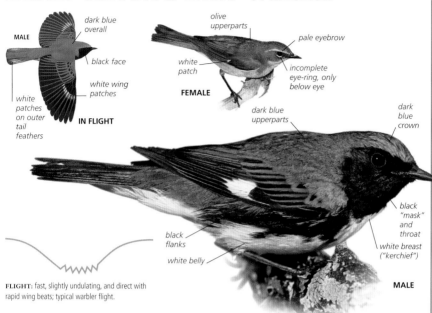

MALE

dark blue overall

black face

white wing patches

white patches on outer tail feathers

IN FLIGHT

olive upperparts

pale eyebrow

white patch

incomplete eye-ring, only below eye

FEMALE

dark blue upperparts

dark blue crown

black "mask" and throat

white breast ("kerchief")

black flanks

white belly

MALE

FLIGHT: fast, slightly undulating, and direct with rapid wing beats; typical warbler flight.

Male and female Black-throated Blue Warblers look so dissimilar that early ornithologists thought they were different species. Many of the females have a blue wash to their wings and tail, and almost all have a subdued version of the male's white "kerchief," so identification is not difficult. This beautiful eastern North American species migrates northward in spring, along the eastern flank of the Appalachians, but a small number of birds fly, along an imaginary line, northwestward to the Great Lakes. This "line" is so clearly defined that this bird is common in Chicago but extremely rare in St. Louis.

VOICE Call a husky junco-like *tchunk*; flight call a distinctive, drawn-out, metallic *ssiiink*, reminiscent of some Northern Cardinal calls; song a relatively low-pitched series of upslurred buzzes *zu zu zo zhray zhree*, or slower *zhray zhray zhreee*.

NESTING Bulky cup of plant material a meter off ground in dense forest; 3–5 eggs; 1–2 broods; May–August.

FEEDING Gleans arthropods, mainly caterpillars, from mid-low level in forest; takes small fruit and nectar.

BLACK, WHITE, AND BLUE
Males are gorgeous year-round, especially when viewed against contrasting, fall foliage.

SIMILAR SPECIES

YELLOW-RUMPED WARBLER (MYRTLE) ♀
see p.326

yellow rump

two wing bars

OCCURRENCE
Breeds in relatively undisturbed deciduous and mixed hardwood forests from southern Ontario and northern Minnesota to Nova Scotia and into the Appalachians of Georgia. Fall migration through wooded habitats; a Caribbean migrant. Winters in Central and South America.

| Length **5in (13cm)** | Wingspan **7½in (19cm)** | Weight **⁹⁄₃₂–⁷⁄₁₆oz (8–12g)** |
| Social **Migrant flocks** | Lifespan **Up to 10 years** | Status **Secure** |

DATE: _____ TIME: _____ LOCATION: _____

| Order **Passeriformes** | Family **Parulidae** | Species **Setophaga palmarum** |

Palm Warbler

yellow eyestripe

chestnut crown

dull gray upperparts

grayish green "mustache"

ring below eye

ADULT (EASTERN)

yellow undertail feathers

chestnut streaks on breast

yellow throat

white-edged tail

dark upperparts

rich yellow underparts

IN FLIGHT

ADULT S. p. hypochrysea (EASTERN; BREEDING)

dark gray upperparts

dusky streaks on breast and belly

dull grayish brown overall

whitish below with brown streaks

ADULT S. p. palmarum (WESTERN MALE; BREEDING)

yellowish rump

yellow under tail

ADULT S. p. palmarum (WESTERN; NONBREEDING)

The Palm Warbler is one of North America's most abundant warblers. Its tail-pumping habits make it easy to identify in any plumage. It was named *palmarum* (meaning "palm") in 1789 because it was first recorded among palm thickets on the Caribbean island of Hispaniola. The western subspecies (*S. p. palmarum*) is found in Western and Central Canada. It is grayish brown above and lacks the chestnut streaks of the eastern subspecies (*S. p. hypochrysea*), which has a yellower face, and breeds in southeastern Canada and northeastern US.

VOICE Call a husky *chik* or *tsip*; flight call a light *ziint*; slow, loose, buzzy trill: *zwi zwi zwi zwi zwi zwi zwi zwi.*

NESTING Cup of grasses on or near ground in open area of conifers at forest edge of a bog; 4–5 eggs; 1 brood; May–July.

FEEDING Eats insects, sometimes caught in flight; also takes seeds and berries.

FLIGHT: fast, slightly undulating, and direct with rapid wing beats.

SIMILAR SPECIES

CAPE MAY WARBLER ♀
see p.314

olive gray back

thin patch of yellow on throat and neck

YELLOW-RUMPED WARBLER (MYRTLE) ♀
see p.326

streaking on back

white throat

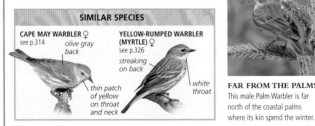

FAR FROM THE PALMS
This male Palm Warbler is far north of the coastal palms where its kin spend the winter.

OCCURRENCE
In North America, breeds in spruce bogs within the northerly forest zone, across Canada from Yukon to the Maritimes and Labrador, and in the US from Minnesota to Maine. Often migrates through central portions of eastern US; winters in southeastern US, Florida, and Central America.

| Length **5½in (14cm)** | Wingspan **8in (20cm)** | Weight **¼–⁷⁄₁₆oz (7–13g)** |
| Social **Flocks** | Lifespan **Up to 6 years** | Status **Secure** |

DATE: _____ TIME: _____ LOCATION: _____

| Order **Passeriformes** | Family **Parulidae** | Species **Setophaga pinus** |

Pine Warbler

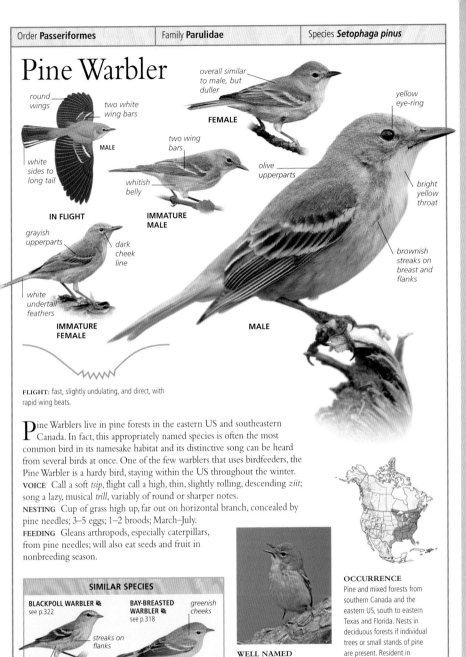

overall similar to male, but duller

yellow eye-ring

round wings

two white wing bars

FEMALE

MALE

two wing bars

olive upperparts

white sides to long tail

whitish belly

IN FLIGHT

IMMATURE MALE

bright yellow throat

grayish upperparts

dark cheek line

brownish streaks on breast and flanks

white undertail feathers

IMMATURE FEMALE

MALE

FLIGHT: fast, slightly undulating, and direct, with rapid wing beats.

Pine Warblers live in pine forests in the eastern US and southeastern Canada. In fact, this appropriately named species is often the most common bird in its namesake habitat and its distinctive song can be heard from several birds at once. One of the few warblers that uses birdfeeders, the Pine Warbler is a hardy bird, staying within the US throughout the winter.

VOICE Call a soft *tsip*, flight call a high, thin, slightly rolling, descending *ziit*; song a lazy, musical *trill*, variably of round or sharper notes.

NESTING Cup of grass high up, far out on horizontal branch, concealed by pine needles; 3–5 eggs; 1–2 broods; March–July.

FEEDING Gleans arthropods, especially caterpillars, from pine needles; will also eat seeds and fruit in nonbreeding season.

SIMILAR SPECIES

BLACKPOLL WARBLER ❧
see p.322

streaks on flanks

larger overall

BAY-BREASTED WARBLER ❧
see p.318

greenish cheeks

buff underparts

WELL NAMED
In many areas, Pine Warblers are the most common breeding birds in mature pine woods.

OCCURRENCE
Pine and mixed forests from southern Canada and the eastern US, south to eastern Texas and Florida. Nests in deciduous forests if individual trees or small stands of pine are present. Resident in southern half of its US range. Breeds and winters in the Bahamas and Hispaniola.

| Length **5in (13cm)** | Wingspan **9in (23cm)** | Weight **⁵⁄₁₆–½oz (9–15g)** |
| Social **Migrant/Winter flocks** | Lifespan **Up to 7 years** | Status **Secure** |

Order **Passeriformes**	Family **Parulidae**	Species **Setophaga coronata**

Yellow-rumped Warbler

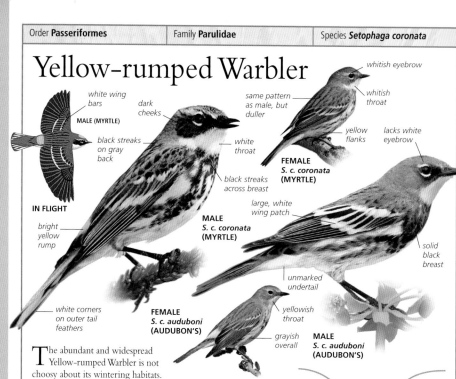

whitish eyebrow

white wing bars

dark cheeks

MALE (MYRTLE)

black streaks on gray back

IN FLIGHT

bright yellow rump

same pattern as male, but duller

whitish throat

white throat

yellow flanks

lacks white eyebrow

FEMALE S. c. coronata (MYRTLE)

black streaks across breast

large, white wing patch

MALE S. c. coronata (MYRTLE)

solid black breast

unmarked undertail

white corners on outer tail feathers

FEMALE S. c. auduboni (AUDUBON'S)

yellowish throat

grayish overall

MALE S. c. auduboni (AUDUBON'S)

The abundant and widespread Yellow-rumped Warbler is not choosy about its wintering habitats. It was often considered to consist of two species, "Myrtle" (*S. c. coronata*) in the East, and "Audubon's" (*S. c. auduboni*) in the West. Because they interbreed freely in a narrow zone of contact in British Columbia and Alberta, the American Ornithologists Union merged them. Recent evidence, however, suggests that they are indeed separate species so the designations may change again.
VOICE Myrtle's call a flat, husky *tchik*; Audubon's a higher-pitched, relatively musical, rising *jip*; flight call of both a clear, upslurred *sviiit*; song loose, warbled trill with an inflected ending; Myrtle's song higher and faster, Audubon's lower and slower.
NESTING Bulky cup of plant matter in conifer; 4–5 eggs; 1 brood; March–August.
FEEDING Feeds mostly on flies, beetles, wasps, and spiders during breeding; takes fruit and berries at other times of the year, often sallies to catch prey.

FLIGHT: fast, slightly undulating, and direct with rapid wing beats.

WIDESPREAD WARBLER
Yellow-rumped Warblers are widespread and are likely to be spotted often.

SIMILAR SPECIES

MAGNOLIA WARBLER ♂
see p.317

yellow throat and breast

more white in tail

CAPE MAY WARBLER ♀
see p.314

dark eye-line

thin, curved bill

OCCURRENCE
Both eastern and western populations are widespread across the continent from Alaska eastward to Quebec and Labrador, and westward in the mountains south to Arizona, New Mexico, and Northern Mexico. Prefers coniferous and mixed hardwood coniferous forests.

Length **5in (13cm)**	Wingspan **9in (23cm)**	Weight **⅜–⅝oz (10–17g)**
Social **Flocks**	Lifespan **Up to 7 years**	Status **Secure**

DATE: _____ TIME: _____ LOCATION: _____

Order **Passeriformes**	Family **Parulidae**	Species ***Setophaga discolor***

Prairie Warbler

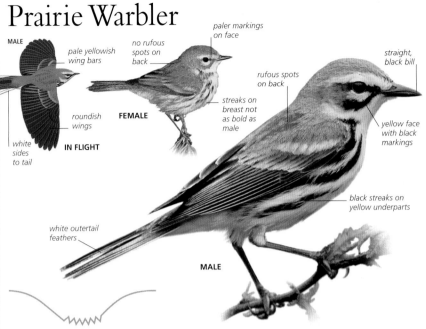

paler markings on face

MALE

pale yellowish wing bars

no rufous spots on back

straight, black bill

rufous spots on back

streaks on breast not as bold as male

roundish wings

FEMALE

yellow face with black markings

white sides to tail

IN FLIGHT

black streaks on yellow underparts

white outertail feathers

MALE

FLIGHT: fast, slightly undulating, and direct, with rapid wing beats.

Contrary to its common name, the Prairie Warbler does not live on the "prairie." Its distinctive song is a quintessential sound of scrubby areas across the eastern US. Although the population of this bird increased in the 19th century due to the widespread clearing of forests, the maturation of this habitat, along with human development, is having a negative impact on local populations.

VOICE Call a thick *tsik* or *tchip*, flight call a high, thin *sssip*; song variable in tempo, but always series of husky, buzzy notes that increase in pitch: *zzu zzu zzu zzo zzo zzo zzee zzee*.

NESTING Cup of plant material in fork of sapling or low trees, often within human reach; 3–5 eggs; 1 brood; May–July.

FEEDING Eats various insects, such as flies and crickets; also berries.

HIGH AND LOUD
Males sing from preferred elevated perches, producing their characteristic buzzy song that increases in pitch and tempo.

SIMILAR SPECIES

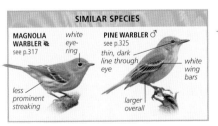

MAGNOLIA WARBLER
see p.317

white eye-ring

less prominent streaking

PINE WARBLER ♂
see p.325

thin, dark line through eye

white wing bars

larger overall

OCCURRENCE
Breeds in shrubby, open-canopied, second-growth habitats, and mangroves; migrant and wintering birds prefer similar brushy habitats. Breeds in parts of southern Ontario. Winters in the Bahamas, Greater and Lesser Antilles, and coasts of southern Mexico to El Salvador.

Length **4¾in (12cm)**	Wingspan **9in (23cm)**	Weight **⁷⁄₃₂–⁵⁄₁₆oz (6–9g)**
Social **Solitary/Winter flocks**	Lifespan **Up to 10 years**	Status **Declining**

DATE: _____ TIME: _____ LOCATION: _____

| Order **Passeriformes** | Family **Parulidae** | Species *Setophaga virens* |

Black-throated Green Warbler

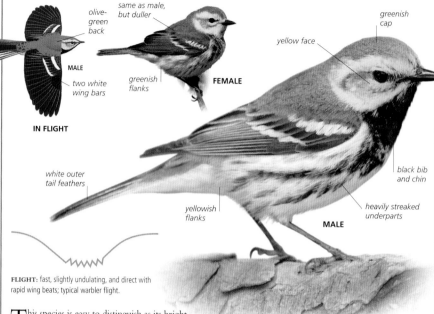

olive-green back

same as male, but duller

greenish cap

yellow face

MALE

two white wing bars

greenish flanks

FEMALE

IN FLIGHT

white outer tail feathers

yellowish flanks

black bib and chin

heavily streaked underparts

MALE

FLIGHT: fast, slightly undulating, and direct with rapid wing beats; typical warbler flight.

This species is easy to distinguish as its bright yellow face is unique among birds inhabiting northeastern North America. It is a member of the *virens* "superspecies," a group of non-overlapping species that are similar in plumage and vocalizations—the Black-throated Green, Golden-cheeked, Townsend's, and Hermit Warblers. Sadly, this species is vulnerable to habitat loss in parts of its wintering range.

VOICE Flat *tchip* call; flight call a rising *siii*; two high-pitched, buzzy songs, fast *zee zee zee zee zoo zee*; and lower, slower *zu zee zu-zu zee*.

NESTING Cup of twigs and grasses around 10–65ft (3–20m) on horizontal branch near trunk in the North, away from trunk in the South; 3–5 eggs; 1 brood; May–July.

FEEDING Gleans arthropods, especially caterpillars; also takes small fruit, including poison ivy berries, in nonbreeding season.

YELLOW-AND-BLACK GEM
From a high perch on a spruce tree, a male bird advertises his territory with a song.

SIMILAR SPECIES

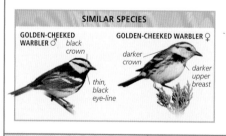

GOLDEN-CHEEKED WARBLER ♂

black crown

thin, black eye-line

GOLDEN-CHEEKED WARBLER ♀

darker crown

darker upper breast

OCCURRENCE
Breeds in many forest types, especially a mix of conifers and hardwood, from British Columbia east to Newfoundland and into southeast US along the Appalachians. Migrants and wintering birds use a variety of habitats. Winters from southern Texas into Venezuela; small numbers in Caribbean.

| Length **5in (13cm)** | Wingspan **8in (20cm)** | Weight ⁹⁄₃₂–³⁄₈oz (8–11g) |
| Social **Migrant/Winter flocks** | Lifespan **Up to 6 years** | Status **Secure** |

DATE: _____ TIME: _____ LOCATION: _____

Order **Passeriformes**	Family **Parulidae**	Species **Cardellina canadensis**

Canada Warbler

paler crown

bicolored eye-ring

faint necklace

yellow patch between eye and bill

dark crown

plain gray tail

MALE

FEMALE

conspicuous yellow eye-ring

white undertail feathers

IN FLIGHT

plain gray upperparts

yellow throat

MALE

black "necklace" across breast

yellow belly

O ne of the last species of wood warblers to arrive in the US and Canada in the spring, and among the first to leave in the fall, the Canada Warbler is sometimes called the "Necklaced Warbler," for the conspicuous black markings on its chest. This uncommon bird is sadly declining, probably because of the maturation and draining of its preferred breeding habitat, consisting of old mixed hardwood forests with moist undergrowth.

VOICE Call a thick *tchip;* flight call a variable, clear *plip;* song a haphazard jumble of sweet notes, often beginning with or interspersed with *tchip,* followed by a pause.

NESTING Concealed cup of leaves, in moss or grass, on or near ground; 4–5 eggs; 1 brood; May–June.

FEEDING Gleans at mid-levels for many species of insects; also flycatches and forages on ground.

FLIGHT: fast, slightly undulating, and direct with rapid wing beats.

TAKING FLIGHT
This species often waits for prey to fly by, before launching into flight to pursue it.

FAMILIAR MEAL
Flying insects, including crane flies, make up the bulk of the Canada Warbler's diet.

OCCURRENCE
Breeds in moist deciduous, mixed, and coniferous forests with well-developed understory, especially swampy woods; migrants use well-vegetated habitats; winters in dense, wet thickets and a variety of tropical woodlands in South America.

SIMILAR SPECIES

MAGNOLIA WARBLER ♀ see p.317	white eyebrow	**KIRTLAND'S WARBLER** ♂ see p.387

streaked mantle and flanks

streaked flanks

Length **5in (13cm)**	Wingspan **8in (20cm)**	Weight **⁹/₃₂–¹/₂oz (8–15g)**
Social **Flocks**	Lifespan **Up to 8 years**	Status **Declining**

DATE: _____ TIME: _____ LOCATION: _____

Order **Passeriformes**	Family **Parulidae**	Species *Cardellina pusilla*

Wilson's Warbler

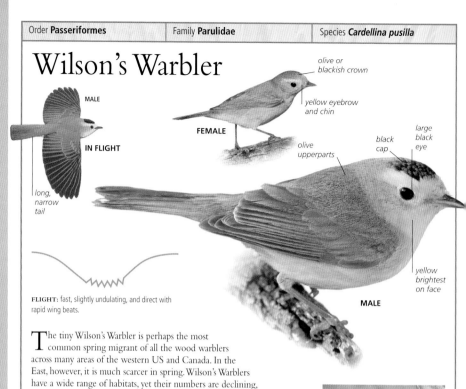

MALE

olive or
blackish crown

yellow eyebrow
and chin

FEMALE

olive
upperparts

black
cap

large
black
eye

IN FLIGHT

long,
narrow
tail

yellow
brightest
on face

MALE

FLIGHT: fast, slightly undulating, and direct with rapid wing beats.

The tiny Wilson's Warbler is perhaps the most common spring migrant of all the wood warblers across many areas of the western US and Canada. In the East, however, it is much scarcer in spring. Wilson's Warblers have a wide range of habitats, yet their numbers are declining, especially in the West, as its riverside breeding habitats are gradually being destroyed by development. This species is named after the renowned early 19th-century ornithologist, Alexander Wilson.

VOICE Call a rich *chimp* or *champ;* flight call a sharp, liquid *tsik;* song a variable, chattering trill, often increases in speed *che che che che chi-chi-chi-chit.*

NESTING Cup of leaves and grass placed on or near ground in mosses or grass, higher along Pacific coast; 4–6 eggs; 1 brood; April–June.

FEEDING Captures insects in foliage, leaf litter, or during flight; also takes berries and honeydew.

BRIGHT WESTERN BIRD
In its western range, male Wilson's Warblers have a glowing yellow-orange face; eastern birds are duller.

EASY IDENTIFICATION
The black cap and yellow face of the otherwise olive-colored Wilson's Warbler are good field marks.

SIMILAR SPECIES

YELLOW WARBLER ♀
see p.320

yellow edges to wing feathers

shorter tail

yellow overall

HOODED WARBLER ♀
see p.312

larger bill

larger body

OCCURRENCE
Breeds in wet shrubby thickets with no canopy, often along streams and lakes; Pacific slope birds use more varied habitats, including moist forests. Widespread in forests south of tundra, from Newfoundland, the Great Lakes, and northern New England; British Columbia to California and New Mexico.

Length **4¾in (12cm)**	Wingspan **7in (17.5cm)**	Weight **7/32–5/16oz (6–9g)**
Social **Flocks**	Lifespan **Up to 6 years**	Status **Declining**

DATE: _____ TIME: _____ LOCATION: _____

| Order **Passeriformes** | Family **Icteriidae** | Species *Icteria virens* |

Yellow-breasted Chat

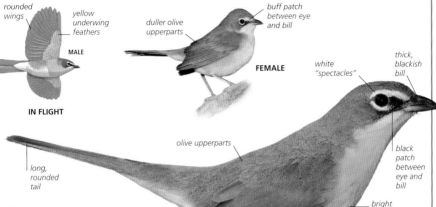

rounded wings

yellow underwing feathers

MALE

IN FLIGHT

duller olive upperparts

buff patch between eye and bill

FEMALE

white "spectacles"

thick, blackish bill

white "spectacles"

black patch between eye and bill

olive upperparts

long, rounded tail

bright yellow breast

black patch between eye and bill

MALE

FLIGHT: fast and direct with rapid wing beats and drooping tail; tends to stay under cover.

black legs and feet

This unique species has puzzled ornithologists and scientists for a long time, as molecular (DNA) studies have given conflicting results about whether it actually belongs to the wood-warbler family or not. Sometimes, it skulks in dense vegetation and is difficult to spot; at other times, it sits in full view, singing atop small trees. One of its behavioral quirks is to suddenly fly upwards, then glides slowly back to earth, while singing.

VOICE Seldom-heard calls include a low, soft *tuk* and nasal, downslurred *tiyew*; song consists of monosyllabic grunts, clucks, and whistles in repeated, decelerating series, with pauses between different series; sometimes sings at night; also mimics other birds.

NESTING Concealed and bulky structure of dead plant matter, in thicket near eye-level; 3–5 eggs; 1–2 broods; May–August.

FEEDING Eats insects; also fruit and berries.

CLUCKS AND WHISTLES
This bird has a remarkably varied vocal repertoire, including loud clucks and whistles.

OCCURRENCE
Breeds in dense shrubby areas, including forest edges; western birds mostly restricted to thickets along riverside corridors; migrants found in varied habitats. Winters in scrubby habitats from Mexico to Panama.

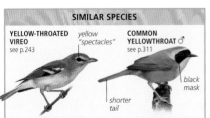

SIMILAR SPECIES

YELLOW-THROATED VIREO see p.243 — yellow "spectacles"

COMMON YELLOWTHROAT ♂ see p.311 — black mask, shorter tail

| Length 7½in (19cm) | Wingspan 9½in (24cm) | Weight ¹¹⁄₁₆–¹¹⁄₁₆oz (20–30g) |
| Social **Solitary** | Lifespan **Up to 9 years** | Status **Declining** |

DATE: _____ TIME: _____ LOCATION: _____

AMERICAN SPARROWS

T HE MALES OF THIS DIVERSE GROUP OF songbirds often have striking head and chest patterns, which help in telling the species apart. They were originally called sparrows because of their similarity to Old World sparrows; however, they are unrelated to them. The Passerellidae probably originated in the Americas, and spread to Europe and Asia, but the relationships between the New World sparrows, Old World buntings, and tangers are still to be resolved.

TYPICAL NEW WORLD SPARROW
A White-crowned Sparrow shows the typical stout emberizid beak.

CARDINALS AND RELATIVES

B IRDS BELONGING to the Cardinalidae family are visually stunning, noisy birds, especially the vivid scarlet-red male Northern Cardinal. However, several smaller species, confusingly called buntings, but not related to the Old World buntings (part of the Emberizidae family), are less striking, especially in dull, brown female plumages.

CARDINALS
Although cardinals are also called "redbirds," only the males have a bright red plumage—females are mostly tan or gray. Cardinals are fairly social birds, and even join flocks that include other species.

TANAGERS
North American tanagers are not closely related to the South American species, few of which reach North America. They are brightly colored, with males being mostly red in the breeding season and females, yellow-green. Tanagers use their pointed but stout bills to feed on a variety of insects as well as fruit.

BUNTINGS
Buntings are mostly small birds. The brightly colored males feature strong blue hues, as seen in the electric-blue plumage of the Indigo Bunting. Females are more cryptically colored. They have stout, triangular bills that are ideal for splitting and peeling seeds.

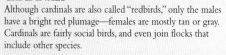

MALE COLORS
Male Scarlet Tanagers are some of North America's most colorful birds.

Order **Passeriformes**	Family **Passerellidae**	Species ***Pipilo erythrophthalmus***

Eastern Towhee

black hood and upperparts

red eye

white corners to tail

single white patch in each wing

ADULT

IN FLIGHT

MALE

white belly

brown hood and upperparts

white wing patches

long tail

small white markings on wings

rusty flanks

FEMALE

The Towhees get their name from the upslurred *chew-eee* (or *to-whee*) call they make. The Eastern Towhee is famous for its vocalizations and has one of the best-known mnemonics for its song: "drink your tea." The Eastern Towhee was once lumped with Spotted Towhees under the name "Rufous-sided Towhee," because they interbreed in the Great Plains. In the southeastern US, Eastern Towhees have paler eyes the further south they are located; individuals with nearly white eyes are found in Florida. Like all towhees, the Eastern Towhee feeds noisily by jumping backwards with both feet at once to move leaves and reveal the insects and seeds that may be hidden underneath.

VOICE Call a nasal, upslurred *chew-eee*; flight call *zeeeooooweeet*; song sounds like *dweee, dyooo di-i-i-i-i-i-i-i-i-i-i-i-i*.

NESTING Large cup in depression on ground under cover, also low in thicket; 3–5 eggs; 1–2 broods; May–August.

FEEDING Eats seeds, fruits, insects, and buds.

FLIGHT: low and direct with much gliding, usually within cover.

TERRESTRIAL LIFE
The bird stays close to the ground, and is usually found not more than a few yards off it.

OCCURRENCE
Found in dense thickets, woodland, dense shrubbery, forest edges and disturbed forests from southeast Saskatchewan, east Nebraska, west Louisiana, east to south Quebec, south Maine, and south Florida. Retreats from areas north of Chicago to winter in east Texas.

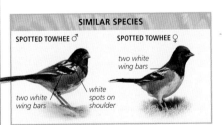

SIMILAR SPECIES

SPOTTED TOWHEE ♂   SPOTTED TOWHEE ♀

two white wing bars

white spots on shoulder

two white wing bars

Length **7½–8in (19–20cm)**	Wingspan **10½in (27cm)**	Weight **1¹⁄₁₆–1¾oz (30–50g)**
Social **Solitary/Small flocks**	Lifespan **Up to 12 years**	Status **Secure**

Order **Passeriformes**	Family **Passerellidae**	Species ***Spizella arborea***

American Tree Sparrow

rufous crown

black-and-yellow bill

rusty tones on shoulder and wings

gray head and nape

rusty stripe behind eye

streaked underparts

ADULT (BREEDING)

JUVENILE

IN FLIGHT

black and rust streaking on back

rust patch on shoulder

dark, central spot

striped back

cleft tail

ADULT (NONBREEDING)

long, squarish tail

ADULT (BREEDING)

The first heavy snowfalls of the winter often bring large flocks of American Tree Sparrows to birdfeeders. This bird is commonly mistaken for the smaller Chipping Sparrow, but the two species look quite dissimilar in the winter. The American Tree Sparrow's central breast spot, bicolored bill, and large size are unique among the *Spizella*. A highly social, vocal, and misnamed species, noisy winter flocks numbering in the hundreds can be found feeding in weedy fields and along the roadsides of the northern US and southern Canada. **VOICE** Call a bell-like *teedle-ee*; flight call a thin, slightly descending *tsiiiu*; song *seee seee di-di-di di-di-di dyew dyew*.
NESTING Neat cup on ground concealed within thicket; 4–6 eggs; 1 brood; June–July.
FEEDING Feeds on seeds, berries, and a variety of insects.

FLIGHT: slightly undulating, often flies to open perch when flushed.

WINTER HABITATS
In winter, this species frequents barren habitats, like old fields and roadsides, as well as feeders.

SIMILAR SPECIES

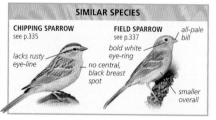

CHIPPING SPARROW
see p.335

lacks rusty eye-line

FIELD SPARROW
see p.337

bold white eye-ring

no central, black breast spot

all-pale bill

smaller overall

OCCURRENCE
Breeds in scrubby thickets of birch and willows in the area between taiga and tundra across Alaska and north Canada. Nonbreeders choose open, grassy, brushy habitats. Winters across south Canada and the northern US. Casual to Pacific coast and southern US.

Length **6¼in (16cm)**	Wingspan **9½in (24cm)**	Weight **⁷⁄₁₆–⁷⁄₈oz (13–25g)**
Social **Flocks**	Lifespan **Up to 11 years**	Status **Secure**

DATE: _____ TIME: _____ LOCATION: _____

| Order **Passeriformes** | Family **Passerellidae** | Species *Spizella passerina* |

Chipping Sparrow

bright rufous crown

blackish bill

white eyebrow

black eye-line

pinkish bill

rusty cast to crown

pale underparts

ADULT

IN FLIGHT

ADULT (WINTER)

ADULT (BREEDING)

gray underparts

heavily streaked, especially on breast

JUVENILE

cleft tail

The Chipping Sparrow is a common, trusting bird, which breeds in backyards across most of North America. While they are easily identifiable in the summer, "Chippers" molt into a drab, nonbreeding plumage during fall, at which point they are easily confused with the Clay-colored and Brewer's Sparrows they flock with. Most reports of this species across the north in winter are actually of the larger American Tree Sparrow. In the winter, Chipping Sparrows can be easily recognized as they lack their bright, rusty crown and are restricted to the south.

VOICE Call a sharp *tsip*; flight call a sharp, thin *tsiiit*; song an insect-like trill of *chip* notes, variable in duration and quality.

NESTING Neat cup usually placed well off the ground in tree or shrub; 3–5 eggs; 1–2 broods; April–August.

FEEDING Eats seeds of grasses and annuals, plus some fruit; when breeding, also eats insects and other invertebrates.

FLIGHT: slightly undulating, often to open perch when flushed.

BACKYARD BIRD
Chipping Sparrows are a very common sight in gardens and backyards all across the continent.

SIMILAR SPECIES

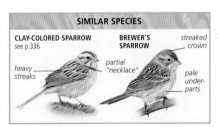

CLAY-COLORED SPARROW see p.336

heavy streaks

BREWER'S SPARROW

partial "necklace"

streaked crown

pale underparts

OCCURRENCE
Found in a wide variety of habitats: open forest, woodlands, grassy, park-like areas, shorelines, and backyards. Breeds in North America south of the Arctic timberline and in Mexico, and in Central America, as far south as Nicaragua. Winters from southern states to Nicaragua.

| Length **5½in (14cm)** | Wingspan **8½in (21cm)** | Weight **⅜–½oz (10–15g)** |
| Social **Large flocks** | Lifespan **Up to 9 years** | Status **Secure** |

| Order **Passeriformes** | Family **Passerellidae** | Species *Spizella pallida* |

Clay-colored Sparrow

bold, dark cheek stripes

white crown stripe

unstreaked, gray nape

long tail

white wing bars

bold, dark brown streaks on upperparts

thick, white eyebrow

brown rump

ADULT

IN FLIGHT

very pale buffy wash across breast

ADULT

whitish gray underparts

notched tail

FLIGHT: slightly undulating, often flies to open perch when flushed.

The little Clay-colored Sparrow is best known for its mechanical, buzzy song. This bird spends much of its foraging time away from the breeding habitat; consequently, males' territories are quite small, allowing for dense breeding populations. Clay-colored Sparrows have shifted their breeding range eastward and northward over the last century, most likely because of changes in land practices. During the nonbreeding season, they form large flocks in open country, associating with other *Spizella* sparrows, especially Chippings and Brewer's.
VOICE Call a sharp *tsip*; flight a call short, rising *sip*; song a series of 2–7 mechanical buzzes on one pitch.
NESTING Cup of grass placed just off the ground in shrub or small tree; 3–5 eggs; 1–2 broods; May–August.
FEEDING Forages on or low to the ground for seeds and insects.

CHRISTMAS PRESENT
The Clay-colored Sparrow is fond of short conifers for breeding, so Christmas tree farms form a perfect habitat.

SIMILAR SPECIES

CHIPPING SPARROW ❋
see p.335

grayish rump

dark stripe through eye

grayer breast

BREWER'S SPARROW

streaked nape

lacks bold, crown stripe

OCCURRENCE
Breeds in open habitats: prairies, shrubland, forest edges, and Christmas tree farms along the US/Canadian border and northward to the southern Northwest Territories. Winters in a large variety of brushy, weedy areas from south Texas to Mexico. Migration takes it to the Great Plains.

| Length 5½in (14cm) | Wingspan 7½in (19cm) | Weight ⅜–½oz (10–15g) |
| Social **Large flocks** | Lifespan **Up to 5 years** | Status **Secure** |

DATE: _____ TIME: _____ LOCATION: _____

| Order **Passeriformes** | Family **Passerellidae** | Species *Spizella pusilla* |

Field Sparrow

small, pink bill

white eye-ring

streaking on back

ADULT (REDDISH FORM)

rusty markings on head

light rust cheek and crown

white wing bars

ADULT (GRAYISH FORM)

long, notched tail

IN FLIGHT

tan underparts

duller overall

dusky chest

JUVENILE

distinctive pink legs

long tail

ADULT (REDDISH FORM)

FLIGHT: slightly undulating; female may use moth-like flight to approach the nest.

The distinctive accelerating trill song of the Field Sparrow is a characteristic sound of shrubby fields and scrubby areas in southeastern Canada and the eastern US. The bird's bright-pink bill, plain "baby face," and white eye-ring make this sparrow one of the easiest to identify. The Field Sparrow has brighter plumage in the East, and drabber plumage in the interior part of its range. Although quite dissimilar at first glance, the Black-chinned Sparrow may in fact be the Field Sparrow's closest relative, sharing its pink bill, relatively unpatterned plumage, and its song.

VOICE Call a sharp *tsik*; flight call a strongly descending *tsiiiu*; song a series of sweet, downslurred whistles accelerating to a rapid trill.

NESTING Grass cup placed on or just above ground in grass or bush; 3–5 eggs; 1–3 broods; March–August.

FEEDING Eats seeds; also insects, insect larvae, and spiders in the summer.

FAMILIAR SONG
Male Field Sparrows sing their familiar and distinctive song throughout the summer.

OCCURRENCE
Breeds in overgrown fields, woodland edges, roadsides, and other shrubby, overgrown areas; occasionally in orchards and parks in southeastern Canada, west to Dakota, east to New England. Winters in similar habitats in the southern US. Casual in Atlantic Canada and on the Pacific Coast.

SIMILAR SPECIES		
WHITE-CROWNED SPARROW ❧ see p.350	**AMERICAN TREE SPARROW** see p.334	lacks bold, white eye-ring
larger body	pale crown stripe	central, black breast spot

| Length **5½in (14cm)** | Wingspan **8in (20cm)** | Weight **⅜–½oz (11–15g)** |
| Social **Solitary/Flocks** | Lifespan **Up to 6 years** | Status **Declining** |

DATE: _____ TIME: _____ LOCATION: _____

Order **Passeriformes**	Family **Passerellidae**	Species ***Pooecetes gramineus***

Vesper Sparrow

bold white eye-ring

dark-bordered ear patches

rusty shoulders

ADULT

IN FLIGHT

pale brown upperparts

streaked breast

uniformly colored and streaked overall

ADULT

bold white-edged long, dark, square tail

white outer tail feathers

ADULT

The Vesper Sparrow got its common name because its pleasant song was considered to sound sweetest in the evening, when prayers known as "vespers" are sung in the Catholic and Eastern Orthodox churches. When Henry David Thoreau wrote of this species, he called it the "Bay-winged Bunting," because of its (sometimes concealed) rusty shoulder patches and its relation to the Old World Emberizidae buntings. The Vesper Sparrow needs areas with bare ground to breed, so it is one of the few species that can successfully nest in areas of intense agriculture; the bird's numbers seem to be declining in spite of this.

VOICE Full *tchup* call, flight call thin *tseent*; song consists of 2 whistles of same pitch, followed by 2 higher-pitched ones, then trills, ends lazily.

NESTING Cup placed on patch of bare ground, against grass, bush, or rock; 3–5 eggs; 1 brood; April–August.

FEEDING Eats insects and seeds.

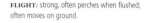

FLIGHT: strong, often perches when flushed; often moves on ground.

SIMILAR SPECIES

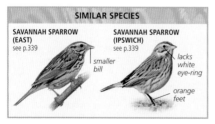

SAVANNAH SPARROW (EAST)
see p.339

smaller bill

SAVANNAH SPARROW (IPSWICH)
see p.339

lacks white eye-ring

orange feet

GIFTED SONGSTER
The sweet song of the Vesper Sparrow is a characteristic sound of more northerly open areas.

OCCURRENCE
Breeds in sparse grassland, cultivated fields, recently burned areas, and mountain parks across south Canada and the northern US. Winters in sparsely vegetated, open habitats from southern US to southwest Mexico. Found in patches of bare earth in all seasons.

Length **6¼in (16cm)**	Wingspan **10in (25cm)**	Weight **¹¹⁄₁₆–1¹⁄₁₆oz (20–30g)**
Social **Flocks**	Lifespan **Up to 7 years**	Status **Declining**

DATE: _____ TIME: _____ LOCATION: _____

Order **Passeriformes**	Family **Passerellidae**	Species ***Passerculus sandwichensis***

Savannah Sparrow

yellow patch between eye and bill

brown overall

ADULT

small bill

short, notched tail

crisp black streaking on underparts

IN FLIGHT

ADULT (EASTERN)

reddish streaks on underparts

pale sandy overall

ADULT
P. s. princeps
(IPSWICH SPARROW)

white belly

ADULT (WESTERN)

FLIGHT: square-tailed with an often undulating or "stair-step" flight pattern.

whitish tail edgings

The Savannah Sparrow is one of the most numerous sparrows in North America. It shows tremendous variation—21 subspecies—across its vast range, but it is always brown, with dark streaks above and white with dark streaks below. The pale "Ipswich Sparrow" (*P. s. princeps*), originally described as a species, breeds on Sable Island, Nova Scotia, and winters along the East Coast. The "Large-billed Sparrow" (*P. s. rostratus* and *P. s. atratus*) breeds in Baja, California, and Sonora, Mexico. Their distinct song consists of three buzzy trills, and their flight calls are lower and more metallic than other populations.

VOICE Call a sharp, but full *stip*; flight call a thin, weak, downslurred *tseew*; song a *sit sit sit suh-EEEEE say*, from perch or in display flight with legs dangling.

NESTING Concealed cup of grass placed in depression on ground, protected by overhanging grass or sedges; 2–6 eggs; 1–2 broods; June–August.

FEEDING Forages on the ground, mostly for insects; in summer also eats seeds; in winter berries and fruit when available; also small snails and crustaceans.

SWEET LOW DOWN
Savannah Sparrows like to vocalize from low vegetation and fenceposts near farms.

OCCURRENCE
Breeds in meadows, grasslands, pastures, bushy tundra, and some cultivated land across northern North America. Also along the Pacific Coast and in Mexican interior. Nonbreeders use varied open habitats. Winters across southern US to Honduras, also Cuba, the Bahamas, and Cayman Islands.

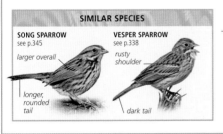

SIMILAR SPECIES

SONG SPARROW
see p.345

larger overall

longer, rounded tail

VESPER SPARROW
see p.338

rusty shoulder

dark tail

Length **5½–6in (14–15cm)**	Wingspan **6¾in (17cm)**	Weight **½–1¹⁄₁₆oz (15–30g)**
Social **Solitary/Loose flocks**	Lifespan **Unknown**	Status **Secure**

| Order **Passeriformes** | Family **Passerellidae** | Species **Ammodramus savannarum** |

Grasshopper Sparrow

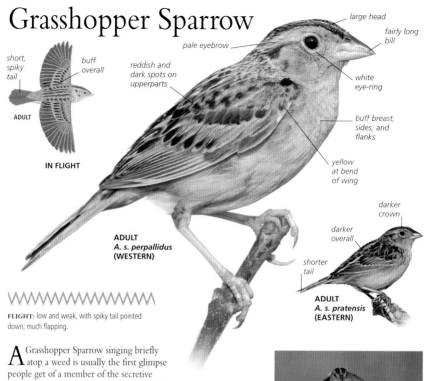

large head

fairly long bill

pale eyebrow

short, spiky tail

buff overall

reddish and dark spots on upperparts

white eye-ring

buff breast, sides, and flanks

yellow at bend of wing

ADULT

IN FLIGHT

ADULT
A. s. perpallidus
(WESTERN)

darker crown

darker overall

shorter tail

ADULT
A. s. pratensis
(EASTERN)

FLIGHT: low and weak, with spiky tail pointed down; much flapping.

A Grasshopper Sparrow singing briefly atop a weed is usually the first glimpse people get of a member of the secretive *Ammodramus* genus. Although its large head and spiky tail are typical of its genus, the Grasshopper Sparrow is the only *Ammodramus* sparrow to have a plain breast and two completely different songs. While it does eat grasshoppers, its common name derives from its song, which resembles the sounds grasshoppers make. It varies geographically, with about 12 subspecies.

VOICE Sharp *tik* call; flight call a long, high *tseeee*; song an insect-like trill *tik'-tok-TREEEE*, or series of quick buzzes.

NESTING Cup of grass placed in clump of grass; 3–6 eggs; 1–2 broods; April–August.

FEEDING Forages on ground for seeds and insects.

YELLOW PATCH
The pale crown stripe and small yellow patch at the bend of its wings are visible here.

SIMILAR SPECIES

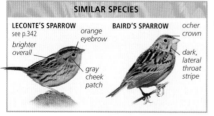

LECONTE'S SPARROW
see p.342

brighter overall

gray cheek patch

orange eyebrow

BAIRD'S SPARROW

ocher crown

dark, lateral throat stripe

OCCURRENCE
Breeds in short grassland, pastures, and even mown areas across much of the US and southern Canada. Locally distributed in the Southwest, also patchily through central US. Winters in similar habitats from southern US to Colombia; also found in the West Indies.

| Length **5in (13cm)** | Wingspan **8in (20cm)** | Weight **½–¹¹⁄₁₆oz (15–20g)** |
| Social **Solitary/Flocks** | Lifespan **Up to 7 years** | Status **Declining** |

DATE: _____ TIME: _____ LOCATION: _____

Henslow's Sparrow

round, spiky tail

dark reddish overall

flat, greenish head with black stripes

whitish scaling on purplish back

heavy bill

rufous-edged wing feathers

black streaks on buffy breast

ADULT

IN FLIGHT

ADULT

The combination of a large, flat, greenish head, and purplish back are unique to Henslow's Sparrow. A bird of the tallgrass prairies and wet grasslands, the breeding range of this sparrow closely mirrors the extent of its habitat. While it has suffered greatly from the drainage, cultivation, and urbanization of much of its preferred breeding grounds, the Henslow's Sparrow has also recently started to use reclaimed strip mines in northwest Missouri and Iowa for breeding.

VOICE Call a sharp *tsik*; flight call a long, high, shrill *tseeeeee*; song a hiccuping sputter with second note higher *tsih-LIK!*

NESTING Cup of grass placed on or near ground; 2–5 eggs; 1–2 broods; May–August.

FEEDING Eats seeds; forages for insects and their larvae, and spiders in the summer.

FLIGHT: low and weak, with spiky tail pointed down; much flapping.

SIMILAR SPECIES

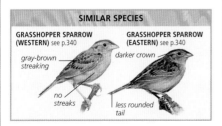

GRASSHOPPER SPARROW (WESTERN) see p.340

gray-brown streaking

no streaks

GRASSHOPPER SPARROW (EASTERN) see p.340

darker crown

less rounded tail

INTO THE AIR
The male puts considerable effort into his short, but surprisingly far-carrying song.

OCCURRENCE
Breeds predominantly in tallgrass prairie and wet grasslands from Oklahoma eastward to New York and up into southeastern Canada, and southward to North Carolina. Winters in weedy, brushy fields, grassy pine woods, and undergrowth along Gulf Coastal Plain from Texas to North Carolina.

Length 4¾–5in (12–13cm)	Wingspan 6½in (16cm)	Weight ⅜–½oz (11–15g)
Social **Solitary/Loose flocks**	Lifespan **Unknown**	Status **Declining**

DATE: _____ TIME: _____ LOCATION: _____

| Order **Passeriformes** | Family **Passerellidae** | Species *Ammodramus leconteii* |

LeConte's Sparrow

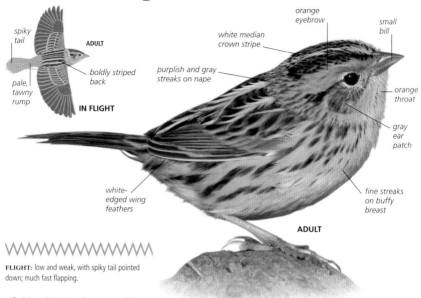

spiky tail

ADULT

boldly striped back

pale, tawny rump

IN FLIGHT

white median crown stripe

orange eyebrow

small bill

purplish and gray streaks on nape

orange throat

gray ear patch

white-edged wing feathers

fine streaks on buffy breast

ADULT

FLIGHT: low and weak, with spiky tail pointed down; much fast flapping.

Although intricately patterned in glowing colors, LeConte's Sparrow is usually very difficult to see. Not only is it tiny—one of the smallest of all sparrows—but in the grasslands and marshes of interior North America where it lives, it prefers to dart for cover under grasses instead of flushing when disturbed. Meanwhile the flight call and song of this elusive little bird are remarkably insect-like. Many people who hear it often then pass off the unseen bird as a grasshopper. Its nest is even harder to find, making this bird a real challenge to study as well as observe.

VOICE Call long, down-slurred *zheeep*; flight call similar to grasshopper; song insect-like, buzzy *tik'-uht-tizz-ZHEEEEEE-k.*

NESTING Concealed little cup placed on or near ground; 3–5 eggs; 1 brood; June–August.

FEEDING Forages on the ground and in grasses for insects and their larvae, spiders, and seeds.

HIDEAWAY BIRD
LeConte's Sparrow is usually found skulking in medium-to-tall grass in all seasons.

OCCURRENCE
Breeds in marshes, wet meadows, and bogs from southwest Yukon to Lake Superior and west Quebec. Migrants or wintering birds found in tall grass and marshes in southwest Kansas to south Indiana, and central Texas to coastal Carolinas.

SIMILAR SPECIES

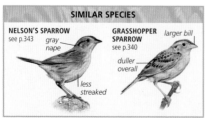

NELSON'S SPARROW see p.343 gray nape — less streaked

GRASSHOPPER SPARROW see p.340 — larger bill — duller overall

| Length **4½–5in (11.5–13cm)** | Wingspan **6½–7in (16–18cm)** | Weight **⁷⁄₁₆–⁹⁄₁₆oz (12–16g)** |
| Social **Solitary/Loose flocks** | Lifespan **Unknown** | Status **Secure** |

DATE: _____ TIME: _____ LOCATION: _____

| Order **Passeriformes** | Family **Passerellidae** | Species ***Ammodramus nelsoni*** |

Nelson's Sparrow

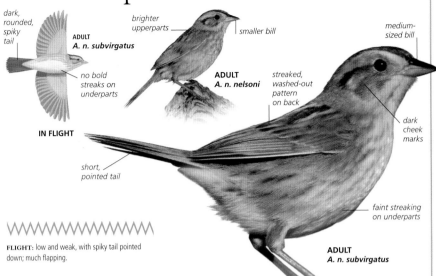

dark, rounded, spiky tail

ADULT
A. n. subvirgatus

brighter upperparts

smaller bill

medium-sized bill

no bold streaks on underparts

ADULT
A. n. nelsoni

streaked, washed-out pattern on back

dark cheek marks

IN FLIGHT

short, pointed tail

faint streaking on underparts

ADULT
A. n. subvirgatus

FLIGHT: low and weak, with spiky tail pointed down; much flapping.

This rather shy species includes three subspecies that differ in plumage, as well as breeding habitat and location. *A. n. nelsoni* is the most brightly colored, and is found from the southern Northwest Territories south to northwest Wisconsin. *A. n. subvirgatus* breeds in coastal Maine and the Maritimes, and along the St. Lawrence River. It is visually duller than *A. n. nelsoni*, with a longer bill and flatter head. The intermediate-looking *A. n. alterus* breeds along the southern and western coasts of Hudson Bay.

VOICE Sharp *tik* call; song a husky *t-SHHHHEE-uhrr*.

NESTING Cup of grass placed on or just above ground; 4–5 eggs; 1 brood; May–July.

FEEDING Forages on the ground mainly for insects, spiders, and seeds.

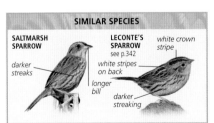

SIMILAR SPECIES

SALTMARSH SPARROW

darker streaks

LECONTE'S SPARROW
see p.342

white stripes on back

longer bill

darker streaking

white crown stripe

IDENTIFYING MARKS
The orange-and-gray facial pattern and streaks on the breast are clearly visible.

OCCURRENCE
Breeds in a variety of marsh habitats across Canada and extreme north, central North America. Nonbreeders found in marshes and wet, weedy fields. *A. n. nelsoni* and *A. n. alterus* winter on coast from Texas northeast to New Jersey; *A. n. subvirgatus* from eastern Florida to New Jersey.

| Length **4¾in (12cm)** | Wingspan **7in (17.5cm)** | Weight **⁷⁄₁₆–¹¹⁄₁₆oz (13–20g)** |
| Social **Solitary/Flocks** | Lifespan **Unknown** | Status **Secure** |

DATE: _____ TIME: _____ LOCATION: _____

Order **Passeriformes**	Family **Passerellidae**	Species ***Passerella iliaca***

Fox Sparrow

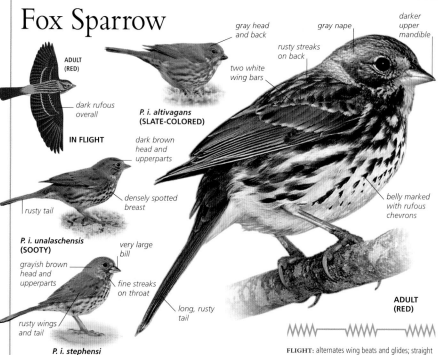

gray head and back

gray nape

darker upper mandible

ADULT (RED)

rusty streaks on back

two white wing bars

dark rufous overall

P. i. altivagans **(SLATE-COLORED)**

IN FLIGHT

dark brown head and upperparts

densely spotted breast

rusty tail

P. i. unalaschensis **(SOOTY)**

very large bill

grayish brown head and upperparts

fine streaks on throat

long, rusty tail

rusty wings and tail

P. i. stephensi **(THICK-BILLED)**

belly marked with rufous chevrons

ADULT (RED)

FLIGHT: alternates wing beats and glides; straight and fluttery, from cover to cover.

L arger, more robust, and more colorful than its close relatives, the Fox Sparrow is a beautiful species. When it appears in backyards, its presence can be detected by its foraging habits; it crouches low in leaf litter, and hops to disturb leaves, under which it finds seeds or insects. It varies considerably over its huge range, from thick-billed birds in the Sierras to dark ones in the Northwest, and distinctive reds in the East.

VOICE Call is sharp, dry *tshak* or *tshuk*; flight call a high-pitched *tzeep!*; song is complex and musical with trills and whistles.

NESTING Dense cup of grasses or moss lined with fine material; usually placed low in shrub; 2–5 eggs; 1 brood; April–July.

FEEDING Forages for insects, seeds, and fruit.

FOXY RED
The Fox Sparrow gets its name from the rusty coloration of the eastern "Red" birds.

OCCURRENCE
Encompasses the entire boreal forest zone, from Alaska in the West to Quebec, Labrador, and Newfoundland in the East. In the West, it occurs in coastal and near-coast thickets within coniferous or mixed woodlands. Winters in the Pacific West, south to Baja California; also from Texas to Massachusetts.

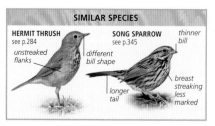

SIMILAR SPECIES		
HERMIT THRUSH see p.284	**SONG SPARROW** see p.345	thinner bill
unstreaked flanks	different bill shape	
	longer tail	breast streaking less marked

Length **6–7½in (15–19cm)**	Wingspan **10½–11½in (27–29cm)**	Weight **⁷⁄₈–1⁹⁄₁₆oz (25–45g)**
Social **Solitary/Small flocks**	Lifespan **Up to 9 years**	Status **Secure**

DATE: _____ TIME: _____ LOCATION: _____

Order **Passeriformes**	Family **Passerellidae**	Species *Melospiza melodia*

Song Sparrow

grayish head with dark chestnut brown crown

central breast spot

grayish head with brown markings

ADULT (WEST COAST)

heavily streaked brownish gray upperparts

streaked underparts

M. m. melodia (EASTERN)

IN FLIGHT

dark "mustache" bordering whitish throat

long, dark, rounded tail

heavily streaked underparts

paler neck

whitish lower belly

more rusty overall

M. m. saltonis (SOUTHWEST)

ADULT (WEST COAST)

The familiar song of this species can be heard in backyards across the continent, including in winter, although it varies both individually and geographically. In the southeastern US, where it does not breed, migrant birds start singing in early spring before departing for northern areas. The Song Sparrow may be the North American champion of geographical variation—about 30 subspecies have been described. These vary from the large, dark birds of the Aleutian Islands (*M. m. maxima*) to the smaller, paler birds of southern Arizona (*M. m. saltonis*). Eastern birds, such as *M. m. melodia*, fall between the two in size.
VOICE A dry *tchip* call; flight call a clear *siiiti*; song a jumble of variable whistles and trills, *deeep deeep deep-deep chrrrr tiiiiiiiiiiiii tyeeur* most common.
NESTING Bulky cup on or near ground, in brush or marsh vegetation; 3–5 eggs; 1–3 broods; March–August.
FEEDING In summer, feeds mainly on insects; in winter, eats mainly seeds, but also fruit.

FLIGHT: low and direct, staying within cover whenever possible.

OCCURRENCE
Widespread in a range of habitats (although not in dense forests) across Canada and the US, from the Atlantic to the Pacific Coasts and north to Alaska. Some populations move south of their breeding range in winter.

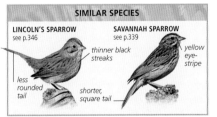

SIMILAR SPECIES	
LINCOLN'S SPARROW see p.346	**SAVANNAH SPARROW** see p.339

thinner black streaks

yellow eye-stripe

less rounded tail

shorter, square tail

BREAST SPOT
The Song Sparrow often sings from exposed perches, showing off its characteristic breast spot.

Length **5–7½in (13–19cm)**	Wingspan **8½–12in (21–31cm)**	Weight **⁷⁄₁₆–1³⁄₄oz (13–50g)**
Social **Solitary/Flocks**	Lifespan **Up to 9 years**	Status **Secure**

DATE: _____ TIME: _____ LOCATION: _____

| Order **Passeriformes** | Family **Passerellidae** | Species **Melospiza lincolnii** |

Lincoln's Sparrow

crested or peaked, rufous crown

broad gray eyebrow

bold eye-ring

small, thin bill

dark brown streak under cheek

streaks on throat

pencil-thin streaking on buffy breast

rounded tail

ADULT

rufous-edged wings

ADULT

IN FLIGHT

A t first glance, Lincoln's Sparrow appears plain, but on close inspection it reveals itself to be a bright-eyed little bird with subtly varying, but crisply outlined, markings. In the breeding season, it seeks out predominantly moist willow scrub at the tundra–taiga timberline; outside the breeding season, Lincoln's Sparrow can be found in scrubby habitats right across North America. It will occasionally visit backyard feeders in winter, but it is generally a secretive bird that stays within fairly dense cover wherever it can. However, Lincoln's Sparrow's rich, musical song is unmistakable, and it varies remarkably little from region to region.

VOICE Call a variable, loud *tchip*, flight call a rolling *ziiiit*; song series of rich, musical trills, *ju-ju-ju dodododo didididididi whrrrr*.

NESTING Grass cup, lined with fine grass, and hidden in depression in ground under overhanging sedges or grasses; 3–5 eggs; 1 brood; June–August.

FEEDING Mainly seeds in winter; in summer, mostly insects, such as beetles, mosquitoes, and moths.

FLIGHT: low and direct, staying within cover whenever possible.

RAISE THE ALARM
When disturbed, Lincoln's Sparrow often raises its central crown feathers, which form a crest.

OCCURRENCE
Breeds in muskeg and wet thickets across northern North America, also south into the western ranges of California and Arizona. Migrants and wintering birds use a variety of scrubby habitats. Winters in southern US (and farther south), and on Pacific Coast north to British Columbia.

SIMILAR SPECIES

SONG SPARROW
see p.345
larger overall

more coarse streaking

short, square, notched tail

SAVANNAH SPARROW
see p.339
yellow stripe above eye

| Length **5¼–6in (13.5–15cm)** | Wingspan **7½–8½in (19–22cm)** | Weight **½–⅞oz (15–25g)** |
| Social **Solitary/Small flocks** | Lifespan **Up to 7 years** | Status **Secure** |

DATE: _____ TIME:_____ LOCATION:_____

| Order **Passeriformes** | Family **Passerellidae** | Species **Melospiza georgiana** |

Swamp Sparrow

rufous crown

gray and rufous face

unstreaked gray nape

rufous flanks

tawny flanks

ADULT (BREEDING)

IN FLIGHT

ADULT (NON-BREEDING)

dark, rounded tail

tan upperparts with dark streaks

gray breast with fine streaking

rusty margins to wing feathers

ADULT (BREEDING)

FLIGHT: low and direct, staying within cover whenever possible.

The Swamp Sparrow is a common breeder in wet habitats across eastern North America and Canada west to the Yukon and British Columbia. It is especially abundant in its preferred habitat of tall reed marshes. A somewhat skittish bird, the Swamp Sparrow is often seen darting rapidly into cover, but usually repays the patient observer with a reappearance, giving its characteristic *chimp* call. Though often confused with both the Song Sparrow and Lincoln's Sparrow, the Swamp Sparrow never shows more than a very faint, blurry streaking on its gray breast, and sports conspicuous rusty-edged wing feathers.

VOICE Call a slightly nasal, forceful *chimp*, flight call a high, buzzy *ziiiiii*; song a slow, monotonous, loose trill of chirps.

NESTING Bulky cup of dry plants placed 1–4ft (30–120cm) above water in marsh vegetation; 3–5 eggs; 1–2 broods; May–July.

FEEDING Mostly insects in the breeding season, especially grasshoppers; seeds in winter; occasionally fruit.

WATCH TOWER
This male Swamp Sparrow is perusing his territory from atop a seeding cattail flower.

OCCURRENCE
Breeds in marshes, cedar bogs, damp meadows, and wet hayfields, from Yukon east to Newfoundland and south to Nebraska and the Delmarva Peninsula; winters in marshes in eastern US and south through Mexico; rare but regular on Pacific coast.

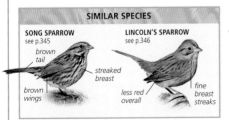

SIMILAR SPECIES

SONG SPARROW
see p.345

brown tail

brown wings

streaked breast

LINCOLN'S SPARROW
see p.346

less red overall

fine breast streaks

| Length **5–6in (12.5–15cm)** | Wingspan **7–7½in (18–19cm)** | Weight **½–⅞oz (15–25g)** |
| Social **Solitary/Small flocks** | Lifespan **Up to 6 years** | Status **Secure** |

DATE: _____ TIME: _____ LOCATION: _____

| Order **Passeriformes** | Family **Passerellidae** | Species *Zonotrichia albicollis* |

White-throated Sparrow

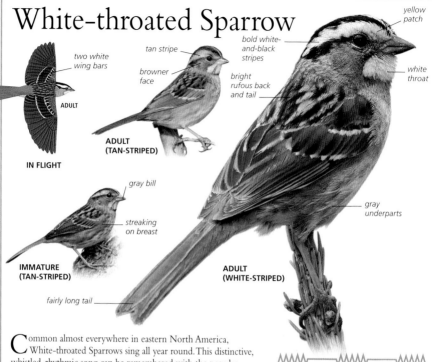

yellow patch

bold white-and-black stripes

tan stripe

two white wing bars

browner face

bright rufous back and tail

white throat

ADULT

IN FLIGHT

ADULT (TAN-STRIPED)

gray bill

streaking on breast

gray underparts

IMMATURE (TAN-STRIPED)

ADULT (WHITE-STRIPED)

fairly long tail

Common almost everywhere in eastern North America, White-throated Sparrows sing all year round. This distinctive, whistled, rhythmic song can be remembered with the popular mnemonics *Oh sweet Canada Canada Canada*, or the less accurate *Old Sam Peabody*. This species has two different color forms, one with a white stripe above its eye, and one with a tan stripe. In the nonbreeding season, large flocks roam the leaf litter of woodlands in search of food. Often the only indication of their presence is the occasional moving leaf or thin, lisping flight call.

VOICE Call loud, sharp *jink*; flight call lisping *tssssst!*; song clear whistle comprising 1–2 higher notes, then three triplets.

NESTING Cup placed on or near ground in dense shrubbery; 2–6 eggs; 1 brood; May–August.

FEEDING Mainly forages on the ground for seeds, fruit, insects, buds, and various grasses.

FLIGHT: low and direct, staying within cover whenever possible.

DIFFERENT COLOR FORMS
The presence of white or tan stripes on White-throated Sparrows is not related to their sex.

OCCURRENCE
Breeds in forests from eastern Yukon to Newfoundland, south into Great Lakes and northern Appalachians. Nonbreeders prefer wooded thickets and hedges. Winters across the eastern US and extreme south of the Southwest. Rare but regular along the Pacific Coast.

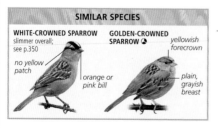

SIMILAR SPECIES

WHITE-CROWNED SPARROW
slimmer overall; see p.350

no yellow patch

orange or pink bill

GOLDEN-CROWNED SPARROW
yellowish forecrown

plain, grayish breast

| Length **6½–7½in (16–17.5cm)** | Wingspan **9–10in (23–26cm)** | Weight **¹¹⁄₁₆–1¼oz (20–35g)** |
| Social **Flocks** | Lifespan **Up to 10 years** | Status **Secure** |

DATE: _____ TIME: _____ LOCATION: _____

Order **Passeriformes**	Family **Passerellidae**	Species *Zonotrichia querula*

Harris's Sparrow

ADULT (NONBREEDING)

IN FLIGHT

indistinct facial markings

two wing bars

ADULT (NONBREEDING)

pinkish bill

gray rump and undertail feathers

pinkish or yellow bill

black crown

gray cheeks

black cheek patch

black chin and throat

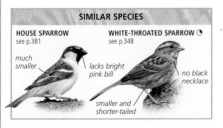

JUVENILE

tan cheek

white chin

concentration of streaks on chest

ADULT (BREEDING)

An unmistakable black-faced, pink-billed bird, Harris's Sparrow is the only breeding bird endemic to Canada. It can be seen in the US during migration or in winter on the Great Plains. This species is occasionally found in large flocks of White-throated and White-crowned Sparrows. Harris's Sparrow is the largest sparrow in the US, approaching the Northern Cardinal in size. Its scientific name, *querula*, comes from the plaintive quality of its whistled song. The first Harris's Sparrow nest was found in 1907 in the Northwest Territories.

VOICE Call a sharp *weeek*; song a melancholy series of 2–4 whistles on the same pitch.

NESTING Bulky cup placed on ground among vegetation or near ground in brush; 3–5 eggs; 1 brood; June–August.

FEEDING Eats seeds, insects, buds, and even young conifer needles in summer.

FLIGHT: low and direct, staying within cover whenever possible.

NORTHERN ACROBAT
This nonbreeding Harris's Sparrow grips two different weeds, one in each foot.

SIMILAR SPECIES

HOUSE SPARROW
see p.381

much smaller

lacks bright pink bill

WHITE-THROATED SPARROW ◑
see p.348

no black necklace

smaller and shorter-tailed

OCCURRENCE
Breeds in scrub-tundra along Canadian taiga–tundra timberline from northern Northwest Territories to north Ontario. Winters in US Great Plains from South Dakota and Iowa south to northern Texas. Nonbreeders found in thickets, hedges. Casual to rare in East and West.

Length 6¾–7½in (17–19cm)	Wingspan 10½–11in (27–28cm)	Weight 1¹⁄₁₆–1⁷⁄₁₆oz (30–40g)
Social **Flocks**	Lifespan **Up to 12 years**	Status **Secure**

| Order **Passeriformes** | Family **Passerellidae** | Species *Zonotrichia leucophrys* |

White-crowned Sparrow

yellowish bill

gray rump and uppertail

ADULT

two wing bars

brown crown

white crown with two black stripes

black line

gray cheek

longish tail

gray breast

IMMATURE

IN FLIGHT

two wing bars

white streaking on brown upperparts

unmarked, grayish underparts

ADULT
Z. l. oriantha
(INTERIOR WEST)

FLIGHT: low and direct, staying within cover whenever possible.

Common in the west, the White-crowned Sparrow has four subspecies. Pacific Coast birds are brown, with a yellowish bill, a gray patch between the eye and bill, and a gray-washed head stripe; western and northwestern birds are gray below, with a gray patch between the eye and bill, an orange bill, and a white head stripe. Eastern and Rocky Mountain birds have a pink bill, a black patch between the eye and bill, and a bright white head stripe; while birds in southwest Canada are darker.
VOICE Call a sharp *tink*; flight call a thin *seep*; song a buzzy whistle followed by buzzes, trills, and whistles.
NESTING Bulky cup of grass placed on or near the ground in bushes; 4–6 eggs; 1–3 broods; March–August.
FEEDING Forages for seeds, insects, fruit, buds, and even grass.

LOOKING RESTED
Perched on a shrub, this sparrow's white eyestreak is highly visible.

SIMILAR SPECIES

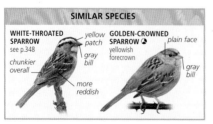

WHITE-THROATED SPARROW see p.348

yellow patch

gray bill

chunkier overall

more reddish

GOLDEN-CROWNED SPARROW ♀

yellowish forecrown

plain face

gray bill

OCCURRENCE
Widespread across the boreal forest and tundra limit, from Alaska eastward to Quebec and Labrador, and southward from British Columbia to coastal California and the interior mountainous west. In the North, breeds in willow thickets, wet forest; in the west, varied habitats include suburbs.

| Length 6½–7in (16–18cm) | Wingspan 9½–10in (24–26cm) | Weight ¹¹⁄₁₆–1¼oz (20–35g) |
| Social **Flocks** | Lifespan **Up to 13 years** | Status **Secure** |

DATE: _____ TIME: _____ LOCATION: _____

Order **Passeriformes**	Family **Passerellidae**	Species *Junco hyemalis*

Dark-eyed Junco

MALE (SLATE-COLORED)

white outer tail feathers

IN FLIGHT

bluish gray hood

dark area between eye and bill

dull, brownish back

pinkish flanks

FEMALE (PINK-SIDED)

gray body with brown wash to back

dark gray head

dark gray head

white belly

MALE (SLATE-COLORED)

reddish brown back

gray rump

black mask

pale gray underparts

MALE (GRAY-HEADED)

rust back

blackish hood

MALE (OREGON)

reddish flanks

The Dark-eyed Junco's appearance at birdfeeders during snowstorms has earned it the colloquial name of "snowbird." They generally prefer to feed on the ground, and can be found hopping about on the forest floor in search of seeds and insects, or on the ground underneath a birdfeeder in backyards across North America. The name "Dark-eyed Junco" is actually used to describe a group of birds that vary geographically in an incredibly diverse way. Sixteen subspecies have been described. "Slate-colored" populations are widespread across Canada and the northeastern US, the "White-winged" nests in the Black Hills, "Pink-sided" birds breed in Idaho, Montana, and Wyoming, and "Oregon" birds breed in the Pacific West, from Alaska to British Columbia and the mountainous western US in the Sierras south to Mexico. "Red-backed" populations reside in the mountains of Arizona and New Mexico, while "Gray-headed" birds range between the "Red-backed" and "Pink-sided" populations. Dark-eyed Juncos can form large flocks in the winter; where ranges overlap, several subspecies may be found foraging together with sparrows and other birds.

VOICE Loud, smacking *tick* and soft *dyew* calls; flight call a rapid, twittering, and buzzy *zzeet*; song a simple, liquid, 1-pitch trill.
NESTING Cup placed on ground hidden under vegetation or next to rocks; 3–5 eggs; 1–2 broods; May–August.
FEEDING Eats insects and seeds; also berries.

FLIGHT: low and direct, staying within cover whenever possible.

PINK-SIDED MALE
Like most juncos, this male is brighter with greater contrasts, darker eye areas, and more vivid colors.

OCCURRENCE
Breeds in coniferous and mixed forests across Canada and the southern US, south in the east Appalachians to Georgia, and in the west, in mountains from Alaska and British Columbia to New Mexico and northern Baja California. Winters from southern Canada to northern Mexico.

Length **6–6¾in (15–17cm)**	Wingspan **8–10in (20–26cm)**	Weight **⅝–1¹⁄₁₆oz (18–30g)**
Social **Flocks**	Lifespan **Up to 11 years**	Status **Secure**

DATE: _____ TIME: _____ LOCATION: _____

| Order **Passeriformes** | Family **Cardinalidae** | Species **Piranga olivacea** |

Scarlet Tanager

black wings

red body

vibrant scarlet head and body

tail appears short in flight

MALE (BREEDING)

IN FLIGHT

black wings

black tail

MALE (BREEDING)

dark brown eyes

yellow patches in red plumage

grayish yellow bill

MALE (MOLTING)

greenish rump and upper tail

overall greenish upperparts

FEMALE

dark gray feet and legs

yellow-green body, head, and rump

MALE (NONBREEDING)

Although the male Scarlet Tanager, in its breeding plumage, is one of the brightest and most easily identified North American birds, its secretive nature and preference for the canopies of well-shaded oak woodlands makes it difficult to spot. The male is most easily located by its distinctive and easily recognizable song. Male Scarlet Tanagers can vary in appearance—some are orange, not scarlet, and others have a faint reddish wing bar.

VOICE Call a hoarse, drawn out *CHIK-breeer*, often shortened to *CHIK*; flight call an upslurred, whistled *pwee*; song a burry, slurred *querit-queer-query-querit-queer*.

NESTING Loosely woven cup of grass, lined with fine material, high up in tree; 3–5 eggs; 1 brood; May–July.

FEEDING Gleans insects, larvae, fruit, buds, and berries.

FLIGHT: strong and direct; rapid wing beats.

STUNNING MALE
Taking a bath away from the treetops, a male Scarlet Tanager can be seen in all its glory.

OCCURRENCE
Breeds in mature deciduous and mixed forests (especially with large oaks) from southern Manitoba and eastern Oklahoma east to the Maritime Provinces and the Carolinas. Trans-Gulf migrant. Winters in varied habitats along the eastern slope of the Andes from eastern Panama to Bolivia.

SIMILAR SPECIES

VERMILION FLYCATCHER ♂

brown wings and tail

SUMMER TANAGER ♀
see p.388

larger bill

olive-yellow upperparts

thinner bill

yellowish underparts

Length **7in (18cm)**	Wingspan **11½in (29cm)**	Weight **¹¹⁄₁₆–1¼oz (20–35g)**
Social **Solitary/Small flocks**	Lifespan **At least 10 years**	Status **Secure**

DATE: _____ TIME: _____ LOCATION: _____

Northern Cardinal

warm red overall

MALE

smaller, duller crest

brownish wings

darker bill

JUVENILE

prominent crest

thick, orange-red bill

bright red back and wings

IN FLIGHT

dark patch not as extensive as male

reddish crest

buff-olive upperparts

red on outer tail feathers

grayish brown underparts

FEMALE

long, red tail

black patch on face, extends onto throat

MALE

brownish toes and legs

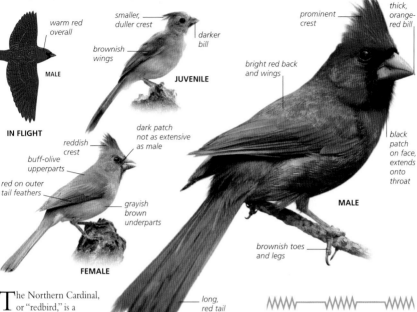

The Northern Cardinal, or "redbird," is a familiar sight across the eastern US and southeastern Canada. Females are less showy, but have a prominent reddish crest and red accents on their tan-colored outer tail and wing feathers. The male aggressively repels intruders and will occasionally attack his reflection in windows and various shiny surfaces.

VOICE Sharp, metallic *tik* call, also bubbly chatters; song a loud, variable, sweet, slurred whistle, *tsee-ew-tsee-ew-whoit-whoit-whoit-whoit-whoit*.

NESTING Loose, flimsy cup of grass, bark, and leaves, in deciduous thicket; 2–4 eggs; 1–3 broods; April–September.

FEEDING Eats seeds and insects, such as beetles and caterpillars; also buds and fruit.

FLIGHT: weak, flapping with downward-angled tail; interrupted by short glides; low within cover.

CONSPICUOUS COLOR
This Northern Cardinal's vivid plumage means that it is often easy to spot on snowy winter days.

SIMILAR SPECIES

SUMMER TANAGER ♂
see p.388

rosy red plumage

no black patch

PYRRHULOXIA ♀

pointed crest

red on outer wing feathers

stubby, yellow bill

OCCURRENCE
Resident in thickets of various relatively moist habitats, such as deciduous woodland, scrub, desert washes, and backyards. Range spans across the eastern US, southernmost Canada, the extreme Southwest, and south into Mexico, northern Guatemala, and northern Belize.

Length **8½in (22cm)**	Wingspan **12in (30cm)**	Weight **1⁷⁄₁₆–1¾oz (40–50g)**
Social **Solitary**	Lifespan **Up to 16 years**	Status **Secure**

DATE: _____ TIME: _____ LOCATION: _____

| Order **Passeriformes** | Family **Cardinalidae** | Species *Pheucticus ludovicianus* |

Rose-breasted Grosbeak

black head and back

bold, white wing patches

rosy or orange breast

white rump

MALE (BREEDING)

IN FLIGHT

IMMATURE MALE (1ST FALL)

short tail with white corners

white marks on head

white wing bars

large, pinkish bill

rose-red breast

thick streaks on underparts

FEMALE

white belly

brown patches on back

streaked underparts

MALE (BREEDING)

MALE (NONBREEDING)

For many birdwatchers in the East, the appearance of a flock of dazzling male Rose-breasted Grosbeaks in early May signals the peak of spring songbird migration. Adult males in their tuxedo attire, with rose-red ties, are unmistakable, but females and immature males are more somber. In the fall, immature male Rose-breasted Grosbeaks often have orange breasts, and are commonly mistaken for female Black-headed Grosbeaks. The difference is in the pink wing lining usually visible on perched birds, pink bill, and streaking across the center of the breast.

FLIGHT: undulating but powerful flight with bursts of wing beats.

VOICE Call a high, sharp, explosive *sink or eeuk*, reminiscent of the squeak of sneakers on floor tiles; flight call an airy *vreee*; song a liquid, flute-like warble, rather slow in delivery, almost relaxed.

NESTING Loose, open cup or platform, usually in deciduous saplings, mid to high level; 2–5 eggs; 1–2 broods; May–July.

FEEDING Eats arthropods, fruit, seeds, and buds.

SIMILAR SPECIES

PURPLE FINCH ♀
see p.373

much smaller

smaller, dark bill

thick, lateral throat stripe

BLACK-HEADED GROSBEAK ♀

tawny breast

pencil-thin streaks on underparts

STUNNING MALE
A striking male Rose-breasted Grosbeak in springtime is quite unmistakable on a tree.

OCCURRENCE
Breeds in deciduous and mixed woods, parks, and orchards across the northeastern quarter of the US, and across Canada westward from Newfoundland through Ontario to southeast Yukon. Winters from Mexico and the Caribbean, south to Guyana and Peru. Rare in the West.

Length **8in (20cm)**	Wingspan **12½in (32cm)**	Weight **1¼–2oz (35–55g)**
Social **Solitary/Small flocks**	Lifespan **Up to 13 years**	Status **Secure**

DATE: _____ TIME: _____ LOCATION: _____

| Order **Passeriformes** | Family **Cardinalidae** | Species **Passerina cyanea** |

Indigo Bunting

blue overall; often appears black in flight

MALE (BREEDING)

IN FLIGHT

intermediate between male and female plumage

bright, cyan-blue body

IMMATURE MALE (1ST SPRING)

darker head

indigo face

MALE (BREEDING)

dull brown overall

small bill

whitish throat

blurry streaks on breast

bluish cast to wings and tail

FEMALE

Few North American birds are more brilliantly colored than the Indigo Bunting. However, it is not particularly well named, because the bird is really not indigo but rather a vibrant, almost cyan-blue. The color only turns to indigo on the male's head before finally becoming a rich violet on the face. Indigo Buntings are specialists of disturbed habitats, originally depending on tree-falls within forests and the grassland-forest edge. Human activity, however, has radically increased suitable breeding habitats. As a result, Indigo Buntings are much more common and widespread than they were a hundred years ago. This adaptable species has even learned to nest in cornfields.

VOICE Call a sharp, dry, rattling *pik!*; flight a call long buzz; song series of simple, high-pitched, paired whistles, often described as "*fire!-fire!*, *where?-where?*, *there!-there!*, *put-it-out!*, *put-it-out!*"

NESTING Open cup above ground in dense tangle or shrub; 3–4 eggs; 1–3 broods; May–September.

FEEDING Eats seeds, insects, fruit, and buds.

FLIGHT: slightly undulating, fast, and direct; gliding and fluttering in territorial encounters.

SIMILAR SPECIES

BLUE GROSBEAK ♂
see p.388

deep indigo-violet overall

much larger bill

rich reddish rust shoulder

VARIED BUNTING ♀

unstreaked underparts

SOUND OF SUMMER
This is one of the most common and cheerful songbirds found in eastern North America.

OCCURRENCE
Breeds in moist disturbed habitats—weedy fields, forest edges, and areas of heavy cultivation across the eastern US, southeastern Canada, and also locally in the Southwest. Winters from Mexico and the Caribbean south to Panama, and in small numbers along the Gulf Coast and in Florida.

| Length **5½in (14cm)** | Wingspan **8in (20cm)** | Weight **⁷⁄₁₆–¹¹⁄₁₆oz (12–19g)** |
| Social **Large flocks** | Lifespan **Up to 11 years** | Status **Secure** |

Order **Passeriformes**	Family **Cardinalidae**	Species **Spiza americana**

Dickcissel

yellow eyebrow

large, pointed bill

yellow-tinged, long eye-line

gray nape

bold braces on back

streaked back

rufous shoulder

black "V" on yellow breast

MALE (BREEDING)

IN FLIGHT

FEMALE

finely streaked underparts

paler gray on face

MALE (BREEDING)

no rufous shoulder

MALE (NONBREEDING)

The Dickcissel is a tallgrass prairie specialist and seldom breeds outside this core range. Known for its dramatic seasonal movements, the Dickcissel winters in Venezuela, with flocks in tens of thousands ravaging rice fields and damaging seed crops, making it a notorious pest. Immature birds, without yellow and rusty plumage, are very similar to female House Sparrows—vagrant and wintering Dickcissels in North America are often mistaken for sparrows.
VOICE Call a flat *chik*; flight call a distinctive, low, electric buzz *frrrrrrt*; song a short series of sharp, insect-like stutters followed by few longer chirps or trill *dick-dick-dick-SISS-SISS-suhl*.
NESTING Bulky cup placed near ground in dense vegetation; 3–6 eggs; 1–2 broods; May–August.
FEEDING Forages on ground for insects, spiders, and seeds.

FLIGHT: strong, direct, and slightly undulating; flocks in tight balls.

UNIQUE SONG
The Dickcissel's onomatopoetic song is the classic sound of a healthy tallgrass prairie.

SIMILAR SPECIES

HOUSE SPARROW ♀
see p.381

shorter bill

EASTERN MEADOWLARK
see p.360

longer bill

shorter tail

no streaking on underparts

bright yellow underparts

OCCURRENCE
Breeds in tallgrass prairie, grassland, hayfields, unmown roadsides, and untilled cropfields across eastern central US. Barely reaches southernmost Canada and northeast Mexico. Winters in huge flocks in Venezuela, in open areas with tall grass-like vegetation, including rice fields.

Length 6½in (16cm)	Wingspan 9½in (24cm)	Weight ⅞–1¼oz (25–35g)
Social **Large flocks**	Lifespan **Up to 5 years**	Status **Secure**

DATE: _____ TIME: _____ LOCATION: _____

ORIOLES AND BLACKBIRDS

T HE ICTERIDS exemplify the wonderful diversity that exists among birds. Its members are common and widespread, occurring from coast to coast in nearly every habitat in North America. The species reveal extremes of color, nesting, and social behavior—from the vibrant, solitary orioles to the vast nesting colonies of comparatively drab blackbirds.

ORIOLES

Generally recognized by their contrasting black and orange plumage, although some species tend more toward yellow or chestnut shades, orioles are common tropical to subtropical seasonal migrants to North America. Their intricate hanging nests are an impressive combination of engineering and weaving. Most species boast a melodious song and tolerance for humans, a combination that makes them popular throughout their range.

COWBIRDS

These strictly parasitic birds have been known to lay eggs in the nests of close to 300 different species in North and South America. The species found in Canada is readily identified by its thick bill and dark, iridescent body contrasting with a brown head.

BLACKBIRDS

As their name suggests, this group of birds is largely covered in dark feathers, and their long, pointed bills and tails add to their streamlined appearance. Not as brilliantly colored as some other Icterids, these are among the most numerous birds on the continent after the breeding season, and form an impressive sight during migration.

SUBTLE BRILLIANCE
Although its plumage is dark, the Common Grackle displays a beautiful iridescence.

MEADOWLARKS

There are just two species in this group, the Eastern and Western Meadowlark, but they are nevertheless distinctive (although difficult to tell apart). Birds of open country, both species have a characteristic bright-yellow chest with a black bib but differing sweet songs.

BIG VOICE
A Meadowlark's melodious voice is a defining feature in many rural landscapes.

NECTAR LOVER
The magnificently colored Baltimore Oriole inserts its bill into the base of a flower, taking the nectar, but playing no part in pollination.

Order **Passeriformes**	Family **Icteridae**	Species *Xanthocephalus xanthocephalus*

Yellow-headed Blackbird

bright yellow head and chest

MALE — yellow head

black, conical bill

black mask and crown on yellow head

JUVENILE MALE

conspicuous white wing patches

IN FLIGHT

brownish overall

yellowish throat and facial patch

black overall

FEMALE

white wing patch

MALE

long tail

FLIGHT: direct with shallow rise and fall pattern; flaps and glides.

The male Yellow-headed Blackbird is unmistakable, with its conspicuous bright yellow head contrasting with a dark body. Females, however, are more drab. Populations of this species fluctuate widely but locally according to available rainfall, which controls the availability and quality of its breeding marshland habitat. In some wetlands, the Yellow-headed Blackbird can be extremely abundant, and is easily noticeable due to its amazing song.

VOICE Call a nasal *whaah*; song a series of harsh, cackling noises, followed by a brief pause, and a high, long, wailing trill.

NESTING Cup of plant strips woven into standing aquatic vegetation; 3–4 eggs; 1 brood; May–June.

FEEDING Eats insects while breeding; agricultural grains and grass seeds in winter.

YELLOW GARLAND
Five evenly spaced yellow-headed males watch over their wetland habitat from a twig.

SIMILAR SPECIES

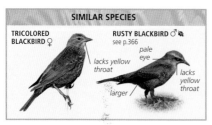

TRICOLORED BLACKBIRD ♀

lacks yellow throat

larger

RUSTY BLACKBIRD ♂ 🐦
see p.366

pale eye

lacks yellow throat

OCCURRENCE
Widely distributed in western Canada and the central and western US, this species breeds in marshes with cattail and bullrush vegetation, and also, locally, in wetlands within wooded areas. Winters in Mexico; resident in Baja California.

Length **8½–10½in (21–27cm)**	Wingspan **15in (38cm)**	Weight **2⅛–3½oz (60–100g)**
Social **Flocks/Colonies**	Lifespan **Up to 9 years**	Status **Localized**

DATE: _____ TIME: _____ LOCATION: _____

| Order **Passeriformes** | Family **Icteridae** | Species ***Dolichonyx oryzivorus*** |

Bobolink

black wings

buff-colored hindneck

MALE (BREEDING)

IN FLIGHT

blackish brown crown

gold-buff overall

pinkish bill

central crown stripe **FEMALE (BREEDING)**

sparrow-like markings

pointed tail feathers

ADULT (FALL)

buffy throat

white rump

black face and crown

white shoulder feathers

black underparts

MALE (BREEDING)

black tail with pointed feathers

FLIGHT: typically direct flight; series of rapid wing beats; glides of varying length.

The Bobolink is a common summer resident of open fallow fields through much of the northern US and southern Canada. In spring, the males perform a conspicuous circling or "helicoptering" display, which includes singing, to establish a territory and to attract females. Bobolink populations have declined on their breeding grounds and in wintering areas because of habitat loss and changing agricultural practices.

VOICE Calls like the end of its name *link*; song a long, complex babbling series of musical notes varying in length and pitch.

NESTING Woven cup of grass close to or on the ground, well hidden in tall grass; 3–7 eggs; 1 brood; May–July.

FEEDING Feeds mostly on insects, spiders, grubs in breeding season, but seasonally variable; also cereal grains and grass seeds.

TAKING A BREAK
This male has fled the sun of the open fields to seek shelter in the shade of a tree.

OCCURRENCE
Breeds in open fields with a mixture of tall grasses and other herbaceous vegetation, especially old hayfields. In Canada from British Columbia to the East Coast; in the US from Idaho to New England. Migrates through the southern US and the Caribbean; winters in northern South America.

SIMILAR SPECIES

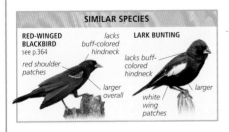

RED-WINGED BLACKBIRD see p.364

red shoulder patches

lacks buff-colored hindneck

LARK BUNTING

lacks buff-colored hindneck

larger overall

larger

white wing patches

| Length **6–8in (15–20cm)** | Wingspan **10–12in (25–30cm)** | Weight **1¹⁄₁₆–2oz (30–55g)** |
| Social **Winter flocks** | Lifespan **Up to 10 years** | Status **Declining** |

DATE: _____ TIME: _____ LOCATION: _____

| Order **Passeriformes** | Family **Icteridae** | Species **Sturnella magna** |

Eastern Meadowlark

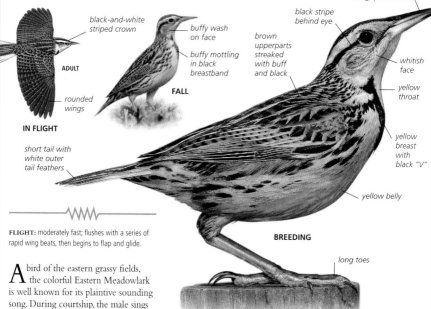

long, pointed bill

black-and-white striped crown

buffy wash on face

buffy mottling in black breastband

ADULT

black stripe behind eye

brown upperparts streaked with buff and black

FALL

whitish face

yellow throat

rounded wings

IN FLIGHT

short tail with white outer tail feathers

yellow breast with black "V"

yellow belly

BREEDING

yellow belly

long toes

FLIGHT: moderately fast; flushes with a series of rapid wing beats, then begins to flap and glide.

A bird of the eastern grassy fields, the colorful Eastern Meadowlark is well known for its plaintive sounding song. During courtship, the male sings enthusiastically from the highest available perch. This species overlaps with the very similar looking Western Meadowlark in the western Great Plains, but is the only meadowlark further east. Where they overlap, these birds are most easily distinguished by their different calls and songs. Throughout its range, numbers of the Eastern Meadowlark have fallen due to human encroachment on its habitat, although in the last decade or so, the species has made a slow (and local) comeback. **VOICE** Call a sharp *dzzeer*; song a series of clear, descending whistles consisting of 3–8 notes, *tseeeoou tseeeeou*; higher pitched than the rattle of the Western Meadowlark.

NESTING Loosely woven, usually domed, cup of grasses and other plants, located on the ground in tall grass fields; 3–8 eggs; 1 brood; March–May.

FEEDING Forages on ground, mainly for insects, especially grasshoppers, but also caterpillars and grubs; seeds and grain in winter.

FAVORITE PERCH
Eastern Meadowlarks are partial to fenceposts as a favorite perch for singing.

OCCURRENCE
Breeds in native tallgrass openings, pastures, and overgrown roadsides. Widespread in eastern North America, from Quebec to New Mexico and Arizona; also in Mexico and Cuba, and locally in South America. Partial migrant in the US, resident in Mexico and South America.

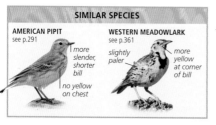

SIMILAR SPECIES

AMERICAN PIPIT
see p.291

more slender, shorter bill

no yellow on chest

WESTERN MEADOWLARK
see p.361

slightly paler

more yellow at corner of bill

| Length **7–10in (18–25cm)** | Wingspan **13–15in (33–38cm)** | Weight **2⅛–4oz (60–125g)** |
| Social **Pairs/Winter flocks** | Lifespan **Up to 9 years** | Status **Declining** |

DATE: _____ TIME: _____ LOCATION: _____

Western Meadowlark

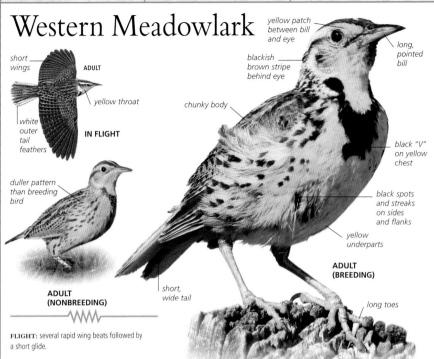

yellow patch between bill and eye

long, pointed bill

blackish brown stripe behind eye

ADULT

short wings

yellow throat

IN FLIGHT

white outer tail feathers

chunky body

black "V" on yellow chest

black spots and streaks on sides and flanks

yellow underparts

duller pattern than breeding bird

ADULT (NONBREEDING)

short, wide tail

ADULT (BREEDING)

long toes

FLIGHT: several rapid wing beats followed by a short glide.

Although the range of the Western Meadowlark overlaps widely with that of its Eastern counterpart, hybrids between the two species are very rare and usually sterile. The larger numbers of this species in the western Great Plains into the Canadian prairies, combined with the male's tendency to sing conspicuously from the tops of shrubs, when fence posts are not available, make this species attractive to birdwatchers. Where the two meadowlarks overlap they are best identified by their song.

VOICE Series of complex, bubbling, whistled notes; lower frequency with no ascending whistles as heard in the Eastern Meadowlark.

NESTING Domed grass cup, well hidden in tall grasses; 3–7 eggs; 1 brood; March–August.

FEEDING Feeds mostly on insects, including beetles, grubs, and grasshoppers; also grains and grass seeds.

A SHRUB WILL DO
With few fenceposts in the Western Meadowlark's habitat, it perches on a shrub to sing.

OCCURRENCE
Common in western North America, across much of southern Canada and the western US, south to Mexico. Breeds primarily in open grassy plains, but also uses agricultural fields with overgrown edges and hayfields. Partial migrant in US, winters south to Mexico.

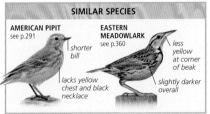

SIMILAR SPECIES

AMERICAN PIPIT
see p.291

shorter bill

lacks yellow chest and black necklace

EASTERN MEADOWLARK
see p.360

less yellow at corner of beak

slightly darker overall

| Length **7–10in (18–26cm)** | Wingspan **13–15in (33–38cm)** | Weight **2⅞–4oz (80–125g)** |
| Social **Pairs/Winter flocks** | Lifespan **Up to 10 years** | Status **Secure** |

Order **Passeriformes**	Family **Icteridae**	Species *Icterus spurius*

Orchard Oriole

slightly curved, blue-gray, black-tipped bill

olive upperparts, very similar to female

black back

MALE

IN FLIGHT

deep orange shoulders

black face, chin, and throat

IMMATURE MALE (1ST SPRING)

olive upperparts

dark, rusty orange belly

dark, rusty orange rump

white-edged flight feathers

MALE

two white wing bars

yellowish underparts

FEMALE

black tail

A small bird, the Orchard Oriole resembles a large warbler in size, color, and the way it flits among leaves while foraging for insects. It flutters its tail, unlike other orioles. It spends less time on the breeding grounds than other migrant orioles, often arriving there as late as mid-May and leaving as early as late-July. The Orchard Oriole tolerates humans and can be found breeding in suburban parks and gardens. In recent years, its numbers have increased in the eastern part of its range.

VOICE Fast, not very melodious, series of high warbling notes mixed with occasional shorter notes ending in slurred *shheere*.
NESTING Woven nest of grass suspended in fork between branches; 4–5 eggs; 1 brood; April–July.
FEEDING Mainly eats insects during breeding season, but will also feed on seeds, fruit, and occasionally, nectar; in winter, mostly fruit and nectar, and some insects.

FLIGHT: quite bouncy flight due to shallow, quick wing beats; interrupted by glides.

RUSTY ORANGE SPLASH
The male Orchard Oriole has distinctive black upperparts and dark, rusty orange underparts.

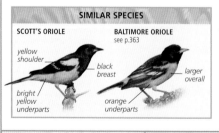

SIMILAR SPECIES		
SCOTT'S ORIOLE	**BALTIMORE ORIOLE** see p.363	
yellow shoulder	black breast	larger overall
bright yellow underparts	orange underparts	

OCCURRENCE
Breeds in the eastern US and south-central Canada, in open forest and woodland edges with a mixture of evergreen and deciduous trees, especially along river bottoms and in shelter belts surrounding agricultural land. Winters in Mexico, Central America, and South America.

Length **7–8in (18–20cm)**	Wingspan **9in (23cm)**	Weight **11/16oz (20g)**
Social **Pairs**	Lifespan **Up to 9 years**	Status **Secure**

DATE: _____ TIME:_____ LOCATION:_____

| Order **Passeriformes** | Family **Icteridae** | Species *Icterus galbula* |

Baltimore Oriole

black and orange tail

white-edged black wings

orange-yellow shoulder patch

MALE

IN FLIGHT

orange-yellow head

MALE (1ST FALL)

black head

black back

straight blue-gray bill

black upper breast

orange underparts

MALE

orange rump

black tail with orange outer tail feathers

yellow-olive rump

olive upperparts

pale orange underparts

two wing bars

FEMALE

The Baltimore Oriole's brilliant colors are familiar to many in eastern North America because this bird is so tolerant of humans. This species originally favored the American Elm for nesting, but Dutch Elm disease decimated these trees. The oriole has since adapted to using sycamores, cottonwoods, and other tall trees as nesting sites. Its ability to use suburban gardens and parks has helped expand its range to incorporate areas densely occupied by humans.

VOICE Loud, clear, melodious song comprising several short notes in series, often of varying lengths.

NESTING Round-bottomed basket usually woven of grass, hung toward the end of branches; 4–5 eggs; 1 brood; May–July.

FEEDING Hops or flits among leaves and branches picking insects and spiders; fond of caterpillars; also eats fruit and sips nectar.

FLIGHT: strong with rapid wing beats; full downstrokes during flight provide great power.

PERFECT FOR FORAGING
The Baltimore Oriole forages alone in dense foliage of trees and bushes or on the ground.

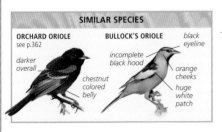

SIMILAR SPECIES

ORCHARD ORIOLE see p.362

darker overall

chestnut colored belly

BULLOCK'S ORIOLE

incomplete black hood

black eyeline

orange cheeks

huge white patch

OCCURRENCE
Forest edges and tall, open mixed hardwoods, especially close to rivers; regularly uses forested parks, suburban and urban areas with abundant tall trees. Small numbers winter in southeastern US and Florida, but most birds move to Mexico, Colombia, and Venezuela.

| Length **8–10in (20–26cm)** | Wingspan **10–12in (26–30cm)** | Weight **1¹/₁₆–1¹/₄oz (30–35g)** |
| Social **Solitary/Pairs** | Lifespan **Up to 11 years** | Status **Secure** |

DATE: _____ TIME: _____ LOCATION: _____

| Order **Passeriformes** | Family **Icteridae** | Species *Agelaius phoeniceus* |

Red-winged Blackbird

MALE

red and yellow "flags"

dark, grayish brown body

no clear yellow edging on red shoulder patches

dull reddish or yellowish shoulder patches

buff to brown edging on feathers

pale throat

JUVENILE (BICOLORED)

black outer wings

IMMATURE

IN FLIGHT

light brown eyebrow

black eye

MALE (BICOLORED)

all-black back and tail

pointed bill

off-white underparts with dark streaks

bright red shoulder patches with yellow edge

FEMALE

MALE

FLIGHT: swift wing beats interrupted by brief bobbing, flapping, and gliding sequences.

One of the most abundant native bird species in North America, the Red-winged Blackbird is also one of the most conspicuous in wetland habitats. The sight and sound of males singing from the tops of cattails is a sure sign that spring is near. This adaptable species migrates and roosts in flocks that may number in the millions. There are numerous subspecies, one of the most distinctive being the "Bicolored" Blackbird (*A. p. gubernator*.)

VOICE Various brusk *chek*, *chit*, or *chet* calls; male song a *kronk-a-rhee* with a characteristic nasal, rolling and metallic "undulating" ending.

NESTING Cup of grasses and mud woven into dense standing reeds or cattails; 3–4 eggs; 1–2 broods; March–June.

FEEDING Forages for seeds and grains; largely insects when breeding.

DENSE FLOCKS
The huge flocks of Red-winged Blackbirds seen in migration are quite an amazing sight.

SIMILAR SPECIES

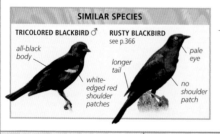

TRICOLORED BLACKBIRD ♂

all-black body

white-edged red shoulder patches

RUSTY BLACKBIRD
see p.366

longer tail

pale eye

no shoulder patch

OCCURRENCE
Widespread across Canada and the US from Alaska to the Maritimes, and south to Mexico, Central America, and the Bahamas. Lives in wetlands, especially freshwater marshes but also saltwater; wet meadows with tall grass cover and open woodlands with reedy vegetation.

Length **7–10in (18–25cm)**	Wingspan **11–14in (28–35cm)**	Weight **1⁹⁄₁₆–2¹⁄₂oz (45–70g)**
Social **Flocks**	Lifespan **At least 14 years**	Status **Secure**

DATE: _____ TIME:_____ LOCATION:_____

Order **Passeriformes**	Family **Icteridae**	Species *Molothrus ater*

Brown-headed Cowbird

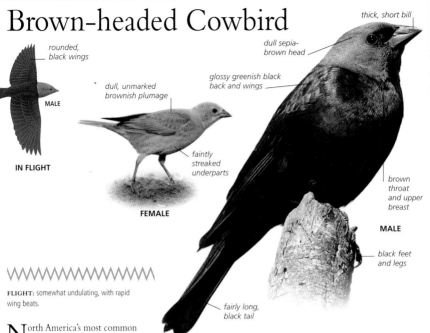

thick, short bill

rounded, black wings

dull sepia-brown head

glossy greenish black back and wings

dull, unmarked brownish plumage

MALE

IN FLIGHT

faintly streaked underparts

brown throat and upper breast

FEMALE

MALE

black feet and legs

FLIGHT: somewhat undulating, with rapid wing beats.

fairly long, black tail

Nnorth America's most common and best-known brood parasite, the Brown-headed Cowbird was once a bird of the Great Plains, following vast herds of bison to prey on insects kicked up by their hooves. Now, due to forest clearance and suburban development, it is found continent-wide. It has recently become a serious threat to North American songbirds, laying its eggs in the nests of more than 220 different species, and having its young raised to fledglings by more than 140 species, including the highly endangered Kirtland's Warbler.

VOICE High-pitched, squeaky whistles and bubbling notes, *dub-dub-come-tzeee*; also various clucks and *cheks*.

NESTING No nest, lays eggs in nests of other species; a single female may lay 25–55 (or more) eggs per season; April–August.

FEEDING Primarily eats grass seeds and cereal grains, but also insects when available, especially grasshoppers and beetles.

AT A FEEDER
A female Brown-headed Cowbird enjoys a snack of seeds at a suburban feeder.

SIMILAR SPECIES

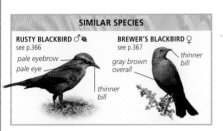

RUSTY BLACKBIRD ♂ 🦅
see p.366

pale eyebrow
pale eye

thinner bill

BREWER'S BLACKBIRD ♀
see p.367

gray brown overall

thinner bill

OCCURRENCE
Favors habitats modified by human activity, such as open wooded patches, low grass fields, fruit orchards, agricultural pastures with livestock, and gardens and residential areas. Widespread across North America.

Length **6–8in (15–20cm)**	Wingspan **11–13in (28–33cm)**	Weight **1⁷⁄₁₆–1³⁄₄oz (40–50g)**
Social **Large flocks**	Lifespan **Up to 16 years**	Status **Secure**

DATE: _____ TIME: _____ LOCATION: _____

| Order **Passeriformes** | Family **Icteridae** | Species **Euphagus carolinus** |

Rusty Blackbird

green sheen on head

pale whitish or yellow eye

MALE (BREEDING)

long tail

MALE (BREEDING)

short, narrow bill

gray-brown eyebrow

pale gray to rusty brown underparts

FEMALE (FALL)

IN FLIGHT

rusty brown crown

pale eyebrow

rusty brown edging to feathers

black overall, with blue-green to greenish sheen

black "mask" between eye and bill

MALE (FALL)

FLIGHT: strong, direct, with slight undulations between flapping and brief gliding.

The Rusty Blackbird is perhaps the least studied of all North American blackbirds. This is mainly because it breeds in remote, inaccessible swampy areas, and is much less of a pest to agricultural operations than some of the other members of its family. Unlike most other blackbirds, the plumage on the male Rusty Blackbird changes to a dull, reddish brown during the fall—giving the species its common name. It is also during the fall migrations that this species is most easily observed, moving south in long, wide flocks that often take several minutes to pass overhead.

VOICE Both sexes use *chuk* call during migration flights; male song a musical *too-ta-lee.*

NESTING Small bowl of branches and sticks, lined with wet plants and dry grass, usually near water; 3–5 eggs; 1 brood; May–July.

FEEDING Eats seasonally available insects, spiders, grains, seeds of trees, and fleshy fruit or berries.

OPEN WIDE
Seldom seen, the male's courtship display includes gaping and tail-spreading.

OCCURRENCE
Breeds in moist to wet forests up to the timberline in the far north (farther north than any other species of North American blackbird); winters in eastern US, in various swampy forests.

SIMILAR SPECIES

BREWER'S BLACKBIRD see p.367
purplish sheen on head

longer tail

COMMON GRACKLE see p.368
bill thicker at base

large tail

bluish sheen on head

glossy bronze body

| Length **8–10in (20–25cm)** | Wingspan **12–15in (30–38cm)** | Weight **1⁹⁄₁₆–2⁷⁄₈oz (45–80g)** |
| Social **Pairs/Winter flocks** | Lifespan **At least 9 years** | Status **Declining** |

DATE: _____ TIME: _____ LOCATION: _____

| Order **Passeriformes** | Family **Icteridae** | Species *Euphagus cyanocephalus* |

Brewer's Blackbird

stout bill

MALE

long, dark tail

IN FLIGHT

brown eyes

gray brown overall

FEMALE

purplish sheen on head

yellow eyes

black body with greenish blue sheen

MALE

black legs and feet

FLIGHT: several wing beats followed by short glides with shallow rise and fall pattern.

The Brewer's Blackbird, unlike the swamp-loving Rusty Blackbird, seems to prefer areas disturbed by humans to natural ones throughout much of its range. It is likely that the relatively recent eastward range expansion of Brewer's Blackbird has been aided by changes in land practices. Interestingly, when its range overlaps with that of the Common Grackle, it wins out in rural areas, but loses out in urban areas. This species can be found feasting on waste grains left behind after the harvest or even in supermarket parking lots.

VOICE Buzzy *tshrrep* song ascending in tone.

NESTING Bulky cup of dry grass, stem and twig framework lined with soft grasses and animal hair; 3–6 eggs; 1–2 broods; April–July.

FEEDING Forages on the ground for many species of insects during breeding season, also snails; seeds, grain, and occasional fruit in fall and winter.

BROWN-EYED BIRD
Brown eyes distinguish the female Brewer's from the yellow-eyed, female Rusty Blackbird.

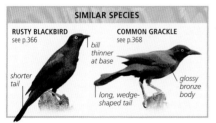

SIMILAR SPECIES

RUSTY BLACKBIRD
see p.366

shorter tail

COMMON GRACKLE
see p.368

bill thinner at base

long, wedge-shaped tail

glossy bronze body

OCCURRENCE
Breeds and winters in open areas, readily adapting to, and preferring, disturbed areas and human developments such as parks, gardens, supermarket parking lots, clear-felled forests, and fallow fields edged with dense trees or shrubs.

| Length **10–12in (25–30cm)** | Wingspan **13–16in (33–41cm)** | Weight **1³/₄–2¹/₂oz (50–70g)** |
| Social **Flocks/Colonies** | Lifespan **Up to 13 years** | Status **Secure** |

DATE: _____ TIME: _____ LOCATION: _____

| Order **Passeriformes** | Family **Icteridae** | Species ***Quiscalus quiscula*** |

Common Grackle

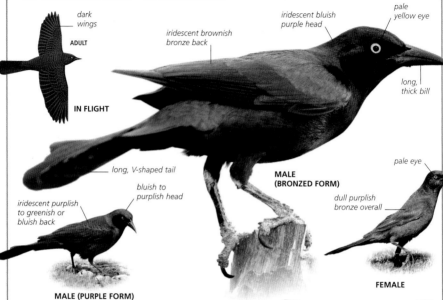

ADULT

dark wings

IN FLIGHT

iridescent brownish bronze back

iridescent bluish purple head

pale yellow eye

long, thick bill

long, V-shaped tail

bluish to purplish head

MALE (BRONZED FORM)

pale eye

dull purplish bronze overall

iridescent purplish to greenish or bluish back

MALE (PURPLE FORM)

FEMALE

This adaptable species has expanded its range rapidly in the recent past, thanks to human land clearing practices. The Common Grackle is so well suited to urban and suburban habitats that it successfully excludes other species from them; it is often a nuisance at bird feeders. During migration and winter, Common Grackles form immense flocks, sometimes numbering over 1 million individuals. This tendency, combined with its preference for cultivated areas, has made this species an agricultural pest in some regions.

VOICE Call a low, harsh *chek*; loud song series of odd squeaks and whistles.
NESTING Small bowl in trees, with a frame of sticks filled with mud and grasses; 4–6 eggs; 1–2 broods; April–July.
FEEDING Eats beetles, flies, spiders, and worms, as well as small vertebrates; also seeds and grain, especially in nonbreeding season; an omnivore.

FLIGHT: straight, level, and direct without the up and down undulation of blackbird species.

OCCURRENCE
The Common Grackle lives in a wide variety of open woodlands, suburban woodlots, city parks, gardens, and hedgerows. It is absent west of the Great Plains. Wintering range extends south to the Gulf Coast.

SIMILAR SPECIES

GREAT-TAILED GRACKLE
larger

BOAT-TAILED GRACKLE

purplish gloss to feathers

very long, deeply wedged tail

longer tail

bluish gloss on black feathers

HIGHLY ADAPTABLE
This grackle is comfortable near human developments, resulting in the expansion of its range.

| Length **11–13¹⁄₂in (28–34cm)** | Wingspan **15–18in (38–46cm)** | Weight **3¹⁄₈–4oz (90–125g)** |
| Social **Flocks** | Lifespan **Up to 20 years** | Status **Secure** |

DATE: _____ TIME: _____ LOCATION: _____

Family **Fringillidae**

FINCHES

T HE NAME "FINCHES" applies to the Fringillidae, a family of seed-eating songbirds that includes sixteen species in North America. They vary in size and shape from the small and fragile-looking redpolls to the robust and chunky Evening Grosbeak. Finch colors range from whitish with some pink (redpolls) to bright red (crossbills), and yellow, white, and black (Evening Grosbeak and American Goldfinch). However, irrespective of body shape, size, and color, all have conical bills with razor-sharp edges. Finches do not crush seeds. Instead, they cut open the hard hull, then seize the seed inside with their tongue and swallow it. The bills of conifer-loving crossbills are crossed at the tip, a unique arrangement that permits them to open tough-hulled pine cones. Roughly 50 percent of crossbills are "left-billed" and 50 percent "right-billed"— lefties are right-footed, and vice versa. Most finches are social. Although they breed in pairs, post-nesting finches form flocks, some of which are huge. Most finch populations fluctuate in size, synchronized with seed production and abundance. All finches are vocal, calling constantly while flying, and singing in the spring. Calls are usually sharp, somewhat metallic sounds, although the American Goldfinch's tinkling calls are sweeter. Songs can be quite musical, clear-sounding melodies, like that of the Purple Finch. Finches make open cup-shaped nests of grasses and lichens, in trees or shrubs, and are remarkably adept at hiding them.

NOT REALLY PURPLE
The inaccurately named Purple Finch actually has a lovely raspberry-red coloration.

CROSSBILL
Perched on a pine tree branch, a female Red Crossbill grinds a seed in her bill to break open the hull and reach the fat-rich kernel inside.

GARDEN GLOW
Even pink flower buds cannot compete with the yellow of a male American Goldfinch.

| Order **Passeriformes** | Family **Fringillidae** | Species **Coccothraustes vespertinus** |

Evening Grosbeak

black wing tips

very dark gray head and shoulders

conspicuous yellow eyebrow

yellow rump

MALE

large white wing patches

huge, yellowish bill

large white wing patch

MALE

IN FLIGHT

black outer wing feathers

large, grayish bill

mustard yellow underparts

grayish wing patch

short, square tail

FEMALE

There is no mistaking a noisy, boisterous winter flock of husky gold-and-black Evening Grosbeaks when they descend on a bird feeder. The bird's outsize yellow bill seems to be made as much for threatening would-be rivals as it is designed for efficiently cracking sunflower seeds. In the breeding season, by contrast, the Evening Grosbeak is secretive and seldom seen, neither singing loudly nor displaying ostentatiously and nesting high in a tree. Once a bird of western North America, it has extended its range eastward in the past 200 years, and now nests as far east as Newfoundland. This may be due to the planting of ornamental box elder, which carries its abundant seeds winter-long, ensuring a ready food supply for the bird.

VOICE Call descending *feeew*; also buzzy notes and beeping chatter.

NESTING Loose, grass-lined twig cup, usually on conifer branch; 3–4 eggs; 1–2 broods; May–July.

FEEDING Eats seeds of pines and other conifers, maple, and box elder seeds; also insects, and their larvae, particularly spruce budworm.

FLIGHT: undulating, with dips between bouts of wing beats, may hover briefly.

OCCURRENCE
Breeds in mixed conifer and spruce forest from Rocky Mountain region to eastern Canada, and on mountain ranges south to Mexico. Winters in coniferous or deciduous woodlands, often in suburban locations; may move south from northern range, depending on food supply.

CAPABLE BILL
This bird's extremely robust bill can deal with all kinds of winter fruits and seeds.

SIMILAR SPECIES

PINE GROSBEAK ♀ *stubby bill* see p.371 — *wing bars* — *gray underparts*

BALTIMORE ORIOLE ♀ see p.363 — *mottled head* — *slender aspect* — *pale orange underparts*

| Length **6½–7in (16–18cm)** | Wingspan **12–14in (30–36cm)** | Weight **2–2½oz (55–70g)** |
| Social **Flocks** | Lifespan **Up to 15 years** | Status **Secure** |

DATE: _____ TIME: _____ LOCATION: _____

| Order **Passeriformes** | Family **Fringillida** | Species **Pinicola enucleator** |

Pine Grosbeak

greenish head

two white
wing bars

greenish
rump

MALE

pale patch
under eye

FEMALE

gray belly

stubby, curved,
blackish bill

pinkish-red head

short neck

IN FLIGHT

pinkish
rump

**IMMATURE
MALE**

long,
blackish
tail

pinkish-red head

MALE

pinkish
red
underparts
(but
regionally
variable)

FLIGHT: undulating, buoyant, calm wing beats
interrupted by glides.

The largest member of the family Fringillidae in North America, and easily distinguished by the male's unmistakable thick, stubby bill, the Pine Grosbeak is a resident of high elevations in the Rocky Mountains in the West. The bird is also found across northern Eurasia, where nine subspecies have been identified, four of which are found in North America. Due to extensive color variation of individual plumages, the age and sex of the bird are not always easily determined.

VOICE Contact calls of eastern birds *tee-tew*, or *tee-tee-tew*; western forms give more complex *tweedle*; warbling song.
NESTING Well-hidden, open cup nest usually in spruce or larch trees; 2–5 eggs, 1 brood; June–July.
FEEDING Eats spruce buds, maple seeds, and mountain ash berries throughout the year; consumes insects in summer.

FRUIT LOVER
This species can often be seen hanging from branches, gorging on ripe fruit.

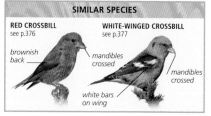

SIMILAR SPECIES

RED CROSSBILL
see p.376

brownish
back

WHITE-WINGED CROSSBILL
see p.377

mandibles
crossed

mandibles
crossed

white bars
on wing

OCCURRENCE
Found in the boreal zone from Alaska to Quebec and Newfoundland, in open, northerly coniferous forests of North America in summer, usually near fresh water. Winters throughout its breeding range, but may move southward to southern Canada and the northeastern US.

| Length **8–10in (20–25cm)** | Wingspan **13in (33cm)** | Weight **2–2¹/₂oz (55–70g)** |
| Social **Flocks** | Lifespan **Up to 10 years** | Status **Secure** |

DATE: _____ TIME: _____ LOCATION: _____

FINCHES

| Order **Passeriformes** | Family **Fringillidae** | Species *Haemorhous mexicanus* |

House Finch

brown cap

grayish
streaks
all over

red face

brown
upperparts

usually
strawberry-
red bib and
head

**MALE
(BREEDING)**

FEMALE

pinkish
head

IN FLIGHT

pale brown
streaking

streaked belly

**MALE
(NON-
BREEDING)**

brown
streaked
undertail
feathers

long tail
feathers

MALE (BREEDING)

FLIGHT: bouncy, undulating flight typical
of finches; usually flies above treetop level.

Historically, the House Finch was a western bird, and was first reported
in the eastern side of the US on Long Island, New York City in 1941.
These birds are said to have originated from the illegal bird trade. The population
of the eastern birds started expanding in the 1960s, and by the late 1990s,
their population had expanded westward to link up with the original western
population. The male House Finch is distinguished from the Purple and
Cassin's finches by its brown streaked underparts, while the females have
plainer faces and generally blurrier streaking.

VOICE Call note *queet*; varied jumble of notes, often starting with husky
notes to whistled and burry notes, and ending with a long *wheeerr*.

NESTING Females build nests from grass stems, thin twigs, and thin weeds
in trees and on man-made structures; 1–6 eggs; 2–3 broods; March–August.

FEEDING Eats, almost exclusively, vegetable matter, such as buds, fruit, and
seeds; readily comes to feeders.

RED IN THE FACE
The breeding male House Finch
can be identified by its stunning
strawberry-red plumage.

OCCURRENCE
Found in urban, suburban,
and settled areas; in the West
also in wilder areas such as
savannas, desert grasslands,
and chaparral, particularly
near people; in the East
almost exclusively in settled
areas, including the centers
of large cities. Resident, some
birds move after breeding.

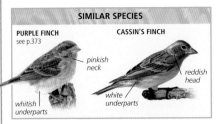

SIMILAR SPECIES

PURPLE FINCH
see p.373

pinkish
neck

whitish
underparts

CASSIN'S FINCH

reddish
head

white
underparts

| Length **5–6in (12.5–15cm)** | Wingspan **8–10in (20–25cm)** | Weight **9/16–1oz (16–27g)** |
| Social **Flocks** | Lifespan **Up to 12 years** | Status **Secure** |

372   DATE: _____ TIME: _____ LOCATION: _____

| Order **Passeriformes** | Family **Fringillidae** | Species *Haemorhous purpureus* |

Purple Finch

pinkish red body

MALE

pale brown overall

lightly streaked overall

darker, streaked wings

FEMALE

brownish, conical bill

pink and brown streaked upperparts

brown stripe between eye and bill

raspberry-red crown

round, brownish wings

IN FLIGHT

pink rump and upper tail

MALE

whitish belly with rosy patches

One of three difficult-to-distinguish members of the genus *Haemorhous* in North America, the Purple Finch is best known as a visitor to winter feeding stations. The western subspecies (*californicus*) is slightly darker and duller than the eastern form (*purpureus*). Only moderately common, the raspberry-red males pose less of an identification challenge than the brown-streaked females. Even on their breeding grounds in open and mixed coniferous forest, Purple Finches are more often heard than seen.

VOICE Flight call single, rough *pikh*; songs rich series of notes, up and down in pitch.
NESTING Cup of sticks and grasses on a conifer branch; 4 eggs; 2 broods; May–July.
FEEDING Eats buds, seeds, flowers of deciduous trees; insects and caterpillars in summer; also seeds and berries.

FLIGHT: rapid wing beats, alternating with downward glides.

RASPBERRY TINTED
On a lichen-covered branch this male's delicate coloring is quite striking.

OCCURRENCE
Breeds in northern mixed conifer and hardwood forests in all Canadian provinces, the Yukon and Northwest Territories, where it is partially migratory. Resident from Baja California north along the Pacific coast up to Yukon Territory.

SIMILAR SPECIES

HOUSE FINCH ♀
western; see p.372

thinner streaks

CASSIN'S FINCH ♀

more marked facial patterning

RED-WINGED BLACKBIRD ♀
see p.364

larger overall

heavily streaked

darker overall

| Length **4³/₄–6in (12–15cm)** | Wingspan **8¹/₂–10in (22–26cm)** | Weight **¹¹/₁₆–1¹/₁₆oz (20–30g)** |
| Social **Flocks** | Lifespan **Unknown** | Status **Declining** |

DATE: _____ TIME: _____ LOCATION: _____

| Order **Passeriformes** | Family **Fringillidae** | Species *Acanthis flammea* |

Common Redpoll

ruby-red cap

small, pointed yellow bill

red cap

MALE

wing bars

IN FLIGHT

rosy-red breast

MALE (BREEDING)

reddish cap

FEMALE

streaked underparts

black streaks on rosy-red breast

pale wing bars

notched tail

pale wing bar

JUVENILE

MALE (NONBREEDING)

Every other year, spruce, birch, and other trees in the northern forest zone fail to produce a good crop of seeds, forcing the Common Redpoll to look for food farther south than usual— as far south as the northern US states. The Common Redpoll is oddly tame around people and is easily attracted to winter feeders. The degree of whiteness in its plumage varies greatly among individuals, due to sex and age. The taxonomy of the Common Redpoll includes four subspecies around the world, and there are suggestions that some may be distinct species.

VOICE Flight call dry *zit-zit-zit-zit* and rattling *chirr*; also high *too-ee* call while perched; song series of rapid trills.

NESTING Cup of small twigs in spruces, larches, willows, alders; 4–6 eggs; 1–2 broods; May–June.

FEEDING Feeds on small seeds from conifers, sedge, birch, willow, alder; also insects and spiders.

FLIGHT: deeply undulating, with dips between bouts of wing beats.

SIMILAR SPECIES

PINE SISKIN see p.378
yellow on tail
two wing bars

HOARY REDPOLL see p.375
brownish upperparts
red cap
pale overall
whitish underparts

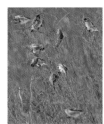

FRIENDLY FLOCK
Common Redpolls are only weakly territorial, sometimes even nesting close together.

OCCURRENCE
Mainly in extreme northern North America from Alaska to Quebec and Labrador, in low forest, subarctic, and shrubby tundra habitats. More southerly winter appearances typically occur every other year, rarely south of northern US states, from Dakota east to New York City and New England.

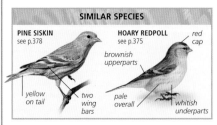

| Length 4³/₄–5¹/₂in (12–14cm) | Wingspan 6¹/₂–6³/₄in (16–17cm) | Weight ³/₈–¹¹/₁₆oz (11–19g) |
| Social **Flocks** | Lifespan **Up to 10 years** | Status **Secure** |

DATE: _____ TIME: _____ LOCATION: _____

Hoary Redpoll

pale upperparts

white rump

MALE

creamy white wing bars

IN FLIGHT

small pinkish red patch on forehead

lightly streaked breast

whitish belly

FEMALE

pinkish red forehead

streaked neck

small conical bill

MALE

pink wash on breast

faint streaks

white uppertail feathers

notched tail

creamy white undertail feathers

W hen a flock of redpolls settles at a feeding station, one or more may stand out as exceptionally white, somewhat fluffier, and with a stubbier bill. These may be Hoary Redpolls, a distinct species from the rest of the redpoll group. This bird of the high Arctic has two recognized subspecies—*A. h. exilipes* and *A. h. hornemanni*. These close relatives of the Common Redpoll often breed in the same areas, but do not interbreed. Like Common Redpolls, chattering flocks of Hoary Redpolls buzz rapidly over trees and fields and are tame around humans, but this species is less well known because of its more limited contact with people.
VOICE Flight calls dry *zit-zit-zit-zit* and rattling *chirr*; also high *too-ee* call while perched; song series of rapid trills.
NESTING Lined cup of twigs, grasses in scrubby trees; 4–6 eggs; 1–2 broods; May–July.
FEEDING Eats seeds, insects, and spiders; in winter, prefers niger thistle seed.

FLIGHT: flurries of energetic wing beats alternating with glides.

GROUND FEEDER
Seeds that fall from trees onto the snow provide a good meal for the Hoary Redpoll.

SIMILAR SPECIES

COMMON REDPOLL
see p.374

more slender shape

SNOW BUNTING
see p.297

larger overall

more heavily streaked

band across chest

OCCURRENCE
Breeds in the High Arctic, including the Canadian Arctic Archipelago; prefers low trees of the open tundra; winters within the boreal forest belt from the Canadian Maritimes and northern New England westward to Alaska.

Length **5–5¹/₂in (12.5–14cm)**	Wingspan **8¹/₂–9¹/₄in (21–23.5cm)**	Weight **⁷/₁₆–¹¹/₁₆oz (12–20g)**
Social **Flocks**	Lifespan **Unknown**	Status **Secure**

DATE: _____ TIME: _____ LOCATION: _____

| Order **Passeriformes** | Family **Fringillidae** | Species *Loxia curvirostra* |

Red Crossbill

black wings

MALE

red body

IN FLIGHT

dark brown wings

red rump

black stripe over eye

streaked belly

JUVENILE

crown usually brick-red

crossed mandibles

some males greenish red overall

MALE

greenish breast

dark wings

MALE

FEMALE

FLIGHT: strong and deeply undulating.

The Crossbill has evolved one of the most efficient mechanisms to unlock the seeds of conifers. The highly adapted bill is used to bite between the scales of a conifer cone and pry them apart, then the seed is lifted out with its tongue. Red Crossbills are further specialized to harvest types of conifer seeds; eight different forms have been recognized, all the same color but different in body size, bill shape and size. Each form has a different flight call and rarely interbreeds with other forms even where they overlap.

VOICE Common call *jit* repeated 2–5 times; song complex, continuous warbling of notes, whistles, and buzzes.

NESTING Cup nest on lateral conifer branch; 3–5 eggs; 2 broods; can breed year-round.

FEEDING Feeds on pine seeds; also insects and larvae, particularly aphids; also other seeds.

PROCESSING SEEDS
The Red Crossbill manipulates seeds with its tongue before swallowing them.

SIMILAR SPECIES

WHITE-WINGED CROSSBILL
see p.377

conspicuous wing bars

SCARLET TANAGER
see p.352

vivid red plumage

pinker plumage

no black stripe

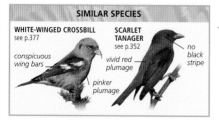

OCCURRENCE
Range covers coniferous or mixed-coniferous, and deciduous forests from Newfoundland to British Columbia and southern Alaska; also mountain forests in the Rockies, south to Mexico; irregular movements, depending on the availability of pine cones.

| Length **5–6³⁄₄in (13–17cm)** | Wingspan **10–10¹⁄₂in (25–27cm)** | Weight **⁷⁄₈–1¹⁄₄oz (25–35g)** |
| Social **Flocks** | Lifespan **Up to 10 years** | Status **Secure** |

DATE: _____ TIME: _____ LOCATION: _____

Order **Passeriformes**	Family **Fringillidae**	Species *Loxia leucoptera*

White-winged Crossbill

crossed mandibles

two conspicuous white wing bars

brownish green head

variable dark patch on cheek

dark brown wings

red body

greenish streaked underparts

MALE

FEMALE

IN FLIGHT

blackish wings

MALE

notched tail

pinkish red underparts

FLIGHT: strong and undulating with quick wing beats alternating with glides.

Cone debris, needles, and whole cones clatter down from a spruce in the otherwise silent winter forest. Some twittering is heard, and then a chorus of metallic, yanking notes reveals that a flock of a dozen White-winged Crossbills has been causing all the commotion. In an instant, the entire flock erupts into the air, calling loudly in flight, only to disappear completely in the distance. Few other creatures of the northerly forest go about their business with such determined energy, and no others accent a winter woodland with hot pink and magenta—the colors of the White-winged Crossbill's head and breast.

VOICE Calls are sharp, chattering *plik*, or deeper *tyoop*, repeated in series of 3–7 notes; song melodious trilling.

NESTING Open cup nest, usually high on end of a spruce branch; 3–5 eggs; 2 broods; July, January–February.

FEEDING Eats seeds from small-coned conifers; spruces, firs, larches; feeds on insects when available.

EATING SNOW
The White-winged Crossbill frequently eats snow to provide essential moisture.

SIMILAR SPECIES

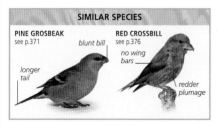

PINE GROSBEAK
see p.371

blunt bill

longer tail

RED CROSSBILL
see p.376

no wing bars

redder plumage

OCCURRENCE
Nomadic; most common in the spruce zone of Canada and Alaska but has bred as far south as Colorado in the West; in the East, from Quebec and Newfoundland southward to New York City and New England.

Length **5¹/₂–6in (14–15cm)**	Wingspan **10–10¹/₂in (26–27cm)**	Weight **¹¹/₁₆–1¹/₁₆oz (20–30g)**
Social **Flocks**	Lifespan **Up to 10 years**	Status **Secure**

DATE: _____ TIME: _____ LOCATION: _____

| Order **Passeriformes** | Family **Fringillidae** | Species *Spinus pinus* |

Pine Siskin

notched tail

conspicuous yellow wing bar

MALE

IN FLIGHT

heavily streaked back

yellow in outer wing feathers

yellow base of tail

ADULT

pale eyebrow

brownish cheek

slender, pointed bill

heavily streaked underparts

FLIGHT: undulating, with quick series of wing beats and closed-winged glides.

This unpredictable little bird of the conifer belt runs in gangs and hordes, zipping over the trees with incessant twittering. An expert at disguise, the Pine Siskin can resemble a cluster of pine needles or cones, and even disappear when a Sharp-shinned Hawk appears. Often abundant wherever there are pines, spruces, and other conifers, Pine Siskins may still disappoint birdwatchers by making a mass exodus from a region if the food supply is not to their liking. A vicious fighter at feeding tables, nomadic by nature, with high energy and fearlessness, the Pine Siskin is a fascinating species.

VOICE Rising *toooeeo*, mostly when perched; also raspy *chit-chit-chit* in flight.

NESTING Shallow cup of grass and lichens near the end of a conifer branch; 3–4 eggs; 1–2 broods; February–August.

FEEDING Eats conifer seeds; gleans insects and spiders; also seen feeding on roadsides, lawns, and weed fields.

FOREST DWELLER
The streaked Pine Siskin inhabits northern and western coniferous forests.

QUARRELSOME
A bird warns off a neighbor at a food source, displaying its yellow wing stripe.

OCCURRENCE
Widespread across North America; occurs in coniferous and mixed coniferous forests, but also seen in parkland and suburbs. In some winters may appear south of regular breeding range to Missouri and Tennessee, also Mexico. Prefers open areas to continuous forest.

SIMILAR SPECIES	
COMMON REDPOLL see p.374	**YELLOW-RUMPED WARBLER** ♀ see p.326

tiny, pale bill

heavier streaking

yellow rump

yellow patches

Length 4¼–5½in (11–14cm)	Wingspan 7–9in (18–23cm)	Weight ⁷⁄₁₆–⁵⁄₈oz (12–18g)
Social **Flocks**	Lifespan **Up to 10 years**	Status **Secure**

DATE: _____ TIME: _____ LOCATION: _____

| Order **Passeriformes** | Family **Fringillidae** | Species *Spinus tristis* |

American Goldfinch

MALE (NONBREEDING)

bright yellow back

IN FLIGHT

tan back

brownish bill

yellow throat and collar

pale tan underparts

MALE (NONBREEDING)

brownish olive back

pinkish bill

FEMALE (BREEDING)

black forehead and crown

short conical pinkish bill

bright yellow underparts

pinkish legs and feet

MALE (BREEDING)

black tail

white rump

white wing bar

brownish overall

dull yellow throat

FEMALE (NONBREEDING)

Often described as a giant yellow-and-black bumblebee, a male American Goldfinch in full breeding plumage is a common summer sight. Even when not seen, the presence of goldfinches in an area is quickly given away by the sound of the birds calling in flight. If there are weed seeds around, goldfinches will find them, whether they are out in the fields or on the feeding table. When a male performs his courtship songs, often singing them while circling his female, he does justice to the nickname "American canary."

VOICE Loud, rising *pter-yee* by males; 3–5-note *tit-tse-tew-tew* by both sexes, usually in flight; song complex warbling.

NESTING Open cup nest of grass, usually shaded from above; 4–5 eggs; 1–2 broods; July–September.

FEEDING Feeds mainly on seeds from annual plants, birch, and alder; some insects; prefers sunflower and thistle seed at feeders.

FLIGHT: deeply undulating; wing beats alternating with closed-wing dips.

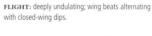

SIMILAR SPECIES

LESSER GOLDFINCH see p.370	EVENING GROSBEAK see p.370	WILSON'S WARBLER see p.330
greenish back	dark gray head and shoulders	black cap
conspicuous wing bars	large white wing patch	yellow face

OCCURRENCE
In low shrubs, deciduous woodlands, farmlands, orchards, suburbs, and gardens across much of North America, from southern Canada to California and Georgia; in winter south to Northern Mexico and Florida; winter habitats similar to those used at other times.

| Length **4¼–5in (11–13cm)** | Wingspan **7–9in (18–23cm)** | Weight **⅜–¹¹⁄₁₆oz (11–20g)** |
| Social **Small flocks** | Lifespan **Up to 11 years** | Status **Secure** |

DATE: _____ TIME: _____ LOCATION: _____

Family **Passeridae**

OLD WORLD SPARROWS

Tⁱ HESE SMALL, SHORT-LEGGED, short-billed, principally seed-eating birds are not closely related to the American sparrows, which are closer to New World buntings than to the sparrows of Europe, Asia, and Africa. The Old World sparrows are more closely related to the weavers of Africa and southern Asia, although they do not have the same highly developed nest-building capabilities.

Sparrows predominantly eat seeds, but during the breeding season require high-protein insect food to feed their growing chicks. Modern intensive farming has reduced the supply of both, so sparrows can find survival difficult through the winter, and also rear fewer young in summer. The only Old World Sparrow to be found in Canada, the House Sparrow was finally introduced successfully to North America during the 1800s after a number of failed attempts. Despite eradication

attempts in the 1900s, this species has successfully expanded its range all over Canada and the US, and its favored habitat is farms and urban settlements where it offers fierce competition for native cavity nesters like martins and swallows. House Sparrows may also create an untidy, domed structure in the open, sometimes around the insulators of a utility pole. They have a variety of simple, cheeping call notes, but also run these together into a more structured, if unmusical, song.

FEEDING FRENZY
House Sparrows feed their chicks on caterpillars, visiting the nest scores of times each day.

DECLINING POPULATIONS
Due to changing land-use patterns and possible competition from the House Finch, which has expanded its range eastward, House Sparrow numbers are on the decline.

| Order **Passeriformes** | Family **Passeridae** | Species ***Passer domesticus*** |

House Sparrow

gray crown

white wing bar

buff eyestripe

yellowish bill

brown nape

black-and-brown streaks on upperparts

black throat

pale rump

drab brown underparts

gray breast

white wing bar

MALE (SUMMER)

IN FLIGHT

FEMALE

MALE (SUMMER)

This is the familiar "sparrow" of towns, cities, suburbs, and farms. The House Sparrow is not actually a sparrow as understood in North America, but rather a member of a Eurasian family called the weaver-finches. It was first introduced in Brooklyn, New York, in 1850. From this modest beginning, and with the help of several other introductions up until the late 1860s, this hardy, and aggressive bird eventually spread right through the North American continent. In a little more than 150 years, the House Sparrow has evolved and shows the same sort of geographic variation as some widespread native birds. It is pale in the arid southwest US, and darker in wetter regions.
VOICE Variety of calls, including a *cheery chirp*, a dull *jurv* and a rough *jigga*; song consists of *chirp* notes repeated endlessly.
NESTING Untidy mass of dried vegetable material in either natural or artificial cavities; 3–5 eggs; 2–3 broods; April–August.
FEEDING Mostly seeds; sometimes gleans insects and fruit.

FLIGHT: fast and bouncing, with rapid wing beats; short wings and tail give it a portly profile.

APTLY NAMED
House Sparrows are often seen near human structures—fences, roofs, curbs, and streetlights.

SIMILAR SPECIES

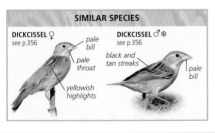

DICKCISSEL ♀
see p.356

pale bill

pale throat

yellowish highlights

DICKCISSEL ♂ ❋
see p.356

black and tan streaks

pale bill

OCCURRENCE
Flourishes in the downtown sections of cities and anywhere near human habitations, including agricultural outbuildings in remote areas of the continent. Found also in Mexico, Central and South America, and the West Indies.

| Length **6in (15.5cm)** | Wingspan **9½in (24cm)** | Weight **⅝–1¹⁄₁₆oz (18–30g)** |
| Social **Flocks** | Lifespan **Up to 7 years** | Status **Declining** |

DATE: _____ TIME: _____ LOCATION: _____

RARE SPECIES

Family **Anatidae**	Species **Mareca penelope**

Eurasian Wigeon

The adult male Eurasian Wigeon is distinctive with its bright chestnut head and broad, creamy yellow forehead. Its bold white forewing, with a green patch bordered in black, is conspicuous in flight. In recent decades, the number of Eurasian Wigeons recorded has increased, particularly in the Pacific Northwest.

OCCURRENCE Winters regularly on both Atlantic and Pacific coasts, with small numbers found inland.

VOICE Males a high-pitched, whistled *wheeeo*; females a low, growling *krrr* or *karr*.

ADULT

pinkish breast

gray body

Length **17½–20in (45–51cm)**	Wingspan **30–34in (75–86cm)**

Family **Anatidae**	Species **Spatula querquedula**

Garganey

The Garganey is a small dabbling duck, the same size and shape as the Blue-winged Teal. A male in breeding plumage is unmistakable, its bold white eyebrow contrasting sharply with its dark brown head. In flight, it has a silver-gray forewing with a broad, white trailing edge.

OCCURRENCE Native to Eurasia, records span North America; prefers wetland habitats with emergent vegetation.

VOICE Male a low, dry rattling *knerek* or *kerrek* call; female a high-pitched quack.

bold white eyebrow extends to nape

gray sides contrast with brown breast

MALE

Length **14½–16in (37–41cm)**	Wingspan **23½–25in (60–64cm)**

Family **Ardeidae**	Species **Egretta thula**

Snowy Egret

The Snowy Egret is very adaptable in estuarine and freshwater habitats. It forages using a wide variety of behaviors, including wing-flicking, foot-stirring, and foot-probing to get its prey moving, making it easier to capture.

OCCURRENCE Found in a wide variety of wetlands throughout North America; rare visitor to the southern provinces in late summer and fall.

VOICE High-pitched *aargaarg* when flushed; low-pitched *arg* and *raah* aggressive calls.

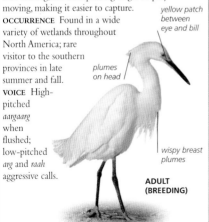

yellow patch between eye and bill

plumes on head

wispy breast plumes

ADULT (BREEDING)

Length **24in (62cm)**	Wingspan **3½ft (1.1m)**

Family **Ardeidae**	Species **Egretta caerulea**

Little Blue Heron

The shy and retreating Little Blue Heron is often overlooked because of its blue-gray color and secretive eating habits. First-year birds, which may be mistaken for Snowy Egrets, are white, and gradually acquire blue-gray, mottled feathers before eventually molting into their all-dark adult plumage.

OCCURRENCE Breeds in various wetlands, such as swamps, marshes, lakes, streams, rivers, and flooded fields. Range has expanded north, particularly into eastern Canada.

VOICE Vocal during courtship; generally silent.

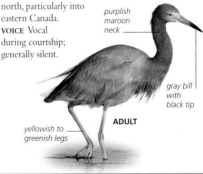

purplish maroon neck

gray bill with black tip

yellowish to greenish legs

ADULT

Length **24in (61cm)**	Wingspan **3ft 3in (100cm)**

Family **Ardeidae**	Species *Nyctanassa violacea*

Yellow-crowned Night-Heron

The Yellow-crowned Night-Heron was unaffected by the 19th century plume hunting trade. It then expanded northward in the 20th century, but has since retreated slightly from the northern edge of its range. It can be seen in wooded areas.

OCCURRENCE Breeds near wetlands in southeastern US and along the coast up to Canadian Maritimes; also likes being near houses in wooded habitat.

VOICE Call an abrupt *quark* or *wok*, higher pitched than Black-crowned Night Heron; most vocal in the mornings, and after dusk.

ADULT

thick, black bill

Length 19½–28in (50–70cm)	Wingspan 3¼–3½ft (1–1.1m)

Family **Cathartidae**	Species *Coragyps atratus*

Black Vulture

Common in the southern and eastern states, the Black Vulture is often seen in large communal roosts in the evening. When not feeding on roadkills along highways and other carrion, Black Vultures sometimes kill the odd prey.

OCCURRENCE Range expanding in the northeast; breeds in dense woodlands, caves, old buildings.

VOICE Usually silent; hisses and barks occasionally.

naked, wrinkled, gray skin

long, grayish legs and feet

ADULT

Length 24–27in (61–68cm)	Wingspan 4½–5ft (1.4–1.5m)

Family **Rallidae**	Species *Porphyrio martinicus*

Purple Gallinule

The Purple Gallinule is conspicuous due to its vibrant coloring. Well known for long-distance vagrancy far outside its normal breeding range, it has been found in Labrador, Switzerland, and South Africa.

OCCURRENCE Breeds and winters in freshwater marshes in the southeastern US; occasionally shows up in southern Ontario east to the Maritimes.

VOICE Call a chicken-like clucking; also grunts and higher-pitched single notes.

ADULT (BREEDING)

dark blue breast and belly

Length 13in (33cm)	Wingspan 22in (56cm)

Family **Charadriidae**	Species *Charadrius wilsonia*

Wilson's Plover

Wilson's Plover is the largest of the North American *Charadrius* species. Its distinctive habit of running horizontally, low to the ground, is a familiar sight on beaches. Wilson's Plover was listed as a species of "high concern" in 2000.

OCCURRENCE Found primarily in coastal habitats (beaches, sand dunes), mostly in the southeast, but sometimes up into Nova Scotia.

VOICE Flight call a short *pip*, or *pi-dit*; alarm calls include slurred whistle *tweet*, and short whistled *peet*.

black breastband

MALE

brownish upperparts

Length 6½–8in (16–20cm)	Wingspan 15½–19½in (39–49cm)

Family **Scolopacidae**	Species *Calidris pugnax*

Ruff

The Ruff is well known for the elaborately colored head ruffs and tufts of breeding male birds. Males are 20 percent larger than the females (known as Reeves), which are more muted in appearance.

OCCURRENCE Rare migrant along Pacific coast, occasional in St. Lawrence River and Great Lakes.

VOICE Mostly silent; occasionally gives a soft *krruk*.

short, slightly drooped bill

JUVENILE (FALL)

Length **8–12in (20–30cm)**	Wingspan **19–23in (48–58cm)**

Family **Stercorariidae**	Species *Stercorarius skua*

Great Skua

Similar to the South Polar Skua, this large and aggressive predator and scavenger can be differentiated by its heavier streaking and more reddish tones to its brown body. The Great Skua is closely related to several species of Southern Hemisphere skuas including the South Polar Skua.

OCCURRENCE Rare visitor, mostly in fall through spring, to pelagic waters off the Atlantic Coast of North America.

VOICE Rough, cackling *rah-rah-rah*.

dark nape

hooked, dark bill

mottled gray to warm brown plumage

ADULT

Length **19½–23in (50–58cm)**	Wingspan **4–4½ft (1.2–1.4m)**

Family **Stercorariidae**	Species *Stercorarius maccormicki*

South Polar Skua

The South Polar Skua is a large, aggressive relative of the jaegers. Away from its breeding areas in the South Shetland Islands and along the coast and islands of the Antarctic, it is a daunting presence on the ocean, lurking menacingly on the water when not badgering other seabirds for food, or battling for scraps behind fishing boats.

OCCURRENCE A scarce visitor to seas on east and west coasts; most numerous in the spring and fall in the Pacific, and in spring in the Atlantic far offshore.

VOICE Deep gull-like burbling; generally silent at sea in North America.

hooked bill

cold brown toned body and head

ADULT

Length **21in (53cm)**	Wingspan **4¹⁄₄ft (1.3m)**

Family **Laridae**	Species *Larus schistisagus*

Slaty-backed Gull

This rare visitor from eastern Russia and Japan is most likely to be confused with the Western Gull. Adults have a series of white spots on the outer wing feather tips, referred to as "a string of pearls." Winter adults have heavily streaked heads with white linings to their underwings that contrast with the gray outer and inner wing feathers.

OCCURRENCE Occurs occasionally in northern and southwestern British Columbia; accidental in winter across Canada and US.

VOICE Slow *aah-aah-aah*.

ADULT (BREEDING)

Length **24–26in (61–66cm)**	Wingspan **4½–5ft (1.4–1.5m)**

Family **Laridae**	Species ***Rhodostethia rosea***

Ross's Gull

In adult breeding plumage, this small, delicate gull is unmistakable. Dove-gray upperparts, pale-pink underparts, red legs, and a black collar, make it an elegant and beautiful-looking bird.

OCCURRENCE Siberian breeder found only along Alaskan north coast in fall; expanded as a breeding bird into Arctic Canada; winter strays found across Canada and to northeast and northwest US.

VOICE Rarely heard in winter; tern-like *kik-kik-kik*.

black "necklace"

wedge-shaped tail

ADULT (BREEDING)

Length **11½–12in (29–31cm)**	Wingspan **35–39in (90–100cm)**

Family **Laridae**	Species ***Pagophila eburnea***

Ivory Gull

The Ivory Gull, all white with black legs, is unlikely to be confused with any other gull. Adults are pure white in summer and winter. Juveniles are patterned to varying degrees with black spots on the tips of their flight feathers, and tail and wing outer feathers, and they have a smudgy black face.

OCCURRENCE High Arctic breeder; rarely strays far south of the pack ice, even in winter; casual in winter to British Columbia and Maritime Provinces; accidental elsewhere.

VOICE Tern-like, harsh *keeuur*; rarely heard away from breeding grounds.

pure white plumage

yellow-tipped slate-blue bill

ADULT

black legs

Length **15½–17in (40–43cm)**	Wingspan **3½–4ft (1.1–1.2m)**

Family **Laridae**	Species ***Sternula antillarum***

Least Tern

The Least Tern is the smallest of the North American terns and, in summer, its distinctive black cap and white forehead distinguish it from other members of its family. In the 19th century their numbers declined. They have rebounded but are now threatened by ongoing habitat loss.

OCCURRENCE Breeds along both coasts, major rivers, lakes, reservoirs; favors sandy areas such as beaches and sandbars. Scattered sightings across Canada.

VOICE Extremely vocal during breeding; a high-pitched *ki-deek, ki-deek*; also a rapid, almost non-stop chatter.

ADULT (BREEDING)

yellow bill

two dark outer wing feathers

Length **8½–9in (21–23cm)**	Wingspan **19–21in (48–53cm)**

Family **Columbidae**	Species ***Zenaida asiatica***

White-winged Dove

This large gray-colored dove is best identified in flight by the conspicuous white bands on its wings. Perched birds display bright blue skin around orange eyes and longish, square tails with white tips. This species has been expanding its population northwards into Canada in recent decades.

OCCURRENCE Breeds and winters in dense, thorny woodlands, deserts, orchards, and residential areas. It is now expanding north into Canada.

VOICE Distinctive, drawn-out cooing: *who-cooks-for-you*; also makes five-note variation from the nest: *la-coo-kla-coo-kla*.

black mark below ear feathers

ADULT

longish, square, gray tail

Length **11½in (29cm)**	Wingspan **19in (48cm)**

Family **Caprimulgidae**	Species *Antrostomus carolinensis*

Chuck-will's-widow

The larger of the two species of North American nightjar and least known, the Chuck-will's-widow is very tolerant of human development and nests in suburban and urban areas. It often feeds by flying continuously and catching its prey in the air, hunting mostly at dawn and dusk but also during a full moon.

OCCURRENCE Breeds in mixed forests and in open fields. Found mainly in the eastern US; sometimes seen in Ontario and the Maritimes.

VOICE Whistled *chuck-will's-wid-ow*, begins softly, then increases in volume with emphasis on the two middle syllables.

ADULT
tawny buff-brown upperparts

Length **11–12½in (28–32cm)**	Wingspan **25–28in (63–70cm)**

Family **Tyrannidae**	Species *Tyrannus forficatus*

Scissor-tailed Flycatcher

Often perched on a wire or fence, the Scissor-tailed Flycatcher also has a spectacular aerial courtship display, with its long tail streaming behind it. Its nest incorporates many human products, such as string, cloth, and paper. Pre-migratory roosting flocks during late summer consist of 100 to 1,000 birds.

OCCURRENCE Breeds in southern states and into Mexico; savanna, open grasslands, pastures, and golf courses. Sporadically appears from coast to coast in Canada.

VOICE Male song variable number of *pups* followed by *perleep* or *peroo* in breeding territories and communal roots.

pale gray head

ADULT
black rump and inner wing feathers

Length **9–15in (23–38cm)**	Wingspan **15in (38cm)**

Family **Parulidae**	Species *Setophaga kirtlandii*

Kirtland's Warbler

One of the rarest songbirds in North America, Kirtland's Warbler is threatened by habitat loss and brood parasitism from the Brown-headed Cowbird. Its pale, lemon-yellow underparts can be seen as it sings from the top of a young Jack Pine.

OCCURRENCE Breeds in Jack Pine stands regrowing after forest fires; rare in Ontario and Quebec.

VOICE Song a loud series of staccato *chips*, ending with bubbly, whistled *tup-CHUP-chup tup-CHEEP-cheep chew-EEP.*

interrupted, white eye-ring

MALE

pale, lemon-yellow underparts with marked streaks on flanks

streaked, blue-gray upperparts

Length **6in (15cm)**	Wingspan **9in (23cm)**

Family **Parulidae**	Species *Setophaga dominica*

Yellow-throated Warbler

The Yellow-throated Warbler is perhaps best known for its habit of creeping along branches, much like the Black-and-white Warbler. The species occasionally interbreeds with the Northern Parula, creating the so-called "Sutton's Warbler."

OCCURRENCE Breeds in the eastern half of North America, in woods with cypress, sycamore, or live oak. Its range has extended northwards with sightings in the southern parts of most provinces.

VOICE Flight call high, thin *siit*; song long, descending cascade of clear whistles, sometimes jumbled.

ADULT

unmarked white undertail feathers

white line from bill to nape

Length **5in (13cm)**	Wingspan **8in (20cm)**

Family **Parulidae**	Species ***Helmitheros vermivorum***

Worm-eating Warbler

The Worm-eating Warbler often hangs upside down, searching suspended dead leaves for inchworms and other caterpillars. Although this bird nests on the ground and tends to forage fairly low, singing males may perch quite high in trees.

OCCURRENCE Breeds in mature, deciduous forests with abundant leaf litter and dense undergrowth; mostly in eastern US but occasionally up into Ontario.

VOICE Thick *chip* call; flight call an upslurred, thin, rolling *ziiit*; song a thin, dry trill.

ADULT

blurry pattern on undertail feathers

tawny wash on breast

Length **5in (13cm)**	Wingspan **8½in (21cm)**

Family **Cardinalidae**	Species ***Piranga rubra***

Summer Tanager

The stunning male Summer Tanager is the only North American bird that is entirely bright red. Immature males in their first spring plumage wear a patchwork of bright yellow-and-red plumage. Of the two subspecies, *P. r. rubra* breeds in the East while *P. r. cooperi* breeds in the West.

OCCURRENCE *P. r. rubra* breeds in deciduous and mixed woodlands in the east up into Canada; *P. r. cooperi* in cottonwood-willow habitats near streams in the west.

VOICE Call an explosive *PIT-tuck!* or *PIT-a TUK*; flight call a muffled, airy *vreee*.

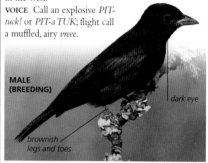

MALE (BREEDING)

dark eye

brownish legs and toes

Length **8in (20cm)**	Wingspan **12in (31cm)**

Family **Cardinalidae**	Species ***Passerina caerulea***

Blue Grosbeak

Blue Grosbeaks have expanded their range northward in recent years, especially in the Great Plains. However, they are still a rare find. Features that can help identification are the Grosbeak's huge bill, uniformly dark plumage, black face, and reddish shoulder.

OCCURRENCE Breeds in dense undergrowth of disturbed habitats: old fields, hedgerows, and desert scrub across all of southern US and expanding north into eastern Canada.

VOICE Call a loud, sharp, metallic *tchink*; similar to Indigo Bunting; song rambling, husky.

black patch between eye and bill

rufous shoulder

MALE

Length **6¾in (17cm)**	Wingspan **11in (28cm)**

Family **Fringillidae**	Species ***Fringilla montifringilla***

Brambling

Widespread in northern Eurasia, from Scandinavia to the far east of Russia, the Brambling is unlike any native North American finch. In all seasons, males and females have a conspicuous white rump and orange outer wing feathers.

OCCURRENCE Regular migrant to the Aleutian and Pribilof Islands, and mainland western Alaska. Occasionally seen elsewhere in Canada and the US.

VOICE Call a characteristic, mewing *jee-eek*; song a trilled *zhreeeee*.

head blackish, with white spots

bill yellow with black tip

MALE

white rump and uppertail feathers

orange chin and breast

Length **5¾in (14.5cm)**	Wingspan **10–11in (25–28cm)**

GLOSSARY

Many terms defined here are illustrated in the general introduction (pp.10–21).

adult A fully developed, sexually mature bird. It is in its final plumage, which no longer changes pattern with age and remains the same after yearly molt, although it may change with season. *See also* **immature**, **juvenile**.

aerie The nest of birds of prey, like eagles or peregrine falcons, usually on a cliff, and often used by the same pair of adult birds in successive years.

alarm call A call made by a bird to signal danger. Alarm calls are often short and urgent in tone, and a few species use different calls to signify the precise nature of the threat. *See also* **call**.

allopreening Mutual preening between two birds, the main purpose of which is to reduce the instinctive aggression when birds come into close contact. In the breeding season, allopreening helps to strengthen the pair bond between the male and female. *See also* **preening**.

altitudinal migrant *see* **vertical migrant**

alula A small group of two to six feathers projecting from a bird's "thumb," at the bend of its wing that reduces turbulence when raised.

Audubon, John James (1785–1851) American naturalist and wildlife illustrator, whose best known work was his remarkable collection of prints, *Birds of North America*.

axillary A term describing feathers at the base of the underwing. Axillary feathers often form small patches, with coloration differing from the rest of the underwing.

barred With marks crossing the body, wing, or tail; the opposite of streaked. *See also* **streaks**.

bastard wing *see* **alula**

beak *see* **bill**

bill A bird's jaws. A bill is made of bone, with a hornlike outer covering of keratin.

bird of prey Any of the predatory birds in the orders Accipitriformes (eagles, hawks, kites, and osprey), Falconiformes (falcons), and Strigiformes (owls). They are characterised by their acute eyesight, powerful legs, strongly hooked bill, and sharp talons. These birds are also known as raptors. *See also* **talon**, **raptor**.

body feather *see* **contour feather**

booming A sound produced by bitterns and some species of grouse. The booming of male bitterns is a deep, resonant, hollow sound that can carry for several miles. The booming of male grouse is produced by wind from air pouches in the sides of the bird's neck.

brackish Containing a mixture of saltwater and freshwater.

breeding plumage A general term for the plumage worn by adult birds when they display and form breeding pairs. It is usually (but not always) worn in the spring and summer. *See also* **nonbreeding plumage**.

brood (noun) The young birds produced from a single clutch of eggs and incubated together. *See also* **clutch**. **(verb)** In birds, to sit on nestlings to keep them warm. Brooding is usually carried out by the adult female. *See also* **incubate**.

brood parasite A bird that lays its eggs in the nest of other birds. Some brood parasites always breed this way, while others do so only occasionally.

brood patch An area of bare skin on the belly of a parent bird, usually the female, that is richly supplied with blood vessels and thus helps keep the eggs warm during incubation. This area loses its feathers in readiness for the breeding season and is fully feathered at other times.

caged-bird A species of bird commonly kept in captivity.

call A sound produced by the vocal apparatus of a bird to communicate a variety of messages to other birds. Calls are often highly characteristic of individual species and can help to locate and identify birds in the field. Most bird calls are shorter and simpler than songs. *See also* **alarm call**, **booming**, **contact call**, **song**.

casque A bony extension on a bird's head.

cere A leathery patch of skin that covers the base of a bird's bill. It is found only in a few groups, including birds of prey, pigeons, and parrots.

claw In birds, the nail that prolongs their toes.

cloaca An opening toward the rear of a bird's belly. It is present in both sexes and is used in reproduction and excretion.

clutch The group of eggs in a single nest, usually laid by one female and incubated together.

cock A term sometimes used to describe the adult male in gamebirds and songbirds. *See also* **hen**.

collar The area around a bird's neck, which in some species is a prominent feature of its plumage pattern and can be used for identification.

color form One of two or more clearly defined plumage variations found in the same species. Also known as a color morph or phase, a color form may be restricted to part of a species's range or occur side by side with other color forms over the entire range. Adults of different color forms are able to interbreed, and these mixed pairings can produce young of either form.

comb A fleshy growth of bare skin usually above the eyes.

contact call A call made by a bird to give its location as a means of staying in touch with others of the same species. Contact calls are used by birds in flocks and by breeding pairs. Contact calls are crucial for nocturnal migrants. *See also* **call**.

contour feather A general term for any feather that covers the outer surface of a bird, including its wings and tail. Contour feathers are also known as body feathers, and help streamline the bird.

cooperative breeding A breeding system in which a pair of parent birds are helped in raising their young by several other birds, which are often related to them and may be young birds from previous broods.

courtship display Ritualized, showy behavior used in courtship by the male, and sometimes by the female, involving plumage, sound (vocal and non-vocal), and movements.

covert A small feather covering the base of a bird's flight feather. Together, coverts form a well-defined feather tract on the wing or at the base of the tail. *See also* **feather tract**.

creche A group of young birds of about the same age, produced by different parents but tightly packed together. One or more adults guards the entire creche.

crepuscular Relating to the period just before dawn, when many birds are active, especially during courtship. When used in connection with birds, the term is often used to refer to both dawn and twilight.

crest A group of elongated feathers on top of a bird's head, which may be raised during courtship or to indicate alarm.

crown The area on top of a bird's head. It is often a prominent plumage feature, with a different color from the feathers on the rest of the head.

dabble To feed in shallow water by sieving water and obtain food through comblike filters in the bill; used mostly for ducks (dabbling ducks or dabblers).

decurved A term describing a bird's bill that curves downward from the forehead toward the tip.

dimorphism *see* **sexual dimorphism**

display *see* **courtship display**, **distraction display**, **threat display**

distraction display A display in which a bird deliberately attempts to attract a predator's attention in order to lure it away from its nest or nestlings.

diurnal Active during the day.

down feather A soft, fluffy feather, lacking the system of barbs of contour or flight feathers, that provides good insulation. Young birds are covered by down feathers until they molt into their first juvenile plumage. Adult birds have a layer of down feathers under their contour feathers. *See also* **contour feather**, **juvenile**.

drake An adult male duck. The adult female is known as the duck.

drift The diversion of migrating birds from their normal migration route by strong winds.

dynamic soaring *see* **soaring**

ear tuft A distinct tuft of feathers on each side of a bird's forehead, with no connection to the true ears, which can be raised as a visual signal. Many owls have ear tufts.

echolocation A method of sensing nearby objects using pulses of high-frequency sound. Echoes bounce back from obstacles, enabling the sender to build up a "picture" of its surroundings.

eclipse plumage A female-like plumage worn in some birds, especially waterfowl, by adult males for a short period after the breeding season is over. The eclipse plumage helps camouflage them during their molt, when they are flightless.

elevational migrant *see* **vertical migrant**

endemic A species (or subspecies) native to a particular geographic area—such as an island, a forest patch,

a mountain, or province, or country —and found nowhere else.

escape An individual bird that has escaped from a zoo or other collection to live in the wild. *See also* **exotic**

eye-ring A ring of color, usually narrow and well defined, around the eye of a bird.

eyestripe A stripe of color running as a line through the eye of a bird.

eyrie *see* **aerie**

exotic A bird found in a region from which it is not native. Some of these are escapes, or were originally, but now live as wild birds.

feather tract A well-defined area on a bird's skin where feathers grow, leaving patches of bare skin in between.

fledge In young birds, to leave the nest or acquire the first complete set of flight feathers. Known as fledglings, these birds may still remain dependent on their parents for some time. *See also* **flight feather**.

fledging period The average time taken by the young of a species to fledge, timed from the moment they hatch. Fledging periods in birds range from 11 days in some small songbirds to as long as 280 days in the Wandering Albatross.

fledgling *see* **fledge**

flight feather A collective term for a bird's wing and tail feathers, used in flight. More specifically, it refers to the largest feathers on the outer part of the wing, the primaries and secondaries.

forewing The front section of a bird's wing, including the primary coverts and secondary coverts. *See also* **hindwing**.

gamebird Generally, any bird that is legally hunted, including some doves and waterfowl. This name is generally used for members of the order Galliformes.

gular sac Also known as a gular pouch, it is a large, fleshy, extendable sac just below the bill of some birds, especially fish-eaters such as pelicans. It forms part of the throat.

habitat The geographical and ecological area where a particular organism usually lives.

hen A term sometimes used to describe the adult female in gamebirds, especially grouse and songbirds. *See also* **cock**.

hindwing The rear section of a bird's spread wing, including the secondary feathers, especially when it has a distinctive color or pattern. *See also* **forewing**.

hybrid The offspring produced when two species, sometimes from different genera, interbreed. Hybrids are usually rare in the wild. Among birds, they are most frequent in gamebirds and waterfowl, especially ducks. Hybrid progeny may or may not be fertile.

immature In birds, an individual that is not yet sexually mature or able to breed. Some birds pass through a series of immature plumages over several years before adopting their first adult plumage and sexual maturity. *See also* **adult**, **juvenile**.

incubate In birds, to sit on eggs to keep them warm, allowing the embryo inside to grow. Incubation is often carried out by the female. *See also* **brood**.

incubation period In birds, the period when a parent incubates its eggs. It may not start until the clutch is completed.

injury feigning *see* **distraction display**

inner wing The inner part of the wing, comprising the secondaries and rows of coverts (typically marginal, lesser, median, and greater coverts).

introduced species A species that humans have accidentally or deliberately brought into an area where it does not normally occur.

iridescent plumage Plumage that shows brilliant, luminous colors, which seem to sparkle and change color when seen from different angles.

irruption A sporadic mass movement of animals outside their normal range. Irruptions are usually short-lived and occur in response to food shortage. Also called irruptive migration.

juvenile A term referring to the plumage worn by a young bird at the time it makes its first flight and until it begins its first molt. *See also* **adult**, **immature**.

keratin A tough but lightweight protein. In birds, keratin is found in the claws, feathers, and outer part of the bill.

kleptoparasite A bird that gets much of its food by stealing it from other birds, usually by following them in flight and forcing them to disgorge their food.

lamellae Delicate, comblike structures on the sides of the bill of some birds used for filtering tiny food particles out of water.

leap-frog migration A pattern of migration in which some populations of a species travel much further than the other populations, by "leap-frogging" over the area where these sedentary (nonmigratory) birds are found. *See also* **migration**.

lek An area, often small, used by males as a communal display arena, where they show off special plumage features accompanied by vocal and non-vocal sounds, to attract females. Females wait along the lek and select the male or males that they will mate with.

lobed feet Feet with loose, fleshy lobes on the toes, adapted for swimming.

lore A small area between a bird's eye and the base of its upper bill.

mandible The upper or lower part of a bird's bill, known as the upper or lower mandible respectively.

mantle The loose term used to define the back of a bird, between its neck and rump.

migrant A species that regularly moves between geographical areas. Most migrants move on an annual basis between a breeding area and a wintering area. *See also* **partial migrant, sedentary**.

migration A journey to a different region, following a well-defined route. *See also* **leap-frog migration, partial migrant, reverse migration, sedentary, vertical migrant**.

mobbing A type of defensive behavior in which a group of birds gang up to harass a predator, such as a bird of prey or an owl, swooping repeatedly to drive it away.

molt In birds, to shed old feathers so that they can be replaced. Molting enables birds to keep their plumage in good condition, change their level of insulation, and change their coloration or markings so that they are ready to breed or display.

monogamous Mating with a single partner, either in a single breeding season or for life. *See also* **polygamous**.

morph *see* **color form**

nape The back of the neck.

nestling A young bird still in the nest.

New World The Americas, from Alaska to Cape Horn, including the Caribbean and offshore islands in the Pacific and Atlantic oceans. *See also* **Old World**.

nictitating membrane A transparent or semiopaque "third eyelid," which moves sideways across

the eye. Waterbirds often use the membrane as an aid to vision when swimming underwater.

nocturnal Active at night.

nomadic Being almost constantly on the move. Birds of deserts, grasslands, and the coniferous forests of the far north are commonly nomadic.

nonbreeding plumage The plumage worn by adult birds outside the breeding season. In many species, particularly in temperate regions, it is also known as winter plumage. *See also* **breeding plumage**.

nonmigrant *see* **sedentary**

nonpasserine Any bird that is not a member of the order Passeriformes (or passerines). *See also* **passerine**.

oil gland Also called the preen gland, a gland at the base of a bird's tail that secretes oils that are spread over the feathers for waterproofing them during preening.

Old World Europe, Asia, Africa, and Australasia. *See also* **New World**.

orbital ring A thin, bare, fleshy ring around the eye, sometimes with a distinctive color. *See also* **eye-ring**.

outer wing The outer half of the wing, comprising the primaries, their coverts, and the alula (the "thumb").

partial migrant A species in which some populations migrate while others are sedentary. This situation is common in broadly distributed species that experience a wide range of climatic conditions. *See also* **migration, sedentary**.

passerine A bird belonging to the vast order Passeriformes (the passerines). This group contains more species than all other orders of birds combined. Passerines are also called songbirds or perching birds. *See also* **nonpasserine**.

pelagic Relating to the open ocean. Pelagic birds spend most of their life at sea and only come to land to nest.

phase *see* **color form**

polygamous Mating with two or more partners during the course of a single breeding season. *See also* **monogamous**.

population A group of individual birds of the same species living in a geographically and ecologically circumscribed area.

preening Routine behavior by which birds keep their feathers in good condition. A bird grasps a feather at its base and then "nibbles" upward toward the tip, and repeats the process with different feathers. This helps smooth and clean the

plumage. Birds often also smear oil from their preen gland onto their feathers at the same time. *See also* **allopreening**.

primary feather One of the large outer wing feathers, growing from the digits of a bird's "hand." *See also* **secondary feather**.

race *see* **subspecies**

range A term to indicate the geographical distribution of a species or population.

raptor A general name for birds belonging to the orders Accipitriformes, Falconiformes, and Strigiformes. Often used interchangeably with bird of prey. *See also* **bird of prey**.

ratite A member of an ancient group of flightless birds that includes the ostrich, cassowaries, emus, rheas, and kiwis. In the past, the group was larger and more diverse.

resident *see* **sedentary**

reverse migration A phenomenon that occurs when birds from a migratory species mistakenly travel in the opposite direction from normal, causing birds to turn up in places far outside their normal range. *See also* **migration**.

roost A place where birds sleep, either at night or by day.

rump The area between a bird's back and the base of its upper tail coverts. In many species, the rump is a different color from the rest of the plumage and can be a useful diagnostic character for identification.

sally A feeding technique (sallying), used especially by tyrant flycatchers, in which a bird makes a short flight from a perch to catch an insect, often in midair, followed by a return to a perch, often the same one.

salt gland A gland located in a depression in the skull, just above the eye of some birds, particularly seabirds. This enables them to extract the fluids they need from saltwater and then expel the excess salts through the nostrils.

scapular Any one of a group of feathers on the "shoulder," forming a more or less oval patch on each side of the back, at the base of the wing.

scrape A simple nest that consists of a shallow depression in the ground, which may be unlined or lined with material such as feathers, bits of grass, or pebbles.

secondary feather One of the row of long, stiff feathers along the rear edge of a bird's wing, between the body and the primary feathers at the wingtip. *See also* **primary feather**.

sedentary Having a settled lifestyle that involves little or no geographic movement. Sedentary birds are also said to be resident or nonmigratory. *See also* **migration**.

semipalmated The condition in which two or more of the toes are partially joined by an incomplete membrane at their base.

sexual dimorphism The occurrence of physical differences between males and females. In birds, the most common differences are in size and plumage.

shield In birds, a hard structure on the forehead that joins the bill and often appears to be an extension of it.

shorebird Also known as a wader, any member of several families in the order Charadriiformes, including plovers, sandpipers, godwits, snipe, avocets, stilts, oystercatchers, and curlews. Not all species actually wade in water and some live in dry habitats.

soaring In birds, flight without flapping of the wings. A soaring bird stays at the same height or gains height. Updraft soaring is a type of soaring in which a bird benefits from rising currents that form at cliffs or along mountain ridges. Seabirds are expert at dynamic soaring, repeatedly diving into the troughs between waves and then using the rising air deflected off the waves to wheel back up into the air.

song A vocal performance by a bird, usually the adult male, to attract and impress a potential mate, advertise ownership of a territory, or drive away rival birds. Songs are often highly characteristic of individual species and can be a major aid in locating and identifying birds in the field. *See also* **call**.

songbird A general term used to describe a member of the suborder Passeri (or oscines), a subdivision of the largest order of birds, the Passeriformes (passerines).

species A group of similar organisms that are capable of breeding among themselves in the wild and producing fertile offspring that resemble themselves, but that do not interbreed in the wild with individuals of another similar group, are called a species. *See also* **subspecies**.

speculum A colorful patch on the wing of a duck, formed by the secondary feathers. *See also* **secondary feather**.

spur A sharply pointed, clawlike structure at the back of the leg of some birds, like the Wild Turkey.

staging ground A stopover area where migrant birds regularly pause while on migration, to rest and feed.

stoop A near-vertical and often very fast dive made by falcons and some other birds of prey when chasing prey in the air or on the ground.

streaks Marks that run lengthwise on feathers; opposite of bars.

subspecies When species show geographical variation in color, voice, or other characters, these differentiated populations are recognized by ornithologists as subspecies (formerly also called races). *See also* **species**.

syrinx A modified section of a bird's trachea (windpipe), equivalent to the voicebox in humans, that enables birds to call and sing.

talon One of the sharp, hooked claws of a bird of prey.

territory An area that is defended by an animal, or a group of animals, against other members of the same species. Territories often include useful resources, such as good breeding sites or feeding areas, which help a male attract a mate.

tertial Any one of a small group of feathers, sometimes long and obvious, at the base of the wing adjacent to the inner secondaries.

thermal A rising bubble or column of warm air over land that soaring birds can use to gain height with little effort. *See also* **soaring**.

threat display A form of defense in which a bird adopts certain postures, sometimes accompanied by loud calls, to drive away a rival or a potential predator.

trachea The breathing tube in animals, also known as the windpipe.

tubenose A general term used to describe members of the order Procellariiformes, including albatrosses, petrels, and shearwaters; their nostrils form two tubes on the upper mandible.

underwing The underside of a bird's wing, usually visible only in flight or when a bird is preening, displaying, or swimming.

upperwing The upper surface of a bird's wing clearly exposed in flight but often mostly hidden when the bird is perched.

vagrant A bird that has strayed far from its normal range. Usually, vagrants are long-distance migrants that have been blown off course by storms, have overshot their intended destination due to strong winds, or have become disoriented.

vent Also called the crissum, the undertail feathers between the lower belly feathers and tail feathers, which in some species are differently colored from either belly or tail feathers. Can be helpful in identification.

vertical migrant A species that migrates up and down mountains, usually in response to changes in the weather or food supply. *See also* **migration**.

wader *see* shorebird.

waterfowl A collective term for members of the family Anatidae, including ducks, geese, and swans.

wattle A bare, fleshy growth that hangs loosely below the bill in some birds. It is often brightly colored, and may play a part in courtship.

wildfowl *see* waterfowl

Wilson, Alexander (1766–1813) A contemporary of J.J. Audubon, Wilson's seminal *American Ornithology* marks the start of scientific ornithology in the US.

wingbar A line or bar of color across the upper surface of a bird's wing. Wingbars can often be seen when a bird is on the ground or perched and its wings are in the closed position, but they are normally much more obvious in flight. Wingbars may be single or in groups of two or more.

wingspan The distance across a bird's outstretched wings and back, from one wingtip to the other.

Acknowledgments

For this edition, Dorling Kindersley would like to thank Priyanjali Narain for editorial assistance.

Dorling Kindersley would like to thank the following people for their help in compiling this book: Lucy Baker, Aditi Batra, Rachel Booth, Kim Bryan, Tanya Desai, Arti Finn, Peter Frances, Rahul Ganguly, Lynn Hassett, Riccie Janus, Megan Jones, Maxine Lea, Kokila Manchanda, Ritu Mishra, Megha Nayar, Alka Ranjan, Ruth O'Rourke, Surya Sankash Sarangi, Yen-Mai Tsang.

Producing such a comprehensive book would be impossible without the research and observations of hundreds of field and museum ornithologists and birdwatchers. The Editor-in-Chief would like to name four who have been especially inspirational and supportive over the years: the late Paul Géroudet, the late Ernst Mayr, Patricia Stryker Joseph, and Helen Hays. In addition, we acknowledge *Birds of North America Online*, edited by Alan Poole, a joint project of the American Ornithologists' Union and Cornell's Laboratory of Ornithology, and The Howard Moore *Complete Checklist of the Birds of the World*, 3rd edition.

The publisher would like to thank the following for their kind permission to reproduce their photographs:

Almost without exception, the birds featured in the profiles in this book were photographed in the wild.

(Key: a-above; b-below/bottom; c-center; f-far; l-left; r-right; t-top)

Alamy Images: AfriPics.com 11cra; Derrick Alderman 18cl; Blickwinkel 19cr; Rick & Nora Bowers, 208t; Bruce Coleman Inc. 14tr, 19crb; Gay Bumgarner 18cb; Nancy Camel 19clb; Redmond Durrell 15cb; Elvele Images Ltd 18-19c; David Hosking 13fcrb; Juniors Bildachiv 13tr; Don Kates 16cla; Charles Melton 29fbl; Renee Morris 379; Rolf Nussbaumer 16clb; Peter Arnold, Inc. 16cl; Stock Connection Blue 13clb; © tbkmedia.de 16-17c.
Ardea: Ian Beames 11cr; Peter Steyn 87ca.
Doug Backlund: 12-13ca, 27cb, 28crb, 108crb, 113cra, 120tr, 225cra, 225tc, 279cla, 279cra, 279crb.
The Barn Owl Centre, UK: 192cla.
Giff Beaton: 318tr.
Corbis: Joe McDonald 14cla, 103cra; Neil Bowman/ Frank Lane Picture Library 121cla, 121crb; Glenn Bartley / BIA / Minden Pictures 136cr.
Mike Danzenbaker: 73tc, 84ca, 88cra, 163cla, 206ca, 206tl, 228cb, 294tr, 296tc, 323tc, 383bl, 383cla, 383cra.
DK Images: Robin Chittenden 58tr; Chris Gomersall Photography 38ca, 38crb, 38tr, 55crb, 68crb, 68tr, 86ca, 86tr, 89tr, 90crb, 98crb, 105cra, 105tc, 134crb, 135crb, 139bc, 162cla, 162cra, 164cra, 165crb, 166crb, 166tc, 170ca, 175cra, 182ca, 182crb, 184cb, 187cra, 224ca, 224crb, 252cla, 290tc, 381cra, 381tc; David Cottridge 277cla; David Tipling Photo Library 34ca, 45cr, 45cra, 58tc, 60tc, 79tc, 105crb, 126cla, 138cla, 171cla, 175cla, 177cra, 179cl, 179cra, 187cla, 254tc; Mark Hamblin 40ca, 45cla, 72c, 92cra, 193cra, 201cra, 277tc; Chris Knights 59crb; Mike Lane 45tr, 53cla, 60tr, 64tc, 68cla, 68cra, 68ca, 78ca, 90cra, 137cla, 139tr, 144tc, 160cra, 160crb, 164crb, 165ca, 166ca, 170cra, 182tc, 183ca, 252ca, 385cra, 387cra; Gordon Langsbury 90tr, 99cla, 127cra, 130tc, 136tr, 150cla; Tim Loseby 40crb, 157crb, George McCarthy 64tr, 67crb, 99cra, 101ca, 134cla, 159ca, 177bc, 184tc; Natural History Museum, London 10cla, 12cl; Kim Taylor 241tr; Roger Tidman 30ca, 30tc, 33ca, 41tr, 49ca, 55ca, 60ca, 72tr, 90cla, 102ca, 134tr, 139tc, 145tc, 156ca, 157ca, 157tr, 158cra, 161ca, 165tc, 179tc, 183crb, 207cra, 277cra, 290cla, 297cla, 297tc, 385cla; Steve Young 41cr, 45crb, 45tc, 53cra, 53tr, 55tc, 55tr, 59ca, 59tc, 68tc, 86tc, 88crb, 88tc, 92tc, 138tc, 158tc, 160cla, 170cla, 171crb, 171fcla, 177fcla, 179crb, 183tc, 183tr, 209cla, 269ca, 297cra.
Dudley Edmondson: 24b, 24cra, 24tl, 27tc, 32tr, 61cra, 67cla, 80ca, 80tc, 94cla, 95cb, 106ca, 106cb, 106cla, 106tc, 108cla, 108cra, 108tc, 110crb, 113crb, 120crb, 123crb, 124tc, 140tc, 173crb, 174tr, 181crb, 197cb, 199tl, 202cla, 202cra, 205crb, 216bc, 238crb, 249ca, 270crb, 278crb, 305bc, 335cra, 344cra, 364crb.
Tom Ennis: 143ca.
Hanne & Jens Eriksen: 131crb, 161crb, 161tc, 180tc, 385br.
Neil Fletcher: 24cla, 26bc, 26cla, 29tc, 32ca, 32cra, 40tr, 42tc, 43crb, 43tr, 68tr, 186cla, 290cra, 380b.
FLPA: Tui De Roy/Minden Pictures 17ca; Goetz Eichhorn/ Foto Natura 74fbl, 75ca; John Hawkins 17cla; David Hosking, 83bl; S Jonasson 81cra; Daphne Kinzler 17tr; S & D & K Maslowski 18clb; Geoff Moon; Roger Tidman 81tr; Winfried Wisniewski/ Foto Natura 17cr; Jim Brandenburg / Minden Pictures 121tr.
Joe Fuhrman: 91cra, 131ca, 316crb.
Getty Images: Marc Moritsch 14-15c; Brad Sharp 18c. Bob Glover: 171fcra, 179fcra.
Melvin Grey: 34crb, 93bc,96ca, 96tr, 97cla, 99crb, 100crb, 122cra, 125tr, 135ca, 137cra, 225cla, 263crb, 383tr, 385cb; Tom Grey: 85cr, 93cra, 95cra, 104crb, 109crb, 113cla, 122crb, 180crb, 188ca, 224cra, 251cra, 293tc, 361cla, 361cra, 383tr, 384br, 384tr, 384bl.
Josef Hlasek: 156crb.
Barry Hughes: 162crb.
Arto Juvonen: 63tc, 83ca, 83crb, 83tc, 92crb, 114cra.
Kevin T. Karlson: 27cla, 52ca, 52crb, 66tc, 73ca, 112cla, 112tc, 132ca, 132cra, 146cr, 146cra, 146crb, 146fcla, 158tc, 164ca, 222tr, 225crb, 327tc, 339cla, 382.
Garth McElroy: 4-5, 15cl, 27cla, 39crb, 47tr, 51tc, 52tc, 53ca, 54tc, 56cla, 57crb, 66tc, 74tc, 78tc, 80cla, 89bc, 91crb, 91tc, 91tl, 97tc, 98ca, 100cla, 101tr, 102crb, 102crb, 116tr, 119cra, 119crb, 125cra, 127cla, 127crb, 128cla, 128crb, 129ca, 130crb, 132crb, 132tc, 137crb, 137tr, 140ca, 141tc, 142crb, 142tc, 145cb, 146ca, 147tr, 149cr, 148ca, 149tc, 150cra, 151crb, 152cra, 153ca, 153cra, 154ca, 154cra, 154crb, 157tc, 169cra, 172crb, 174ca, 176ca, 176cla, 176cra, 176crb, 178crb, 178tc, 178tl, 189cra, 191crb, 198cr, 200cla, 201bc, 201tc, 203crb, 209cla, 209tc, 218cb, 218cla, 218cra, 234cla, 234crb, 235crb, 235tc, 238ca, 247bc, 248cla, 248cra, 248crb, 254cr, 256ca, 256crb, 257cra, 259bc, 259ca, 259crb, 261crb, 262bc, 262ca, 262crb, 263ca, 264ra, 264br, 266cra, 266crb, 267bc, 267cra, 269bc, 272crb, 273tc, 274crb, 276b, 278ca, 278cra, 280cb, 280tc, 282ca, 282crb, 283cb, 283crb, 284cb, 284cra, 286crb, 286tc, 287cb, 287crb, 288bc, 291cra, 292cla, 292cra, 292tc, 293cla, 299ca, 299crb, 300crb, 301crb, 304cb, 304cra, 308bc, 310crb, 311cra, 311crb, 313bl, 316cra, 317cla, 317crb, 317tc, 318crb, 319cla, 321cra, 321crb, 321tc, 322cra, 322tc, 323crb, 325bc, 327cra, 328cra, 329cb, 333ca, 333crb, 334cra, 335crb, 335tc, 336ca, 337crb, 338ca, 340cra, 343bc, 343tc, 344crb, 345bc, 345tc, 346ca, 347tc, 348cla, 348crb, 348tc, 351cra, 353crb, 354cra, 355bc, 359crb, 359tc, 361cra, 363crb, 366crb, 366tr, 368bc, 369tr, 370bc, 370ca, 371crb, 373cb, 373cra, 373tc, 374bc, 375crb, 376cr, 377cra, 377crb, 377tc, 378crb, 379cra, 379tc, 383br.
Arthur Morris/Birds As Art: 182tr.
Bob Moul: 78cla, 129crb, 242crb, 285crb, 311tc, 368cla.
Alan Murphy: 61cl, 77ca, 186b, 189cl, 190crb, 207cl, 210bl, 210br, 211ca, 211cb, 212l, 231crb, 243cb, 243crb, 253b, 261ca, 298b, 320cla, 332br, 337cra, 337tr, 352cra, 352crb, 357b.
Tomi Muukonen: 36crb, 71cl, 79tr, 107tr, 114cla,167cla, 167crb, 170crb, 175fcla, 176bc, 184ca, 295crb, 297crb.
naturepl.com: Vincent Munier 10-11c; Barry Mansell 23c; Tom Vezo 17crb; Markus Varesvuo 294b.
NHPA/Photoshot: Bill Coster 76bc, 124bc; Dhritiman Mukherjee; Kevin Schafer 81cb; NHPA / Lee Dalton 239b.
Photoshot: Picture Alliance 222b.
Judd Patterson: 22, 112bc, 112cra.
E. J. Peiker: 25cra, 30fcra, 30tr, 33tc, 34tc, 37cb, 39ca, 41cla, 41cra, 42ca, 42crb, 42tr, 43ca, 43cb, 43tc, 44cb, 44crb, 46ca, 46crb, 56crb, 57tc, 70cra, 71tr, 73crb, 74crb, 91fcra, 97cra, 98cra, 102tc, 111cra, 121tc, 124cr, 126cra, 126crb, 128cra, 134cr, 147tc, 150crb, 163cb, 167cra, 185tr, 188bc, 193cla, 193tc, 195cra, 209crb, 212br, 215cb, 223ca, 223cla, 227cl, 237cb, 242cra, 249cb, 250crb, 268bc, 275c, 275crb, 293cra, 307cla, 320crb, 326tr, 331bc, 332tr, 352tr, 354bc, 357tr, 358bc, 360fcla, 362crb, 365tr, 372crb, 372tr, 379tr, 386br.
Jari Peltomäki: 26ca, 47crb, 53crb, 63cra, 67tc, 71bc, 103bc, 115ca, 115cra, 115crb, 121cla, 121cra, 121crb, 184crb, 187crb, 192b, 199cb, 241crb, 258cra, 258crb, 295cra, 369cla, 384tl, 385tr.
Mike Read: 82crb, 226crb.
George Reszeter: 386cra.
Robert Royse: 29crb, 30cla, 51ca, 66cla, 67cra, 118ca, 118crb, 131cra, 135tr, 142ca, 152ca, 154cla, 178cra, 180ca, 180tr, 189bc, 191cra, 234cra, 268tc, 296cra, 296crb, 297tr, 309crb, 309tr, 310cla, 324cra, 336crb, 337ca, 342ca, 342crb, 352ca, 385bl.
Chris Schenk: 53fcla.
Bill Schmoker: 27cra, 28ca, 30crb, 32tc, 75cla, 75tc, 80crb, 82cr, 84crb, 85ca, 85crb, 85tr, 87crb, 87tc, 95ca, 113tc, 143crb, 240ca.
Brian E. Small: 1c, 2c, 11fcra, 24tc, 24tr, 26tc, 26tr, 29ca, 30tr, 31ca, 31tc, 32crb, 37ca, 37tc, 40tc, 44ca, 44tc, 46tc, 50tc, 51tr, 54ca, 57ca, 66cra, 70cr, 72ca, 73cla, 76tr, 94cra, 96tc, 104ca, 104tc, 106cra, 107ca, 109cra, 111bc, 117ca, 117crb, 123c, 123cla, 125tc, 126tc, 128tc, 133ca, 133tc, 135tc, 141tr, 145ca, 150ca, 151ca, 152cla, 156fcla, 168ca, 172ca, 172cra, 173tr, 174cra, 181ca, 185ca, 188tc, 190ca, 190cra, 194cra, 195cla, 197cla, 197cra, 198ca, 198cra, 199cra, 204tr, 204cl, 206crb, 208crb, 211cra, 211tr, 212cra, 213bc, 213cra, 214bc, 214tc, 215cla, 215cra, 217cb, 217cla, 217cra, 219cb, 220ca, 220cb, 220cra, 220fcla, 221cla, 221cra, 227tr, 227b, 228ca, 229cb, 229cra, 231ca, 232ca, 232crb, 233cra, 235cb, 236bc, 236ca, 238cra, 239cla, 240crb, 243ca, 244ca, 244crb, 246ca, 246crb, 247ca, 248tc, 254tr, 255cra, 257crb, 258ca, 260ca, 263crb, 265cra, 265tc, 266cla, 270cra, 271crb, 272bc, 272cra, 273ca, 274bc, 274cra, 275cla, 276ra, 278tr, 280ca, 281bc, 281ca, 283cra, 283tc, 284cla, 284tc, 285cra, 287ca, 289ca, 289crb, 289tc, 291tc, 293crb, 298tr, 300ca, 301ca, 302cla, 302cra, 302crb, 303bc, 303cla, 303cra, 304cla, 305cla, 305cra, 306cra, 306tc, 307crb, 308tr, 309ca, 310tc, 310tr, 312ca, 313cra, 313tc, 314cra, 314crb, 314tc, 315ca, 315crb, 315tc, 315tr, 316cla, 317tr, 318ca, 318tc, 319tr, 320cra, 322crb, 323ca, 324bc, 324cla, 324tc, 325ca, 325cla, 325cra, 325tc, 326cla, 327crb, 328tc, 329tc, 330ca, 330tc, 331ca, 331tc, 333cra, 335cla, 338cra, 339tr, 340ca, 341bc, 341ca, 343cra, 344cl, 345cra, 346crb, 347cra, 347crb, 348cra, 349cra, 350cra, 350crb, 350tc, 351cl, 351crb, 351fcla, 351tc, 353cla, 353cra, 353tc, 354cl, 354cla, 354tc, 355cla, 355tc, 355tr, 356cla, 356cr, 356crb, 356tr, 358cra, 362cla, 362cra, 362tr, 371cla, 371tc, 376ca, 376cra, 376tl, 378ca, 379cla, 383crb, 384cra, 386crb, 387br, 388cla, 388cra, 388clb.
Michelle Lynn St.Sauveur: 148crb.
Bob Steele: 13cb, 24tc, 26cla, 26crb, 26cra, 27ca, 28tc, 28tr, 29ca, 29crb, 29tc, 32crb, 33tr, 34tr, 37crb, 38tc, 41cla, 41crb, 44crb, 46tr, 50crb, 50tr, 54crb, 56tc, 57tr, 61cla, 70tr, 74tr, 77crb, 77tc, 82ca, 94tc, 96cb, 99tc, 101crb, 107cra, 109ca, 111cla, 111tc, 114crb, 116b, 119cla, 120ca, 120tc, 122cla, 123cra, 125ca, 127tc, 130ca, 133crb, 136bc, 136ca, 138cra, 140crb, 141ca, 141crb, 144ca, 144bc, 147ca, 147crb, 155ca, 155crb, 155tc, 155tr, 156fcra, 158bc, 158fcla, 160tc, 160cra, 168cla, 168crb, 169cla, 169tc, 173ca, 174cla, 174crb, 174tc, 175crb, 175tc, 181tc, 185crb, 185tc, 192tr, 195cb, 196cra, 196tc, 200crb, 203cra,203tc, 204b, 205ca, 209cra, 214cra, 216ca, 216tr, 219cla, 219cra, 223crb, 223tr, 228crb, 229cr, 230cra, 230crb, 230tc, 233crb, 235cra, 237ca, 237cra, 237crb, 240cra, 241tc, 247crb, 249crb, 250ca, 251ca, 251crb, 252crb, 253a, 254bc, 254cla, 255crb, 255tc, 256cra, 256tr, 257tc, 259tc, 260crb, 260tc, 265crb, 266ca, 268cra, 271cra, 272tc, 273crb, 274tc, 275bc, 275tr, 279tc, 281crb, 286cla, 286cra, 288ca, 290fcla, 291crb, 298cl, 304crb, 306cla, 306crb, 307cra, 308cla, 312crb, 312tc, 313bc, 313cla, 319cb, 319crb, 320tc, 321cla, 322cla, 326c, 326cra, 326crb, 328crb, 329ca, 329crb, 330cb, 330crb, 334cla, 334crb, 334tc, 338bc, 339crb, 339tc, 340crb, 344cla, 344tc, 345cl, 349cla, 349crb, 349tc, 357cr, 365crb, 366cla, 367cra, 367tc, 369b, 370cra, 372cla, 372cra, 374cl, 374tc, 378cb, 387cla, 387bl.
Matthew Studebaker: 385clb.
Andy & Gill Swash: 82tr, 94crb, 100cra.
Markus Varesvuo: 12-13bc, 23cra, 26crb, 30crb, 35ca, 35cb, 35tr, 47ca, 47tc, 49cb, 49crb, 49tc, 51crb, 56ca, 58ca, 58crb, 61cb, 63crb, 64cra, 64fbr, 68ca, 72crb, 74ca, 74cb, 76cl, 78crb, 79ca, 79crb, 107crb, 110cra, 110tr, 114ca, 114tr, 138crb, 139ca, 157cb, 159crb, 159tc, 162tc, 196crb, 200cra, 226cla, 241cra,Vireo: Dr.Yuri Artukhin, Rick and Nora Bowers 259fbl, 269crb, 290crb, 292crb, 295cla, 295tc, 375cra, 375tc, 376crb, 383tl; Robert L. Pitman 86bc; Harold Stiver, 84fbl.
Cal Vornberger: 352cr.
Peter S Weber: 25tc, 50ca, 62crb, 70crb, 97ca, 100tr, 194crb, 202crb, 205tr, 213cla, 215fcla, 216tc, 221clb, 265crb.
Ian Whetton: 86crb.
Roger Wilmshurst: 226cra.

All other images © Dorling Kindersley
For further information see: www.dkimages.com